"This volume, by a trustworthy and immensely careful scholar, is an essential addition to the desk of any serious biblical scholar or student."

—Ann Jervis, professor of New Testament and advanced degree director, Wycliffe College, and senior fellow, Massey College

"The EGGNT series is a must-have addition to the library of pastors, faculty, and students. These volumes present the reader with excellent exegesis of each particular New Testament book. The work on Romans is provided by John D. Harvey, whose highly competent exegetical skills are well-known in evangelical circles. Harvey's analysis of the Greek text of Romans is superb, contemporary, and clear. He discusses the sacred text word by word, phrase by phrase, and sentence by sentence, producing an illuminating outline of the Greek passage under consideration. The exegesis is all there at the fingertips of the reader: vocabulary, syntax, grammatical outline, as well as further resources for advanced study on that particular passage in Romans. Add to this a very practical section on homiletics in terms of possible outlines for sermons, and the reader has at his or her disposal an invaluable commentary. At the same time, Harvey's objective exegesis grants readers the opportunity to develop their own respective theological messages and applications to today's world. John Harvey's work is a masterful study of Romans that will endear itself to readers for years to come!"

—C. Marvin Pate, chair of the department of Christian theology and the Elma Cobb Professor of Christian Theology, Ouachita Baptist University

"In this volume on the Greek text of Romans, John Harvey provides an excellent guide for anyone wishing to work their way through Paul's epic epistle. Harvey strikes just the right balance between giving readers insights and information on Greek forms, grammar, and syntax and leaving ample space for readers to consider interpretive options for themselves. For students ready to take the next step in Greek exegesis, pastors who want to make good use of the Greek text for sermon preparation, and scholars needing a compendium of the major issues in the Greek text of Romans, this book is a must-have."

—Brian Vickers, professor of New Testament interpretation and biblical theology, The Southern Baptist Theological Seminary

The Exegetical Guide to the Greek New Testament

Volumes Available

Luke	Alan J. Thompson
John	Murray J. Harris
Romans	John D. Harvey
Ephesians	Benjamin L. Merkle
Philippians	Joseph H. Hellerman
Colossians, Philemon	Murray J. Harris
James	Chris A. Vlachos
1 Peter	Greg W. Forbes

Forthcoming Volumes

Matthew	Charles L. Quarles
Mark	Joel F. Williams
Acts	L. Scott Kellum
1 Corinthians	Jay E. Smith
2 Corinthians	Colin G. Kruse
Galatians	David A. Croteau
1–2 Thessalonians	David W. Chapman
1–2 Timothy, Titus	Ray Van Neste
Hebrews	Dana M. Harris
2 Peter, Jude	Terry L. Wilder
1–3 John	Robert L. Plummer
Revelation	Bruce N. Fisk

EXEGETICAL GUIDE TO THE GREEK NEW TESTAMENT

Romans

John D. Harvey

EXEGETICAL GUIDE TO THE GREEK NEW TESTAMENT

ROMANS

Andreas J. Köstenberger
Robert W. Yarbrough
GENERAL EDITORS

Exegetical Guide to the Greek New Testament: Romans

Published by B&H Academic

Brentwood, Tennessee

ISBN: 978-1-4336-7613-0

Dewey Decimal Classification: 227.1

Subject Heading: BIBLE. N.T. Romans—STUDY\BIBLE N.T. ROMANS—CRITICISM

Printed in the United States of America

5 6 7 8 9 10 • 29 28 27 26 25

To Dr. Richard N. Longenecker, who graciously passed on to all his students a love for Paul and his letter to the Romans

Contents

Romans

Acknowledgments

I am grateful for the opportunity I have had to spend the past five years thinking about Paul's letter to the Romans. This project has given me a fresh appreciation for those scholars with whose work I have been able to interact, as well as a deeper love for the gospel that is "the power of God for salvation to everyone who believes" (Rom 1:16, NASB).

I would like to thank Andreas Köstenberger, who invited me to contribute to this series and regularly offered his assistance with procedural matters; the team at B&H Academic, who provided consistent support and practical guidance; and my wife, Anita, who patiently lived with piles of books in various places around the house while this project was in progress.

My prayer is that this volume will help others more effectively fulfill the calling reflected in the motto of Columbia International University: "To know Christ, and to make him known."

Publisher's Preface

It is with great excitement that we publish this volume of the Exegetical Guide to the Greek New Testament series. When the founding editor, Dr. Murray J. Harris, came to us seeking a new publishing partner, we gratefully accepted the offer. With the help of the coeditor, Andreas J. Köstenberger, we spent several years working together to acquire all of the authors we needed to complete the series. By God's grace we succeeded and contracted the last author in 2011. Originally working with another publishing house, Murray's efforts spanned more than twenty years. As God would have it, shortly after the final author was contracted, Murray decided God wanted him to withdraw as coeditor of the series. God made clear to him that he must devote his full attention to taking care of his wife, who faces the daily challenges caused by multiple sclerosis.

Over the course of many years, God has used Murray to teach his students how to properly exegete the Scriptures. He is an exceptional scholar and professor. But even more importantly, Murray is a man dedicated to serving Christ. His greatest joy is to respond in faithful obedience when his master calls. "There can be no higher and more ennobling privilege than to have the Lord of the universe as one's Owner and Master and to be his accredited representative on earth."[1] Murray has once again heeded the call of his master.

It is our privilege to dedicate the Exegetical Guide to the Greek New Testament series to Dr. Murray J. Harris. We pray that our readers will continue the work he started.

B&H Academic

1. Murray J. Harris, *Slave of Christ: A New Testament Metaphor for Total Devotion to Christ* (Downers Grove: InterVarsity, 1999), 155.

General Introduction to the EGGNT Series

Studying the New Testament in the original Greek has become easier in recent years. Beginning students will work their way through an introductory grammar or other text, but then what? Grappling with difficult verb forms, rare vocabulary, and grammatical irregularities remains a formidable task for those who would advance beyond the initial stages of learning Greek to master the interpretive process. Intermediate grammars and grammatical analyses can help, but such tools, for all their value, still often operate at a distance from the Greek text itself, and analyses are often too brief to be genuinely helpful.

The Exegetical Guide to the Greek New Testament (EGGNT) aims to close the gap between the Greek text and the available tools. Each EGGNT volume aims to provide all the necessary information for understanding of the Greek text and, in addition, includes homiletical helps and suggestions for further study. The EGGNT is not a full-scale commentary. Nevertheless these guides will make interpreting a given New Testament book easier, in particular for those who are hard-pressed for time and yet want to preach or teach with accuracy and authority.

In terms of layout, each volume begins with a brief introduction to the particular book (including such matters as authorship, date, etc.), a basic outline, and a list of recommended commentaries. At the end of each volume, you will find a comprehensive exegetical outline of the book. The body of each volume is devoted to paragraph-by-paragraph exegesis of the text. The treatment of each paragraph includes:

1. The Greek text of the passage, phrase by phrase, from the fifth edition of the United Bible Societies' *Greek New Testament* (UBS^5).
2. A structural analysis of the passage. Typically, verbal discussion of the structure of a given unit is followed by a diagram, whereby the verbal discussion serves to explain the diagram and the diagram serves to provide a visual aid illumining the structural discussion. While there is no one correct or standard way to diagram Greek sentences, the following format is typically followed in EGGNT volumes:
   a. The original Greek word order is maintained.
   b. When Greek words are omitted, this is indicated by ellipses (. . .).

c. The diagramming method, moving from left to right, is predicated upon the following. In clauses with a finite verb, the default order is typically verb-subject-object. In verbless clauses or clauses with nonfinite verb forms, the default order is typically subject-(verb)-object. Departures from these default orders are understood to be pragmatically motivated (e.g., contrast, emphasis, etc.).
d. Indents are used to indicate subordination (e.g. in the case of dependent clauses).
e. Retaining original word order, modifiers are centered above or below the word they modify (e.g., a prepositional phrase in relation to the verb).
f. Where a given sentence or clause spans multiple lines of text, drawn lines are used, such as where a relative pronoun introduces a relative clause (often shifting emphasis).
g. Underline is used to indicate imperatives; dotted underline is used to indicate repetition (the same word or cognate used multiple times in a given unit); the symbol ⋮ may be used where an article is separated from a noun or participle by interjected material (such as a prepositional phrase).
h. In shorter letters diagrams are normally provided for every unit; in longer letters and Revelation, ellipses may be used to show less detail in diagramming (keeping larger blocks together on the same line) in order to focus primarily on the larger structure of a given unit; in the Gospels and Acts, detailed diagrams will usually not be provided, though less detailed diagrams may be used to illustrate important or more complex structural aspects of a given passage.

3. A discussion of each phrase of the passage with discussion of relevant vocabulary, significant textual variants, and detailed grammatical analysis, including parsing. When more than one solution is given for a particular exegetical issue, the author's own preference is indicated by an asterisk (*). When no preference is expressed, the options are judged to be evenly balanced, or it is assumed that the text is intentionally ambiguous. When a particular verb form may be parsed in more than one way, only the parsing appropriate in the specific context is supplied; but where there is difference of opinion among grammarians or commentators, both possibilities are given and the matter is discussed.
4. Various translations of significant words or phrases.
5. A list of suggested topics for further study with bibliography for each topic. An asterisk (*) in one of the "For Further Study" bibliographies draws attention to a discussion of the particular topic that is recommended as a useful introduction to the issues involved.
6. Homiletical suggestions designed to help the preacher or teacher move from the Greek text to a sermon outline that reflects careful exegesis. The first suggestion for a particular paragraph of the text is always more exegetical

than homiletical and consists of an outline of the entire paragraph. These detailed outlines of each paragraph build on the general outline proposed for the whole book and, if placed side by side, form a comprehensive exegetical outline of the book. All outlines are intended to serve as a basis for sermon preparation and should be adapted to the needs of a particular audience.[2]

The EGGNT volumes will serve a variety of readers. Those reading the Greek text for the first time may be content with the assistance with vocabulary, parsing, and translation. Readers with some experience in Greek may want to skip or skim these sections and focus attention on the discussions of grammar. More advanced students may choose to pursue the topics and references to technical works under "For Further Study," while pastors may be more interested in the movement from grammatical analysis to sermon outline. Teachers may appreciate having a resource that frees them to focus on exegetical details and theological matters.

The editors are pleased to present you with the individual installments of the EGGNT. We are grateful for each of the contributors who has labored long and hard over each phrase in the Greek New Testament. Together we share the conviction that "all Scripture is inspired by God and is profitable for teaching, for rebuking, for correcting, for training in righteousness" (2 Tim 3:16 CSB) and echo Paul's words to Timothy: "Be diligent to present yourself approved to God, a worker who doesn't need to be ashamed, correctly teaching the word of truth" (2 Tim 2:15 CSB).

Thanks to David Croteau, who served as assistant editor for this volume.

Andreas J. Köstenberger
Robert W. Yarbrough

2. As a Bible publisher, B&H Publishing follows the "Colorado Springs Guidelines for Translation of Gender-Related Language in Scripture." As an academic book publisher, B&H Academic asks that authors conform their manuscripts (including EGGNT exegetical outlines in English) to the B&H Academic style guide, which affirms the use of singular "he/his/him" as generic examples encompassing both genders. However, in their discussion of the Greek text, EGGNT authors have the freedom to analyze the text and reach their own conclusions regarding whether specific Greek words are gender specific or gender inclusive.

Abbreviations

For abbreviations used in discussion of text critical matters, the reader should refer to the abbreviations listed in the Introduction to the United Bible Societies' *Greek New Testament*.

*	indicates the reading of the original hand of a manuscript as opposed to subsequent correctors of the manuscript, *or*
	indicates the writer's own preference when more than one solution is given for a particular exegetical problem, *or*
	in the "For Further Study" bibliographies, indicates a discussion of the particular topic that is recommended as a useful introduction to the issues involved
§, §§	paragraph, paragraphs

Books of the Old Testament

Gen	Genesis	Song	Song of Songs (Canticles)
Exod	Exodus	Isa	Isaiah
Lev	Leviticus	Jer	Jeremiah
Num	Numbers	Lam	Lamentations
Deut	Deuteronomy	Ezek	Ezekiel
Josh	Joshua	Dan	Daniel
Judg	Judges	Hos	Hosea
Ruth	Ruth	Joel	Joel
1–2 Sam	1–2 Samuel	Amos	Amos
1–2 Kgs	1–2 Kings	Obad	Obadiah
1–2 Chr	1–2 Chronicles	Jonah	Jonah
Ezra	Ezra	Mic	Micah
Neh	Nehemiah	Nah	Nahum

Esth	Esther	Hab	Habakkuk
Job	Job	Zeph	Zephaniah
Ps(s)	Psalm(s)	Hag	Haggai
Prov	Proverbs	Zech	Zechariah
Eccl	Ecclesiastes	Mal	Malachi

Books of the New Testament

Matt	Matthew	1–2 Thess	1–2 Thessalonians
Mark	Mark	1–2 Tim	1–2 Timothy
Luke	Luke	Titus	Titus
John	John	Phlm	Philemon
Acts	Acts	Heb	Hebrews
Rom	Romans	Jas	James
1–2 Cor	1–2 Corinthians	1–2 Pet	1–2 Peter
Gal	Galatians	1–3 John	1–3 John
Eph	Ephesians	Jude	Jude
Phil	Philippians	Rev	Revelation
Col	Colossians		

General Abbreviations

ABD	D. N. Freedman, ed., *The Anchor Bible Dictionary*, 6 vols. New York: Doubleday, 1992.
abs.	absolute(ly)
acc.	accusative
act.	active (voice)
adj.	adjective, adjectival(ly)
adv.	adverb, adverbial(ly)
anar.	anarthrous
aor.	aorist
apod.	apodosis
appos.	apposition, appositional
art.	(definite) article, articular
attrib.	attributive, attributive(ly)
AThR	*Anglican Theological Review*
AusBR	*Australian Biblical Review*
AUSS	*Andrews University Seminary Studies*
BAR	*Biblical Archaeology Review*

Barrett	C. K. Barrett, *A Commentary on the Epistle to the Romans*, 2nd ed. New York: Harper, 1991.
BBR	*Bulletin for Biblical Research*
BDAG	F. W. Danker, ed., *A Greek-English Lexicon of the New Testament and Other Early Christian Literature*. Chicago/London: University of Chicago Press, 2000. Based on W. Bauer's *Griechisch-deutsches Wörterbuch* (6th ed.) and on previous English ed. W. F. Arndt, F. W. Gingrich, and F. W. Danker. References to BDAG are by page number and quadrant on the page, *a* indicating the upper half and *b* the lower half of the left-hand column, and *c* and *d* the upper and lower halves of the right-hand column. With the use of dark type, biblical references are now clearly visible within each subsection.
BDF	F. Blass and A. Debrunner, *A Greek Grammar of the New Testament and Other Early Christian Literature*, ET and rev. by R. W. Funk. Chicago: University of Chicago Press, 1961.
BGk.	Biblical Greek (i.e., LXX and NT Greek)
Bib	*Biblica*
BibT	*Bible Today*
BJRL	*Bulletin of the John Rylands University Library of Manchester*
BR	*Biblical Research*
BSac	*Bibliotheca Sacra*
BT	*Bible Translator*
BTB	Biblical Theology Bulletin
Burton	E. de W. Burton, *Syntax of the Moods and Tenses in New Testament Greek*, 3rd ed. Edinburgh: T & T Clark, 1898.
CBQ	*Catholic Biblical Quarterly*
CEV	Contemporary English Version (1995)
cf.	*confer* (Lat.), compare
CJT	*Canadian Journal of Theology*
comp.	comparative, comparison
cond.	condition(al)
conj.	conjunctive, conjunction
Cranfield	C. E. B. Cranfield, *A Critical and Exegetical Commentary on the Epistle to the Romans*, 2 vols. Edinburgh: T & T Clark, 1980.
CSB	Christian Standard Bible (2017)
cstr.	construction, construe(d)

CTJ	*Calvin Theological Journal*
CTQ	*Concordia Theological Quarterly*
CTR	*Criswell Theological Review*
dat.	dative
decl.	declension, decline
def.	definite
dep.	deponent
DJG	J. B. Green, J. K. Brown, and N. Perrin, eds., *Dictionary of Jesus and the Gospels*. Downers Grove: InterVarsity, 2013.
DLNT	R. P. Martin and P. H. Davids, eds., *Dictionary of the Later New Testament and Its Developments*. Leicester / Downers Grove: InterVarsity, 1997.
DNTB	C. A. Evans and S. E. Porter, eds., *Dictionary of New Testament Background*. Leicester / Downers Grove: InterVarsity, 2000.
DPL	G. F. Hawthorne, R. P. Martin, and D. G. Reid, eds., *Dictionary of Paul and His Letters*. Downers Grove: InterVarsity, 1993.
dir.	direct
Dunn	J. D. G. Dunn, *Romans*, 2 vols. Waco, TX: Word, 1988.
EDT	W. A. Elwell, ed., *Evangelical Dictionary of Theology*. Grand Rapids: Baker 1984.
EDBT	W. A. Elwell, ed., *Evangelical Dictionary of Biblical Theology*. Grand Rapids: Baker, 2001.
EDNT	H. Balz and G. Schneider, eds., *Exegetical Dictionary of the New Testament*, 3 vols. Grand Rapids: Eerdmans, 1990–93.
ed(s).	edited by, edition(s), editor(s)
e.g.	*exempli gratia* (Lat.), for example
Eng.	English
epex.	epexegetic, epexegetical(ly)
esp.	especially
ESV	English Standard Version (2011)
et al.	*et alii* (Lat.), and others
ETL	*Ephemerides Theologicae Lovanienses*
EvQ	*Evangelical Quarterly*
EvRevTh	*Evangelical Review of Theology*
EVV	English versions of the Bible
ExpTim	*Expository Times*
fem.	feminine

fig. figurative(ly)

FilNeot *Filología Neotestamentaria*

Funk R. W. Funk, "The Apostolic 'Parousia': Form and Significance. Pages 249–68 in *Christian History and Interpretation: Studies Presented to John Knox*. Edited by W. R. Farmer, C. F. D. Moule, and R. R. Niebuhr. Cambridge: Cambridge University Press, 1967.

fut. future

gen. genitive

Gamble H. Y. Gamble, Jr., *The Textual History of the Letter to the Romans: A Study in Textual and Literary Criticism*. Grand Rapids: Eerdmans, 1977.

Gk. Greek

GNB Good News Bible (1976)

Harris M. J. Harris, *Prepositions and Theology in the Greek New Testament*. Grand Rapids: Zondervan, 2012.

Harvey J. D. Harvey, *Listening to the Text: Oral Patterning in Paul's Letters*. Grand Rapids: Baker 1998.

HBT *Horizons in Biblical Theology*

Heb. Hebrew, Hebraism

HTR *Harvard Theological Review*

IBS *Irish Biblical Studies*

IDB G. A. Buttrick, ed., *Interpreter's Dictionary of the Bible*, 4 vols. Nashville/New York: Abingdon, 1962–76.

IDBSup *Interpreter's Dictionary of the Bible (Supplement Volume)*

i.e. *id est* (Lat.), that is

impers. impersonal

impf. imperfect (tense)

impv. imperative (mood), imperatival(ly)

incl. including

indef. indefinite

indic. indicative (mood)

indir. indirect

inf. infinitive

instr. instrument, instrumental(ly)

Int *Interpretation*

interr. interrogative

ISBE	G. W. Bromiley, et al. eds., *International Standard Bible Encyclopedia*, 4 vols. Grand Rapids: Eerdmans, 1979–88.
iter.	iterative
JAC	*Jahrbuch für Antike und Christentum*
Jewett	R. Jewett, *Romans*. Minneapolis: Fortress, 2007.
JBL	*Journal of Biblical Literature*
JBR	*Journal of Bible and Religion*
JETS	*Journal of the Evangelical Theological Society*
JSNT	*Journal for the Study of the New Testament*
JSOT	*Journal for the Study of the Old Testament*
JTS	*Journal of Theological Studies*
Käsemann	E. Käsemann, *Commentary on Romans*, trans. G. W. Bromiley. Grand Rapids: Eerdmans, 1980.
KJV	King James Version (= "Authorized Version") (1611)
Kuss	O. Kuss, *Der Römerbrief übersetzt und erklärt*, 3 vols. Regensburg: Pustet, 1957–78.
lit.	literal(ly)
LN	J. P. Louw and E. A. Nida, eds., *Greek-English Lexicon of the New Testament Based on Semantic Domains, Vol. I: Introduction and Domains*. New York: United Bible Societies, 1988.
locat.	locative
Longenecker	R. N. Longenecker, *The Epistle to the Romans*. New International Greek Testament Commentary. Grand Rapids: Eerdmans, 2016.
LQ	*Lutheran Quarterly*
LTJ	*Lutheran Theological Journal*
LXX	Septuagint (= Greek Old Testament)
Macc	Maccabees
masc.	masculine
Metzger	B. M. Metzger, *A Textual Commentary on the Greek New Testament*. Stuttgart: Deutsche Bibelgesellschaft / New York: United Bible Societies, 1994; second ed. of 1994 based on UBS^4.
Meyer	H. A. W. Meyer, *Critical and Exegetical Handbook to the Epistle to Romans*, trans. J. C, Moore, 3 vols. Edinburgh: T & T Clark, 1876.

mid.	middle
mng.	meaning
Moo	D. J. Moo, *The Epistle to the Romans*. New International Commentary on the New Testament. Grand Rapids: Eerdmans, 1996.
Moule	C. F. D. Moule, *An Idiom Book of New Testament Greek*, 2nd ed. Cambridge: Cambridge University Press, 1960.
ms(s).	manuscript(s)
MT	Masoretic Text
MThZ	*Münchener Theologische Zeitschrift*
MGWJ	*Monatsschrift für die Geschichte und Wissenschaft des Judentums*
Murray	J. Murray, *The Epistle to the Romans*, 2 vols. Grand Rapids: Eerdmans, 1965
n.	note
NASB	New American Standard Bible (1995)
NCV	New Century Version (1987)
NEB	New English Bible (1970)
neg.	negative, negation
Neot	*Neotestamentica*
NET	New English Translation Bible (2005)
neut.	neuter
NIDNTT	C. Brown, ed., *The New International Dictionary of New Testament Theology*, 3 vols. Grand Rapids: Zondervan, 1975–78.
NIDNTTE	M. Silva, ed., *New International Dictionary of New Testament Theology and Exegesis*, 5 vols. Grand Rapids: Zondervan, 2014.
NIV	New International Version (2011)
NIRV	New International Readers Version (1996)
NJB	New Jerusalem Bible (1985)
NKJV	New King James Version (1982)
NLT	New Living Translation of the Bible (1996)
nom.	nominative
NovT	*Novum Testamentum*
NRSV	New Revised Standard Version (1990)
NSBT	New Studies in Biblical Theology

NT	New Testament
NTS	*New Testament Studies*
obj.	object(ive)
opt.	optative
orig.	origin, original(ly)
OT	Old Testament
p(p).	page(s)
pass.	passive
periph.	periphrastic
pers.	person(al)
pf.	perfect
pl.	plural
Porter	S. E. Porter, *Idioms of the Greek New Testament*. Sheffield: *JSOT*, 1992.
poss.	possessive, possession
pred.	predicate, predicative
pref.	prefix
prep.	preposition(al)
pres.	present
pron.	pronoun
prot.	protasis
ptc.	participle, participial(ly)
R	A. T. Robertson, *A Grammar of the Greek New Testament in the Light of Historical Research*, 4th ed. Nashville: Broadman, 1934.
RB	*Revue Biblique*
rdg(s).	(textual) reading(s)
ref.	reference
refl.	reflexive
rel.	relative
rev.	revised
RevExp	*Review and Expositor*
ResQ	*Restoration Quarterly*
RSV	Revised Standard Version (1952)
RTR	*Reformed Theological Review*

S-H	W. Sanday and A. C. Headlam, *A Critical and Exegetical Commentary on the Epistle to the Romans*. Edinburgh: T & T Clark, 1895.
SBT	*Studies in Biblical Theology*
Schreiner	T. R. Schreiner, *Romans*. Grand Rapids: Baker, 1998.
SE	*Studia Evangelica*
Sem.	Semitic, Semitism
sg.	singular
sim.	similar(ly)
SJT	*Scottish Journal of Theology*
ST	*Studia theological*
subj.	subject(ive)
subjunc.	subjunctive
subord.	subordinate, subordination
subst.	substantive, substantival(ly)
superl.	superlative
SwJT	*Southwestern Journal of Theology*
T	N. Turner, *A Grammar of New Testament Greek*. Edited by J. H. Moulton, vol. 3: *Syntax*. Edinburgh: Clark, 1963.
TDNT	G. Kittel and G. Friedrich, eds., *Theological Dictionary of the New Testament*, 9 vols. Translated by G. W. Bromiley. Grand Rapids: Eerdmans, 1964–74.
TE	*Theologica Evangelica*
temp.	temporal(ly)
TJ	*Trinity Journal*
TJT	*Toronto Journal of Theology*
TLZ	*Theologische Literaturzeitung*
TS	*Theological Studies*
tr	translate(d), translation(s)
TynBul	*Tyndale Bulletin*
TZ	*Theologische Zeitschrift*
UBS[5]	B. Aland, K. Aland, J. Karavidopoulos, C. M. Martini, and B. M. Metzger, eds., *The Greek New Testament*, 5th rev. ed. Stuttgart: Deutsche Bibelgesellschaft; New York: United Bible Societies, 2014.
USQR	*Union Seminary Quarterly Review*

v(v).	verse(s)
var.	variant (form or reading)
vb.	verb
VE	*Vox Evangelica*
voc.	vocative
vol(s).	volume(s)
Wallace	D. B. Wallace, *Greek Grammar Beyond the Basics: An Exegetical Syntax of the New Testament*. Grand Rapids: Zondervan, 1996.
WesThJ	*Wesleyan Theological Journal*
WTJ	*Westminster Theological Journal*
ZNW	*Zeitschrift für die neutestamentliche Wissenschaft und die Kunde der älteren Kirche*
ZTK	*Zeitschrift für Theologie und Kirche*

Romans

Introduction

AUTHORSHIP

Romans has been accepted as Pauline since post-apostolic times (1 Clem 32.2; 35.5; 50.6; Polycarp 3.3; 4.1; 6.2; 10.1; Ignatius, *Eph.* 19.3; *Magn.* 6.2; 9.1; *Trall.* 9.2; *Smyr.* 1.1). That conclusion is seldom disputed, and the internal evidence supports it:

1. The salutation identifies Paul as the author (1:1).
2. The author's background fits that of Paul (11:1; cf. 2 Cor 11:22; Phil 3:5).
3. The author's companions, travels, and ministry all fit the record of Paul's activities in Acts (15:14–33; 16:21–23).
4. The language and style are similar to other letters ascribed to Paul.
5. The content of the letter reflects others ascribed to Paul.

PLACE OF ORIGIN AND DATE

Internal statements suggest that the letter was written close to the end of Paul's third missionary journey, most likely from Corinth.

1. Acts places Paul in Achaia for three months before he traveled to Jerusalem (Acts 20:1–3).
2. Gaius, whose household Paul baptized in Corinth (1 Cor 1:14), was Paul's host (16:23).
3. The collection had been completed (15:25–29), and Paul was ready to leave for Jerusalem (15:25).
4. Timothy and Sopater, who accompanied Paul when he left Greece for Jerusalem (Acts 20:4), were present with Paul when he wrote (16:23).

Gallio's time as proconsul in Achaia dates Paul's first visit to Corinth at AD 50–52 (Acts 18:12–17). His subsequent ministry in Ephesus for three years (Acts 18:18–19:10) places his second visit to Corinth at AD 56–57. Paul's departure for Jerusalem after the Feast of Unleavened Bread (Acts 20:4–6) makes early AD 57 the most likely date for the letter.

AUDIENCE, OCCASION, AND PURPOSE

By the first century, Rome's population was at least one million and consisted of people of all socioeconomic levels from across the empire. As early as 139 BC Rome had a Jewish population estimated at 40,000. Both Julius Caesar and Octavius declared Judaism a legal religion, but the Jews in Rome still experienced racial discrimination. Tiberius expelled all Jews in AD 19, and Claudius did the same in AD 49. Jews from Rome were present at Pentecost (cf. Acts 2:10) and most likely carried the gospel back to Italy with them. Claudius's expulsion of all Jews probably reflects an initial Christian presence in the synagogues of Rome. Nero allowed the Jews to return after Claudius's death (AD 54), and Paul expected to encounter an active Christian church when he passed through Rome on his way to Spain (1:8–12; 15:22–24; 16:3–16).

Much of Romans is devoted to issues of particular interest to Jewish readers (2:1–3:8; 3:19–20, 27–31; 4:12–15; 5:13–14, 20; 6:14; 7:1–8:4; 9:30–10:8; 13:8–10). Yet the epistolary sections of the letter are styled for Gentiles (1:1–17; 15:14–16:27), and Paul includes his readers among the Gentiles to whom he was called to minister (1:5–6, 13; 15:14–21). It is probably best to see Romans as written to a mixed congregation of Jews and Gentiles, with Gentiles in the majority.

Paul anticipated traveling and ministering in the western Mediterranean area after he had delivered the collection to the church in Jerusalem (15:14–33). With those travel plans in mind, he wrote to introduce himself to the church in Rome, clarify the nature of his "gospel to the Gentiles," and correct the attitudes and behavior of the Jewish and Gentile believers in the church. Rather than trying to identify a single purpose for the letter, it is probably better to think of a cluster of purposes that address missionary, theological, and pastoral concerns.

OUTLINE

The following outline is informed by epistolary analysis (1:1–17; 15:14–16:27) as well as an analysis of the argument of Romans (1:18–15:13). Note that 16:24 is omitted in key early manuscripts. See the discussion of 16:21–23.

- I. Letter Opening (1:1–17)
  - A. Salutation (1:1–7)
  - B. Thanksgiving (1:8–12)
  - C. Occasion for Writing (1:13–15)
  - D. Thesis (1:16–17)
- II. Letter Body (1:18–15:13)
  - A. The revelation of God's righteousness (1:18–4:25)
    - 1. God reveals his righteousness through wrath (1:18–3:20)
      - a. Because humankind suppresses God's truth (1:18–23)
      - b. Because the Gentiles practice unrighteousness (1:24–32)
      - c. Because the moral person judges others (2:1–16)
      - d. Because the Jews transgress the law (2:17–29)
      - e. Because God always acts righteously (3:1–8)
      - f. Because all are under sin (3:9–20)

2. God reveals his righteousness apart from law (3:21–31)
    a. Through faith in Christ (3:21–26)
    b. Apart from works (3:27–31)
3. God reveals his righteousness in response to faith (4:1–25)
    a. Apart from works or circumcision (4:1–12)
    b. Apart from law (4:13–25)

B. The provision of God's righteousness (5:1–8:39)
1. God's righteousness is imputed in Christ (5:1–21)
    a. Bringing peace, hope, and reconciliation (5:1–11)
    b. Counteracting the effects of Adam's sin (5:12–21)
2. God's righteousness is appropriated in Christ (6:1–23)
    a. By understanding our death with Christ (6:1–14)
    b. By serving our new master (6:15–23)
3. God's righteousness is not lived out according to the law (7:1–25)
    a. Because dying with Christ brings release from the law (7:1–6)
    b. Because the law brings knowledge of sin (7:7–12)
    c. Because sin uses the law to produce death (7:13–25)
4. God's righteousness is lived out according to the Spirit (8:1–30)
    a. Who gives us life and assurance (8:1–17)
    b. Who gives us hope of glory (8:18–30)
5. God's righteousness results in victory (8:31–39)

C. The vindication of God's righteousness (9:1–11:36)
1. Paul's concern for Israel (9:1–5)
2. God's righteousness is vindicated by his sovereign working (9:6–29)
    a. According to his sovereign calling (9:6–13)
    b. Out of his sovereign mercy (9:14–18)
    c. Under his sovereign authority (9:19–29)
3. God's righteousness is vindicated despite Israel's unresponsiveness (9:30–10:21)
    a. Reflected in their failed pursuit (9:30–10:4)
    b. Rooted in their flawed understanding (10:5–13)
    c. Resulting in their frustrating disobedience (10:14–21)
4. God's righteousness is vindicated by his plan for salvation history (11:1–32)
    a. To preserve a Jewish remnant (11:1–10)
    b. To bring salvation to the Gentiles (11:11–24)
    c. To restore Israel (11:25–32)
5. Paul's praise to God (11:33–36)

D. The practice of God's righteousness (12:1–15:13)
1. God's righteousness is practiced in Christian living (12:1–13:14)
    a. By giving ourselves wholly to God (12:1–2)
    b. By humbly exercising spiritual gifts (12:3–8)
    c. By pursuing total transformation (12:9–21)

d. By being subject to authorities (13:1–7)
e. By loving one another (13:8–10)
f. By living in light of Jesus's return (13:11–14)
2. God's righteousness is practiced in Christian liberty (14:1–15:13)
a. By accepting one another (14:1–12)
b. By pursuing peace with one another (14:13–23)
c. By pleasing one another (15:1–6)
d. By following Christ's example (15:7–13)
III. Letter Closing (15:14–16:27)
A. Paul's mission (15:14–21)
B. Paul's travel plans (15:22–29)
C. Paul's prayer request (15:30–33)
D. Commendation of Phoebe (16:1–2)
E. Greetings from Paul (16:3–16)
F. Final advice (16:17–20)
G. Greetings from others (16:21–23)
H. Doxology (16:25–27)

RECOMMENDED COMMENTARIES

The discussion that follows refers regularly to six commentaries as primary resources. They are cited throughout by the author's last name except where noted:

Cranfield, C. E. B. *A Critical and Exegetical Commentary on the Epistle to the Romans*. International Critical Commentary. 2 volumes. Edinburgh: T & T Clark, 1980.
Dunn, J. D. G. *Romans*. Word Biblical Commentary. 2 volumes. Waco, TX: Word, 1988.
Jewett, R. *Romans*. Hermeneia. Minneapolis: Fortress, 2007.
Longenecker, R. N. *The Epistle to the Romans*. New International Greek Testament Commentary. Grand Rapids: Eerdmans, 2016.
Moo, D. J. *The Epistle to the Romans*. New International Commentary on the New Testament. Grand Rapids: Eerdmans, 1996.
Schreiner, T. R. *Romans*. Baker Exegetical Commentary on the New Testament. Grand Rapids: Baker, 1998.

Cranfield excels at setting out possible options on interpretive issues. His commentary is still a benchmark for the study of Romans. Dunn includes a relevant bibliography (through 1987) at the beginning of each section of his commentary. His focus on the "new perspective" on Paul tends to influence his interpretative decisions. Jewett provides bibliographic information through 2007. He uses rhetorical criticism to understand the letter's structure and provides a detailed analysis of the structure of each paragraph. Longenecker's commentary is the most recent and is particularly strong on providing Jewish and Jewish Christian background. He also interacts extensively with the history of scholarship on interpretive issues. Although Moo focuses on the English text, he includes extensive discussions of the Greek text in footnotes. Schreiner is particularly helpful in understanding the overall argument of the letter.

I. Letter Opening (1:1–17)

A. SALUTATION (1:1–7)

STRUCTURE

The salutation follows the normal letter pattern of "A (writer) to B (recipient), greeting." Paul expands the writer section (1:1–6) considerably, most likely because he had neither planted the church nor visited it. He uses that section to introduce both himself and the gospel he proclaims. The recipient (1:7a) and the greeting (1:7b) sections are comparable to those in Paul's other letters.

```
Παῦλος  δοῦλος Χριστοῦ Ἰησοῦ,
        κλητὸς ἀπόστολος
        ἀφωρισμένος εἰς εὐαγγέλιον θεοῦ,

ὃ προεπηγγείλατο
    διὰ τῶν προφητῶν αὐτοῦ
    ἐν γραφαῖς ἁγίαις
    περὶ τοῦ υἱοῦ αὐτοῦ
            τοῦ γενομένου
                ἐκ σπέρματος Δαυὶδ
                κατὰ σάρκα,
            τοῦ ὁρισθέντος υἱοῦ θεοῦ ἐν δυνάμει
                κατὰ πνεῦμα ἁγιωσύνης
                ἐξ ἀναστάσεως νεκρῶν,
            Ἰησοῦ Χριστοῦ τοῦ κυρίου ἡμῶν,
                    δι᾽ οὗ ἐλάβομεν χάριν καὶ ἀποστολὴν
                        εἰς ὑπακοὴν πίστεως
                        ἐν πᾶσιν τοῖς ἔθνεσιν
                        ὑπὲρ τοῦ ὀνόματος αὐτοῦ,
                            ἐν οἷς ἐστε καὶ ὑμεῖς κλητοὶ Ἰησοῦ Χριστοῦ,

πᾶσιν τοῖς οὖσιν ἐν Ῥώμῃ   ἀγαπητοῖς θεοῦ,
                            κλητοῖς ἁγίοις,
```

χάρις ὑμῖν καὶ εἰρήνη
ἀπὸ θεοῦ πατρὸς ἡμῶν καὶ κυρίου Ἰησοῦ Χριστοῦ.

VERSE 1

Παῦλος δοῦλος Χριστοῦ Ἰησοῦ

On Παῦλος, see Longenecker (48–50). Δοῦλος (nom. sg. masc. of δοῦλος, -οῦ, ὁ, "slave") stands in apposition to Παῦλος—as do κλητός and ἀφωρισμένος—and is best understood in the positive sense of one subject to a superior, especially God (BDAG 260b). Paul also introduces himself as δοῦλος in Philippians and Titus; the term suggests total ownership and obedience. The genitive phrase Χριστοῦ Ἰησοῦ modifies δοῦλος and is possessive ("belonging to") as well as objective ("one who serves"). Χριστός Ἰησοῦς occurs fifteen times elsewhere in Romans (cf. thirteen times for Ἰησοῦς Χριστός and thirty-six times for Χριστός) and is best understood as a title, "Messiah Jesus" (Longenecker 52–53). Despite comparatively weak manuscript support ($\mathfrak{P}^{10}$, B, 81), UBS[5] gives the reading a {B} rating (cf. Metzger 446), which agrees with Paul's tendency to prefer Χριστοῦ Ἰησοῦ (85 times) over Ἰησοῦ Χριστοῦ (25 times). Among others, the LXX describes Moses (2 Kgs 18:12; Rev 15:3), Joshua (Josh 24:29), and David (Ps 35:1) as δοῦλος κυρίου.

κλητὸς ἀπόστολος

Κλητός, -ή, -όν designates "God's gracious call to life and salvation, which is always at the same time a call to faith, obedience, service" (Cranfield 51). Dunn (and most EVV) understand κλητὸς ἀπόστολος as "called to be an apostle" (8); Porter suggests "a called apostle" (84). God issues the divine summons (1 Cor 1:1; Gal 1:15; 2 Tim 1:9). Paul uses ἀπόστολος with three nuances: (1) a messenger sent on a specific task (Phil 2:25), (2) a commissioned missionary (Rom 16:7), and (3) one of the Twelve called directly by Christ (1 Cor 15:7). Here, Paul aligns himself with the third group as one who saw the risen Christ (cf. 1 Cor 9:1–2), received his commission directly from Christ (cf. Gal 1:1), and had his ministry validated by the signs and wonders of an apostle (cf. 2 Cor 12:12). "Apostle" is the most common self-designation in Paul's salutations (1 Cor 1:1; 2 Cor 1:1; Gal 1:1; Eph 1:1; Col 1:1; 1 Tim 1:1; 2 Tim 1:1).

ἀφωρισμένος εἰς εὐαγγέλιον θεοῦ

The substantival participle ἀφωρισμένος (nom. sg. masc. of pf. pass. ptc. of ἀφορίζω, "set apart") further explains Παῦλος as "one who has been set apart" (divine pass.) for the work to which he was called (Gal 1:15; cf. Acts 13:2). In the LXX, God set apart both the Levites and Israel for special service (Num 8:11; Lev 20:26). The specific purpose (εἰς + acc.) for which Paul has been set apart relates to the εὐαγγέλιον (acc. sg. neut. of εὐαγγέλιον, -ου, τό, "gospel") that originates with (gen. of source) and is about (obj. gen.) θεοῦ (Schreiner 37). Cranfield suggests that εὐαγγέλιον includes both the message of the good news and the activity of preaching that message (54 n. 2). Prepositional phrases commonly omit the article when the object is sufficiently definite (cf. BDF §255).

VERSE 2

ὃ προεπηγγείλατο διὰ τῶν προφητῶν αὐτοῦ ἐν γραφαῖς ἁγίαις

The relative clause introduced by ὅ (acc. sg. neut. of rel. pron. ὅς, ἥ, ὅ) further describes εὐαγγέλιον. The prefix προ- and the indirect middle make προεπηγγείλατο (3 sg. aor. mid. indic. of dep. προεπαγγέλλομαι, "promise from the beginning") doubly emphatic ("he himself promised ahead of time"); the only other NT occurrence is in 2 Corinthians 9:5. The agents (διά + gen.) God used to "pre-promise" the gospel were τῶν προφητῶν αὐτοῦ ("his prophets"). The article points to the prophets as a class (generic); αὐτοῦ is possessive ("belonging to") as well as subjective ("sent by"). These prophets are the OT writers, because the means (ἐν + dat.) by which the promise was recorded is γραφαῖς ἁγίαις ("the holy Scriptures"). This verse is Paul's only use of the full phrase, although γραφαῖς (dat. pl. fem. of γραφή, -ῆς, ἡ, "writing") occurs elsewhere (Rom 15:5; 16:26; 1 Cor 15:3, 4). The absence of the art. might be qualitative (Murray 4) or, more likely, continues the style of 1:1 (Cranfield 56 n. 8).

VERSE 3

περὶ τοῦ υἱοῦ αὐτοῦ

The gospel concerns (περί + gen.) God's Son. The article identifies the Son as one-of-a-kind (monadic); αὐτοῦ is anaphoric, referring back to θεοῦ (1:1). Paul calls Jesus υἱός 17 times, using various modifiers; "his Son" (Rom 1:3, 9; 5:10; 8:29; 1 Cor 1:9; Gal 1:16; 4:4, 6; Col 1:13) and "his own Son" (Rom 8:3, 32) are the most common. The focus is on the close relationship between God and Jesus (Dunn 11). See 1:4 on the title "Son of God."

τοῦ γενομένου ἐκ σπέρματος Δαυὶδ κατὰ σάρκα

The adjectival participle τοῦ γενομένου (gen. sg. masc. of aor. mid. ptc. of dep. γίνομαι, "be, exist, come into being") modifies υἱοῦ. The repetition of the article is common with the attributive participle (cf. R 778) and places emphasis on it (cf. BDF §270). Γίνομαι is more general than γεννάω ("to give birth") and highlights the state of being rather than the event of giving birth (Dunn 12). In one respect (κατά + acc.), Jesus's origin was human, with σάρκα (acc. sg. fem. of σάρξ, σαρκός, ἡ, "flesh") indicating human lineage (cf. Rom. 4:1; 9:3, 5, 8; 11:14), not human nature that is hostile to God (cf. Rom 8:4, 5, 12, 13). Specifically, he was a descendant (ἐκ σπέρματος) of Δαυίδ (indecl. gen.) and, therefore, in the messianic line (2 Sam 7:12–16; cf. John 7:42). Longenecker notes that the connection between Christ and David is rare in Paul's letters (65).

VERSE 4

τοῦ ὁρισθέντος υἱοῦ θεοῦ

The participle τοῦ ὁρισθέντος (gen. sg. masc. of aor. pass. ptc. of ὁρίζω, "appoint, determine") is parallel to τοῦ γενομένου and, therefore, adjectival. Elsewhere in the NT, ὁρίζω consistently means "to appoint, determine" (Luke 22:22; Acts 2:23; 10:42; 11:29; 17:26, 31; Heb 4:7). The anarthrous phrase υἱοῦ θεοῦ ("Son of God") is monadic. Υἱοῦ is a predicate genitive, and θεοῦ is a genitive of relationship. Paul uses the full title "Son of God" four other times (2 Cor 1:19; Gal 2:20; Eph 4:13; 1 Thess 1:10). Jewett designates it a royal title and proposes that both υἱός θεοῦ and ὁρίζω are derived from the royal decree language of Psalm 2:7 (104).

ἐν δυνάμει

Although Jewett links ἐν δυνάμει to ὁρισθέντος as instrumental (107), most other commentators link it to υἱοῦ θεοῦ (Cranfield 62; Dunn 14; Longenecker 69; Schreiner 42). Cranfield notes that elsewhere in the NT the phrase has the sense "invested with power" (62); Dunn suggests "in executive authority" (14). The preposition ἐν designates state/condition and could be translated "clothed with" (cf. BDAG 327b); the absence of the article makes δυνάμει (dat. sg. fem. of δύναμις, -εως, ἡ, "power") qualitative. The noun itself carries the sense of might that works wonders (BDAG 262d) and is also used to describe Jesus's earthly ministry (Acts 10:38). When the prepositional phrase is linked with ὁρισθέντος υἱοῦ θεοῦ, it highlights the power inherent in Jesus's enthronement as messianic king.

κατὰ πνεῦμα ἁγιωσύνης

The parallel between this phrase and κατὰ σάρκα (1:3) has been understood as a contrast between Jesus's human and divine natures, a contrast between Jesus's outward qualifications and inward perfection, or a contrast between Jesus's preresurrection (physical) and postresurrection (spiritual) modes of existence. Each of these interpretations sees πνεῦμα (acc. sg. neut. of πνεῦμα, -ατος, τό, "spirit") as referring to Jesus's personal spirit, with ἁγιωσύνης (gen. sg. fem. of ἁγιωσύνη, -ης, ἡ, "holiness") attributing that quality to his spirit (e.g., Longenecker 72–75, "his spirit of holiness"). Since πνεῦμα ἁγιωσύνης is a literal translation of the Hebrew *ruach qodesh* (MT, Ps 51:13; Isa 63:10–11), however, it should be understood as a reference to the Holy Spirit (cf. Cranfield 62–64). When taken with the preceding phrase's reference to power and the following phrase's reference to the resurrection, therefore, the contrast is between Jesus's humiliation in taking on "flesh" and his exaltation as the one with all power who sends the Holy Spirit.

ἐξ ἀναστάσεως νεκρῶν

Having previously referred to Jesus's human birth (1:3), Paul now refers to his resurrection. (Note the parallel with ἐκ σπέρματος Δαυίδ.) Ἐκ + genitive marks temporal sequence (Schreiner 44; cf. BDAG 297d) and may be translated "at the time of." Even without the article, *ἀναστάσεως* (gen. sg. fem. of *ἀναστάσις*, -εως, ἡ, "resurrection") is definite (cf. Longenecker 76). The genitive *νεκρῶν* indicates separation—"out of, from among dead ones"—and is comparable to the more common *ἐκ νεκρῶν* (cf. Rom 4:24; 6:4, 9; 7:4; 8:11; 10:7, 9). Jesus's resurrection inaugurates his exaltation and marks the key turning point in salvation history.

Ἰησοῦ Χριστοῦ τοῦ κυρίου ἡμῶν

Ἰησοῦ Χριστοῦ (gen. sg. masc.) is in apposition to *τοῦ υἱοῦ αὐτοῦ* (1:3) and frames the extended description of Jesus. *Τοῦ κυρίου* (gen. sg. masc. of *κύριος*, -ου, ὁ, "lord") is in apposition to *Ἰησοῦ Χριστοῦ* and serves as the concluding title in Paul's list. The article identifies Jesus Christ as the only *κύριος* worthy of consideration (*par excellence*). The personal pronoun *ἡμῶν* denotes those who are subject to Jesus (gen. of subord.). LXX regularly translates the divine name using *κύριος* (*TDNT* 3.1058–59). Paul calls Jesus *κύριος* 200+ times and incorporates it into the longer title frequently, using both the word order here (cf. 5:21; 7:25) and different word order (e.g., 6:23; 8:39). Cranfield says it "designates the glorified Christ, the incarnate Son of God, placed close to the Father and at the right hand of His majesty, to whom His believers render adoring worship" (65).

VERSE 5

δι' οὗ ἐλάβομεν χάριν καὶ ἀποστολήν

Christ (antecedent of *οὗ*, gen. sg. masc. of rel. pron. *ὅς, ἥ, ὅ*) is also the agent (*διά* + gen.) "through whom" Paul received his role as an apostle. *Ἐλάβομεν* (1 pl. aor. act. ind. of *λαμβάνω*, "receive") is an epistolary aorist and refers to Paul alone (cf. Rom 3:8–9; 1 Cor 9:11; 2 Cor 1:12; 1 Thess 3:1–2); the aorist tense is constative and refers to the event as a whole. Schreiner translates the compound direct object *χάριν καὶ ἀποστολήν* as "gracious apostleship" to reflect the hendiadys (33; cf. BDF §442.16). A parallel construction in Romans 15:15 suggests "grace given in order to become an apostle" (cf. Jewett 109). *Ἀποστολή*, -ῆς, ἡ is the office of an apostle/special emissary (BDAG 121d); it is also a "ministry" (cf. Acts 1:25). See 1:7 for *χάρις*.

εἰς ὑπακοὴν πίστεως

The purpose (*εἰς* + acc.) for which Christ placed Paul in the office of apostle relates to "the obedience of faith" (elsewhere only in Rom 16:26). Cranfield lists seven possible interpretations of *ὑπακοὴν πίστεως* (66). Most commentators lean toward a combination of genitive functions for *πίστεως* (gen. sg. fem. of *πίστις*, -εως, ἡ, "faith"). A "plenary genitive" (both subj. gen. and obj. gen.) understanding might be best: "obedience to the call of faith (the gospel) that results in a lifestyle of faithful obedience" (cf. Wallace 119–21). The ambiguity honors both Jewish (obedience) and Gentile (faith) concerns in Rome (Jewett 110). By repeating the same phrase in 16:26, Paul creates an *inclusio* that frames the letter (Longenecker 82).

ἐν πᾶσιν τοῖς ἔθνεσιν ὑπὲρ τοῦ ὀνόματος αὐτοῦ

The sphere (ἐν + dat.) of Paul's ministry is "among all the Gentiles." Πᾶσιν (dat. pl. neut. of πᾶς, πᾶσα, πᾶν, "all") highlights universal scope; τοῖς points to the class (generic) of non-Jewish groups within Rome and the empire (Jewett 111); ἔθνεσιν (dat. pl. neut. of ἔθνος, -ους, τό, "nation, people") occurs twenty-nine times in Romans and is best translated "Gentiles" (cf. Rom 11:13; Gal 1:16; 2:8). Paul ministers "for the sake of" (ὑπέρ + gen.) Jesus's name, which Dunn equates with his "reputation" (18) and Cranfield equates with his "glory" (67). Paul's perspective is a reminder that all ministry has God's glory as its focus.

VERSE 6

ἐν οἷς ἐστε καὶ ὑμεῖς κλητοὶ Ἰησοῦ Χριστοῦ

The relative pronoun οἷς (dat. pl. neut. of rel. pron. ὅς, ἥ, ὅ) refers back to the ἔθνεσιν "among whom" the readers are included. Most commentators see an indication that the Roman church is predominantly Gentile (e.g., Schreiner 36; contra Cranfield 68). Ἐστε (2 pl. pres. act. indic. of εἰμί, "be") is a simple equative; καί is adjunctive ("also," cf. R 1180); ὑμεῖς ("you") adds emphasis. See 1:1 for κλητός. The genitive Ἰησοῦ Χριστοῦ denotes possession ("belonging to Jesus Christ") rather than source "because God the Father always issues a divine call" (Longenecker 83; contra Cranfield 68). The expressed agent who calls is Ἰησοῦ Χριστοῦ. Cranfield notes that this verse is parenthetic but allows Paul to remind the Roman church that they are also within the scope of his apostolic ministry (67).

VERSE 7

πᾶσιν τοῖς οὖσιν ἐν Ῥώμῃ

The dative phrase πᾶσιν τοῖς οὖσιν identifies the recipients. Placing πᾶσιν first makes it emphatic and includes both the Gentile and Jewish Christians in Rome. The article is generic and is best understood with οὖσιν (masc. pl. dat. of pres. act. ptc. of εἰμί, "be"), although Jewett takes it with ἀγαπητοῖς (113). Ἐν Ῥώμῃ identifies the readers' location. Metzger gives the reading an {A} rating, attributing the variant either to an accident in transmission or to a deliberate omission to show the general application of the letter (446).

ἀγαπητοῖς θεοῦ, κλητοῖς ἁγίοις

Paul adds two appositives to describe the recipients. Ἀγαπητοῖς (dat. pl. masc. of ἀγαπητός, -ή, -όν, "beloved") is a verbal adjective of ἀγαπάω and denotes those who are dearly loved (BDAG 7b); θεοῦ is a genitive of agency (BDF §183) as seen in the fuller construction with a passive participle elsewhere (Col 3:12; 1 Thess 1:4; 2 Thess 2:13). See 1:1 for κλητός. Ἁγίοις (dat. pl. masc. of ἅγιος, -α, -ον, "holy") is also a verbal adjective that pertains to being separated or consecrated to the service of God (BDAG 11c) and is best translated "saints." Paul uses it elsewhere in reference to believers as a whole (Rom 8:27; 12:13; 15:25); LXX uses it in reference to those who have been specially chosen and set apart (Ps 15:3; 33:10; Isa 4:3; Dan 7:18; 8:24).

χάρις ὑμῖν καὶ εἰρήνη

The conventional greeting in Greek letters was χαίρειν ("to wish well, greeting," BDAG 1075b). Paul replaced χαίρειν with χάρις (nom. sg. fem. of χάρις, -ιτος, ἡ, "grace") and added εἰρήνη (nom. sg. fem. of εἰρήνη, -ης, ἡ, "peace") to it. Both are nominative absolutes found in introductory material. The personal pronoun ὑμῖν (dat. pl.) is anaphoric, pointing back to πᾶσιν τοῖς οὖσιν. Robertson suggests that the optative verb εἴη ("be") has dropped out (396); πληθυνείη ("be multiplied") occurs in 1 Peter 1:2; 2 Peter 1:2; Jude 2. In general, χάρις connotes a benevolent disposition toward someone (BDAG 1079b); the NT use focuses on divine unmerited favor, encompassing both an event and a state (*TDNT* 10.393–99). Εἰρήνη corresponds to the Hebrew *shalom* and connotes a state of well-being and wholeness (BDAG 287d). The combination χάρις . . . καὶ εἰρήνη, therefore, incorporates both Greek and Hebrew concepts.

ἀπὸ θεοῦ πατρὸς ἡμῶν καὶ κυρίου Ἰησοῦ Χριστοῦ

The sources (ἀπό + gen.) of grace and peace are the Father and the Son (cf. Cranfield 72; Longenecker 89). God is specifically designated πατρὸς ἡμῶν ("our Father")—Jesus's own way of addressing the Father (Matt 6:9; Luke 11:2; cf. Rom 8:14–17)—and occurs regularly in Paul's salutations (1 Cor 1:3; 2 Cor 1:2; Gal 1:3–4; Eph 1:2; Phil 1:2; Col 1:2; 1 Thess 1:1, 3; 2 Thess 1:1–2; Phlm 3). The connective καί ("and") places Jesus on an equal level with God the Father. The title κυρίου Ἰησοῦ Χριστοῦ differs only in form from the similar title in 1:4.

FOR FURTHER STUDY

1. Slave and Slavery (1:1)

Bartchy, S. S. *ABD* 6.65–73.

Bradley, K. *Slaves and Masters in the Roman Empire: A Study in Social Control*. Oxford: Oxford University Press, 1987.

Byron, J. *Slavery Metaphors in Early Judaism and Pauline Christianity*. Tübingen: Mohr Siebeck, 2003.

Combes, I. A. H. *The Metaphor of Slavery in the Writings of the Early Church from the New Testament to the Beginning of the Fifth Century*. Sheffield: Sheffield University Press, 1998.

Glancy, J. *Slavery in Early Christianity*. Oxford: Oxford University Press, 2002.

Harril, J. A. *Slaves in the New Testament: Literary, Social, and Moral Dimensions*. Minneapolis: Fortress, 2006.

Harris, M. J. *Slave of Christ: A New Testament Metaphor for Total Devotion to Christ.* Downers Grove, IL: InterVarsity, 2001.
Lyall, F. *Slaves, Citizens, Sons: Legal Metaphors in the Epistles*. Grand Rapids: Zondervan, 1984.
________. "Roman Law in the Writings of Paul—The Slave and the Freedman." *NTS* 17 (1970–71): 73–79.
Rengstorf, K. *TDNT* 2.261–80.
Rupprecht, A. W. "Attitudes on Slavery among the Church Fathers." Pages 261–77 in *New Dimensions in New Testament Studies*. Edited by R. N. Longenecker and M. C. Tenney. Grand Rapids: Zondervan, 1974.
________. *DPL* 881–83.
Russel, K. C. *Slavery as Reality and Metaphor in the Pauline Letters*. Rome: Catholic Book Agency, 1968.
Westermann, W. L. *The Slave Systems of Greek and Roman Antiquity*. Philadelphia: American Philosophical Society, 1955.
Wiedemann, T. *Greek and Roman Slavery*. London: Croom Helm, 1981.

2. Apostle and Apostleship (1:1)

Agnew, F. H. "On the Origin of the Term *Apostolos*." *CBQ* 38 (1976): 49–53.
________. "The Origin of the New Testament Apostle-Concept: A Review of Research." *JBL* 105 (1986): 75–96.
Ashcraft, M. "Paul's Understanding of Apostleship." *RevExp* 55 (1958): 400–12.
Barnett, P. W. *DPL* 45–51.
Barrett, C. K. *The Signs of an Apostle*. Philadelphia: Fortress, 1972.
________. "Shaliaḥ and Apostle." Pages 88–102 in *Donum Gentilicum: New Testatment Studies in Honor of David Daube*. Edited by E. Bammel, C. K. Barrett, and W. D. Davies. Oxford: Clarendon, 1978.
Brown, S. "Apostleship in the New Testament as an Historical and Theological Problem." *NTS* 30 (1984): 474–80.
Buhner, J.-A. *EDNT* 1.142–46.
Clark, A. C. "Apostleship: Evidence from the New Testament and Early Christian Literature." *EvRevTh* 13 (1989): 344–82.
Dorsey, D. "Paul's use of Ἀπόστολος." *ResQ* 28 (1986): 193–99.
Gavin, F. "Shaliach and *Apostolos*" *AThR* 9 (1927): 250–59.
Geldenhuys, J. N. *Supreme Authority*. London: Marshall, 1953.
Kirk, J. A. "Apostleship since Rengstorf: Towards a Synthesis." *NTS* 21 (1974–1975): 249–64.
Mosbech, H. "*Apostolos* in the New Testament." *Studia Theologica* 2 (1948): 166–200
Müller, D. and C. Brown. *NIDNTT* 1.126–37.
Rengstorf, K. H. *TDNT* 1.407–47.
Schmithals, W. *The Office of Apostle in the Early Church*. Translated by J. E. Steely. Nashville: Abingdon, 1969.
Schnackenburg, R. "Apostles Before and During Paul's Time." Pages 287–303 in *Apostolic History and the Gospel*. Edited by W. W. Gasque and R. P. Martin. Grand Rapids: Eerdmans, 1970.

3. Gospel (1:1)

Becker, U. *NIDNTT* 2.107–15.
Broyles, C. C. *DJG* 282–86.
Burrows, M. "The Origin of the Term 'Gospel.'" *JBL* 44 (1925): 21–33.
Dodd, C. H. *The Apostolic Preaching and Its Developments*. London: Hodder, 1936.
Fitzmyer, J. A. "The Gospel in the Theology of Paul." Pages 149–161 in *To Advance the Gospel*. Grand Rapids: Eerdmans, 1998.
Friedrich, G. *TDNT* 2.707–36.
Jervis, L. A., and P. Richardson. *Gospel in Paul: Studies on Corinthians, Galatians and Romans for Richard N. Longenecker*. Sheffield: Sheffield Academic Press, 1994.
Luter, A. B. *DPL* 369–72.
Martin, R. P. *ISBE* 2.529–32.
Spallek, A. J. "The Origin and Meaning of *Euangelion* in the Pauline Corpus." *CTQ* 57 (1993): 177–90.
Stagg, F. "Gospel in Biblical Usage." *RevExp* 63 (1966): 5–13.
Stuhlmacher, P. "The Pauline Gospel." Pages 149–72 in *The Gospel and the Gospels*. Edited by P. Stuhlmacher. Grand Rapids: Eerdmans, 1991.

4. Resurrection (1:4)

Adams, E. W. *EDBT* 593–97.
Callan, T. *Dying and Rising with Christ: The Theology of Paul the Apostle*. Mahwah, NJ: Paulist, 2006.
Charlesworth, J. H., C. D. Elledge, and J. L. Crenshaw. *Resurrection: The Origin and Future of a Biblical Doctrine*. New York: T&T Clark, 2006.
Dunn, J. D. G. *The Theology of Paul the Apostle*. Grand Rapids: Eerdmans, 2006.
Faw, C. E. "Death and Resurrection in Paul's Letters." *JBR* 27 (1959): 291–98.
Gaffin, R. B. *The Centrality of the Resurrection: A Study in Paul's Soteriology*. Grand Rapids: Baker, 1978.
Glasson, T. F. "Dying and Rising with Christ." *London Quarterly and Holborn Review* 186 (1961): 286–91.
Grundmann, W. *TDNT* 7.781–97.
Harris, M. J. *Raised Immortal: The Relation Between Resurrection and Immortality in New Testament Teaching*. Grand Rapids: Eerdmans, 1985.
Kreitzer, L. *DPL* 805–12.
Longenecker, R. N. *Life in the Face of Death: The Resurrection Message of the New Testament*. Grand Rapids: Eerdmans, 1998.
Meyer, B. F. "Did Paul's View of the Resurrection of the Dead Undergo Development?" *TS* 47 (1986): 363–87.
Nickelsberg, G. *Resurrection, Immortality, and Eternal Life in Intertestamental Judaism*. Cambridge, MA: Harvard University Press, 1972.
Stanley, D. M. *Christ's Resurrection in Pauline Soteriology*. Rome: Pontifico Instituto Biblico, 1961.
Tannehill, R. C. *Dying and Rising with Christ: A Study in Pauline Theology*. Berlin: Töpelmann, 1967.
Wilson, W. E. "The Development of Paul's Doctrine of Dying and Rising Again with Christ." *ExpTim* 42 (1930–31): 562–65.

Wedderburn, A. J. M. *Baptism and Resurrection: Studies in Pauline Theology against Its Graeco-Roman Background*. Tübingen: Mohr, 1987.

5. Gentiles (1:5)

Boers, H. *The Justification of the Gentiles: Paul's Letters to the Galatians and Romans*. Peabody, MA: Hendrickson, 1994.
Brown, R. E. "Not Jewish Christianity and Gentile Christianity but Types of Jewish/Gentile Christianity." *CBQ* 45 (1983): 74–79.
Campbell, W. S. *Paul's Gospel in an Intercultural Context: Jew and Gentile in the Letter to the Romans*. Frankfurt am Main: Peter Lang, 1991.
Chae, D. J.-S. *Paul as Apostle to the Gentiles: His Apostolic Self-Awareness and Its Influence on the Soteriological Argument in Romans*. Carlisle, UK: Paternoster, 1997.
de Lacy, D. R. *DPL* 335–39.
Donaldson, T. *Paul and the Gentiles: Remapping the Apostle's Convictional World*. Philadelphia: Fortress, 1997.
Downs, D. J. "'The Offering of the Gentiles' in Romans 15.16." *JSNT* 29 (2006): 173–86.
Gathercole, S. J. "A Law unto Themselves: The Gentiles in Romans 2.14–15 Revisited." *JSNT* 85 (2002): 27–49.
Hengel, M. *Jews, Greeks, and Barbarians: Aspects of the Hellenization of Judaism in the pre-Christian Period*. Philadelphia: Fortress, 1980.
Kaylor, R. D. *Paul's Covenant Community: Jew and Gentile in Romans*. Atlanta: John Knox, 1988.
Lieu, H. *Neither Jew nor Greek? Constructing Early Christianity*. Edinburgh: T & T Clark, 2002.
Stendahl, K. *Paul Among Jews and Gentiles*. Philadelphia: Fortress, 1976.
Stowers, S. *A Rereading of Romans: Justice, Jews and Gentiles*. New Haven, CT: Yale University Press, 1994.
Watson, F. *Paul, Judaism, and the Gentiles: Beyond the New Perspective*. Grand Rapids: Eerdmans, 2007.

6. Grace (1:7)

Breytenbach, C. *"Charis" and "Eleos" in Paul's Letter to the Romans*. Leuven: Peeters, 2009.
Conzelmann, H., and W. Zimmerli. *TDNT* 9.372–402.
Doughty, D. J. "The Priority of *Charis*: An Investigation of the Theological Language of Paul." *NTS* 19 (1972–73): 163–80.
Eastman, B. *The Significance of Grace in the Letters of Paul*. New York: Peter Lang, 1999.
Esser, H.-H. *NIDNTT* 2.115–24.
Hardman, O. *The Christian Doctrine of Grace*. New York: Macmillan, 1947.
Harrison, J. R. *Paul's Language of Grace in its Graeco-Roman Context*. Tübingen: Mohr Siebeck, 2003.
Lieu, J. M. "'Grace to you and Peace': The Apostolic Greeting." *BJRL* 68 (1985): 161–78.
Luter, A. B. *DPL* 372–74.
Manson, W. "Grace in the New Testament." Pages 33–60 in *The Doctrine of Grace*. Edited by W. T. Whitley. London: SCM, 1932.
Moffatt, J. *Grace in the New Testament*. New York: Long & Smith, 1932.
Smith, C. R. *The Bible Doctrine of Grace and Related Doctrines*. London; Epworth, 1956.

Torrance, T. F. *The Doctrine of Grace in the Apostolic Fathers*. Grand Rapids: Eerdmans, 1959.

HOMILETICAL SUGGESTIONS

Introductory Salutation (1:1–7)

1. The writer: the apostle Paul (1:1–5)
2. The recipients: the saints in Rome (1:6–7a)
3. The greeting: grace and peace (1:7b)

Paul, the Gospel, and Jesus (1:1–5)

1. Paul: a slave, separated for the gospel, an apostle to the Gentiles (1:1, 5)
2. The gospel: concerning Jesus, promised by the prophets, recorded in the Old Testament (1:2)
3. Jesus: Davidic Messiah, Son of God, our Lord (1:3–4)

B. THANKSGIVING (1:8–12)

STRUCTURE

The thanksgiving section consists of both the thanksgiving proper and a prayer report. The thanksgiving proper includes the expression of thanksgiving (1:8a) and the reason for it (1:8b). The prayer report includes the expression of prayer (1:9a–b), the content of the prayer (1:9c), and Paul's desire for a visit as the reason for the prayer (1:11–12).

Πρῶτον μὲν εὐχαριστῶ τῷ θεῷ μου
διὰ Ἰησοῦ Χριστοῦ
περὶ πάντων ὑμῶν
ὅτι ἡ πίστις ὑμῶν καταγγέλλεται ἐν ὅλῳ τῷ κόσμῳ.

μάρτυς γάρ μού ἐστιν ὁ θεός
ᾧ λατρεύω ἐν τῷ πνεύματί μου ἐν τῷ εὐαγγελίῳ τοῦ υἱοῦ αὐτοῦ

ὡς ἀδιαλείπτως μνείαν ὑμῶν ποιοῦμαι
πάντοτε
ἐπὶ τῶν προσευχῶν μου,
δεόμενος εἴ πως ἤδη ποτὲ εὐοδωθήσομαι
ἐν τῷ θελήματι τοῦ θεοῦ
ἐλθεῖν πρὸς ὑμᾶς.

ἐπιποθῶ γὰρ ἰδεῖν ὑμᾶς,
ἵνα τι μεταδῶ χάρισμα ὑμῖν πνευματικὸν
εἰς τὸ στηριχθῆναι ὑμᾶς
τοῦτο δέ ἐστιν συμπαρακληθῆναι ἐν ὑμῖν
διὰ τῆς ἐν ἀλλήλοις πίστεως ὑμῶν τε καὶ ἐμοῦ.

VERSE 8

Πρῶτον μὲν εὐχαριστῶ τῷ θεῷ μου

Used as an adverb of time, πρῶτον (neut. sg. acc. of πρῶτος, -η, -ον, "first") marks the first item in a sequence and may be translated "to begin with" (BDAG 893d). Jewett's suggestion that it denotes Paul's main purpose in writing seems unlikely (117). The postpositive particle μέν without δέ following adds emphasis (BDAG 630c; cf. Rom 3:2; 1 Cor 11:18). Εὐχαριστῶ (1 sg. pres. act. indic. of εὐχαριστέω, "give thanks") is a customary present denoting an action that happens on a regular basis; it takes a dative direct object (BDAG 415d). The definite article is monadic denoting "one of a kind." Cranfield notes that Paul uses τῷ θεῷ μου comparatively rarely (74; cf. 1 Cor 1:4; 2 Cor 12:21; Phil 1:3; 4:19; Phlm 4). The genitive pronoun μου denotes personal devotion rather than ownership or possession (cf. Dunn 28).

δὶα Ἰησοῦ Χριστοῦ περὶ πάντων ὑμῶν

The phrase διὰ Ἰησοῦ Χριστοῦ denotes the agent (διά + gen.) through whom Paul gives thanks and highlights his apostolic authority (Schreiner 49). It displaces the adverb πάντοτε, which subsequently appears in verse 10. He gives thanks "on behalf of" (περί + gen.) all the Roman believers (cf. BDF §229.1). Πάντων (gen. pl. masc. of πᾶς, πᾶσα, πᾶν, "all") echoes 1:5 and 1:7 and highlights Paul's inclusive focus (Longenecker 105).

ὅτι ἡ πίστις ὑμῶν καταγγέλλεται ἐν ὅλῳ τῷ κόσμῳ

Ὅτι introduces the reason for Paul's thanksgiving. The definite article frequently precedes abstract nouns. Some aspect of the recipients' faith is a common element in Paul's thanksgiving sections (cf. Eph 1:15–16; Col 1:3–4; 1 Thess 1:2–3; 2 Thess 1:3–4). Here, it is both the Romans' initial exercise of faith and their faithful life-style (cf. 1:5) that is repeatedly (iter. pres.) being proclaimed (3 sg. pres. pass. indic. of καταγγέλλω, "proclaim, announce"). The sphere (ἐν + dat.) in which that proclamation occurs is ὅλῳ τῷ κόσμῳ. Ὅλος, -η, -ον ("whole, entire, complete") regularly occurs before nouns with the art. (BDAG 704b). Although Cranfield views the phrase as hyperbolic (75 n. 2), Jewett notes that events in Rome were commonly reported throughout the empire (120). Schreiner suggests either the Pauline churches (cf. Rom 16:19) or the area from Jerusalem to Illyricum (Rom 15:19) as options (49).

VERSE 9

μάρτυς γάρ μού ἐστιν ὁ θεός

As further explanation (γάρ) of his interest in the Romans, Paul describes his prayers for them. Paul uses similar "witness formulas" (Moo 58) when he is particularly concerned to attest to the truth of what he is saying (cf. 2 Cor 1:23; Phil 1:8; 1 Thess 2:5, 10). Placing μάρτυς (nom. sg. masc. of μάρτυς, -υρος, ὁ, "witness") first makes it emphatic. Μου (obj. gen.) indicates that God testifies on Paul's behalf. The article marks θεός as the subject of εἰμί.

ᾧ λατρεύω ἐν τῷ πνεύματί μου ἐν τῷ εὐαγγελίῳ τοῦ υἱοῦ αὐτοῦ

The relative pronoun ᾧ (dat. sg. masc.) introduces a parenthetical comment about Paul's devotion to God. Λατρεύω (1 sg. pres. act. indic. of λατρεύω, "serve, worship") often describes the act of carrying out religious duties (*TDNT* 4.59–61) and includes Paul's prayers for the Romans within the scope of his apostolic ministry (cf. Rom 15:16). The manner (ἐν + dat.) by which Paul serves is τῷ πνεύματί μου ("by/with my spirit"). The definite article occurs regularly with the possessive pronoun Cranfield notes that πνεύματι (dat. sg. neut. of πνεῦμα, -ατος, τό, "spirit") can be understood in at least seven ways (76). Paul's own spirit is more likely than the Holy Spirit (e.g., KJV, RSV, NASB, NEB; contra Jewett 121); Schreiner understands it as "wholehearted service with all his being" (51; cf. Longenecker 110; cf. GNB, NIV, CEV). The sphere (ἐν + dat.) of that service is τῷ εὐαγγελίῳ (R 589). The definite article is anaphoric, pointing back to 1:1 where εὐαγγέλιον is anarthrous. Τοῦ υἱοῦ is an objective genitive ("about"); see 1:3 for "his Son."

ὡς ἀδιαλείπτως μνείαν ὑμῶν ποιοῦμαι

The particle ὡς serves as a marker of discourse content ("that") after μάρτυς (BDAG 1105c; cf. Phil 1:8; 1 Thess 2:10) and is equivalent to ὅτι (R 1032; Moo 59 n. 24). Paul uses the adverb ἀδιαλείπτως ("constantly, unceasingly") to describe prayer three other times (1 Thess 1:2; 2:13; 5:17). Placing μνείαν (acc. sg. fem. of μνεία, -ας, ἡ, "mention, remembrance") before the verb gives it emphasis; the content of what Paul prays regularly follows μνεία (cf. Eph 1:16–17; Phil 1:3–5; 1 Thess 1:2–3; 1 Tim 1:3–5; Phlm 4–6). The genitive pronoun ὑμῶν is objective ("about you"). The present of ποιοῦμαι (1 sg. pres. mid. indic. of ποιέω, "make") is either iterative or customary; the indirect middle shows that Paul takes special interest in the action.

VERSE 10

πάντοτε ἐπὶ τῶν προσευχῶν μου

Although Longenecker (112) and most EVV connect 1:10a with 1:9c (e.g., KJV, ASV, RSV, GNB, NIV), it is better understood with what follows. Jewett suggests that doing so recognizes the distinction between intercession and petition (122). Paul also uses πάντοτε ("always, at all times") in 1 Corinthians 1:4; Philippians 1:4; Colossians 1:3; 1 Thessalonians 1:2; and 2 Thessalonians 1:3. Ἐπί + genitive is temporal, denotes a period of time (R 603), and may be translated "at the time of" or "during." Προσευχή, -ῆς, ἡ ("prayer") is a general word for making requests of God (LN 33.178). The article is common with the possessive pronoun, and μου (subj. gen.) indicates that Paul himself is praying.

δεόμενος εἴ πως ἤδη ποτὲ εὐοδωθήσομαι

The participle δεόμενος (nom. sg. masc. of pres. mid. ptc. of dep. δέομαι, "ask, plead") is adverbial of time ("while"; contra Longenecker 112) and modifies ποιοῦμαι in 1:9. The present tense is either customary or iterative; the middle-voice emphasizes Paul's personal involvement. Δέομαι is a stronger word for prayer that denotes asking with urgency based on perceived need (LN 33.170). Εἴ πως ("if somehow") expresses hope rather than uncertainty (cf. Acts 27:12; Phil 3:11); ἤδη ποτέ ("now at last") is a marker of culmination (R 1147; BDAG 434d). Jewett notes that the combination both honors the audience and forestalls potential criticism if Paul is delayed (123). Εὐοδωθήσομαι (1 sg. fut. pass. indic. of εὐοδόω, "lead along a good road") may be understood either figuratively ("I will succeed/have things go well") or literally ("I will be granted a good journey"). Most commentators choose the former (e.g., Moo 59 n. 30), but Tobit 5:16 supports the latter.

ἐν τῷ θελήματι τοῦ θεοῦ ἐλθεῖν πρὸς ὑμᾶς

The means (ἐν + dat.) by which Paul will be granted a good journey is τῷ θελήματι τοῦ θεοῦ. The definite articles make the entire phrase monadic (cf. Wallace 224) and emphasize that his plans are dependent on God's will rather than his own. (Contrast the more common anarthrous construction; e.g., Rom 15:32; 2 Cor 8:5; 1 Thess 4:3; Col 4:12.) The infinitive ἐλθεῖν (aor. act. inf. of ἔρχομαι, "come") is constative and denotes result (R 1090). Πρὸς ὑμᾶς ("to you") marks Paul's anticipated destination.

VERSE 11

ἐπιποθῶ γὰρ ἰδεῖν ὑμᾶς

The reason (γάρ) Paul wants to go to Rome is his strong desire to see the letter's recipients. The progressive present of ἐπιποθῶ (1 sg. pres. act. indic. of ἐπιποθέω, "long for, desire") indicates action in progress at the time of writing. Paul uses the verb multiple times to denote "ardent desire" for his readers (Rom 15:23; 2 Cor 5:2; 9:14; Phil 1:8; 2:26; 1 Thess 3:6; 2 Tim 1:4). Jewett notes that Paul's use in connection with Christians goes beyond the more common reference to family members (123). The infinitive ἰδεῖν (aor. act. inf. of ὁράω, "see") is a constative aorist and completes ἐπιποθῶ; ὑμᾶς is the obj. of the inf.

ἵνα τι μεταδῶ χάρισμα ὑμῖν πνευματικόν

Paul introduces the purpose (ἵνα) of his visit in this verse and clarifies it in the next. The aorist subjunctive of μεταδῶ (1 sg. aor. act. subjunc. of μεταδίδωμι, "share") is normal with ἵνα (R 983; contra Jewett who says it is opt.). The dative of ὑμῖν expresses advantage ("for your benefit"). Pulling apart the words in the phrase τι χάρισμα πνευματικόν is a rhetorical technique that gives greater emphasis to the separated elements (BDF §473.1). The indefinite pronoun τι ("some kind of") suggests that Paul is reluctant to spell out explicitly what he wants to say until he develops his argument more fully in the letter body (Longenecker 118). Dunn notes that πνευματικόν (acc. sg. neut. of πνευματικός, -ή, -όν, "spiritual") is redundant and therefore emphatic (30). The adjective corresponds to the divine Spirit but is used of impersonal things (BDAG 837a). Χαρισμά, -τος, τό ("gift") denotes something that is freely and graciously given (BDAG 1081a) and occurs in Romans with at least four nuances (Longenecker 114). In this context it most likely refers to a general spiritual benefit rather than a specific gift from the list in Romans 12:3–8. Longenecker follows Denney and Fee in suggesting that Paul is referring to the understanding of the gospel he presents in the letter (117).

εἰς τὸ στηριχθῆναι ὑμᾶς

Εἰς τό + infinitive indicates purpose (R 991); the accusative pronoun ὑμᾶς functions as the subject of στηριχθῆναι (aor. pass. inf. of στηρίζω, "confirm, establish, strengthen"); the translation is "in order for you to be strengthened" (cf. BDF §406). Στηρίζω carries the idea of causing to be inwardly firm or committed (BDAG 945b).

God is the one who strengthens (divine pass., Dunn 31), although the means of strengthening is specified in the next verse.

VERSE 12

τοῦτο δέ ἐστιν συμπαρακληθῆναι ἐν ὑμῖν

Τοῦτο δέ ἐστιν occurs only here in the NT (τοῦτ' ἔστιν elsewhere). Inserting δέ ("but, now") indicates that Paul is expanding what he has written in verse 11 rather than simply repeating it. The infinitive συμπαρακληθῆναι (aor. pass. inf. of συμπαρακαλέω, "encourage together") is parallel to στηριχθῆναι and also indicates purpose. Adding the preposition συμ- ("with") is the first of more than twenty such compounds in Romans, highlighting close identification both with other believers (e.g., 15:30) and with Christ (e.g., 6:4–8; 8:17, 29). Ἐν ὑμῖν ("among you") is local (Cranfield 81).

διὰ τῆς ἐν ἀλλήλοις πίστεως ὑμῶν τε καὶ ἐμοῦ

The means (διά + gen.) by which Paul and the Romans will be encouraged is the faith they share (Moo 60 n. 41). The article agrees with the abstract noun πίστις and brackets the prepositional phrase that modifies it. Ἐν ἀλλήλοις is best translated "mutual" (cf. BDAG 326d). That mutuality is highlighted by the correlated subjective genitives that follow ("both yours and mine"). The possessive pronoun ἐμοῦ is emphatic and always occurs with another genitive (BDF §284).

FOR FURTHER STUDY

7. Pauline Thanksgivings (1:8)

Arzt, P. "The 'Epistolary Introductory Thanksgiving' in the Papyri and in Paul." *NovT* 36 (1994): 29–46.

Mullins, T. Y. "The Thanksgivings of Philemon and Colossians." *NTS* 30 (1984): 288–93.

O'Brien, P. T. *DPL* 68–71.

________. "Thanksgiving and the Gospel in Paul." *NTS* 21 (1974–75): 144–55.

________. *Introductory Thanksgivings in the Letters of Paul*. Leiden: Brill, 1977.

________. "Thanksgiving within the Structure of Pauline Theology." Pages 50–66 in *Pauline Studies*. Edited by D. A. Hagner and M. J. Harris. Grand Rapids: Eerdmans, 1980.

Pao, D. W. *Thanksgiving: An Investigation of a Pauline Theme*. Downers Grove, IL: InterVarsity, 2003.

Reed, J. T. "Are Paul's Thanksgivings 'Epistolary'?" *JSNT* 61 (1996): 87–99.

Sanders, J. T. "The Transition from Opening Epistolary Thanksgiving to Body in the Letters of the Pauline Corpus." *JBL* 81 (1962): 348–62.

Schubert, P. *Form and Function of the Pauline Thanksgivings*. Berlin: Topelmann, 1939.

8. Prayer in Paul (1:9)

Balentine, S. E. *Prayer in the Hebrew Bible: The Drama of the Divine-Human Dialogue*. Minneapolis: Fortress, 1993.

Bradshaw, P. F. *Daily Prayer in the Early Church.* London: SPCK, 1981.
Brown, C. *NIDNTT* 2.882–86.
Carson, D. A. *A Call to Spiritual Reformation: Priorities from Paul and His Prayers.* Grand Rapids: Baker, 1992.
Clowney, E. P. "A Biblical Theology of Prayer." Pages 136–73 in *Teach Us to Pray: Prayer in the Bible and the World.* Edited by D. A. Carson. Grand Rapids: Baker, 1990.
Coggan, F. D. *The Prayers of the New Testament.* New York: Harper and Row, 1967.
Hunter, W. B. *DPL* 725–34.
Longenecker, R. N. "Prayer in the Pauline Letters." Pages 28–52 in *Studies in Paul: Exegetical and Theological.* Sheffield: Sheffield Phoenix, 2004.
Mullins, T. Y. "Petition as a Literary Form." *NovT* 5 (1962): 46–54.
Peterson, D. G. "Prayer in Paul's Writings." Pages 84–101 in *Teach Us to Pray: Prayer in the Bible and the World.* Edited by D. A. Carson. Grand Rapids: Baker, 1990.
Schonweiss, H., and C. Brown. *NIDNTT* 2.873–75.
Stanley, D. M. *Boasting in the Lord. The Phenomenon of Prayer in Saint Paul.* New York: Paulist, 1973.
Wiles, G. P. *Paul's Intercessory Prayers.* Cambridge: Cambridge University, 1974.

HOMILETICAL SUGGESTIONS

Paul's Concern for the Romans (1:8–12)

1. He thanks God for them (1:8)
    a. Reason: Their faith is proclaimed (1:8b)
2. He prays for them (1:9–10)
    a. Manner: Constantly mentioning (1:9c)
    b. Time: During his prayers (1:10a)
    c. Request: For a good journey (1:10b)
3. He longs to see them (1:11–12)
    a. Purpose: To share a spiritual benefit (1:11b)
    b. Purpose: To be mutually encouraged (1:12)

The Fellowship of the Church Universal (1:8–12)

1. It is founded on faith (1:8, 12)
2. It is promoted by prayer (1:9–10)
3. It is strengthened through sharing (1:11–12)

C. OCCASION FOR WRITING (1:13–15)

STRUCTURE

Jewett labels this paragraph the *narratio* that states the facts on which the following appeals are based (127). Longenecker discusses at length the relationship between this paragraph and its context and concludes that the opening disclosure formula marks the start of the letter body (127–30). The paragraph consists of three sentences grouped into two sub-subsections: Paul's plan to visit (1:13) and how that visit relates to Paul's apostolic calling (1:14–15).

οὐ θέλω δὲ ὑμᾶς ἀγνοεῖν, ἀδελφοί,
    ὅτι πολλάκις προεθέμην ἐλθεῖν πρὸς ὑμᾶς, καὶ ἐκωλύθην ἄχρι τοῦ δεῦρο,
        ἵνα τινὰ καρπὸν σχῶ καὶ ἐν ὑμῖν
            καθὼς καὶ ἐν τοῖς λοιποῖς ἔθνεσιν.

  Ἕλλησίν τε καὶ βαρβάροις,
  σοφοῖς τε καὶ ἀνοήτοις
ὀφειλέτης εἰμί,

οὕτως τὸ κατ᾽ ἐμὲ πρόθυμον καὶ ὑμῖν τοῖς ἐν Ῥώμῃ εὐαγγελίσασθαι.

VERSE 13

οὐ θέλω δὲ ὑμᾶς ἀγνοεῖν, ἀδελφοί

Elsewhere in his letters, Paul uses similar disclosure formulas to introduce information of special importance (cf. Rom 11:25; 1 Cor 10:1; 12:1; 1 Thess 4:13). In several letters a disclosure formula marks the body opening (2 Cor 1:8; Gal 1:11; Phil 1:12; Col 2:1; 1 Thess 2:1; 2 Thess 2:1). The conjunction δέ is transitional ("now") rather than adversative. Θέλω (1 sg. pres. act. indic. of θέλω, "wish, want") is a gnomic present and has considerably stronger manuscript support than the variant οἴομαι (Metzger 447). The complementary infinitive ἀγνοεῖν (pres. act. inf. of ἀγνοέω) is a progressive present ("to continue being ignorant") and has the accusative pronoun ὑμᾶς as its subject. Ἀδελφοί ("brothers") is nominative plural but functions as a vocative of direct address. Cranfield notes that throughout Romans Paul uses direct address to heighten the sense of intimacy of what he is communicating (81–82; cf. 7:1; 8:12; 10:1; 11:25; 15:14; 16:17).

ὅτι πολλάκις προεθέμην ἐλθεῖν πρὸς ὑμᾶς

The content (ὅτι) of the information Paul wants to disclose concerns his plan to visit them. The adverb πολλάκις ("frequently, often") refers to a number of repeated points in time (BDAG 846b) and is placed emphatically (Longenecker 135). The verb προτίθημι ("plan, purpose, intend") is stronger than either θέλω or βούλομαι (Jewett 129; Cranfield 82) and denotes a clear sense of purpose (Moo 61 n. 44). The indirect middle intensifies Paul's personal commitment to the plan. The infinitive ἐλθεῖν (aor. act. inf. of dep. ἔρχομαι, "come") is complementary; the prepositional phrase πρὸς ὑμᾶς is spatial ("toward you").

καὶ ἐκωλύθην ἄχρι τοῦ δεῦρο

The conjuction καί is adversative (Longenecker 135) and introduces a parenthetical comment (BDF §465.1; R 1182). The aorist of ἐκωλύθην (1 sg. aor. pass. indic. of κωλύω, "hinder, prevent") is consummative and stresses the end of the hindrances Paul has encountered. The simple passive without an expressed agent is for rhetorical effect; Jewett suggests it indicates "circumstantial hindrance" (129 n. 27). Paul's comments later in the letter (15:22–24, 28–29) point to his missionary work in the eastern Mediterranean as the reason for his delay. The prepositional phrase ἄχρι τοῦ δεῦρο is a standard expression of time ("until now"); the article with an adverb acting as a noun is a common construction (R 547).

ἵνα τινὰ καρπὸν σχῶ καὶ ἐν ὑμῖν

The purpose (ἵνα + 1 sg. aor. act. subjunc. of ἔχω) of Paul's planned visit is τινὰ καρπόν. The indefinite pronoun (acc. sg. masc. of τις, "any, some") is adjectival and indicates a member of a class ("some kind of"). It might acknowledge that God gives the increase (cf. 1 Cor 3:6), or it might continue the deference of the previous verses. Paul uses the noun καρπός, -οῦ, ὁ eleven times in his letters, the adjective ἄκαρπος, -ον three times (1 Cor 14:14; Eph 5:11; Titus 3:14) and the compound verb καρποφορέω three times (Rom 7:4; Col 1:6, 10). The two literal uses occur in analogies (1 Cor 9:7; 2 Tim 2:6). The remaining uses are metaphorical and refer to the conduct of believers (e.g., Rom 6:22; Eph 5:9; Phil 1:11) or to the result of ministry (e.g., Rom 15:28; Phil 1:22; 4:17). The latter nuance best fits this verse. Καί is adjunctive ("also"); ἐν ὑμῖν is again local ("among you").

καθὼς καὶ ἐν τοῖς λοιποῖς ἔθνεσιν

The purpose for Paul's visit to Rome is not unique; it is comparable (καθώς) to his ministry elsewhere. That ministry is "even" (ascensive καί) "among" (local dat.) "the rest of the Gentiles." The article is anaphoric, pointing back to ἔθνεσιν in vv. 5–6; λοιπός, -ή, -όν includes the Romans within Paul's apostolic scope because he is the apostle to the Gentiles (cf. Rom 11:13).

VERSE 14

Ἕλλησίν τε καὶ βαρβάροις

The absence of a connecting conjunction (asyndeton) calls attention to the content of the sentence; placing the two pairs of datives first makes them emphatic (Longenecker 137). The paired conjunctions τε . . . καί ("both . . . and") bring together opposites (R 179) and echo the same pairing at the end of 1:12. Names of peoples are normally anarthrous (BDF §262.2; T 189). Ἕλλην, -ηνος, ὁ encompasses all those who had come under the influence of Greco-Roman culture (BDAG 318c) and expands ἔθνεσιν in 1:13. Βάρβαρος, -ον describes the uncultured alien tribes that could not speak Greek or Latin, including some of the inhabitants of Spain (*TDNT* 1.547–48).

σοφοῖς τε καὶ ἀνοήτοις

Adjectives used as nouns are frequently anarthrous (BDF §264.1); when they are, they identify a class (R 764). Σοφός, -ή, -όν denotes understanding that results in wise attitudes and conduct (BDAG 935c). In this context it might well point to those individuals shaped by Greco-Roman culture (Jewett 131). In contrast, ἀνόητος, -ον describes a person who is unintelligent, foolish, or dull-witted (BDAG 82a). Such a person was worthy of contempt because he or she could not make a constructive contribution to society (Jewett 132). Cranfield identifies five possible interpretations for the two pairs of opposites (83–85). The most natural sees all humanity described from two perspectives: culture and education.

ὀφειλέτης εἰμί

Paul uses ὀφειλέτης, -ου, ὁ two other times in Romans (8:12; 15:27). The noun describes a person who is under moral or social obligation (BDAG 742d). Schreiner concludes that the word underlines Paul's divine call as the apostle to the Gentiles (55). The use of the dative (Ἕλλησίν . . . βαρβάροις . . . σοφοῖς . . . ἀνοήτοις) with εἰμί indicates credit or discredit (T 239).

VERSE 15

οὕτως τὸ κατ᾽ ἐμὲ πρόθυμον

The adverb οὕτως ("so, in this manner") draws an inference from what precedes (BDAG 742c; Moo 62 n. 55) and makes clear that Paul's eagerness to visit Rome grows out of his sense of obligation to all humankind (cf. Cranfield 85). Jewett sets out three possible ways of understanding τὸ κατ᾽ ἐμὲ πρόθυμον (133); the most natural is that the phrase is the subject of the infinitive that follows. The article turns the neuter adjective (acc. sg. neut. of πρόθυμος, -ον, "eager, willing") into a noun and pulls the phrase together into a unit. Κατ᾽ ἐμέ is the equivalent of a genitive (R 608; BDF §224.1; cf. Phil 1:12), and the phrase may be translated "my eagerness" (NEB, NRSV) or, perhaps, "I am ready/eager" (KJV, ASV, RSV, NASB, GNB, NIV).

καὶ ὑμῖν τοῖς ἐν Ῥώμῃ εὐαγγελίσασθαι

Καί is ascensive ("also"); ὑμῖν is a dative of indirect object ("to you"). The definite article turns ἐν Ῥώμῃ into a noun (BDF §266.2) that stands in apposition to ὑμῖν ("to you who are in Rome"). Although two manuscripts omit the phrase, it is more likely that the original reading included it (Metzger 447). The infinitive εὐαγγελίσασθαι (aor. mid. inf. of εὐαγγελίζω, "proclaim the gospel") is epexegetical and explains πρόθυμον.

The middle voice is common with a mention of one who receives the message (BDAG 402c). The idea of "preaching the gospel" goes beyond the initial act of winning converts to include challenging believers to live in a manner worthy of the gospel (cf. Phil 1:27).

FOR FURTHER STUDY

9. Letters and Letter Writing (1:13)

Archer, R. L. "The Epistolary Form in the New Testament." *ExpTim* 68 (1951–52): 296–98.
Bahr, G. J. "Paul and Letter Writing in the First Century." *CBQ* 28 (1966): 465–77.
Bryskog, S. "Epistolography, Rhetoric and Letter Prescript: Romans 1.1–7 as a Test Case." *JSNT* 65 (1997): 27–46.
Doty, W. G. "The Classification of Epistolary Literature." *CBQ* 31 (1969): 183–99.
________. *Letters in Primitive Christianity.* Philadelphia: Fortress, 1973.
Exler, F. X. J. *The Form of the Ancient Greek Letter: A Study in Greek Epistolography.* Washington, DC: Catholic University of America, 1923.
Harvey, J. D. *Interpreting the Pauline Letters.* Grand Rapids: Kregel, 2012.
Jewett, R. "Romans as an Ambassadorial Letter." *Int* 36 (1982): 5–20.
Kerns, V. "Letter Writing—St. Paul's Way." *BibT* 68 (1973): 1326–28.
Klauck, H.-J. *Ancient Letters and the New Testament: A Guide to Context and Exegesis.* Waco, TX: Baylor University Press, 2006.
Longenecker, R. N. "On Reading a New Testament Letter: Devotionally, Homiletically, Academically." *Them* 20 (1994): 4–8.
________. "On the Form, Function and Authority of the New Testament Letters." Pages 281–97 in *Scripture and Truth.* Edited by D. A. Carson and J. D. Woodbridge. Grand Rapids: Zondervan, 1983.
O'Brien, P. T. *DPL* 550–53.
Roller, O. *Das Formular der paulinischen Briefe. Ein Beitrag zur Lehre vom antiken Briefe.* Stuttgart: Kohlhammer, 1933.
Stowers, S. K. *Letter Writing in Graeco-Roman Antiquity.* Philadelphia: Westminster, 1986.
Stirewalt, M. L. "The Form and Function of the Greek Letter-Essay." Pages 175–206 in *The Romans Debate.* Edited by K. Donfried. Minneapolis: Augsburg, 1977.
________. *Paul, the Letter Writer.* Grand Rapids: Eerdmans, 2003.
Weima, J. A. D. *DNTB* 640–44.
________. "Preaching the Gospel in Rome: A Study of the Epistolary Framework of Romans." Pages 337–66 in *Gospel in Paul: Studies on Corinthians, Galatians and Romans for Richard N. Longenecker.* Edited by L. A. Jervis and P. Richardson. Sheffield: Sheffield Academic Press, 1994.
White, J. L. *Light from Ancient Letters.* Philadelphia: Fortress, 1986.
________. "Saint Paul and the Apostolic Letter Tradition." *CBQ* 45 (1983): 433–44.
________. "Introductory Formulae in the Body of the Pauline Letter." *JBL* 90 (1971): 91–97.
_________. *The Form and Function of the Body of the Greek Letter.* Missoula, MT: Scholars Press, 1972.

HOMILETICAL SUGGESTIONS

Paul's Planned Visit to Rome (1:13–15)

1. Paul's intention to visit (1:13)
   a. Often planned
   b. Circumstantially hindered
   c. With an eye to fruit
2. Paul's reason to visit (1:14–15)
   a. Obligated to all humankind
   b. Eager to preach the gospel

Paul's Understanding of His Ministry (1:13–15)

1. Its Nature: An obligation to fulfill (1:14)
2. Its Scope: All the Gentiles (1:13d)
3. Its Purpose: To cultivate fruit (1:13c)
4. Its Means: Preaching the gospel (1:15)

D. THESIS (1:16–17)

STRUCTURE

Jewett labels these verses the *propositio* that sets out the basic contention of the argument (135). Most commentators agree that the verses state the thesis or theme for the letter (e.g., Dunn 35). Grammatically, they consist of four clauses that develop Paul's thesis step-by-step, concluding with scriptural confirmation from the OT.

Οὐ γὰρ ἐπαισχύνομαι τὸ εὐαγγέλιον,
δύναμις γὰρ θεοῦ ἐστιν εἰς σωτηρίαν παντὶ τῷ πιστεύοντι,
Ἰουδαίῳ τε πρῶτον καὶ Ἕλληνι.
δικαιοσύνη γὰρ θεοῦ ἐν αὐτῷ ἀποκαλύπτεται ἐκ πίστεως εἰς πίστιν,
καθὼς γέγραπται, Ὁ δὲ δίκαιος ἐκ πίστεως ζήσεται.

VERSE 16

Οὐ γὰρ ἐπαισχύνομαι τὸ εὐαγγέλιον

The gospel is the reason (γάρ) Paul is eager to go to Rome, and he is not ashamed to preach it, even in the capital of the empire. Οὐ ἐπαισχύνομαι (1 sg. pres. mid. indic. of dep. ἐπαισχύνομαι, "be ashamed") echoes God's promise in Isa 28:16 (cf. Rom 9:33; 10:11) as well as Jesus's statement in Mark 8:38. Schreiner notes that elsewhere Paul contrasts being ashamed with suffering for the gospel (2 Tim 1:8, 12), and so the idea must include the overcoming of fear (60). Longenecker argues that it is best to view Paul's statement in the context of criticisms of his message and explores possible options (159–63). The article with εὐαγγέλιον is *par excellence* (cf. 1:1, 9, 15). See 1:1 for εὐαγγέλιον.

δύναμις γὰρ θεοῦ ἐστιν εἰς σωτηρίαν

The saving power of the gospel is the reason (γάρ) Paul is not ashamed. A definite predicate nominative is usually anarthrous (Wallace 264); θεοῦ is a genitive of source. Εἰς + accusative denotes result (Schreiner 60). God's power is a recurring theme in Paul's letters (Rom 1:20; 9:17; 1 Cor 1:18, 24; 2:5; 6:14; 2 Cor 4:7; 6:7; 13:4; 2 Tim 1:8). Cranfield describes it as "God's effective power active in the world of men to bring about deliverance from His wrath in the final judgment and reinstatement in that glory of God which was lost through sin" (89). Paul always uses σωτηρία, -ας, ἡ and σῴζω to speak of spiritual deliverance (Moo 67; cf. *TDNT* 8:992), especially deliverance from final destruction (e.g., Rom 5:9; 13:11).

παντὶ τῷ πιστεύοντι

The adjective πᾶς, πᾶσα, πᾶν ("all, every") occurs sixty-eight times in Romans and highlights the universal scope of Paul's gospel. It is usually articular when used with a substantival participle (R 773, T 151). Since the participle is singular (dat. sg. masc. of pres. act. ptc. of πιστεύω, "believe"), the phrase should be translated "to every one who is believing." The progressive present highlights "continuing orientation and motivation for life" (Dunn 40). The cognate noun has already occurred in 1:5, 8, 12; see 1:17 for πιστίς.

Ἰουδαίῳ τε πρῶτον καὶ Ἕλληνι

Two nouns in apposition further specify the participle. Ἰουδαῖος, -αία, -αῖον refers to one who is Jewish with respect to birth (BDAG 478d); see 1:15 for Ἕλλην, -ηνος, ὁ. Moo suggests that Paul uses the latter word because, for him, ἔθνη is always plural (68 n. 25; e.g., 2:14; 9:30; 15:9–12). The paired conjunctions τε . . . καί continue the style of 1:14 and emphasize the basic equality between Jew and Greek (Longenecker 167). The adverb πρῶτον (neut. sg. acc. of πρῶτος, -η, -ον, "first") balances παντί and, according to Schreiner, brings together both salvation historical reality and Paul's missiological practice (62).

VERSE 17

δικαιοσύνη γὰρ θεοῦ ἐν αὐτῷ ἀποκαλύπτεται

The way the gospel reveals God's righteousness explains (γάρ) why it is God's saving power. Δικαιοσύνη, -ης, ἡ regularly translates *tsadak* and its cognates in the LXX (Cranfield 94). The genitive of θεοῦ can be understood either as source (T 211) or as subjective (BDF §449). Cranfield gives four arguments for the former and five arguments for the latter (96–97). If the genitive denotes source, the phrase "God's righteousness" is forensic and describes a gift that results in a changed status. If the genitive is subjective, the phrase is transformative and describes an activity that results in a changed life. Schreiner concludes that the best understanding includes both aspects (64–66; cf. Longenecker 175–76; Wallace suggests the term "plenary genitive," although he does not cite this verse as an example). The instrument (ἐν + dat.) by which God's righteousness is revealed is the gospel; αὐτῷ is anaphoric, pointing back to εὐαγγέλιον at the beginning of 1:16. Ἀποκαλύπτεται (3 sg. pres. pass. indic. of ἀποκαλύπτω, "reveal") is a progressive present (Schreiner 62) and a divine passive (Dunn 43). The verb itself denotes the activity of causing something to be known fully (BDAG 112a). Moo distinguishes between a cognitive understanding (disclosing aspects of God's redemptive plan) and a historical understanding (unfolding God's redemptive plan in human history); he concludes that the latter should be preferred (69).

ἐκ πίστεως εἰς πίστιν

Cranfield sets out twelve interpretations of this phrase (99–100). Schreiner (citing Silva) notes that in ambiguous constructions the interpretation adding the least to the meaning of a phrase should be preferred (72). If the two prepositions denote source/starting point (ἐκ + gen.) and extent/end (εἰς + acc.), the combination means "from first to last" (NIV) or "from beginning to end" (GNB). Paul uses the noun πίστις, -εως, ἡ forty times and the verb πιστεύω twenty-one times in Romans. The idea includes both acceptance of truth (e.g., 4:3; 6:8; 10:9, 16) and reliance upon truth (e.g., 4:5, 24; 9:33; 10:11). As part of Paul's thesis, the phrase highlights the centrality of faith in the letter.

καθὼς γέγραπται, Ὁ δὲ δίκαιος ἐκ πίστεως ζήσεται

In support of his statement that the revelation of God's righteousness relates solely to faith, Paul quotes Habakkuk 2:4 (cf. Gal 3:11; Heb 10:38). He uses the phrase καθὼς γέγραπται ("just as it has been written") thirteen other times in Romans to introduce direct OT quotations. Longenecker notes that most occurrences "appear in sections where Paul is arguing in a Jewish and/or Jewish Christian manner" (181). The intensive perfect of γέγραπται (3 sg. pf. pass. indic. of γράφω, "write") emphasizes the present results of God's past action (divine pass.). Paul retains the conjunction δέ (without its adversative nuance) but omits the pronoun μου (present in the LXX). The article marks the adjective δίκαιος ("righteous, just") as the subject; ἐκ πίστεως ("out of/by faith") denotes cause (R 599); ζήσεται (3 sg. fut. mid. indic. of ζάω, "live") is a gnomic future ("will live"). Although ζάω can denote the way a person behaves, the idea here is more likely "to live in a transcendent sense" (BDAG 425d); Longenecker views it as equivalent to the experience of salvation (186). RSV, NEB, GNB, CEV, and NJB (along with Cranfield 102) take ἐκ πίστεως with ὁ δίκαιος, while KJV, NASB, NIV, and ESV (along with Jewett 146) take it with ζήσεται. Dunn argues that Jewish interpretive practices of Paul's day would include the possibility of taking the phrase with both the subject and the verb (45).

FOR FURTHER STUDY

10. Righteousness (1:17)

Barnett, P. *Romans: The Revelation of God's Righteousness*. Fearn: Christian Focus, 2003.
Brown, C. and H. Seebass. *NIDNTT* 3.360–73.
Bultmann, R. "ΔΙΚΑΙΟΣΥΝΗ ΘΕΟΥ." *JBL* 83 (1964): 12–16.
Käsemann, E. "The Righteousness of God in Paul." Pages 168–82 in E. Käsemann, *New Testament Questions of Today*. Philadelphia: Fortress, 1969.
Kertelge, K. *EDNT* 1.325–34.
Ladd, G. E. "Righteousness in Romans." *SwJT* 19 (1976): 6–17.
Longenecker, R. N. "'The Righteousness of God' and 'Righteousness' in Paul." Pages 168–76 in *The Epistle to the Romans*. Grand Rapids: Eerdmans, 2016.
McGrath, A. E. *DPL* 517–23.
Moo, D. J. "'Righteousness' Language in Paul." Pages 79–90 in *The Epistle to the Romans*. Grand Rapids: Eerdmans, 1996.
Moxnes, H. "Honour and Righteousness in Romans." *JSNT* 32 (1988): 61–77.
Onesti, K. L., and M. T. Brauch. *DPL* 827–37.
Piper, J. *Counted Righteous in Christ: Should We Abandon the Imputation of Christ's Righteousness?* Wheaton, IL: Crossway, 2002.
Quell, G., and G. Schrenk. *TDNT* 2.174–225.

Reumann, J. *ABD* 5.736–73.

Seifrid, M. A. "Paul's Use of Righteousness Language against its Hellenistic Background." Pages 39–74 in *Justification and Variegated Nomism*. Volume 2. Grand Rapids: Baker, 2004.

Soards, M. L. "The Righteousness of God in the Writings of the Apostle Paul." *BTB* 15 (1985): 104–9.

Southall, D. *Rediscovering Righteousness in Romans: Personified dikaiosynē within Metaphoric and Narratorial Settings*. Tübingen: Mohr Siebeck, 2008.

Toon, P. *EDBT* 687–87.

Turner, G. "The Righteousness of God in Psalms and Romans." *SJT* 63 (2010): 285–301.

Vickers, B. *Jesus' Blood and Righteousness: Paul's Theology of Imputation*. Wheaton, IL: Crossway, 2006.

Watson, N. W. "Review Article: *The Meaning of Righteousnesss in Paul: A Linguistic and Theological Investigation*." *NTS* 20 (1973–74): 217–28.

Wright, S. K. "'The Righteousness of God' in Romans." *JBL* 99 (1980): 241–90.

Ziesler, J. A. *The Meaning of Righteousness in Paul: A Linguistic and Theological Investigation*. Cambridge: Cambridge University Press, 1972.

11. Faith (1:17)

Barth, G. *EDNT* 3.91–98.

Blackmon, E. C. *IDB* 2.222–34.

Bultmann, R. *TDNT* 6.174–222.

Campbell, D. A. "The Meaning of ΠΙΣΤΙΣ and ΝΟΜΟΣ in Paul: A Linguistic and Structural Perspective." *JBL* 111 (1992): 91–103.

Daalen, D. H. van. "Faith according to Paul." *ExpT* 87 (1975): 83–85.

Davies, G. N. Pages 25–30 in *Faith and Obedience in Romans: A Study in Romans 1–4*. Sheffield: *JSOT*, 1990.

Garlington, D. B. "The Obedience of Faith in the Letter to the Romans." *WTJ* 52 (1990): 201–24.

________. *The Obedience of Faith: A Pauline Phrase in Historical Context*. Tübingen: Mohr Siebeck, 1991.

________. *Faith, Obedience, and Perseverance: Aspects of Paul's Letter to the Romans*. Tübingen: Mohr Siebeck, 1994.

Lindsay, D. R. "The Roots and Development of the πιστ- Word Group as Faith Terminology." *JSNT* 49 (1993); 103–18.

Ljungman, H. *Pistis: A Study of Its Presuppositions and Its Meaning in Pauline Use*. Lund: Gleerup, 1964.

Machen, J. G. *What is Faith?* Grand Rapids: Eerdmans, 1962.

McBride, M. A. "Meaning of Faith." *CJT* 9 (1963): 20–28.

Michel, O. *NIDNTT* 1.587–606.

Morris, L. *DPL* 285–91.

Seifrid, M. A. *Justification by Faith: The Origin and Development of a Central Pauline Theme*. Leiden: Brill, 1992.

Swartz, H. L. *EDBT* 236–39.

12. Paul's Use of the Old Testament (1:17)

Beale, G. K. *The Right Doctrine from the Wrong Texts? Essays on the Use of the Old Testament in the New*. Grand Rapids: Baker, 1994.

________, and D. A. Carson. *Commentary on the New Testament Use of the Old Testament*. Grand Rapids: Baker, 2007.

Bruno, C. R. "Readers, Authors, and the Divine Author: An Evangelical Proposal for Identifying Paul's Old Testament Citations." *WTJ* 71 (2009): 311–21.

Dodson, J. R. "The Voices of Scripture: Citations and Personifications in Paul." *BBR* 20 (2010): 419–31.

Ellis, E. E. *Paul's Use of the Old Testament.* Edinburgh: Oliver and Boyd, 1957.

Evans, C. A., and J. A. Sanders. *Paul and the Scriptures of Israel.* Sheffield: Sheffield Academic Press, 1993.

Fitzmyer, J. A. "The Use of Explicit Old Testament Quotations in Qumran Literature and in the New Testament." *NTS* 7 (1960–1961): 297–333.

Hays, R. B. *Echoes of Scripture in the Letters of Paul.* Yale University Press, 1993.

Hooker, M. D. "Beyond the Things that are Written: St Paul's Use of Scripture." *NTS* 27 (1981): 295–309.

Hirss, I. "Paul's Understanding of the Old Testament in Romans: Some Exploratory Comments." *Journal of European Baptist Studies* 2 (2002): 23–28.

Kaiser, W. C., Jr. *Uses of the Old Testament in the New.* Chicago: Moody, 1985.

Litwak, K. D. "Echoes of Scripture? A Critical Survey of Recent Works on Paul's Use of the Old Testament." *Currents in Research* 6 (1998): 260–88.

Longenecker, R. N. *Biblical Exegesis in the Apostolic Period.* Grand Rapids: Eerdmans, 1975.

________. "Prolegomena to Paul's Use of Scripture in Romans." Pages 67–93 in *Studies in Paul: Exegetical and Theological.* Sheffield: Sheffield Phoenix, 2004.

Moyise, S. *Paul and Scripture: Studying the New Testament use of the Old Testament.* Grand Rapids: Baker, 2010.

Porter, S. E., and C. D. Stanley. *As It Is Written: Studying Paul's Use of Scripture.* Atlanta: Society of Biblical Literature, 2008.

Seifrid, M. A. "Romans." Pages 607–94 in *Commentary on the New Testament Use of the Old Testament.* Edited by G. K. Beale and D. A. Carson. Grand Rapids: Baker, 2007.

Silva, M. *DPL* 630–42.

Watson, F. "Scripture in Pauline Theology: How Far Down Does It Go?" *Journal of Theological Interpretation* 2 (2008): 181–92.

HOMILETICAL SUGGESTIONS

Paul's Confidence in the Gospel (1:16–17)

1. It is the expression of God's power (1:16)
   a. Resulting in salvation
   b. To everyone who believes
2. It is the revelation of God's righteousness (1:17)
   a. Entirely by faith
   b. Affirmed by God's Word

II. Letter Body (1:18–15:13)

A. THE REVELATION OF GOD'S RIGHTEOUSNESS (1:18–4:25)

1. God Reveals His Righteousness Through Wrath (1:18–3:20)

a. Because Humankind Suppresses God's Truth (1:18–23)

STRUCTURE

The opening paragraph of the letter body consists of three sentences (1:18–19; 1:20–21; 1:22–23). The first two have parallel structures, with opening statements supported by causal clauses phrased in terms of "knowing" God. The third sentence further explains the second and makes the transition to the next paragraph by introducing the "exchange" language that forms a key part of it.

Ἀποκαλύπτεται γὰρ ὀργὴ θεοῦ ἀπ' οὐρανοῦ ἐπὶ πᾶσαν ἀσέβειαν καὶ ἀδικίαν ἀνθρώπων τῶν τὴν ἀλήθειαν ἐν ἀδικίᾳ κατεχόντων,
    διότι τὸ γνωστὸν τοῦ θεοῦ φανερόν ἐστιν ἐν αὐτοῖς·
        ὁ θεὸς γὰρ αὐτοῖς ἐφανέρωσεν.

τὰ γὰρ ἀόρατα αὐτοῦ ἀπὸ κτίσεως κόσμου τοῖς ποιήμασιν νοούμενα καθορᾶται, ἥ τε ἀΐδιος αὐτοῦ δύναμις καὶ θειότης, εἰς τὸ εἶναι αὐτοὺς ἀναπολογήτους,
    διότι γνόντες τὸν θεὸν   οὐχ ὡς θεὸν ἐδόξασαν ἢ ηὐχαρίστησαν
        ἀλλ' ἐματαιώθησαν ἐν τοῖς διαλογισμοῖς αὐτῶν
        καὶ ἐσκοτίσθη ἡ ἀσύνετος αὐτῶν καρδία.

φάσκοντες εἶναι σοφοὶ ἐμωράνθησαν καὶ ἤλλαξαν τὴν δόξαν τοῦ ἀφθάρτου θεοῦ ἐν ὁμοιώματι εἰκόνος φθαρτοῦ ἀνθρώπου καὶ πετεινῶν καὶ τετραπόδων καὶ ἑρπετῶν.

VERSE 18

Ἀποκαλύπτεται γὰρ ὀργὴ θεοῦ ἀπ᾽ οὐρανοῦ

Paul now explains (γάρ) why the righteous person must live by faith: humankind's actions earn God's wrath rather than his righteousness (cf. Cranfield 108). Ὀργὴ θεοῦ is parallel to δικαιοσύνη θεοῦ in 1:17, with the genitive understood as both source (a judgment) and subjective (an action). Ὀργή, -ῆς, ἡ occurs eleven times in Romans, all denoting divine indignation directed at injustice, cruelty, and corruption (BDAG 720d; cf. *TDNT* 5.383–409). See Longenecker for a helpful discussion of God's wrath (201–2). Ἀποκαλύπτεται (3 sg. pres. pass. indic. of ἀποκαλύπτω, "reveal")—also parallel to 1:17—is a progressive present and a divine passive. Cranfield sees the parallelism extending to the gospel as the instrument by which God's wrath is revealed (110), but Longenecker disagrees (203). The location (ἀπό + gen.) from which the wrath is revealed is "heaven" (οὐρανός, -ου, ὁ), the transcendent dwelling place where God's throne is located (BDAG 738d; cf. Cranfield 111 n. 1). Jewett thinks it "improbable" that it is simply a way of referring to God himself (151 n. 22).

ἐπὶ πᾶσαν ἀσέβειαν καὶ ἀδικίαν ἀνθρώπων

The object against which (ἐπί + acc.) God's wrath is revealed is human irreligion and injustice. Καί pulls the nouns together so that πᾶσαν (acc. sg. fem. of πᾶς, πᾶσα, πᾶν, "all") encompasses both. The nouns also occur together in the LXX (Ps 73:6; Prov 11:5; Ezek 18:30; Hos 10:13; Mic 7:18). Ἀσέβεια, -ας, ἡ ("ungodliness") reflects the vertical dimension of lack of reverence for God (BDAG 141b), while ἀδικία, -ας, ἡ ("unrighteousness") reflects the horizontal dimension of lack of respect for his just order (Cranfield 112; contra Longenecker 204). The genitive of ἀνθρώπων is subjective.

τῶν τὴν ἀλήθειαν ἐν ἀδικίᾳ κατεχόντων

The genitive article marks the participle κατεχόντων (gen. pl. masc. of pres. act. ptc. of κατέχω, "suppress") as adjectival and serves to bracket the participial phrase. The present tense is progressive (Jewett 153), and the verb carries the idea of "hold down, stifle" (BDAG 532c). Τὴν ἀλήθειαν (acc. sg. fem. of ἀλήθεια, -ας, ἡ, "truth") is the object of the participle and denotes the ultimate truth of Christianity (BDAG 42c). The ἀδικία against which God reveals his wrath is also the means (ἐν + dat.) through which humankind suppresses his truth (Moo 103 n. 51).

VERSE 19

διότι τὸ γνωστὸν τοῦ θεοῦ φανερόν ἐστιν ἐν αὐτοῖς

The classical conjunction διότι ("for") provides a loose subordination (BDF §456.1) that indicates why something just stated can reasonably be considered valid (BDAG 251c). The neuter article with a substantized adjective is common (BDF §263.2, R 763); γνωστός, -ή, -όν denotes something that is capable of being known (BDAG 204b;

cf. Gen 2:9; Sir 21:7). Wallace argues that the passive ending of γνωστόν eliminates τοῦ θεοῦ as an objective genitive because God is not directly known (118 n. 128). The genitive is better understood as denoting reference, and the phrase may be translated as "that which can be known with reference to God." Bringing φανερόν ("readily evident") forward adds emphasis. Longenecker argues that ἐν + dative is parallel to the simple dative ("to them") in the next line and, therefore, is equivalent to an indirect object (206).

ὁ θεὸς γὰρ αὐτοῖς ἐφανέρωσεν

God's initiative is the reason (γάρ) information about him can be readily known. The article with θεός is anaphoric and marks it as the subject. Αὐτοῖς (dat. pl. masc. of αὐτός, -ή, -ό) is a dative of indirect object ("to them"). Moo suggests that φανερόω ("to cause to become known") is as strong as ἀποκαλύπτω when Paul uses it elsewhere (104 n. 57; cf. Rom 3:21; Eph 5:13–14; Col 1:16; 3:4; 1 Tim 3:16; 2 Tim 1:10; Titus 1:3). The aorist of ἐφανέρωσεν (3 sg. aor. act. indic. of φανερόω) is most likely gnomic. (See 1:21 below.)

VERSE 20

τὰ γὰρ ἀόρατα αὐτοῦ ἀπὸ κτίσεως κόσμου

As an explanation (γάρ) of 1:18–19 Paul describes the way in which humankind suppresses what can be known about God (1:20–23). The neuter plural article is generic and allows the adjective to function as a noun. Ἀόρατος, -ον ("invisible") denotes that which is not subject to being seen (BDAG 95a); the possessive pronoun is common after adjectives ending in -τος (cf. 1:21; 2:4; 6:12; 8:11; 9:22). NASB, NEB, and ESV translate the phrase "his invisible attributes," while GNB and NIV render it "his invisible qualities." Robertson notes that the phrase makes what follows more concrete (654). The prepositional phrase ἀπὸ κτίσεως κόσμου is temporal (ἀπό + gen.) and best translated as "since the creation of the world" (Cranfield 114; Longenecker 208). Κτίσις, -εως, ἡ describes the act of creation (BDAG 573a); κόσμου is an objective genitive; although anarthrous, both genitive nouns are definite (cf. Wallace 250–51).

τοῖς ποιήμασιν νοούμενα καθορᾶται

Τοῖς ποιήμασιν (dat. pl. neut. of ποίημα, -ατος, τό, "what is created/made") is an instrumental dative ("by means of the things that are being made") and modifies νοούμενα (nom. pl. neut. of pres. pass. ptc. of νοέω, "understand"). The participle, in turn, is adverbial of attendant circumstance ("and are being understood") and modifies καθορᾶται (3 sg. pres. pass. indic. of καθοράω, "perceive, notice"). The prefix intensifies καθοράω ("clearly seen"), which echoes τὰ ἀόρατα and creates the rhetorical device *annominato* by using words with both similar sound and similar sense (R 1201)—"His unseen attributes . . . are being clearly seen."

ἥ τε ἀΐδιος αὐτοῦ δύναμις καὶ θειότης

The noun phrase stands in apposition to τὰ ἀόρατα (Jewett 155). The correlative conjunctions (τέ . . . καί) continue the style Paul used earlier (1:12, 14, 16), and the article establishes a close connection between the two nouns that follow (R 787). In this instance, the first noun is a subset of the second (cf. Wallace 287). The adjective ἀΐδιος (nom. sg. fem. of ἀΐδιος, -ον, "eternal") modifies both nouns; the genitive of αὐτοῦ is possessive. See 1:4 for δύναμις. Θειότης, -τος, ἡ, denotes a quality or characteristic pertaining to deity and can be translated "divine nature" (BDAG 446d). Dunn suggests that Paul uses the language of Hellenistic Judaism (ἀόρατος, ποίημα, καθοράω, ἀΐδιος, θειότης) to build a bridge to non-Jewish philosophy (58).

εἰς τὸ εἶναι αὐτοὺς ἀναπολογήτους

Εἰς τὸ εἶναι (pres. act. infin. of εἰμί) is adverbial of result (R 1002; T 43). The accusative commonly occurs as the subject of an infinitive, especially with personal pronouns (cf. 3:26; 4:11, 18; 7:4; 8:29; 11:11; 12:2; 15:13, 16). The adjective ἀναπολόγητος, -ον ("without excuse") also occurs in 2:1.

VERSE 21

διότι γνόντες τὸν θεόν

The conjunction διότι repeats 1:19, and the rest of the phrase echoes it. The participle γνόντες (nom. pl. masc. of aor. act. ptc. of γινώσκω, "know") is adverbial of concession (R 1129) and modifies the verbs that follow. The article is anaphoric; θεόν (acc. sg. masc.) is the object of the participle. The gnomic aorist of γνόντες denotes timeless action (Porter, 39; cf. BDF §333), and the other aorists in verses 21–23 should also be understood as gnomic (cf. GNB and CEV).

οὐχ ὡς θεὸν ἐδόξασαν ἢ ηὐχαρίστησαν

The particle οὐχ ("not") negates the verbs that follow. The phrase ὡς θεόν is elliptical of manner ("in the manner that God should be"), and the direct object ("him") must be supplied for both verbs (cf. EVV). Δοξάζω occurs four other times in Romans, twice to indicate the response owed to God (15:6, 9); it carries the idea of influencing opinion so as to enhance a reputation (BDAG 258c). The conjunction ἤ ("or") is disjunctive (R 1188). Εὐχαριστέω expresses appreciation for benefits or blessings (BDAG 415c).

ἀλλ' ἐματαιώθησαν ἐν τοῖς διαλογισμοῖς αὐτῶν

In contrast (ἀλλά) to what humankind did is what was done to them. Jewett translates the divine passive of ἐματαιώθησαν (3 pl. aor. pass. indic. of ματαιόω, "be futile") as "were made futile" (158). Ἐν + dat. is local ("in their reasonings"); the article with a possessive pronoun is common; αὐτῶν is a subjective genitive. Διαλογισμός, -ου, ὁ denotes the process of reasoning (BDAG 232d).

καὶ ἐσκοτίσθη ἡ ἀσύνετος αὐτῶν καρδία

Καί ("and") connects ἐσκοτίσθη (3 sg. aor. pass. indic. of σκοτίζω, "make dark") with the preceding verb. The singular (ἡ καρδία) is distributive and represents a group (T 23) as the plural possessive pronoun (αὐτῶν) makes clear. Καρδία, -ας, ἡ denotes the "inward, hidden self as a thinking, willing, and feeling subject" (Cranfield 118; *NIDNTT* 2.182). Ἀσύνετος, -ον describes humankind's heart as void of understanding (BDAG 146d).

VERSE 22

φάσκοντες εἶναι σοφοὶ ἐμωράνθησαν

By using asyndeton to introduce the third sentence Paul highlights humankind's lack of understanding. The participle φάσκοντες (nom. pl. masc. of pres. act. ptc. of φάσκω, "state with confidence") is adverbial of means (Murray 42), and the gnomic present denotes timeless truth. See Acts 24:9 and 25:19 for other uses of φάσκω. The infinitive (pres. act. inf. of εἰμί) completes the participle, and the nominative (σοφοί) is expected with the infinitive when it has the same subject as the main verb (R 457; T 146; cf. Wallace 599). Ἐμωράνθησαν (3 pl. aor. pass. indic. of μωραίνω, "make foolish") parallels the aorist passive verbs in verse 21 ("they were made foolish").

VERSE 23

καὶ ἤλλαξαν τὴν δόξαν τοῦ ἀφθάρτου θεοῦ

Καί ("and") connects this clause to verse 22. Ἤλλαξαν (3 pl. aor. act. indic. of ἀλλάσσω, "exchange") anticipates the strengthened cognate verbs in verses 25 and 26 (cf. Longenecker 213). The article with the direct object δόξαν (sg. acc. fem.) is simple identification. See Cranfield for δόξα, -ης, ἡ (119–20; cf. *TDNT* 2.235–58). The article with θεοῦ is anaphoric; the genitive is possessive. The adjective ἄφθαρτος, -ον denotes something that is impervious to corruption and death (BDAG 156a).

ἐν ὁμοιώματι εἰκόνος φθαρτοῦ ἀνθρώπου καὶ πετεινῶν καὶ τετραπόδων καὶ ἑρπετῶν

The object for which God's incorruptible glory is exchanged (ἐν + dat.; cf. Cranfield 120) is a mere "copy" (ὁμοίωμα) of an "image" (εἰκών) that represents the basic form and features of the original (BDAG 282d). That image is the antithesis of God in that it is subject to decay and death (φθαρτός, -ή, -όν). The four genitives joined by καί are possessive; the nouns are anarthrous because they highlight essence/quality. The singular of ἀνθρώπου is best translated "a human being" (NJB) or "humans" (CEV). Πετεινόν, -οῦ, τό refers to any kind of wild or domestic bird (BDAG 809a); τετράπους, -ουν denotes four-footed animals (BDAG 1001b); ἑρπετόν, -οῦ, τό is a general term for animals that crawl (e.g., NASB, Acts 10:12; 11:6). The combination echoes the creation account (Gen 1:20–27).

FOR FURTHER STUDY

13. God's Wrath (1:18)

Ashmon, S. A. "The Wrath of God: A Biblical Overview." *Concordia Journal* (2005): 348–58.
Bedenbaugh, J. B. "Paul's Use of 'Wrath of God.'" *LQ* 6 (1954): 154–57.
Borchert. G. L. *DPL* 991–93.
Bornkamm, G. "The Revelation of God's Wrath (Romans 1–3)." Pages 44–70 in *Early Christian Experience*. Translated by P. L. Hammer. Philadelphia: Westminster, 1969.
Carson, D. A. "God's Love and God's Wrath." *BSac* 156 (1999): 387–98.
Erlandsson, S. "The Wrath of YHWH." *TynBul* 23 (1972): 111–16.
Hahn, H. C. *NIDNTT* 1.107–13.
Hanson, A. T. *The Wrath of the Lamb*. London: SPCK, 1957.
Kratz, R. G., and H. Spieckermann. *Divine Wrath and Divine Mercy in the World of Antiquity*. Tübingen: Mohr Siebeck, 2008.
MacGregor, G. H. C. "The Concept of the Wrath of God in the New Testament." *NTS* 7 (1960–61): 101–109.
Stählin, G. *TDNT* 5.419–47.
Smith, T. C. "The Wrath of God." *RevExp* 45 (1948): 193–208.
Tasker, R. V. G. *The Biblical Doctrine of the Wrath of God*. London: Tyndale, 1957.
Travis, S. H. *ABD* 6.996–98.

14. Heaven (1:18)

Alcorn, R. *Heaven*. Wheaton, IL: Tyndale, 2004.
Baxter, J. S. *The Other Side of Death: What the Bible Teaches about Heaven and Hell*. Grand Rapids: Kregel, 1987.
Bietentard, H. *NIDNTT* 2.188–96.
Blamires, H. *Knowing the Truth about Heaven and Hell*. Ann Arbor, MI: Servant, 1988.
Boa, K. D., and R. M. Bowman, Jr. *Sense and Nonsense about Heaven and Hell*. Grand Rapids: Zondervan, 2007.
Grider, J. K. *EDT* 499–500.
Hoekema, A. A. *The Bible and the Future*. Grand Rapids: Eerdmans, 1979.
Lincoln, A. T. *Paradise Now and Not Yet: Studies in the Role of the Heavenly Dimension in Paul's Thought With Special Reference to His Eschatology*. New York: Cambridge, 1981.
Maile, J. F. *DPL* 381–83.
McDannell, C., and B. Lang. *Heaven: A History*. New York: Vintage, 1988.
McGrath, A. *A Brief History of Heaven*. Oxford: Blackwell, 2003.
Milne, B. *The Message of Heaven and Hell*. Downers Grove, IL: InterVarsity, 2002.
Smith, W. M. *The Biblical Doctrine of Heaven*. Chicago: Moody, 1968.
Ware, J. P. "Paul's Hope and Ours: Recovering Paul's Hope of the Renewed Creation." *Concordia Journal* 35 (2009): 129–39.
Wright, N. T. *Surprised by Hope: Rethinking Heaven, Resurrection and the Mission of the Church*. Grand Rapids: Zondervan, 2010.

15. General Revelation (1:20)

Berkouwer, G. C. *General Revelation*. Grand Rapids: Eerdmans, 1955.

Byl, J. "General Revelation and Evangelicalism." *Mid-America Journal of Theology* 5 (1989): 1–13.

Demarest, B. *General Revelation: Historical Views and Contemporary Issues*. Grand Rapids: Zondervan, 1982.

________. *EDT* 944–45.

Diehl, D. W. "Evangelicalism and General Revelation: An Unfinished Agenda." *JETS* 30 (1987): 441–55.

Gooties, N. H. "General Revelation in Its Relation to Special Revelation." *WTJ* 51 (1989): 359–68.

Hoffmeier, J. K. "'The Heavens Declare the Glory of God': The Limits of General Revelation." *TJ* 21 (2000): 17–24.

Howard, D. "A Critical Analysis of General Revelation." *CTR* 8 (2010): 53–75.

Johnson, D. "Between Two Wor(l)ds: Worldview and Observation I: The Use of General Revelation to Interpret Scripture, and Vice Versa." *JETS* 41 (1998): 69–84.

Moore, R. D. "Natural Revelation." Pages 67–101 in *A Theology for the Church*. 2nd ed. Edited by D. L. Akin. Nashville: B&H, 2014.

Oden, T. C. "Without Excuse: Classic Christian Exegesis of General Revelation." *JETS* 41 (1998): 55–68.

Snodgrass, K. "The Gospel in Romans: A Theology of Revelation." Pages 288–314 in *Gospel in Paul: Studies on Corinthians, Galatians and Romans for Richard N. Longenecker*. Edited by L. A. Jervis and P. Richardson. Sheffield: Sheffield Academic Press, 1994.

Thomas, R. L. "General Revelation and Biblical Hermeneutics." *Master's Seminary Journal* 9 (1998): 5–23.

16. Heart (1:21)

Behm, J. *TDNT* 3.611–14.

Brandon, O. R. *EDT* 944–45.

Jewett, R. *Paul's Anthropological Terms: A Study of their Use in Conflict Settings*. Leiden: Brill, 1971.

Mitchell, C. "Heart and Mind in the Hebrew Scriptures." *Touchstone* 23 (2005): 5–13.

Richards, W. A. "Head and Heart in the New Testament: The Philippian Correspondence as a Case Study." *Touchstone* 23 (2005): 14–19.

Sorg, T. *NIDNTT* 180–84.

Waltke, B. K. *EDBT* 331–32.

17. God's Glory (1:23)

Aalen, S. *NIDNTT* 2.44–48.

deSilva, D. A. *The Hope of Glory: Honor Discourse and New Testament Interpretation*. Collegeville, MN: Liturgical Press, 1999.

Gaff, R. B., Jr. *DPL* 348–50.

Giblin, C. H. *In Hope of God's Glory: Pauline Theological Perspectives*. New York: Herder, 1970.

Harrison, E. F. *EDT* 443–44.

Harrison, J. R. "Paul and the Roman Ideal of Glory in the Epistle to the Romans." Pages 329–69 in *Letter to the Romans*. Edited by U. Schnelle. Leuven: Peeters, 2009.

Hegemann, H. *EDNT* 1.344–49.

Morgan, C., and R. Peterson. *The Glory of God.* Wheaton, IL: Crossway, 2010.
Von Rad, G., and G. Kittel. *TDNT* 2.233–55.

HOMILETICAL SUGGESTIONS

The Revelation of God's Wrath (1:18–23)

1. Because humankind unrighteously suppresses his truth (1:18–19)
   a. Despite knowing about God (1:19a)
   b. Despite God making truth manifest (1:19b)
2. Because humankind inexcusably ignores his power and divine nature (1:20–21)
   a. Although seeing it clearly in creation (1:20)
   b. Resulting in foolish thinking and darkened hearts (1:21)
3. Because humankind foolishly discards his glory (1:22–23)
   a. Although claiming to be wise (1:22)
   b. Exchanging incorruptible reality for copies of the corruptible (1:23)

b. Because the Gentiles Practice Unrighteousness (1:24–32)

STRUCTURE

The second paragraph also consists of three sentences (1:24–25; 1:26–27; 1:28–32), each introduced by παρέδωκεν αὐτοὺς ὁ θεός. Jewett suggests that the first sentence addresses the religious level in the form of perverted worship, the second sentence addresses the sexual level in the form of perverted relationships, and the third sentence addresses the public level in the form of perverted behavior (165).

Διὸ παρέδωκεν αὐτοὺς ὁ θεὸς
ἐν ταῖς ἐπιθυμίαις τῶν καρδιῶν αὐτῶν
εἰς ἀκαθαρσίαν
τοῦ ἀτιμάζεσθαι τὰ σώματα αὐτῶν ἐν αὐτοῖς
οἵτινες μετήλλαξαν τὴν ἀλήθειαν τοῦ θεοῦ ἐν τῷ ψεύδει
καὶ ἐσεβάσθησαν καὶ ἐλάτρευσαν τῇ κτίσει παρὰ τὸν κτίσαντα,
ὅς ἐστιν εὐλογητὸς εἰς τοὺς αἰῶνας, ἀμήν.

διὰ τοῦτο παρέδωκεν αὐτοὺς ὁ θεὸς
εἰς πάθη ἀτιμίας,
αἵ τε γὰρ θήλειαι αὐτῶν μετήλλαξαν τὴν φυσικὴν χρῆσιν εἰς τὴν παρὰ φύσιν,
ὁμοίως τε καὶ οἱ ἄρσενες ἀφέντες τὴν φυσικὴν χρῆσιν τῆς θηλείας ἐξεκαύθησαν
ἐν τῇ ὀρέξει αὐτῶν εἰς ἀλλήλους, ἄρσενες ἐν ἄρσεσιν τὴν ἀσχημοσύνην
κατεργαζόμενοι καὶ τὴν ἀντιμισθίαν ἣν ἔδει τῆς πλάνης αὐτῶν ἐν ἑαυτοῖς
ἀπολαμβάνοντες.

καὶ καθὼς οὐκ ἐδοκίμασαν τὸν θεὸν ἔχειν ἐν ἐπιγνώσει,
παρέδωκεν αὐτοὺς ὁ θεὸς
εἰς ἀδόκιμον νοῦν,
ποιεῖν τὰ μὴ καθήκοντα,
πεπληρωμένους πάσῃ ἀδικίᾳ πονηρίᾳ πλεονεξίᾳ κακίᾳ,
μεστοὺς φθόνου φόνου ἔριδος δόλου κακοηθείας,
ψιθυριστὰς καταλάλους
θεοστυγεῖς ὑβριστὰς ὑπερηφάνους ἀλαζόνας,
ἐφευρετὰς κακῶν, γονεῦσιν ἀπειθεῖς,
ἀσυνέτους ἀσυνθέτους ἀστόργους ἀνελεήμονας

οἵτινες τὸ δικαίωμα τοῦ θεοῦ ἐπιγνόντες ὅτι οἱ τὰ τοιαῦτα πράσσοντες ἄξιοι θανάτου εἰσίν,
οὐ μόνον αὐτὰ ποιοῦσιν ἀλλὰ καὶ συνευδοκοῦσιν τοῖς πράσσουσιν.

VERSE 24

Διὸ παρέδωκεν αὐτοὺς ὁ θεός

The inferential conjunction διό ("therefore") introduces God's response to 1:22–23, which is captured by the statement Paul repeats three times in the paragraph: "God handed them over." The anaphoric article with the subject θεός continues the pattern present throughout the preceding paragraph. The personal pronoun αὐτούς is also anaphoric, pointing back to those described in verses 22–23. The verb παρέδωκεν (3 sg. aor. act. indic. of παραδίδωμι, "hand over") is a constative aorist summarizing God's action as a whole. BDAG identifies it as a technical term used to describe handing over to the judicial custody of the police, the courts, or prison (762c). In the OT, it describes being delivered for punishment or retribution (Exod 23:31; Deut 7:23). Cranfield concludes that it describes God's deliberate act of forsaking in order to show mercy (121).

ἐν ταῖς ἐπιθυμίαις τῶν καρδιῶν αὐτῶν εἰς ἀκαθαρσίαν

The custody to which humans are handed over (ἐν + dat.) is "the lusts of their hearts" (Jewett 168). The article accompanies the abstract noun ἐπιθυμίαις (dat. pl. fem.), which denotes a craving or lust for something forbidden (BDAG 372c). The article regularly occurs with the possessive personal pronoun; the genitive of καρδιῶν indicates the origin of the desires. See 1:21 for καρδία. The final punishment for which they are delivered (εἰς + acc.) is the state of moral corruption described as ἀκαθαρσίαν (acc. sg. fem. of ἀκαθαρσία, -ας, ἡ, "immorality").

τοῦ ἀτιμάζεσθαι τὰ σώματα αὐτῶν ἐν αὐτοῖς

The result (τοῦ + inf.) of the handing over is the dishonoring of their bodies (BDF §400.2; T 141). The present of ἀτιμάζεσθαι (pres. pass. inf. ἀτιμάζω, "dishonor") is iterative (Wallace 521); Cranfield classifies the voice as passive (122). If the infinitive is passive, τὰ σώματα (acc. pl. neut. of σῶμα, -ατος, τό, "body") is its subject. The article again occurs with the possessive pronoun (αὐτῶν). Cranfield lists five possible interpretations of ἐν αὐτοῖς and decides on "among them" (122; cf. NASB). The textual variant ἑαυτοῖς that appears in some manuscripts explains the translation "among themselves" in several EVV (e.g., RSV, ESV).

VERSE 25

οἵτινες μετήλλαξαν τὴν ἀλήθειαν τοῦ θεοῦ ἐν τῷ ψεύδει

The relative pronoun οἵτινες (nom. pl. masc. of ὅστις, ἥτις, ὅ τι) is qualitative and intensive; Wallace (344) suggests translating it "who indeed"; Longenecker (216) suggests a causal nuance ("because they . . ."). The prefix on μετήλλαξαν (3 pl. aor. act. indic. of μεταλλάσσω, "exchange") intensifies it; the aorist is constative. Robertson notes that the verb is more commonly followed by εἰς as in 1:26 (561). The article occurs frequently with abstract nouns such as τὴν ἀλήθειαν (acc. sg. fem. of ἀλήθεια,

-ας, ἡ, "truth"). Τοῦ θεοῦ is an objective genitive, which Moo understands as the fact of God as he has revealed himself (112). Humankind has exchanged "the truth about God" ἐν τῷ ψεύδει ("for the lie"), which Jewett defines as the fundamental tendency to replace God with ourselves (170).

καὶ ἐσεβάσθησαν καὶ ἐλάτρευσαν τῇ κτίσει παρὰ τὸν κτίσαντα

Continuing (*καί*) the description of humankind's turning away from God, Paul highlights the way in which they perverted worship with two constative aorist verbs linked by *καί*. The deponent σεβάζομαι is more general and denotes showing reverential awe (BDAG 917c), while λατρεύω (with dat. dir. obj.) is more specific and denotes rendering religious service (BDAG 587c). The article with τῇ κτίσει is simple identification, while the noun itself (dat. sg. fem. of κτίσις, -εως, ἡ, "creation") points to the sum of everything created (BDAG 573b). The preposition παρά should be translated "instead of" (BDF §236.3; R 616) or "rather than" (Moule, 51). The accusative article marks the participle as substantival and the object of the preposition. Κτίσαντα (acc. sg. masc. of aor. act. ptc. of κτίζω, "create") is a word play on the preceding noun and points to the creator of the universe (BDAG 572d).

ὅς ἐστιν εὐλογητὸς εἰς τοὺς αἰῶνας, ἀμήν

The relative pronoun ὅς (nom. sg. masc. of ὅς, ἥ, ὅ) links the preceding participle to the descriptive clause it introduces (R 960). Εὐλογητός, -ή, -όν ("blessed") is a predicate adjective (cf. T 89). For the temporal εἰς τοὺς αἰῶνας, BDAG suggests "to all eternity" (32b). Ἀμήν ("amen") signifies agreement with something that is sure and valid (Dunn 64; cf. *TDNT* 1.335–37).

VERSE 26

διὰ τοῦτο παρέδωκεν αὐτοὺς ὁ θεὸς εἰς πάθη ἀτιμίας

Because (διά) of what precedes (τοῦτο), God takes the second step in "handing over" humankind. See 1:24 for παρέδωκεν αὐτοὺς ὁ θεός. As in verse 24, εἰς + accusative denotes the punishment to which they are delivered. Πάθος, -ους, τό points to a strong desire (BDAG 748b), which Jewett describes as an involuntary state that comes over a person (172). Robertson classifies ἀτιμίας (gen. sg. fem. of ἀτιμία, -ας, ἡ, "dishonor") as an attributive genitive (496), while Turner (213), Moo (113 n. 111), and Cranfield (125) classify it as a genitive of quality. EVV uniformly choose the former ("dishonorable passions").

αἵ τε γὰρ θήλειαι αὐτῶν μετήλλαξαν τὴν φυσικὴν χρῆσιν εἰς τὴν παρὰ φύσιν

Paul provides further explanation (γάρ) of the "handing over" by describing the sexual perversion that results. The correlative pronoun (τε) introduces the first example and creates an inner bond between verse 26b and verse 27 (R 1179). The use of θῆλυς, -εια, -υ ("female") and ἄρσην, -εν, -ενος ("male") in what follows echoes the creation account (Gen 1:27; cf. Matt 19:4; Mark 10:6) and stresses sexual distinction (Moo 114 n. 114). See Schreiner for a concise summary of the discussion of these verses and their bearing on the issue of homosexuality (94–97). Longenecker includes a helpful discussion of the likely reasons Paul chose to highlight homosexuality in this portion of his argument (217–19). The article with the adjective θήλειαι is generic; the pronoun αὐτῶν is a possessive genitive. See verse 25 for μεταλλάσσω. Τὴν φυσικὴν χρῆσιν is the direct object; the definite article is commonly used with an attributive adjective and places emphasis on "natural" (cf. R 776). Χρῆσις, -εως, ἡ denotes intimate involvement with a person (BDAG 1089d); φυσικός, -ή, -όν denotes something in accordance with the basic order of things in nature (BDAG 1069b). Paul uses it elsewhere in a number of contexts (Rom 2:27; 1 Cor 11:14; Gal 2:15; 4:8; Eph 2:3). The more common εἰς follows μεταλλάσσω to describe that for which the "natural use" has been exchanged. The definite article enables the prepositional phrase to function as a substantive; παρά + acc. denotes opposition ("against, contrary to"); φύσις, -εως, ἡ describes the established order of things (BDAG 1070b) set by reason of intrinsic state or birth (Moo 114). The phrase παρὰ φύσιν also occurs in Romans 11:24 to describe a wild olive branch grafted into a cultivated olive tree. Both Philo (*Spec. Leg.* 3.39) and Josephus (*Ap.* 2.37) use the phrase to describe homosexuality. Josephus also uses the contrasting phrase κατὰ φύσιν to describe something "in accordance with nature" (2.24). See also *TDNT* 9.262–65, 273.

VERSE 27

ὁμοίως τε καὶ οἱ ἄρσενες ἀφέντες τὴν φυσικὴν χρῆσιν τῆς θηλείας

The correlative conjunction τε introduces the second example and connects it with the first. The adverb ὁμοίως ("likewise") points out a similarity in some respect (BDAG 708a); καί is adjunctive ("also") and commonly follows ὁμοίως. The article with ἄρσενες ("males") is generic. Passages in Leviticus use the adjective when discussing homosexuality (18:22; 20:13). The participle ἀφέντες (nom. pl. masc. of pres. act. ptc. of ἀφίημι, "abandon, leave behind") may be understood as adjectival* or adverbial of time (Jewett 163). See verse 26 for τὴν φυσικὴν χρῆσιν. The article with θηλείας ("females") is anaphoric; the genitive is objective.

ἐξεκαύθησαν ἐν τῇ ὀρέξει αὐτῶν εἰς ἀλλήλους

The verb ἐξεκαύθησαν (3 pl. aor. pass. indic. of ἐκκαίω) describes being enflamed with sexual desire (BDAG 303b). The passive has an active sense; the aorist is constative. The manner (ἐν + dat.) with which the males are enflamed is described as "strong desire" (ὄρεξις, -εως, ἡ). The genitive of αὐτῶν is subjective. Their desire is directed εἰς ἀλλήλους ("toward one another").

ἄρσενες ἐν ἄρσεσιν τὴν ἀσχημοσύνην κατεργαζόμενοι

The phrase ἄρσενες ἐν ἄρσεσιν ("males with males") is best taken with the participle (Moo 116 n. 127); ἐν + dative indicates association. The article accompanies the abstract noun ἀσχημοσύνην, which describes behavior resulting in disgrace (BDAG 147d). The participle κατεργαζόμενοι (nom. pl. masc. of pres. mid. ptc. of dep. κατεργάζομαι, "achieve, accomplish") is adverbial of result; the present tense is iterative ("with the result that they are repeatedly committing what is disgraceful").

καὶ τὴν ἀντιμισθίαν ἣν ἔδει τῆς πλάνης αὐτῶν ἐν ἑαυτοῖς ἀπολαμβάνοντες

The continuative καί joins the parallel adverbial participles κατεργαζόμενοι and ἀπολαμβάνοντες. The noun ἀντιμισθίαν (acc. sg. fem. of ἀντιμιθία, -ας, ἡ, "recompense") is the object of the participle that follows; the article with it is simple identification; the best translation is "penalty." The relative clause ἣν ἔδει further defines ἀντιμισθίαν. Ἔδει is an impersonal verb (3 sg. impf. act. indic. of δεῖ, "it is necessary/fitting"); EVV tend to translate the relative clause as an adjective "the due penalty" (RSV, NASB, NEB, NIV, NJB, ESV). The genitive τῆς πλάνης is best understood as subjective, modifying ἀντιμισθίαν; αὐτῶν is a possessive genitive. The location (ἐν + dat.) where the penalty is received is "themselves" (dat. pl. masc. of the reflexive pronoun ἑαυτοῦ, -ῆς, -οῦ).

VERSE 28

καὶ καθὼς οὐκ ἐδοκίμασαν τὸν θεὸν ἔχειν ἐν ἐπιγνώσει

Καὶ καθώς . . . ἐπιγνώσει resumes the theme of rejecting the truth about God (cf. 1:21, 23, 25) as the fundamental sin that leads both to other sins (Käsemann 47) and to God's judgment. Καθώς is causal (BDF §453.2; R 968) and provides the grounds for the third statement of God's "handing over." Δοκιμάζω means to draw a conclusion about something on the basis of testing (BDAG 255d); Moo notes that it should be translated "see fit" when followed by an infinitive (117 n. 138). The article with θεόν is anaphoric; the noun functions as the object of ἔχειν (pres. act. inf. of ἔχω, "have"). The infinitive completes the thought of ἐδοκίμασαν; the present tense is progressive. Ἐν + dative is local; ἐπιγνώσει (dat. sg. fem. of ἐπίγνωσις, -εως, ἡ, "knowledge") is definite even though it is anarthrous; BDAG suggests that the phrase is equivalent to "to recognize God" (369d).

παρέδωκεν αὐτοὺς ὁ θεὸς εἰς ἀδόκιμον νοῦν

See verses 24 and 26 for παρέδωκεν αὐτοὺς ὁ θεὸς εἰς. Νοῦς, νοός, ὁ denotes an attitude or way of thinking (BDAG 680d); Paul uses it elsewhere in Romans as the organ of moral reasoning and willing (7:23, 25; 11:34; 12:2; 14:5). The absence of the article is qualitative; the adjective ἀδόκιμος, -ον echoes ἐδοκίμασαν. Jewett captures the word play as "did not see fit . . . an unfitting mind" (163). The idea of "not fitting" continues with τὰ μὴ καθήκοντα in the infinitive phrase that follows.

ποιεῖν τὰ μὴ καθήκοντα

Wallace classifies ποιεῖν (pres. act. inf. of ποιέω, "commit") as result (502),* although others label it epexegetical (R 1086; Porter 198); the present tense is iterative. The definite article marks the participle as substantival and the object of the infinitive; the negative particle μή is commonly used with participles (BDF §430.3). Καθήκοντα (acc. pl. neut. of pres. act. ptc. of καθήκω) denotes what is not appropriate, proper, or fitting (cf. *TDNT* 3.438–40) and continues that theme ("what is not fitting").

VERSES 29–31

πεπληρωμένους πάσῃ ἀδικίᾳ πονηρίᾳ πλεονεξίᾳ κακίᾳ

The asyndeton that begins verse 29 serves to draw attention to the vice list that follows (R 427). Schreiner suggests that it is best not to draw precise distinctions between the terms in the list because Paul is seeking to paint a picture of comprehensive wickedness (98). See Longenecker for the use of vice lists in antiquity (229–30). The participle πεπληρωμένους (acc. pl. masc. of pf. pass. ptc. from πληρόω, "fill") stands in apposition to αὐτούς in verse 28 (Cranfield 128) and is an intensive perfect, focusing on the resulting state (Moo 118 n. 144). The first four terms are all modified by πάσῃ (dat. sg. fem. of πᾶς, πᾶσα, πᾶν, "all"), are in the dative case, and denote content (Wallace 171). See verse 18 for ἀδικία. Πονηρία, -ας, ἡ describes a condition lacking in moral values (BDAG 851b); πλεονεζία, -ας, ἡ denotes a desire to have more than is one's due (BDAG 824d); κακία, -ας, ἡ points to a mean-spirited disposition (BDAG 500b). Dunn seeks to capture the *homoioteleuton* of the endings by translating the sequence "unrighteousness, wickedness, greediness, badness" (67).

μεστοὺς φθόνου φόνου ἔριδος δόλου κακοηθείας

The next five terms are all genitive singular of content and depend on the adjective μεστούς (acc. pl. masc. of μεστός, -ή, -όν, "full"), which also stands in apposition to αὐτοὺς and denotes being thoroughly characterized by something (BDAG 636a). Cranfield suggests that φθονός, -ου, ὁ ("envy") and φόνος, -ου, ὁ ("murder") are connected both by assonance and inwardly, with the first leading ultimately to the second as in Genesis 4 (130). Ἔρις, -ιδος, ἡ ("strife") points to engagement in rivalry, strife, or contention (BDAG 392c); δόλος, -ου, ὁ ("deceit") describes taking advantage through craft and underhanded methods (BDAG 256d). Κακοήθεια, -ας, ἡ ("meanness") points to a basic defect in character that leads one to be hurtful to others (BDAG 500c; cf. *TDNT* 3.486); Aristotle uses it to refer to an attitude that sees the worst in everything (*Rhet.* 2.13).

ψιθυριστὰς καταλάλους

According to Cranfield, both of these accusative plural nouns denote people who destroy the reputations of others by misrepresentation (130). Someone who passes on rumors as secret slander fits the term ψιθυριστής, -ου, ὁ (cf. BDAG 1098b), while someone who openly slanders others by speaking ill of them fits the term κατάλαλος, -ου, ὁ (cf. BDAG 519d). ESV translates the nouns "gossips [and] slanderers"; NEB has "whisperers and scandal-mongers."

θεοστυγεῖς ὑβριστὰς ὑπερηφάνους ἀλαζόνας

Although Moo suggests that these four accusative plural nouns all relate to arrogance (119), the first seems to fit that category least well. Θεοστυγής, -ές may be understood as "hateful to God" (e.g., NEB, GNB), or "haters of God" (e.g., NLT, ESV); given the context, the latter seems preferable (cf. BDAG 452c). Trench sees the remaining three terms as denoting activity, thought, and speech respectively (98–105). Ὑβριστής, -οῦ, ὁ describes a violent or insolent person (BDAG 1023d) who treats others with contempt (Cranfield 131); ὑπερήφανος, -ον describes someone who is haughty or proud (BDAG 1033d); ἀλαζών, -όνος, ὁ describes someone who is boastful (BDAG 41a) and seeks to impress others by making big claims (Cranfield 132). Most EVV translate the words as "insolent, arrogant, boastful."

ἐφευρετὰς κακῶν, γονεῦσιν ἀπειθεῖς

These terms each consist of two words. The first, "inventors of evil," combines one who forms strategies to effect something (BDAG 418b) with something that is socially or morally reprehensible (BDAG 501d); the genitive of κακῶν is objective. The second, "disobedient to parents," uses the dative of person as equivalent to an objective genitive. Since the dative noun usually follows the adjective in this construction, placing γονεῦσιν first adds emphasis. Both anarthrous nouns are qualitative (R 794).

ἀσυνέτους ἀσυνθέτους ἀστόργους ἀνελεήμονας

The final four adjectives, all accusative plural, are linked by assonance (BDF §488.2) and denote the absence of positive qualities. Ἀσύνετος, -ον describes one who is void of understanding (BDAG 146d); ἀσύνθετος, -ον describes one who does not keep his or her word (BDAG 146d); ἄστοργος, -ον describes one who is lacking in good feelings for others (BDAG 146a); ἀνελεήμων, -ον describes one who lacks mercy (BDAG 76d). Moo suggests translating the terms as "without understanding, without faithfulness, without affection, without mercy" (120), while Dunn suggests "senseless, faithless, loveless, merciless" (68).

VERSE 32

οἵτινες τὸ δικαίωμα τοῦ θεοῦ ἐπιγνόντες

The relative pronoun οἵτινες is again qualitative (cf. 1:25) to denote humans in general. The article with δικαίωμα (acc. sg. neut. of δικαίωμα, -ατος, τό, "regulation, requirement") marks the noun, which serves as the object of the participle, as well-known but not previously mentioned. The article with θεοῦ is anaphoric, and the genitive is possessive. The participle ἐπιγνόντες (nom. pl. masc. of aor. act. ptc.) is adverbial of concession (Moo 121 n. 165) modifying οὐ μόνον αὐτὰ ποιοῦσιν ἀλλὰ καὶ συνευδοκοῦσιν at the end of the verse. The aorist is gnomic; the verb ἐπιγινώσκω suggests having exact or complete knowledge of someone or something (BDAG 369b).

ὅτι οἱ τὰ τοιαῦτα πράσσοντες ἄξιοι θανάτου εἰσίν

The conjunction ὅτι ("that") provides the substance of what humans know but reject. The article οἱ (nom. pl. masc.) agrees with πράσσοντες (nom. pl. masc. of pres. act. ptc. of πράσσω, "practice") and marks the participle as the subject of the clause. The article usually occurs with τοιαῦτα (R 710), which points back at least to 1:29–31 (Schreiner 99), or possibly to all of 1:24–31 (Moo 121).* The predicate adjective ἄξιοι (nom. pl. masc. of ἄξιος, -α, -ον, "worthy, deserving") denotes something that is correspondingly fitting (BDAG 94a). The genitive of θανάτου is objective (Wallace 135); the phrase "worthy of death" also occurs in Matthew 26:66.

οὐ μόνον αὐτὰ ποιοῦσιν ἀλλὰ καὶ συνευδοκοῦσιν τοῖς πράσσουσιν

The combination οὐ μόνον . . . ἀλλὰ καὶ ("not only . . . but also") marks a sharp antithesis (R 1166). Αὐτά (acc. pl. neut. of αὐτός, -ή, -ό) is anaphoric, points back to τοιαῦτα, and is the direct object of ποιοῦσιν (3 pl. pres. act. indic. of ποιέω, "do"). The present tenses of ποιοῦσιν and συνευδοκοῦσιν are iterative. Συνευδοκέω means to join in approval of something and occurs with the dative of person (BDAG 970c). The article with πράσσουσιν (dat. pl. masc. of pres. act. ptc. of πράσσω) marks the participle as substantival, serving as the direct object of συνευδοκοῦσιν.

FOR FURTHER STUDY

18. Mind (1:28)

Behm, J. *TDNT* 6.958–59.
Feinberg, P. D. *EDT* 718–20.
Goetzmann, J. *NIDNTT* 2.616–20.
Herder, G. *NIDNTT* 3.122–30.
Jewett, R. *Paul's Anthropological Terms: A Study of their Use in Conflict Settings.* Leiden: Brill, 1971.
Ladd, G. E. "The Pauline Psychology." Pages 457–78 in *A Theology of the New Testament.* Grand Rapids: Eerdmans, 1974.
Macdonald, P. S. *The History of the Concept of the Mind.* England: Ashgate, 2003.
Towner, P. H. *EDBT* 527–30.

19. Vice and Virtue Lists (1:29–31)

Charles, J. D. *DNTB* 1252–57.
________. *Virtue Amidst Vice: The Catalog of Virtues in 2 Peter 1.* Sheffield: Sheffield Academic Press, 1997.
Easton, B. S. "New Testament Ethical Lists." *JBL* 51 (1932): 1–12.

Engberg-Petersen, T. "Paul, Virtues, and Vices." Pages 608–33 in *Paul and the Greco-Roman World: A Handbook*. Edited by J. P. Sampley. Harrisburg, PA: Trinity Press International, 2003.

Fitzgerald, J. F. *ABD* 6.857–59.

Kruse, C. G. *DPL* 962–63.

López, R. "Views on Paul's Vice Lists and Inheriting the Kingdom." *BSac* 168 (2011): 81–97.

________. "Vice Lists in Non-Pauline Sources." *BSac* 168 (2011): 178–95.

________. "A Study of Pauline Passages with Vice Lists." *BSac* 168 (2011): 301–16.

Malherbe, A. J. *Moral Exhortation: A Greco-Roman Sourcebook*. Philadelphia: Westminster, 1986.

Martin, R. P. *NIDNTT* 1.928–30.

McEleney, N. J. "The Vice Lists of the Pastoral Epistles." *CBQ* 36 (1974): 203–19.

Schweizer, E. "Traditional Ethical Patterns in the Pauline and Post-Pauline Letters and their Development (Lists of Vices and House-tables)." Pages 195–209 in *Text and Interpretation*. Edited by E. Best and R. McL. Wilson. Cambridge: Cambridge University Press, 1979.

20. Death and Life (1:32)

Barrosse, T. "Death and Sin in Saint Paul's Epistle to the Romans." *CBQ* 15 (1953): 438–59.

Bieder, W. *EDNT* 2.129–33.

Blackwell, B. C. "Immortal Glory and the Problem of Death in Romans 3.23." *JSNT* 32 (2010): 285–308.

Daniel, F. H. "Perspectives on Death in the New Testament." *Journal for Preachers* 5 (1982): 17–21.

de Boer, M. D. *The Defeat of Death*. Sheffield, *JSOT*, 1988.

Bruce, F. F. "Paul on Immortality." *SJT* 24 (1974): 457–72.

Bultmann, R. *TDNT* 3.7–25.

________, and G. Bertram. *TDNT* 2.832–75.

Grundmann, W. *TDNT* 7.776–97.

Harris, M. J. *Raised Immortal: The Resurrection and Immortality in the New Testament*. London: Marshall, Morgan & Scott, 1983.

Kreitzer, L. J. *DPL* 438–41.

Link, H.-G. *NIDNTT* 474–83.

Longenecker, R. N. *Life in the Face of Death: The Resurrection Message of the New Testament*. Grand Rapids: Eerdmans, 1998.

Minear, P. S. "The Truth about Sin and Death: The Meaning of Atonement in the Epistle to the Romans." *Int* 7 (1953): 142–55.

Schmithals, W. *NIDNTT* 1.430–41.

Schottroft, L. *EDNT* 2.105–09.

Seeley, D. *The Noble Death: Graeco-Roman Martyrology and Paul's Concept of Salvation*. Sheffield: Sheffield Academic Press, 1990.

Scott, J. J., Jr. *DPL* 553–55.

HOMILETICAL SUGGESTIONS

God "Hands Over" Humankind (1:24–32)

1. God hands over to perverted worship (παρέδωκεν αὐτοὺς ὁ θεός, 1:24–25)
   a. State: lusts of hearts (1:24b)
   b. Punishment: uncleanness (1:24c)
   c. Result: dishonoring bodies (1:24d)
   d. Reason: exchange truth of God for a lie (1:25)
2. God hands over to perverted sex (παρέδωκεν αὐτοὺς ὁ θεός, 1:26–27)
   a. Punishment: dishonorable passions (1:26a)
   b. Result: exchanging natural for unnatural (1:26b–27)
3. God hands over to perverted conduct (παρέδωκεν αὐτοὺς ὁ θεός, 1:28–32)
   a. Reason: did not recognize God (1:28a)
   b. Punishment: unfitting mind (1:28b)
   c. Result: doing what is not fitting (1:28c)
   d. State: filled with every imaginable vice (1:29–31)
   e. Summary: practice and approve things contrary to God's regulation (1:32)

Humankind's Fundamental Sin: Rejecting God

1. They do not glorify God or give him thanks (1:21)
2. They exchange God's glory for idols (1:23)
3. They exchange truth about God for a lie (1:25a)
4. They worship and serve creation rather than the Creator (1:25b)
5. They do not recognize God (1:28)

c. Because the Moral Person Judges Others (2:1–16)

STRUCTURE

The next paragraph may be divided into three sections (2:1–5; 2:6–11; 2:12–16). The shift from third person to second person at 2:1 marks a clear discourse boundary (Porter 301) and introduces a five-verse diatribe section in which words related to "judgment" appear eight times. The relative pronoun at 2:6 introduces an inverted structure (A-B-C-C′-B′-A′) in the third person that extends through 2:11 and describes God's righteous and impartial judgment. The final section continues in the third person, further explains the concept of God's impartial judgment, and uses both Hebrew parallelism and Greek syntactic construction. Longenecker proposes an alternate understanding of the passage's structure based on antithetic Hebrew paralleism (253–54) and includes a discussion of possible traditional materials (238–39).

Διὸ ἀναπολόγητος εἶ, ὦ ἄνθρωπε πᾶς ὁ κρίνων·
  ἐν ᾧ γὰρ κρίνεις τὸν ἕτερον, σεαυτὸν κατακρίνεις,
    τὰ γὰρ αὐτὰ πράσσεις ὁ κρίνων.

οἴδαμεν δὲ ὅτι τὸ κρίμα τοῦ θεοῦ ἐστιν κατὰ ἀλήθειαν ἐπὶ τοὺς τὰ τοιαῦτα πράσσοντας.

λογίζῃ δὲ τοῦτο, ὦ ἄνθρωπε ὁ κρίνων τοὺς τὰ τοιαῦτα πράσσοντας καὶ ποιῶν αὐτά,
  ὅτι σὺ ἐκφεύξῃ τὸ κρίμα τοῦ θεοῦ;

ἢ τοῦ πλούτου τῆς χρηστότητος αὐτοῦ καὶ τῆς ἀνοχῆς καὶ τῆς μακροθυμίας καταφρονεῖς,
  ἀγνοῶν ὅτι τὸ χρηστὸν τοῦ θεοῦ εἰς μετάνοιάν σε ἄγει;

κατὰ δὲ τὴν σκληρότητά σου καὶ ἀμετανόητον καρδίαν θησαυρίζεις σεαυτῷ ὀργὴν ἐν ἡμέρᾳ ὀργῆς καὶ ἀποκαλύψεως δικαιοκρισίας τοῦ θεοῦ,

A ὃς ἀποδώσει ἑκάστῳ κατὰ τὰ ἔργα αὐτοῦ·

B τοῖς μὲν καθ' ὑπομονὴν ἔργου ἀγαθοῦ δόξαν καὶ τιμὴν καὶ ἀφθαρσίαν ζητοῦσιν ζωὴν αἰώνιον,

C τοῖς δὲ ἐξ ἐριθείας καὶ ἀπειθοῦσιν τῇ ἀληθείᾳ πειθομένοις δὲ τῇ ἀδικίᾳ ὀργὴ καὶ θυμός.

C′ θλῖψις καὶ στενοχωρία ἐπὶ πᾶσαν ψυχὴν ἀνθρώπου τοῦ κατεργαζομένου τὸ κακόν,
  Ἰουδαίου τε πρῶτον καὶ Ἕλληνος·

B′ δόξα δὲ καὶ τιμὴ καὶ εἰρήνη παντὶ τῷ ἐργαζομένῳ τὸ ἀγαθόν,
  Ἰουδαίῳ τε πρῶτον καὶ Ἕλληνι·

A′ οὐ γάρ ἐστιν προσωπολημψία παρὰ τῷ θεῷ.

ὅσοι γὰρ	ἀνόμως ἥμαρτον,	ἀνόμως καὶ ἀπολοῦνται,
καὶ ὅσοι	ἐν νόμῳ ἥμαρτον,	διὰ νόμου κριθήσονται·
οὐ γὰρ	οἱ ἀκροαταὶ νόμου	δίκαιοι παρὰ [τῷ] θεῷ,
ἀλλ'	οἱ ποιηταὶ νόμου	δικαιωθήσονται.

ὅταν γὰρ ἔθνη τὰ μὴ νόμον ἔχοντα φύσει τὰ τοῦ νόμου ποιῶσιν,
οὗτοι νόμον μὴ ἔχοντες ἑαυτοῖς εἰσιν νόμος

οἵτινες ἐνδείκνυνται τὸ ἔργον τοῦ νόμου γραπτὸν ἐν ταῖς καρδίαις αὐτῶν,
συμμαρτυρούσης αὐτῶν τῆς συνειδήσεως
καὶ μεταξὺ ἀλλήλων τῶν λογισμῶν κατηγορούντων ἢ καὶ ἀπολογουμένων,
ἐν ἡμέρᾳ ὅτε κρίνει ὁ θεὸς τὰ κρυπτὰ τῶν ἀνθρώπων κατὰ τὸ εὐαγγέλιόν μου διὰ Χριστοῦ Ἰησοῦ.

VERSE 1

Διὸ ἀναπολόγητος εἶ, ὦ ἄνθρωπε πᾶς ὁ κρίνων

Paul looks back to 1:18–32 as a whole and draws an inference (διό) from that discussion of human sinfulness (Cranfield 141; Longenecker 245; Schreiner 106): the person who passes judgment on that sinfulness is also "without excuse" (ἀναπολόγητος, -ον; cf. 1:20). The shift to direct address in the second person increases the vividness of the argument (Cranfield 142) and introduces the diatribe style that Paul also uses later in the chapter (2:17–24). Longenecker suggests that by using a diatribal form Paul presents himself to the Romans as their teacher (243–44). The interjection ὦ ("O!") adds emphasis to the vocative of direct address (ἄνθρωπε). The nominative participial phrase πᾶς ὁ κρίνων ("everyone who is judging") stands in apposition to the preceding vocative (R 464). See the similar construction in 1:16; the present tense is customary. Κρίνω carries the idea of passing unfavorable judgment on the life or action of another (BDAG 567d).

ἐν ᾧ γὰρ κρίνεις τὸν ἕτερον, σεαυτὸν κατακρίνεις

The reason (γάρ) Paul draws his inference resides in the nature of passing judgment: judging another person condemns the one who judges. The prepositional phrase ἐν ᾧ is short for ἐν τούτῳ (R 721) and refers to the act of judging. Κρίνεις (2 sg. pres. act. indic.) is a customary present. The definite article with ἕτερον (acc. sg. masc. of ἕτερος, -α, -ον, "another") allows the adjective to function as a noun and emphasize the distinctness from the one doing the judging (BDAG 399d suggests the translation "one's neighbor"). Placing the direct object σεαυτόν (acc. sg. masc. of reflex. pron. σεαυτοῦ, -ῆς, "yourself") before its verb creates a chiasmus; κατακρίνεις (2 sg. pres. act. indic.) is a word play on κρίνεις. Κατακρίνω denotes the act of pronouncing a sentence on someone after determining guilt (BDAG 519a).

τὰ γὰρ αὐτὰ πράσσεις ὁ κρίνων

The explanation (γάρ) of this self-condemnation comes from the actions of the one who judges (ὁ κρίνων). The word order of the clause calls attention to its content. Placing the object first gives it emphasis, and placing the subject last brackets the sentence. The article with the pronoun (τὰ αὐτά) marks its identifying function, best translated as "the same things." Cranfield notes that the actions involved are of the same sort rather than necessarily being identical (142). Πράσσεις (2 sg. pres. act. indic. of πράσσω) echoes 1:32 and denotes actions that are not praiseworthy (BDAG 860c).

VERSE 2

οἴδαμεν δὲ ὅτι τὸ κρίμα τοῦ θεοῦ ἐστιν κατὰ ἀλήθειαν

The disclosure formula introduces an accepted fact that establishes common ground between Paul and his audience (Jewett 198; cf. Rom 3:19; 7:14; 8:22, 28). The conjunction δέ is transitional ("now"); οἴδαμεν (1 pl. pf. act. indic. of οἶδα, "know"; pf. with act. mng.) is gnomic; ὅτι introduces a substantival clause of content ("that"). The article with κρίμα (nom. sg. neut.) identifies it as distinct from the act of human judgment previously discussed; the noun itself denotes a judicial verdict (BDAG 567b) that comes from God (subj. gen.). That verdict is in accordance with the standard (κατά + acc.) of truth and, therefore, is just (Moo 131).

ἐπὶ τοὺς τὰ τοιαῦτα πράσσοντας

That judgment comes "upon" (ἐπί + acc.) those who are judging because they are practicing the same sort of actions they judge. See 1:32 for a similar construction. The correlative pronoun τοιαῦτα (acc. pl. neut. of τοιοῦτος, -αύτη, -οῦτον, "of such kind") is a stylistic variant on τὰ αὐτά at the end of verse 1 that reinforces the nature of the actions rather than their specific identity.

VERSE 3

λογίζῃ δὲ τοῦτο, ὦ ἄνθρωπε ὁ κρίνων τοὺς τὰ τοιαῦτα πράσσοντας καὶ ποιῶν αὐτά

Rhetorical questions are a standard feature of diatribe and serve to set out false premises that will be refuted. In contrast (δέ) to the principle Paul has just established is the idea that it is possible to escape judgment. Λογίζῃ (2 sg. pres. mid. indic. of dep. λογίζομαι) is used in the LXX to denote thinking that involves feelings and the will (Cranfield 143 n. 4). Wallace suggests that the present tense of verbs of thinking may be lexically influenced and therefore describes action that is completed at the moment of action ("instantaneous present," 517). Τοῦτο points forward to the content of the ὅτι clause that follows. The extended direct address repeats content from verses 1 and 2, using the synonym ποιέω (for πράσσω) and the anaphoric personal pronoun αὐτά ("them").

ὅτι σὺ ἐκφεύξῃ τὸ κρίμα τοῦ θεοῦ;

The conjunction ὅτι ("that") introduces a noun clause in apposition to τοῦτο. Σύ is emphatic (Moo 132 n. 28); ἐκφεύξῃ (2 sg. fut. mid. indic.) is a future deponent. Ἐκφεύγω describes becoming free from danger by avoiding peril and is followed by the accusative of what is escaped (BDAG 312a). See verse 2 for τὸ κρίμα τοῦ θεοῦ.

VERSE 4

ἢ τοῦ πλούτου τῆς χρηστότητος αὐτοῦ καὶ τῆς ἀνοχῆς καὶ τῆς μακροθυμίας καταφρονεῖς

The disjunctive conjunction ἤ ("or") introduces a second rhetorical question and drives home the point Paul has just made (Cranfield 144; cf. 1 Cor 9:6). Jewett notes the "rhetorical sophistication" of the word order Paul uses in framing the question (200). Τοῦ πλούτου (gen. sg. masc. of πλοῦτος, -ου, ὁ, "riches") is genitive because καταφρονέω takes a genitive direct object (cf. Matt 6:24; 18:10; Luke 16:13; 1 Cor 11:22). Πλοῦτος, in turn, takes the genitive of the content described (BDAG 832b); a definite article accompanies each of the abstract nouns dependent on it. Χρηστότης, -ητος, ἡ denotes the quality of kindness or generosity (BDAG 1090b); ἀνοχή, -ῆς, ἡ describes the act of being forbearing or tolerant (BDAG 86c); μακροθυμία, -ας, ἡ describes the virtue of being able to bear up under provocation (BDAG 613a). Moo notes the use of the same nouns in Wisdom of Solomon 15:1–2 and suggests that the second and third explain God's goodness in patiently withholding judgment (132–33). The present tense of καταφρονεῖς (2 sg. pres. act. indic.) is customary; the verb carries the sense of looking on something with contempt because it has little value (BDAG 529d).

ἀγνοῶν ὅτι τὸ χρηστὸν τοῦ θεοῦ εἰς μετάνοιάν σε ἄγει;

The adverbial participle ἀγνοῶν (nom. sg. masc. of pres. act. ptc. of ἀγνοέω, "be uninformed about") is causal, and the conjuction ὅτι ("that") introduces a noun clause of content. Blass notes that a neuter singular adjective preceded by the definite article (τὸ χρηστόν) functions as an abstract noun and is peculiar to Paul (§263.2). The dependent genitive that follows it (τοῦ θεοῦ) is possessive. The objective toward which God's kindness is directed (εἰς + acc.) is μετάνοιαν (acc. sg. fem. of μετάνοια, -ας, ἡ, "repentance"). See Wallace's note on the μετανο- word group (289 n. 92). The personal pronoun (σε) continues the second person focus of the section and is placed before the verb for emphasis. Ἄγει (3 sg. pres. act. indic. of ἄγω, "lead") is a conative present (R 880; T 63); the verb can carry the nuance of guiding morally or spiritually (BDAG 16c). Jewett suggests that the entire participial clause heightens the "outrageous behavior" described.

VERSE 5

κατὰ δὲ τὴν σκληρότητά σου καὶ ἀμετανόητον καρδίαν θησαυρίζεις σεαυτῷ ὀργὴν

Paul contrasts (δέ) the intent of God's kindness with humankind's actual response to it. That response is in accordance with (κατά + acc.) a condition characterized by two distinct qualities that the article-noun-καί-noun construction unites (cf. Wallace 286–90). Σκληρότης, -ητος, ἡ denotes stubbornness or hardness of heart (BDAG 930c), while ἀμετανόητος, -ον ("unrepentant, impenitent") contrasts with μετάνοια in the preceding verse. See 1:21 for καρδία. Θησαυρίζεις (2 sg. pres. act. indic. of θησαυρίζω, "store up") is a progressive present. The verb carries the idea of doing something that will bring about a future condition (BDAG 456b); Schreiner suggests that Paul uses it ironically (109). Moo classifies σεαυτῷ as a dative of disadvantage (134 n. 46). See 1:18 for ὀργή.

ἐν ἡμέρᾳ ὀργῆς καὶ ἀποκαλύψεως δικαιοκρισίας τοῦ θεοῦ

The time (ἐν + dat.) when the wrath will be unleashed is the "day" (ἡμέρᾳ), a term Paul uses elsewhere as shorthand for the day of Christ's return (e.g., 1 Cor 1:8; 2 Cor 1:14; Phil 1:6; 1 Thess 5:2; 2 Thess 1:10; 2 Tim 1:12). That day will be characterized by wrath and revelation (attrib. gens., R 497), specifically, the revelation of a just verdict (obj. gen.). The eighth occurrence of a word related to judgment (δικαιοκρισία) rounds out the first section, and τοῦ θεοῦ (subj. gen.) leads naturally to the second section. Longenecker suggests the translation "the day of wrath when God's righteous judgment will be revealed" (250).

VERSE 6

ὃς ἀποδώσει ἑκάστῳ κατὰ τὰ ἔργα αὐτοῦ

The relative pronoun ὅς (nom. sg. masc.) connects directly to τοῦ θεοῦ and introduces an extended discussion of God's just verdict. Ἀποδώσει (3 sg. fut. act. indic. of ἀποδίδωμι, "recompense, repay") is a predictive future; ἑκάστῳ (dat. sg. masc. of ἕκαστος, -η, -ον, "each one") is a dative of disadvantage; the standard (κατά + acc.) of repayment is "works"; the definite article with ἔργα (acc. pl. neut.) is simple identification; αὐτοῦ is a subjective genitive. Cranfield notes that Paul echoes Psalm 61:13 (LXX) and Proverb 24:2 (LXX) and provides a good review of OT and NT passages that address the idea of judgment according to works (146).

VERSE 7

τοῖς μὲν καθ' ὑπομονὴν ἔργου ἀγαθοῦ δόξαν καὶ τιμὴν καὶ ἀφθαρσίαν ζητοῦσιν ζωὴν αἰώνιον

The correlative conjunction μέν introduces the first category of individuals Paul describes. The definite article τοῖς (dat. pl. masc.) is generic and, with the substantival participle ζητοῦσιν (dat. pl. masc. of pres. act. ptc. of ζητέω, "seek"), brackets the description of the category. The participle stands in apposition to ἑκάστῳ in the preceding verse. Moo views κατά as causal (137 n. 10), while Cranfield suggests manner (147; cf. Moule 58). The parallel with verse 6, however, makes standard ("according/corresponding to") more likely. Ὑπομονή, -ῆς, ἡ denotes the capacity to bear up in the face of adversity (BDAG 1039a); Longenecker suggests "steadfast endurance" (256); ἔργου ἀγαθοῦ is an objective genitive ("perseverance that produces a good work"). The three anarthrous abstract nouns are qualitative and function as the objects of the participle. See 1:23 for δόξα and ἀφθαρσία. Τιμή, -ῆς, ἡ is a manifestation of esteem and can be a heavenly possession (BDAG 1005c); ζητέω describes devoting serious effort to realizing a desire (BDAG 428c). Ζωὴν αἰώνιον is the direct object of ἀποδώσει in verse 6 and describes transcendent life in a period of unending duration that follows the final judgment (BDAG 430d). Longenecker provides intertestamental background to support the idea that the phrase refers to the final destination of the righteous (257; cf. 2 Macc 7:9; 4 Macc 15:3).

VERSE 8

τοῖς δὲ ἐξ ἐριθείας καὶ ἀπειθοῦσιν τῇ ἀληθείᾳ πειθομένοις δὲ τῇ ἀδικίᾳ ὀργὴ καὶ θυμός

The second category of individuals (δέ) stands in antithetic parallelism to the first (R 1200). The dative definite article (τοῖς) introduces three descriptions in apposition to ἑκάστῳ. The first is the substantival prepositional phrase (ἐξ ἐριθείας) that characterizes their motivation (ἐκ + gen.) as "selfishness" (ἐριθεία, -ας, ἡ; cf. Longenecker 257). The conjunction καί adds the substantival participle ἀπειθοῦσιν (dat. pl. masc. of pres. act. ptc. of ἀπειθέω, "disobey"), which is then contrasted (δέ) with the substantival participle πειθομένοις (dat. pl. masc. of pres. mid. ptc. of πείθω, "obey"). The play on words (ἀπειθέω . . . πείθω) is heightened by the contrast in the dependent datives (τῇ ἀληθείᾳ . . . τῇ ἀδικίᾳ), which also occur together in 1:18. Ὀργή, -ῆς, ἡ ("wrath") occurs in both 1:18 and 2:5. It is also paired with θυμός, -οῦ, ὁ ("fury") in the LXX, so that the second noun strengthens and emphasizes the first (Cranfield 149). Instead of the accusative (cf. ζωὴν αἰώνιον in v. 7), ὀργὴ καὶ θυμός are in the nominative, perhaps anticipating the nominative nouns that begin the second half of the inverted structure in the next sentence.

VERSE 9

θλῖψις καὶ στενοχωρία ἐπὶ πᾶσαν ψυχὴν ἀνθρώπου τοῦ κατεργαζομένου τὸ κακόν

Paul now retraces his argument in reverse order. The absence of a conjunction (asyndeton) calls attention both to the beginning of a new sentence and to the repeated idea of judgment (cf. Moo 138 n. 15). Based on LXX uses, Jewett views θλῖψις καὶ στενοχωρία as a formula for divine wrath (207), although Paul's other uses do not appear to support that conclusion (cf. Rom 8:35; 2 Cor 6:4). Cranfield sees θλῖψις ("tribulation") as outward and στενοχωρία ("distress") as inward (149), while Moo sees θλῖψις as objective and στενοχωρία as subjective (139). In either case, they represent the effects of ὀργὴ καὶ θυμός in verse 8 and are the subject of an understood future tense of εἰμί. The preposition ἐπί ("upon") is spatial, and the anarthrous noun ἀνθρώπου is generic (R 757). Jewett translates πᾶσαν ψυχὴν ἀνθρώπου as "every single person" and notes that the use of πᾶς in this sentence and the next eliminates the possibility that preference could be given to any group (208). The articular participle τοῦ κατεργαζομένου is adjectival and modifies ἀνθρώπου; the construction as a whole is characteristic of Hellenistic Greek (Z 192). The neuter singular adjective with a definite article (τὸ κακόν) functions as an abstract noun (cf. 1:19; 2:4) and is the object of the participle.

Ἰουδαίου τε πρῶτον καὶ Ἕλληνος

See the discussion in 1:16. The phrase stands in apposition to τοῦ κατεργαζομένου and is repeated in the following sentence where it stands in apposition to τῷ ἐργαζομένῳ. In both sentences, Paul uses the phrase to eliminate any notion of Jewish precedence and, therefore, to anticipate his conclusion in verse 11.

VERSE 10

δόξα δὲ καὶ τιμὴ καὶ εἰρήνη παντὶ τῷ ἐργαζομένῳ τὸ ἀγαθόν, Ἰουδαίῳ τε πρῶτον καὶ Ἕλληνι

In contrast (δέ) to the judgment that comes upon those who perform evil are the blessings promised to those who perform good. Paul adds εἰρήνη ("peace," cf. 1:7) to δόξα ("glory") and τιμή ("honor") that both occur in 2:7. Παντὶ τῷ ἐργαζομένῳ is a dative of advantage and parallel to the ἐπί phrase in the previous sentence. The change from κατεργάζομαι to ἐργάζομαι is for variety; τὸ ἀγαθόν provides the antithesis to τὸ κακόν; the concluding phrase stands in apposition to ἐργαζομένῳ.

VERSE 11

οὐ γάρ ἐστιν προσωπολημψία παρὰ τῷ θεῷ

The final explanation (γάρ) of why God acts as he does resides in his impartiality. Paul also uses προσωπολημψία, -ας, ἡ ("partiality, favoritism") in Ephesians 6:9 and Colossians 3:25. The idea occurs in Galatians 2:6 as well, although in a form that more nearly reflects the concept's Hebraic background (cf. Jewett 209–10). Moule classifies παρὰ τῷ θεῷ as spatial and translates it "in the presence of God" (52).

How best to understand Paul's affirmation of judgment according to works in verses 6–11 has generated considerable discussion. Cranfield identifies ten possible interpretations and concludes that Paul is speaking of good works that are the expression of Christian faith (151–52). Schreiner reaches the same conclusion (115), while Moo leans toward "the unrealizable condition for salvation apart from Christ" (140–42).

Dunn sees Paul placing a check on Jewish self-assurance growing out of their priority in God's working (93). Jewett argues that Paul uses traditional biblical language to secure his audience's assent to the principle of God's impartiality as it advances his rhetorical purpose. For that reason, he views any perceived disparity between this passage and Paul's later emphasis on justification by faith as irrelevant (210).

VERSE 12

ὅσοι γὰρ ἀνόμως ἥμαρτον, ἀνόμως καὶ ἀπολοῦνται

Paul begins the third section of the paragraph with an explanation (*γάρ*) of the principle of God's impartiality structured in synonymous parallelism (cf. Longenecker 265). The first line applies the principle to those who have had no access to the law. The relative adjective *ὅσοι* (nom. pl. masc. of *ὅσος, -η, -ον*, "as many as") introduces a subordinate clause of condition (Wallace 664). The adverb *ἀνόμως* denotes someone without awareness of a legal system (BDAG 86b); the context suggests the system of the Mosaic law (cf. Longenecker 264; Moo 145). The aorist of *ἥμαρτον* (3 pl. aor. act. indic. of *ἁμαρτάνω*, "sin") is a collective aorist of the indefinite past (Burton §54). *Καί* is adjunctive ("also"); the future middle *ἀπολοῦνται* (3 pl. fut. mid. indic. of *ἀπόλλυμι*) carries the force of the passive (Wallace 416 n. 18) and is translated "will perish."

καὶ ὅσοι ἐν νόμῳ ἥμαρτον, διὰ νόμου κριθήσονται

The second line applies the principle to those who have had regular access to the law and is joined to the first line by the connective *καί* ("and"). *Ἐν νόμῳ* places this second group within the sphere of the law; *διὰ νόμου* identifies the intermediate agency of the judgment they receive. *Κριθήσονται* (3 pl. fut. pass. indic. of *κρίνω*, "judge") is a divine passive (Jewett 211).

VERSE 13

οὐ γὰρ οἱ ἀκροαταὶ νόμου δίκαιοι παρὰ [τῷ] θεῷ

The reason (*γάρ*) those who have had regular access to the law will not automatically avoid judgment resides in the principle set out in the antithetic parallelism of this sentence (cf. Jas 1:22–25). The strength of the contrast is introduced by *οὐ* in the first line and reinforced by *ἀλλά* in the second line. The article with *ἀκροαταί* (nom. pl. masc. of *ἀκροατής, -οῦ, ὁ*, "hearer") is generic (R 757), and *νόμου* is an objective genitive. Robertson notes that the anarthrous noun is definite (796), and Blass notes that Paul tends to omit the article with *νόμος* (§258.2). *Δίκαιοι* (nom. pl. masc. of *δίκαιος, -α, -ον*, "just") stands in a verbless predicate construction (art.-noun-adj.) that makes a statement about the noun that precedes it. *Παρὰ τῷ θεῷ* echoes the same phrase in verse 11.

ἀλλ' οἱ ποιηταὶ νόμου δικαιωθήσονται

Οἱ ποιηταὶ νόμου is directly parallel to the first line, with "doers" replacing "hearers." Δικαιωθήσονται (3 pl. fut. pass. indic. of δικαιόω, "justify") parallels and stands in contrast to κριθήσονται at the end of verse 12; it is another divine passive (Wallace 438). Longenecker examines this statement at length and concludes that Paul "speaks as he does in ch. 2 (1) in order to gain rapport with his Christian addressees in Rome, who themselves use such teaching . . . in their own worship, proclamation, and instruction, and (2) because [it] served, when rightly understood, to support and enforce the points he wants to make in this section of his letter: that God judges people on the basis of what they do, not just what they possess and know, and that God judges people impartially, not according to any special privilege of race, religion, or circumstance" (266–69).

VERSE 14

ὅταν γὰρ ἔθνη τὰ μὴ νόμον ἔχοντα φύσει τὰ τοῦ νόμου ποιῶσιν

Paul now explains (γάρ) how the principle he has enunciated can be extended to the Gentiles (ἔθνη). The subordinate conjunction ὅταν ("whenever") followed by the present subjunctive (ποιῶσιν) introduces a temporal clause that sets out a general case; the present tense is iterative (T 112). The absence of the article with ἔθνη makes it clear that Paul is not describing all Gentiles (Cranfield 155 n. 3; cf. Longenecker 273). The neuter plural definite article τά marks the participle ἔχοντα (nom. pl. neut. of pres. act. ptc. of ἔχω) as adjectival and brackets μὴ νόμον with it ("who are not having the law"). Although Cranfield (156), Jewett (214), and Schreiner (123) all take φύσει with the preceding participial phrase, Moo (149), Dunn (98), Longenecker (274), and most EVV take it with the main verb that follows as a dative of cause ("on the basis of nature").* The article with a genitive phrase functioning as a substantive ("the things of the law") is a common construction (cf. Wallace 236); delaying the verb until the end of the clause gives it emphasis. Longenecker concludes that Paul intends his readers to understand that he is referring to Gentiles doing "some of the law's commands" (275).

οὗτοι νόμον μὴ ἔχοντες ἑαυτοῖς εἰσιν νόμος

Although the gender of οὗτοι (nom. pl. masc.) does not agree with its antecedent (ἔθνη), the connection is one according to sense (R 704) and, therefore, clear enough. The participle ἔχοντες (nom. pl. masc. of pres. act. ptc. of ἔχω) is adverbial of concession ("although they are not having law"); ἑαυτοῖς is a dative of advantage (Moo 151 n. 39); νόμος is a predicate nominative. Cranfield notes that the phrase ἑαυτῷ εἶναι νόμος is a stereotyped description of a person of superior moral virtue who does not need guidance from external law (157).

VERSE 15

οἵτινες ἐνδείκνυνται τὸ ἔργον τοῦ νόμου γραπτὸν ἐν ταῖς καρδίαις αὐτῶν

The relative pronoun οἵτινες (nom. pl. masc.) is generic ("who all"); Longenecker gives it a causal nuance (276). The present tense of ἐνδείκνυνται (3 pl. pres. mid. indic. of ἐνδείκνυμι, "show") is customary, while the indirect middle voice highlights the subject's interest in the action. The verb means to direct attention to something or to cause to become known (BDAG 331d); it commonly takes an object-complement (Wallace 188). The object (τὸ ἔργον) is accompanied by a generic definite article and the subjective genitive τοῦ νόμου ("the kind of work the law requires"); the complement (γραπτόν) is accompanied by a prepositional phrase of location ("written in their hearts").

συμμαρτυρούσης αὐτῶν τῆς συνειδήσεως

The first of two genitive absolutes is adverbial of time ("while"). Συμμαρτυρέω describes the action of providing supporting evidence by testifying; the present tense is customary (cf. Cranfield 159–60; *TDNT* 7.904). The definite article marks the genitive noun as the subject of the participle.

καὶ μεταξὺ ἀλλήλων τῶν λογισμῶν κατηγορούντων ἢ καὶ ἀπολογουμένων

The connective καί joins the two genitive absolutes, although the relationship between them is debated. Jewett is probably correct that the constructions are parallel (215) rather than seeing the second as explaining the first (e.g., Cranfield 161). The preposition μεταξύ ("between") takes the genitive case and reinforces the reciprocal relationship inherent in the pronoun ἀλλήλων ("one another"). Longenecker understands the prepositional phrase as "referring to the inner debate that goes on within the conscience of a person . . . concerning right and wrong in their own works" (278). The definite article marks λογισμῶν (gen. pl. masc. of λογισμός, -οῦ, ὁ, "thought, reasoning") as the subject of the genitive participles that follow. Κατηγορέω ("accuse") can be used without legal connotations (BDAG 533c). When it is joined with ἀπολογέομαι ("speak in defense"), however, the terms point to prosecution and defense in a law court (Moo 153 n. 60).

VERSE 16

ἐν ἡμέρᾳ ὅτε κρίνει ὁ θεὸς τὰ κρυπτὰ τῶν ἀνθρώπων

With the temporal ἐν ἡμέρᾳ, Paul reintroduces the idea of a "day" when (ὅτε) God will judge (cf. 2:5). The present tense of κρίνει is futuristic (BDF §323) and explains the variant (κρινεῖ) that occurs in a few manuscripts. The article with θεός is anaphoric; the neuter plural article with κρυπτά (acc. pl. neut. of κρυπτός, -ή, -όν, "hidden") allows the adjective to stand as the direct object ("the hidden things"); τῶν ἀνθρώπων is a subjective genitive. Longenecker suggests that this verse connects logically with 2:13 (281).

κατὰ τὸ εὐαγγέλιόν μου διὰ Χριστοῦ Ἰησοῦ

The standard (κατά + acc.) for God's judgment is the gospel that Paul proclaims (subj. gen.) and was given through the agency (διά + gen.) of Christ Jesus. A decision on the textual variant is difficult because of the variety of combinations Paul uses in referring to Jesus. Metzger chooses Χριστοῦ Ἰησοῦ because it is supported by "the oldest extant witnesses" (448; cf. Longenecker 234), but Paul's tendency to use Ἰησοῦ Χριστοῦ with διά (1:8; 5:1, 21; 7:25; 15:30; 16:27) and Χριστῷ Ἰησοῦ with ἐν (3:24; 6:11, 23; 8:1, 2, 39; 14:14; 15:17; 16:3) suggests otherwise.

FOR FURTHER STUDY

21. Diatribe (2:1–5)

Bultmann, R. *Der Stil der Paulinischen Predigt und die kynish-stoische Diatribe.* Göttingen, Vandenhock & Ruprecht, 1910.
Carras, G. P. "Romans 2,1–29: A Dialogue on Jewish Ideals." *Bib* 73 (1992): 183–207.
Kustas, G. I. *Diatribe in Ancient Rhetorical Theory*. Berkeley, CA: Center for Hermeneutical Studies, 1976.
Malherbe, A. "ME GENOITO in the Diatribe and Paul." *HTR* 73 (1980): 231–40.
Porter, S. E. *DNTB* 296–98.
Schmeller, T. *Paulus und die "Diatribe." Eine vergleichende Stilinterpretation.* Münster: Aschendorff, 1987.
Song, C. *Reading Romans as a Diatribe: Studies in Biblical Literature.* New York: Peter Lang, 2004.
Spitaler, P. "Diatribe and the Construction of a Negative Pauline Anthropology." *ETL* 84 (2008): 445–75.
Stowers, S. K. *The Diatribe and Paul's Letter to the Romans.* Chico, CA: Scholars Press, 1981.
________. "Paul's Dialogue with a Fellow Jew in Romans 3:1–9." *CBQ* 46 (1984): 707–22.
________. "The Diatribe." Pages 71–83 in *Greco-Roman Literature and the New Testament*. Edited by D. E. Aune. Atlanta: Scholars Press, 1988.
Watson, D. F. *DPL* 213–14.

22. God's Judgment (2:2)

Bird, Michael F. "Judgment and Justification in Paul: A Review Article." *BBR* 18 (2008): 299–313.
Büchsel, H. M. F. *TDNT* 3.933–54.
Donfried, K. P. "Justification and Last Judgment in Paul." *Interp* 30 (1976): 140–52.
Hamilton, J. M., Jr. *God's Glory in Salvation through Judgment: A Biblical Theology.* Wheaton, IL: Crossway, 2010.

Jewett, R. "The Anthropological Implications of the Revelation of Wrath in Romans." Pages 24–38 in *Reading Paul in Context*. Edited by W. S. Campbell. London: T & T Clark, 2010.

Keillor, S. *God's Judgments: Interpreting History and the Christian Faith*. Downers Grove: InterVarsity, 2007.

Morris, L. *The Biblical Doctrine of Judgment.* Grand Rapids: Eerdmans, 1960.

________. *EDBT* 436–40.

Roetzel, C. J. "Judgment Form in Paul's Letters." *JBL* 88 (1969): 305–12.

________. *Judgment in the Community: A Study of the Relationship between Eschatology and Ecclesiology in Paul*. Leiden: Brill, 1972.

Schneider, W. *NIDNTT* 2.362–67.

Travis, S. H. *Christ and the Judgment of God: The Limits of Divine Retribution in New Testament Thought*. London: Marshall Pickering, 1986.

VanLandingham, C. *Judgment & Justification in Early Judaism and the Apostle Paul*. Peabody, MA: Hendrickson, 2006.

Youngblood, R. *EDT* 590–91.

23. Repentance (2:4)

Behm, J. *TDNT* 4.999–1008.

Boda, M., and G. Smith. *Repentance in Christian Theology.* Collegeville, MN: Liturgical Press, 2006.

Dunnett, W. M. *EDBT* 761–62.

Ferguson, S. *The Grace of Repentance.* Wheaton, IL: Crossway, 2010.

Healey, J. P. *ABD* 5.671–72.

Kromminga, C. G. *EDT* 936–37.

Neusner, J. "Sin, Repentance, Atonement and Resurrection: The Perspective of Rabbinic Theology on the Views of James 1–2 and Paul in Romans 3–4." Pages 409–34 in *Missions of James, Peter, and Paul*. Edited by B. Chilton, C. A. Evans, and B. Evans. Leiden: Brill, 2005.

Wilkin, R. N. "Repentance and Salvation, Part 3: New Testament Repentance: Lexical Considerations." *Journal of the Grace Evangelical Society* 2 (1989): 13–21.

________. "Repentance and Salvation, Part 5: New Testament Repentance: Repentance in the Epistles and Revelation." *Journal of the Grace Evangelical Society* 3 (1990): 19–32.

24. Paul and the Law (2:12)

Adeyemi, F. "Paul's 'Positive' Statements about the Mosaic Law." *BSac* 164 (2007): 49–58.

Bruce, F. F. "Paul and the Law in Recent Research." Pages 115–25 in *Law and Religion.* Edited by B. Lindars. Cambridge: James Clarke, 1988.

Das, A. A. *Paul, the Law, and the Covenant.* Peabody. MA: Hendrickson, 2001.

Esser, H.-H. *NIDNTT* 2.438–53.

Gundry, S. N. *Five Views on Law and Gospel*. Grand Rapids: Zondervan, 1999.

Hays, R. B. "Three Dramatic Roles." Pages 151–64 in *Paul and the Mosaic Law*. Edited by J. D. G. Dunn. Tübingen: Mohr Siebeck, 1996.

Hübner, H. *Law in Paul's Thought*. Edinburgh: T & T Clark, 1984.

Jewett, R. "The Law and the Coexistence of Jews and Gentiles in Romans." *Int* 39 (1985): 341–56.

Kuula, K. *The Law, the Covenant and God's Plan, 2: Paul's Treatment of the Law and Israel in Romans*. Göttingen: Vandenhoeck & Ruprecht, 2003.
Marcus, J. "'Under the Law' The Background of a Pauline Expression." *CBQ* 63 (2001): 72–83.
Martin, B. L. "Paul on Christ and the Law." *JETS* 26 (1983): 271–82.
________. *Christ and the Law in Paul*. Leiden: Brill, 1989.
Moo, D. J. "'Law,' 'Works of the Law,' and Legalism in Paul." *WTJ* 45 (1983): 73–100.
Räisänen, H. *Paul and the Law*. Tübingen: Mohr Siebeck, 1983.
Sanders, E. P. *Paul, the Law and the Jewish People*. Philadelphia: Fortress, 1983.
Schreiner, T. R. *40 Questions about Christians and Biblical Law*. Grand Rapids: Kregel, 2010.
________. *The Law & Its Fulfillment: A Pauline Theology of Law*. Grand Rapids: Baker, 1993.
________. "The Abolition and Fulfillment of the Law in Paul." *JSNT* 35 (1989): 47–74.
Sloan, R. B. "Paul and the Law: Why the Law Cannot Save." *NovT* 33 (1991): 35–60.
Snodgrass, K. "Spheres of Influence: A Possible Solution to the Problem of Paul and the Law." *JSNT* 32 (1988): 93–113.
Thielman, F. *DPL* 529–42.
________. *From Plight to Solution: A Jewish Framework for Understanding Paul's View of the Law in Galatians and Romans*. Leiden: Brill, 1989.
________. *Paul and the Law*. Downers Grove, IL: InterVarsity, 1994.
Tomson, P. J. *Paul and the Jewish Law: Halakah in the Letters of the Apostle to the Gentiles*. Minneapolis: Fortress, 1990.
Westerholm, S. *Israel's Law and the Church's Faith: Paul and His Recent Interpreters*. Grand Rapids: Eerdmans, 1988.
Winger, J. M. *By What Law? The Meaning of* Νόμος *in the Letters of Paul*. Atlanta: Scholars Press, 1992.
Wright, N. T. *The Climax of the Covenant: Christ and the Law in Pauline Theology*. Edinburgh: T & T Clark, 1991.

25. Conscience (2:15)

Bosman, P. *Conscience in Philo and Paul: A Conceptual History of the Synoida Word Group*. Tübingen: Mohr Siebeck, 2003.
Cook, E. "'Conscience' in the New Testament." *Journal of the Adventist Theological Society* 15 (2004): 142–58.
Davies, W. D. *IDB* 1.671–76.
Eckstein, H.-J. *Der Begriff Syneidesis bei Paulus*. Tübingen: Mohr Siebeck, 1983.
Gundry-Volf, J. M. *DPL* 153–56.
Harris, B. F. "SYNEIDĒSIS (Conscience) in the Pauline Writings." *WTJ* 24 (1962): 173–86.
Jewett, R. *Paul's Anthropological Terms: A Study of Their Use in Conflict Settings*. Leiden: Brill, 1971.
Maurer, C. *TDNT* 7.914–19.
Meaders, G. T. *EDBT* 113–15.
Pierce, C. A. *Conscience in the New Testament: A Study of Syneidēsis in the New Testament in the Light of its Sources*. London: SCM, 1955.
Reicke, B. I. "Syneidesis in Rom 2:15." *TZ* 12 (1956): 157–61.
Renwinkel, A. M. *EDT* 267–78.

Spicq, C. "La conscience dans le Nouveau Testament." *RB* 47 (1938): 50–80.
Stepień, J. "Syneidesis: la conscience dans l'anthropologie de Saint-Paul." *Revue d'histoire et de philosophie religieuses* 60 (1980): 1–20.
Thrall, M. E. "Pauline Use of *Syneidēsis*." *NTS* 14 (1967): 118–25.
Wall, R. W. *ADB* 1.1128–30.

HOMILETICAL SUGGESTIONS

God's Judgment (2:1–16)

1. God's judgment is deserved (2:1–5)
   a. By those who practice what they judge (2:1–3)
      1) Judging others condemns the one who judges (2:1)
      2) God judges those who practice the actions they judge (2:2)
      3) Those who practice what they judge should not think they can escape God's judgment (2:3)
   b. By those who despise God's goodness (2:4–5)
      1) God intends his kindness to lead to repentance (2:4)
      2) Rejecting his kindness stores up judgment (2:5)
2. God's judgment is based on works (2:6–11)
   a. Premise: The criterion for judgment is works (2:6)
      1) Eternal life to those who seek good (2:7)
      2) Wrath and fury to those who pursue evil (2:8)
      3) Tribulation and distress to both Jews and Greeks who do evil (2:9)
      4) Glory, honor, and peace to both Jews and Greeks who do good (2:10)
   b. Conclusion: God's judgment is impartial (2:11)
3. God's judgment is impartially applied (2:12–16)
   a To those who have the law (2:12–13)
      1) They are judged for sinning, without the law or with the law (2:12)
      2) They are not justified for hearing the law but for doing the law (2:13)
   b. To those who do not have the law (2:14–16)
      1) They affirm the validity of the law when they do it (2:14)
      2) They show the law written on their hearts when they listen to their consciences (2:15–16)

d. Because the Jews Transgress the Law (2:17–29)

STRUCTURE

Paul returns to the second person diatribe style in this paragraph, which divides into two sections (2:17–24; 2:25–29). The first centers on the law, divides further into three subsections—each with four descriptions of Jewish advantage/obligation/transgression—and concludes with an Old Testament quotation. The second centers on circumcision, divides further into three subsections—each built on a series of antitheses—and concludes with a statement on the proper source of praise.

Εἰ δὲ σὺ Ἰουδαῖος ἐπονομάζῃ
καὶ ἐπαναπαύῃ νόμῳ
καὶ καυχᾶσαι ἐν θεῷ
καὶ γινώσκεις τὸ θέλημα
καὶ δοκιμάζεις τὰ διαφέροντα
κατηχούμενος ἐκ τοῦ νόμου,

πέποιθάς τε σεαυτὸν ὁδηγὸν εἶναι τυφλῶν,
φῶς τῶν ἐν σκότει,
παιδευτὴν ἀφρόνων,
διδάσκαλον νηπίων,
ἔχοντα τὴν μόρφωσιν τῆς γνώσεως καὶ τῆς ἀληθείας ἐν τῷ νόμῳ·

ὁ οὖν διδάσκων ἕτερον σεαυτὸν οὐ διδάσκεις;
ὁ κηρύσσων μὴ κλέπτειν κλέπτεις;
ὁ λέγων μὴ μοιχεύειν μοιχεύεις;
ὁ βδελυσσόμενος τὰ εἴδωλα ἱεροσυλεῖς;
ὃς ἐν νόμῳ καυχᾶσαι, διὰ τῆς παραβάσεως τοῦ νόμου τὸν θεὸν ἀτιμάζεις·

τὸ γὰρ ὄνομα τοῦ θεοῦ δι’ ὑμᾶς βλασφημεῖται ἐν τοῖς ἔθνεσιν, καθὼς γέγραπται.

περιτομὴ μὲν γὰρ ὠφελεῖ
ἐὰν νόμον πράσσῃς·
ἐὰν δὲ παραβάτης νόμου ᾖς,
ἡ περιτομή σου ἀκροβυστία γέγονεν.

ἐὰν οὖν ἡ ἀκροβυστία τὰ δικαιώματα τοῦ νόμου φυλάσσῃ,
οὐχ ἡ ἀκροβυστία αὐτοῦ εἰς περιτομὴν λογισθήσεται;
καὶ κρινεῖ ἡ ἐκ φύσεως ἀκροβυστία τὸν νόμον τελοῦσα σὲ
τὸν διὰ γράμματος καὶ περιτομῆς παραβάτην νόμου.

οὐ γὰρ ὁ ἐν τῷ φανερῷ Ἰουδαῖός ἐστιν οὐδὲ ἡ ἐν τῷ φανερῷ ἐν σαρκὶ περιτομή,
ἀλλ’ ὁ ἐν τῷ κρυπτῷ Ἰουδαῖος, καὶ περιτομὴ καρδίας ἐν πνεύματι οὐ γράμματι,

οὗ ὁ ἔπαινος οὐκ ἐξ ἀνθρώπων ἀλλ’ ἐκ τοῦ θεοῦ.

VERSE 17

Εἰ δὲ σὺ Ἰουδαῖος ἐπονομάζῃ

A transitional δέ ("now") begins the next paragraph in Paul's argument. Εἰ ("if") introduces the protasis of a first class condition that assumes the premise is true for the sake of argument (R 451, 694; T 115). Longenecker suggests that Paul's use of the first class condition sets out what Paul believes characterizes "the self-identity and self-consciousness of many Jews of his day" (298). The resulting construction (2:17–20) is one of the instances of extended anacoluthon that Blass describes as "numerous and flagrant in Paul" (BDF §467). The personal pronoun σύ is emphatic and resumes the diatribe style from 2:1–5. See 1:16 for Ἰουδαῖος, which is a nominative of appellation and forms an *inclusio* with verses 28–29 (Schreiner 125). Most EVV understand ἐπονομάζῃ (2 sg. pres. mid. indic. of ἐπονομάζω, "call, name") as a direct middle translated "call yourself" (cf. Jewett 221; Longenecker 299).

καὶ ἐπαναπαύῃ νόμῳ

A connective καί begins a series of clauses that set out four perceived advantages of being a Jew (cf. Jewett 222). The present tense of the verbs in each clause is customary, describing action that regularly occurs. Ἐπαναπαύῃ (2 sg. pres. mid. indic. of the dep. ἐπαναπαύομαι, "rest, rely upon") suggests the idea of finding well-being or inner security in something (BDAG 358d). The dative of νόμῳ denotes sphere. Robertson notes that the anarthrous noun refers to the Mosaic law (R 796).

καὶ καυχᾶσαι ἐν θεῷ

Καί continues the series of perceived advantages. Καυχᾶσαι (2 sg. pres. mid. indic. of dep. καυχάομαι, "boast") denotes the idea of finding glory or taking pride (BDAG 536c). It commonly occurs with ἐν + dat. of the person or thing that is the source of pride. The verb occurs thirty-five times in Paul, including three others that speak of boasting in God (Rom 5:11; 1 Cor 1:31; 2 Cor 10:17).

VERSE 18

καὶ γινώσκεις τὸ θέλημα

A connective καί adds a third advantage to the list. Γινώσκεις (2 sg. pres. act. indic. of γινώσκω, "know") denotes knowledge that is acquired by repeated exposure (BDAG 200d). The definite article with θέλημα functions as a possessive pronoun ("his will"; cf. Dunn 111). The noun θέλημα, -τος, τό denotes what one wishes or wills to happen (BDAG 447a).

καὶ δοκιμάζεις τὰ διαφέροντα

Καί again introduces the final clause. Δοκιμάζεις (2 sg. pres. act. indic. of δοκιμάζω, "test, examine, approve") denotes the action of making a critical examination to determine the genuineness of something (BDAG 255c; cf. 1:28). The definite article regularly accompanies substantival participles. The participial phrase τὰ διαφέροντα (acc. pl. neut. of pres. act. ptc. of διαφέρω) can mean "the things that matter" (Cranfield 166, Dunn 111), "the things that are important" (Jewett 224), or "the things that are excellent" (Longenecker 302, Moo 161, Schreiner 130). The parallel in Philippians 1:10 suggests the third understanding.

κατηχούμενος ἐκ τοῦ νόμου

Paul uses a participial phrase to modify the preceding clauses and round out the list of perceived advantages of being a Jew. Κατηχούμενος (nom. sg. masc. of pres. pass. ptc. of κατηχέω, "instruct") is an adverbial participle of cause (Schreiner 130). The verb also occurs in Acts 18:25, 1 Corinthians 14:19, and Galatians 6:6. The source (ἐκ + gen.) out of which the Jew is instructed is τοῦ νόμου; the definite article with νόμος is anaphoric and points back to the Mosaic law in verse 17.

VERSE 19

πέποιθάς τε σεαυτὸν ὁδηγὸν εἶναι τυφλῶν

The conjunction τέ joins πέποιθας (nom. sg. masc. of pf. act. ptc. of πείθω, "persuade") to verses 17–18 and introduces a new list that describes the Jews' obligations to others, especially the Gentiles (Jewett 225). Dunn notes that the verb denotes conviction rather than knowledge (112). The participle is adverbial of cause; the perfect tense is intensive, emphasizing the resulting state (Wallace 576). The complementary infinitive εἶναι (pres. act. inf. of εἰμί) is the direct object of πέποιθας and serves as the verb in indirect discourse (Moo 161 n. 22; cf. Porter 270). The reflexive pronoun σεαυτόν ("yourself") is an accusative of general reference and serves as the subject of the infinitive (R 489). Ὁδηγόν (sg. acc. masc.) is the object of the infinitive and denotes one who assists another in following a path (BDAG 690c). The genitive τυφλῶν is objective. BDAG suggests that the noun refers to those not converted to the Mosaic way of life (1021b).

φῶς τῶν ἐν σκότει

Φῶς (sg. acc. neut.) is a second object of the infinitive and denotes one who brings light that illumines the human soul (BDAG 1073b). The definite article allows the prepositional phrase to serve as a noun; ἐν + dative is spatial; the resulting genitival phrase is objective. The concept of the Jews as guides to the blind echoes Isaiah 42:9 while the idea of being a light to the Gentiles occurs in Isaiah 42:6; 49:6 (Schreiner 131).

VERSE 20

παιδευτὴν ἀφρόνων, διδάσκαλον νηπίων

The third obligation is to be an "instructor" (παιδευτής, -οῦ, ὁ) of those who lack prudence or good judgment (BDAG 159d). The fourth obligation is to be a "teacher" (διδάσκαλος, -ου, ὁ) of those who view spiritual things from the standpoint of a child (BDAG 671b). The adjective νήπιος, -ια, -ιον also occurs in 1 Corinthians 3:1 and Ephesians 4:14.

ἔχοντα τὴν μόρφωσιν τῆς γνώσεως καὶ τῆς ἀληθείας ἐν τῷ νόμῳ

A causal participial phrase again modifies the preceding items and concludes the subsection. The definite article with μόρφωσιν (sg. acc. fem. of μόρφωσις, -εως, ἡ, "embodiment") is *par excellence*. The article also accompanies two abstract nouns (γνώσεως and ἀληθείας) joined by a connective καί. The genitive of both nouns is descriptive. Ἐν + dative denotes sphere; the article with νόμῳ is anaphoric, pointing back to verses 17–18.

VERSE 21

ὁ οὖν διδάσκων ἕτερον σεαυτὸν οὐ διδάσκεις;

The inferential οὖν draws a conclusion from what precedes and introduces the third subsection, consisting of four rhetorical questions that do not indicate whether the expected answer is positive or negative (Porter 277). The subject of each question is a substantival participle in the customary present. Each question uses the interrogative indicative for the main verb (R 915). Jewett notes that the use of the second person forces the readers to condemn themselves (227). The verb διδάσκω echoes the cognate noun in verse 20. See 2:1 on ἕτερος, which is the object of the participle. The reflexive pronoun σεαυτόν is the object of διδάσκεις (2 sg. pres. act. indic.). The negative particle οὐ regularly occurs with the indicative.

ὁ κηρύσσων μὴ κλέπτειν κλέπτεις;

Κηρύσσω denotes the action of making a public declaration or telling widely (BDAG 543d). The negative particle μή regularly occurs with non-indicative moods and modes. The complementary infinitive κλέπτειν (pres. act. inf. of κλέπτω, "steal") is the direct object of the participle and functions as indirect discourse. See Exodus 20:15 for the commandment not to steal.

VERSE 22

ὁ λέγων μὴ μοιχεύειν μοιχεύεις;

Μὴ μοιχεύειν (pres. act. inf. of μοιχεύω, "commit adultery") repeats the previous construction. See Exodus 20:14 for the commandment not to commit adultery.

ὁ βδελυσσόμενος τὰ εἴδωλα ἱεροσυλεῖς;

Βδελύσσομαι carries the idea of detesting something because it is utterly offensive (BDAG 172c). The definite article is generic; εἴδωλον, -ου, τό denotes a fabricated deity (BDAG 281d). Ἱεροσυλέω also occurs in Acts 19:37 and refers to objects taken from a temple by force (T 132). See Exodus 20:4–5 for the commandment related to idolatry; the verb occurs elsewhere in the LXX (cf. 2 Macc 4:39, 42; 9:2; 13:6).

VERSE 23

ὃς ἐν νόμῳ καυχᾶσαι, διὰ τῆς παραβάσεως τοῦ νόμου τὸν θεὸν ἀτιμάζεις·

Paul rounds off the subsection with a different construction, this time a relative clause (cf. Moule 106). The relative pronoun assumes an embedded antecedent (σύ) understood from verse 17 (R 712). Ἐν + dative is causal (T 253); νόμῳ without the article refers to the Mosaic law (R 796). See verse 17 on καυχάομαι and 1:24 on ἀτιμάζω. The latter verb places the Jews in the same category as the pagan Gentiles (Jewett 230). The means (διά + gen.) by which they bring dishonor to God is transgression ("your breaking the law"). The definite article functions as a possessive pronoun (cf. NASB, NJB, CEV), and παράβασις, -εως, ἡ describes the act of deviating from an established norm (BDAG 758d). Τοῦ νόμου is again the Mosaic law; the genitive is objective.

VERSE 24

τὸ γὰρ ὄνομα τοῦ θεοῦ δι' ὑμᾶς βλασφημεῖται ἐν τοῖς ἔθνεσιν, καθὼς γέγραπται.

The explanation (γάρ) of Paul's conclusion is found in the OT. See Moo for the form of the quotation and its likely source (166 n. 48; cf. Schreiner 134). Ὄνομα, -τος, τό can refer to the divine name (BDAG 712c), which the possessive genitive makes explicit. The combination of definite article with ὄνομα plus the adjunct τοῦ θεοῦ makes the entire phrase monadic (cf. Wallace 224). Βλασφημεῖται (3 sg. pres. pass. indic. of βλασφημέω, "blaspheme") is an iterative present and a simple passive. It is the Jews and their actions that are the cause (διά + acc.) of the Gentiles speaking disrespectfully about God's name. See 1:5 for ἐν τοῖς ἔθνεσιν and 1:17 for καθὼς γέγραπται. Longenecker concludes that in 2:17–24 Paul "is asserting that the Jews of his day have broken the covenant and therefore are not to be considered any better than the Gentiles whom they despise" (312).

VERSE 25

περιτομὴ μὲν γὰρ ὠφελεῖ ἐὰν νόμον πράσσῃς

The explanatory conjunction γάρ makes the connection to what precedes and addresses the implied Jewish objection that circumcision functions as a protection against God's wrath (Moo 167; Schreiner 136). The correlative μέν introduces the first half of an A-B-B′-A′ construction (circumcision-law-law-circumcision). The anarthrous subject περιτομή is definite and refers to Jewish circumcision. The present of ὠφελεῖ (3 sg. pres. act. indic. of ὠφελέω, "be of value") is gnomic. Ἐάν followed by the present subjunctive (πράσσῃς) is a third class general condition that says nothing about the likelihood of fulfillment. The anarthrous object νόμον is also definite and refers to the Mosaic law.

ἐὰν δὲ παραβάτης νόμου ᾖς, ἡ περιτομή σου ἀκροβυστία γέγονεν

The correlative δέ introduces the second half of the A-B-B′-A′ construction. Ἐάν followed by the present subjunctive (ᾖς) is another third class general condition. The indefinite noun παραβάτης (nom. sg. masc.) is a predicate nominative; νόμου is an objective genitive. The definite article with περιτομή is both anaphoric, pointing back to the beginning of the verse, and possessive ("your circumcision"; cf. KJV, RSV, NASB, NEB, ESV). Ἀκροβυστία, -ας, ἡ denotes the state of being uncircumcised (BDAG 39d) and, therefore, describes a Gentile outside the covenant (Schreiner 138). Γέγονεν (3 sg. pf. act. indic. of dep. γίνομαι, "become") is an intensive perfect that emphasizes the existing state.

VERSE 26

ἐὰν οὖν ἡ ἀκροβυστία τὰ δικαιώματα τοῦ νόμου φυλάσσῃ

The inferential οὖν draws a conclusion from verse 25 that also employs a third class general condition (ἐάν + pres. subjunc.). The abstract noun ἡ ἀκροβυστία is a metonymy (part for the whole) that refers to the person rather than the condition (cf. R 683). The article with δικαιώματα (acc. pl. neut.) is generic, and the noun denotes regulations relating to right or just action (BDAG 249d). The article with νόμου is anaphoric; the genitive is subjective. Φυλάσσω ("keep, obey, follow") is regularly used in the OT for keeping the Mosaic law (e.g., Deut 4:40; 6:2; 17:19; 28:45; 30:10, 16) and is synonymous with πράσσω (2:25) and τελέω (2:27).

οὐχ ἡ ἀκροβυστία αὐτοῦ εἰς περιτομὴν λογισθήσεται;

The particle οὐχ introduces a question that anticipates an affirmative answer. Ἡ ἀκροβυστία repeats the subject from the protasis. Although the genitive pronoun αὐτοῦ ("his") has no expressed personal antecedent, the construction according to sense reflects the metonymy of the first clause (BDF §282.2). The prepositional phrase εἰς περιτομήν is a Hebraism that serves as a predicate nominative (R 481) and occurs elsewhere with λογίζομαι (cf. Rom 4:3, 5, 9). Λογισθήσεται (3 sg. fut. pass. indic.) is a simple future and a divine passive (Schreiner 141).

VERSE 27

καὶ κρινεῖ ἡ ἐκ φύσεως ἀκροβυστία τὸν νόμον τελοῦσα σὲ

Paul connects (καί) the preceding question with a statement to emphasize the consequences of Jewish transgression. Κρινεῖ is a simple future (cf. 2:1 on the meaning of the verb). The definite article is anaphoric and with its noun frames the phrase that serves as the subject. Ἐκ + genitive denotes the source of uncircumcision (cf. 1:26 and 2:14 on φύσις). Τὸν νόμον is the object of the participle. Although Wallace takes τελοῦσα (nom. sg. fem. of pres. act. ptc. of τελέω, "fulfill, carry out") as adverbial of condition (633; cf. KJV, NASB), most EVV take it as adjectival, which seems more natural (cf. RSV, GNB, NIV, NJB, CEV, ESV). The second person pronoun σέ is the object of κρινεῖ; its position at the end of the construction is emphatic.

τὸν διὰ γράμματος καὶ περιτομῆς παραβάτην νόμου

The definite article and its noun παραβάτην (acc. sg. masc.) frame an extended phrase that stands in apposition to σέ. Διά + genitive ("through") has been interpreted as means (BDF §223.3; R 583), manner (T 267), or attendant circumstances (Moule 57; cf. Cranfield 174, Moo 173 n. 38, Schreiner 139); the third understanding is preferable. Γράμμα, -τος, τό denotes the literally correct form of the law (BDAG 205d). Schreiner notes that the word focuses on the externality of the law and the commandments contained in it (142; cf. Rom 7:5–7; 2 Cor 3:3, 6–7). Παραβάτης, -ου, ὁ denotes one who commits the act of transgression; νόμου is an objective genitive.

VERSE 28

οὐ γὰρ ὁ ἐν τῷ φανερῷ Ἰουδαῖός ἐστιν

Paul's summary explanation (γάρ) is so elliptical that Cranfield supplies eight words to clarify the A-B-A′-B′ double antithetic parallelism of verses 28–29a (175). The contrast between φανερός, -ά, -όν ("evident, visible") in this verse and κρυπτός, -ή, -όν ("secret, hidden") in the next reinforces the strong contrast established by οὐ . . . οὐδέ (2:28) and ἀλλ' . . . καί (2:29a). The nominative definite article allows the prepositional phrase ἐν τῷ φανερῷ ("the one who is visible") to function as the subject and assumes the gender of Ἰουδαῖος, which is a predicate nominative.

οὐδὲ ἡ ἐν τῷ φανερῷ ἐν σαρκὶ περιτομή

The connective οὐδέ ("and not") introduces the second part of the parallelism. The nominative definite article assumes the feminine gender of περιτομή (predicate nominative) and allows the first prepositional phrase to function as the subject. Ἐν + dative specifies the location ("in flesh") of the circumcision (R 590); the anarthrous noun σαρκί is qualitative, stressing nature or essence ("that which is visible in flesh"). The verb ἐστιν is understood from the first clause.

VERSE 29

ἀλλ' ὁ ἐν τῷ κρυπτῷ Ἰουδαῖος

The adversative ἀλλά introduces the second half of the strong contrast. The construction parallels the first clause of verse 28 but replaces φανερῷ with κρυπτῷ and omits ἐστιν.

καὶ περιτομὴ καρδίας ἐν πνεύματι οὐ γράμματι

Another connective (καί) introduces the second part of the parallelism, which again omits ἐστιν. The anarthrous phrase περιτομὴ καρδίας ("circumcision of heart") is qualitative, and the genitive is objective. See Leviticus 26:41; Deuteronomy 10:16; 30:6; Jeremiah 4:4; 9:26 for OT occurrences of the same idea. Ἐν πνεύματι οὐ γράμματι is more likely instrumental (cf. NIV, NEB, ESV) than locative (cf. KJV, CEV), and πνεῦμα is best understood as the Holy Spirit (Cranfield 175 n. 3; cf. GNB, NJB).

οὗ ὁ ἔπαινος οὐκ ἐξ ἀνθρώπων ἀλλ' ἐκ τοῦ θεοῦ

The relative pronoun οὗ (gen. sg. masc.) is qualitative ("who indeed") and gathers up the first half of the verse (i.e., the "true" Jew and the "true" circumcision). The article with ἔπαινος (nom. sg. masc, of ἔπαινος, -ου, ὁ, "praise") marks that noun as the subject. The verb ἐστιν is again understood. Schreiner notes that "praise" sometimes points to an eschatological reward from God (144; cf. 1 Cor 4:5; 1 Pet 1:7). Οὐκ . . . ἀλλά again marks a strong contrast so that the two uses of ἐκ + genitive identify contrasting sources of praise: men (anarthrous, emphasizing class traits) and God (with the definite article, emphasizing identity).

FOR FURTHER STUDY

26. Circumcision (2:27)

Barclay, J. M. G. "Paul and Philo on Circumcision: Romans 2:25–9 in Social and Cultural Context." *NTS* 44 (1998): 536–56.

Berkley, T. W. *From a Broken Covenant to Circumcision of the Heart: Pauline Intertextual Exegesis in Romans 2:17–29*. Atlanta: Society of Biblical Literature, 2000.

Borgen, P. "Debates on Circumcision in Philo and Paul." Pages 15–32 in *Paul Preaches Circumcision and Pleases Men*. Trondheim: Tapir, 1983.

Carras, G. P. "Romans 2,1–29: A Dialogue on Jewish Ideals." *Bib* 73 (1992): 183–207.

Forshey, H. O. "Circumcision: An Initiatory Rite in Ancient Israel?" *ResQ* 16 (1973): 150–58.

Goldingay, J. "The Significance of Circumcision." *JSOT* 88 (2000): 3–18.

Hahn, H. C. *NIDNTT* 1.307–11.

Hall, R. G. *ABD* 1.1025–31.

Harrison, R. K. *EDBT* 98–99.

Marcus, J. "The Circumcision and Uncircumcision in Rome." *NTS* (1989): 67–81.

Mark, E. W. *The Covenant of Circumcision: New Perspectives on an Ancient Jewish Rite*. Lebanon, NH: University Press of New England, 2003.

McEleney, N. J. "Conversion, Circumcision and the Law." *NTS* 20 (1973–74): 319–41.
Meyer, R. *TDNT* 6.72–84.
Sasson, J. M. "Circumcision in the Ancient Near East." *JBL* 85 (1966): 473–76.
Schreiner, T. R. *DPL* 137–39.

HOMILETICAL SUGGESTIONS

The Case Against the Jews (2:17–29)

1. Possession of the law does not exempt from judgment (2:17–24)
   a. Four advantages of being instructed from the Mosaic law (2:17–18)
      1) Rest in the law (2:17b)
      2) Boast in God (2:17c)
      3) Know God's will (2:18a)
      4) Approve what is important (2:18b)
   b. Four obligations that result from possessing the Mosaic law (2:19–20)
      1) Guide to the blind (2:19a)
      2) Light to those in darkness (2:19b)
      3) Instructor to those who lack judgment (2:20a)
      4) Teacher of the immature (2:20b)
   c. Four transgressions of the Mosaic law (2:21–23)
      1) Not teaching self (2:21a)
      2) Stealing (2:21b)
      3) Committing adultery (2:22a)
      4) Robbing temples (2:22b)
   d. Proof of guilt from the Mosaic law (2:24)
2. Possession of circumcision does not exempt from judgment (2:25–29)
   a. The relation of circumcision to the law (2:25)
      1) Practicing the law confirms circumcision (2:25a)
      2) Transgressing the law negates circumcision (2:25b)
   b. The relation of uncircumcision to the law (2:26–27)
      1) Keeping the law is reckoned as circumcision, even for the uncircumcised person (2:26)
      2) The uncircumcised person who keeps the law will judge the circumcised person who transgresses it (2:27)
   c. The nature of true Jewishness and true circumcision (2:28–29a)
      1) It is not external in flesh (2:28)
      2) It is internal in Spirit (2:29a)
   d. The legitimate source of praise (2:29b)

e. Because God Always Acts Righteously (3:1–8)

STRUCTURE

Paul continues his question-and-answer style in this paragraph. It consists of four double questions; each (except the fourth pair) is followed by a double answer. The four parts of the paragraph, therefore, are 3:1–2; 3:3–4; 3:5–6; 3:7–8. See Longenecker for a helpful analysis of the structure (337–38).

Τί οὖν τὸ περισσὸν τοῦ Ἰουδαίου
ἢ τίς ἡ ὠφέλεια τῆς περιτομῆς;
    πολὺ κατὰ πάντα τρόπον.
    πρῶτον μὲν [γὰρ] ὅτι ἐπιστεύθησαν τὰ λόγια τοῦ θεοῦ.

τί γάρ;
εἰ ἠπίστησάν τινες, μὴ ἡ ἀπιστία αὐτῶν τὴν πίστιν τοῦ θεοῦ καταργήσει;
    μὴ γένοιτο·
    γινέσθω δὲ ὁ θεὸς ἀληθής, πᾶς δὲ ἄνθρωπος ψεύστης,
        καθὼς γέγραπται, Ὅπως ἂν δικαιωθῇς ἐν τοῖς λόγοις σου
                καὶ νικήσεις ἐν τῷ κρίνεσθαί σε.

εἰ δὲ ἡ ἀδικία ἡμῶν θεοῦ δικαιοσύνην συνίστησιν, τί ἐροῦμεν;
μὴ ἄδικος ὁ θεὸς ὁ ἐπιφέρων τὴν ὀργήν; κατὰ ἄνθρωπον λέγω.
    μὴ γένοιτο·
    ἐπεὶ πῶς κρινεῖ ὁ θεὸς τὸν κόσμον;

εἰ δὲ ἡ ἀλήθεια τοῦ θεοῦ ἐν τῷ ἐμῷ ψεύσματι ἐπερίσσευσεν εἰς τὴν δόξαν αὐτοῦ, τί ἔτι κἀγὼ ὡς ἁμαρτωλὸς κρίνομαι;
καὶ μὴ καθὼς βλασφημούμεθα καὶ καθώς φασίν τινες ἡμᾶς λέγειν ὅτι Ποιήσωμεν τὰ κακά, ἵνα ἔλθῃ τὰ ἀγαθά;
    ὧν τὸ κρίμα ἔνδικόν ἐστιν.

VERSES 1–2

Τί οὖν τὸ περισσὸν τοῦ Ἰουδαίου

Paul has argued that neither the law nor circumcision provides any inherent benefit (2:17–29). The logical inference (οὖν) would be that there is no benefit to being a Jew, and Paul raises that objection by posing another question. Elsewhere in the letter τί οὖν ("what then?") occurs in a question with ἐροῦμεν (4:1; 6:1; 7:7; 8:31; 9:14, 30), and alone (3:9; 6:15; 11:7). Longenecker concludes that Paul uses the question to further his argument by raising a question about what he has taught (332). The adjective περισσός, -ή, -όν denotes something not ordinarily encountered (BDAG 805d). The article with the neuter singular allows the adjective to function as a noun with the sense of "special advantage" (cf. Longenecker 340). The article with Ἰουδαίου (gen. sg.

masc.) is generic and is common with ethnic names (BDF §139). The singular noun is representative for a class (R 408), and the genitive is subjective.

ἢ τίς ἡ ὠφέλεια τῆς περιτομῆς;

The disjunctive ἤ separates the first question from the second. By mentioning circumcision, Paul focuses on the specific sign of God's covenant with Israel and echoes the discussion at the end of the preceding section. Ὠφέλεια, -ας, ἡ denotes gain or advantage (BDAG 1107c). Schreiner suggests that use of the cognate verb in 2:25 implies "saving advantage" (148); Longenecker prefers "value" (340). The article with περιτομῆς is anaphoric; the genitive is subjective.

πολὺ κατὰ πάντα τρόπον

The adjective πολύ (acc. sg. neut.) functions as an adverb (R 659). Κατά + accusative denotes standard. The adjective πᾶς with an anarthrous noun is translated "every" (cf. R 771). Τρόπος, -ου, ὁ denotes the manner in which something is done (BDAG 1017a). Since περισσόν is also neuter, Jewett connects his translation to it and suggests "high in every respect" (242); Cranfield prefers "much in every respect" (177). Either translation highlights the great privilege of being a Jew. Longenecker responds to the criticism by Dodd and Räisänen that Paul's answer here is inconsistent with his denunciation of the Jews in chapter 2 (341).

πρῶτον μὲν [γὰρ] ὅτι ἐπιστεύθησαν τὰ λόγια τοῦ θεοῦ

Cranfield concludes that reading γάρ is more difficult and should be understood as original (178). It explains ("for") the statement Paul has just made about the great privilege of being a Jew. Although ἔπειτα δέ usually follows πρῶτον μέν to indicate a contrast, the partial construction also functions as an adverb and carries the idea "of chief importance" (Schreiner 148; Jewett 243). The specific advantage is introduced by ὅτι ("that") functioning as a conjunction of content. The aorist of ἐπιστεύθησαν (3 pl. aor. pass. indic. of πιστεύω) is constative and the passive is a divine passive. In this context, the verb should be understood as "they were entrusted with" (cf. 1 Cor 9:17; Gal 2:7; 1 Thess 2:4; 1 Tim 1:11), with the object of the passive (τὰ λόγια) retained (R 816). Cranfield notes five possible interpretations of τὰ λόγια and takes it in the broadest sense of God's self-revelation in the OT and NT (179). The article with λόγια is individualizing; the article with θεοῦ is monadic; the genitive of θεοῦ is subjective. The Jews' advantage is also a responsibility: to be the custodians of God's special revelation.

VERSES 3–4

τί γάρ;

Most EVV (with the exception of the NASB), Schreiner (147), and Jewett (244) incorporate these words into the first question. UBS[5], Cranfield (181), Moo (183 n.

30), and Dunn (131), however, punctuate them as a separate question (cf. Phil 1:18). BDF suggests "What difference does it make?" (§299.3).

εἰ ἠπίστησάν τινες

The first class condition (εἰ + indic.) assumes the protasis is true and establishes an evidence-inference argument (cf. Wallace 663). Ἠπίστησαν (3 pl. aor. act. indic. of ἀπιστέω, "be unfaithful") is a constative aorist and begins a triple word play that extends into the apodosis. Following Calvin, Cranfield notes that the indefinite pronoun τινες (nom. sg. masc.) lessens the harshness of the censure (181).

μὴ ἡ ἀπιστία αὐτῶν τὴν πίστιν τοῦ θεοῦ καταργήσει;

The particle μή anticipates a negative answer (cf. Longenecker 344). Ἡ ἀπιστία αὐτῶν ("their unfaithfulness") echoes the preceding verb and contrasts with the following noun. The article regularly occurs in conjunction with the possessive pronoun. The article also accompanies the abstract noun πίστιν. With the subjective genitive τοῦ θεοῦ, the phrase is best translated "God's faithfulness" (Cranfield 181). Καταργέω carries the sense of "make ineffective" (Dunn 132; cf. *TDNT* 1.453–55); the future indicative substitutes for the deliberative subjunctive (Wallace 465).

μὴ γένοιτο·

Paul uses this phrase nine other times in Romans to express strong denial, always after a question (3:6, 31; 6:2, 15; 7:7, 13; 9:14; 11:1, 11). Γένοιτο (3 sg. aor. mid. opt. of dep. γίνομαι, "be") is best understood as a voluntative optative, although Wallace notes that it has lost that nuance in this stereotyped formula (487–88). The negative μή is normal with non-indicative moods. Longenecker discusses possible translations and settles on "God forbid!" (344–45; cf. KJV).

γινέσθω δὲ ὁ θεὸς ἀληθής

Paul explains (δέ, untranslated in most EVV) his strong denial with an affirmation of God's character. The imperative of γινέσθω (3 sg. pres. mid. impv. of dep. γίνομαι) is an emphatic way of stating the true situation (Cranfield 181; cf. Longenecker 347); γίνομαι is equivalent to εἰμί (BDF §99). Ἀληθής, -ές denotes something that is in accordance with fact (BDAG 43b). Cranfield believes the adjective highlights God's faithfulness to his promises (181); Dunn notes the connection to Paul's indictment of humankind in chapters 1 and 2 (133). GNB and NEB translate the clause "God must be true."

πᾶς δὲ ἄνθρωπος ψεύστης

The character of humankind ("liar") stands in direct contrast to God's character ("true"). EVV tend to translate δέ as concessive ("though" e.g., NASB, ESV). The adjective πᾶς with the anarthrous ἄνθρωπος is translated "every man."

καθὼς γέγραπται

Paul supports his answer with a quotation of Psalm 51:4b (LXX). See 1:17 on the introductory formula.

Ὅπως ἂν δικαιωθῇς ἐν τοῖς λόγοις σου καὶ νικήσεις ἐν τῷ κρίνεσθαί σε

Elsewhere in the NT Luke uses ὅπως ἄν with the aorist subjunctive to denote purpose (Luke 2:35; Acts 3:20; 8:15; 9:2; 15:17), although Longenecker prefers result (348). Ἐν τοῖς λόγοις σου identifies the impersonal means for δικαιωθῇς (2 sg. aor. pass. subjunc.). Δικαιόω carries the sense of "prove to be right." Καί ("and") adds νικήσεις (2 sg. fut. act. indic. of νικάω, "conquer, win, overcome") as a second verb of purpose. BDAG suggests that νικάω carries the nuance of winning in the face of legal obstacles (673a). Although ὅπως ἄν occurs with the future indicative frequently in the LXX, this verse is the only NT occurrence of that combination (R 986; T 105). The infinitival phrase ἐν τῷ κρίνεσθαί σε gives the time when God will "go to law" (Moo 188 n. 53). See 2:1 for κρίνω.

VERSES 5–6

εἰ δὲ ἡ ἀδικία ἡμῶν θεοῦ δικαιοσύνην συνίστησιν, τί ἐροῦμεν;

The adversative δέ ("but") introduces the third pair of questions. Εἰ . . . συνίστησιν (3 sg. pres. act. indic. of συνίστημι, "demonstrate") is a first class condition; the present tense is gnomic. Ἡ ἀδικία ἡμῶν ("our unrighteousness") corresponds to ἡ ἀπιστία αὐτῶν in verse 3, while θεοῦ δικαιοσύνην ("God's righteousness") corresponds to τὴν πίστιν τοῦ θεοῦ in verse 3. In this context, Moo defines δικαιοσύνη as "God's faithfulness in his person and word, particularly in judging sin" (190). Paul uses the rhetorical question τί ἐροῦμεν six other times in the letter (4:1; 6:1; 7:7; 8:31; 9:14, 30); the future tense (1 pl. fut. act. indic. of λέγω, "say") is deliberative.

μὴ ἄδικος ὁ θεὸς ὁ ἐπιφέρων τὴν ὀργήν;

The particle μή anticipates a negative answer (cf. 3:3). Placing ἄδικος (nom. sg. masc.) in the first predicate position gives it emphasis (cf. Wallace 307). The articular participle (nom. sg. masc. of pres. act. ptc. of ἐπιφέρω, "inflict") is adjectival and equivalent to a relative clause (R 1108; T 152); the present tense is futuristic and points to the time when God will inflict wrath (cf. GNB, NJB). The definite article accompanies the abstract noun ὀργήν, which is the object of the participle; Wallace suggests that the noun ὀργή regularly has an "eschatological tinge" (cf. Rom 2:5, 8; Eph 5:6; Col 3:6; 1 Thess 1:10; 5:9). See also 1:18.

κατὰ ἄνθρωπον λέγω

Paul inserts a parenthetical apology, lest what he has just said gives offense (BDF §465.2; 495.3). He uses similar phrases elsewhere to note that he is speaking from a purely human perspective (Rom 6:19; 1 Cor 9:8; Gal 3:15). The present tense of λέγω is best understood as instantaneous (cf. Wallace 517).

μὴ γένοιτο (see 3:4)

ἐπεὶ πῶς κρινεῖ ὁ θεὸς τὸν κόσμον;

The causal conjunction ἐπεί ("otherwise") introduces the reason the proposed objection should be rejected so strongly (cf. 11:16, 22; 1 Cor 16:16; 15:29). Κρινεῖ (3 sg. fut. act. indic. of κρίνω) is a predictive future; the article with θεός is monadic as is the article with κόσμον.

VERSES 7–8

εἰ δέ ἡ ἀλήθεια τοῦ θεοῦ ἐν τῷ ἐμῷ ψεύσματι ἐπερίσσευσεν εἰς τὴν δόξαν αὐτοῦ

Metzger argues that the parallel with verse 5 means δέ should be preferred as original over the variant γάρ (448; cf. Moo 177 n. 1). Εἰ introduces another first class condition that assumes the truth of Paul's statement (cf. 1:3, 5). The definite article accompanies the abstract noun ἀλήθεια; see 1:18 for ἀλήθεια. The article with θεοῦ is monadic; the genitive is probably plenary (both subj. and obj.) reflecting the affirmation that God is true in verse 4. Paul ironically characterizes the means (ἐν + dat.) by which he glorifies God as τῷ ἐμῷ ψεύσματι ("my lie"). The possessive pronoun (ἐμός, -ή, -όν) is more formal and emphatic than the possessive genitive μου (R 288); it always occurs in the attributive position (R 685). Ψεῦσμα, -τος, τό echoes verse 4 and denotes engagement in the act of lying (BDAG 1097d). Ἐπερίσσευσεν (3 sg. aor. act. indic. of περισσεύω, "abound, overflow") is a gnomic aorist that RSV, NIV, and ESV translate as present. The advantage (εἰς + acc.) of Paul's teaching accrues to God's glory. See 1:23 for δόξα. The article regularly occurs in conjunction with the possessive pronoun.

τί ἔτι κἀγὼ ὡς ἁμαρτωλὸς κρίνομαι;

Moo notes that ἔτι highlights the logical inference Paul draws (194 n. 87). Crasis (κἀγώ) occurs more than twenty times in his letters (e.g., Rom 11:3; 1 Cor 15:8; 16:4). The καί is emphatic, and the first person represents one of a class (R 678). Jewett suggests that the combination τί ἔτι κἀγώ may be translated as "Why am I of all people?" (249). The conjunction ὡς introduces an elliptical clause of manner with ἁμαρτωλός as the subject ("in the way that a sinner {would be judged}"). The anarthrous noun is qualitative and emphasizes the class trait of "sinners." Κρίνομαι (1 sg. pres. pass. indic. of κρίνω, "judge") is an iterative present and a simple passive with an implied generic agent (cf. Wallace 434).

καὶ μὴ καθὼς βλασφημούμεθα καὶ καθώς φασίν τινες ἡμᾶς λέγειν

Cranfield writes that the construction of verse 8 is "unusually clumsy and tangled" (186); to resolve it, Jewett proposes an ellipse of ὡς ἁμαρτωλὸς κρινόμεθα from the previous verse (250). The best solution is to understand a rhetorical question that begins at καί, ends at ἀγαθά, and includes an extended parenthesis (καθὼς . . . λέγειν) that paraphrases one of the charges against Paul's teaching. Καί adds a second parallel apodosis to the initial conditional clause in verse 7. The particle μή agrees with ποιήσωμεν and continues the pattern that runs throughout the paragraph rather than anticipating a negative answer. The rhetorical question is best understood as καὶ {τί} μὴ {λέγομεν} . . . (cf. NASB, GNB, NIV).

The double use of the comparative conjunction καθώς ("just as") complicates the parenthesis but occurs because of the change from passive to active voice (Moo 195 n. 94). Βλασφημέω denotes speaking in a disrespectful way that demeans, denigrates, or maligns (BDAG 178a). The present tense is iterative; the simple passive keeps the focus on the subject. Paul uses φημί seven times in his letters and the plural only to report statements by others (cf. 1 Cor 6:16; 2 Cor 10:10). The indefinite pronoun τινες ("some") generalizes the accusation rather than identifying specific opponents. The accusative (ἡμᾶς) is normal with the infinitive when its subject differs from that of the main verb (R 1039). The infinitive λέγειν (pres. act. infin. of λέγω) is the object of φασίν (indirect discourse); the present tense is customary.

ὅτι Ποιήσωμεν τὰ κακά, ἵνα ἔλθῃ τὰ ἀγαθά;

The combination of φημί, infinitive, and recitative ὅτι is classical (R 1036). Ποιήσωμεν (1 pl. aor. act. subjunc. of ποιέω, "do") is a hortatory subjunctive. The articles with the neuter plural adjectives (τὰ κακά . . . τὰ ἀγαθά) are generic and allow the adjectives to function as nouns (T 14; R 763). See 1:29–30 and 2:7–10 for κακός and ἀγαθός. Ἵνα + subjunctive commonly indicates purpose; aorist is the normal tense (R 983). Neuter plural subjects regularly take singular verbs.

ὧν τὸ κρίμα ἔνδικόν ἐστιν

Unlike the first three sets of questions, Paul dismisses the fourth set abruptly: "Whose condemnation is justly deserved" (Dunn 143). The relative pronoun ὧν (gen. pl. masc.) most naturally refers back to τινες. Κρίμα denotes "a formal judicial decision by the divine judge" (Jewett 251). Ἔνδικος, -ον ("just/deserved") occurs only one other time in the NT (Heb 2:2); Dunn suggests "based on what is right" (137).

FOR FURTHER STUDY

See For Further Study §§ 10 ("Righteousness"), 13 ("God's Wrath"), 17 ("God's Glory"), 22 ("God's Judgment"), 26 ("Circumcision")

HOMILETICAL SUGGESTIONS

Four Accusations Against Paul's Teaching (3:1–8)

1. Paul's teaching impugns God's covenant with Israel (3:1–2)
    a. The objector's questions (3:1)
        1) What is the advantage of being a Jew? (3:1a)
        2) What is the benefit of circumcision? (3:1b)
    b. Paul's answers (3:2)
        1) Much in every way (3:2a)
        2) Israel was entrusted with God's revelation (3:2b)
2. Paul's teaching impugns God's faithfulness (3:3–4)
    a. The objector's questions (3:3)
        1) What difference does it make? (3:3a)
        2) Is God's faithfulness negated? (3:3b)
    b. Paul's answers (3:4)
        1) God forbid (3:4a)
        2) God must be true (3:4b)
3. Paul's teaching impugns God's justice (3:5–6)
    a. The objector's questions (3:5)
        1) Does human unrighteousness promote God's righteousness? (3:5a)
        2) Is God unjust when he inflicts wrath? (3:5b)
    b. Paul's answers (3:6)
        1) God forbid (3:6a)
        2) How will God judge the world? (3:6b)
4. Paul's teaching impugns God's truth (3:7–8)
    a. The objector's questions (3:7–8a)
        1) Does Paul promote God's truth by teaching a lie? (3:7)
        2) Does Paul promote doing evil? (3:8a)
    b. Paul's answer: Those who suggest such things receive the condemnation they deserve (3:8b).

f. Because All Are Under Sin (3:9–20)

STRUCTURE

A fifth pair of questions and answers (3:9) concludes both the preceding diatribe section and Paul's entire discussion of humankind's guilt before God (1:18–3:20). The paired answers are supported by a string of OT proofs (3:10–18). A two-sentence conclusion explains the implications of the OT proofs for Paul's teaching on the revelation of God's righteousness (3:19–20).

Τί οὖν;
προεχόμεθα;
οὐ πάντως·
προῃτιασάμεθα γὰρ Ἰουδαίους τε καὶ Ἕλληνας πάντας ὑφ' ἁμαρτίαν εἶναι,
καθὼς γέγραπται ὅτι

Οὐκ ἔστιν δίκαιος οὐδὲ εἷς,
οὐκ ἔστιν ὁ συνίων,
οὐκ ἔστιν ὁ ἐκζητῶν τὸν θεόν.

πάντες ἐξέκλιναν
ἅμα ἠχρεώθησαν·
οὐκ ἔστιν ὁ ποιῶν χρηστότητα,
[οὐκ ἔστιν] ἕως ἑνός.

τάφος ἀνεῳγμένος ὁ λάρυγξ αὐτῶν,
ταῖς γλώσσαις αὐτῶν ἐδολιοῦσαν,
ἰὸς ἀσπίδων ὑπὸ τὰ χείλη αὐτῶν·
ὧν τὸ στόμα ἀρᾶς καὶ πικρίας γέμει,

ὀξεῖς οἱ πόδες αὐτῶν ἐκχέαι αἷμα,
σύντριμμα καὶ ταλαιπωρία ἐν ταῖς ὁδοῖς αὐτῶν,
καὶ ὁδὸν εἰρήνης οὐκ ἔγνωσαν.
οὐκ ἔστιν φόβος θεοῦ ἀπέναντι τῶν ὀφθαλμῶν αὐτῶν.

Οἴδαμεν δὲ ὅτι ὅσα ὁ νόμος λέγει τοῖς ἐν τῷ νόμῳ λαλεῖ,
ἵνα πᾶν στόμα φραγῇ καὶ ὑπόδικος γένηται πᾶς ὁ κόσμος τῷ θεῷ·
διότι ἐξ ἔργων νόμου οὐ δικαιωθήσεται πᾶσα σὰρξ ἐνώπιον αὐτοῦ,
διὰ γὰρ νόμου ἐπίγνωσις ἁμαρτίας.

VERSE 9

Τί οὖν; (See 3:1)

προεχόμεθα;

Moo notes the variants connected with this word and concludes that the UBS[5] reading has the best support (197 n. 1; cf. Longenecker 328). Προεχόμεθα can be either middle or passive (R 816). Cranfield chooses middle with active meaning (189; cf. Longenecker 352–53; Schreiner 162): "Are we having an advantage?" Jewett prefers the passive (257; cf. Moule 168): "Are we being excelled?" (i.e., "Are we at a disadvantage?"); EVV uniformly choose the former. Moo sets out five possibilities for the identity of "we" (1 pl.) and chooses "we Jews" (199–200). Dunn adjusts that understanding slightly to Jews in solidarity with humankind (146–47).

οὐ πάντως

Blass notes this unusual combination (§433.2). Robertson (423) and Jewett (257) translate the phrase "Not at all." Turner (287) and Schreiner (163) prefer "Certainly not." Either way, the emphatic refusal is clear (cf. 1 Cor 5:10).

προῃτιασάμεθα γὰρ Ἰουδαίους τε καὶ Ἕλληνας πάντας ὑφ' ἁμαρτίαν εἶναι

The explanation (γάρ) for Paul's emphatic rejection of the idea that one group holds an advantage over another is found in his preceding discussion (1:18–2:29). Προῃτιασάμεθα (1 pl. aor. mid. indic. of dep. προαιτιάομαι) means to reach a charge of guilt prior to an implied point in time (BDAG 865b); this verse is the only occurrence of the verb in the NT. The middle voice is indirect (R 812); it is followed by an infinitive of indirect discourse (R 1036). See 1:16 for Ἰουδαίους τε καὶ Ἕλληνας. Longenecker argues that, in this context, the phrase is inclusive, although without "the particularistic thrust signaled . . . by πρῶτον in 1:16 and 2:9-10" (354). Πάντας (acc. pl. masc.) stands in apposition to "both Jews and Greeks" and is the subject of the infinitive. Ὑπό + accusative denotes subordination ("under the rule of sin").

VERSES 10–12

καθὼς γέγραπται ὅτι

See 1:17 for the introductory formula. The conjunction ὅτι ("that") introduces direct discourse (Wallace 455). The scriptural proofs in verses 10–12 demonstrate the universality of sin. Their source is the LXX version of Psalm 13:1–3d (cf. Eccl 7:20a; Ps 52:3b–4d).

Οὐκ ἔστιν δίκαιος οὐδὲ εἷς

Five of the seven lines in these verses begin with οὐκ ἔστιν (anaphora). The section is framed by the *inclusio* οὐδὲ εἷς . . . ἕως ἑνός (Jewett 254). Robertson notes both that οὐδὲ εἷς ("not even") is more emphatic than οὐδεις (751) and that the double negative (οὐκ . . . οὐδε) has an intensifying effect (1164). See 1:16 for δίκαιος.

οὐκ ἔστιν ὁ συνίων

The article is typical with a substantival participle (BDF §413.1). Συνίημι denotes the act of having an intelligent grasp of something that challenges thought or practice (BDAG 972b). The present tense of the participle is customary.

οὐκ ἔστιν ὁ ἐκζητῶν τὸν θεόν

Ἐκζητέω denotes the act of exerting effort to find out or learn something (BDAG 302d). The present tense of the participle is again customary. Θεόν (acc. sg. masc.) is the object of the participle; the definite article is monadic.

πάντες ἐξέκλιναν

Ἐκκλίνω can mean to avoid, but here it means to turn aside (BDAG 304d). The aorist is consummative and emphasizes the end of the action. EVV reflect this sense by translating "All have turned aside" (e.g., ESV).

ἅμα ἠχρεώθησαν

The adverb ἅμα ("together") is common in the LXX and occurs ten times in the NT (R 638); it highlights association in something (BDAG 49b). Ἠχρεώθησαν (3 pl. aor. pass. indic. of ἀχρειόω, "make worthless") is also a consummative aorist. No agent is expressed with the passive voice because the focus is on the subjects.

οὐκ ἔστιν ὁ ποιῶν χρηστότητα

The substantival participle ὁ ποιῶν is also a customary present. Χρηστότης, -ητος, ὁ ("good") denotes uprightness in relations with others (BDAG 1090b).

[οὐκ ἔστιν] ἕως ἑνός

UBS[5] gives οὐκ ἔστιν a {C} rating because B (fourth century) omits it. Metzger notes, however, that the longer reading is supported by most manuscripts and could have been deleted as superfluous (448). Robertson notes that ἕως is a preposition accompanied by the genitive (643). The phrase ἕως ἑνός forms an *inclusio* with οὐδὲ εἷς in verse 10.

VERSES 13–14

The scriptural proofs in verses 13–14 demonstrate the extent of humankind's sin as expressed in speech. Their source is the LXX version of Psalm 13:3e–h (cf. Ps 5:10c–d; 139:4b; 9:28a). The first and third lines of this section end with the possessive pronoun αὐτῶν (*antistrophe*).

τάφος ἀνεῳγμένος ὁ λάρυγξ αὐτῶν

The definite article with λάρυγξ ("throat") marks it as the subject. The noun τάφος ("tomb") is in the predicate position (noun-article-noun) and makes a statement about the subject. The participle ἀνεῳγμένος (nom. sg. masc. of pf. pass. ptc. of ἀνοίγω, "open") is adjectival; the perfect tense is intensive.

ταῖς γλώσσαις αὐτῶν ἐδολιοῦσαν

The dative of γλώσσαις ("tongues") is instrumental. The article regularly occurs in conjunction with the possessive pronoun. Ἐδολιοῦσαν (3 pl. impf. act. indic. of δολιόω, "deceive") is an iterative imperfect.

ἰὸς ἀσπίδων ὑπὸ τὰ χείλη αὐτῶν

The anarthrous noun ἰός ("poison") is generic; the genitive of ἀσπίδων ("of asps") is possessive. Ὑπό + accusative denotes "to rest beneath" (Moule 66). The verb ἔστιν is understood.

ὧν τὸ στόμα ἀρᾶς καὶ πικρίας γέμει

The relative pronoun ὧν ("whose") replaces αὐτῶν but also points back to πάντες in verse 12. The definite article marks στόμα ("mouth") as the subject. The genitives ἀρᾶς ("curses") and πικρίας ("bitterness") indicate content (cf. Wallace 92 n. 59) in conjunction with γέμει (3 sg. pres. act. indic. of γέμω, "be full"). The present tense is progressive.

VERSES 15–18

The scriptural proofs in verses 15–18 demonstrate the extent of humankind's sin as expressed in action. Their source is the LXX version of Psalm 13:3i–l (cf. Isa 59:7a, 7c, 8a; Ps 35:2b). The second and fourth lines of this section also end with αὐτῶν (*antistrophe*).

ὀξεῖς οἱ πόδες αὐτῶν ἐκχέαι αἷμα

Ὀξεῖς (nom. pl. masc. of ὀξύς, -εῖα, -ύ, "swift") is the predicate nominative. The definite article marks πόδες ("feet") as the subject. The infinitive ἐκχέαι (aor. act. inf. of ἐκχέω, "pour out in quantity") denotes purpose (R 1062); aorist is the natural tense for such an infinitive (R 1080). Αἷμα ("blood") is the object of the infinitive.

σύντριμμα καὶ ταλαιπωρία ἐν ταῖς ὁδοῖς αὐτῶν

Σύντριμμα ("destruction") and ταλαιπωρία ("misery") are the subjects of an understood εἰσίν. Ἐν + dative is spatial ("in their ways/paths").

καὶ ὁδὸν εἰρήνης οὐκ ἔγνωσαν

Καί ("and") adds one more description before the summary statement in verse 18. Ὁδόν echoes the previous line and is definite even though anarthrous. See 1:7 for εἰρήνη; the genitive is attributive and highlights a specific quality. Ἔγνωσαν (3 pl. aor. act. indic. of γινώσκω, "know") is a consummative aorist (ESV, "they have not known").

οὐκ ἔστιν φόβος θεοῦ ἀπέναντι τῶν ὀφθαλμῶν αὐτῶν

The sixth occurrence of οὐκ ἔστιν brings the list of proofs to a conclusion that highlights the root sin underlying all the others: a lack of reverence for God (cf. 1:21, 28). The anarthrous φόβος is qualitative; θεοῦ is an objective genitive (R 500). Ἀπέναντι occurs four times in the NT and means "in the presence of" (Moule 82); Blass notes that the cognate improper preposition ἐναντίον is an alternative to πρό (§214.6). Moo notes that Paul has changed αὐτοῦ in the LXX to αὐτῶν (204 n. 37).

VERSE 19

Οἴδαμεν δὲ ὅτι ὅσα ὁ νόμος λέγει τοῖς ἐν τῷ νόμῳ λαλεῖ

A transitional δέ ("now") introduces the conclusion to Paul's argument. Οἴδαμεν is a perfect with present force (cf. Wallace 579). See 2:2 on the disclosure formula οἴδαμεν δὲ ὅτι. The correlative pronoun ὅσα (acc. pl. neut. of ὅσος, -η, -ον, "as many {things} as") gathers up the preceding verses; the article with νόμος marks it as well-known. The article preceding ἐν τῷ νόμῳ allows the prepositional phrase to function as the indirect object of λαλεῖ (3 sg. pres. act. indic. of λαλέω, "speak"). Ἐν + dative denotes sphere. Moo distinguishes between λέγω as content and λαλέω as act (204 n. 40). Both present tenses are gnomic.

ἵνα πᾶν στόμα φραγῇ καὶ ὑπόδικος γένηται πᾶς ὁ κόσμος τῷ θεῷ

The purpose (ἵνα) for which the law speaks is to create accountability. Πᾶν (nom. sg. neut.) without the article is "every" (R 771). The aorist subjunctive is the normal tense with ἵνα (R 983). The agent of the passive φραγῇ (3 sg. aor. pass. subjunc. of φράσσω, "close, shut") is suppressed because it is obvious from the context. Longenecker notes that πᾶν στόμα φραγῇ is "a biblical idiom that refers to God . . . silencing . . . all those who are unrighteous and practice injustice" (358). Καί ("and") adds a second purpose more closely connected with God's righteousness. The position of ὑπόδικος ("accountable") is emphatic; it occurs only here in the NT and denotes the condition of being under divine indictment (Jewett 265). Γένηται (3 sg. aor. mid. subjunc. of dep. γίνομαι) parallels φραγῇ. Πᾶς with an articular noun is "the entire world." The dative τῷ θεῷ identifies God as the injured party with a right to satisfaction (Cranfield 197).

VERSE 20

διότι ἐξ ἔργων νόμου οὐ δικαιωθήσεται πᾶσα σὰρξ ἐνώπιον αὐτοῦ

Jewett notes that διότι ("because") usually introduces causal clauses within sentences and, so, provides the underlying reason for God's action in verse 19 (265; contra Longenecker who understands it as inferential, 360). The impersonal means (ἐκ + gen.) that fails to justify is ἔργων νόμου ("works of law"). The same phrase occurs in 3:28 and six times in Galatians (2:16 [3x]; 3:2, 5, 10) and is best understood as "works commanded by the law" (Schreiner 177; cf. the excursus in Moo 211–17).

Longenecker argues that the phrase refers to deeds "viewed in a legalistic manner as gaining 'righteousness' before God and so acceptance by him" (369). Schreiner adequately refutes Dunn's suggestion that the phrase denotes "boundary markers" separating Jew from Gentile (204). The future of δικαιωθήσεται is predictive; God is the unexpressed ultimate agent of the passive voice. Here, δικαιόω carries the sense of "declare righteous." The combination οὐ . . . πᾶσα σάρξ is a Hebraism equivalent to οὐδεις (R 752; T 196). Σάρξ ("flesh") denotes humankind as a whole (Cranfield 198). EVV regularly translate ἐνώπιον αὐτοῦ as "in his sight."

διὰ γὰρ νόμου ἐπίγνωσις ἁμαρτίας

The reason (γάρ) works of law do not justify relates to what the law accomplishes. It is the means (διά + gen.) through which humankind comes to know sin. As the object of a preposition, νόμου is definite although it is anarthrous. Ἐπίγνωσις carries the nuance of "recognition" (Jewett 266); ἁμαρτίας is an objective genitive. Longenecker provides a helpful comparison with Paul's argument in Galatians 3:19–25 (371–72).

FOR FURTHER STUDY

27. Sin (3:9)

Bell, R. H. *No One Seeks for God: An Exegetical and Theological Study of Romans 1.18–3.20*. Tübingen: Mohr Siebeck, 1998.

Biddle, M. E. *Missing the Mark: Sin and Its Consequences in Biblical Theology*. Nashville: Abingdon, 2005.

Doriani, D. *EDBT* 736–39.

Gaventa, B. R. "The Cosmic Power of Sin in Paul's Letter to the Romans: Toward a Widescreen Edition." *Int* 58 (2004): 229–40.

Günther, W., and W. Bauder. *NIDNTT* 3.573–87.

Lyonnet, S., and L. Sabourin. *Sin, Redemption, and Sacrifice: A Biblical and Patristic Study*. Rome: Biblical Institute Press, 1970.

Malina, B. J. "Some Observations on the Origin of Sin in Judaism and St. Paul." *CBQ* 31 (1969): 18–34.

Morris, L. *DPL* 877–81.

Neusner, J. "Sin, Repentance, Atonement and Resurrection: The Perspective of Rabbinic Theology on the Views of James 1–2 and Paul in Romans 3–4." *Annali di storia dell' esegesi* 18 (2001): 409–31.

Röhser, G. *Metaphorik und Personification der Sünde*. Tübingen: Mohr, 1987.

Quell, C. *TDNT* 1.267–335.

Sanders, E. P. *ABD* 6.46–47.

Schneider, J. *TDNT* 5.736–44.

Smith, C. R. *The Bible Doctrine of Sin*. London: Epworth, 1953.

28. Works of Law (3:20)

Abegg, M. G. "Paul, 'Works of the Law' and MMT." *BAR* 20 (1994): 52–55, 82.

Abernathy, D. "A Critique of James D. G. Dunn's View of Justification by Faith as Opposed to the 'Works of the Law.'" *LTJ* 35 (2001): 139–44.

Barrick, W. D. "The New Perspective and 'Works of the Law' (Gal 2:16 and Rom 3:20)." *Master's Seminary Journal* 16 (2005): 277–92.

Bertram, G. *TDNT* 2.633–55.

Bowsher, H. "To Whom Does the Law Speak? Romans 3:19 and the Works of the Law Debate." *WTJ* 68 (2006): 295–303.

Cranfield, C. E. B. "'The Works of the Law' in the Epistle to the Romans." *JSNT* 43 (1991): 89–101.

deRoo, J. C. R. *Works of the Law at Qumran and in Paul.* Sheffield: Sheffield Phoenix, 2007.

Dunn, J. D. G. "Works of the Law and the Curse of the Law (Galatians 3:10–14)." *NTS* 31 (1985): 523–42.

Fuller, D. P. "Paul and the Works of the Law." *WTJ* 38 (1975): 28–42.

Gaston, L. "Works of Law as a Subjective Genitive." *Studies in Religion/Sciences religieuses* 13 (1984): 39–46.

Hahn, H. C. *NIDNTT* 3.1147–51.

Ito, A. "NOMOS (TON) ERGON and NOMOS PISTEOS: The Pauline Rhetoric and Theology of NOMOS." *NovT* 45 (2003): 237–59.

Longenecker, R. N. "Excursus: 'The Law,' 'Works of the Law,' and 'The New Perspective.'" Pages 362–70 in *The Epistle to the Romans*. Grand Rapids: Eerdmans, 2016.

Moo, D. J. "Excursis: Works of Law." Pages 211–17 in *The Epistle to the Romans*. Grand Rapids: Eerdmans, 1996.

________. "'Law,' 'Works of the Law,' and Legalism in Paul." *WTJ* 45 (1983): 73–100.

O'Neill, J. C. "'Did You Receive the Spirit by the Works of the Law?' (Gal 3:2): The Works of the Law in Judaism and the Pauline Corpus." *AusBR* 46 (1998): 70–84.

Owen, P. L. "The 'Works of the Law' in Romans and Galatians: A New Defense of the Subjective Genitive." *JBL* 126 (2007): 553–77.

Rapa, R. K. *The Meaning of "Works of the Law" in Galatians and Romans*. New York: Peter Lang, 2001.

Sanders, E. P. *Paul, the Law, and the Jewish People.* Philadelphia: Fortress, 1983.

Schreiner, T. R. *DPL* 975–79.

Schreiner, T. "Did Paul Believe in Justification by Works? Another Look at Romans 2." *BBR* 3 (1993): 131–55.

Westerholm, S. *Perspectives Old and New on Paul: the "Lutheran" Paul and His Critics*. Grand Rapids: Eerdmans, 2004.

29. Flesh (3:20)

Burton, E. D. *Spirit, Soul, and Flesh: pneuma, psyche, and sarx in Greek Writings and Translated Works from the Earliest Period to 225 AD; and of Their Equivalents rûah, nepeš and baśar in the Hebrew Old Testament*. Chicago: University of Chicago Press, 1918.

Dayton, W. T. "The New Testament Conception of Flesh." *WesThJ* 2 (1967): 7–17.

Deasley, A. R. G. *EDBT* 259–60.

Dunn, J. D. G. "Jesus—Flesh and Spirit." *JTS* 24 (1973): 40–68.

Erickson, R. J. *DPL* 303–06.

Frey, J. "Die paulinische Antithese von 'Fleisch' und 'Geist' und die palästinisch-jüdische Weisheitstradition." *ZNW* 90 (1999): 45–77

Jewett, R. *Paul's Anthropological Terms: A Study of Their Use in Conflict Settings*. Leiden: Brill, 1971.
Marshall, I. H. "Living in the 'Flesh.'" *BSac* 159 (2002): 387–403.
Moo, D. J. "Flesh in Romans: A Challenge for the Translator." Pages 365–79 in *The Challenge of Bible Translation*. Edited by G. G. Scorgie and M. L. Strauss. Grand Rapids: Zondervan, 2003.
Moyter, J. A. *EDT* 417–18.
Sand, A. Der Begriff "Fleisch" in den paulinischen Hauptbriefen. Regensburg: Pustet, 1967.
Schweitzer, E., R. Meyer, and F. Baumgärtel. *TDNT* 7.98–151.
Scornaienchi, L. *Sarx und Soma bei Paulus: Der Mensch zwischen Destruktivität und Konstruktivität*. Göttingen: Vandenhoeck & Ruprecht, 2008.
Seebass, H., and A. C. Thiselton. *NIDNTT* 1.671–82.

HOMILETICAL SUGGESTIONS

The Case Against Humankind (3:9–20)

1. Thesis: Jews and Greeks are both under sin (προῃτιασάμεθα γάρ, 3:9)
   a. Jews have no advantage (3:9a)
   b. Jews and Greeks are both under sin (3:9b)
2. Proof: OT teaching (καθὼς γέγραπται, 3:10–18; cf. Ps 13:1–3)
   a. None is righteous (3:10b–12)
   b. Their speech condemns them (3:13–14)
   c. Their actions condemn them (3:15–17)
   d. They do not fear God (3:18)
3. Implication: The law makes accountable and exposes sin (οἴδαμεν δέ, 3:19–20)
   a. It makes all accountable (3:19)
   b. It brings the recognition of sin (3:20)

We Sin Daily . . . (3:10–18)

1. In thought (3:10b–12, 18)
2. In word (3:13–14)
3. In deed (3:15–17)

The Role of the Law (3:19–20)

1. It silences everyone (3:19b)
2. It justifies no one (3:20a)
3. It exposes sin (3:20b)

2. God Reveals His Righteousness Apart from Law (3:21–31)

a. Through Faith in Christ (3:21–26)

STRUCTURE

Campbell notes the elegant style and "extended periodic syntax" that characterize this paragraph (*Rhetoric of Righteousness* 81). It consists of a single sentence divided into three parts. The first part (3:21–22a) reconnects to 1:16–17 and identifies faith as the key component in the revelation of God's righteousness. The second part (3:22b–24) explains the divine impartiality governing that revelation. The third part (3:25–26) is an extended relative clause that highlights the way in which Jesus's propitiatory work provides justification without violating God's justice. Jewett provides a concise discussion of what some consider a pre-Pauline formula in 3:25–26 (270–71; cf. Longenecker 397–98); Cranfield argues the other side of that issue (200 n. 1). See Longenecker for an extended discussion of the relationship between 3:21–4:25 and 1:16–3:20 (381–87).

Νυνὶ δὲ χωρὶς νόμου δικαιοσύνη θεοῦ πεφανέρωται
μαρτυρουμένη ὑπὸ τοῦ νόμου καὶ τῶν προφητῶν,
δικαιοσύνη δὲ θεοῦ διὰ πίστεως Ἰησοῦ Χριστοῦ εἰς πάντας τοὺς πιστεύοντας.

οὐ γάρ ἐστιν διαστολή,
πάντες γὰρ ἥμαρτον καὶ ὑστεροῦνται τῆς δόξης τοῦ θεοῦ
δικαιούμενοι δωρεὰν τῇ αὐτοῦ χάριτι διὰ τῆς ἀπολυτρώσεως τῆς ἐν Χριστῷ Ἰησοῦ·

ὃν προέθετο ὁ θεὸς ἱλαστήριον διὰ [τῆς] πίστεως ἐν τῷ αὐτοῦ αἵματι
εἰς ἔνδειξιν τῆς δικαιοσύνης αὐτοῦ
διὰ τὴν πάρεσιν τῶν προγεγονότων ἁμαρτημάτων ἐν τῇ ἀνοχῇ τοῦ θεοῦ,
πρὸς τὴν ἔνδειξιν τῆς δικαιοσύνης αὐτοῦ ἐν τῷ νῦν καιρῷ,
εἰς τὸ εἶναι αὐτὸν δίκαιον καὶ δικαιοῦντα τὸν ἐκ πίστεως Ἰησοῦ.

VERSE 21

Νυνὶ δὲ χωρὶς νόμου δικαιοσύνη θεοῦ πεφανέρωται

Paul marks the beginning of a new element in his discussion of the revelation of God's righteousness with a double contrast. Νυνὶ δέ ("but now") occurs fifteen other times in Paul's letters, sometimes with logical force (cf. Rom 7:17; 1 Cor 12:18; 13:13; 15:20); sometimes with temporal force (cf. Rom 15:23, 25; 2 Cor 8:11, 22; Phlm 9, 11); and sometimes as a soteriological contrast between "what was" in Adam and "what is" in Christ (cf. Rom 6:22; 7:6; Eph 2:13; Col 1:22; 3:8). The latter is most natural here (cf. Dunn 164). Χωρὶς νόμου ("apart from law") contrasts with ἐν τῷ νόμῳ (3:19) and ἐξ ἔργων νόμου (3:20) to point out that the discussion has moved beyond what the law is able to accomplish. Jewett argues that the anarthrous νόμου denotes "every kind of law" (274), but Longenecker concludes that "there can hardly be any doubt" Paul is referring to the Mosaic law (400; cf. Moo 223). See 1:17 for δικαιοσύνη θεοῦ (cf. Longenecker 403–05). Πεφανέρωται (3 sg. pf. pass. indic. of φανερόω, "manifest") echoes ἀποκαλύπτεται at the beginning of 1:18–3:20 and is also a divine passive; the perfect tense is intensive. See 1:19 on the relationship between ἀποκαλύπτω and φανερόω.

μαρτυρουμένη ὑπὸ τοῦ νόμου καὶ τῶν προφητῶν

The participle μαρτυρουμένη (nom. sg. fem. of pres. pass. ptc. of μαρτυρέω, "bear witness") could be adverbial (RSV, NIV, and ESV translate it as adv. of concession) but is more likely adjectival ("which is being witnessed") modifying δικαιοσύνη θεοῦ (cf. Jewett 268). The present tense is progressive; ὑπό + genitive indicates the agency of the simple passive. The article with νόμου is anaphoric; the article with προφητῶν is generic. "Law and Prophets" occurs nowhere else in Paul; see Longenecker for Jewish background on the phrase (417); "Prophets" is a metonymy for their writings (BDAG 891b).

VERSE 22

δικαιοσύνη δὲ θεοῦ διὰ πίστεως Ἰησοῦ Χριστοῦ εἰς πάντας τοὺς πιστεύοντας

Paul repeats δικαιοσύνη θεοῦ for clarity and introduces it with an explanatory δέ ("that is"). Longenecker writes that, in this context, the conjunction introduces "a fuller and more significant definition" of δικαιοσύνη θεοῦ in 3:21 (407). The means (διά + gen.) through which God's righteousness is communicated is "faith" (cf. 1:17). Wallace takes Ἰησοῦ Χριστοῦ as a subjective genitive (114–16), and Longenecker presents an extended defense of such an understanding (408–13). Most grammars and commentators take it as objective (R 500; Cranfield 203; Dunn 166–67; Moo 225; Jewett 275), and Schreiner offers an extended discussion of that position (181–86).* The righteousness accrues to the advantage (εἰς + acc.) of "all" (πάντας) who exercise faith. Εἰς πάντας has far stronger manuscript support than ἐπί πάντας, and the third variant (εἰς πάντας καὶ ἐπί πάντας) is most likely a conflation. The article marks πιστεύοντας (acc. pl. masc. of pres. act. ptc. of πιστεύω) as a substantival participle; the present tense is progressive (cf. 1:16).

οὐ γάρ ἐστιν διαστολή

Divine impartiality ("there is no difference") is the reason (γάρ) God's righteousness is universally available. See 10:12–13 for a fuller statement using διαστολή and 2:11 for a parallel statement using προσωπολημψία ("favoritism"). See BDAG 327a for διαστολή, -ῆς, ἡ.

VERSE 23

πάντες γὰρ ἥμαρτον καὶ ὑστεροῦνται τῆς δόξης τοῦ θεοῦ

Divine impartiality, in turn, is explained (γάρ) by human sinfulness. The substantival adjective πάντες (nom. pl. masc.) emphasizes the universality of sin (Cranfield 204). Ἥμαρτον (3 pl. aor. act. indic. of ἁμαρτάνω, "sin") is either historic (Cranfield 204; cf. Longenecker 416) or, more likely, gnomic (R 837; cf. Porter 38). Under either analysis, the verb stresses the "decisive and universal character of the fall" (Dunn 167). The connective καί ("and so") adds the consequences of ἥμαρτον (Moo 226). The gnomic present ὑστεροῦνται (3 pl. pres. mid. indic. of ὑστερέω, "fall short of") highlights the timelessness of the truth, and the indirect middle calls special attention to it. Ὑστερέω denotes a deficiency in something advantageous or desirable (BDAG 1044a), in this instance "the glory of God." See 1:23 for δόξα. The ablative of δόξης indicates separation, and the genitive of θεοῦ is possessive. The combination of the definite article with δόξης plus the adjunct τοῦ θεοῦ makes the entire phrase monadic (cf. Wallace 224). The glory in question is the divine glory that was lost in the fall and that humankind can never possess apart from Christ (Dunn 168; Schreiner 187; Moo 226).

VERSE 24

δικαιούμενοι δωρεὰν τῇ αὐτοῦ χάριτι

Cranfield sets out four possible ways in which verse 24 could relate to the preceding context and decides that δικαιούμενοι (nom. pl. masc. of pres. pass. ptc. of δικαιόω, "declare righteous") is adjectival, modifying πάντες in verse 23 (205; cf. Jewett 281).* Longenecker views the participle both as the beginning of preformed material and as adjectival of attendent circumstance (421). Δωρεάν (acc. sg. fem. of δωρέα, -ᾶς, ἡ, "gift") is used as an adverb to denote manner (BDAG 266c). The dative τῇ χάριτι ("by his grace") is impersonal means. The article accompanies the abstract noun, and placing the possessive pronoun αὐτοῦ in the attributive position gives it greater emphasis (cf. BDF §284.3).

διὰ τῆς ἀπολυτρώσεως τῆς ἐν Χριστῷ Ἰησοῦ

The intermediate agency (διά + gen.) through which the declaration of righteousness is made possible is τῆς ἀπολυτρώσεως (gen. sg. fem. of ἀπολύτρωσις, -εως, ἡ, "redemption"). The first article is *par excellence* and is expected because of the article that follows. Jewett describes "redemption" as "a specialized theological concept of salvation through the forgiveness of sins" (282). Ἀπολύτρωσις carries the idea of release from a captive condition (BDAG 117a); other NT uses support the notion that it involves the payment of a ransom (cf. Mark 10:45; Acts 20:28; Rom 7:23; 1 Cor 6:20; 1 Tim 2:6; 1 Pet 1:18; 2 Pet 2:1; Rev 5:9). See also Longenecker for background (422–24). The second article allows the prepositional phrase to function as an adjective (R 782); ἐν

+ dative is most likely spatial ("that is in Christ Jesus"; cf. Wallace 375),* although Longenecker argues for source/agency ("that came by Christ Jesus"; 424).

VERSE 25

ὃν προέθετο ὁ θεὸς ἱλαστήριον

An extended relative clause describes the details of how God is able to declare sinners righteous without violating his own righteousness. Christ Jesus is the antecedent for the relative pronoun ὅν (acc. sg. masc.), which in turn is the object in an object-complement double accusative (R 480; Moule 35). Προέθετο (3 sg. aor. mid. indic. of προτίθημι) is a constative aorist and an indirect middle. Although the verb can mean to have something in mind beforehand (e.g., 1:13; Eph 1:9), here it means to display/set forth publicly (Cranfield 208–09; Longenecker 426; cf. Gal 3:1). The article with θεός is monadic; ἱλαστήριον is definite although anarthrous and is the complement in the double accusative construction. The noun itself has generated considerable discussion (e.g., Schreiner 191–94; Longenecker 426–29). Twenty-one of twenty-seven LXX occurrences refer to the mercy seat as the place of sacrifice (cf. Heb 9:5), and Moo concludes that it is "inevitable" that the word refers to turning away God's wrath (235). "Propitiation" is therefore the preferred translation (ESV).

διὰ [τῆς] πίστεως ἐν τῷ αὐτοῦ αἵματι

Metzger notes the balance in external and internal considerations related to the textual variant [τῆς] (449). If the article with πίστεως is original, it is anaphoric (cf. v.22). Ἐν τῷ αὐτοῦ αἵματι ("by his blood") is instrumental (BDF §219.3; cf. Longenecker 432) and modifies ἱλαστήριον (v. 24), not πίστεως (Cranfield 210). The attributive possessive pronoun is emphatic (cf. v. 24). Αἷμα, -τος, τό is a metonymy for the life of an individual (BDAG 26d); its sacrificial significance is clear from elsewhere in the NT (e.g., 1 Cor 11:25; Eph 1:7; Col 1:20).

εἰς ἔνδειξιν τῆς δικαιοσύνης αὐτοῦ

The purpose (εἰς + acc.) of God's displaying Jesus as a means of propitiation is the demonstration (ἔνδειξιν) of his righteousness. Ἔνδειξις, -εως, ἡ denotes something that compels acceptance (BDAG 332a); Cranfield suggests "proving" (211). Although anarthrous, ἔνδειξιν is definite as the object of εἰς. Δικαιοσύνης refers to God's righteous character (Moo 240) and is an objective genitive. The article is anaphoric and occurs regularly with a possessive pronoun (αὐτοῦ).

διὰ τὴν πάρεσιν τῶν προγεγονότων ἁμαρτημάτων

The reason (διά + acc.) for Christ's propitiatory work relates to God's postponement of punishment for sin. Πάρεσις, -εως, ἡ describes a deliberate disregard of something (BDAG 776c), in this context God's decision to let sin go unpunished for a time (Dunn 173). Ἁμάρτημα, -τος, τό denotes sin as a serious moral defect (BDAG 50b).

Προγεγονότων (gen. pl. neut. of pf. act. ptc. of dep. προγίνομαι, "originate previously") is adjectival; its attributive position gives it emphasis; the extensive perfect emphasizes past completed action. Moo concludes, "God 'postponed' the full penalty due sins in the Old Covenant, allowing sinners to stand before him without their having provided an adequate 'satisfaction' of the demands of his holy justice" (240).

VERSE 26

ἐν τῇ ἀνοχῇ τοῦ θεοῦ

God passed over sins because of (ἐν + dat.) his forbearance. See 2:4 for ἀνοχή; the article accompanies the abstract noun. The article with θεοῦ is anaphoric; the genitive is possessive.

πρὸς τὴν ἔνδειξιν τῆς δικαιοσύνης αὐτοῦ ἐν τῷ νῦν καιρῷ

Πρὸς τὴν ἔνδειξιν reinforces the purpose of Christ's propitiatory work (Jewett 291); the change from εἰς to πρός is "purely stylistic" (Moo 240 n. 107). Moo concludes that the εἰς phrase points to God's past act of postponing judgment on sin, while the πρός phrase points to his present act of declaring those sinners righteous (241). Ἐν + dative is temporal. Νῦν is an adverb used as a descriptive adjective (R 547); placing it in the attributive position gives it emphasis. The phrase also occurs in 8:18 and 11:5 (cf. 2 Cor 8:14) and marks the time of the gospel events and proclamation as "specially significant and critical" (Cranfield 212 n. 2).

εἰς τὸ εἶναι αὐτὸν δίκαιον καὶ δικαιοῦντα τὸν ἐκ πίστεως Ἰησοῦ

The ultimate objective (εἰς τό + inf.) of God's public display of Christ as a propitiation is the vindication of his righteousness. The intensive pronoun αὐτόν is the subject of the infinitive; Longenecker suggests that the emphasis is comparable to "God himself and not anyone else" (436); δίκαιον is a predicate accusative (Wallace 192). Jewett notes four options on καί (292): copulative ("and"), concessive ("even while"), instrumental ("by means of"), explicative ("in that").* Δικαιοῦντα (acc. sg. masc. of pres. act. ptc. of δικαιόω, "declare righteous") is a second predicate accusative (Longenecker 437); the present tense is progressive. The article marks the prepositional phrase as an adjective; ἐκ + genitive denotes source; Ἰησοῦ is an objective genitive (cf. v. 22; contra Longenecker 440).

FOR FURTHER STUDY

30. Prophets and Prophecy (3:21)

Aune, D. E. *Prophecy in Early Christianity and the Ancient Mediterranean World*. Grand Rapids: Eerdmans, 1983. See pages 189–217.

Boring, E. M. *The Continuing Voice of Jesus: Christian Prophecy in the Gospel Tradition*. Louisville: John Knox, 1991.

Crone, T. M. *Early Christian Prophecy: A Study of Its Origin and Function*. Baltimore: St. Mary's University Press, 1973.

Dautzenberg, G. *Urchristliche Prophetie*. Stuttgart: Kohlhammer, 1975.
Ellis, E. E. *Prophecy and Hermeneutic in Early Christianity: New Testament Essays*. Tübingen: Mohr Siebeck, 1978.
________. "The Role of the Christian Prophets in Acts." Pages 55–67 in *Apostolic History of the Gospel*. Edited by W. W. Gasque and R. P. Martin. Grand Rapids: Eerdmans, 1970.
Evans, C. A. "Paul and the Prophets: Prophetic Criticism in the Epistle to the Romans (with Special Reference to Romans 9–11)." Pages 115–28 in *Romans and the People of God*. Grand Rapids: Eerdmans, 1999.
Forbes, C. *Prophecy and Inspired Speech in Early Christianity and Its Hellenistic Environment*. Tübingen: Mohr Siebeck, 1995.
Friedrich, G. *TDNT* 6.828–61.
Grudem, W. A. *The Gift of Prophecy in 1 Corinthians*. Washington, DC: University Press of America, 1982.
________. *The Gift of Prophecy in the New Testament and Today*. Westchester, IL: Crossway, 1988.
Guy, H. A. *New Testament Prophecy: Its Origin and Significance*. London: Epworth, 1947.
Hill, C. *Prophecy Past and Present: An Exploration of the Prophetic Ministry in the Bible and the Church Today*. Ann Arbor, MI: Servant, 1989.
Hill, D. *New Testament Prophecy*. London: Marshall, Morgan & Scott, 1979.
Hui, A. "The Spirit of Prophecy and Pauline Pneumatology." *TynBul* 50 (1999): 93–115.
Kaiser, W. C., Jr. *EDBT* 641–47.
LaMorte, A., and G. F. Hawthorne. *EDT* 886–87.
Müller, U. B. *Prophetie und Predigt im Neuen Testament*. Gütersloh: Mohn, 1975.
Robeck, C. M., Jr. *DPL* 755–62.
Silva, M. *NIDNTTE* 4.161–74.
Turner, M. "Spiritual Gifts Then and Now." *VE* 15 (1985): 7–64.

31. Faith of Jesus Christ (3:22)

Bird, M. F., and P. M. Sprinkle, eds. *The Faith of Jesus Christ: Exegetical, Biblical, and Theological Studies*. Peabody, MA: Hedrickson, 2009.
Campbell, D. A. "False Presuppositions in the *Pistis Christou* Debate: A Response to Brian Dodd." *NTS* 116 (1997): 713–19.
________. "Romans 1:17—A Crux Interpretum for the *Pistis Christou* Debate." *JBL* 113 (1994): 265–85.
Dodd, B. "Romans 1:17—A Crux Interpretum for the *Pistis Christou* Debate?" *JBL* 114 (1995): 470–73.
Dunn, J. D G. "*Ek Pisteōs*: A Key to the Meaning of *Pistis Christou*." Pages 351–66 in *The Word Leaps the Gap*. Edited by J. R. Wagner, C. K. Rowe, and A. K. Grieb. Grand Rapids: Eerdmans, 2008.
________. "Once More, ΠΙΣΤΙΣ ΧΡΙΣΤΟΥ." Pages 61–81 in *Pauline Theology*. Volume 4. Edited by E. E. Johnson and D. M. Hay. Atlanta: SBL, 1997.
Dunnill, J. "Saved by Whose Faith?—The Function of *Pistis Christou* in Pauline Theology." *Colloquium* 30 (1998): 3–25.
Easter, M. C. "The *Pistis Christou* Debate: Main Arguments and Responses in Summary." *Currents in Biblical Research* 9 (2010): 33–47.
Harrisville, R. A. "*Pistis Christou* and the New Perspective on Paul." *Logia* 19 (2010): 19–28.
________. "Before *Pistis Christou*: The Objective Genitive as Good Greek." *NovT* 48 (2006): 353–58.

________. "ΠΙΣΤΙΣ ΧΡΙΣΤΟΥ: The Witness of the Fathers." *NovT* 36 (1994): 233–41.
Hays, R. B. *The Faith of Jesus Christ: The Narrative Substructure of Galatians 3:1–4:11*. Grand Rapids: Eerdmans, 2002.
________. "ΠΙΣΤΙΣ and Pauline Christology: What Is At Stake?" Pages 35–60 in *Pauline Theology*. Volume 4. Edited by E. E. Johnson and D. M. Hay. Atlanta: SBL, 1997.
Hooker, M. "ΠΙΣΤΙΣ ΧΡΙΣΤΟΥ." *NTS* 35 (1989): 321–49.
Howard, G. E. "On the Faith of Christ." *HTR* 60 (1967): 459–65.
________. "The 'Faith of Christ.'" *ExpTim* 85 (1974): 212–15.
Hultgren, A. J. "The ΠΙΣΤΙΣ ΧΡΙΣΤΟΥ Formulation in Paul." *NovT* 22 (1980): 248–63.
Just, A. A., Jr., "The Faith of Christ: a Lutheran Appropriation of Richard Hay's Proposal." *Concordia Theological* Quarterly 70 (2006): 3–15.
Longenecker, B. N. "ΠΙΣΤΙΣ in Romans 3.25: Neglected Evidence for the 'Faithfulness of Christ?'"*NTS* 39 (1993): 478–80.
Matlock, R. B. "The Rhetoric of *Pistis* in Paul: Galatians 2:16, 3:22, Romans 3:22, and Philippians 3:9." *JSNT* 30 (2007): 173–203.
________. "Detheologizing the ΠΙΣΤΙΣ ΧΡΙΣΤΟΥ Debate: Cautionary Remarks from a Lexical Semantic Perspective." *NovT* 42 (2000): 1–23.
Ota, S. "Absolute Use of PISTIS and PISTIS CHRISTOU in Paul." *Annual of the Japanese Biblical Institute* 23 (1997): 64–82.
Pollard, P. "The 'Faith of Christ' in Current Discussion." *Concordia Journal* 23 (1997): 213–28.
Whitenton, M. R. "After *Pistis Christou*: Evidence from the Apostolic Fathers." *JTS* 61 (2010): 82–109.
Williams, Sam K. "Again *Pistis Christou*." *CBQ* 49 (1987): 431–47.

32. Justification (3:24)

Aune, D. E., ed. *Rereading Paul Together: Protestant and Catholic Perspectives on Justification*. Grand Rapids: Baker, 2006 .
Beilby, J. K., and P. R. Eddy, eds. *Justification: Five Views*. Downers Grove, IL: InterVarsity, 2011.
Bird, M. F. "Incorporated Righteousness: A Response to Recent Evangelical Discussion Concerning the Imputation of Christ's Righteousness in Justification." *JETS* 47 (2004): 253–75.
________. "'Raised for our Justification': A Fresh Look at Romans 4:25." *Colloquium* 35 (2003): 31–46.
Boers, H. *The Justification of the Gentiles: Paul's Letters to the Galatians and Romans*. Peabody, MA: Hendrickson, 1994.
Boice, J. M. Romans, *Vol. 1: Justification by Faith, Romans 1–4*. Grand Rapids: Baker, 1991.
Campbell, D. A. *The Deliverance of God: An Apocalyptic Rereading of Justification in Paul*. Grand Rapids: Eerdmans, 2009.
________. "Towards a New, Rhetorically Assisted Reading of Romans 3.27–4:25." Pages 355–402 in *Rhetorical Criticism and the Bible*. Edited by S. E. Porter and D. L. Stamps. Sheffield: Sheffield Academic Press, 2002.
Carson, D. A. "Why Trust a Cross? Reflections on Romans 3:21–26." *Evangelical Review of Theology* 28 (2004): 345–62.
________, O'Brien, P. T., and M. A. Seifrid, eds. *Justification and Variegated Nomism. Volume 2, The Paradoxes of Paul*. Grand Rapids: Baker, 2004.

Chow, S. "Justification by Faith Reconsidered." *Theology* 27 (2004): 117–31.
Conzelmann, H. "Paul's Doctrine of Justification: Theology or Anthropology." Pages 108–23 in *Theology of the Liberating Word*. Edited by F. Herzog. Nashville: Abingdon, 1971.
Cosgrove, C. H. "Justification in Paul." *JBL* 106 (1987): 653–70.
Gathercole, S. "After the New Perspective: Works, Justification and Boasting in Early Judaism and Romans." *TynBul* 52 (2001): 303–306.
Gatiss, L. "Justified Hesitation? J. D. G. Dunn & the Protestant Doctrine of Justification." *Churchman,* 115 (2001): 29–48.
Gorman, M. J. *Inhabiting the Cruciform God: Kenosis, Justification, and Theosis in Paul's Narrative Soteriology*. Grand Rapids: Eerdmans, 2009.
Gyllenberg, R. *Rechtfertigung und Altes Testament bei Paulus*. Stuttgart: Kohlhammer, 1973.
Husbands, M., and J. T. Daniel. *Justification: What's at Stake in the Current Debates*. Downers Grove, IL: InterVarsity, 2004.
Kertelge, K. *"Rechtfertigung" bei Paulus. Studien zur Struktur und zum Bedeutungesgehalt des paulinischen Rechtfertigungsbetriffs*. Münster: Aschendorff, 1971.
Kirk, J. R. D. *Unlocking Romans: Resurrection and the Justification of God*. Grand Rapids: Eerdmans, 2008.
Kruse. G. G. *Paul, the Law and Justification*. Peabody, MA: Hendrickson, 1997.
Lambrecht, J., and R. W. Thompson, eds. *Justification by Faith: The Implications of Romans 3:27–31*. Wilmington, DE: Michael Glazier, 1989.
Leithart, P. J. "Justification as Verdict and Deliverance: A Biblical Perspective." *Pro Ecclesia* 16 (2007): 56–72.
Maier, W. A. "Paul's Concept of Justification, and Some Recent Interpretations of Romans 3:21–31." *Springfielder* 37 (1974): 248–64.
Maxwell, D. R. "Justified by Works and not by Faith Alone: Reconciling Paul and James." *Concordia Journal* 33 (2007): 375–78.
Moore, R. K. *Rectification ("Justification") in Paul, in Historical Perspective and in the Bible: God's Gift of Right Relationship*. 3 Volumes. Lewiston, NY: Edwin Mellen, 2002.
Morris, L. *EDBT* 441–43.
Ortlund, D. "Justified by Faith, Judged according to Works: Another Look at a Pauline Paradox." *JETS* 52 (2009): 323–39.
Packer, J. I. *EDT* 593–97.
Piper, J. *The Future of Justification: A Response to N.T. Wright*. Wheaton, IL: Crossway, 2007.
Plevnik. J. "Recent Developments in the Discussion Concerning Justification by Faith." *TJT* 2 (1986): 47–62.
Stuhlmacher, P., and D. A. Hagner, eds. *Revisiting Paul's Doctrine of Justification: A Challenge to the New Perspective*. Downers Grove, IL: InterVarsity, 2001.
Ryken, P. G., D. A. Carson, and T. Keller, eds. *Justification*. Wheaton, IL: Crossway, 2011.
Schreiner, T. R. "An Old Perspective on the New Perspective." *Concordia Journal* 35 (2009): 140–55.
Seifrid, M. A. *Christ, Our Righteousness: Paul's Theology of Justification*. Downers Grove, IL: InterVarsity, 2000.
________. *Justification by Faith: The Origin and Development of a Central Pauline Theme*. Leiden: Brill, 1992.

Stegman, T. D. "Paul's Use of *dikaio*-Terminology: Moving beyond N. T. Wright's Forensic Interpretation." *TS* 72 (2011): 496–524.
Westerholm, S. "Justification by Faith is the Answer: What is the Question?" *CTQ* 70 (2006): 197–217.
Wright, N. T. "Justification: Yesterday, Today, and Forever." *JETS* 54 (2011): 49–63.
________. *Justification: God's Plan and Paul's Vision*. Downers Grove, IL: InterVarsity, 2009.

33. Redemption (3:24)

Bockmuehl, M., and J. C. Paget, eds. *Redemption and Resistance: The Messianic Hopes of Jews and Christians in Antiquity*. London: T&T Clark, 2007.
Bolt, J. "The Relation between Creation and Redemption in Romans 8:18–27." *CTJ* 30 (1995): 34–51.
Brondos, D. A. *Paul on the Cross: Reconstructing the Apostle's Story of Redemption*. Minneapolis: Fortress, 2006.
________. "The Cross and the Curse: Galatians 3.13 and Paul's Doctrine of Redemption." *JSNT* 81 (2001): 3–32.
Brown, C. *NIDNTT* 3.177–200.
Brunt, J. *Redemption in Romans*. Nampa, ID: Pacific Press Publishing Association, 2010.
Buchanan, G. W. "The Day of Atonement and Paul's Doctrine of Redemption." *NovT* 32 (1990): 236–49.
Büchsel, F. *TDNT* 4.351–56.
Gaffin, R. B. *Resurrection and Redemption: A Study in Paul's Soteriology*. Phillipsburg, NJ: Presbyterian and Reformed, 1987.
Harrison, E. F. *EDT* 918–19.
Hill, D. *Greek Words and Hebrew Meanings: Studies in the Semantics of Soteriological Terms*. Cambridge: Cambridge University Press, 1967.
Howell, D. N. "The Center of Pauline Theology." *BSac* 151 (1994): 50–70.
Marshall, I. H. "The Development of the Concept of Redemption in the New Testament." Pages 153–69 in *Reconciliation and Hope*. Edited by R. Banks. Exeter: Paternoster, 1974.
McKnight, S. *Jesus and His Death: Historiography, the Historical Jesus, and Atonement Theory*. Waco, TX: Baylor University Press, 2005.
Morris, L. *DPL* 784–86.
________. *The Atonement: Its Meaning and Significance*. Downers Grove: InterVarsity, 1983.
________. *The Apostolic Preaching of the Cross*. Grand Rapids: Eerdmans, 1965.
Piper, J. *Counted Righteous in Christ: Should We Abandon the Imputation of Christ's Righteousness*? Wheaton, IL: Crossway, 2002.
Searle, D. "The Cross of Christ. 3, Justified and Redeemed Romans 3:24." *European Journal of Theology* 8 (1999): 115–22.
Silva, M. *NIDNTTE* 3.179–87.
Swartz, H. L. *EDBT* 664–65.
Tolmie, D. F. "Salvation as Redemption: The Use of 'Redemption' Metaphors in Pauline Literature." Pages 247–69 in *Salvation in the New Testament*. Edited by J. G. van der Watt. Leiden: Brill, 2005.
Torrance, T. F., and R. T. Walker. *Atonement: The Person and Work of Christ*. UK: Paternoster, 2009.

34. "In Christ" (3:24)

Allan, J. A. "The 'In Christ' Formula in the Pastoral Epistles." *NTS* 10 (1963): 115–21.
Barcley, W. B. *Christ in You: A Study in Paul's Theology and Ethics*. Lanham, MD: University Press of America, 1999.
Best, E. *One Body in Christ*. London: SPCK, 1955.
Bouttier, M. *En Christ*. Paris: Presses Universitares de France, 1962.
Büchsel, F. I. "'In Christus' bei Paulus." *ZNW* 42 (1949): 143–56.
Campbell, C. R. *Paul and Union with Christ: An Exegetical and Theological Study*. Grand Rapids: Zondervan, 2012.
Colijn, B. B. "Paul's Use of the 'In Christ' Formula." *Ashland Theological Journal* 23 (1991): 9–26.
Longenecker, R. N. "Excursus: Paul's Use of 'in Christ Jesus' and Its Cognates." Pages 686–94 in *The Epistle to the Romans*. Grand Rapids: Eerdmans, 2016.
Moule, C. F. D. *The Origin of Christology*. New York: Cambridge University Press, 1977.
Neugebauer, F. *In Christus/EN ΧΡΙΣΤΩ: Eine Untersuchung zum paulinischen Glaubensverständnis*. Göttingen: Vandenhoech & Ruprecht, 1961.
________. "Das paulinischen 'in Christo.'" *NTS* 4 (1958): 124–38.
Oepke, A. *TDNT* 2.537–43.
Seifrid, M. A. *DPL* 433–36.
Schweitzer, A. *The Mysticism of Paul the Apostle*. New York: Henry Holt, 1931.
Woodhouse, H. F. "Life in Christ and Life in the Spirit." *AThR* 47 (1965): 289–93.
Wedderburn, A. J. M. "Some Observations on Paul's Use of the Phrases 'In Christ' and 'With Christ.'" *JSNT* 25 (1985): 83–97.

35. Propitiation (3:25)

Beilby, J., and P. R. Eddy, eds. *The Nature of the Atonement: Four Views*. Downers Grove, IL: InterVarsity, 2006.
Boice, J. M. "The Nature of the Atonement: Propitiation." Pages 31–47 in *Atonement*. Phillipsburg, NJ: P & R, 2010.
________. *Our Saviour God: Man, Christ, and the Atonement*. Grand Rapids: Baker, 1980.
Büchsel, H. M. F., and J. Herrmann. *TDNT* 3.301–23.
Dalton, W. J. "Expiation or Propitiation: (Rom 3:25)." *AusBR* 8 (1960): 3–18.
Dever, M., and L. Michael, eds. *It Is Well: Expositions on Substitutionary Atonement*. Wheaton, IL: Crossway, 2010.
Dodd, C. H. "ΙΛΑΣΚΕΣΘΑΙ, Its Cognates, Derivatives and Synonyms in the Septuagint." *JTS* 32 (1931): 352–60.
Fluhrer, G. N. E. *Atonement*. Phillipsburg, NJ: P & R, 2010.
Fryer, N. S. L. "The Meaning and Translation of *Hilastērion* in Romans 3:25." *EvQ* 59 (1987): 99–116.
Gundry-Volff, J. M. *DPL* 279–84.
Hengel, M. *The Atonement: The Origins of the Doctrine in the New Testament*. Translated by J. Bowden. London: SCM, 1977.
Hill, D. H. *Greek Words and Hebrew Meanings*. Cambridge: Cambridge University Press, 1967.
Judisch, D. M. L. "Propitiation in Old Testament Prophecy." *CTQ* 49 (1985): 1–17.

________. "Propitiation in the Language and Typology of the Old Testament." *CTQ* 48 (1984): 21–43.
Link, H.-G., and C. Brown. *NIDNTT* 3.148–66.
Manson, T. W. "ΙΛΑΣΤΗΡΙΟΝ." *JTS* 46 (1945): 1–10.
Morris, L. *EDT* 888.
________. *The Atonement: Its Meaning and Significance.* Downers Grove, IL: InterVarsity, 1983.
________. *The Apostolic Preaching of the Cross.* London: Tyndale, 1965.
________. "The Meaning of ΙΛΑΣΤΗΡΙΟΝ' in Romans iii,25." *NTS* 2 (1955–56): 33–43.
________. "The Use of Hilaskesthai etc. in Biblical Greek." *ExpTim* 62 (1951): 227–33.
Nicole, R. R. "C. H. Dodd and the Doctrine of Propitiation." *WTJ* 17 (1955): 117–57.
Seume, R. H. "Divine Propitiation." *BSac* 100 (1943): 289–300.
Stott, J. R. W., and A. E. McGrath. *The Cross of Christ.* Downers Grove, IL: InterVarsity, 2006.
Thornton, T. C. G. "Propitiation or Expiation." *ExpTim* 80 (1968): 53–55.
Trotter, H. T., Jr. *EDBT* 42–45.
Tuckett, C. M. *ABD* 1.519.
Young, N. "C. H. Dodd, *Hilaskesthai* and His Critics." *EvQ* 48 (1976): 67–78.

HOMILETICAL SUGGESTIONS

God's Righteousness Through Faith (3:21–26)

1. It is manifested in the new epoch (νυνί δέ, 3:21–22b)
   a. Apart from law (3:21a)
   b. Witnessed by law and prophets (3:21b)
   c. Through faith in Christ (3:22a)
   d. To all who believe (3:22b)
2. It is available to all (οὐ γάρ ἐστιν διαστολή, 3:22c–24)
   a. Who sin and lack God's glory (3:23)
   b. Who are declared righteous (3:24)
      1) Freely (3:24a)
      2) By grace (3:24b)
      3) Through redemption in Christ (3:24c)
3. It is displayed in Jesus's propitiatory sacrifice (ὃν προέθετο ὁ θεός, 3:25–26)
   a. Through faith (3:25b)
   b. By blood (3:25c)
   c. To demonstrate God's righteousness (3:25d, 26b)
   d. Because of passing over sins (3:25e)
   e. To be just and justifier (3:26c)

The Gospel (3:21–26)

a. It upholds God's promise (3:21–22)
b. It upholds God's impartiality (3:23–24)
c. It upholds God's righteousness (3:25–26)

b. Apart from Works (3:27–31)

STRUCTURE

Paul returns to his question-and-answer diatribe style. Dunn notes the abrupt change and suggests that Paul intentionally varies his style to hold his audience's attention (185). The paragraph consists of four dialogical interchanges. The first (3:27a–b) and the fourth (3:31) consist of a single question and brief answer. The second (3:27c–28) and the third (3:29–30) consist of a double question, a brief answer, and supporting rationale.

Ποῦ οὖν ἡ καύχησις;
    ἐξεκλείσθη.

διὰ ποίου νόμου;
τῶν ἔργων;
    οὐχί, ἀλλὰ διὰ νόμου πίστεως.
        λογιζόμεθα γὰρ δικαιοῦσθαι πίστει ἄνθρωπον χωρὶς ἔργων νόμου.

ἢ Ἰουδαίων ὁ θεὸς μόνον;
οὐχὶ καὶ ἐθνῶν;
    ναὶ καὶ ἐθνῶν,
        εἴπερ εἷς ὁ θεός ὃς δικαιώσει περιτομὴν ἐκ πίστεως καὶ ἀκροβυστίαν διὰ τῆς πίστεως.

νόμον οὖν καταργοῦμεν διὰ τῆς πίστεως;
    μὴ γένοιτο· ἀλλὰ νόμον ἱστάνομεν.

VERSES 27–28

Ποῦ οὖν ἡ καύχησις; ἐξεκλείσθη

Paul's explanation of how God's righteousness is manifested (3:21–26; Longenecker suggests 2:17–3:26, 442) has implications (οὖν), especially in regard to the role of the law. His first question is elliptical with ἐστιν understood. See 2:17 for καύχησις. The verb (καυχάομαι) and its cognates occur thirty times in Paul; the noun that describes the cause of boasting (καύχημα) occurs ten times; and the noun that describes the act of boasting in this verse (καύχησις) occurs nine other times (cf. Longenecker 442–43). The article accompanies the abstract noun and is anaphoric to 2:17 and 2:23 (Longenecker 443). Ἐξεκλείσθη (3 sg. aor. pass. indic. of ἐκκλείω, "exclude") is a consummative aorist and a divine passive (Schreiner 200 n. 1). Jewett notes that the verb can mean "to have the door shut in one's face" (296).

διὰ ποίου νόμου; τῶν ἔργων; οὐχί, ἀλλὰ διὰ νόμου πίστεως

Two elliptical questions explore the means (διά + gen.) that excludes boasting. Paul's use of "law" (νόμος) is probably a deliberate play on words, since the interrogative pronoun ποῖος is qualitative ("what kind of") and stresses membership in a class rather than identity (Moo 250). The article with ἔργων is generic, and the genitive of apposition describes a specific kind of "law." The negative particle οὐχί ("never"; Longenecker 444) with the adversative conjunction ἀλλά ("but") forms a strong contrast to emphasize the answer. Διὰ νόμου echoes the question with πίστεως added as a genitive of definition (Longenecker 444); both nouns are definite (R 780). Cranfield explains νόμου πίστεως as the OT law that summons to faith (220; cf. 9:31; 10:6–8); Longenecker concludes that νόμος should be understood as "principle" (445). Jewett suggests that the combination νόμου ἔργων . . . νόμου πίστεως distinguishes between an understanding of the law (νόμου ἔργων) that enhances boasting and an understanding of the law (νόμου πίστεως) that excludes it (297).*

λογιζόμεθα γὰρ δικαιοῦσθαι πίστει ἄνθρωπον χωρὶς ἔργων νόμου

Both manuscript evidence and grammatical context favor γάρ ("for") over the variant οὖν (Metzger 450), because the sentence it introduces provides the reason faith excludes boasting. EVV translate λογιζόμεθα (1 pl. pres. mid. indic. of dep. λογίζομαι) variously as "conclude" (KJV), "hold" (RSV, NRSV, ESV), "maintain" (NASB, NIV). Cranfield calls it "a faith conviction reached in light of the gospel" (220). The use of the first person plural has been explained as epistolary (Wallace 396), apostolic (Schreiner 203),* or referring to all believers (Moo 250). The infinitive δικαιοῦσθαι (pres. pass. inf. of δικαιόω, "declare righteous") is complementary to the main verb with the indefinite ἄνθρωπον as its subject. The present tense is gnomic; the passive is a divine passive. Πίστει (dat. sg. fem.) describes the means by which a person is declared righteous; its placement between the infinitive and its subject is emphatic. Χωρὶς ἔργων νόμου ("apart from works of law") is equivalent to both χωρὶς νόμου (3:21) and χωρὶς ἔργων (4:6) and is a distinctive Pauline theme found elsewhere only in James 2:26.

VERSES 29–30

ἢ Ἰουδαίων ὁ θεὸς μόνον; οὐχὶ καὶ ἐθνῶν; ναὶ καὶ ἐθνῶν

The disjunctive ἤ ("or") introduces a fresh argument (Schreiner 205); ἐστιν is again understood. See 1:16 for Ἰουδαῖος; the genitive is possessive. The article with θεός is anaphoric; the accusative adjective μόνον is used adverbially. The negative οὐχί anticipates a positive response; καί is adjunctive ("also"). Ἔθνος often occurs without the article (BDF §254.3); the genitive is possessive. The combination ναὶ καί ("certainly also") leaves no room for doubt (Jewett 299). The possessive genitive ἐθνῶν parallels Ἰουδαίων and makes it clear that God is the God of both ethnic groups.

εἴπερ εἷς ὁ θεός ὃς δικαιώσει περιτομὴν ἐκ πίστεως καὶ ἀκροβυστίαν διὰ τῆς πίστεως

The intensive conjunction εἴπερ ("if after all"; Longenecker 449) gives the reason God is the God of both Jew and Gentile (BDF §456.3): "God is one." Εἷς ὁ θεός echoes the Shema: Ἄκουε, Ἰσραηλ· κύριος ὁ θεὸς ἡμῶν κύριος εἷς ἐστιν (Deut 6:4, LXX). A clause introduced by the definite relative pronoun ὅς ("who") further describes θεός. Δικαιώσει (3 sg. fut. act. indic. of δικαιόω) has gnomic significance (Moo 252 n. 33). See 2:25–26 for περιτομή and ἀκροβυστία; the anarthrous nouns are indefinite, indicating membership in a class. Both ἐκ πίστεως and διὰ τῆς πίστεως indicate means; the change in prepositions is stylistic with no fine distinction between them (Moule 195). The article with the second occurrence of πίστεως is anaphoric to 3:22 ("the same faith"). Longenecker again argues that the reference is to divine faithfulness (450–51).

VERSE 31

νόμον οὖν καταργοῦμεν διὰ τῆς πίστεως;

The final question raises a false inference (οὖν) from the preceding discussion. Longenecker views it as stating an objection Paul knows his readers will raise in response to 3:21–23 (451). Placing the direct object νόμον (sg. acc. masc.) first makes it emphatic. Although anarthrous, the referent is the Mosaic law in its entirety (cf. 3:21). See 3:4 for καταργέω ("abolish/render ineffective"); the present tense is voluntative, suggesting desire. Διὰ τῆς πίστεως repeats the concluding phrase from the preceding sentence.

μὴ γένοιτο· (see 3:4)

ἀλλὰ νόμον ἱστάνομεν

Μή . . . ἀλλά establishes a strong contrast (cf. 3:27). Νόμον is again brought forward for emphasis. Ἱστάνομεν (1 pl. pres. act. indic. of ἱστάνω, "establish") is a later form of the more common ἵστημι; it describes the act of validating something that is in force (BDAG 482c). Schreiner sets out three views of the way in which faith establishes the law (206–208); he concludes that those who have faith in Christ will keep the law (cf. 13:8–10). Longenecker adds that this statement highlights the way in which both specific OT texts and the entire OT narrative support Paul's teaching (452).

FOR FURTHER STUDY

See For Further Study §§ 5 ("Gentiles"), 11 ("Faith"), 24 ("Paul and the Law"), 26 ("Circumcision"), 28 ("Works of Law")

HOMILETICAL SUGGESTIONS

The Implications of Righteousness Through Faith (3:27–31)

1. It shuts the door on boasting (ἐξεκλείσθη, 3:27–28)
    a. Through the law of faith (3:27)
    b. Because it justifies by faith apart from works (3:28)

2. It establishes God as the God of both Jew and Gentile (3:29–30)
   a. He is also the God of the Gentiles (3:29)
   b. Because he justifies both by faith (3:30)
3. It confirms the role of the Law (ἱστάνομεν, 3:31)

3. God Reveals His Righteousness in Response to Faith (4:1–25)

a. Apart from Works or Circumcision (4:1–12)

STRUCTURE

Paul introduces the example of Abraham in 4:1–2 and continues the discussion through 4:25. The first paragraph in his discussion centers on two OT quotations: Genesis 15:6 (4:3–5) and Psalm 32:1–2 (4:6–12). Jewett notes both the parallelism Paul uses in developing his argument and the way in which qualifying material creates imbalances within that parallelism (305).

Τί οὖν ἐροῦμεν εὑρηκέναι Ἀβραὰμ τὸν προπάτορα ἡμῶν κατὰ σάρκα;
εἰ γὰρ Ἀβραὰμ ἐξ ἔργων ἐδικαιώθη, ἔχει καύχημα, ἀλλ᾽ οὐ πρὸς θεόν.

τί γὰρ ἡ γραφὴ λέγει;
    Ἐπίστευσεν δὲ Ἀβραὰμ τῷ θεῷ
    καὶ ἐλογίσθη αὐτῷ εἰς δικαιοσύνην.
        τῷ δὲ ἐργαζομένῳ
            ὁ μισθὸς οὐ λογίζεται κατὰ χάριν ἀλλὰ κατὰ ὀφείλημα,
        τῷ δὲ μὴ ἐργαζομένῳ πιστεύοντι δὲ ἐπὶ τὸν δικαιοῦντα τὸν ἀσεβῆ
            λογίζεται ἡ πίστις αὐτοῦ εἰς δικαιοσύνην·

καθάπερ καὶ Δαυὶδ λέγει τὸν μακαρισμὸν τοῦ ἀνθρώπου ᾧ ὁ θεὸς λογίζεται δικαιοσύνην χωρὶς ἔργων,
    Μακάριοι ὧν ἀφέθησαν αἱ ἀνομίαι καὶ ὧν ἐπεκαλύφθησαν αἱ ἁμαρτίαι·
    μακάριος ἀνὴρ οὗ οὐ μὴ λογίσηται κύριος ἁμαρτίαν.
        ὁ μακαρισμὸς οὖν οὗτος ἐπὶ τὴν περιτομὴν
                ἢ καὶ ἐπὶ τὴν ἀκροβυστίαν;
    λέγομεν γάρ, Ἐλογίσθη τῷ Ἀβραὰμ ἡ πίστις εἰς δικαιοσύνην.

        πῶς οὖν ἐλογίσθη; ἐν περιτομῇ ὄντι ἢ ἐν ἀκροβυστίᾳ;
                οὐκ ἐν περιτομῇ ἀλλ᾽ ἐν ἀκροβυστίᾳ·

καὶ σημεῖον ἔλαβεν περιτομῆς σφραγῖδα τῆς δικαιοσύνης τῆς πίστεως τῆς ἐν τῇ ἀκροβυστίᾳ,
    εἰς τὸ εἶναι αὐτὸν πατέρα πάντων τῶν πιστευόντων δι᾽ ἀκροβυστίας,
                εἰς τὸ λογισθῆναι αὐτοῖς [τὴν] δικαιοσύνην,
        καὶ πατέρα περιτομῆς
                τοῖς οὐκ ἐκ περιτομῆς μόνον
        ἀλλὰ καὶ τοῖς στοιχοῦσιν τοῖς ἴχνεσιν τῆς ἐν ἀκροβυστίᾳ πίστεως
                τοῦ πατρὸς ἡμῶν Ἀβραάμ.

VERSE 1

Τί οὖν ἐροῦμεν εὑρηκέναι Ἀβραὰμ τὸν προπάτορα ἡμῶν κατὰ σάρκα;

UBS[5] gives εὑρηκέναι Ἀβραὰμ τὸν προπάτορα ἡμῶν a {B} rating over three other variants. The rare προπάτορα is to be preferred over πατέρα as the more difficult reading with stronger MSS support (ℵ, A, B, C; cf. Cranfield 226). Although the omission of εὑρηκέναι is shorter (B; cf. BDF §480.5), it appears to be an isolated reading. Schreiner suggests that the variant with εὑρηκέναι following Ἀβραὰμ τὸν προπάτορα ἡμῶν (33) is an attempt to correct a syntactical difficulty (221).

Paul introduces his rhetorical question with the interrogative pronoun τί and links it to 3:27–31 with the inferential οὖν (Porter 305; cf. Dunn 198). Ἐροῦμεν (1 pl. fut. act. indic. of λέγω) is a deliberative future. The full phrase appears five other times in Romans (6:1; 7:7; 8:31; 9:14, 30; cf. 3:5). Εὑρηκέναι (pf. act. inf.) is an infinitive in indirect discourse; the intensive perfect highlights completed action. Εὑρίσκω denotes discovery through reflection, observation, or investigation (BDAG 412a); Dunn notes its frequent OT use in the phrase "to find mercy/grace" (198). The indeclinable Ἀβραάμ is the accusative subject of the infinitive (T 168). The article with προπάτορα (acc. sg. masc.) is natural with the possessive pronoun; the noun ("forefather") denotes the primary founder of a family (BDAG 873c). Although Jewett takes κατὰ σάρκα with the infinitive (308), it is more naturally connected to προπάτορα (Moo 260). The preposition denotes reference; the anarthrous noun is qualitative.

VERSE 2

εἰ γὰρ Ἀβραὰμ ἐξ ἔργων ἐδικαιώθη, ἔχει καύχημα, ἀλλ' οὐ πρὸς θεόν

Paul goes on to explain (γάρ) the relevance of verse 1 to his overall argument (Cranfield 227). The first class condition (εἰ + indic.) assumes the protasis is true for the sake of argument (Wallace 694). Ἀβραάμ (indecl.) is nominative of subject; ἐδικαιώθη (3 sg. aor. pass. indic.) is a simple passive with the impersonal means expressed by ἐξ ἔργων (cf. 3:20). See 2:13 for δικαιόω and 3:27 for καύχημα (acc. sg. neut.) and its cognates. The combination of adversative conjunction (ἀλλά) and negative particle (οὐ) rejects the previous suggestion (Cranfield 228). EVV understand πρός ("before") as orientation toward something (BDAG 874b); θεόν is definite although anarthrous.

VERSE 3

τί γὰρ ἡ γραφὴ λέγει;

The reason (γάρ) works did not justify Abraham is found in ἡ γραφή, which denotes the OT Scripture in its entirety (BDAG 206c; contra Longenecker [494] who argues that it refers only to Gen 15:6). The phrase ἡ γραφὴ λέγει also introduces OT quotations in 9:17; 10:11; 11:2 (cf. Gal 4:30; 1 Tim 5:18) and is equivalent to καθὼς γέγραπται (fourteen times). The quotation it introduces (Gen 15:6) is taken directly from the LXX. Cranfield notes that Paul appeals to a verse his fellow Jews assumed would support their view that Abraham was justified on the basis of his works (229).

Ἐπίστευσεν δὲ Ἀβραὰμ τῷ θεῷ καὶ ἐλογίσθη αὐτῷ εἰς δικαιοσύνην.

The OT context suggests that δέ is connective ("and"); ἐπίστευσεν (3 sg. aor. act. indic.) is constative; Ἀβραάμ (indecl.) is nominative of subject; a dative direct object is common with πιστεύω; the article with θεῷ is monadic. Καί is connective ("and"); ἐλογίσθη (3 sg. aor. pass. indic.) is a divine passive; αὐτῷ (dat. sg. masc.) is the indirect object. Λογίζομαι ("place to one's account"; cf. Jewett 312) occurs eleven times in Romans 4, four times followed by εἰς δικαιοσύνην (cf. 4:5, 9, 22) as a substitute for a predicate nominative (R 458; T 253). See 1:17 for δικαιοσύνη.

VERSE 4

τῷ δὲ ἐργαζομένῳ

From the scriptural proof of Genesis 15:6, Paul transitions (δέ) to its implications, using λογίζομαι plus the dative to unify the antithetic parallelism of his argument. The substantival participle ἐργαζομένῳ (dat. sg. masc. of pres. mid. ptc.) serves as the indirect object, echoes the dative αὐτῷ in the OT quotation, and is brought forward to make the connection clear. See 2:10 for ἐργάζομαι, which echoes the ἐξ ἔργων of verse 3. Each of the present tense verbs in this verse is gnomic as Paul states general, timeless principles.

ὁ μισθὸς οὐ λογίζεται κατὰ χάριν ἀλλὰ κατὰ ὀφείλημα

The individualizing article with μισθός denotes the reward that is given to each one to whom the principle applies (R 757); the noun describes recognition for laudable conduct (BDAG 653d). Λογίζεται is a true passive (T 58). The negative particle οὐ followed by the adversative ἀλλά establishes a strong contrast between the standards (κατά + acc.) involved. Ὀφείλημα, –τος, τό denotes that which is owed in a financial sense (BDAG 743a); see 1:7 for χάρις. Both nouns are objects of prepositions as well as abstract and, therefore, are definite.

VERSE 5

τῷ δὲ μὴ ἐργαζομένῳ πιστεύοντι δὲ ἐπὶ τὸν δικαιοῦντα τὸν ἀσεβῆ

The first δέ introduces the second half of the antithetic parallelism and is adversative. The negative particle μή is expected with a participle. Paul expands the line by adding the contrasting (δέ) substantival participle πιστεύοντι (dat. sg. masc. of pres. act. ptc.). The initial article holds the two participles together: "to the one who is not working but is believing." Paul uses πιστεύω ἐπί four times in Romans—twice with the accusative (4:5, 24) and twice with the dative (9:33; 10:11)—more frequently than other constructions. Harris suggests that the accusative reflects metaphorical movement "directed toward" someone or something and usually refers to the initial act of conversion (235). The article with the substantival participle δικαιοῦντα (acc. sg. masc. of pres. act. ptc.) marks it as the object of ἐπί. The article enables ἀσεβής, -ες ("ungodly") to function as the object of the participle. The adjective describes the violation of norms for a proper relationship with God (BDAG 141a; see also 1:18). Harris notes that Christ, rather than God, is far more frequently the object of faith in Paul's letters (237).

λογίζεται ἡ πίστις αὐτοῦ εἰς δικαιοσύνην

Having established that believing is the antithesis to working, Paul incorporates the noun πίστις into the formula from Genesis 15:6. The article is normally present with a possessive pronoun; λογίζεται is passive; εἰς δικαιοσύνην repeats the construction of the OT quotation (cf. 4:3). Dunn concludes that πίστις must mean "faith" in this context (204).

VERSE 6

καθάπερ καὶ Δαυὶδ λέγει τὸν μακαρισμὸν τοῦ ἀνθρώπου

Paul adds (adjunctive καί) to his argument that righteousness is reckoned apart from works by introducing a second OT quotation. Eleven of the twelve NT occurrences of καθάπερ ("just as") are in Paul's letters; it introduces an OT quotation four other times in Romans (3:4; 9:13; 10:15; 11:8). Δαυίδ (indecl.) is nominative; λέγει ("speaks of," EVV) is a perfective present (cf. Wallace 532–33). An article accompanies the abstract noun μακαρισμός, -οῦ, ὁ ("blessing"), which describes the pronouncement of special favor (BDAG 611c; cf. 4:9; Gal 4:15). The blessing is pronounced upon (obj. gen.) the person (individualizing article) described in the following relative clause.

ᾧ ὁ θεὸς λογίζεται δικαιοσύνην χωρὶς ἔργων

The relative pronoun ᾧ (dat. sg. masc.) further describes ἀνθρώπου in the preceding clause and functions as the indirect object in its own clause. The article with the subject θεός is monadic; λογίζεται is a deponent middle, translated as active voice; the anarthrous abstract noun δικαιοσύνην is qualitative. Χωρὶς ἔργων ("apart from works") returns to the thesis of verse 2 and makes it clear that the reckoning of righteousness is independent of works just as it was independent of law (cf. 3:21).

VERSE 7

Μακάριοι ὧν ἀφέθησαν αἱ ἀνομίαι καὶ ὧν ἐπεκαλύφθησαν αἱ ἁμαρτίαι

The second OT quotation (Ps 32:1–2) is also taken directly from the LXX and highlights the blessing that results from the forgiveness of sins by placing the predicate adjective μακάριος, -α, -ον ("blessed") first in both lines. The understood subject of the verbless clause is οὗτοι (R 720), which is also the embedded antecedent of both genitive relative pronouns (ὧν). Ἀφέθησαν (3 pl. aor. pass. indic. of ἀφίημι, "cancel/

pardon") and ἐπεκαλύφθησαν (3 pl. aor. pass. indic. of ἐπικαλύπτω, "cover") are both divine passives (Wallace 438). The former describes release from legal and/or moral consequences (BDAG 156c), while the latter occurs only here in the NT but carries the idea of forgiving sins in Psalm 85:2 (Cranfield 234). Jewett states that both verbs describe "a single event now completed" (316). The article accompanies both abstract nouns that function as subjects of the compound relative clause. Ἀνομία, -ας, ἡ denotes a lawless deed produced by a lawless disposition (BDAG 85c); Cranfield describes it as "rebellion against the divine authority, the deliberate and open violation of God's commandment" (233). Ἁμαρτία, -ας, ἡ denotes a departure from the divine standard of uprightness and can in certain contexts communicate the commercial metaphor of a debt (BDAG 50d).

VERSE 8

μακάριος ἀνὴρ οὗ οὐ μὴ λογίσηται κύριος ἁμαρτίαν

The second line of the OT quotation also begins with μακάριος ("blessed") as the predicate adjective of a verbless clause. The anarthrous subject ἀνήρ (nom. sg. masc.) is indefinite and best understood as "someone/a person" (BDAG 79d). See Cranfield for why the genitive relative pronoun οὗ is the preferred reading (234). Οὐ μὴ λογίσηται (3 sg. aor. mid. subjunc. of dep. λογίζομαι) is emphatic negation (T 96). Κύριος is definite and monadic; ἁμαρτίαν (acc. sg. fem.) is indefinite and qualitative.

VERSE 9

ὁ μακαρισμὸς οὖν οὗτος ἐπὶ τὴν περιτομὴν ἢ καὶ ἐπὶ τὴν ἀκροβυστίαν;

Paul uses the vividness of a rhetorical question to begin drawing out his inference (οὖν) from the OT quotation. Ὁ μακαρισμός οὗτος ("this blessing") refers back to the near context of verse 6 as developed in verses 7–8. The understood verb may be λέγεται ("spoken about"; cf. R 394) or δίδοται ("bestowed upon"; cf. Moo 267 n. 2). Ἐπί + accusative marks the one to/for/about whom something is done or said (BDAG 366b). Τὴν περιτομήν and τὴν ἀκροβυστίαν are anaphoric, resuming the designation of two classes begun in 3:30. Jewett's suggestion that the terms were "abusively hurled back and forth between Jews and Gentiles in Rome" is purely speculative (318). The conjunction ἤ is disjunctive ("or"), while καί is adjunctive ("also").

λέγομεν γάρ, Ἐλογίσθη τῷ Ἀβραὰμ ἡ πίστις εἰς δικαιοσύνην

The reason (γάρ) for Paul's question resides in the OT proof of Genesis 15:6. Two adjustments clarify his premise that Abraham was justified on the basis of faith alone. The abstract noun πίστις substitutes for the verb (ἐπίστευσεν) with the article serving as a mild possessive pronoun ("his faith"). The dative τῷ Ἀβραάμ (indecl.) replaces the pronoun (αὐτῷ) and makes the reference to Abraham clear. See verse 3 for ἐλογίσθη . . . εἰς δικαιοσύνην.

VERSE 10

πῶς οὖν ἐλογίσθη; ἐν περιτομῇ ὄντι ἢ ἐν ἀκροβυστίᾳ;

Two more rhetorical questions continue drawing out Paul's inference (οὖν) and enhance the dialectical vividness of his argument (R 1198). The interrogative particle πῶς ("how") probes the circumstances in which something is done (BDAG 901a). Although Moo understands the participle ὄντι (dat. sg. masc. of pres. act. ptc. from εἰμί) as adjectival to τῷ Ἀβραάμ in verse 9 (268 n. 9), EVV and other commentators uniformly translate it as adverbial of time ("while"). Ἐν + dative denotes state; the conjunction ἤ is again disjunctive ("or").

οὐκ ἐν περιτομῇ ἀλλ' ἐν ἀκροβυστίᾳ

The answer is framed as a strong contrast (οὐκ . . . ἀλλ') stating unequivocally that God declared Abraham righteous before he was circumcised (ἐν ἀκροβυστίᾳ).

VERSE 11

καὶ σημεῖον ἔλαβεν περιτομῆς

The conjunction καί is more nearly explanatory ("for") than connective ("and") in that it introduces an extended discussion of the relationship between Abraham's faith and his circumcision. Jewett notes that verses 11–12 paraphrase the LXX of Genesis 17:11–13, which highlights the extended time between the two events (318). Σημεῖον (acc. sg. neut.) denotes a distinguishing mark by which something is known (BDAG 920c); placing the direct object before the verb and separating it from the genitive that depends on it gives it emphasis. Περιτομῆς (gen. sg. fem.) is a genitive of apposition ("the sign which is circumcision"; cf. R 498; T 214); both nouns are definite although anarthrous (R 780). Ἔλαβεν (3 sg. aor. act. indic. from λαμβάνω) is a consummative aorist, highlighting the conclusion of the action.

σφραγῖδα τῆς δικαιοσύνης τῆς πίστεως τῆς ἐν τῇ ἀκροβυστίᾳ

The indefinite noun σφραγῖδα (acc. sg. fem. from σφραγίς, -ιδος, ἡ, "seal") stands in apposition to σημεῖον; it denotes something that confirms the validity of a reality already present (Jewett 319; cf. BDAG 980d). Δικαιοσύνης is an objective genitive; πίστεως is subjective; definite articles accompany both abstract nouns as is normal in genitive phrases (Wallace 239). The third article marks the prepositional phrase as adjectival modifying πίστεως (R 782) and functions as a relative pronoun ("the faith that was [his while] in uncircumcision").

εἰς τὸ εἶναι αὐτὸν πατέρα πάντων τῶν πιστευόντων δι' ἀκροβυστίας

The divine purpose (εἰς τό + infin.) of Abraham's circumcision was to make him "the point of union between all who believe, whether circumcised or uncircumcised" (Cranfield 236). Αὐτόν (acc. sg. masc.) is the subject of the infinitive, while πατέρα (acc. sg. masc.) is the predicate accusative (R 782). Abraham's descendants (gen. of rel.) are "all those who are believing." The article marks πιστευόντων (gen. pl. masc. of pres. act. ptc.) as a substantival participle; the present tense is progressive and denotes continuing belief (cf. Wallace 621 n. 22). Δι' ἀκροβυστίας is most likely a stylistic variation on ἐν τῇ ἀκροβυστίᾳ (Harris 77; cf. 113).

εἰς τὸ λογισθῆναι αὐτοῖς τὴν δικαιοσύνην

The omission of καί after λογισθῆναι is supported by ℵ, A, and 33; Metzger suggests that it might have been added in an attempt to sharpen the argument (450). Εἰς τό + infinitive may be understood as purpose (Dunn 210) or result (Cranfield 237; Moo 270 n. 20); the latter seems more likely. Λογισθῆναι (aor. pass. infin.) is a divine passive; αὐτοῖς is a dative of indirect object; the accusative τὴν δικαιοσύνην is the subject of the infinitive.

VERSE 12

καὶ πατέρα περιτομῆς τοῖς οὐκ ἐκ περιτομῆς μόνον

The connective καί ("and") adds a second predicate accusative to εἰς τὸ εἶναι αὐτόν in verse 11, so that Abraham is designated as father (πατέρα) of both uncircumcised and circumcised believers. Περιτομῆς is another genitive indicating descendants; the anarthrous genitive noun is normal when it occurs with an anarthrous head noun (cf. 3:30; 15:8); Cranfield notes the use of the abstract for the concrete (237). The article τοῖς (dat. pl. masc.) allows the prepositional phrase ἐκ περιτομῆς to function as a noun; the dative denotes reference; the separation of οὐκ . . . μόνον ("not only") is a instance of hyperbaton (R 423).

ἀλλὰ καὶ τοῖς στοιχοῦσιν τοῖς ἴχνεσιν τῆς ἐν ἀκροβυστίᾳ πίστεως τοῦ πατρὸς ἡμῶν Ἀβραάμ

Ἀλλά καί ("but also") establishes a strong contrast with the preceding dative phrase. The inclusion of the article before στοιχοῦσιν complicates the question of whether one or two groups are in view in this verse. Jewett argues for two groups (320); Cranfield views the article as a mistake and argues for one group (237). Schreiner offers a nuanced argument in favor of one group (226), which supports the more natural understanding that verse 11 refers to uncircumcised individuals who believe (Gentiles) and verse 12 refers to individuals who not only are circumcised but also believe (Jews).

The article τοῖς marks the participle στοιχοῦσιν (dat. pl. masc. of pres. act. ptc. of στοιχέω, "walk") as substantival; the dative again denotes reference; the present tense is progressive. Στοιχέω describes the activity of holding to what is considered a standard for conduct (BDAG 946d); it occurs with similar meaning three other times in Paul's letters (Gal 5:25; 6:16; Phil 3:16). Τοῖς ἴχνεσιν is a dative of rule ("in conformance with the footsteps"; Wallace 158). Πίστεως may be understood as an attributive genitive ("faithful footsteps") or a descriptive genitive ("footsteps characterized by faith").* Most EVV choose the latter and translate the phrase τοῖς ἴχνεσιν τῆς ἐν ἀκροβυστίᾳ πίστεως as "in the footsteps of the faith [Abraham] had before he was circumcised." Τοῦ πατρὸς ἡμῶν is a subjective genitive; Ἀβραάμ (indecl.) is a genitive of simple apposition ("our father who is Abraham").

FOR FURTHER STUDY

36. Abraham (4:1–25)

Adams, E. "Abraham's Faith and Gentile Disobedience: Textual Links between Romans 1 and 4." *JSNT* 65 (1997): 47–66.

Baird, W. "Abraham in the New Testament: Tradition and New Identity." *Int* 42 (1988): 63–77.

Berger, K. "Abraham in den paulinischen Hauptbriefen." *MThZ* 17 (1966): 47–89.

Byrne, B. *"Sons of God"—"Seed of Abraham"; A Study of the Idea of the Sonship of All Christians in Paul against the Jewish Background.* Rome: Pontifical Biblical Institute, 1979.

Calvert, N. L. *DPL* 1–8.

Cranford, M. "Abraham in Romans 4: The Father of All Who Believe." *NTS* 41 (1995): 71–88.

Holst, R. "The Meaning of 'Abraham Believed God' in Romans 4:3." *WTJ* 59 (1997): 319–26.

Hunt, S. A., ed. *Perspectives on Our Father Abraham: Essays in Honor of Marvin R. Wilson.* Grand Rapids: Eerdmans, 2010.

Jipp, J. W. "Rereading the Story of Abraham, Isaac, and 'Us' in Romans 4." *JSNT* 32 (2009): 217–42.

Lincoln, A. T. "Abraham Goes to Rome: Paul's Treatment of Abraham in Romans 4." Pages 163–79 in *Worship, Theology and Ministry in the Early Church: Essays in Honor of Ralph P. Martin.* Edited by M. J. Wilkins and T. Paige. Sheffield: Sheffield Academic Press, 1993.

Neubrand, M. *Abraham—Vater von Juden und Nichtjuden. Eine exegetische Studie zu Röm 4.* Würzburg: Echter, 1997.

Schliesser, B. "'Abraham did not doubt in unbelief' (Rom 4:20): Faith, Doubt, and Dispute in Paul's Letter to the Romans." *JTS* 62 (2012): 492–522.

________. *Abraham's Faith in Romans 4: Paul's Concept of Faith in Light of the History of Reception of Genesis 15:6.* Tübingen: Mohr Siebeck, 2007.

Schmitz, O. "Abraham im Spätjudentum und im Urchristentum." Pages 99–123 in *Aus Schrift und Geschichte: Theologische Abhandlungen Adolf Schlatter zu seinem 70. Geburtstag dargebracht von Freunden und Schülern.* Edited by K. Bornhaüser, et al. Stuttgart: Calwer, 1922.

Tobin, T. H. "What Shall We Say that Abraham Found? The Controversy behind Romans 4." *HTR* 88 (1995): 437–52.

Waetjen, H. C. "The Trust of Abraham and the Trust of Jesus Christ: Rom 1:17." *Currents in Theology and Mission* 30 (2003): 446–54.

Williams, G. J. "Abraham in Christian Tradition." *Scripture Bulletin* 37 (2007): 1–11.

Wright, N. T. "Paul and the Patriarch: The Role of Abraham in Romans 4." *JSNT* 35 (2013): 207–41.

HOMILETICAL SUGGESTIONS

Lessons from Abraham's Experience, Part 1 (4:1–12)

1. Question: How was Abraham declared righteous? (4:1–2)
2. Answer #1: Abraham was declared righteous apart from works (4:3–5)
   a. OT proof: Genesis 15:6 (ἡ γραφὴ λέγει, 4:3)
   b. Explanation (δέ, 4:4–5)
      1) The one who works is owed a reward (4:4)
      2) The one who believes is credited with righteousness (4:5)
3. Answer #2: Abraham was declared righteous apart from circumcision (4:6–12)
   a. OT proof: Psalm 32:1–2 (καθάπερ καὶ Δαυὶδ λέγει, 4:6–8)
   b. Explanation (οὖν, 4:9–12)
      1) Does the proof apply to circumcised or uncircumcised individuals? (4:9)
      2) Abraham was declared righteous before he was circumcised (4:10)
         a) He is the father of all uncircumcised individuals who believe (4:11)
         b) He is the father of all circumcised individuals who believe (4:12)

b. Apart from Law (4:13–25)

STRUCTURE

The second paragraph in Paul's discussion of Abraham's experience also breaks into two sections held together by the theme of "promise" (4:13, 14, 16, 20, 21). The first section is a shorter rejection of the law (4:13–15); the second section is a longer affirmation of faith (4:16–21). A quotation of Genesis 15:6 marks the end of the paragraph and brackets the exposition (4:22; cf. 4:3). A brief concluding paragraph applies the lessons from Abraham's experience to the readers (4:23–25).

Οὐ γὰρ διὰ νόμου ἡ ἐπαγγελία τῷ Ἀβραὰμ ἢ τῷ σπέρματι αὐτοῦ, τὸ κληρονόμον αὐτὸν εἶναι κόσμου,
ἀλλὰ διὰ δικαιοσύνης πίστεως.
εἰ γὰρ οἱ ἐκ νόμου κληρονόμοι, κεκένωται ἡ πίστις καὶ κατήργηται ἡ ἐπαγγελία·
ὁ γὰρ νόμος ὀργὴν κατεργάζεται·
οὗ δὲ οὐκ ἔστιν νόμος οὐδὲ παράβασις.

διὰ τοῦτο ἐκ πίστεως, ἵνα κατὰ χάριν,
εἰς τὸ εἶναι βεβαίαν τὴν ἐπαγγελίαν παντὶ τῷ σπέρματι,
οὐ τῷ ἐκ τοῦ νόμου μόνον
ἀλλὰ καὶ τῷ ἐκ πίστεως Ἀβραάμ,

ὅς ἐστιν πατὴρ πάντων ἡμῶν,
καθὼς γέγραπται ὅτι Πατέρα πολλῶν ἐθνῶν τέθεικά σε,
κατέναντι οὗ ἐπίστευσεν θεοῦ τοῦ ζῳοποιοῦντος τοὺς νεκροὺς
καὶ καλοῦντος τὰ μὴ ὄντα ὡς ὄντα·

ὃς παρ' ἐλπίδα ἐπ' ἐλπίδι ἐπίστευσεν
εἰς τὸ γενέσθαι αὐτὸν πατέρα πολλῶν ἐθνῶν
κατὰ τὸ εἰρημένον· Οὕτως ἔσται τὸ σπέρμα σου,
καὶ μὴ ἀσθενήσας τῇ πίστει κατενόησεν τὸ ἑαυτοῦ σῶμα . . . καὶ τὴν νέκρωσιν τῆς μήτρας Σάρρας·
εἰς δὲ τὴν ἐπαγγελίαν τοῦ θεοῦ οὐ διεκρίθη τῇ ἀπιστίᾳ
ἀλλ' ἐνεδυναμώθη τῇ πίστει,
δοὺς δόξαν τῷ θεῷ καὶ πληροφορηθεὶς ὅτι ὃ ἐπήγγελται δυνατός ἐστιν καὶ ποιῆσαι.
διὸ [καὶ] ἐλογίσθη αὐτῷ εἰς δικαιοσύνην.

Οὐκ ἐγράφη δὲ δι' αὐτὸν μόνον ὅτι ἐλογίσθη αὐτῷ,
ἀλλὰ καὶ δι' ἡμᾶς, οἷς μέλλει λογίζεσθαι,
τοῖς πιστεύουσιν ἐπὶ τὸν ἐγείραντα Ἰησοῦν τὸν κύριον ἡμῶν ἐκ νεκρῶν,

ὃς παρεδόθη διὰ τὰ παραπτώματα ἡμῶν
καὶ ἠγέρθη διὰ τὴν δικαίωσιν ἡμῶν.

VERSE 13

Οὐ γὰρ διὰ νόμου ἡ ἐπαγγελία τῷ Ἀβραὰμ ἢ τῷ σπέρματι αὐτοῦ

Paul introduces (*γάρ*) the third "not" in his argument with a strong antithetical thesis (*οὐ διὰ νόμου . . . ἀλλὰ διὰ δικαιοσύνης πίστεως*) that highlights "promise" as one of the key words in the paragraph (5x). Ἐπαγγελία, -ας, ἡ involves a declaration to do something with the implication of an obligation to carry out what is stated (BDAG 355d). Διά + genitive indicates means; as the object of the preposition *νόμου* is definite and refers to the Mosaic law (Cranfield 238). The article marks *ἐπαγγελία* as well known; Longenecker concludes that it refers to the particular promise of Genesis 15:4–5 (509); the dative article with Ἀβραάμ (indecl.) marks it as the indirect object. The conjunction *ἤ* is disjunctive (R 1188); Longenecker notes that it is equivalent to *καί* (510); the article with *σπέρματι* is expected with the possessive pronoun. In this context *σπέρμα, -τος, τό* denotes descendant, child, or posterity (BDAG 937b).

τὸ κληρονόμον αὐτὸν εἶναι κόσμου

The infinitival phrase stands in apposition to and explains *ἐπαγγελία* (R 1059). With the infinitive (*εἶναι*), the pronoun (*αὐτόν*) is the object, and the noun (*κληρονόμον*) is the predicate accusative (Wallace 196). Κληρονόμος, -ου, ὁ denotes a beneficiary who receives a possession (BDAG 548b). The article with *κληρονόμον* marks it as well known; the anarthrous *κόσμου* is monadic.

ἀλλὰ διὰ δικαιοσύνης πίστεως

Ἀλλά ("but") completes the contrast; *διά* + genitive again indicates means. Both *δικαιοσύνης* and *πίστεως* are qualitative; *πίστεως* is a subjective genitive (T 211).

VERSE 14

εἰ γὰρ οἱ ἐκ νόμου κληρονόμοι

Paul's reason (*γάρ*) that the promise must be through faith rather than through law begins with an elliptical first class condition (R 1023) that heightens the vividness of his argument (Cranfield 240). The article with *ἐκ νόμου* allows the prepositional phrase to function as a noun that describes individuals who have a common origin and hold to a common persuasion (T 15; R 599); Longenecker suggests "those people who base their lives on the Mosaic law" (512). The verb *εἰσιν* is understood, so that *κληρονόμοι* functions as the predicate nominative.

κεκένωται ἡ πίστις καὶ κατήργηται ἡ ἐπαγγελία

Placing *κεκένωται* (3 sg. pf. pass. indic. from *κενόω*, "cause to be without result") and *κατήργηται* (3 sg. pf. pass. indic. from *καταργέω*, "render ineffective") ahead of their subjects adds emphasis. Both verbs are gnomic perfects that set out timeless truths; the passive voice of both keeps the focus on the subjects with an implicit generic agent.

The articles with πίστις and ἐπαγγελία are anaphoric with abstract nouns; Jewett suggests that the article with the first noun functions as a possessive pronoun that refers to Abraham's faith (326); Longenecker agrees and concludes that the article with the second noun refers to God's promise (512).

VERSE 15

ὁ γὰρ νόμος ὀργὴν κατεργάζεται·

The explanation (γάρ) for why inheritance through the law would nullify both faith and promise lies in the law's effect: it produces wrath. Ὁ νόμος refers to the Torah (Dunn 215; cf. Longenecker 512); ὀργήν is qualitative; κατεργάζεται is a gnomic present (Schreiner 229 n. 5). See 1:18 for ὀργή; κατεργάζομαι carries the nuance of "produce/bring about" and emphasizes the result of the action (Moo 276 n. 32).

οὗ δὲ οὐκ ἔστιν νόμος οὐδὲ παράβασις

The presence of γάρ at the beginning of verses 13, 14, and 15 might have led either to its insertion after οὗ or to its replacement with δέ. The manuscript support (א*, A, B, C) for the connective δέ ("and"), however, is solid. Οὗ ("where") is a local conjunction (T 344) and introduces a parenthetical explanation of why the law produces wrath: it points out acts that deviate from God's established norm and demand his punishment (Moo 276). Παράβασις, -εως, ἡ denotes a violation of a written and specified commandment (Schreiner 230; cf. *TDNT* 5.739–40). Longenecker offers this alternate understanding of Paul's statement: "Because the Gentiles were not given the Mosaic law, their status of righteousness before God . . . must depend solely on God's grace, God's promise, and their response of faith" (513).

VERSE 16

διὰ τοῦτο ἐκ πίστεως, ἵνα κατὰ χάριν

Having rejected the role of the law (vv. 13–15), Paul moves on to affirm the role of faith (vv. 16–21). Διὰ τοῦτο ("for this reason") most likely points forward rather than backward (Cranfield 241; cf. 2 Cor 13:10; Phlm 15; 1 Tim 1:16). Ἡ ἐπαγγελία ἐστιν may be understood from verse 13 (Longenecker 514); ἐκ + genitive denotes the reason on which something is based (BDAG 296d; πίστεως is definite as the object of the preposition; ἵνα ("in order that") indicates purpose, and γένηται may be supplied as the verb. Κατά + accusative indicates standard; χάριν is definite as the object of the preposition.

εἰς τὸ εἶναι βεβαίαν τὴν ἐπαγγελίαν παντὶ τῷ σπέρματι

Εἰς τὸ εἶναι sets out the purpose that the promise is based on faith (T 143): that the promise might be valid (βεβαίαν; cf. BDAG 172d) to Abraham's descendants. The article marks ἐπαγγελίαν as the subject of the infinitive; βεβαίαν is the predicate accusative.

Jewett suggests translating the adjective as "guaranteed" (330; cf. Longenecker 514). The placement of παντί is emphatic; the article is regularly present with πᾶς; σπέρματι has collective force (Moo 278 n. 46). KJV translates the phrase "to all the seed," NASB "to all the descendants," and ESV "to all his offspring."

οὐ τῷ ἐκ τοῦ νόμου μόνον ἀλλὰ καὶ τῷ ἐκ πίστεως Ἀβραάμ

Οὐ . . . μόνον ("not only") begins a strong contrast followed by ἀλλὰ καί ("but also"), with the entire combination further describing παντὶ τῷ σπέρματι. Both definite articles allow their respective prepositional phrases to function as nouns. Ἐκ + genitive designates source in both phrases; Ἀβραάμ (indecl.) is a subjective genitive (Wallace 116). Deciding on the identity of the two groups mentioned is a challenge. Jewett sees the first group as ethnic Jews and the second group as believing Jews (331; cf. Dunn 216). This interpretation, however, could imply that it is possible for ethnic Jews to have a claim on the inheritance based on their ability to keep the law, which would run counter to Paul's overall argument. Cranfield and most other commentators see the first group as Jewish Christians and the second group as Gentile Christians (242).

ὅς ἐστιν πατὴρ πάντων ἡμῶν

A relative clause further describes Ἀβραάμ and repeats verses 11b–12. Πατήρ is the predicate nominative and, therefore, definite even though it is anarthrous. Πάντων adds emphasis; ἡμῶν is a possessive genitive.

VERSE 17

καθὼς γέγραπται ὅτι Πατέρα πολλῶν ἐθνῶν τέθεικά σε

Καθὼς γέγραπται ("just as it has been written") introduces an OT quotation (Gen 17:5, LXX) as it has elsewhere (cf. 1:17; 2:24; 3:4, 10), and ὅτι marks it as direct discourse (R 1028). In this context, τέθεικά (1 sg. pf. act. indic. from τίθημι, "make") is a futuristic perfect and denotes a change in condition (BDAG 1004b). The verb takes a double accusative with σε ("you") as the object and πατέρα ("father") as the complement (T 246). Πολλῶν ἐθνῶν is a genitive of relationship (descendants). The quotation is offered as proof of the statement in the previous relative clause that Abraham is the father of all who believe.

κατέναντι οὗ ἐπίστευσεν θεοῦ

The exact relationship of this phrase to the preceding quotation and the immediate context is difficult to determine. Moo lists five possible solutions (279–80). The most common is to understand attraction of the relative pronoun, to reconstruct the wording as κατέναντι τοῦ θεοῦ ᾧ ἐπίστευσεν (BDF §294.2), and to connect the phrase back to the statement about Abraham in verse 16b. NJB reflects this solution: "Abraham is our father in the eyes of God, in whom he put his faith." Campbell offers a minority solution that is somewhat more straightforward when he suggests that the antecedent of οὗ is the OT quotation (Jewett 333). The translation would read "In the face of which [promise] he believed God."

τοῦ ζῳοποιοῦντος τοὺς νεκροὺς καὶ καλοῦντος τὰ μὴ ὄντα ὡς ὄντα

The God in whose promise Abraham believed is described by two participles (gen. sg. masc. of pres. act. ptc.) introduced by a single article and connected by *καί* (Granville Sharp). The present tense of both participles is iterative and highlights God's continuing activity. *Ζῳοποιέω* denotes the act of giving life to someone or something, in this instance "the dead." *Καλέω* denotes the act of summoning or inviting; Dunn suggests it is best understood as indicating an effectual summons (218). The summons is issued to *τὰ μὴ ὄντα* (NEB, "things that are not yet in existence") and the consequence is that they become *ὡς ὄντα* (NEB, "as if they already were"). Moo (282) and Schreiner (237) reject the suggestion that Paul is alluding to creation; Cranfield (244) and Dunn (218) affirm it. Jewett views the language of both participles as affirming God's power to do the impossible (334).

VERSE 18

ὃς παρ' ἐλπίδα ἐπ' ἐλπίδι ἐπίστευσεν

The relative pronoun *ὅς* resumes the description of Abraham (verse 16b) and continues to develop his act of faith: he believed (constative aor.) *παρ' ἐλπίδα ἐπ' ἐλπίδι*. The combination is translated in various ways; the most common is "against hope in hope" (KJV, RSV, NASB, NIV, ESV). Dunn notes that although the content is not explicit, the combination makes the point and is pleasing to the ear (219). *Ἐλπίς, -ίδος, ἡ* describes the act of looking forward to something with reason for confidence in its fulfillment (BDAG 319d).

εἰς τὸ γενέσθαι αὐτὸν πατέρα πολλῶν ἐθνῶν

The result (*εἰς τό* + inf.) of Abraham's belief (Cranfield 246; Moo 283 n. 70) was that he (*αὐτόν*) became (*γενέσθαι*, aor. mid. inf. of dep. *γίνομαι*) the father of many nations as God had promised.

κατὰ τὸ εἰρημένον· Οὕτως ἔσται τὸ σπέρμα σου

Paul returns to God's original promise (Gen 15:5, LXX) to reinforce the long-term nature of Abraham's faith. *Κατά* + accusative indicates the standard to which Abraham's status corresponds: that which "has been spoken" in Scripture. The article with *εἰρημένον* (acc. sg. neut. of pf. pass. ptc. of *λέγω*) marks it as the substantival object of the preposition; the intensive perfect emphasizes the continuing validity of what has been spoken; the passive voice is a divine passive. *Οὕτως* ("so") is an adverb used as a predicate (T 226); *ἔσται* (3 sg. fut. mid. indic. of *εἰμί*) is a predictive future. Moo concludes that the "many nations" of which Abraham became the father (Gen 17:5) are, in fact, the spiritual "seed" (believing Jews and Gentiles) of Genesis 15:5 (283).

VERSE 19

καὶ μὴ ἀσθενήσας τῇ πίστει

The conjunction καί ("and") adds another element to the relative clause begun in verse 18. Μή is the expected negative with a participle; ἀσθενήσας (nom. sg. masc. of aor. act. ptc. of ἀσθενέω, "be weak") is adverbial of cause. Dunn notes that ἀσθενέω points to religious or moral weakness (220; cf. 14:1–2; 1 Cor 8:11–12; 2 Cor 11:29). The article accompanies the abstract noun πίστει, which is a dative of reference (cf. BDF §197).

κατενόησεν τὸ ἑαυτοῦ σῶμα [ἤδη] νενεκρωμένον

Western and Byzantine manuscripts (D, G. K, P, Ψ) include οὐ before κατενόησεν, while Alexandrian manuscripts (ℵ, A, B, C) omit it. Both readings make good sense, but the context suggests that Paul wants to highlight Abraham's active consideration of the obstacles (Metzger 451; cf. Schreiner 239–40). A few manuscripts omit ἤδη, which would be the shorter reading, and Cranfield views it as secondary (248). Jewett, however, notes the broader manuscript support for its inclusion (322).

Κατανοέω carries the idea of looking at something in a reflective manner (BDAG 522d). Abraham "considered" (constative aor.) two factors, first, τὸ ἑαυτοῦ σῶμα ("his own body"), which he evaluated as already (ἤδη) "worn out" (BDAG 668c). The reflexive pronoun ἑαυτοῦ (gen. sg. masc.) adds emphasis and distinguishes Abraham's condition from the subsequent comment about Sarah. The intensive perfect of νενεκρωμένον (acc. sg. neut. of pf. pass. ptc. of νεκρόω, "put to death") highlights the established state of deadness (Moo 283 n. 74).

ἑκατονταετής που ὑπάρχων

A parenthetical comment adds detail to Abraham's hopeless state: his body was "about one hundred years old" (ἑκατονταετής που). The enclitic adverb πού is a marker of numerical approximation ("about, approximately") that aligns with the statement in Genesis 17:1 that Abraham was ninety-nine. The participle ὑπάρχων (nom. sing. masc. of pres. act. ptc. of ὑπάρχω, "be") is adverbial of cause and gives the reason Abraham reached the conclusion he did about his own body.

καὶ τὴν νέκρωσιν τῆς μήτρας Σάρρας

The second consideration (καί) was Sarah's condition. Νέκρωσις, -εως, ἡ ("deadness") denotes the cessation of activity (BDAG 668d). The genitive τῆς μήτρας (gen. sg. fem. of μήτρα, -ας, ἡ, "womb") is best understood as an attributed genitive (cf. Wallace 89–90), which results in the translation "Sarah's dead womb." Both Abraham's worn-out body and Sarah's dead womb stood in the way of God's promise; yet, Abraham believed that promise.

VERSE 20

εἰς δὲ τὴν ἐπαγγελίαν τοῦ θεοῦ

The weak connective δέ ("and") allows the focus to fall on God's promise (τὴν ἐπαγγελίαν τοῦ θεοῦ), which is brought forward for emphasis. Εἰς + accusative can denote reference (Harris 91; cf. Cranfield 248; Moo 284 n. 78). The combination of definite article with ἐπαγγελίαν plus the adjunct τοῦ θεοῦ makes the entire phrase monadic (cf. Wallace 224); the genitive is subjective.

οὐ διεκρίθη τῇ ἀπιστίᾳ

The negative οὐ establishes a strong contrast with ἀλλά in the next clause. Διεκρίθη (3 sg. aor. pass. indic. of διακρίνω, "doubt") is a deponent passive that carries an active sense (R 334). The dative of τῇ ἀπιστίᾳ denotes cause (R 532; T 242; BDF §196); see 3:3 for ἀπιστία.

ἀλλ' ἐνεδυναμώθη τῇ πίστει

The second half of the contrast (ἀλλ') sets out the positive side of Abraham's experience. 'Ενεδυναμώθη (3 sg. aor. pass. indic. of ἐνδυναμόω, "grow strong") is an antonym for ἀσθενέω in verse 19 (Schreiner 238). The passive form can be translated either actively as "he grew strong" (RSV, NASB, ESV) or passively as "he was strengthened" (NIV, NKJV); Longenecker prefers the latter, with God as the understood agent (521).* Robertson (532) and Turner (242) view τῇ πίστει as a dative of cause ("because of his faith"), while Moo (285 n. 85) views it as respect ("with respect to his faith"). Longenecker (521) and EVV (e.g., NET, CSB), however, understand it as locative ("in his faith").*

δοὺς δόξαν τῷ θεῷ

The participle δούς (nom. sg. masc. of aor. act. ptc. of δίδωμι) is adverbial of manner, highlighting Abraham's attitude; Robertson notes that the aorist tense indicates simultaneous action (861; cf. Moo 286 n. 86). The act of Abraham giving glory to God contrasts sharply with the response of humankind in general (1:21). Cranfield writes, "A man gives glory to God when he acknowledges God's truthfulness and goodness and submits to his authority" (249).

VERSE 21

καὶ πληροφορηθεὶς ὅτι ὃ ἐπήγγελται δυνατός ἐστιν καὶ ποιῆσαι

Καί adds a second adverbial participle of manner (nom. sg. masc. of aor. pass. ptc.) that describes Abraham's attitude. Πληροφορέω conveys the idea of being fully persuaded, not limited at all by doubt (BDAG 827d; cf. *TDNT* 6.309–10). The conjunction ὅτι is declarative (R 1035) and introduces a relative clause that might well allude to Gen 18:14. The relative pronoun includes an embedded demonstrative ("[that one] who"); ἐπήγγελται (3 sg. pf. mid. indic. of dep. ἐπαγγέλλομαι) is an intensive perfect. See verse 13 for ἐπαγγελλία. Moving the predicate adjective (δυνατός) forward gives it emphasis; καί is adjunctive ("also"); ποιῆσαι (aor. act. inf. of ποιέω) completes the thought of δυνατός ("is able also to do [it]").

VERSE 22

διὸ [καὶ] ἐλογίσθη αὐτῷ εἰς δικαιοσύνην

The manuscript evidence on whether to include (ℵ, A, C, D[1])* or omit (B, D*) καί is balanced, and UBS[5] gives it a {C} rating. If it is included, is it emphatic ("indeed"), and Dunn writes that its presence after διό ("therefore") makes the inference "self-evident" (221; cf. Rom 15:22; 2 Cor 1:20; 5:9). The quotation of Genesis 15:6 forms an inclusion with verse 3 and brackets the body of Paul's argument (4:3–22).

VERSE 23

Οὐκ ἐγράφη δὲ δι' αὐτὸν μόνον ὅτι ἐλογίσθη αὐτῷ

As Paul makes the transition (δέ) to his concluding paragraph that applies the lessons from Abraham's experience, he begins with his third οὐκ μόνον . . . ἀλλὰ καί contrast (cf. 4:12, 16). 'Εγράφη (3 sg. aor. pass. indic. from γράφω) is a variation of καθὼς γέγραπται in verse 17. Διά + accusative denotes the reason ("for the sake of") the statement that follows was included in the Genesis account. Abraham is the antecedent of both αὐτόν and αὐτῷ; ὅτι introduces indirect discourse. The aorist indicative of ἐλογίσθη (3 sg. aor. pass. indic. of dep. λογίζομαι) highlights the past action of God crediting righteousness to Abraham's account.

VERSE 24

ἀλλὰ καὶ δι' ἡμᾶς, οἷς μέλλει λογίζεσθαι

The parallelism of the second half of the contrast (ἀλλὰ καί) moves the lesson from the historical (δι' αὐτόν) to the personal (δι' ἡμᾶς) and from the past (ἐλογίσθη) to the present (μέλλει λογίζεσθαι). Διά + accusative again makes it clear that the lesson was "for our sake"; the relative pronoun οἷς (dat. pl. masc.) further explains ἡμᾶς and serves as the indirect object of the clause. Μέλλει (3 sg. pres. act. indic. of μέλλω, "be about") is a "helper" verb that requires an infinitive to complete its meaning; the complementary infinitive λογίζεσθαι (pres. pass. infin.) is a true passive (T 58). Although μέλλω has a future nuance inherent in its lexical meaning ("to take place at a future point in time," BDAG 628b), Paul is referring to the present justification of believers rather than to the future act of final judgment (Cranfield 250; Schreiner 242). Jewett accurately notes that the action Paul describes was future from the standpoint of the statement recorded (ἐγράφη) about Abraham (341).

τοῖς πιστεύουσιν ἐπὶ τὸν ἐγείραντα Ἰησοῦν τὸν κύριον ἡμῶν ἐκ νεκρῶν

The substantival participle τοῖς πιστεύουσιν (dat. pl. masc. of pres. act. ptc) stands in apposition to the preceding relative pronoun (οἷς) and expands the description of the "us" to whom the lesson applies. The progressive present tense of the participle emphasizes continuing belief (Wallace 621 n. 22). That belief is directed toward (ἐπί + acc.; cf. Harris 235) "the one who raised Jesus our Lord." The article with ἐγείραντα (acc. sg. masc. of aor. act. ptc. of ἐγείρω, "raise") allows the participle to function substantivally as the object of the preposition; the verb carries the nuance of "cause to return to life" (BDAG 271d). Ἰησοῦν (acc. sg. masc.) is the object of ἐγείραντα and is explained by placing τὸν κύριον ἡμῶν in apposition to it. Ἐκ + genitive denotes separation, and the anarthrous substantival adjective νεκρῶν is definite as the object of the preposition ("from among the dead ones").

VERSE 25

Paul concludes both his discussion of Abraham's experience (4:1–25) and his exposition of the revelation of God's righteousness (1:18–4:25) with a statement on Jesus's death and resurrection that is carefully constructed using synonymous parallelism. Cranfield believes the statement is a quotation of a traditional formula (251). Longenecker provides a concise defense of the verse as an early Christian confessional statement (535). Jewett notes that the terminology is traditional but also affirms that the style is "distinctively Pauline" (342). See H.-J. van der Minde, *Schrift und Tradition bei Paulus*, 90–99 for a survey of scholarship.

ὃς παρεδόθη διὰ τὰ παραπτώματα ἡμῶν

The antecedent of the relative pronoun (ὅς) is Ἰησοῦν τὸν κύριον ἡμῶν. Παρεδόθη (3 sg. aor. pass. indic. from παραδίδωμι, "hand over to custody") is a constative aorist and a divine passive (Moo 288). See 1:24 on παραδίδωμι. Διά + accusative in this line and the next has generated considerable discussion. Harris summarizes three interpretations and decides that causal is the best choice in both lines (81–82; cf. Schreiner 252). Παράπτωμα, -τος, τό denotes the violation of moral standards, usually against God (BDAG 770d). The line might be paraphrased as "Who was handed over because we sinned against God."

καὶ ἠγέρθη διὰ τὴν δικαίωσιν ἡμῶν

The connective καί ("and") introduces the second line of the synonymous parallelism. Ἠγέρθη (3 sg. aor. pass. indic. of ἐγείρω, "raise") is also a constative aorist and a divine passive. Δικαίωσις, -εως, ἡ refers to the act of executing righteous judgment and can be translated as "justification," "acquittal," or "vindication" (Jewett 343; cf. BDAG 250b; Moo 288 n. 8). If διά + accusative is also causal in this line, the paraphrase might be "and was raised because God declared us righteous."

FOR FURTHER STUDY

37. Promise (4:13)

Bailey, K. E. "St Paul's Understanding of the Territorial Promise of God to Abraham: Romans 4:13 in Its Historical and Theological Context." *Theological Review* 15 (1994): 59–69.

Barclay, W. B. "The Law and the Promise: God's Covenant with Abraham in Pauline Perspective." Pages 138–52 in *Perspectives on our Father Abraham*. Edited by S. A. Hunt. Grand Rapids: Eerdmans, 2010.

Bruce, F. F. "Promise and Fulfillment in Paul's Presentation of Jesus." Pages 36–50 in *Promise and Fulfillment; Essays Presented to S H Hooke in Celebration of his 90th Birthday*. Edinburgh: T & T Clark, 1963.

Dever, M. *The Message of the New Testament: Promises Kept*. Wheaton, IL: Crossway, 2005.

Forman, M. *The Politics of Inheritance in Romans*. Cambridge: Cambridge University Press, 2011.

________. "The Politics of Promise: Echoes of Isaiah 54 in Romans 4.19–21." *JSNT* 31 (2009): 301–24.

Gray, R. W. "A Comparison between the Old Covenant and the New Covenant." *WTJ* 4 (1941): 1–30.

Harrison, E. F. *EDBT* 638–39.

Hoffmann, E. *NIDNTT* 3.68–74.

Juncker, G. H. "'Children of Promise': Spiritual Paternity and Patriarch Typology in Galatians and Romans." *BBR* 17 (2007): 131–60.

Klein, R. W. "Promise and Fulfillment." Pages 47–63 in *Contesting Texts*. Edited by M. D. Knowles, E. Menn, J Powlikoski, and T. J. Sandoval. Minneapolis: Fortress, 2007.

Kruger, M. A. "Law and Promise in Galatians." *Neot* 26 (1992): 311–27.

Kümmel, W. G. *Promise and Fulfillment: The Eschatological Message of Jesus*. Translated by D. M. Barton. London: SCM, 1956.

Martin, O. R. *Bound for the Promised Land: The Land Promise in God's Redemptive Plan*. Downers Grove, IL: InterVarsity, 2015.

Pester, J. "The Gospel of the Promised Seed in Romans: Transformation for Designation unto Inheritance." *Affirmation & Critique* 6 (2001): 35–50.

Schniewind, J., and G. Friedrich. *TDNT* 2.576–86.

Smith, W. M. *EDT* 885–86.

Visscher, G. H. *Romans 4 and the New Perspective on Paul: Faith Embraces the Promise*. New York: Peter Lang, 2009.

Williams, S. K. "Promise in Galatians: A Reading of Paul's Reading of Scripture." *JBL* 107 (1988): 709–20.

Williamson, P. R. "Historical Roots of the Gospel: The Promise behind the Promise." *RTR* 70 (2011): 73–106.

Wrightman, Paul. *Paul's Later Letters: From Promise to Fulfillment*. New York: Alba House, 1984.

38. Seed (4:13)

Alexander, T. D. "Further Observations on the Term 'Seed' in Genesis." *TynBul* 48 (1997): 363–67.

Beach, J. M. "Calvin and the Dual Aspect of Covenant Membership: Galatians 3:15–22—The Meaning of 'The Seed is Christ'—and Other Key Texts." *Mid-America Journal of Theology* 20 (2009): 49–73.

Chance, J. B. "The Seed of Abraham and the People of God: A Study of Two Pauls." *SBL Seminar Papers* 32 (1993): 384–411.

Chung, S.-W. "Paul's Portraits of Jesus in Romans: 'The Seed of David.'" *Yonsei Journal of Theology* 5 (2000): 263–80.

Demarest, B. A. *NIDNTT* 3.521–24.

DeRouchie, J. S., and J. C. Meyer. "Christ or Family as the 'Seed' of Promise? An Evaluation of N. T. Wright on Galatians 3:16." *Southern Baptist Journal of Theology* 14 (2010): 36–48.

Kagarise, R. J. "The 'Seed' in Galatians 3:16—A Window to Paul's Thinking." *Evangelical Journal* 18 (2000): 67–73.

Pester, J. "The Gospel of the Promised Seed in Romans: Transformation for Designation unto Inheritance." *Affirmation & Critique* 6 (2001): 35–50.

________. "The Gospel of the Promised Seed: Deification according to the Organic Pattern in Romans 8 and Philippians 2." *Affirmation & Critique* 7 (2002): 55–69.

Pyne, R. A. "The 'Seed,' the Spirit, and the Blessing of Abraham." *BSac* 152 (1995): 211–22.

Whitsett, C. G. "Son of God, Seed of David: Paul's Messianic Exegesis in Romans 1:3–4." *JBL* 119 (2000): 661–81.

39. Heir, Inheritance (4:13)

Ahern, B. "The Indwelling Spirit, Pledge of Our Inheritance (Eph. 1:14)." *CBQ* 9 (1947): 179–89.

Bevere, A. R. *Sharing in the Inheritance: Identity and the Moral Life in Christians.* Sheffield: Sheffield Academic Press, 2003.

Boers, H. "We Who are by Inheritance Jews, not from the Gentiles, Sinners." *JBL* 111 (1992): 273–81.

Brown, W. E. *EDBT* 374–75.

Craston, R. C. *EDT* 561.

Denton, D. R. "Inheritance in Paul and Ephesians." *EvQ* 54 (1982): 157–62.

Eichler, J. *NIDNTT* 2.295–303.

Forman, M. *The Politics of Inheritance in Romans.* Cambridge: Cambridge University Press, 2011.

Herrmann, J., and W. Foerster. *TDNT* 3.781–85.

Hammer, P. J. *ABD* 3.415–17.

________. "A Comparison of κληρονομία in Paul and Ephesians." *JBL* 79 (1960): 267–72.

Hester, J. D. *Paul's Concept of Inheritance. A Contribution to the Understanding of Heilsgeschichte.* Edinburgh: Oliver & Boyd, 1968.

Kerr, A. J. "Ἀρραβών." *JTS* 39 (1988): 92–97.

López, R. "A Study of Pauline Passages on Inheriting the Kingdom." *BSac* 168 (2011): 443–59.

Naizer, E. R. "The 'Heir' through Faith and the 'Slave' under the Law: Galatians 4:1–7." *Bangalore Theological Forum* 41 (2009): 198–209.

Pester, J. "The Gospel of the Promised Seed in Romans: Transformation for Designation unto Inheritance." *Affirmation & Critique* 6 (2001): 35–50.

Sherwin-White, A. N. *Roman Society and Roman Law in the New Testament*. Oxford: Clarendon, 1963.
Silva, M. *NIDNTTE* 1.404–5.
________. *NIDNTTE* 2.693–701.
Wright, N. T. "New Exodus, New Inheritance: The Narrative Substructure of Romans 3–8." Pages 26–38 in *Romans and the People of God: Essays in Honor of Gordon D. Fee on the Occasion of His 65th Birthday*. Edited by S. K. Soderlund and N. T. Wright. Grand Rapids: Eerdmans, 1999.
________. "The New Inheritance According to Paul: The Letter to the Romans Re-enacts for all Peoples the Israelite Exodus from Egypt to the Promised Land—from Slavery to Freedom." *BR* 14 (1998): 16–47.

HOMILETICAL SUGGESTIONS

Lessons from Abraham's Experience, Part 2 (4:13–25)

1. The promise was not given to Abraham through the law (4:13–15)
   a. Explanation #1: The law would nullify the promise (γάρ, 4:14)
   b. Explanation #2: The law provokes wrath and reveals sin (γάρ, 4:15)
2. The promise was given to Abraham on the basis of faith (4:16–22)
   a. Purpose: To guarantee the promise to his spiritual descendants (4:16b)
   b. Abraham's example (4:16c–21)
      1) OT Promise: Genesis 17:5 (καθὼς γέγραπται, 4:17a)
      2) Response #1: He believed God who does the impossible (4:17b–18)
      3) Response #2: He considered the obstacles (4:19)
      4) Response #3: He became strong in faith (4:20–21)
   c. Conclusion: Faith was reckoned for righteousness (διὸ, 4:22)
3. The promise was given for our sakes (4:23–25)
   a. Not written for Abraham alone (4:23)
   b. Written also for us (4:24–25)

Abraham's Example of Faith (4:16–22)

1. He believed in God's power (4:16–17)
2. He believed in God's providence (4:18–19)
3. He believed in God's promise (4:20–22)

B. THE PROVISION OF GOD'S RIGHTEOUSNESS (5:1–8:39)

1. God's Righteousness Is Imputed in Christ (5:1–21)

a. Bringing Peace, Hope, and Reconciliation (5:1–11)

STRUCTURE

Paul begins the second section of the letter body with a paragraph consisting of three parts (5:1–5; 5:6–8; 5:9–11). The first sentence summarizes and builds upon 1:18–4:25, focuses on the present, and is unified by the threefold repetition of ἐλπίς. The second gives the reason for 5:1–5, focuses on the past, and is unified by the fourfold repetition of ἀποθνῄσκω + ὑπέρ. The third draws the conclusion from 5:6–8, focuses on the future, and is unified by the threefold repetition of καταλλάσσω/καταλλαγή. The paragraph is bracketed by the participle δικαιωθέντες, a form of καυχάομαί, and the phrase διὰ τοῦ κυρίου ἡμῶν Ἰησοῦ Χριστοῦ. The latter phrase also occurs at the end of each major section in chapters 5–8 (cf. 5:21; 6:23; 7:25; 8:39).

Δικαιωθέντες οὖν ἐκ πίστεως εἰρήνην ἔχομεν πρὸς τὸν θεὸν διὰ τοῦ κυρίου ἡμῶν Ἰησοῦ Χριστοῦ

δι' οὗ καὶ τὴν προσαγωγὴν ἐσχήκαμεν [τῇ πίστει] εἰς τὴν χάριν ταύτην

ἐν ᾗ ἑστήκαμεν καὶ καυχώμεθα ἐπ' ἐλπίδι τῆς δόξης τοῦ θεοῦ.

οὐ μόνον δέ, ἀλλὰ καὶ καυχώμεθα ἐν ταῖς θλίψεσιν,
εἰδότες ὅτι ἡ θλῖψις ὑπομονὴν κατεργάζεται,
ἡ δὲ ὑπομονὴ δοκιμήν,
ἡ δὲ δοκιμὴ ἐλπίδα.
ἡ δὲ ἐλπὶς οὐ καταισχύνει,
ὅτι ἡ ἀγάπη τοῦ θεοῦ ἐκκέχυται ἐν ταῖς καρδίαις ἡμῶν διὰ πνεύματος ἁγίου τοῦ δοθέντος ἡμῖν.

ἔτι γὰρ Χριστὸς ὄντων ἡμῶν ἀσθενῶν ἔτι κατὰ καιρὸν ὑπὲρ ἀσεβῶν ἀπέθανεν.
μόλις γὰρ ὑπὲρ δικαίου τις ἀποθανεῖται·
ὑπὲρ γὰρ τοῦ ἀγαθοῦ τάχα τις καὶ τολμᾷ ἀποθανεῖν·
συνίστησιν δὲ τὴν ἑαυτοῦ ἀγάπην εἰς ἡμᾶς ὁ θεὸς, ὅτι ἔτι ἁμαρτωλῶν ὄντων ἡμῶν Χριστὸς ὑπὲρ ἡμῶν ἀπέθανεν.

πολλῷ οὖν μᾶλλον δικαιωθέντες νῦν ἐν τῷ αἵματι αὐτοῦ σωθησόμεθα δι' αὐτοῦ ἀπὸ τῆς ὀργῆς.
εἰ γὰρ ἐχθροὶ ὄντες κατηλλάγημεν τῷ θεῷ διὰ τοῦ θανάτου τοῦ υἱοῦ αὐτοῦ,
πολλῷ μᾶλλον καταλλαγέντες σωθησόμεθα ἐν τῇ ζωῇ αὐτοῦ·
οὐ μόνον δέ, ἀλλὰ καὶ καυχώμενοι ἐν τῷ θεῷ διὰ τοῦ κυρίου ἡμῶν Ἰησοῦ Χριστοῦ,

δι' οὗ νῦν τὴν καταλλαγὴν ἐλάβομεν.

VERSE 1

Δικαιωθέντες οὖν ἐκ πίστεως

Paul uses the inferential conjunction οὖν ("therefore") to gather up the preceding discussion and connect it to the next step in his exposition. The adverbial participle of cause δικαιωθέντες (nom. pl. masc. of aor. pass. ptc. of δικαιόω, "declare righteous") followed by ἐκ πίστεως (means) summarizes 3:21–4:25 (cf. 3:26, 30; 4:16). The consummative aorist of the participle highlights the completion of action (R 859) and marks it as happening in the past (Dunn 246). God is the ultimate agent of the action (Jewett 348). See 2:13 for δικαιόω.

εἰρήνην ἔχομεν πρὸς τὸν θεὸν

The variant readings ἔχομεν and ἔχωμεν reflect a common interchange between ο and ω (T 74; cf. 14:19; 1 Cor 15:49). Although the subjunctive reading (ἔχωμεν) has stronger manuscript support (א*, A, B*, 33), the subjunctive tends to occur more often in the "practical" sections of Paul's letters (cf. 15:4). The presence of the indicative ἐσχήκαμεν in 5:2 and the fact that elsewhere in Paul's letters peace is something God gives (2 Cor 13:11; Phil 4:7, 9; 1 Thess 3:16) suggest that the indicative reading (ἔχομεν) is to be preferred. Moo has an extended discussion in which he decides for the indicative (295 n. 17); Jewett (344 n. a.) and Longenecker (554–55) opt for the subjunctive. For a detailed, two-way interchange see V. D. Verbrugge, "The Grammatical Internal Evidence for ῎EXOMEN in Romans 5:1," *JETS* 54 (2011): 559–72; S. E. Porter, "Not Only That (οὐ μόνον), But It Has Been Said Before: A Response to Verlyn Verbrugge, or Why Reading Previous Scholarship Can Avoid Scholarly Misunderstandings," *JETS* 56 (2013): 577–83; V. B. Verbrugge, "Response to Stanley Porter," *JETS* 56 (2013): 585–87.

The placement of εἰρήνην is emphatic; see 1:7 on the meaning (cf. Longenecker 556 n. 40). Cranfield notes that the noun refers to an objective state rather than to a subjective emotion (258). Jewett suggests that Paul is addressing differences within the congregations in Rome (348; cf. 14:19). The present tense of ἔχομεν is progressive and highlights the continuing state of peace that now exists (R 823, 850). Πρός + accusative denotes relationship (Harris 190) and highlights the reciprocal fellowship that now exists between God and the one who is declared righteous by faith (cf. Moo 299 n. 29).

διὰ τοῦ κυρίου ἡμῶν Ἰησοῦ Χριστοῦ

Διά + genitive identifies the agent through whom peace is achieved (R 583; cf. Jewett 349). The article "invariably" occurs when a possessive pronoun is attached to a noun (cf. Wallace 239); Ἰησοῦ Χριστοῦ is a genitive of simple apposition. The full phrase (and a variation using ἐν + dat.) also occurs in 5:11, 5:21, 6:23, 7:25, and 8:39. It gives unity to the section as a whole, marks the ends of divisions within the section, brackets 5:1–11, and serves as ring-composition framing 5:1–8:39 (Harvey 125).

VERSE 2

δι᾽ οὗ καὶ τὴν προσαγωγὴν ἐσχήκαμεν [τῇ πίστει]

A relative clause continues the description of Jesus Christ by adding (adjunctive καί) a second way in which he functions as an agent (δι᾽ οὗ): providing access into grace. Προσαγωή, -ῆς, ἡ denotes a way of approach (BDAG 876a); Cranfield describes it as the privilege of being introduced into the presence of someone of high station (259; cf. Harris 194–95). Ἐσχήκαμεν (1 pl. pf. act. indic. of ἔχω, "have") is an intensive perfect that includes initial entrance and highlights continuing availability (Dunn 248; cf. BDF §343.2; Wallace 576).

Of the three variants related to τῇ πίστει, Moo concludes that it is "suspect as a later addition" and should be omitted (296 n. 18). Metzger explains the variant with ἐν as a result of dittography (452), although the preposition is more likely a clarifying addition. The UBS[5] decision to enclose τῇ πίστει in brackets with a {C} rating reflects the tension between external and internal considerations. Schreiner (258) and Jewett (344 n. b) both argue that manuscript support for including τῇ πίστει is stronger than for omitting it, and their conclusion seems most likely. The dative indicates means; the article is anaphoric to ἐκ πίστεως in verse 1. Dunn notes that this verse is the last occurrence of πίστις until 9:30 (248).

εἰς τὴν χάριν ταύτην ἐν ᾗ ἑστήκαμεν

Access is "into" (εἰς + acc.) "this grace" (τὴν χάριν ταύτην). Dunn suggests that the use of χάρις is unusual and refers to "a sphere or state (a secure area) into which one enters" (248); Cranfield views it as referring to the state of being declared righteous (259). The continuing experience of the state of grace in which (ἐν ᾗ) believers exist is highlighted by the intensive perfect of ἑστήκαμεν (1 pl. pf. act. indic. of ἵστημι, "stand"). Cranfield suggests "abide" as the translation (259); Jewett connects the idea with the OT congregation or priests "standing before" God (350; cf. Lev 9:5; Ps 24:3–4; 2 Chron 29:11, LXX).

καὶ καυχώμεθα ἐπ᾽ ἐλπίδι τῆς δόξης τοῦ θεοῦ

Καυχώμεθα (1 pl. aor. act.) can be indicative or subjunctive, and καί can join it either to ἔχομεν/ἔχωμεν in verse 1 or to ἑστήκαμεν in the immediately preceding clause. Commentators are unanimous in connecting it to verse 1, although they are divided on whether it is indicative (e.g., Cranfield 259) or subjunctive (e.g., Jewett 351). The repeated use of the present and perfect tenses in verses 1–5 suggests that indicative is more likely (cf. Longenecker 559). Καυχάομαι echoes 2:17 (cf. 2:23; 3:27; 4:2), but Paul gives the verb a new, positive basis (ἐπί + dat.). See Dunn for a discussion of the reversal of ideas that have occurred previously (249). See 4:18 for ἐλπίς as confident expectation; Schreiner suggests that it is an eschatological possession (254); the noun is definite as the object of a preposition. The article with δόξης (obj. gen.) refers back to 4:20; τοῦ θεοῦ is possessive. The combination of the definite article with δόξης plus the adjunct τοῦ θεοῦ makes the entire phrase monadic. TEV translates the phrase as "the hope we have of sharing God's glory." "Hope" becomes the key word in the verses that follow (cf. 5:3–5).

VERSE 3

οὐ μόνον δέ, ἀλλὰ καὶ καυχώμεθα ἐν ταῖς θλίψεσιν

Paul connects to (δέ) and builds on the first sentence with the strong contrast he used three times in chapter 4: οὐ μόνον . . . ἀλλὰ καί ("not only . . . but also"; cf. 4:12, 16, 23). Robertson suggests supplying καυχώμεθα before ἀλλὰ καί (394). The present tense is iterative; ἐν + dative gives the cause for boasting (T 463); the definite article functions as a possessive pronoun ("our tribulations"). Θλῖψις, -εως, ἡ denotes trouble brought about by outward circumstances that inflict distress (BDAG 457c; cf. 2:9). Dunn views it as eschatological troubles (250; cf. 2:9), but Schreiner's suggestion that it points to the pressures and troubles of the present age seems more likely (cf. 8:35; 12:12). In either case, it "piques the readers' curiosity, thereby preparing them for the explanation that follows" (Schreiner 255).

εἰδότες ὅτι ἡ θλῖψις ὑπομονὴν κατεργάζεται

The perfect participle εἰδότες (nom. pl. masc. of pf. act. ptc. of οἶδα, "know") is adverbial of cause (Wallace 631 n. 47) and introduces "a knowledge given to faith . . . for which absolute validity is claimed (Cranfield 261); ὅτι identifies the content of that knowledge. The article with θλῖψις is anaphoric of renewed mention (Moule 117) and is the first of four such uses. See 1:27, 2:9, and 4:5 for κατεργάζεται. Ὑπομονή, -ῆς, ἡ describes the capacity to hold out or bear up in the face of difficulty (BDAG 1039d; cf. Dunn 251 for possible translations).

VERSE 4

ἡ δὲ ὑπομονὴ δοκιμήν, ἡ δὲ δοκιμὴ ἐλπίδα

Both uses of δέ are connective ("and"), and both articles are anaphoric. Δοκιμή, -ῆς, ἡ describes the result of going through a test (BDAG 256a; cf. 2 Cor 2:19; 8:2; 13:3; Phil 2:22); NEB translates it as "proof that we have stood the test." See 4:18 and 5:2 for ἐλπίς.

VERSE 5

ἡ δὲ ἐλπὶς οὐ καταισχύνει

Paul reaches the climax of his argument (R 1200; BDF §493.3) with a statement that echoes the LXX (Ps 21:6; 24:3, 30; 119:116; Isa 28:16). The article with ἐλπίς is anaphoric and refers back to the end of verse 2 (Longenecker 561). Schreiner suggests that καταισχύνει should be accented as future (καταισχυνεῖ, 256), but a gnomic present is more likely (cf. Jewett 356). The prefix κατά intensifies the verb (Harris 160), which denotes shame and disappointment that come to one whose faith is shown to be vain (BDAG 517b; cf. *TDNT* 1.189–90).

ὅτι ἡ ἀγάπη τοῦ θεοῦ ἐκκέχυται ἐν ταῖς καρδίαις ἡμῶν

The reason (ὅτι) hope does not disappoint rests in God's work in our hearts. The article accompanies the abstract noun ἀγάπη. Although Robertson views τοῦ θεοῦ as an objective genitive (499), most commentators see it as subjective (e.g., Cranfield 262; Dunn 252; Schreiner 257). Wallace offers it as a possible example of a "plenary" genitive that is both subjective and objective (121), and his explanation makes good sense. The extensive perfect of ἐκκέχυται (3 sg. pf. pass. indic. of ἐκχέω, "pour out") emphasizes the continuing effect of a past action (Wallace 577); the ultimate, unstated agent is God. 'Εν + dative indicates location; the article accompanies the possessive pronoun.

διὰ πνεύματος ἁγίου τοῦ δοθέντος ἡμῖν

Διά + genitive indicates the intermediate agent (R 583). Πνεύματος ἁγίου is definite as the object of the preposition; the full title occurs four other times in Romans (9:1; 14:17; 15:13, 16). The article with δοθέντος (gen. sg. neut. of aor. pass. ptc. of δίδωμι, "give") marks it as adjectival, modifying πνεύματος; the consummative aorist stresses the completion of the act; the passive is a divine passive; ἡμῖν is the object of the participle. Dunn notes that the giving of the Spirit is a mark of the new age (253; cf. Isa 32:15; 34:16; 44:3; Ezek 11:14; 36:26–27; 37:4–14; Joel 2:28–32).

VERSE 6

ἔτι γὰρ Χριστὸς ὄντων ἡμῶν ἀσθενῶν

Six textual variants add to the complexity of this verse. Metzger (453), Moo (296 n. 19), and Jewett (345 n. d–e) all have extended discussions. The variant included in UBS[5] (ἔτι γάρ . . . ἔτι) has the strongest mss. support (א, A, C, D) and best explains the others. The emphatic placement of both Χριστός and ἀπέθανεν (Dunn 254) suggests that Paul repeated ἔτι for emphasis.

The postpositive conjunction γάρ ("for") establishes verses 6–8 as the reason for what has preceded. Ἔτι ("still") marks a period of time that extends until the moment of an action or event (Jewett 358). Moule describes the placement of Χριστός as "an impressive example" of prolepsis for emphasis (166; cf. BDF §476.1). The genitive absolute ὄντων (gen. sg. masc. of pres. act. ptc. of εἰμί) is adverbial of time with ἡμῶν as the subject and ἀσθενῶν as the predicate adjective. See 4:19 for the cognate verb ἀσθενέω.

ἔτι κατὰ καιρὸν ὑπὲρ ἀσεβῶν ἀπέθανεν

The repetition of ἔτι highlights our condition prior to Christ's death on our behalf. Κατὰ καιρόν is best taken with the verb that follows (Jewett 358); NJB translates the phrase "at the appointed time," while GNB renders it "at the time God chose." See similar ideas in Mark 1:15 and Galatians 4:4. Ὑπέρ + genitive ("on behalf of") occurs four times in verses 6–8 as a synonym for ἀντί with the nuance of substitution (Porter 177); Harris suggests both representation and substitution (215–16). Ἀσεβῶν is qualitative; see 1:18 for the meaning. Ἀπέθανεν (3 sg. aor. act. indic. of ἀποθνῄσκω, "die") is a constative aorist and stands in the place of final emphasis.

VERSE 7

μόλις γὰρ ὑπὲρ δικαίου τις ἀποθανεῖται

As an explanation (γάρ) of the magnitude of what Christ has done, Paul offers two examples from human experience. Μόλις is a adverb of manner that describes something rare on a scale of occurrences (BDAG 657c). Ὑπὲρ δικαίου ("on behalf of a righteous person") contrasts with ὑπὲρ ἀσεβῶν in the preceding verse; the substantival adjective δικαίου is qualitative. The indefinite pronoun τις (nom. sg. masc.) is the subject of the clause; ἀποθανεῖται (3 sg. fut. mid. indic. of ἀποθνῄσκω) is a gnomic future (Wallace 527; R 876); the middle voice focuses attention on the subject.

ὑπὲρ γὰρ τοῦ ἀγαθοῦ τάχα τις καὶ τολμᾷ ἀποθανεῖν

A second explanation (γάρ) reinforces Paul's point. Ὑπὲρ τοῦ ἀγαθοῦ parallels ὑπὲρ δικαίου in the preceding clause but also draws a distinction with it. Schreiner offers five views of the distinction between δικαίου and ἀγαθοῦ and concludes that ἀγαθοῦ denotes a "benefactor" (261); NJB translates it as "the truly good person." The article with ἀγαθοῦ is generic (R 763). Τάχα ("perhaps/possibly") is an adverb of manner that expresses contingency ranging from probability to possibility (BDAG 992b). Τις ("someone") is again the subject; καί is ascensive ("even"). Τολμάω describes the act of showing boldness or resolution in the face of danger, opposition, or a problem (BDAG 1010b); ἀποθανεῖν (aor. act. inf.) completes the action of the main verb.

VERSE 8

συνίστησιν δὲ τὴν ἑαυτοῦ ἀγάπην εἰς ἡμᾶς ὁ θεός

Divine concrete action, however, stands in sharp contrast (δέ) to human possible (but unlikely) action. Συνίστησιν (3 sg. pres. act. indic. of συνίστημι, "prove, demonstrate") describes the action of providing evidence of a personal characteristic or claim through action (BDAG 973a; cf. 3:5). The present tense is possibly an example of "past into present" (cf. Wallace 519). The use of the reflexive pronoun ἑαυτοῦ ("his own love") highlights the subject and is emphatic (Cranfield 265). Εἰς ἡμᾶς should be taken with ἀγάπην (Moo 309 n. 84; cf. Eph 1:15; Col 1:14; 1 Thess 3:2; 2 Thess 1:3) rather than with the verb (contra R 789). The placement of ὁ θεός is emphatic (Dunn 256); the article is monadic.

ὅτι ἔτι ἁμαρτωλῶν ὄντων ἡμῶν Χριστὸς ὑπὲρ ἡμῶν ἀπέθανεν

The explanatory ὅτι (Wallace 460) may be short for ἐν τούτῳ ὅτι (R 1034) and should be translated "in that" (BDF §394). Ἔτι ("still") echoes verse 6 as does the genitive absolute ἁμαρτωλῶν ὄντων ἡμῶν ("while we were sinful"), which is adverbial of time. See 3:7 for ἁμαρτωλός. Placing ὑπὲρ ἡμῶν between the subject (Χριστός) and the verb gives it emphasis; ἀπέθανεν (3 sg. aor. act. indic. of ἀποθνῄσκω) is a constative aorist. The overall structure of verses 6–8 is an A–B–B′–A′ pattern: divine-human-human-divine, and the repeated ὑπέρ phrases "drive home the point that Christ died, not on behalf of the righteous or good, but on behalf of the weak, ungodly, and sinful—specifically on behalf of us" (Harvey 126).

VERSE 9

πολλῷ οὖν μᾶλλον δικαιωθέντες νῦν ἐν τῷ αἵματι αὐτοῦ

Paul begins his conclusion (οὖν) from verses 6–8 with an emphatic comparison that combines a dative of degree (πολλῷ; cf. Wallace 167) and an adverb μᾶλλον ("more") that indicates a greater or higher degree (BDAG 613d); NEB translates the combination as "all the more certainly." The form of argument reflects both the Jewish "light and heavy" pattern (Cranfield 265) and the Greco-Roman "from lesser to greater" pattern (Jewett 362). Δικαιωθέντες repeats the accomplished reality already mentioned in verse 1; νῦν ("now") marks it as a reality in present time (cf. 3:21). The prepositional phrase ἐν τῷ αἵματι αὐτοῦ echoes 3:25 and may be understood either as impersonal means ("by means of his blood"; cf. Moule 77)* or as instrumental of price ("at the price of his blood"; cf. BDF §219.3).

σωθησόμεθα δι' αὐτοῦ ἀπὸ τῆς ὀργῆς

Σωθησόμεθα (1 pl. fut. pass. indic. of σῴζω, "save") is a temporal fut. (Moo 310) and a divine passive. See 1:16 for the cognate noun σωτηρία. Διά + genitive indicates the intermediate agent (Harris 70); ἀπό + ablative indicates separation (R 518); ὀργή makes it clear that the salvation is eschatological (Schreiner 263; cf. 2:8).

VERSE 10

εἰ γὰρ ἐχθροὶ ὄντες κατηλλάγημεν τῷ θεῷ διὰ τοῦ θανάτου τοῦ υἱοῦ αὐτοῦ

Paul restates verse 9 (γάρ; cf. Schreiner 263) using a first class condition (εἰ + indic.) that introduces the third key link word in the paragraph (καταλλάσσω). The participle ὄντες is adverbial of time, with the predicate nominative brought forward for emphasis. Although Jewett views ἐχθρός, -ά, -όν as denoting deliberate human rebellion (364; cf. 1:18–3:20), Schreiner argues for mutual hostility between God and humans (264; cf. Dunn 258). The prefix κατά intensifies κατηλλάγημεν (1 pl. aor. pass. indic. of καταλλάσσω, "reconcile"), which is a consummative aorist of antecedent action and a simple passive. Τῷ θεῷ is dative of the indirect object; διὰ τοῦ θανάτου indicates the means of reconciliation; τοῦ υἱοῦ αὐτοῦ is an objective genitive.

πολλῷ μᾶλλον καταλλαγέντες σωθησόμεθα ἐν τῇ ζωῇ αὐτοῦ

Introducing the second half of the sentence with πολλῷ μᾶλλον is the more usual construction for the "light and heavy" argument (Dunn 258). The participle καταλλαγέντες (nom. pl. masc. of aor. pass. ptc.) is adverbial of time (Wallace 627; cf. Longenecker 566) and makes the argument clear by repeating καταλλάσσω. Paul then repeats σωθησόμεθα from verse 9; ἐν τῇ ζωῇ αὐτοῦ indicates the means of salvation. Dunn notes the interchange of prepositions in verse 9 (ἐν τῷ αἵματι αὐτοῦ . . . δι' αὐτοῦ) and verse 10 (διὰ τοῦ θανάτου . . . ἐν τῇ ζωῇ αὐτοῦ) and concludes that the variation is primarily stylistic (260). In any event, the argument is clear: if God has done the "lesser" act of reconciling us while we were his enemies, he will certainly do the "greater" act of saving us when we are his friends.

VERSE 11

οὐ μόνον δέ, ἀλλὰ καὶ καυχώμενοι ἐν τῷ θεῷ διὰ τοῦ κυρίου ἡμῶν Ἰησοῦ Χριστοῦ

To conclude his argument Paul connects it (δέ) to everything that has preceded by repeating the strong adversative of verse 3: οὐ μόνον . . . ἀλλὰ καί. Robertson suggests supplying σωθησόμεθα before ἀλλὰ καί (394). The participle καυχώμενοι (nom. pl. masc. of pres. mid. ptc.) repeats the iterative present of καυχάομαι in verse 3 and functions as the main verb in the clause (Wallace 653; cf. Moule 179). Ἐν τῷ θεῷ denotes the object of pride/boasting (Harris 132); διὰ τοῦ κυρίου ἡμῶν denotes agency; Ἰησοῦ Χριστοῦ is simple apposition. It is more likely that Christ is the agent of all the benefits we receive from God rather than the agent through whom we boast. See GNB: "We rejoice because of what God has done through our Lord Jesus Christ."

δι' οὗ νῦν τὴν καταλλαγὴν ἐλάβομεν

Specifically, Christ is the agent through whom (δι' οὗ) we experience reconciliation in the present age (νῦν). Καταλλαγή, -ῆς, ἡ describes the reestablishment of an interrupted or broken relationship (BDAG 521b; cf. Cranfield 267; Jewett 365–66; Longenecker 566–70). Paul uses the noun elsewhere three times (Rom 11:15; 2 Cor 5:18, 19) and cognate verb forms seven times (1 Cor 7:11; 2 Cor 5:18, 19, 20; Eph 2:16; Col 1:20, 22). Of ἐλάβομεν (1 pl. aor. act. indic. of λαμβάνω) Dunn writes, "The final aorist brings the whole talk of hope and boasting back to the firm point that the decisive action has already taken place on the cross and in their lives" (261).

FOR FURTHER STUDY

40. Peace (5:1)

Arichea, D. C. "Peace in the New Testament." *BT* 38 (1987): 201–206.

Beck, H., and C. Brown. *NIDNTT* 2.776–83.
Bray, G. L. "Peace with God (Romans 5:1–11)." *Evangel* 17 (1999): 70–73.
DeVilliers, P. G. R. "Peace in the Pauline Letters: A Perspective on Biblical Spirituality." *Neot* 43 (2009): 1–26.
Hasler, V. *EDNT* 1.394–97.
Jewett, R. "The God of Peace in Romans: Reflections on Crucial Lutheran Texts." *Currents in Theology and Mission* 25 (1998): 186–94.
Love, M. "Living in the Peace of God: Perspectives from Romans." *Leaven* 9 (2001): 205–209.
Minear, P. S. "The Peace of God: Conceptions of Peace in the New Testament." Pages 118–31 in *Celebrating Peace*. Edited by L. S. Rouner. Notre Dame, IN: University of Notre Dame Press, 1990.
Porter, S. E. *DPL* 695–99.
Reimer, R. H. "Living out the Peace of God: The Apostle Paul's Theology and the Practice of Peace." Pages 91–101 in *Vital Christianity*. Edited by D. L. Weaver-Zercher and W. H. Willmon. London: T & T Clark, 2005.
Roth, W. "Language of Peace: shalom and eirene." *Explore: A Journal of Theology* 3 (1977): 69–74.
Schaeffer, G. E. *EDBT* 597–98.
Stuhlmacher, P. "'He Is Our Peace' (Eph. 2:14): On the Exegesis and Significance of Eph. 2:14–18." Pages 182–200 in *Reconciliation, Law, and Righteousness: Essays in Biblical Theology*. Translated by E. R. Kalin. Philadelphia: Fortress, 1986.
Swartley, W. M. *Covenant of Peace: The Missing Peace in New Testament Theology and Ethics*. Grand Rapids: Eerdmans, 2006.
Von Rad, G., and W. Foerster. *TDNT* 2.400–20.
Yoder, P. B., and W. M. Swartley. *The Meaning of Peace: Biblical Studies*. Louisville, KY: Westminster/John Knox, 1992.
Wengst, K. *Pax Romana and the Peace of Christ*. Philadelphia: Fortress, 1987.

41. Hope (5:2)

Ateek, N. S. "Hope in a Hopeless World." *Evangelical Review of Theology* 10 (1986): 33–38.
Banks, R., ed. *Reconciliation and Hope*. Grand Rapids: Eerdmans, 1974.
Beker, J. C. *Suffering and Hope: The Biblical Vision and the Human Predicament*. Philadelphia: Fortress, 1987.
Bossman, D. M. "Paul's Mediterranean Gospel: Faith, Hope, Love." *BTB* 25 (1995): 71–78.
Currie, S. D. "Hope in its Biblical Settings." *Austin Seminary Bulletin* 84 (1969): 29–39.
Denbeaux, F. J. "Biblical Hope." *Int* 5 (1951): 285–303.
Everts, J. M. *DPL* 415–17.
Gibbs, J. A. "Regaining Biblical Hope: Restoring the Prominence of the Parousia." *Concordia Journal* 27 (2001): 310–22.
Harrington, W. J. "Paul's Word of Hope." *Spirituality* 15 (2009): 23–27.
Hebblethwaite, B. *The Christian Hope*. Grand Rapids: Eerdmans, 1984.
Heil, J. P. *Romans—Paul's Letter of Hope*. Rome: Biblical Institute Press, 1987.
Hoffmann, E. *NIDNTT* 2.238–44.
Hubbard, D. A. "Hope in the Old Testament." *TynBul* 34 (1983): 33–59.

Ito, A. "The 'Hope' in the Pauline Epistles: Between 'Already' and 'Not Yet.'" *Exegetica* 19 (2008): 93–113.
Moule, C. F. D. *The Meaning of Hope*. Philadelphia: Fortress, 1963.
Nebe, G. *"Hoffnung" bei Paulus. Elpis und ihre Synonyme im Zusammenhang der Eschatologie*. Göttingen: Vandenhoeck & Ruprecht, 1983.
Neyrey, J. H. "Hope Against Hope." *Way* 27 (1987): 264–73.
Rengstorf, K. H., and R. Bultmann. *TDNT* 2.517–35.
Robertson, A. C. "'Hope' in Ephesians 1:18: A Contextual Approach." *Journal of Theology for Southern Africa* 55 (1986): 62–63.
Stuhlmacher, P. "Eschatology and Hope in Paul." *EvQ* 72 (2000): 315–33.
Thompson, M. D. "Groan but not as those who have no hope." *St Mark's Review* 212 (2010): 51–63.

42. Reconciliation (5:11)

Banks, R., ed. *Reconciliation and Hope*. Grand Rapids: Eerdmans, 1974.
Barclay, W. "The One, New Man." Pages 73–81 in *Unity and Diversity in New Testament Theology: Essays in Honor of George E. Ladd*. Edited by R. A. Guelich. Grand Rapids: Eerdmans, 1978.
Büchsel, F. *TDNT* 1.258–59.
Fitzmyer, J. A. "Reconciliation in Pauline Theology." Pages 155–77 in *No Famine in the Land*. Edited by J. W. Flanagan and A. W. Robinson. Missoula, MT: Scholars Press, 1975.
Fong, B. W. "Addressing the Issue of Racial Reconciliation according to the Principles of Eph 2:11–22." *JETS* 38 (1995): 565–80.
Gunton, C. E., ed. *The Theology of Reconciliation*. London: T&T Clark, 2003.
Horrell, D. G. "From ἀδελφοί to οἶκος θεοῦ: Social Transformation in Pauline Christianity." *JBL* 120 (2001): 293–311.
Kim, S. "2 Cor 5:11–21 and the Origin of Paul's Conception of 'Reconciliation.'" *NovT* 39 (1997): 360–84.
Käsemann, E. "Some Thoughts on the Theme 'The Doctrine of Reconciliation in the New Testament.'" Pages 49–64 in *The Future of Our Religious Past*. Edited by J. M. Robinson. New York: Harper & Row, 1971.
Lincoln, A. T. "The Church and Israel in Ephesians 2." *CBQ* 49 (1987): 605–24.
Link, H.-G., C. Brown, and H. Vorländer. *NIDNTT* 3.145–76.
Marshall, I. H. "The Meaning of 'Reconciliation.'" Pages 117–32 in *Unity and Diversity in New Testament Theology: Essays in Honor of George E. Ladd*. Edited by R. A. Guelich. Grand Rapids: Eerdmans, 1978.
Martin, R. P. *Reconciliation: A Study of Paul's Theology*. Revised edition. Grand Rapids: Eerdmans, 1990.
Moore, M. S. "Ephesians and 2:14–16: A History of Recent Interpretations." *EvQ* 54 (1982): 163–68.
Porter, S. E. *Καταλλάσσω in Ancient Greek Literature, with Reference to the Pauline Writings*. Cordoba: Ediciones el Almendro, 1994.
________. *DPL* 695–99.
Ridderbos, H. "The Biblical Message of Reconciliation." Pages 72–90 in *Studies in Scripture and Its Authority*. Grand Rapids: Eerdmans, 1978.
Silva, M. *NIDNTTE* 1.242–49.

Stuhlmacher, P. "'He Is Our Peace' (Eph. 2:14): On the Exegesis and Significance of Eph. 2:14–18." Pages 182–200 in *Reconciliation, Law, and Righteousness: Essays in Biblical Theology*. Translated by E. R. Kalin. Philadelphia: Fortress, 1986.
Taylor, V. *Forgiveness and Reconciliation*. London: Macmillan, 1946.
White, R. E. O. *EDT* 917–18.

HOMILETICAL SUGGESTIONS

Three Dimensions of Justification by Faith (5:1–11)

1. The Present Results of Justification: Peace, grace, and hope (5:1–5)
   a. We have peace with God (5:1)
   b. We have access into grace (5:2a)
   c. We hope in God's glory (5:2b–5)
      1) Because we know what tribulation produces (5:3–4)
      2) Because God's love is poured out in our hearts (5:5)
2. The Past Basis of Justification: Christ's death for us (5:6–8)
   a. We were not righteous or good (5:7)
   b. We were weak, ungodly, and sinful (5:6, 8)
3. The Future Promise of Justification: Salvation from wrath (5:9–11)
   a. Because we are declared righteous by Christ's blood (5:9)
   b. Because we are reconciled through Christ's death (5:10)

b. Counteracting the Effects of Adam's Sin (5:12–21)

STRUCTURE

The second paragraph of chapter 5 is complicated by the fact that Paul twice interrupts his train of thought to clarify what he has just written. The result is five parts (5:12; 5:13–14; 5:15–17; 5:18–19; 5:20–21), with the fourth part resuming the thought begun in the first. Paul begins a comparison intended to provide the reason Christ's death was necessary for God to impute his righteousness to us: Adam's sin (5:12). He breaks off the comparison, however, in order to explain the situation that existed between Adam's sin and the giving of the Mosaic law (5:13–14). He then identifies the ways in which the comparison between Adam and Christ does *not* apply (5:15–17) before setting out the way in which it does (5:18–19). Finally, he explains how the law fits into this understanding of human history (5:20–21).

Διὰ τοῦτο ὥσπερ δι' ἑνὸς ἀνθρώπου ἡ ἁμαρτία εἰς τὸν κόσμον εἰσῆλθεν καὶ διὰ τῆς ἁμαρτίας ὁ θάνατος, καὶ οὕτως εἰς πάντας ἀνθρώπους ὁ θάνατος διῆλθεν, ἐφ' ᾧ πάντες ἥμαρτον·

    ἄχρι γὰρ νόμου ἁμαρτία ἦν ἐν κόσμῳ, ἁμαρτία δὲ οὐκ ἐλλογεῖται μὴ ὄντος νόμου,
    ἀλλ' ἐβασίλευσεν ὁ θάνατος ἀπὸ Ἀδὰμ μέχρι Μωϋσέως καὶ ἐπὶ τοὺς μὴ ἁμαρτήσαντας
    ἐπὶ τῷ ὁμοιώματι τῆς παραβάσεως Ἀδὰμ ὅς ἐστιν τύπος τοῦ μέλλοντος.

        Ἀλλ' οὐχ ὡς τὸ παράπτωμα, οὕτως καὶ τὸ χάρισμα·
        εἰ γὰρ τῷ τοῦ ἑνὸς παραπτώματι οἱ πολλοὶ ἀπέθανον,
        πολλῷ μᾶλλον ἡ χάρις τοῦ θεοῦ καὶ ἡ δωρεὰ ἐν χάριτι τῇ τοῦ ἑνὸς ἀνθρώπου
        Ἰησοῦ Χριστοῦ εἰς τοὺς πολλοὺς ἐπερίσσευσεν.

        καὶ οὐχ ὡς δι' ἑνὸς ἁμαρτήσαντος τὸ δώρημα·
        τὸ μὲν γὰρ   κρίμα   ἐξ ἑνὸς   εἰς κατάκριμα,
        τὸ δὲ   χάρισμα   ἐκ πολλῶν παραπτωμάτων   εἰς δικαίωμα.

        εἰ γὰρ τῷ τοῦ ἑνὸς παραπτώματι ὁ θάνατος ἐβασίλευσεν διὰ τοῦ ἑνός,
        πολλῷ μᾶλλον οἱ τὴν περισσείαν τῆς χάριτος καὶ τῆς δωρεᾶς τῆς δικαιοσύνης
        λαμβάνοντες ἐν ζωῇ βασιλεύσουσιν διὰ τοῦ ἑνὸς Ἰησοῦ Χριστοῦ.

Ἄρα οὖν ὡς   δι' ἑνὸς παραπτώματος   εἰς πάντας ἀνθρώπους   εἰς κατάκριμα,
οὕτως καὶ   δι' ἑνὸς δικαιώματος   εἰς πάντας ἀνθρώπους   εἰς δικαίωσιν ζωῆς·

ὥσπερ γὰρ   διὰ τῆς παρακοῆς . . .   ἁμαρτωλοὶ   κατεστάθησαν   οἱ πολλοί,
οὕτως καὶ   διὰ τῆς ὑπακοῆς . . .   δίκαιοι   κατασταθήσονται   οἱ πολλοί.

νόμος δὲ παρεισῆλθεν, ἵνα πλεονάσῃ τὸ παράπτωμα·
οὗ δὲ ἐπλεόνασεν ἡ ἁμαρτία, ὑπερεπερίσσευσεν ἡ χάρις,
    ἵνα ὥσπερ   ἐβασίλευσεν   ἡ ἁμαρτία   ἐν τῷ θανάτῳ,
    οὕτως καὶ   ἡ χάρις   βασιλεύσῃ   διὰ δικαιοσύνης εἰς ζωὴν αἰώνιον
                                              διὰ Ἰησοῦ Χριστοῦ τοῦ κυρίου ἡμῶν.

VERSE 12

Διὰ τοῦτο ὥσπερ δι' ἑνὸς ἀνθρώπου ἡ ἁμαρτία εἰς τὸν κόσμον εἰσῆλθεν

"Because of this" (*διὰ τοῦτο*) introduces the reason for what precedes (Wallace 334; cf. Moo 317 n. 17 for an extended discussion of the phrase). The conceptual antecedent for *τοῦτο* is best understood as all of 5:1–11 (Longenecker 586; Schreiner 270). Ὥσπερ ("just as") is a marker of similarity (BDAG 1106d), usually followed by *οὕτως καί* ("so also"). In this instance, however, the comparison is left unfinished (cf. Cranfield 262 n. 5). *Διά* + genitive denotes agency (Porter 149); *ἑνὸς ἀνθρώπου* ("one man") refers to Adam (Dunn 272). See 3:9, 20 for ἁμαρτία. *Εἰς τὸν κόσμον* denotes entry ("into the world"); the definite article is monadic; *κόσμος* is a metonymy for "all people" of the world (Moo 319 n. 26). Εἰσῆλθεν (3 sg. aor. act. indic. of dep. εἰσέρχομαι, "enter") is a consummative aorist and stresses the conclusion of action.

καὶ διὰ τῆς ἁμαρτίας ὁ θάνατος

Καί is connective ("and"); *διά* + genitive is instrumental; the article with *ἁμαρτία* is anaphoric. "Death" (*ὁ θάνατος*) encompasses both physical and spiritual death (Moo 320). Schreiner describes sin and death as "twin powers that entered the world when Adam transgressed" (272).

καὶ οὕτως εἰς πάντας ἀνθρώπους ὁ θάνατος διῆλθεν

Καὶ οὕτως ("and so") differs from *οὕτως καί* ("so also") and denotes the natural consequence of sin entering the world (Cranfield 274). *Εἰς πάντας ἀνθρώπους* (GNB, "to the whole human race") denotes entry; its placement gives it stress. The article with *θάνατος* is anaphoric; διῆλθεν (3 sg. aor. act. indic. of dep. διέρχομαι, "spread/pass through") is a consummative aorist.

ἐφ' ᾧ πάντες ἥμαρτον·

The prepositional phrase *ἐφ' ᾧ* has been widely discussed. Although Jewett understands it as spatial ("on which [world]," 376), most grammars and commentators view it as short for *ἐπὶ τούτῳ ὅτι* (Harris 139–40; cf. 2 Cor 5:4; Phil 3:12; 4:10) and interpret it as cause (Wallace 342–43; Moo 321),* ground (R 604, 963), or reason (BDF §235.2). Schreiner's understanding that the conceptual antecedent of *ᾧ* (dat. sg. neut.) is the first part of the verse seems likely (274; cf. Longenecker 589). The resulting idea would be "because sin entered the world through Adam, all sinned." The anarthrous use of *πάντες* (nom. pl. masc.) is rare (R 773) and highlights humankind as a whole. Ἥμαρτον (3 pl. aor. act. indic. from ἁμαρτάνω, "sin") is a constative aorist (R 833; Longenecker 590). The dash (cf. EVV) marks the break in Paul's thought (anacoluthon, R 438).

Cranfield discusses six main interpretations of "all sinned" (274–79), of which three are most common: (1) Pelagius held that all people sin after Adam's example; (2) Cranfield (279), Longenecker (591), and Schreiner (276) hold that all people sin as the result of the nature inherited from Adam; (3) following Augustine, Murray (186), Stott (151–54), and Moo (326) hold that all people sinned in Adam's transgression. Dunn remains agnostic because he does not view the issue as one Paul addresses (290). In any event, Paul's point is that Adam's one act had far-reaching consequences for all humankind.

VERSE 13

ἄχρι γὰρ νόμου ἁμαρτία ἦν ἐν κόσμῳ

Paul breaks off his initial train of thought to explain (*γάρ*) the dynamics of sin and death during the period between Adam's sin and the giving of the law. Moo has an extended discussion of how verses 13–14 relate to their context and concludes they are best understood as reinforcing the universality of sin even when the law was not present to define it (329–32). Ἄχρι + genitive ("until") marks the endpoint of a continuous extent of time (BDAG 160d); *νόμου* is definite and refers to Torah rather than to a generic "law" (Dunn 274). The anarthrous subject *ἁμαρτία* is qualitative; *ἦν* (3 sg. impf. act. indic. from *εἰμί*) is a progressive imperfect; *ἐν* + dative is local; *κόσμῳ* is definite as one-of-a-kind (R 796).

ἁμαρτία δὲ οὐκ ἐλλογεῖται μὴ ὄντος νόμου

Δέ ("but") introduces a possible objection based on Paul's statement in 4:15 that there is no violation apart from law. Ἐλλογεῖται (3 sg. pres. pass. indic. from *ἐλλογέω*, "charge to an account") is a gnomic present (Moo 332 n. 78) and a divine passive; it carries the idea of charging a financial obligation to someone's account (BDAG 319a). Μή is the usual negative with participles; *ὄντος νόμου* is a genitive absolute of time ("when there is no law").

VERSE 14

ἀλλ' ἐβασίλευσεν ὁ θάνατος ἀπὸ Ἀδὰμ μέχρι Μωϋσέως

The stronger adversative *ἀλλά* ("but") introduces Paul's answer to the objection: the fact that men and women died before the law was given proves they sinned. Ἐβασίλευσεν (3 sg. aor. act. indic. from *βασιλεύω*, "rule") is a constative aorist (R 833). The verb carries the idea of exercising authority at a royal level (BDAG 170c); Jewett suggests the exercise of "dominion" (377). The article with *θάνατος* is anaphoric; *ἀπό* ("from") and *μέχρι* ("until") mark the boundaries of the time period defined by Adam and Moses.

καὶ ἐπὶ τοὺς μὴ ἁμαρτήσαντας ἐπὶ τῷ ὁμοιώματι τῆς παραβάσεως Ἀδάμ

Καί is ascensive ("even"); *ἐπί* + accusative indicates those "over" whom death exercised its authority (BDAG 365d). The article marks the participle as substantival, and *μή* is the usual negative particle; *ἁμαρτήσαντας* (acc. sg. masc. of aor. act. ptc. from ἁμαρτάνω, "sin") is a constative aorist. Most EVV condense ἐπὶ τῷ ὁμοιώματι into "like" (cf. KJV "after the likeness") reflecting the fact that ὁμοίωμα, -τος, τό denotes the state of having common characteristics or experiences (BDAG 707c; cf. Thayer 233). Τῆς παραβάσεως is a descriptive genitive; Ἀδάμ (indecl.) is a subjective genitive. Adam's sin consisted of a violation of a clear divine command. GNB renders the entire line as "even over those who did not sin in the same way that Adam did when he disobeyed God's command."

ὅς ἐστιν τύπος τοῦ μέλλοντος

Paul uses a relative pronoun (ὅς) with Adam (the "one man" of v. 12a) as its antecedent to return to his primary line of thought. Τύπος, -ου, ὁ ("type") refers to a person or thing that prefigures another person or thing related to future redemption (Cranfield 283; cf. *TDNT* 8.246–47). The substantival participle τοῦ μέλλοντος (gen. sg. masc. of pres. act. ptc. from μέλλω, "be about to") is a descriptive genitive ("of the one who was to come") and connects Adam to Christ. See Dunn for a discussion of the history of the Adam/Christ parallel (277–79).

VERSE 15

Ἀλλ' οὐχ ὡς τὸ παράπτωμα, οὕτως καὶ τὸ χάρισμα

Having established the connection between Adam and Christ, Paul begins to clarify the ways in which they differ (ἀλλ'). Moo notes that ἐστιν is assumed (335 n. 91; cf. ESV). Οὐχ ὡς ("not as") . . . οὕτως καί ("so also") establishes a contrast between what characterizes Adam's work (τὸ παράπτωμα) and what characterizes Christ's work (τὸ χάρισμα). See 4:25 for παράπτωμα, which Moo views as synonymous with ἁμαρτία and παράβασις (335 n. 92; cf. Cranfield 284 and Schreiner 283 n. 1). Χάρισμα, -τος, τό denotes a favor or gift that is freely and graciously given (BDAG 1081a). Schreiner identifies the gift as the righteous status granted to God's people (283 n. 2; cf. Cranfield 284; contra Moo 335). Along with δωρήμα, κρίμα, κατάκριμα, and δικαίωμα, both nouns are part of a word play (*homoioteleuton*) that extends through verse 18 (cf. BDF §488.3).

εἰ γὰρ τῷ τοῦ ἑνὸς παραπτώματι οἱ πολλοὶ ἀπέθανον

Paul explains (γάρ) the first difference using "lesser to greater" argumentation (cf. 5:9–11). Εἰ . . . ἀπέθανον (aor. act. indic.) establishes a first class condition that assumes the truth of the "if" clause. The instrumental dative τῷ παραπτώματι (Moule 44) is brought forward to establish a close connection to what precedes. Inserting the subjective genitive τοῦ ἑνός between the dative article and noun gives it greater stress than the noun. The substantival adjective οἱ πολλοί ("the many") is intended to designate a large number in contrast to "the one" (Cranfield 285 n. 1). Attempting to draw fine distinctions from the synonymous uses of "many" and "all" loses track of Paul's main argument (cf. Jewett 380): Adam's work ("the sin of the one") had a widespread impact ("the many died").

πολλῷ μᾶλλον ἡ χάρις τοῦ θεοῦ καὶ ἡ δωρεὰ ἐν χάριτι τῇ τοῦ ἑνὸς ἀνθρώπου Ἰησοῦ Χριστοῦ

See 5:9 on the comparison of degree established by πολλῷ μᾶλλον. See 1:5 for ἡ χάρις (abstract). Τοῦ θεοῦ is a subjective genitive; καί is connective ("and"); δωρεά, -ᾶς, ἡ denotes something that is given or transferred freely by one person to another (BDAG 266c). Ἐν χάριτι is best taken with δωρεά as instrumental (Cranfield 285); χάριτι is definite as the object of a preposition. The article (τῇ) allows the genitive phrase τοῦ ἑνὸς ἀνθρώπου to act as a noun modifying grace; Ἰησοῦ Χριστοῦ is a genitive of simple apposition. NEB captures the idea well: "the gift that came to so many by the grace of the one man, Jesus Christ."

εἰς τοὺς πολλοὺς ἐπερίσσευσεν

Εἰς + accusative denotes advantage. Τοὺς πολλούς ("the many") echoes the same phrase in the apodosis; Moo notes that it refers to "all who respond to the gift of grace" (336). Ἐπερίσσευσεν (3 sg. aor. act. indic. from περισσεύω, "abound"; cf. 3:7) is a constative aorist; placing it last (in parallel to ἀπέθανον) gives it emphasis. In contrast to Adam's work, Christ's work ("the gift of the one man") had an even greater impact ("abounded to the many"). The first key difference Paul highlights between Adam and Christ relates to *degree*: although Adam's work brought widespread death, Christ's work brings far more abundant grace.

VERSE 16

καὶ οὐχ ὡς δι' ἑνὸς ἁμαρτήσαντος τὸ δώρημα

Paul adds (καί) a second difference (οὐχ ὡς) between Adam's work (ἁμαρτάνω) and Christ's work (δώρημα). Διά + genitive is instrumental. The participle ἁμαρτήσαντος (gen. sg. masc. of aor. act. ptc. from ἁμαρτάνω) is definite and substantival ("the one who sinned") and denotes antecedent action; the reference is to Adam (R 860). Δώρημα, -τος, τό is synonymous with χάρισμα and occurs elsewhere only in Jas 1:17 to describe God's gift of wisdom. The parallelism with verse 15 suggests that in this context it refers to the gift of righteous status. CEV renders the clause as "There is a lot of difference between Adam's sin and God's gift."

τὸ μὲν γὰρ κρίμα ἐξ ἑνὸς εἰς κατάκριμα

Paul explains (γάρ) his elliptical statement with parallel verbless clauses introduced by the correlative conjunctions μέν . . . δέ ("on the one hand . . . on the other hand"). "Judgment" is the judicial verdict rendered for sin (Moo 338 n. 105); see 2:2–3 for κρίμα. Ἐκ + genitive denotes source; the parallel with πολλῶν παραπτωμάτων that follows suggests that ἑνός refers to "one sin" (Schreiner 285 n. 5). Εἰς + accusative gives the ultimate end of sin ("condemnation"). Κατάκριμα, -τος, τό refers to a judicial pronouncement upon a guilty person (BDAG 518d).

τὸ δὲ χάρισμα ἐκ πολλῶν παραπτωμάτων εἰς δικαίωμα

Χάρισμα repeats the "gift" noun from verse 15 as παράπτωμα repeats the "sin" noun. Ἐκ + genitive again indicates source, and εἰς + accusative again indicates the ultimate end. See 1:32 and 2:26 for δικαίωμα; it is best understood here as the result of God's action (Cranfield 287 n. 2), i.e., his judicial verdict. "Acquittal" (NEB, NJB; cf. "not guilty" in GNB) is probably a better parallel to condemnation than "justification" (KJV, RSV, NIV, ESV). The second key difference Paul highlights between Adam and Christ relates to *consequence*: Adam's work led to condemnation, while Christ's work leads to acquittal.

VERSE 17

εἰ γὰρ τῷ τοῦ ἑνὸς παραπτώματι ὁ θάνατος ἐβασίλευσεν διὰ τοῦ ἑνός

Although Schreiner views this verse as the support for verse 16b–c (285), it is better understood as a parallel explanation (γάρ) that sets out a third difference between Adam and Christ (cf. Cranfield 287). See verse 15 for the "lesser to greater" argumentation (εἰ . . . πολλῷ μᾶλλον) and for τῷ τοῦ ἑνὸς παραπτώματι. The article with θάνατος is anaphoric; see verse 14 on ἐβασίλευσεν; διά + genitive denotes agency; τοῦ ἑνός refers to Adam.

πολλῷ μᾶλλον οἱ τὴν περισσείαν τῆς χάριτος καὶ τῆς δωρεᾶς τῆς δικαιοσύνης λαμβάνοντες

The plural masculine article (οἱ) agrees with the substantival participle λαμβάνοντες (nom. pl. masc. of pres. act. ptc. from λαμβάνω, "receive"), which serves as the subject of the clause. The present tense of the participle is gnomic. Dunn notes that the "piling up of language in superfluous repetition" between the article and participle mirrors "the superabundant quality of grace given and received" (281). Τὴν περισσείαν (acc. sg. fem. from περισσεία, -ας, ἡ, "abundance, surplus") is the object of the participle; the verb carries the sense of what is beyond the regular or expected amount (BDAG 805a; cf. 2 Cor 8:2; 10:15; Jas 1:21). The article with χάριτος (gen. sg. fem.) is anaphoric; the noun is an attributed genitive with the result that περισσείαν functions as an attributive adjective (cf. Wallace 89–90); GNB captures the sense with "the abundant grace." The conjunction καί adds a second attributive genitive, τῆς δωρεᾶς, followed by an epexegetical genitive, τῆς δικαιοσύνης, that further describes the gift. The full participial phrase may be translated "the ones who receive the abundant grace and gift that is righteousness."

ἐν ζωῇ βασιλεύσουσιν διὰ τοῦ ἑνὸς Ἰησοῦ Χριστοῦ

Placing ἐν ζωῇ before the verb gives it stress; ἐν + dative denotes sphere (cf. v. 21); see 1:17 for ζωή. Βασιλεύσουσιν (3 pl. fut. act. indic.) may be a logical future denoting a present reality (cf. Moo 288) or an eschatological future pointing to the future (cf. Cranfield 288), although the NT concept of "now and not yet" suggests both are true. Διὰ τοῦ ἑνός (agency) parallels the same phrase at the beginning of the verse; adding Ἰησοῦ Χριστοῦ (apposition) makes the reference clear. The third key difference Paul highlights between Adam and Christ relates to *result*: Adam's work inaugurated the reign of death, while Christ's work inaugurates the reign of life.

VERSE 18

Ἄρα οὖν ὡς δι' ἑνὸς παραπτώματος εἰς πάντας ἀνθρώπους εἰς κατάκριμα

Robertson notes that Paul is "especially fond" of the emphatic inferential combination *ἄρα οὖν (*1190). It occurs seven other times in Romans (7:3, 25; 8:12; 9:16, 18; 14:12, 19) and four times elsewhere in his letters (Gal 6:10; Eph 2:19; 1 Thess 5:6; 2 Thess 2:15). He uses the combination ("consequently," NIV) to resume the comparison (ὡς) he began in 5:12 but broke off to engage in the clarifications of verses 13–17. Blass notes that the elliptical nature of this verse is "unintelligible without the long exposition preceding it" (§481). Διά + genitive is causal (BDF §481); ἑνός is masculine (Cranfield 289; cf. NRSV, "one man's trespass"; contra Longenecker 597). Εἰς πάντας ἀνθρώπους ("for all people") denotes advantage, while εἰς κατάκριμα denotes result ("resulting in condemnation"; cf. Moule 70). The sense is "because of one man's trespass [the verdict was pronounced] resulting in condemnation for all people." Longenecker (597) suggests supplying the verb ἀπέβη ("has resulted").

οὕτως καὶ δι' ἑνὸς δικαιώματος εἰς πάντας ἀνθρώπους εἰς δικαίωσιν ζωῆς

Οὕτως καί ("in this way also") introduces the second part of the comparison; οὕτως is an adverb used to draw an inference (Porter 215); καί is adjunctive. Διά + genitive is again causal; ἑνός is again masculine (NRSV, "one man's act of righteousness"). Εἰς πάντας ἀνθρώπους again denotes advantage ("for all people"), while εἰς δικαίωσιν ζωῆς again denotes result ("resulting in justification of life"). In contrast to verse 16, δικαίωμα refers to conduct ("righteous act"; cf. Jewett 385); see 4:25 for δικαίωσις ("justification"). Ζωῆς is a genitive of result ("justification that leads to life"; cf. Moo 341 n. 126). Longenecker (597) suggests supplying the verb ἀποβήσεται ("will result in").

VERSE 19

ὥσπερ γὰρ διὰ τῆς παρακοῆς τοῦ ἑνὸς ἀνθρώπου ἁμαρτωλοὶ κατεστάθησαν οἱ πολλοί

Γάρ ("for") explains the mechanics behind verse 18. There is no significant difference between ὥσπερ . . . οὕτως καί in this verse and ὡς . . . οὕτως καὶ in the preceding verse (Moo 344 n. 136). Διά + genitive denotes intermediate agency; the article with παρακοῆς is simple identification; παρακοή, -ῆς, ἡ describes a refusal to listen and obey (BDAG 767a); τοῦ ἑνὸς ἀνθρώπου ("of the one man") is a subjective genitive.

Ἁμαρτωλοί is the retained complement of what would be a double accusative (person + thing) with an active voice verb of making or appointing (cf. Wallace 186); the nominative case agrees with the subject (οἱ πολλοί). Κατεστάθησαν (3 pl. aor. pass. indic. from καθίστημι, "appoint") is a constative aorist and a divine passive. Moo concludes that the verb has a forensic nuance and should be translated "judged" or "declared" (345). The reversed word order of the entire clause calls attention to the way in which one act of disobedience affects "the many" (οἱ πολλοί).

οὕτως καὶ διὰ τῆς ὑπακοῆς τοῦ ἑνὸς δίκαιοι κατασταθήσονται οἱ πολλοί

The syntactical parallelism between the two halves of the comparison is exact except for the omission of ἀνθρώπου. Commentators are divided on whether ὑπακοή ("obedience") refers to the passive obedience of Christ's death (Dunn 284; Moo 368; Schreiner 287; Jewett 386) or the active obedience of his whole life (Cranfield 291; Murray 204), but it might be best not to make a sharp distinction between the two options. The wordplay between παρακοή and ὑπακοή is an example of *annominatio* (words with similar sounds but different senses). See 1:17 for δίκαιοι, which functions in the same way ἁμαρτωλοί did in the first half of the verse. Κατασταθήσονται (3 pl. fut. pass. indic. from καθίστημι) may be understood as a logical future, or an eschatological future. The NT concept of "now and not yet" suggests that both are true (cf. βασιλεύσουσιν in verse 17). The passive is a divine passive. See Schreiner for a discussion of the universal language in verses 15–19 (290–92).

VERSE 20

νόμος δὲ παρεισῆλθεν, ἵνα πλεονάσῃ τὸ παράπτωμα

Having concluded his comparison of Adam and Christ, Paul resumes (δέ) the topic of the law initially introduced in verse 13. Although anarthrous, νόμος is definite and refers to the Mosaic law (Dunn 285). Παρεισῆλθεν (3 sg. aor. act. indic. of dep. παρεισέρχομαι, "come in beside") has generated considerable discussion. Jewett views it as a derogatory term (387), while Robertson says it carries no notion of stealth (613). The best understanding is probably one of coming in as a side issue (BDAG 774c); that is, the law had a subordinate role in salvation history (Morris 241). Even in its subordinate role, however, the law had a purpose (ἵνα + subjunc.): to cause sin (τὸ παράπτωμα) to increase. Πλεονάζω carries the idea of becoming more and more so as to be in abundance (BDAG 824b). Cranfield notes three ways in which the law causes sin to become abundant: (1) by making it known, (2) by making it more sinful, and (3) by increasing its quantity (293); Moo adds a fourth: by intensifying its seriousness (348).

οὗ δὲ ἐπλεόνασεν ἡ ἁμαρτία, ὑπερεπερίσσευσεν ἡ χάρις

In contrast (δέ) to the increase of sin is the superabundance of grace. Οὗ ("where") is a relative adverb of sphere. It has no explicit antecedent (R 722), but commentators regularly understand it to point to Israel's history (e.g., Cranfield 293; Moo 349 n.

164; Schreiner 296). Ἁμαρτία is synonymous with παράπτωμα (cf. Dunn 286); the articles with ἁμαρτία and χάρις are anaphoric. Ὑπερεπερίσσευσεν (3 sg. aor. act. indic. from ὑπερπερισσεύω, "increase much more") forms a climax to the terms expressing abundance (Cranfield 294); the prefix ὑπέρ denotes excess ("beyond measure"). The only other NT occurrence of the verb is in 2 Cor 7:4; Dunn points to 4 Ezra 4:50 as an indication that it refers to eschatological abundance (287; cf. Jewett 388 n. 237; *TDNT* 6.60).

VERSE 21

ἵνα ὥσπερ ἐβασίλευσεν ἡ ἁμαρτία ἐν τῷ θανάτῳ

The purpose (ἵνα) of grace increasing beyond measure is that the reign of grace and life might replace the reign of sin and death. Ὥσπερ . . . οὕτως καί echoes the comparison language running throughout the paragraph. Ἐβασίλευσεν echoes verses 14 and 17, but now it is sin (ἡ ἁμαρτία) rather than death that reigns. Ἐν τῷ θανάτῳ indicates sphere (NIV, NET, CSB, "in death") rather than instrument (NEB, GNB, "by means of death").

οὕτως καὶ ἡ χάρις βασιλεύσῃ διὰ δικαιοσύνης εἰς ζωὴν αἰώνιον

See 1:17 for χάρις. The subjunctive βασιλεύσῃ (3 sg. aor. act. subjunc.) follows naturally from ἵνα at the beginning of the verse; the aorist is constative. Διά δικαιοσύνης is instrumental ("through righteousness"); εἰς ζωὴν αἰώνιον indicates result (ESV, "leading to eternal life").

διὰ Ἰησοῦ Χριστοῦ τοῦ κυρίου ἡμῶν (See 5:1)

FOR FURTHER STUDY

43. Adam/Christ Typology (5:12–21)

Barrett, C. K. *From First Adam to Last: A Study in Pauline Theology*. London: Black, 1962.

Barth, K. *Christ and Adam: Man and Humanity in Romans 5*. Translated by T. A. Smail. Edinburgh: Oliver & Boyd, 1956.

Bray, G. "Adam and Christ (Romans 5:12–21)." *Evangel* 18 (2000): 4–8.

Brandenberger, E. *Adam und Christus. Exegetisch-religions-geschichtliche Untersuchungen zu Römer 5,12–21 (1. Kor.15)*. Neukirchen-Vluyn: Neukirchener, 1962.

Bultmann, R. "Adam and Christ according to Rom. 5." Pages 143–65 in *Current Issues in New Testament Interpretation. Essays in Honor of Otto A. Piper.* Edited by W. Klassen and G. F. Snyder. London: SCM, 1962.

Byrne, B. "'The Type of the One to Come' (Rom 5:14): Fate and Responsibility in Romans 5:12–21." *AusBR* 36 (1988): 19–30.

Caragounis, C. C. "Romans 5.15–16 in the Context of 5.12–21: Contrast or Comparison?" *NTS* 31 (1985): 142–48.

Hofius, O. "Die Adam-Christus-Antithese und das Gesetz. Erwägungen zu Röm 5,12–21." Pages 165–206 in *Paul and the Mosaic Law*. Edited by J. D. G. Dunn. Tübingen: Mohr Siebeck, 1996.
Hooker, M. D. *From Adam to Christ. Essays on Paul*. Cambridge: Cambridge University Press, 1990.
Kertelge, K. "The Sin of Adam in the Light of Christ's Redemptive Act according to Romans 5:12–21." *Communio/International Catholic Review* 18 (1991); 502–13.
Kister, M. "Romans 5:12–21 against the Background of Torah-Theology and Hebrew Usage." *HTR* 100 (2007): 391–424.
Kreitzer, L. J. *DPL* 9–15.
________. "Christ and Second Adam." *Communio Vistorum* 32 (1989): 55–101.
________. "Adam as Analogy: Help or Hindrance?" *King's Theological Review* 11 (1988): 59–62.
Lee, Y. *The Son of Man as the Last Adam: The Early Church Tradition as a Source of Paul's Adam Christology*. Eugene, OR: Pickwick, 2012.
O'Neill, J. "Adam 'who is the figure of him that was to come'—A Reading of Rom 5:12–21." Pages 183–99 in *Crossing the Boundaries: Essays in Biblical Interpretation in Honour of Michael D. Goulder*. Edited by S. E. Porter, P. Joyce, and D. E. Orton. Leiden: Brill, 1994.
Scroggs, R. *The Last Adam: A Study in Pauline Anthropologie*. Oxford: Blackwell, 1966.

HOMILETICAL SUGGESTIONS

Salvation History in a Nutshell (5:12–21)

1. The impact of Adam's sin (5:12)
   a. Sin entered the world (5:12a)
   b. Death passed to all (5:12b)
2. The period before the law (5:13–14)
   a. Sin was not charged (5:13)
   b. Death reigned (5:14)
3. The differences between Adam and Christ (5:15–17)
   a. Degree (5:15)
      1) Adam: Many died (5:15b)
      2) Christ: Grace abounds to many (5:15c)
   b. Consequence (5:16)
      1) Adam: Judgment leads to condemnation (5:16b)
      2) Christ: Grace gift leads to acquittal (5:16c)
   c. Result (5:17)
      1) Adam: Death reigned (5:17a)
      2) Christ: Those receiving grace and righteousness reign in life (5:17b)
4. The impact of Christ's gift (5:18–19)
   a. Righteous act leads to life (5:18)
   b. Many declared righteous (5:19)
5. The impact of the law (5:20–21)
   a. Sin increased (5:20a)

b. Grace increased even more (5:20b)
    1) To replace the reign of death with the reign of life (5:21)

Adam and Christ (5:15–19)

1. Character of the work: Sin vs. gift (5:15, 16)
2. Nature of the act: Disobedience vs. obedience (5:19)
3. Judicial verdict: Condemnation vs. acquittal (5:16, 18)
4. Resulting status: Sinners vs. righteous (5:19)
5. Ultimate outcome: Death vs. life (5:15, 17, 18)

2. God's Righteousness Is Appropriated in Christ (6:1–23)

a. By Understanding Our Death with Christ (6:1–14)

STRUCTURE

Paul uses a double rhetorical question (6:1) to link this paragraph to the previous discussion (Porter 305; Cranfield 297) and acknowledge the potentially controversial nature of that discussion (Dunn 306; cf. Longenecker 609). After an emphatic denial (6:2a), Paul addresses the false inference in four parts. The first introduces the ideas of dying and rising with Christ using a diatribal exchange that draws an analogy to baptism (6:2b–4). The second focuses on the theological implications of dying with Christ (6:5–7); the third focuses on the theological implications of rising with him (6:8–11). The fourth moves to practical admonition with three verbs in the imperative mood (6:12–14).

Τί οὖν ἐροῦμεν;
ἐπιμένωμεν τῇ ἁμαρτίᾳ, ἵνα ἡ χάρις πλεονάσῃ;

μὴ γένοιτο.
οἵτινες ἀπεθάνομεν τῇ ἁμαρτίᾳ, πῶς ἔτι ζήσομεν ἐν αὐτῇ;
ἢ ἀγνοεῖτε ὅτι ὅσοι ἐβαπτίσθημεν εἰς Χριστὸν Ἰησοῦν,
εἰς τὸν θάνατον αὐτοῦ ἐβαπτίσθημεν;
συνετάφημεν οὖν αὐτῷ διὰ τοῦ βαπτίσματος εἰς τὸν θάνατον,
ἵνα ὥσπερ ἠγέρθη Χριστὸς ἐκ νεκρῶν διὰ τῆς δόξης τοῦ πατρός,
οὕτως καὶ ἡμεῖς ἐν καινότητι ζωῆς περιπατήσωμεν.

εἰ γὰρ σύμφυτοι γεγόναμεν τῷ ὁμοιώματι τοῦ θανάτου αὐτοῦ,
ἀλλὰ καὶ τῆς ἀναστάσεως ἐσόμεθα·
τοῦτο γινώσκοντες, ὅτι ὁ παλαιὸς ἡμῶν ἄνθρωπος συνεσταυρώθη,
ἵνα καταργηθῇ τὸ σῶμα τῆς ἁμαρτίας,
τοῦ μηκέτι δουλεύειν ἡμᾶς τῇ ἁμαρτίᾳ·
ὁ γὰρ ἀποθανὼν δεδικαίωται ἀπὸ τῆς ἁμαρτίας.

εἰ δὲ ἀπεθάνομεν σὺν Χριστῷ, πιστεύομεν ὅτι καὶ συζήσομεν αὐτῷ,
εἰδότες ὅτι Χριστὸς ἐγερθεὶς ἐκ νεκρῶν οὐκέτι ἀποθνήσκει, θάνατος αὐτοῦ οὐκέτι κυριεύει.
ὃ γὰρ ἀπέθανεν, τῇ ἁμαρτίᾳ ἀπέθανεν ἐφάπαξ·
ὃ δὲ ζῇ, ζῇ τῷ θεῷ.
οὕτως καὶ ὑμεῖς λογίζεσθε ἑαυτοὺς [εἶναι] νεκροὺς μὲν τῇ ἁμαρτίᾳ
ζῶντας δὲ τῷ θεῷ ἐν Χριστῷ Ἰησοῦ.

Μὴ οὖν βασιλευέτω ἡ ἁμαρτία ἐν τῷ θνητῷ ὑμῶν σώματι εἰς τὸ ὑπακούειν ταῖς ἐπιθυμίαις αὐτοῦ,

μηδὲ παριστάνετε τὰ μέλη ὑμῶν ὅπλα ἀδικίας τῇ ἁμαρτίᾳ,
ἀλλὰ παραστήσατε ἑαυτοὺς τῷ θεῷ ὡσεὶ ἐκ νεκρῶν
ζῶντας
καὶ τὰ μέλη ὑμῶν ὅπλα δικαιοσύνης τῷ θεῷ.
ἁμαρτία γὰρ ὑμῶν οὐ κυριεύσει·
οὐ γάρ ἐστε ὑπὸ νόμον ἀλλ' ὑπὸ χάριν.

VERSE 1

Τί οὖν ἐροῦμεν; (see 4:1)

ἐπιμένωμεν τῇ ἁμαρτίᾳ, ἵνα ἡ χάρις πλεονάσῃ;

A second rhetorical question follows the introductory question of general inference and specifies the issue at hand (Jewett 393). Ἐπιμένωμεν (1 pl. pres. act. subjunc. from ἐπιμένω, "continue") is a customary present and a deliberative subjunctive. Dunn suggests the translation "persist" (306; cf. BDAG 375d); Schreiner discusses the variant forms (327). The definite article occurs regularly with ἁμαρτία throughout the paragraph and highlights sin as a power (cf. Schreiner 304); the dative denotes sphere. Ἵνα + subjunctive indicates purpose (Moule 143); see 5:20 for πλεονάζω; the aorist is constative. The article accompanies the abstract noun χάρις.

VERSE 2

μὴ γένοιτο (see 3:4)

οἵτινες ἀπεθάνομεν τῇ ἁμαρτίᾳ, πῶς ἔτι ζήσομεν ἐν αὐτῇ;

The indefinite relative pronoun οἵτινες is generic, denoting those who share an essential quality (Jewett 395); Moo suggests "we who are of such a nature" (357 n. 24). The clause it introduces functions adverbially to indicate cause (Wallace 662; R 728; cf. Longenecker 611); placing the clause at the beginning of the question gives it emphasis (298). Ἀπεθάνομεν (1 pl. aor. act. indic. of ἀποθνῄσκω, "die") is a constative aorist. The dative ἁμαρτίᾳ has been understood as reference (Wallace 140; Porter 98), respect (Jewett 395), advantage (Longenecker 611), disadvantage (Moo 357 n. 25), or possession (Schreiner 327); reference/respect is most likely. Ζήσομεν (1 pl. fut. act. indic. of ζάω, "live") is a deliberative future; Schreiner discusses the variant subjunctive form (327). Ἐν + dative could be location (Jewett 396) or, more likely, standard (cf. Wallace 372). In either event, the possibility of living a sinful lifestyle is one to be avoided.

VERSE 3

ἢ ἀγνοεῖτε ὅτι, ὅσοι ἐβαπτίσθημεν εἰς Χριστὸν Ἰησοῦν, εἰς τὸν θάνατον αὐτοῦ ἐβαπτίσθημεν;

Ἀγνοέω occurs five other times in Romans, three times as part of a disclosure formula (1:13; 7:1; 11:25). The formula ("or are you being ignorant") implies that the readers are likely to know the information (Cranfield 300), but it also suggests there is a further element to understand (Dunn 308; Jewett 396). Ἢ is disjunctive ("or"), and ὅτι ("that") introduces the object clause of the verb ἀγνοεῖτε. The correlative pronoun ὅσοι (nom. pl. masc. of ὅσος, -η, -ον) is quantitative ("as many of us as"). Ἐβαπτίσθημεν (1 pl. aor. pass. indic. of βαπτίζω, "baptize") is an ingressive aorist, denoting entrance into a state; the passive is a divine passive (Dunn 311). Harris argues that εἰς Χριστὸν Ἰησοῦν ("into Christ Jesus") is equivalent to εἰς τὸ ὄνομα τοῦ Χριστοῦ (229; cf. Cranfield 301), which occurs in Matthew 28:19; Acts 8:16; 19:5. Although Moo argues that the phrase denotes spatial union (360), Harris's conclusion that it denotes relationship and belonging is more persuasive. Εἰς τὸν θάνατον αὐτοῦ ("into his death") more clearly points to the benefits of Christ's death (Cranfield 303) and is reminiscent of Galatians 2:20 and Philippians 3:10. Schreiner provides an extended discussion of baptism as it relates to this passage (306–10), and Dunn ably refutes any connection to the mystery cults (308–11; see also Cranfield 301–302).

VERSE 4

συνετάφημεν οὖν αὐτῷ διὰ τοῦ βαπτίσματος εἰς τὸν θάνατον

Paul now states the logical inference (οὖν) from his preceding questions. Metzger gives οὖν an {A} rating because of its strong manuscript support (453). Συνετάφημεν (1 pl. aor. pass. indic. from συνθάπτω, "bury together with"; cf. Col 2:12) is an ingressive aorist and a simple passive. The συν- prefix denotes association and explains the dative of αὐτῷ, which refers back to Χριστὸν Ἰησοῦν in verse 3. Διά + genitive indicates intermediate agency; the article with βαπτίσματος is anaphoric, referring back to ἐβαπτίσθημεν in verse 3 (Wallace 219; Moo 361 n. 46); Jewett translates it as an unemphatic possessive pronoun ("through our death," 398). See verse 3 for εἰς τὸν θάνατον; the article is anaphoric and possessive ("into his death"); the phrase modifies βάπτισμα (Moo 361 n. 46).

ἵνα ὥσπερ ἠγέρθη Χριστὸς ἐκ νεκρῶν διὰ τῆς δόξης τοῦ πατρός

The conjunction ἵνα marks the purpose of being buried with Christ (Cranfield 304). The correlative pair ὥσπερ . . . οὕτως καί was a regular feature of the preceding paragraph (5:12, 18, 19, 21). Moo concludes that ὥσπερ carries a causal sense in this context (357). Ἠγέρθη (3 sg. aor. pass. indic. of ἐγείρω, "raise") is a constative aorist and a divine passive (cf. 4:25). Χριστός is a nominative of subject; ἐκ + genitive denotes separation; διά + genitive indicates the efficient cause of Christ's resurrection (Jewett 399). The phrase τῆς δόξης τοῦ πατρός is monadic, denoting "one of a kind"; in a genitive phrase both nouns either have or lack the article; πατρός is a possessive genitive. Δόξα is the power of God that accomplished the resurrection (Schreiner 311; cf. Phil 3:21; Col 1:11).

οὕτως καὶ ἡμεῖς ἐν καινότητι ζωῆς περιπατήσωμεν

Ἡμεῖς is emphatic and provides subject focus; ἐν + dative indicates sphere (cf. BDAG 803d). Καινότης, -ητος, ἡ is distinct from νέος (Cranfield 305) and denotes "newness with a connotation of something extraordinary" (BDAG 497b). Ζωῆς is an attributed genitive (Wallace 90; cf. Schreiner 311) and should be translated adjectivally as "new life" (cf. R 493). Περιπατήσωμεν (1 pl. aor. act. subjunc. of περιπατέω, "walk") is an ingressive aorist (R 850) and a subjunctive of purpose. Jewett writes that the verb is a "characteristic term for ethical behavior" (399); Cranfield provides OT background (305).

VERSE 5

εἰ γὰρ σύμφυτοι γεγόναμεν τῷ ὁμοιώματι τοῦ θανάτου αὐτοῦ

Γάρ ("for") introduces the first explanation of what it means to die and rise with Christ. Εἰ + indicative is a first class condition (Moo 368 n. 77); γεγόναμεν (1 pl. pf. act. indic. of dep. γίνομαι, "be") is an intensive perfect emphasizing the resulting state (Dunn 316). Σύμφυτοι (nom. pl. masc. of σύμφυτος, -ον, "united with") should be understood as "united with" (e.g., ESV, NIV) rather than "planted with" (KJV). The συν- prefix denotes association (R 528), which explains the dative that follows as the object with which we have been united (Moo 368; cf. Dunn 316). Moo argues that ὁμοίωμα is best understood as "form" and that the sense is close to "conformity" in Romans 8:29 and Philippians 3:10, 21 (368–70). The genitive τοῦ θανάτου αὐτοῦ is comparison.

ἀλλὰ καὶ τῆς ἀναστάσεως ἐσόμεθα

Ἀλλά is emphatic ("indeed"), and καί is adjunctive ("also"). It is most natural to understand σύμφυτοι τῷ ὁμοιώματι before τῆς ἀναστάσεως (comparative gen.). The article with ἀναστάσεως is a mild possessive pronoun ("his resurrection"). Ἐσόμεθα (1 pl. fut. mid. indic. of εἰμί) is a genuine future (Schreiner 312) and a deponent middle.

VERSE 6

τοῦτο γινώσκοντες ὅτι ὁ παλαιὸς ἡμῶν ἄνθρωπος συνεσταυρώθη

Τοῦτο is accusative as the object of the participle and points forward to the ὅτι clause of content (Wallace 333). Γινώσκοντες (nom. pl. masc. of pres. act. ptc. of γινώσκω, "know") is adverbial of cause (R 1128) and introduces shared knowledge (Jewett 402). Placing παλαιὸς ἡμῶν between the article and ἄνθρωπος gives greater emphasis to the adjective. "Our old man" (cf. Eph 4:22–24; Col 3:9–11) describes who we were in Adam prior to conversion (Schreiner 307; Dunn 318). Συνεσταυρώθη (3 sg. aor. pass. indic. of συσταυρόω, "crucify together with") is a constative aorist describing a decisive event (Dunn 319), and absence of an agent with the passive voice keeps the focus on the subject. The συν- prefix continues the close association of believers with Christ (cf. Gal 2:19).

ἵνα καταργηθῇ τὸ σῶμα τῆς ἁμαρτίας

The purpose (ἵνα) of being crucified with Christ is that "the sinful body might be rendered ineffective." See 3:4, 31; 4:14 for καταργηθῇ (3 sg. aor. pass. subjunc. of καταργέω). The aorist is again constative; the absence of an agent again keeps the focus on the subject. Τὸ σῶμα τῆς ἁμαρτίας denotes the whole person as controlled by sin (Cranfield 309); ἁμαρτίας is an attributed genitive (Wallace 87).

τοῦ μηκέτι δουλεύειν ἡμᾶς τῇ ἁμαρτίᾳ

Although Cranfield and others understand τοῦ + infinitive as purpose, Turner views it as result (141), which seems more likely as the consequence of the preceding purpose clause. Δουλεύειν (pres. act. infin. of δουλεύω, "serve") is a customary present; the verb carries the idea of conducting oneself in total service to another (BDAG 259d). Ἡμᾶς (acc. pl.) is the subject of the infinitive; τῇ ἁμαρτίᾳ is a dative of the direct object.

VERSE 7

ὁ γὰρ ἀποθανὼν δεδικαίωται ἀπὸ τῆς ἁμαρτίας

Γάρ ("for") introduces a gnomic explanation of the preceding sentence (Moo 376; Jewett 404). The substantival participle ὁ ἀποθανών (nom. sg. masc. of aor. act. ptc. of ἀποθνῄσκω, "die") gathers up the idea of dying with Christ. Δεδικαίωται (3 sg. pf. pass. indic. of δικαιόω, "declare righteous") is a divine passive. The idea is more likely "has been declared righteous" (cf. Stott 177; Cranfield 311 n. 1) than "has been set free" (cf. Moo 377), since Paul uses ἐλευθερόω in 6:15–23 for the latter idea. The idea of being declared right in regard to something (ἀπό + gen.) occurs elsewhere in Acts 13:38 (cf. Sir 26:29; TSim 6:1).

VERSE 8

εἰ δὲ ἀπεθάνομεν σὺν Χριστῷ

The transitional δέ ("now") introduces a second explanation of what it means to die and rise with Christ. Although 𝔓[46] replaces δέ with γάρ, Moo concludes that the manuscript evidence is "too slight" to support that variant reading (353 n. 9). The first class condition (εἰ + indic.) parallels the same construction at the beginning of verse 5 and might provide a reason for a scribe to insert γάρ and bring the clause into agreement with the earlier verse. Ἀπεθάνομεν (1 pl. aor. act. indic. of ἀποθνῄσκω) is a constative aorist summarizing the events of Christ's crucifixion (6:6), death (6:5), and burial (6:4). Σὺν Χριστῷ makes explicit the association already present in the συν- compounds of verses 4–6.

πιστεύομεν ὅτι καὶ συζήσομεν αὐτῷ

Πιστεύομεν (1 pl. pres. act. indic. of πιστεύω, "believe") is a customary present and points to unbroken confident trust. Ὅτι ("that") introduces indirect discourse (R 872); καί is adjunctive ("also"). Συζήσομεν (1 pl. fut. act. indic. of συζάω, "live together with") is a genuine future (Schreiner 320; cf. Moo 377) and the fourth συν-compound in the paragraph, which explains the associative dative of αὐτῷ. The pronoun is anaphoric, pointing back to Christ in the preceding clause.

VERSE 9

εἰδότες ὅτι Χριστὸς ἐγερθεὶς ἐκ νεκρῶν οὐκέτι ἀποθνῄσκει

Εἰδότες (nom. pl. masc. of pf. act. ptc. of οἶδα, "know") is adverbial of cause (R 1128; Schreiner 320; Moo 378 n. 136; contra Cranfield 313); the perfect is used as a present (Wallace 631). With ὅτι of content the phrase introduces something that is common knowledge (Dunn 322; cf. 5:3; 6:3, 6). The participle ἐγερθείς (nom. sg. masc. of aor. pass. ptc. of ἐγείρω) is adverbial of cause ("after Christ was raised," Jewett 390); the aorist is constative; the passive is a divine passive. Ἐκ νεκρῶν describes separation (cf. v.4); ἀποθνῄσκει is a futuristic present (Wallace 536).

θάνατος αὐτοῦ οὐκέτι κυριεύει

Θάνατος is a nominative of subject; αὐτοῦ is a genitive of direct object. Κυριεύει (3 sg. pres. act. indic. of κυριεύω) is a gnomic present; the verb denotes the exercise of authority or control over someone or something (BDAG 576c).

VERSE 10

ὃ γὰρ ἀπέθανεν, τῇ ἁμαρτίᾳ ἀπέθανεν ἐφάπαξ

Γάρ ("for") introduces another gnomic explanation similar to verse 7 (Jewett 407). The relative pronoun ὅ (acc. sg. neut.) stands for τὸν θάνατον ὅν (Cranfield 313) and is the object of ἀπέθανεν (e.g., ESV: "the death he died"). Τῇ ἁμαρτίᾳ is a dative of reference (R 541; T 238; Moule 46); commentators uniformly connect it with the second occurrence of ἀπέθανεν. The adverb ἐφάπαξ ("once for all") occurs elsewhere in Hebrews 7:27; 9:12, 26, 28; 10:10; and 1 Peter 3:18. It denotes something that takes place "once for all and never again" (BDAG 417d).

ὃ δὲ ζῇ, ζῇ τῷ θεῷ

Christ's life stands in contrast (δέ) to his death. He died (aorist tense) "to sin," but he lives (present tense) "to God" (τῷ θεῷ). His death will never be repeated ("once for all"), but his life continues forever.

VERSE 11

οὕτως καὶ ὑμεῖς λογίζεσθε ἑαυτοὺς [εἶναι] νεκροὺς μὲν τῇ ἁμαρτίᾳ

Although the adverb οὕτως usually indicates manner ("in this way"), both Cranfield (315) and Schreiner (300) view it as inferential here ("so then"). Καί is adjunctive ("also"), and ὑμεῖς provides subject focus. Although Jewett understands λογίζεσθε as indicative (408), it is more likely imperative (Cranfield 315). The present tense is progressive (Moo 380; Dunn 323; contra Wallace 525); the middle form is deponent. See 3:28 for λογίζομαι. The reflexive pronoun ἑαυτούς (acc. 3 pl.) is the object in a double accusative construction (BDF §157.3); the use of the third person pronoun with a second person verb is a common idiom (R 689). Schreiner notes that the manuscript evidence for εἶναι is ambiguous, but the sense is the same whether it is included or omitted (327). The correlative μέν introduces the first of two complements. The anarthrous adjective νεκρούς (acc. pl. masc.) is qualitative; τῇ ἁμαρτίᾳ is a dative of reference (Wallace 146).

ζῶντας δὲ τῷ θεῷ ἐν Χριστῷ Ἰησοῦ

The correlative δέ introduces the second complement. The participle ζῶντας (acc. pl. masc. of pres. act. ptc. of ζάω) is adjectival and should be translated "alive" (e.g., ESV). Τῷ θεῷ is a second dative of reference. Ἐν Χριστῷ Ἰησοῦ is the second of thirteen occurrences of "in Christ" in Romans (cf. 3:24; 6.23; 8:1, 2, 39; 9:1; 12:5; 15:17; 16:3, 7, 9, 10). Harris argues that the phrase is causal ("because of your union with Christ," 124). Dunn identifies three senses of the phrase: being in Christ, doing something in Christ, and redemptive power enacted in Christ (324); the third sense is in view here. The longer variant that includes τῷ κυρίῳ ἡμῶν is supported by 𝔓[94], א, C, and 33, but there would be no apparent reason to delete it if it were original. It most likely reflects assimilation to 5:1, 21; 6:33. Moo describes it as "surely secondary" (353 n. 10).

VERSE 12

Μὴ οὖν βασιλευέτω ἡ ἁμαρτία ἐν τῷ θνητῷ ὑμῶν σώματι

For Paul, the truth of our dying and rising with Christ leads logically (οὖν) to a call to action (Jewett 408). The negative particle μή with βασιλευέτω (3 sg. pres. act. impv. of βασιλεύω, "rule") forms a prohibition (cf. Wallace 487). See 5:14 for βασιλεύω. Jewett (408) and Blass (§513.3.2) agree that the present imperative states a general command/prohibition. Moo suggests "make it your practice not to . . ." and has a balanced discussion of the present and aorist imperatives (382 n. 154). Cranfield writes that Paul calls his readers to "revolt in the name of their rightful ruler, God, against sin's usurping rule" (316). Ἐν + dative denotes sphere; τῷ θνητῷ ὑμῶν σώματι ("your mortal body") describes the whole person as vulnerable to the power of sin (Dunn 336); placing the adjective in the first attributive position gives it emphasis.

εἰς τὸ ὑπακούειν ταῖς ἐπιθυμίαις αὐτοῦ

Of the three textual variants, ταῖς ἐπιθυμίαις αὐτοῦ has strong Alexandrian manuscript support (𝔓[94], ℵ, A, B, C*) and understands σώματι as the antecedent of αὐτοῦ. Metzger gives it a {B} rating (454). The second reading (αὐτῇ) is supported by 𝔓[46] and Western manuscripts (D, G); it understands ἁμαρτία as the antecedent. The third reading is supported by Byzantine manuscripts and conflates the other two; Schreiner considers it "the most improbable" (328).

The result (εἰς τό + inf.; cf. R 1090) of living under sin's rule is obedience to the body's lusts. Wallace understands the present tense of the infinitive as gnomic (535). Ὑπακούω occurs eleven times in Romans and eleven times elsewhere in Paul (Dunn 336); it describes the act of complying with a set of instructions (BDAG 1029a). Ταῖς ἐπιθυμίαις is a dative of direct object; the article regularly accompanies a noun with a possessive pronoun (αὐτοῦ). See 1:24 for ἐπιθυμία.

VERSE 13

μηδὲ παριστάνετε τὰ μέλη ὑμῶν ὅπλα ἀδικίας τῇ ἁμαρτίᾳ

Μηδέ with παριστάνετε (2 pl. pres. act. impv. of παριστάνω, "put at one's disposal") is a second prohibition (T 76); the present tense is customary and describes an action Paul expects to occur regularly; παριστάνω is a later form of παρίστημι (BDAG 778a). Τὰ μέλη ὑμῶν ("your members") is the object of an object-complement double accusative and denotes any natural capacity (Cranfield 317). The anarthrous ὅπλα (acc. pl. neut. of ὅπλον, -ου, τό, "instrument") is qualitative and is the complement to μέλη. It can describe any instrument or tool one uses to prepare or make something ready (BDAG 716d); Jewett suggests the translation "weapons" (410). Ἀδικίας (gen. sg. fem.) is an objective genitive describing the purpose for which the "weapons" are used (Moo 385 n. 170; Cranfield 318); τῇ ἁμαρτίᾳ is a pure dative of indirect object.

ἀλλὰ παραστήσατε ἑαυτοὺς τῷ θεῷ ὡσεὶ ἐκ νεκρῶν ζῶντας

Ἀλλά ("but") establishes a strong contrast with μηδέ in the preceding clause. Παραστήσατε (2 pl. aor. act. impv. of παρίστημι) is an ingressive aorist (Wallace 720; BDF §337.1) and an imperative of command. Ἑαυτούς is the direct object, and τῷ θεῷ is a pure dative of indirect object. The particle ὡσεί ("as") is comparative (R 968, 1140), although it probably has a causal nuance here ("since you are"; cf. Moo 385 n. 177). Ἐκ νεκρῶν indicates separation; ζῶντας (acc. pl. masc. of pres. act. ptc. of ζάω) is an adjectival participle and should be translated "alive" (cf. v. 11).

καὶ τὰ μέλη ὑμῶν ὅπλα δικαιοσύνης τῷ θεῷ

The continuative καί adds a double accusative that parallels the construction in the first clause of the verse. In this clause, the objective genitive δικαιοσύνης replaces ἀδικίας, and the pure dative τῷ θεῷ replaces τῇ ἁμαρτίᾳ. See above for the analysis.

VERSE 14

ἁμαρτία γὰρ ὑμῶν οὐ κυριεύσει

The reason (*γάρ*) we should present ourselves to God rather than to sin is that sin is not our ruler. The absence of the article with *ἁμαρτία* differs from the pattern in the rest of the paragraph. The noun still denotes sin as a power (T 177), although with a qualitative nuance (Moo 387 n. 184). Ὑμῶν is a genitive of direct object with *κυριεύσει* (3 sg. fut. act. indic. of *κυριεύω*; cf. v. 9). Cranfield sets out four possible interpretations of this clause and concludes it is a promise that sin will no longer "be lord," because as Christ's subjects believers now have the resources "to fight against sin's usurped power and to demonstrate their true allegiance" (319).

οὐ γάρ ἐστε ὑπὸ νόμον ἀλλ' ὑπὸ χάριν

Paul adds an explanation (*γάρ*) that focuses on eras rather than on rulers and uses the strong contrast between law and grace established by *οὐ . . . ἀλλά* ("not . . . but"). Ὑπό + accusative denotes subordination; Harris suggests "under the rule of" (221). Both *νόμον* and *χάριν* are definite as objects of prepositions, and Robertson notes that words in pairs are often anarthrous (793). Νόμος refers to the Mosaic law (R 796), and Schreiner argues that it refers to the Mosaic era as a whole (326; cf. Moo 389). It is possible, therefore, to conclude that the contrast points to the two eras of salvation history: the era of the old covenant, administered according to law and characterized by sin and death, and the era of the new covenant, administered according to grace and characterized by righteousness and life. The individual who has exercised faith has been transferred from the former era to the latter.

FOR FURTHER STUDY

44. Baptism (6:3)

Beasley-Murray, G. R. *DPL* 60–66.

________. *NIDNTT* 1.144–50.

________. *Baptism in the New Testament*. Grand Rapids: Eerdmans, 1962.

Bieder, W. *EDNT* 1.192–96.

Bornkamm, G. "Taufe und neues Leben bei Paulus (Röm. 6)." Pages 34–50 in *Das Endes des Gesetzes: Paulusstudien*. Munich: Kaiser, 1958.

Bridge, D., and D. Phypers. *The Water That Divides: The Baptism Debate*. Downers Grove, IL: InterVarsity, 1977.

Carlson, R. P. "The Role of Baptism in Paul's Thought." *Int* 47 (1993): 255–66.

Dockery, D. S. *DJG*. First edition. 55–58.

Dunn, J. D. G. "Baptism and the Unity of the Church in the New Testament." Pages 78–103 in *Baptism and the Unity of the Church*. Edited by M. Root and R. Saarinen. Grand Rapids: Eerdmans, 1998.

Fape, M. O. *Paul's Concept of Baptism and Its Present Implications for Believers: Walking in the Newness of Life*. Lewiston, NY: Mellen, 1999.

Ferguson, E. *DJG*. Second edition. 66–69.

________. *Baptism in the Early Church: History, Theology, and Liturgy in the First Five Centuries*. Grand Rapids: Eerdmans, 2008.
Hammett, J. S. *40 Questions about Baptism and the Lord's Supper*. Grand Rapids: Kregel, 2015.
Hartman, L. *ABD* 1.583–94.
________. *"Into the Name of the Lord Jesus": Baptism in the Early Church*. Edinburgh: T&T Clark, 1997.
Jeremias, J. *Infant Baptism in the First Four Centuries*. Translated by D. Cairns. Philadelphia: Westminster, 1960.
Jewett, P. K. *Infant Baptism and the Covenant of Grace*. Grand Rapids: Eerdmans, 1978.
Moody, D. *Baptism: Foundation for Christian Unity*. Philadelphia: Westminster, 1967.
Murray, J. *Christian Baptism*. Grand Rapids: Baker, 1952.
Oepke, A. *TDNT* 1.529–46.
Petersen, A. K. "Shedding New Light on Paul's Understanding of Baptism: A Ritual-Theoretical Approach to Romans 6." *Studia Theologica* 52 (1998): 3–28.
Porter, S. E., and A. R. Cross, eds. *Baptism, the New Testament, and the Church*. Sheffield: Academic Press, 1999.
Schnabel, E. "The Meaning of βαπτίζειν in Greek, Jewish, and Patristic Literature." *FilNeot* 44 (2011): 3–40.
Schnackenburg, R. *Baptism in the Thought of St. Paul: A Study in Pauline Theology*. Translated by G. R. Beasley-Murray. Oxford: Blackwell, 1964.
Schreiner, T. R., and D. W. Shawn, eds. *Believer's Baptism: Sign of the New Covenant in Christ*. Nashville: B&H, 2006.
Silva, M. *NIDNTTE* 1.460–67.
Wagner, G. *Pauline Baptism and the Pagan Mysteries: The Problem of the Pauline Doctrine of Baptism in Romans VI.1–11, in the Light of Its Religio-Historical "Parallels."* Translated by J. P. Smith. Edinburgh: Burns & Oates, 1967.
Wedderburn, A. J. M. *Baptism and Resurrection: Studies in Pauline Theology against Its Graeco-Roman Background*. Tübingen: Mohr Siebeck, 1987.

45. "With Christ" (6:8)

Callan, T. *Dying and Rising with Christ: The Theology of Paul the Apostle*. Mahway, NJ: Paulist, 2006.
Gaffin, R. B. "Union with Christ: Some Biblical and Theological Reflections." Pages 271–88 in *Always Reforming*. Edited by A. T. B. McGowan. Downers Grove, IL: InterVarsity, 2006.
Garcia, M. A. "Imputation and the Christology of Union with Christ: Calvin, Osiander, and the Contemporary Quest for a Reformed Model." *WTJ* 68 (2006): 219–51.
Grundmann, W. *TDNT* 7.781–94.
Harris, M. J. *NIDNTT* 3.1206–07.
Harvey, J. D. "The 'With Christ' Motif in Paul's Thought." *JETS* 35 (1992): 329–40.
Lohmeyer, E. "Syn Christō." Pages 218–57 in *Festgabe für Adolf Deissmann*. Edited by K. L. Schmidt. Tübingen: Mohr, 1927.
Moo, D. J. "Paul's 'With Christ' Conception." Pages 391–95 in *The Epistle to the Romans*. Grand Rapids: Eerdmans, 1996.
Schnackenburg, R. *Baptism in the Thought of St. Paul: A Study in Pauline Theology*. Translated by G. R. Beasley-Murray. Oxford: Blackwell, 1964.
Schweizer, E. "Dying and Rising with Christ." *NTS* 14 (1967–68): 1–14.

Smedes, L. B. *All Things Made New: A Theology of Man's Union with Christ*. Grand Rapids: Eerdmans, 1970.

Tannehill, R. C. *Dying and Rising with Christ: A Study in Pauline Theology*. Berlin: Töpelmann, 1967.

Wedderburn, A. J. M. "Some Observations on Paul's Use of the Phrases 'In Christ' and 'With Christ.'" *JSNT* 25 (1985): 83–97.

HOMILETICAL SUGGESTIONS

Dead to Sin; Alive to God (6:1–14)

1. Introduction (τί οὖν ἐροῦμεν, 6:1–4)
   a. False conclusion: Continue in sin to increase grace (6:1)
   b. Emphatic rejection: Cannot live in sin when dead to it (6:2)
   c. Theological truth: Buried with Christ to walk in new life (6:3–4)
2. First Explanation: United in the likeness of Christ's death (γάρ, 6:5–7)
   a. Premise: Old man was crucified with Christ (6:6a)
      1) Purpose: To render the sinful body ineffective (6:6b)
         a) Result: To stop serving sin (6:6c)
   b. Principle: Death declares righteous from sin (6:7)
3. Second Explanation: Will live with Christ (δέ, 6:8–11)
   a. Premise: Death no longer rules Christ (6:9b)
      1) Time: After raised from the dead (6:9a)
   b. Principle: Christ died to sin and lives to God (6:10)
   c. Command: Consider selves dead to sin and alive to God (6:11)
4. Application (οὖν, 6:12–14)
   a. Prohibition: Sin must not reign (6:12)
   b. Prohibition: Do not present members to sin and unrighteousness (6:13a)
   c. Command: Present members to God and righteousness (6:13b)
   d. Rationale: Under grace, not law (6:14)

Our Union "With Christ" (6:4–8)

1. Crucified with him (6:6)
2. Died with him (6:8)
3. Buried with him (6:4)
4. Made alive with him (6:8)

b. By Serving Our New Master (6:15–23)

STRUCTURE

Paul again uses a double question to raise a possible false conclusion from what he has just written (6:15a). After an emphatic denial (6:15b), he uses a third question to introduce a general teaching on obedience and slavery (6:16). He develops that teaching in two parts. The first sets out the change in status that takes place at conversion and the conduct that should result from that change (6:17–19). The second contrasts the two "slaveries" and ends with an antithetical summary statement that concludes the entire chapter (6:20–23).

Τί οὖν;
ἁμαρτήσωμεν, ὅτι οὐκ ἐσμὲν ὑπὸ νόμον ἀλλ' ὑπὸ χάριν;

μὴ γένοιτο.
οὐκ οἴδατε ὅτι ᾧ παριστάνετε ἑαυτοὺς δούλους εἰς ὑπακοήν,
δοῦλοί ἐστε ᾧ ὑπακούετε,
ἤτοι ἁμαρτίας εἰς θάνατον ἢ ὑπακοῆς εἰς δικαιοσύνην;

χάρις δὲ τῷ θεῷ ὅτι ἦτε δοῦλοι τῆς ἁμαρτίας
ὑπηκούσατε δὲ ἐκ καρδίας εἰς ὃν παρεδόθητε τύπον διδαχῆς,
ἐλευθερωθέντες δὲ ἀπὸ τῆς ἁμαρτίας ἐδουλώθητε τῇ δικαιοσύνῃ.
ἀνθρώπινον λέγω διὰ τὴν ἀσθένειαν τῆς σαρκὸς ὑμῶν.

ὥσπερ γὰρ	παρεστήσατε . . . τῇ ἀκαθαρσίᾳ καὶ τῇ ἀνομίᾳ	εἰς τὴν ἀνομίαν,
οὕτως νῦν	παραστήσατε . . . τῇ δικαιοσύνῃ	εἰς ἁγιασμόν.

ὅτε γὰρ δοῦλοι ἦτε τῆς ἁμαρτίας, ἐλεύθεροι ἦτε τῇ δικαιοσύνῃ.
τίνα οὖν καρπὸν εἴχετε τότε; ἐφ' οἷς νῦν ἐπαισχύνεσθε,
τὸ γὰρ τέλος ἐκείνων θάνατος.

νυνὶ δὲ ἐλευθερωθέντες ἀπὸ τῆς ἁμαρτίας δουλωθέντες δὲ τῷ θεῷ,
ἔχετε τὸν καρπὸν ὑμῶν εἰς ἁγιασμόν,
τὸ δὲ τέλος ζωὴν αἰώνιον.

τὰ γὰρ	ὀψώνια τῆς ἁμαρτίας	θάνατος,	
τὸ δὲ	χάρισμα τοῦ θεοῦ	ζωὴ αἰώνιος	ἐν Χριστῷ Ἰησοῦ τῷ κυρίῳ ἡμῶν.

VERSE 15

Τί οὖν; (See 4:1)

ἁμαρτήσωμεν, ὅτι οὐκ ἐσμὲν ὑπὸ νόμον ἀλλ' ὑπὸ χάριν;

Ἁμαρτήσωμεν (1 pl. aor. act. subjunc. of ἁμαρτάνω) is a deliberative subjunctive that parallels the rhetorical question in verse 1; the aorist is constative, describing sinning in general (Schreiner 329). Schreiner addresses the variant readings ἁμαρτήσομεν and ἡμαρτήσαμεν (341). Moo sees no significant difference between the present tense in verse one and the aorist tense in this verse (397 n. 5). The conjunction ὅτι is causal (Jewett 415). The remainder of the question repeats the final clause of verse 14, replacing ἐστε with ἐσμέν (1 pl. pres. act. indic. of εἰμί).

μὴ γένοιτο (See 3:4)

VERSE 16

οὐκ οἴδατε ὅτι ᾧ παριστάνετε ἑαυτοὺς δούλους εἰς ὑπακοήν

Οὐκ οἴδατε ὅτι ("are you not knowing that") is a disclosure formula that assumes a degree of common knowledge (cf. 6:9; 11:2). The relative pronoun ᾧ (dat. sg. masc.) has no expressed antecedent and introduces a clause EVV translate either as abverbial of condition (RSV, NEB, NJB, ESV, NET)* or time (NASB, NIV). Παριστάνετε is a customary present (cf. 6:13); ἑαυτοὺς δούλους is an object-complement double accusative; εἰς ὑπακοήν denotes result (cf. 1:16).

δοῦλοί ἐστε ᾧ ὑπακούετε

Δοῦλοί (nom. pl. masc.) is a predicate nominative; ᾧ introduces a relative clause that functions substantivally as the indirect object (R 720); ὑπακούετε (2 pl. pres. act. indic.) is a customary present.

ἤτοι ἁμαρτίας εἰς θάνατον ἢ ὑπακοῆς εἰς δικαιοσύνην

The inclusion of εἰς θάνατον is strongly supported by ℵ, A, B, C, and 33 and stands in parallel to εἰς δικαιοσύνην. Metzger concludes that the omission of the phrase in D and a few other manuscripts is an "unintentional oversight" (454). The paired disjunctives ἤτοι . . . ἤ ("whether . . . or") establish a correlation (T 334). Δοῦλοί should be understood before the subjective genitives ἁμαρτίας and ὑπακοῆς (Moo 399 n. 12). Εἰς + accusative establishes the contrasting results of being slaves of sin or obedience; θάνατος refers to ultimate condemnation while δικαιοσύνη refers to ultimate vindication (Schreiner 332).

VERSE 17

χάρις δὲ τῷ θεῷ ὅτι ἦτε δοῦλοι τῆς ἁμαρτίας

The adversative conjunction δέ makes it clear that believers are not neutral in regard to the question of whom they obey (Schreiner 333). Although χάρις is translated "thanks" in this context (cf. 7:25; 2 Cor 2:14; 8:16; 9:15), the word is a reminder that God's grace makes the change of masters possible. The verb ἔστω should be understood (Jewett 417); τῷ θεῷ is a pure dative of indirect object. Although EVV translate ὅτι as "that," it is causal and introduces the reason for giving thanks (Schreiner 334; cf. GNB; BDAG 1080c). The customary imperfect of ἦτε (2 pl. impf. act. indic. of εἰμί) indicates action in progress in the past (Wallace 548); Blass suggests "were then but no longer are" (§327). Δοῦλοί is a predicate nominative; the article with ἁμαρτίας is anaphoric; the genitive is subjective. Cranfield (323), Moo (400 n. 21), and Schreiner (334) all understand the clause as concessive (cf. GNB "though at one time you were slaves of sin").

ὑπηκούσατε δὲ ἐκ καρδίας εἰς ὃν παρεδόθητε τύπον διδαχῆς

Δέ is again adversative; ὑπηκούσατε (2 pl. aor. act. indic.) is a constative aorist; ἐκ + genitive indicates source; καρδίας is definite as the object of a preposition (R 792). The manuscripts that add καθαρᾶς probably reflect an assimilation to 1 Tim 1:5 and 2 Tim 2:22 (Schreiner 341; Jewett 413). The relative clause is awkward because it incorporates the antecedent and τύπον is attracted to the relative pronoun. Robertson suggests τῷ τύπῳ διδαχῆς εἰς ὃν παρεδόθη (719); Moo suggests τύπον διδαχῆς εἰς ὃν παρεδόθητε (400 n. 22). Blass notes that the sense is equivalent to ὃς παρεδόθη ὑμιν (§294.5), but that understanding seems to downplay Paul's focus on God's work in the believer's life. Schreiner concludes that "the clumsy syntax . . . is deliberate" to emphasize God's role (336), and Longenecker has an extended discussion (622–25). Παρεδόθητε (2 pl. aor. pass. indic.) is an ingressive aorist and a divine passive. See 1:24, 26, 28 for παραδίδωμι + εἰς. Τύπος, -ου, ὁ describes a model or pattern (cf. BDAG 1020a); διδαχῆς (gen. sg. fem.) describes the source from which the model is derived (Schreiner 336).

VERSE 18

ἐλευθερωθέντες δὲ ἀπὸ τῆς ἁμαρτίας ἐδουλώθητε τῇ δικαιοσύνῃ

The continuative δέ reinforces the previous idea. Ἐλευθερωθέντες (nom. pl. masc. of aor. pass. ptc. of ἐλευθερόω, "set free") is adverbial of time (contra Longenecker who argues for attendent circumstance, 625) and a divine passive. The verb suggests being freed from domination (BDAG 317b); Robertson notes that it always occurs with ἀπό to denote separation (518). Ἐδουλώθητε (2 pl. aor. pass. indic. of δουλόω, "enslave") is an ingressive aorist and a divine passive. The verb describes the act of making someone subservient to another's intersts (BDAG 260d). Elsewhere, the enslavement is to

God (6:22) and the elementary principles of the world (Gal 4:3); here, it is to righteousness (dat. of advantage).

VERSE 19

ἀνθρώπινον λέγω διὰ τὴν ἀσθένειαν τῆς σαρκὸς ὑμῶν

Asyndeton marks the start of a parenthetical comment explaining why Paul uses the metaphor of slavery (Moo 403). Ἀνθρώπινον (acc. sg. neut.) is an adjective used adverbially; λέγω is an instantaneous present (cf. Wallace 517). NJB translates the first two words of the clause as "I am putting it in human terms." Διά + accusative indicates cause; ἀσθένεια, -ας, ἡ denotes weakness, inadequacy, or poor judgment (BADG 142c). The entire phrase ("the weakness of your flesh") describes the limitation of human understanding as the result of sin (Schreiner 333).

ὥσπερ γὰρ παρεστήσατε τὰ μέλη ὑμῶν δοῦλα τῇ ἀκαθαρσίᾳ καὶ τῇ ἀνομίᾳ εἰς τὴν ἀνομίαν

Paul now explains (γάρ) what it means to be enslaved to righteousness using a comparison (ὥσπερ) structured in two parallel lines—one using the indicative, the other using the imperative—and echoing the language of verse 13. Παρεστήσατε is a constative aorist describing past conduct as a whole (cf. Cranfield 326); τὰ μέλη ὑμῶν δοῦλα is an object-complement double accusative; καί links two datives of indirect object. See 1:24 for ἀκαθαρσία (sexual sin) and 4:7 for ἀνομία (sin in general). Εἰς + accusative denotes result ("which results in more lawlessness," NJB); the article with ἀνομίαν is generic, denoting the general condition produced by the specific acts (Jewett 420).

οὕτως νῦν παραστήσατε τὰ μέλη ὑμῶν δοῦλα τῇ δικαιοσύνῃ εἰς ἁγιασμόν

The corrollary (οὕτως) to the past is "now" (νῦν), which Cranfield calls "the time of opportunity and decision" (327); Longenecker highlights the eschatological aspect (626). Παραστήσατε is an imperative of command and an ingressive aorist; τὰ μέλη ὑμῶν δοῦλα repeats the double accusative of the previous line; τῇ δικαιοσύνῃ ("to righteousness") replaces uncleanness and lawlessness as the indirect object; the article accompanies the abstract noun. In contrast to ἀνομία, the result of believers presenting themselves to righteousness is ἁγιασμός ("sanctification"). Moo concludes that the word focuses on the process of becoming holy rather than on the final state of holiness (405).

VERSE 20

ὅτε γὰρ δοῦλοι ἦτε τῆς ἁμαρτίας, ἐλεύθεροι ἦτε τῇ δικαιοσύνῃ

The reason (γάρ) for presenting ourselves to righteousness rather than to sin lies in the consequences of obeying the two masters. "When you were slaves of sin" (ὅτε . . . δοῦλοι ἦτε τῆς ἁμαρτίας) echoes verse 17 and begins to develop the consequences of the preconversion pattern of conduct described in verse 19b. Paul will contrast the past with the present (νυνὶ δέ) in verse 22. The imperfect of both occurrences of ἦτε is again customary, and the genitive of ἁμαρτίας is again subjective. The predicate adjective ἐλεύθεροι (nom. pl. masc.) echoes the cognate verb in verse 18 (BDAG 317a); τῇ δικαιοσύνῃ is a dative of reference/respect (Moule 46; BDF §197).

VERSE 21

τίνα οὖν καρπὸν εἴχετε τότε; ἐφ' οἷς νῦν ἐπαισχύνεσθε,

UBS[5] and most commentators punctuate this line with a question mark after τότε (cf. Moo 406), but Schreiner's conclusion that a question mark after ἐπαισχύνεσθε makes better sense of the causal clause that follows is preferable (339; cf. Murray 236, KJV, RSV, NASB, GNB, NIV, ESV).

Used in a question, οὖν is more nearly transitional ("then") than logical ("therefore"). The interrogative pronoun τίνα (acc. sg. masc. of τίς, τί) is used adjectivally to modify καρπόν and has a qualitative nuance ("what sort of fruit"); see 1:13 for καρπός. Εἴχετε (2 pl. impf. act. indic. of ἔχω) is a customary imperfect; the temporal adverb τότε ("at that time") points to a time in the past (BDAG 1012d) and continues the time frame begun in verse 20. 'Επί + dative supplies the basis of the readers' shame; the prepositional phrase is abbreviated from ἐπί τούτοις ἐφ' οἷς (R 714, 721). 'Επαισχύνεσθε (2 pl. pres. mid. indic. of dep. ἐπαισχύνομαι, "be ashamed") is a progressive present and a deponent middle; the verb describes the experience of a loss of status because of some event or activity (BDAG 357d); Murray notes the psychological aspect present in this context (236). The adverb νῦν ("now") highlights the readers' present attitude toward their past conduct.

τὸ γὰρ τέλος ἐκείνων θάνατος

The reason (γάρ) for their shame is the ultimate consequence of their conduct. The article marks τέλος as the subject; the noun describes the final goal toward which something is directed (BDAG 999a). 'Εκείνων is a genitive of production ("the end brought about by those things"); the placement of the pronoun is emphatic (BDF §284.3). The verb ἐστίν is understood; θάνατος stands in antithesis to ζωὴν αἰώνιον in verse 23 and denotes future death.

VERSE 22

νυνὶ δὲ ἐλευθερωθέντες ἀπὸ τῆς ἁμαρτίας

"But now" (νυνὶ δέ) moves the discussion into the readers' post-conversion reality (cf. 3:21) and should be taken with the main verb (Cranfield 328). It introduces a restatement of verse 18 and begins to develop the consequences of the post-conversion pattern of conduct commanded in verse 19c. See 6:18 for ἐλευθερωθέντες ἀπὸ τῆς ἁμαρτίας.

δουλωθέντες δὲ τῷ θεῷ

The contrasting half of the statement (δέ) uses a second adverbial participle of time (nom. pl. masc. of aor. pass. ptc. of δουλόω) and τῷ θεῷ as the dative of reference. Moo notes that the aorist tense of both participles highlights the status believers attained in the past (407 n. 74).

ἔχετε τὸν καρπὸν ὑμῶν εἰς ἁγιασμόν

The progressive present of ἔχετε contrasts with the imperfect εἴχετε in verse 21, and "your fruit" (τὸν καρπὸν ὑμῶν) contrasts with shameful fruit in the same verse (Jewett 424). See 6:19 for εἰς ἁγιασμόν.

τὸ δὲ τέλος ζωὴν αἰώνιον

Δέ is continuative ("and"). See 6:21 for τὸ τέλος. The verb ἐστίν is understood. See 2:7 for ζωὴν αἰώνιον; Moo highlights the eschatological connotation (408 n. 78).

VERSE 23

τὰ γὰρ ὀψώνια τῆς ἁμαρτίας θάνατος

A carefully crafted summary statement provides a summary explanation (γάρ) of verses 20–22 and concludes the entire chapter. Ὀψώνιον, -ου, τό describes pay, wages, or compensation paid (BDAG 747a); see Jewett for the background (425). Τῆς ἁμαρτίας is a subjective genitive ("wages which sin pays," Cranfield 329); the verb ἐστίν is understood; θάνατος is a predicate nominative.

τὸ δὲ χάρισμα τοῦ θεοῦ ζωὴ αἰώνιος

In contrast (δέ) to the wages sin pays, God (subject. gen.) offers a "gift" (χάρισμα) that is freely and graciously given (Jewett 4:26; cf. 1:11). See 2:7 for ζωὴ αἰώνιος.

ἐν Χριστῷ Ἰησοῦ τῷ κυρίῳ ἡμῶν (See 5:1)

FOR FURTHER STUDY

46. Sanctification and Holiness (6:19, 22)

Alexander, D., ed. *Christian Spirituality: Five Views of Sanctification*. Downers Grove, IL: InterVarsity, 1988.

Berkhower, G. C. *Faith and Sanctification*. Translated by J. Vriend. Grand Rapids: Eerdmans, 1952.

Brady, P. J. *The Process of Sanctification in the Christian Life: An Exegetical-Theological Study of 1 Thess 4,1–8 and Rom 6,15–23*. Rome: Editrice Pontificia Università Gregoriana, 2008.

Combs, W. W. "Romans 12:1–2 and the Doctrine of Sanctification." *Detroit Baptist Seminary Journal* 11 (2006): 3–22.

Cranfield, C. E. B. "Paul's Teaching on Sanctification." *Reformed Review* 48 (1995): 217–29.
Dieter, M. E., et al. *Five Views of Sanctification*. Grand Rapids: Zondervan, 1987.
Earle, R. *Sanctification in the New Testament*. Kansas City, MO; Beacon Hill Press, 1988.
Katoppo, P. G. "Translating *Hagiasmos* 'Sanctification' in Paul's Letters." *Bible Translator* 38 (1987): 429–32.
Kinghorn, K. C. "Holiness: The Central Plan of God." *Evangelical Journal* 15 (1997): 57–70.
Klaiber, W. F. "Sanctification in the New Testament." *Asbury Theological Journal* 51 (1996): 11–21.
Mullen, B. A. *EDBT* 708–13.
Peterson, D. *Possessed by God: A New Testament Theology of Sanctification and Holiness*. Grand Rapids: Eerdmans, 1995.
Porter, S. E. *DPL* 397–402.
Procksch, O., and K. G. Kuhn. *TDNT* 1.88–115.
Purkeiser, W. T., et al. *Exploring Christian Holiness*. Three volumes. Kansas City, MO: Beacon Hill Press, 1983–85.
Raabe, P. R. "The Law and Christian Sanctification: A Look at Romans." *Concordia Journal* 22 (1996): 178–85.
Seebas, H., and C. Brown. *NIDNTT* 2.224–32.
White, R. E. O. *EDT* 969–71.

47. Honor and Shame in Paul's World (6:21)

Aalen, S. *NIDNTT* 2.48–52.
Bultmann, R. *TDNT* 1.189–91.
Corrigan, G. M. "Paul's Shame for the Gospel." *BTB* 16 (1986): 23–27.
deSilva, D. A. *DNTB* 518–22.
________. *Honor, Patronage, Kinship and Purity: Unlocking New Testament Culture*. Downers Grove, IL: InterVarsity, 2000.
________. *The Hope of Glory: Honor Discourse and New Testament Interpretation*. Collegeville, MN: Liturgical Press, 1999.
Domeris, W. R. "Honor and Shame in the New Testament." *Neot* 27 (1993): 283–97.
Georges, J. "From Shame to Honor: A Theological Reading of Romans for Honor-Shame Contexts." *Missiology* 38 (2010): 295–307.
Hellerman, J. H. *Reconstructing Honor in Roman Philippi*. Cambridge: Cambridge University Press, 2005.
Link, H.-G., and E. Tiedtke. *NIDNTT* 3.561–64.
Malina, B. J. and J. H. Neyrey. "Honor and Shame in Luke-Acts: Pivotal Values of the Mediterranean World." Pages 25–65 in *The Social World of Luke-Acts*. Edited by J. H. Neyrey. Peabody, MA: Hendrickson, 1991.
Moxnes, H. "Honor and Shame." Pages 19–40 in *The Social Sciences and New Testament Interpretation*. Edited by R. Rohrbaugh. Peabody, MA: Hendrickson, 1996.
________. "Honor and Shame: A Reader's Guide." *BTB* 23 (1993): 167–76.
________. "Honor and Righteousness in Romans." *JSNT* 21 (1988): 61–77.
________. "Honor, Shame and the Outside World in Paul's Letter to the Romans." Pages 207–18 in *The Social World of Formative Christianity and Judaism*. Edited by J. Neusner, et al. Philadelphia: Fortress, 1988.

Peristiany, J. G., ed. *Honor and Shame: The Values of Mediterranean Society*. London: Weidenfeld & Nicholson, 1965.
Pilch, J. J. "Honor/Shame." Pages 95–104 in *Biblical Social Values and Their Meaning*. Edited by J. J. Pilch and B. J. Malina. Peabody, MA: Hendrickson, 1993.
Schneider, J. *TDNT* 8.174–80.

HOMILETICAL SUGGESTIONS

Freed from Sin; Enslaved to God (6:15–23)

1. Introduction (τί οὖν, 6:15–16)
   a. False conclusion: Sin because under grace (6:15a)
   b. Emphatic negation: Never! (6:15b)
   c. Theological truth: Obedience reveals your master (6:16)
2. Change of masters (χάρις δὲ τῷ θεῷ, 6:17–19)
   a. Reason: Obeyed teaching to which delivered (6:17)
   b. Result: Freed from sin and enslaved to God (6:18)
   c. Response: Present members to righteousness (6:19)
3. Slaveries contrasted (6:20–23)
   a. Slaves of sin (ὅτε, 6:20–21)
      1) Status: Free regarding righteousness (6:20b)
      2) Fruit: Shame (6:21a)
      3) Ultimate end: Death (6:21b)
   b. Slaves of God (νυνὶ δέ, 6:22)
      1) Status: Free from sin (6:22a)
      2) Fruit: Sanctification (6:22c)
      3) Ultimate end: Life (6:22d)
   c. Summary (γάρ, 6:23)

Two Kinds of Slavery (6:19–22)

1. Sin's slavery
   a. Time: "Then" (6:21a)
   b. Status: Free from righteousness (6:20b)
   c. Conduct: Present members to uncleanness (6:19b)
   d. Result: Lawlessness (6:19b)
   e. End: Death (6:21b)
2. God's slavery
   a. Time: "Now" (6:22a)
   b. Status: Free from sin (6:22a)
   c. Conduct: Present members to righteousness (6:19c)
   d. Result: Sanctification (6:19c)
   e. End: Life (6:22d)

3. God's Righteousness Is Not Lived Out According to The Law (7:1–25)

a. Because Dying with Christ Brings Release from the Law (7:1–6)

STRUCTURE

Having raised the issue of the law in each of the four preceding chapters (3:19–21, 27–28, 31; 4:13–16; 5:13, 20; 6:14–15), Paul now turns to an extended discussion (7:1–25). In this first paragraph of the discussion, he explains how it is that believers are no longer "under law" (cf. 6:14). He begins with an analogy from marital law (7:1–3), which he then applies to himself and his readers (7:4–6). In developing that application, he contrasts the experience of living in the flesh (7:5) with the experience of living in the Spirit (7:6) and so previews the remainder of chapter 7 and the entirety of chapter 8.

Ἢ ἀγνοεῖτε, ἀδελφοί, γινώσκουσιν γὰρ νόμον λαλῶ,
ὅτι ὁ νόμος κυριεύει τοῦ ἀνθρώπου ἐφ' ὅσον χρόνον ζῇ;

ἡ γὰρ ὕπανδρος γυνὴ τῷ ζῶντι ἀνδρὶ δέδεται νόμῳ·
ἐὰν δὲ ἀποθάνῃ ὁ ἀνήρ, κατήργηται ἀπὸ τοῦ νόμου τοῦ ἀνδρός.

ἄρα οὖν ζῶντος τοῦ ἀνδρὸς μοιχαλὶς χρηματίσει ἐὰν γένηται ἀνδρὶ ἑτέρῳ·
ἐὰν δὲ ἀποθάνῃ ὁ ἀνήρ, ἐλευθέρα ἐστὶν ἀπὸ τοῦ νόμου,
τοῦ μὴ εἶναι αὐτὴν μοιχαλίδα γενομένην ἀνδρὶ ἑτέρῳ.

ὥστε, ἀδελφοί μου, καὶ ὑμεῖς ἐθανατώθητε τῷ νόμῳ διὰ τοῦ σώματος τοῦ Χριστοῦ,
εἰς τὸ γενέσθαι ὑμᾶς ἑτέρῳ, τῷ ἐκ νεκρῶν ἐγερθέντι,
ἵνα καρποφορήσωμεν τῷ θεῷ.

ὅτε γὰρ ἦμεν ἐν τῇ σαρκί, τὰ παθήματα τῶν ἁμαρτιῶν τὰ διὰ τοῦ νόμου ἐνηργεῖτο ἐν τοῖς μέλεσιν ἡμῶν,
εἰς τὸ καρποφορῆσαι τῷ θανάτῳ·
νυνὶ δὲ κατηργήθημεν ἀπὸ τοῦ νόμου ἀποθανόντες ἐν ᾧ κατειχόμεθα,
ὥστε δουλεύειν ἡμᾶς ἐν καινότητι πνεύματος καὶ οὐ παλαιότητι γράμματος.

VERSE 1

Ἢ ἀγνοεῖτε, ἀδελφοί

See 6:3 for ἢ ἀγνοεῖτε . . . ὅτι. The vocative ἀδελφοί signals the start of a new section (Schreiner 343; cf. 1:13); Jewett suggests that it softens the gentle reprimand implied by the question (430); Longenecker views it as introducing a specific message for Paul's Roman audience (631).

γινώσκουσιν γὰρ νόμον λαλῶ

An explanatory parenthesis (*γάρ*) addresses all who know the law (*νόμον*). Γινώσκουσιν (dat. pl. masc. of pres. act. ptc. of *γινώσκω*, "know") is a substantival participle functioning as the indirect object; the present tense is progressive. The verb itself indicates some measure of understanding (Cranfield 333). Although anarthrous, "law" is the Mosaic law (Dunn 359; Longenecker 631; Moo 412). Λαλῶ (1 sg. pres. act. indic. of *λαλέω*, "speak") is a progressive present.

ὅτι ὁ νόμος κυριεύει τοῦ ἀνθρώπου ἐφ' ὅσον χρόνον ζῇ;

The *ὅτι* is recitative (Longenecker 631); the article with *νόμος* is anaphoric. See 6:9 for *κυριεύω*; the present tense is gnomic. Ἀνθρώπου is a genitive of direct object; the article identifies a category ("a man"; cf. Porter 105). The prepositional phrase *ἐφ' ὅσον χρόνον* ("for as much time as") functions as a temporal conjunction (R 978); EVV translate the phrase "only as long as" (e.g., ESV). Ζῇ (3 sg. pres. act. indic. of *ζάω*) is a gnomic present. Similar expressions occur in 1 Corinthians 7:39 and Galatians 4:1.

VERSE 2

ἡ γὰρ ὕπανδρος γυνὴ τῷ ζῶντι ἀνδρὶ δέδεται νόμῳ

Paul explains (*γάρ*) the principle he has just stated with an example from Jewish marital law (Dunn 360; cf. Deut 24:1–4). The article with *γυνή* identifies a category (Porter 105); placing the adjective between the article and noun gives it emphasis. Ὕπανδρος, -ον describes being legally bound to a man in marriage (BDAG 1029b); EVV translate the phrase "a married woman" (e.g., NEB). The article marks *ζῶντι* (dat. sg. masc. of pres. act. ptc. of *ζάω*) as adjectival, modifying *ἀνδρί* ("to the living husband"). Δέδεται (3 sg. pf. pass. indic. of *δέω*, "bind") is a gnomic perfect that also emphasizes the resulting state (Wallace 581). The dative *νόμῳ* ("by law") identifies the instrument that binds.

ἐὰν δὲ ἀποθάνῃ ὁ ἀνήρ, κατήργηται ἀπὸ τοῦ νόμου τοῦ ἀνδρός

Death, however, provides the exception (*δέ*) to the rule. Ἐάν + subjunctive introduces a third class condition that is undetermined as to fulfillment (Wallace 688; R 1019); *ἀποθάνῃ* (3 sg. aor. act. subjunc. of *ἀποθνῄσκω*, "die") is a gnomic aorist. The article with *ἀνήρ* functions as a possessive pronoun ("her husband"; cf. Longenecker 633). Κατήργηται (3 sg. pf. pass. indic. of *καταργέω*, "be discharged/released") is a gnomic perfect; in this verse the passive voice describes the release of someone from an obligation (BDAG 526a; contrast 3:3, 31; 4:14; 6:6). Ἀπό + ablative denotes separation (cf. R 515); the article regularly appears with both nouns in genitive phrases (cf. Wallace 239). The genitive of *ἀνδρός* is objective (T 212); Cranfield discusses three interpretations and concludes that the phrase describes the law that binds the wife to the husband (333–34).

VERSE 3

ἄρα οὖν ζῶντος τοῦ ἀνδρὸς μοιχαλὶς χρηματίσει ἐὰν γένηται ἀνδρὶ ἑτέρῳ

See 5:18 for ἄρα οὖν (R 1192), which draws out the implications of verse 2; Longenecker suggests that it signals a conclusion and alerts to an implied application (633). Ζῶντος τοῦ ἀνδρός is a genitive absolute of time (Wallace 655); the article functions as a possessive pronoun ("while her husband is living"). Μοιχαλίς ("adulteress") is qualitative; Dunn suggests that the word reinforces the Jewish perspective of the legal discussion (360). Χρηματίσει (3 sg. fut. act. indic. of χρηματίζω, "have the name of") is a gnomic future (BDF §349.1). Ἐάν + subjunctive introduces another third class condition; γένηται (3 sg. aor. mid. subjunc. of dep. γίνομαι, "become") is a gnomic aorist; ἀνδρί is indefinite and a dative of possession (T 239). The phrase γίνομαι ἀνδρί occurs in the LXX with the idea of to "be married to" (Moo 413 n. 23; cf. Lev 22:12; Deut 24:2; Hos 3:3).

ἐὰν δὲ ἀποθάνῃ ὁ ἀνήρ, ἐλευθέρα ἐστὶν ἀπὸ τοῦ νόμου

Another third class condition (ἐάν + subjunc.) sets out a contrasting situation (δέ) in which the woman's husband dies (ἀποθάνῃ). The predicate adjective ἐλευθέρα (nom. sg. fem.) is placed first for emphasis; ἀπό + ablative is common with ἐλεύθερος, -α, -ον to denote separation (T 215); the article with νόμου is anaphoric.

τοῦ μὴ εἶναι αὐτὴν μοιχαλίδα γενομένην ἀνδρὶ ἑτέρῳ

Τοῦ + infinitive states the result (Moule 128); μή is expected with the infinitive; αὐτήν (acc. sg. fem.) is the subject of the infinitive (Wallace 195); μοιχαλίδα is a predicate accusative (Wallace 192). Γενομένην (acc. sg. fem. of aor. mid. ptc. of dep. γίνομαι) is an adverbial participle of condition (Wallace 653); the aorist tense is gnomic. See above for ἀνδρὶ ἑτέρῳ.

VERSE 4

ὥστε, ἀδελφοί μου, καὶ ὑμεῖς ἐθανατώθητε τῷ νόμῳ διὰ τοῦ σώματος τοῦ Χριστοῦ

Paul draws a conclusion (ὥστε) from the principle stated in verse 1 and illustrated in verses 2–3 (Schreiner 345) and states his central point in the paragraph: death severs the relationship between a person and the law (Moo 414). See verse 1 for ἀδελφοί. Καί ("also") connects the clause to verses 2–3, but with a different focus (ὑμεῖς). The aorist of ἐθανατώθητε marks a single event in the past (Jewett 433); the divine passive emphasizes God's role in the action (Cranfield 336); θανατόω ("put to death") is somewhat stronger than ἀποθνήσκω (Dunn 361). Τῷ νόμῳ is a dative of disadvantage (Moo 414 n. 31); διά + genitive denotes the means of death (Jewett 433); τοῦ Χριστοῦ is a possessive genitive. The phrase "the body of Christ" points to his death on the cross (Cranfield 336). Moo sets out three interpretations of "being put to death to the law" (414); the idea of death to the law's condemnation fits well with the reference to the crucifixion.

εἰς τὸ γενέσθαι ὑμᾶς ἑτέρῳ, τῷ ἐκ νεκρῶν ἐγερθέντι

Εἰς τό + infinitive denotes purpose (R 1071; cf. Longenecker 636; contra T 143); ὑμᾶς is the subject of the infinitive; ἑτέρῳ is a dative of possession (BDF §189.2). The substantival participle τῷ ἐγερθέντι (dat. sg. masc. of aor. pass. ptc. of ἐγείρω) stands in apposition to ἑτέρῳ and clarifies "another" as a reference to Christ (Cranfield 336; cf. 4:24). Ἐκ + genitive denotes separation.

ἵνα καρποφορήσωμεν τῷ θεῷ

Although Cranfield connects this ἵνα clause to ἐθανατώθητε (336), it is more naturally understood as modifying to εἰς τὸ γενέσθαι and stating the purpose of being joined to Christ. Καρποφορήσωμεν (1 pl. aor. act. subjunc. of καρποφορέω, "bear fruit") is an ingressive aorist; the verb itself connotes appropriate productivity (BDAG 510c; cf. Dunn 363); it occurs elsewhere in Colossians 1:6, 10 (cf. Rom 6:21–23). Τῷ θεῷ is a dative of advantage (BDF §188.2).

VERSE 5

ὅτε γὰρ ἦμεν ἐν τῇ σαρκί

Verses 5–6 provide a two-part explanation (γάρ) of verse 4. The temporal conjunction ὅτε ("when") refers to the reader's preconversion situation, to which Paul will contrast their present situation in verse 6. Ἦμεν (1 pl. impf. act. indic. of εἰμί) is a progressive imperfect, highlighting continuing action; ἐν + dative denotes domain (Moo 419); ἐν σαρκί describes the preconversion condition, which is in contrast to and at odds with ἐν Χριστῷ (Dunn 364; cf. Rom 8:8–9).

τὰ παθήματα τῶν ἁμαρτιῶν τὰ διὰ τοῦ νόμου ἐνηργεῖτο ἐν τοῖς μέλεσιν ἡμῶν

Although πάθημα, -τος, τό can describe an interest or desire in general (BDAG 748a), in Galatians 5:48 it has a bad connotation. The plural ἁμαρτιῶν points to concrete acts of sin (Cranfield 337); the genitive could be a genitive of source ("passions that come from sins"), an objective genitive ("passions that lead to sins"), or a genitive of quality ("sinful passions"); EVV choose the third (e.g., GNB, NIV, ESV; cf. Longenecker 636). When the head noun in a genitival phrase has the definite article, so does the noun in the genitive. The article (τά, nom. pl. neut.) is repeated to remove any misunderstanding that the prepositional phrase functions adjectivally (T 187; R 782). Διά + genitive identifies the agency through which the sinful passions were stimulated (Cranfield 337). The progressive imperfect of ἐνηργεῖτο (3 sg. impf. mid. indic. of ἐνεργέω, "work") highlights constant activity (Jewett 437); the middle voice occurs regularly with an impersonal subject (cf. 2 Cor 1:6; 4:12; Gal 5:6; 1 Thess 2:13; 2 Thess 2:7). Ἐν + dative denotes location; see 6:13, 19 for τὰ μελή.

εἰς τὸ καρποφορῆσαι τῷ θανάτῳ

Εἰς τό + infinitive states the result of sin's activity; the aorist of καρποφορῆσαι is constative; see verse 4 for καρποφορέω; τῷ θανάτῳ is a dative of advantage.

VERSE 6

νυνὶ δὲ κατηργήθημεν ἀπὸ τοῦ νόμου

The adversative νυνὶ δέ ("but now") marks a shift to the new epoch (cf. 3:21; 6:22). Κατηργήθημεν (1 pl. aor. pass. indic. of καταργέω) is an ingressive aorist and a divine passive. See verse 2 for καταργέω followed by ἀπὸ τοῦ νόμου.

ἀποθανόντες ἐν ᾧ κατειχόμεθα

Ἀποθανόντες (nom. pl. masc. of aor. act. ptc. of ἀποθνῄσκω) is an adverbial participle of cause. Ἐν ᾧ identifies impersonal means and is short for τούτῳ ἐν ᾧ (R 721); the antecedent for the relative pronoun is τοῦ νόμου (Dunn 365). Κατειχόμεθα (1 pl. impf. pass. indic. of κατέχω, "restrain") is a progressive imperfect and a simple passive; the verb describes keeping someone or something within limits in a confining manner (BDAG 533a; cf. 1:18).

ὥστε δουλεύειν ἡμᾶς ἐν καινότητι πνεύματος καὶ οὐ παλαιότητι γράμματος.

The result (ὥστε + inf.) of being released from the law is that we (ἡμᾶς, acc. of subj.) regularly serve (customary pres.) according to a new standard (ἐν + dat.). Τῷ θεῷ is understood as the object of δουλεύειν. See 6:4 for καινότης; πνεύματος is a genitive of source ("the new state determined by the Spirit"; Moo 421 n. 64). Καὶ οὐ ("and not") introduces a sharp double contrast (R 1095) that adds emphasis (Dunn 366). Παλαίοτης, -ητος, ἡ describes a state of being obsolete (BDAG 751d; cf. 6:6) and contrasts with καινότης. Γράμμα, -τος, τό contrasts sharply with πνεύμα in 2 Cor 3:6; the genitive again designates source ("the obsolete state determined by the letter"). Cranfield suggests that "letter . . . is what the legalist is left with as a result of his misunderstanding and misuse of the law" (340).

FOR FURTHER STUDY

48. Paul's Marriage Analogy (7:1–6)

Burchard, C. "Römer 7, 2–3 im Kontext." Pages 443–56 in *Antikes Judentum und Frühes Christentum: Festschrift für Harmut Stegemann zum 65. Geburtstag*. Edited by B. Kollman, W. Reinbold, and A. Steudel. Berlin: de Gruyter, 1999.

Derrett, J. D. M. "Romans vii.1–4: The Relationship with the Resurrected Christ." Pages 463–70 in *Law in the New Testament*. London: Darton, Longman & Todd, 1970.

Earnshaw, J. D. "Reconsidering Paul's Marriage Analogy in Romans 7:1–4." *NTS* 40 (1994): 68–88.

Gale, H. M. *The Use of Analogy in the Letters of Paul*. Philadelphia: Westminster, 1964.

Giensiusz, A. "Rom 7:1–6: Lack of Imagination? Function of the Passage in the Argumentation of Rom 6,1–7,6." *Bib* 74 (1993): 389–400.
Lee, C. W. "Understanding the Law in Rom. 7:1–6: An Enthymemic Analysis." *Scriptura* 88 (2005): 127–32.
Little, J. A. "Paul's Use of an Analogy: A Structural Analysis of Romans 7:1–6." *CBQ* 46 (1984): 82–90.

HOMILETICAL SUGGESTIONS

Released from the Law; Joined to Christ (7:1–6)

1. Analogy from Marital Law (ἢ ἀγνοεῖτε, ἀδελφοί, 7:1–3)
   a. Principle: Law governs a person as long as he/she lives (7:1)
   b. Illustration: Law binds a married woman to her husband (7:2a)
      1) Exception: If her husband dies (7:2b)
   c. Two Implications (7:3)
      1) She is an adulteress if she remarries while her husband lives (7:3a)
      2) She is free to remarry if her husband dies (7:3b)
2. Practical Application (ὥστε, ἀδελφοί μου, 7:4–6)
   a. Conclusion: God severed our obligation to the law through Christ's death (7:4a)
      1) Purpose: To join us to Christ (7:4b)
         a) Purpose: We can bear fruit for God (7:4c)
   b. Two Situations (7:5–6)
      1) Prior Situation: Sinful passions worked in our members (7:5a)
         a) Purpose: Bear fruit to death (7:5b)
      2) Present Situation: Released from the Law (7:6a)
         a) Cause: Died to what confined (7:6b)
         b) Result: Serve in newness of the Spirit (7:6c)

b. Because the Law Brings Knowledge of Sin (7:7–12)

STRUCTURE

Continuing his diatribal question-and-answer style, Paul leads his readers to the next step in his discussion of the law. They should not conclude that the law is sin (7:7a); rather, the law brings the knowledge of sin (7:7b; cf. 3:20). The problem is that sin uses the law as an opportunity to produce death, a point Paul reinforces by using ring-composition to frame the central panel of the paragraph (7:8–11). He concludes with an affirmation of the divine nature of the law (7:12).

Τί οὖν ἐροῦμεν;
ὁ νόμος ἁμαρτία;

μὴ γένοιτο·
ἀλλὰ τὴν ἁμαρτίαν οὐκ ἔγνων εἰ μὴ διὰ νόμου·
τήν τε γὰρ ἐπιθυμίαν οὐκ ᾔδειν εἰ μὴ ὁ νόμος ἔλεγεν, οὐκ ἐπιθυμήσεις.

ἀφορμὴν δὲ λαβοῦσα ἡ ἁμαρτία διὰ τῆς ἐντολῆς κατειργάσατο ἐν ἐμοὶ πᾶσαν ἐπιθυμίαν·
    χωρὶς γὰρ νόμου ἁμαρτία νεκρά.
ἐγὼ δὲ ἔζων χωρὶς νόμου ποτέ, ἐλθούσης δὲ τῆς ἐντολῆς ἡ ἁμαρτία ἀνέζησεν,
ἐγὼ δὲ ἀπέθανον καὶ εὑρέθη μοι ἡ ἐντολὴ ἡ εἰς ζωήν, αὕτη εἰς θάνατον·
ἡ γὰρ ἁμαρτία ἀφορμὴν λαβοῦσα διὰ τῆς ἐντολῆς ἐξηπάτησέν με καὶ δι᾽ αὐτῆς ἀπέκτεινεν.

ὥστε ὁ μὲν νόμος ἅγιος καὶ ἡ ἐντολὴ ἁγία καὶ δικαία καὶ ἀγαθή.

VERSE 7

Τί οὖν ἐροῦμεν; (see 6:1)

ὁ νόμος ἁμαρτία;

In this question without an interrogative word (R 915), the verb ἐστιν is understood. The definite article identifies νόμος as the subject; ἁμαρτία is the predicate nominative. The "law" is the Mosaic law (Schreiner 358).

μὴ γένοιτο (see 3:4)

ἀλλὰ τὴν ἁμαρτίαν οὐκ ἔγνων εἰ μὴ διὰ νόμου

The conjuction ἀλλά is restrictive ("yet," RSV) or emphatic ("indeed," NIV)* rather than adversative (cf. Moo 432; Schreiner 365) and clarifies Paul's emphatic rejection of the idea that the law is sin. The placement of ἁμαρτίαν (acc. sg. fem.) is emphatic; Jewett suggests that the article points to the topic of sin (446). Ἔγνων (1 sg. aor. act. indic. of γινώσκω, "know") is an ingressive aorist; γινώσκω carries the sense of arriving at a knowledge of something (BDAG 199d). NEB translates the clause "I should never have become acquainted with sin." Εἰ μή ("except") introduces an incomplete second class condition without ἄν (BDF §360.1); διά + genitive identifies the instrument through which acquaintance with the law arrived; νόμου is definite although anarthrous. Cranfield suggests that the law brings full recognition of sin for what it is: deliberate disobedience of God's revealed will (349).

τήν τε γὰρ ἐπιθυμίαν οὐκ ᾔδειν εἰ μὴ ὁ νόμος ἔλεγεν οὐκ ἐπιθυμήσεις

Τε γάρ ("for indeed") establishes a close connection between the clauses (BDF §443.3); ἐπιθυμίαν is brought forward for emphasis in parallel with the preceding clause; the article is probably generic ("what it is to covet," ESV). The pluperfect ᾔδειν (1 sg. plpf. act. indic. of οἶδα, "know") has simple past force (cf. Wallace 586) and is equivalent to the imperfect (Cranfield 348). Moo argues that the verb has the same meaning and kind of action as ἔγνων in the preceding clause (433 n. 29), which would suggest an ingressive sense (Dunn 379). See the preceding clause for εἰ μή; the article with νόμος is anaphoric; ἔλεγεν (3 sg. impf. act. indic. of λέγω, "say") is a progressive imperfect. Οὐκ ἐπιθυμήσεις is an abbreviated quotation of Exod 20:19; ἐπιθυμήσεις (2 sg. fut. act. indic. of ἐπιθυμέω, "covet") is a future of command (Wallace 453); see 1:24 for ἐπιθυμία; Jewett sets out the Jewish antecedents for seeing covetousness as a representative summary of the Mosaic law (448; cf. *TNDT* 3.168–72).

VERSE 8

ἀφορμὴν δὲ λαβοῦσα ἡ ἁμαρτία

Verses 8–11 elaborate (δέ) on Paul's premise. Ἀφορμή, -ῆς, ἡ describes a circumstance from which action becomes possible (BDAG 158d); Dunn suggests "opportunity" (380). Jewett notes that the circumstance is not necessarily bad in itself but, in this case, is misused by sin (449; cf. 2 Cor 5:12; 11:12). The noun is brought forward for emphasis. Λαβοῦσα (nom. sg. fem. of aor. act. ptc. of λαμβάνω, "take") is adverbial of manner ("opportunistically"), modifying the verb that follows. The article with the abstract noun ἁμαρτία is also anaphoric.

διὰ τῆς ἐντολῆς κατειργάσατο ἐν ἐμοὶ πᾶσαν ἐπιθυμίαν·

Although most EVV take διὰ τῆς ἐντολῆς ("through the commandment") with the participle (e.g., NIV: "seizing the opportunity afforded by the commandment"), Cranfield sets out four reasons to take it with the finite verb (350; cf. Dunn 380; contra Moo 435 n. 40 and Schreiner 367 n. 14). Ἐντολή, -ῆς, ἡ refers to the specific command against coveting rather than to the entire law (Jewett 449). See 1:27 for κατεργάζομαι; the aorist tense is constative. Ἐν ἐμοί ("in me") is locative (Harris 118); the adjective πᾶσαν (acc. sg. fem.) is qualitative and designates a class ("all kinds of coveting"; cf. Schreiner 367; BDAG 784c).

χωρὶς γὰρ νόμου ἁμαρτία νεκρά

The explanation (γάρ) for how sin takes opportunity through the law begins with the principle that "apart from the law" (χωρὶς νόμου) sin is "dead." LN set out three elements in the semantic domain of the adjective νεκρός, -ά, -όν: being without life (23.121, "dead"; cf. Jas 2:26), being without purpose (65.39, "useless"; cf. Heb 9:14), and being without effect (74.28, "powerless"; cf. Eph 2:5). Here, the third nuance applies: "incapable of achieving its purpose" (Jewett 450).

VERSE 9

ἐγὼ δὲ ἔζων χωρὶς νόμου ποτέ

Paul transitions (δέ) to a brief narrative (v. 9–10) describing how sin comes to life when an individual encounters the law. Ἐγώ is variously interpreted as Adam (Dunn 381–84), Israel (Moo 437–39), or Paul himself (Schreiner 363–65; cf. Longenecker 642, although he argues that the referent changes in 7:14–25). Ἔζων (1 sg. impf. act. indic. of ζάω, "live") is a progressive imperfect; see verse 8 for χωρὶς νόμου; ποτέ is an adverb of time ("once, formerly").

ἐλθούσης δὲ τῆς ἐντολῆς ἡ ἁμαρτία ἀνέζησεν

The change (δέ) happened "when the commandment came." Ἐλθούσης (gen. sg. fem. of aor. act. ptc. of ἔρχομαι, "come") introduces a genitive absolute of time; τῆς ἐντολῆς is the subject of the participle; the article is anaphoric, pointing back to the commandment of verse 7. Ἀνέζησεν (3 sg. aor. act. indic. of ἀναζάω, "come to life") is an ingressive aorist; the verb describes something that begins to function after being dormant (BDAG 62c) and may be translated "spring to life" (Cranfield 352); its use in Luke 11:24 suggests the nuance "again."

VERSE 10

ἐγὼ δὲ ἀπέθανον καὶ εὑρέθη μοι ἡ ἐντολὴ ἡ εἰς ζωήν, αὕτη εἰς θάνατον

In contrast (δέ) to giving life to sin, the law brings death to the individual who encounters it (ἀπέθανον, "I died"), confirming what Paul has already written in chapter 5 (5:12, 15, 17, 21). In addition (καί), the law's intended purpose is perverted—promising to give life, it actually results in death. The passive of εὑρέθη (3 sg. aor. pass. indic. of εὑρίσκω, "find") reflects a Hebraism (Jewett 452) with the sense "prove to be" (Cranfield 352 n. 3; cf. ESV); μοι is a dative of disadvantage (R 531); ἡ ἐντολή is the subject. The article preceding εἰς ζωήν allows the prepositional phrase to function as an adjective (R 398, 782) setting out the "true and proper purpose" for the law (Cranfield 352). That is, the law promises life for the one who obeys it (Moo 439; cf. Lev 18:5; Ps 19:7–10; Ezek 20:11; Luke 20:28). The demonstrative pronoun αὕτη (nom. sg. fem.) is resumptive (R 698), pointing back to ἡ ἐντολή ("this same commandment," Moo 439). Εἰς θάνατον sets out the actual effect of the law (GNB, NJB, CEV, "brought death").

VERSE 11

ἡ γὰρ ἁμαρτία ἀφορμὴν λαβοῦσα διὰ τῆς ἐντολῆς ἐξηπάτησέν με καὶ δι' αὐτῆς ἀπέκτεινεν

Paul returns to the wording of verse 8 (ἡ ἁμαρτία ἀφορμὴν λαβοῦσα διὰ τῆς ἐντολῆς) to state the reason (γάρ) the law results in death: seizing the opportunity provided by the law, sin deceives and kills. Ἐξηπάτησέν (3 sg. aor. act. indic. of ἐξαπατάω, "deceive") is a constative aorist as is ἀπέκτεινεν; the personal pronoun αὐτῆς (gen. sg. fem.) refers back to τῆς ἐντολῆς. The parallel provided by placing δι' αὐτῆς ("through it") before ἀπέκτεινεν supports the previous contention that the prepositional phrases modify their respective verbs rather than the participle λαβοῦσα.

VERSE 12

ὥστε ὁ μὲν νόμος ἅγιος καὶ ἡ ἐντολὴ ἁγία καὶ δικαία καὶ ἀγαθή

The conclusion (ὥστε) Paul draws from verses 7–11 highlights the divine nature of the law. Because the correlative particle μέν lacks the corresponding δέ (R 1152), both Cranfield (353) and Dunn (385) conclude that Paul is implying a contrast between law and sin. Ὁ νόμος refers to the law as a whole (Dunn 385), while ἡ ἐντολή refers to the specific representative commandment Paul has cited in verse 7 (Moo 440). See 1:7 for ἅγιος; 1:17 for δίκαιος; 2:7–10 for ἀγαθός. The first adjective ("holy") points to the law's divine origin; the second ("just") points to its divine character; the third ("good") points to its divine purpose. Despite sin's opportunistic perversion of the law, the law is not sin; it is "a gift of God, given to serve his purposes" (Dunn 402).

FOR FURTHER STUDY

49. "I" in Romans 7 (7:7–25)

Bornkamm, G. "Sin, Law and Death (Romans 7)." Pages 87–104 in *Early Christian Experience*. Translated by P. L. Hammer. Philadelphia: Westminster, 1969.

Bultmann, R. "Römer 7 und die Anthropologie des Paulus." Pages 53–62 in *Exegetica: Aufsätze zur Erforschung des Neuen Testaments*. Tübingen: Mohr Siebeck, 1967.

Campbell, D. H. "The Identity of Ἐγώ in Romans 7:7–25." Pages 57–64 in *Studia Biblica 1978*, vol. 3: *Papers on Paul and Other New Testament Authors*. Edited by E. A. Livingstone. Sheffield: *JSOT*, 1980.

Dockery, D. "Romans 7:14–25: Pauline Tension in the Christian Life." *Grace Theological Journal* 2 (1981): 239–57.

Dodd, B. *Paul's Paradigmatic "I": Personal Example as Literary Strategy*. Sheffield: Academic Press, 1999.

Dunn, J. D. G. "Rom. 7,14–25 in the Theology of Paul." *TZ* 31 (1975): 257–73.

Engberg-Pedersen, T. "The Reception of Graeco-Roman Culture in the New Testament: The Case of Romans 7:7–25." Pages 32–57 in *The New Testament as Reception*. Edited by M. Müller and H. Tronier. Sheffield: Academic Press, 2002.

Fung, R. Y. K. "The Impotence of the Law: Towards a Fresh Understanding of Romans 7:14–25." Pages 34–48 in *Scripture, Tradition and Interpretation: Festschrift for E. F. Harrison*. Edited by W. W. Gasque and W. S. LaSor. Grand Rapids: Eerdmans, 1978.

Gundry, R. H. "The Moral Frustration of Paul before his Conversion: Sexual Lust in Romans 7:7–25." Pages 254–70 in *Pauline Studies: Essays Presented to Professor F. F. Bruce on His 70th Birthday*. Edited by D. A. Hagner and M. J. Harris. Grand Rapids: Eerdmans, 1980.

Jervis, L. A. "'The Commandment Which Is for Life.' (Romans 7:10): Sin's Use of the Obedience of Faith." *JSNT* 27 (2004): 193–216.

Karlberg, M. W. "Israel's History Personified: Romans 7:7–13 in Relation to Paul's Teaching on the 'Old Man.'" *TJ* 7 (1986): 65–74.

Kümmel. W. G. *Römer 7 und das Bild des Menschen in Neuen Testament: Zwei Studien*. Munich: Kaiser, 1974.

________. *Römer 7 und die Bekehrung des Paulus*. Leipzig: Hinrichs, 1929.

Lambrecht, J. *The Wretched "I" and Its Liberation: Paul in Romans 7 and 8*. Louvain: Peeters, 1992.

________. "Man before and without Christ: Romans 7 and Pauline Anthropology." *Louvain Studies* 5 (1974): 18–33.

Martin, B. L. "Some Reflections on the Identity of the Ego in Rom 7:14–25." *SJT* 34 (1981): 39–47.

Middendorf, M. P. *The "I" in the Storm: A Study of Romans 7*. St. Louis: Concordia Academic Press, 1997.

Milne, D. J. W. "Romans 7:7–12, Paul's Pre-conversion Experience." *RTR* 43 (1984): 9–17.

Mitton, C. L. "Romans vii. Reconsidered." *ExpTim* 65 (1953–54): 78–81, 99–103, 132–35.

Moo, D. J. "The History and Experience of Jews under the Law." Pages 423–31 in *The Epistle to the Romans*. Grand Rapids: Eerdmans, 1996.

________. "Israel and Paul in Romans 7:7–12." *NTS* 32 (1986): 122–35.

Packer, J. I. "The 'Wretched Man' in Romans 7." Pages 621–27 in *Studia Evangelica*, vol. 2: *The New Testament Scriptures*. Edited by F. L. Cross. Berlin: Akademie, 1964.

Stowers, S. K. "Romans 7:7–25 as a Speech-in-Character (προσωποποεία)." Pages 180–225 in *Paul in His Hellenistic Context*. Edited by T. Engberg-Pedersen. Minneapolis: Fortress, 1995.

Thiessen, G. *Psychological Aspects of Pauline Theology*. Translated by J. P. Galvin. Philadelphia: Fortress, 1987.

Thurén, L. "Romans 7 Derhetorized." Pages 420–40 in *Rhetorical Criticism and the Bible*. Edited by S. E. Porter and D. L. Stamps. Sheffield: Academic Press, 2002.

Watson, N. M. "The Interpretation of Romans VII." *AusBR* 21 (1973): 27–39.

Wilder, T., ed. *Perspectives on Our Struggle with Sin: Three Views of Romans 7*. Nashville: B&H, 2013.

HOMILETICAL SUGGESTIONS

Law Good; Sin Bad (7:7–12)

1. The Issue: The nature of the law (τί οὖν ἐροῦμεν, 7:7)
    a. Rhetorical Question: Is the law sin? (7:7a)
    b. Emphatic negation: Never! (7:7b)
    c. Refutation: The law makes sin known (7:7c)

2. The Explanation: Sin uses the law to deceive and kill (δέ, 7:8–11)
   a. Apart from the law, sin is powerless (7:8)
   b. When the law comes, sin springs to life (7:9)
   c. The law proves to result in death (7:10)
3. The Conclusion: The law is holy, just, and good (ὥστε, 7:12)

c. Because Sin Uses the Law to Produce Death (7:13–25)

STRUCTURE

The third and longest paragraph in Paul's discussion of the law begins with another false inference (7:13a) and refutation (7:13b) that restate and expand on the earlier rhetorical question in verse 7. He develops his explanation in two parallel sections (7:14–17; 7:18–20), each of which ends with identical wording that identifies indwelling sin as the culprit. The paragraph concludes with a section (7:21–25) that plays on the word "law" (7x), includes both a cry for help and an expression of hope (7:24–25a), and ends with a recapitulation of the paragraph as a whole (7:25b). Longenecker has an extended discussion of the identity of "I" in this paragraph and concludes that it is a generic reference to "people who attempt to live their lives apart from God . . . by means of their own resources and abilities" (651–59).

Τὸ οὖν ἀγαθὸν ἐμοὶ ἐγένετο θάνατος;
μὴ γένοιτο·
ἀλλʼ ἡ ἁμαρτία, ἵνα φανῇ ἁμαρτία, διὰ τοῦ ἀγαθοῦ μοι κατεργαζομένη θάνατον,
    ἵνα γένηται καθʼ ὑπερβολὴν ἁμαρτωλὸς ἡ ἁμαρτία διὰ τῆς ἐντολῆς.

οἴδαμεν γὰρ ὅτι ὁ νόμος πνευματικός ἐστιν,
ἐγὼ δὲ σάρκινός εἰμι πεπραμένος ὑπὸ τὴν ἁμαρτίαν.
    ὃ γὰρ κατεργάζομαι οὐ γινώσκω·
    οὐ γὰρ ὃ θέλω τοῦτο πράσσω, ἀλλʼ ὃ μισῶ τοῦτο ποιῶ.
    εἰ δὲ ὃ οὐ θέλω τοῦτο ποιῶ, σύμφημι τῷ νόμῳ ὅτι καλός.
νυνὶ δὲ οὐκέτι ἐγὼ κατεργάζομαι αὐτὸ ἀλλʼ ἡ οἰκοῦσα ἐν ἐμοὶ ἁμαρτία.

οἶδα γὰρ ὅτι οὐκ οἰκεῖ ἐν ἐμοί, τοῦτʼ ἔστιν ἐν τῇ σαρκί μου, ἀγαθόν·
    τὸ γὰρ θέλειν παράκειταί μοι, τὸ δὲ κατεργάζεσθαι τὸ καλὸν οὔ·
    οὐ γὰρ ὃ θέλω ποιῶ ἀγαθόν, ἀλλʼ ὃ οὐ θέλω κακὸν τοῦτο πράσσω.
εἰ δὲ ὃ οὐ θέλω [ἐγὼ] τοῦτο ποιῶ, οὐκέτι ἐγὼ κατεργάζομαι αὐτὸ ἀλλʼ ἡ οἰκοῦσα ἐν ἐμοὶ ἁμαρτία.

Εὑρίσκω ἄρα τὸν νόμον, τῷ θέλοντι ἐμοὶ ποιεῖν τὸ καλόν, ὅτι ἐμοὶ τὸ κακὸν παράκειται·
συνήδομαι γὰρ τῷ νόμῳ τοῦ θεοῦ κατὰ τὸν ἔσω ἄνθρωπον,
βλέπω δὲ ἕτερον νόμον ἐν τοῖς μέλεσίν μου
    ἀντιστρατευόμενον τῷ νόμῳ τοῦ νοός μου
    καὶ αἰχμαλωτίζοντά με ἐν τῷ νόμῳ τῆς ἁμαρτίας τῷ ὄντι ἐν τοῖς μέλεσίν μου.

ταλαίπωρος ἐγὼ ἄνθρωπος·
τίς με ῥύσεται ἐκ τοῦ σώματος τοῦ θανάτου τούτου;
χάρις δὲ τῷ θεῷ διὰ Ἰησοῦ Χριστοῦ τοῦ κυρίου ἡμῶν.

ἄρα οὖν αὐτὸς ἐγὼ τῷ μὲν νοῒ δουλεύω νόμῳ θεοῦ
τῇ δὲ σαρκὶ νόμῳ ἁμαρτίας.

VERSE 13

Τὸ οὖν ἀγαθὸν ἐμοὶ ἐγένετο θάνατος;

The inferential οὖν ("therefore") connects this rhetorical question to the discussion that precedes. The question both restates the faulty thinking of verse 7 and picks up the idea of the law's "goodness" from verse 12. The article with the adjective ἀγαθόν (nom. sg. neut.) allows it to function as an abstract noun (NIV, "that which is good") and the subject of the question. Ἐμοί is a dative of indirect object (R 537); ἐγένετο (3 sg. aor. mid. indic. of dep. γίνομαι, "become") is a consummative aorist pointing to the completion of the process described in verses 8–11 (cf. v.10); the predicate nominative θάνατος is anarthrous, abstract, and qualitative.

μὴ γένοιτο (See 3:4)

ἀλλ' ἡ ἁμαρτία, ἵνα φανῇ ἁμαρτία, διὰ τοῦ ἀγαθοῦ μοι κατεργαζομένη θάνατον

Ἀλλά is adversative ("but") and introduces Paul's refutation of the opening question (Moo 452). The article with ἁμαρτία marks it as the subject; ἵνα + subjunctive introduces a parenthetical purpose clause highlighting the revelatory role of the law; φανῇ (3 sg. aor. pass. subjunc. of φαίνω, "become known/apparent") is a constative aorist; NEB translates the clause "sin exposed its true character." Διά + genitive marks the law as the instrumental cause of death (Schreiner 372); τοῦ ἀγαθοῦ again refers to the law; μοι is locative. Moo understands ἦν before κατεργαζομένη, making the participle part of the main verb (452 n. 29);* Cranfield suggests ἐγένετο after κατεργαζομένη, making the participle adverbial of manner (354).

ἵνα γένηται καθ' ὑπερβολὴν ἁμαρτωλὸς ἡ ἁμαρτία διὰ τῆς ἐντολῆς

Wallace includes ἵνα γένηται among his examples of purpose-result (474); the clause further explains ἵνα φανῇ ἁμαρτία. Κατά + accusative denotes standard or rule of measure (R 609); ὑπερβολή, -ῆς, ἡ describes the state of exceeding to an extraordinary degree (BDAG 1032c); the prepositional phrase is used adverbially to modify the adjective ἁμαρτωλός (ESV, "sinful beyond measure"). Ἡ ἁμαρτία is the subject; διὰ τῆς ἐντολῆς again denotes instrumentality.

VERSE 14

οἴδαμεν γὰρ ὅτι ὁ νόμος πνευματικός ἐστιν

Metzger gives οἴδαμεν an {A} rating (454). The variant οἶδα μεν has limited support (33) and is probably influenced by the first singular in verses 7–25. Cranfield concludes that the variant is "surely to be rejected" (355). Paul uses the first person plural (οἴδαμεν, 1 pl. pf. act. indic.) to draw his audience into his first explanation (γάρ) of how sin becomes exceedingly sinful (Moo 453; cf. 2:2). Longenecker notes that the disclosure formula introduces content that is common ground between Paul and his addressees (660). Ὅτι introduces content ("that"); placing πνευματικός ("spiritual") before ἐστιν gives the adjective emphasis; Wallace suggests that all the present tense verbs in the paragraph should be understood as gnomic (531–32). Cranfield writes that πνευματικός affirms the divine origin, majesty, and authority of the law, corresponds to the law's mode of operation and effectiveness, and highlights humankind's inability to understand the law apart from the Spirit's help (355–56). Longenecker provides a helpful explanation of why Paul would choose to call the law "spiritual" (661–62).

ἐγὼ δὲ σάρκινός εἰμι πεπραμένος ὑπὸ τὴν ἁμαρτίαν

Humankind's fleshly nature stands in contrast (δέ) to the law's spiritual nature. Σάρκινος, -η, -ον describes the state of being human at a disappointing level of behavior or character (BDAG 914c); in 1 Cor 3:1–3, "fleshly" highlights what is opposite to "spiritual" (i.e., godly) character and conduct. Εἰμι πεπραμένος is a periphrastic construction, with the intensive perfect of the participle (nom. sg. masc. of pf. pass. ptc. of πιπράσκω, "sell") emphasizing the existing state (Wallace 649); ὑπό + accusative indicates subordination ("under the power/authority of sin"; cf. Cranfield 357); the article with ἁμαρτίαν personalizes sin as "a malevolent force that is both hostile to God and alienates people from God" (Longenecker 662). Jewett provides the background behind the slavery metaphor of the verb (461).

VERSE 15

ὃ γὰρ κατεργάζομαι οὐ γινώσκω

In verses 15–16 Paul describes what it means to be "sold under sin" (Jewett 462). Placing the relative clause first gives it emphasis (R 1158). Οὐ negates γινώσκω; EVV uniformly translate the verb as "understand" (cf. Cranfield 358); Schreiner suggests the phrase denotes the inability fully to comprehend the depth of indwelling sin (373). Cranfield suggests there is little difference between κατεργάζομαι and ποιέω, while πράσσω is distinct and less definite (358; cf. *TDNT* 6.636–37). Moo, however, sees no important difference between ποιέω and πράσσω but views κατεργάζομαι as slightly stronger (455 n. 40; cf. 460 n. 58).

οὐ γὰρ ὃ θέλω τοῦτο πράσσω ἀλλ' ὃ μισῶ τοῦτο ποιῶ

Γάρ continues his explanation by using a strong contrast (οὐ . . . ἀλλά) to describe the conflict between "willing" and "doing" (cf. 7:18). Οὐ stands outside the relative clause and negates the main verb (πράσσω). Θέλω describes the resolve to accomplish something (Moo 457 n. 45; cf. BDAG 448b). Μισέω describes a strong aversion to something (BDAG 653a); NEB translates it as "detest." Both instances of τοῦτο are resumptive (R 698), referring to the preceding relative clauses.

VERSE 16

εἰ δὲ ὃ οὐ θέλω τοῦτο ποιῶ, σύμφημι τῷ νόμῳ ὅτι καλός

The transitional conjunction δέ ("now") adds a first class condition (εἰ + indic.) that introdues a preliminary conclusion (Schreiner 373). The negative particle οὐ stands inside the relative clause and modifies θέλω; τοῦτο is again resumptive. Σύμφημι ("concur, agree with") occurs only here in the NT (R 319); Bauer suggests "I concur . . . and thus bear witness" (960b). Τῷ νόμῳ is an associative dative ("with the law"); ὅτι introduces content. Καλός is its own clause (Porter 85, 287) with ἐστιν understood ("that it is good"); the adjective describes high moral quality (BDAG 504d).

VERSE 17

νυνὶ δὲ οὐκέτι ἐγὼ κατεργάζομαι αὐτὸ ἀλλ' ἡ οἰκοῦσα ἐν ἐμοὶ ἁμαρτία

Νυνί δέ is logical ("So now," EVV; cf. Longenecker 664) rather than temporal or adversative (Cranfield 360; Moo 457; Schreiner 374) and draws verses 14–17 to a conclusion. Ἐγώ is emphatic (T 37); including it at the beginning of the sentence and delaying ἁμαρτία to the end heightens the strong contrast established by οὐκέτι . . . ἀλλά. See verse 15 for κατεργάζομαι. The pronoun αὐτό (acc. sg. neut.) refers back to ὃ οὐ θέλω in verse 16. The article preceding οἰκοῦσα (nom. sg. fem. of pres. act. ptc. of οἰκέω, "dwell") accompanies ἁμαρτία and brackets the noun phrase in which the participle is adjectival and ἐν ἐμοί is locative (Harris 118). CEV translates the phrase as "the sin that lives in me."

VERSE 18

οἶδα γὰρ ὅτι οὐκ οἰκεῖ ἐν ἐμοί, τοῦτ' ἔστιν ἐν τῇ σαρκί μου, ἀγαθόν

The second explanation (γάρ) builds on the idea of indwelling sin in the preceding verse (Schreiner 374). Οἶδα (1 sg. pf. act. indic.) is a perfect used as present; ὅτι ("that") introduces the content of what Paul knows; οὐκ negates οἰκεῖ rather than ἀγαθόν (Jewett 467; cf. GNB); ἐν ἐμοί is locative (Harris 118). Τοῦτ' ἔστιν ἐν τῇ σαρκί μου ("that is, in my flesh," ESV) stands in apposition to and specifies more precisely ἐν ἐμοί (R 399). Σάρξ is best understood as the material ("fleshly") body (Moo 459). Placing the subject ἀγαθόν (nom. sg. neut.) at the end of the clause gives it emphasis; the noun echoes the same word in verses 12–13. Here, however, it refers to the capacity to do good rather than to the law.

τὸ γὰρ θέλειν παράκειταί μοι

In verses 18b–19 Paul describes what it means that good does not dwell in him. Τὸ θέλειν (pres. act. inf.) is a substantival infinitive of subject (T 140); the article is anaphoric, pointing back to the same verb in verses 15–16 (BDF §399.1); the present tense is progressive (R 890). Παράκειμαι carries the idea of being present and ready for action (BDAG 766a); μοι is a dative of association ("with me").

τὸ δὲ κατεργάζεσθαι τὸ καλὸν οὔ·

In contrast (δέ) to the "willing" that is present, the "working" is not. Τὸ κατεργάζεσθαι (pres. mid. inf. of dep. κατεργάζομαι) is a substantival infinitive of subject (Wallace 601); the present tense is progressive (R 890). See 7:16 for καλός. The reading οὔ has good manuscript support (א, A, B, C) and is more difficult than either οὐχ εὑρίσκω (D, 33) or οὐ γινώσκω. Metzger gives it a {B} rating (454). The additions probably reflect either attempts to smooth the reading or assimilations to verse 21 or verse 15 respectively.

VERSE 19

οὐ γὰρ ὃ θέλω ποιῶ ἀγαθόν ἀλλ' ὃ οὐ θέλω κακὸν τοῦτο πράσσω

This sentence repeats the substance of verse 15b (Cranfield 361) with a number of differences. Οὐ . . . ποιῶ ἀγαθόν (GNB, "I don't do the good") replaces οὐ . . . τοῦτο πράσσω and specifies the antecedent of the first relative clause (ὃ θέλω) as "doing good." Κακὸν τοῦτο πράσσω (GNB, "I do the evil") replaces τοῦτο ποιῶ and specifies the antecedent of the second relative clause (ὃ οὐ θέλω) as "doing evil." The use of θέλω in both relative clauses (contrast μισῶ in 7:15c) repeats the infinitive in verse 18b and reinforces the positive desire to do good. See 1:30 for κακός.

VERSE 20

εἰ δὲ ὃ οὐ θέλω [ἐγὼ] τοῦτο ποιῶ (See 7:16a)

The external evidence on whether to include ἐγώ (א, A, 33) or omit it (B, C, D) is divided. Metzger notes that it could either have been accidentally omitted or deliberately added (455). Jewett argues that "the inclusion of this seemingly redundant term . . . is so hard to explain that it is likely original" (455 n. i).

οὐκέτι ἐγὼ κατεργάζομαι αὐτὸ ἀλλ' ἡ οἰκοῦσα ἐν ἐμοὶ ἁμαρτία (See 7:17)

VERSE 21

Εὑρίσκω ἄρα τὸν νόμον

Paul draws a conclusion (ἄρα) from verses 14–20 (Moo 460). Εὑρίσκω suggests a new experience (Jewett 469; cf. 7:10). Τὸν νόμον has been explained as an adverbial accusative of reference ("I find with reference to the law," Schreiner 377), the object of θέλοντι ("while my will is directed toward the law," Jewett 469), or the object of εὑρίσκω ("I find the law," Moo 460 n. 62). The third is most natural, and νόμος is best understood as "principle" (Cranfield 362; cf. KJV, NASB, NEB).

τῷ θέλοντι ἐμοὶ ποιεῖν τὸ καλόν

Moo sets out three options for the way in which the participial phrase relates to the rest of the sentence (460 n. 60). It is best taken with the ὅτι clause that follows but brought forward for emphasis (Cranfield 362) and as adverbial of time ("when I want to do what is good," GNB). Ἐμοί functions as the subject of the participle; ποιεῖν (pres. act. infin.) is a complementary infinitive; καλόν is the object of the infinitive; the article is anaphoric (cf. 7:18)

ὅτι ἐμοὶ τὸ κακὸν παράκειται

Ὅτι introduces the content of εὑρίσκω (R 1035, 1041); ἐμοί is variously understood as a dative of advantage ("for me," R 539), a dative of location ("in me," NASB, CEV), or a dative of association ("with me," KJV, NIV); the article with κακόν is anaphoric. See 7:18 for παράκειμαι.

VERSE 22

συνήδομαι γὰρ τῷ νόμῳ τοῦ θεοῦ κατὰ τὸν ἔσω ἄνθρωπον

The explanation (γάρ) for the principle Paul describes resides in what Dunn calls "the divided I" (409). The "inner man" (ὁ ἔσω ἄνθρωπος; cf. 2 Cor 4:16; Eph 3:16) experiences joy in connection with the law (συνήδομαι, cf. BDAG 971c). Τῷ νόμῳ is a dative of association; τοῦ θεοῦ (poss. gen.) clarifies that Paul is talking about the Mosaic law (Schreiner 375). One manuscript replaces θεοῦ (א, A, C, D, 33) with νοός (B). Metzger gives θεοῦ an {A} rating (455). The variant is most likely either an assimilation to verse 23 or an inadvertent jump to the same verse (Schreiner 394).

VERSE 23

βλέπω δὲ ἕτερον νόμον ἐν τοῖς μέλεσίν μου

In contrast (δέ) to the inner man, there is "a different law" at work in the members of a person's physical body (cf. Schreiner 377). Βλέπω refers to developing an awareness of something (BDAG 179c); ἐν + dative denotes location; the article regularly occurs with the possessive pronoun. Ἕτερον νόμον is clearly distinct from τῷ νόμῷ τοῦ θεοῦ in verse 22, but its meaning is debated, especially given the other uses of νόμος in verses 21–25. The best understanding is (a) that τὸν νόμον in verse 21 refers to a general principle; (b) that τῷ νόμῳ τοῦ θεοῦ in verse 22 along with τῷ νόμῳ τοῦ νοός later in this verse and νόμῳ θεοῦ in verse 25 all refer to the Mosaic law, and (c) that ἕτερον νόμον along with τῷ νόμῳ τῆς ἁμαρτίας later in this verse and νόμῳ ἁμαρτίας in verse 25 all refer to the authority or power of sin. See Moo 462–64 and Schreiner 375–79 for detailed discussions but differing conclusions.

ἀντιστρατευόμενον τῷ νόμῳ τοῦ νοός μου

The adjectival participle (acc. sg. masc. of pres. mid. ptc. of dep. ἀντιστρατεύομαι) describes the different law that is "waging war" (NIV, ESV) "against" (dat. of disadvantage; cf. NJB) "the law of my mind." Cranfield renders the latter phrase "the law my mind acknowledges" (364; cf. GNB, NEB).

καὶ αἰχμαλωτίζοντά με ἐν τῷ νόμῳ τῆς ἁμαρτίας τῷ ὄντι ἐν τοῖς μέλεσίν μου

Paul adds (καί) a second adjectival participle (acc. sg. masc. of pres. act. ptc. of αἰχμαλωτίζω, "take captive") to his description of the different law. The verb refers to the action of causing someone to become a prisoner of war (BDAG 31d); με is the object of the participle. Ἐν + dative here is equivalent to εἰς + accusative following the same verb in 2 Cor 10:5 (Cranfield 365) and probably reflects the use of the dative after verbs implying personal relation (e.g., δουλεύω; cf. Wallace 171–72). If τῷ νόμῳ τῆς ἁμαρτίας denotes the authority or power that sin exercises (see above), the genitive is subjective. The articular participle τῷ ὄντι (dat. sg. masc. of pres. act. ptc. of εἰμί) is substantival (R 1109) in apposition to νόμῳ; ἐν τοῖς μέλεσίν μου is locative (see above).

VERSE 24

ταλαίπωρος ἐγὼ ἄνθρωπος

Robertson notes that this combination is an example of the conscious suppression of part of a sentence under the influence of strong emotion (*aposiopesis*, 1203). The adjective ταλαίπωρος ("wretched, miserable") is brought forward for emphasis. CEV translates "What a miserable person I am!"

τίς με ῥύσεται ἐκ τοῦ σώματος τοῦ θανάτου τούτου;

The interrogative pronoun τίς (nom. sg. masc. "who") poses a rhetorical question that suggests the answer "No one!" (Jewett 471); με is the direct object brought forward for emphasis. Ῥύσεται (3 sg. fut. mid. indic. of dep. ῥύομαι, "rescue") is a predictive future; ἐκ + ablative denotes release (R 518). Τοῦ θανάτου is an attributive genitive (Wallace 87); τούτου modifies σώματος (T 214); the resulting translation is "this dead body" (cf. CEV, "this dead corpse"). Cranfield writes "That from which the speaker longs to be delivered is the condition of life in the body as we know it under the occupation of sin . . . a life which, because of sin, must succumb to death" (367; cf. Longenecker 669–70).

VERSE 25

χάρις δὲ τῷ θεῷ (See 6:17)

MSS attest to four additional readings. Metzger argues that χάρις δὲ τῷ θεῷ best explains the others and gives it a {B} rating (455). Schreiner agrees and has a concise summary of what others have written (394).

διὰ Ἰησοῦ Χριστοῦ τοῦ κυρίου ἡμῶν (See 5:1, 11, 21; 6:23)

ἄρα οὖν αὐτὸς ἐγὼ τῷ μὲν νοΐ δουλεύω νόμῳ θεοῦ

The inferential combination ἄρα οὖν ("So then," RSV, NIV) introduces a summarizing recapitulation of 7:14–23 (Moo 467; cf. 5:18). Αὐτὸς ἐγώ ("I myself") is doubly emphatic (cf. Longenecker 672); the correlative conjunction μέν introduces the first (positive) half of the equation. The article with νοΐ (dat. sg. masc. of νοῦς, νοός, ὁ, "mind") functions as a possessive pronoun (R 770); the dative is instrumental (R 540); the phrase should be translated as "with my mind." Νοῦς corresponds to ὁ ἔσω ἄνθρωπος in verse 22. Δουλεύω describes the action of conducting oneself in total service to another (BDAG 259b; cf. 6:6); the present tense is customary; the dative of direct object regularly follows δουλεύω. Νόμῳ is definite although anarthrous; in a genitive phrase both nouns either have or lack the article (R 780).

τῇ δὲ σαρκὶ νόμῳ ἁμαρτίας

The correlative pronoun δέ introduces the second (negative) half of the equation, which parallels the first without δουλεύω. Τῇ σαρκί is instrumental ("in my flesh"); see verse 23 for νόμῳ ἁμαρτίας. Σάρξ echoes verses 14 and 18, gathers up the references to "in me" (7:17, 18, 20), "in my members" (7:23), and "this dead body" (7:24), and denotes the fleshly material body in its weakness and opposition to God (NEB, "my unspiritual nature").

FOR FURTHER STUDY

See For Further Study §§ 24 ("Paul and the Law"), 29 ("Flesh"), 49 ("I" in Romans 7)

HOMILETICAL SUGGESTIONS

The Role of Indwelling Sin (7:13–25)

1. The Issue (οὖν, 7:13)
   a. Rhetorical Question: Does the law cause death? (7:13a)
   b. Emphatic Negation: Never! (7:13b)
   c. Refutation: Sin uses the law to produce death (7:13c)
2. The First Explanation (οἴδαμεν γάρ, 7:14–17)
   a. The law is spiritual, but human beings are fleshly (7:14–16)
      1) Detested acts replace desired acts (7:15)
      2) The result is an affirmation of the law's goodness (7:16)
   b. Indwelling sin is responsible for producing detested acts (7:17)
3. The Second Explanation (οἶδα γάρ, 7:18–20)
   a. No good dwells in the fleshly body (7:18–19)
      1) The desire to do good is present, but the ability is not (7:18b)

        2) The result is doing evil, not good (7:19)
    b. Indwelling sin is responsible for producing evil (7:20)
4. The Conclusion (ἄρα, 7:21–25)
    a. Principle: Evil is present despite the desire to do good (7:21–23)
        1) The "inner self" delights in the law (7:22)
        2) The "members" are captive to sin (7:23)
    b. Cry for Help: Who will deliver? (7:24)
    c. Expression of Hope: Jesus Christ! (7:25a)
    d. Recapitulation: The mind serves the law of God, but the flesh serves the law of sin (ἄρα οὖν, 7:25b)

The Two "Laws" (7:13–25)

1. The "law" of sin
    a. Appeals to the members of the body (7:23, 25b)
    b. Promotes the practice of doing evil (7:15–17, 19–20)
    c. Leads to captivity to sin (7:23)
2. The law of God
    a. Appeals to the inner man of the mind (7:22, 25a)
    b. Promotes the desire for doing good (7:15–17, 19–20)
    c. Leads to delight in the law (7:22)

4. God's Righteousness Is Lived Out According to the Spirit (8:1–30)

a. Who Gives Us Life and Assurance (8:1–17)

STRUCTURE

Returning to the new epoch (νῦν) in which believers are released from the law (7:6), Paul declares their status (8:1) and then builds his argument in four parts (8:2–4; 8:5–8; 8:9–11; 8:12–17). The first opens with a verbless clause to catch the listeners' attention and uses νόμος to connect to the preceding discussion (7:1–25). The second develops the contrast between flesh and spirit introduced at the end of verse 4. The third uses a fourfold "if . . . then" pattern to build to a climax in discussing the indwelling Spirit. The fourth draws out the consequences of daily living for those who are indwelt by the Spirit and consists of three subsections (8:12–13; 8:14–15; 8:16–17).

Οὐδὲν ἄρα νῦν κατάκριμα τοῖς ἐν Χριστῷ Ἰησοῦ.

ὁ γὰρ νόμος τοῦ πνεύματος τῆς ζωῆς ἐν Χριστῷ Ἰησοῦ ἠλευθέρωσέν σε ἀπὸ τοῦ νόμου τῆς ἁμαρτίας καὶ τοῦ θανάτου.
τὸ γὰρ ἀδύνατον τοῦ νόμου ἐν ᾧ ἠσθένει διὰ τῆς σαρκός, ὁ θεὸς τὸν ἑαυτοῦ υἱὸν πέμψας ἐν
ὁμοιώματι σαρκὸς ἁμαρτίας καὶ περὶ ἁμαρτίας κατέκρινεν τὴν ἁμαρτίαν ἐν τῇ σαρκί,
ἵνα τὸ δικαίωμα τοῦ νόμου πληρωθῇ ἐν ἡμῖν τοῖς μὴ κατὰ σάρκα περιπατοῦσιν ἀλλὰ κατὰ πνεῦμα.

οἱ γὰρ κατὰ σάρκα ὄντες τὰ τῆς σαρκὸς φρονοῦσιν,
οἱ δὲ κατὰ πνεῦμα τὰ τοῦ πνεύματος.
τὸ γὰρ φρόνημα τῆς σαρκὸς θάνατος,
τὸ δὲ φρόνημα τοῦ πνεύματος ζωὴ καὶ εἰρήνη·
διότι τὸ φρόνημα τῆς σαρκὸς ἔχθρα εἰς θεόν,
τῷ γὰρ νόμῳ τοῦ θεοῦ οὐχ ὑποτάσσεται, οὐδὲ γὰρ δύναται·
οἱ δὲ ἐν σαρκὶ ὄντες θεῷ ἀρέσαι οὐ δύνανται.

ὑμεῖς δὲ οὐκ ἐστὲ ἐν σαρκὶ ἀλλ' ἐν πνεύματι, εἴπερ πνεῦμα θεοῦ οἰκεῖ ἐν ὑμῖν.
εἰ δέ τις πνεῦμα Χριστοῦ οὐκ ἔχει,
οὗτος οὐκ ἔστιν αὐτοῦ.
εἰ δὲ Χριστὸς ἐν ὑμῖν,
τὸ μὲν σῶμα νεκρὸν διὰ ἁμαρτίαν
τὸ δὲ πνεῦμα ζωὴ διὰ δικαιοσύνην.
εἰ δὲ τὸ πνεῦμα τοῦ ἐγείραντος τὸν Ἰησοῦν ἐκ νεκρῶν οἰκεῖ ἐν ὑμῖν,
ὁ ἐγείρας Χριστὸν ἐκ νεκρῶν ζῳοποιήσει καὶ τὰ θνητὰ σώματα ὑμῶν διὰ τοῦ ἐνοικοῦντος αὐτοῦ πνεύματος ἐν ὑμῖν.

Ἄρα οὖν, ἀδελφοί, ὀφειλέται ἐσμὲν οὐ τῇ σαρκὶ τοῦ κατὰ σάρκα ζῆν,
εἰ γὰρ κατὰ σάρκα ζῆτε, μέλλετε ἀποθνῄσκειν·

εἰ δὲ πνεύματι τὰς πράξεις τοῦ σώματος θανατοῦτε, ζήσεσθε.

ὅσοι γὰρ πνεύματι θεοῦ ἄγονται, οὗτοι υἱοὶ θεοῦ εἰσιν
οὐ γὰρ ἐλάβετε πνεῦμα δουλείας πάλιν εἰς φόβον
ἀλλ' ἐλάβετε πνεῦμα υἱοθεσίας
└── ἐν ᾧ κράζομεν, Αββα ὁ πατήρ.

αὐτὸ τὸ πνεῦμα συμμαρτυρεῖ τῷ πνεύματι ἡμῶν ὅτι ἐσμὲν τέκνα θεοῦ.
εἰ δὲ τέκνα, καὶ κληρονόμοι·
κληρονόμοι μὲν θεοῦ,
συγκληρονόμοι δὲ Χριστοῦ,
εἴπερ συμπάσχομεν ἵνα καὶ συνδοξασθῶμεν.

VERSE 1

Οὐδὲν ἄρα νῦν κατάκριμα τοῖς ἐν Χριστῷ Ἰησοῦ

Longenecker suggests that the absence of a verb highlights this clause as "a theological pronouncement" (684). Placing the adjective *οὐδέν* (nom. sg. neut.) first gives it special emphasis. Dunn writes that *ἄρα* ("therefore/then") suggests a less direct connection and ties this verse back to 5:12–21 (415; cf. Moo 469). The more likely connection is to 7:6 (Cranfield 372; Jewett 479; Schreiner 398). See 3:21 for *νῦν* as a soteriological contrast (cf. 3:26; 5:9, 11; 6:19, 22; 7:6, 17). See 5:16 for *κατάκριμα*; Jewett suggests a nuance of "doom" (480). The definite article allows the prepositional phrase to function as a noun; ἐν + dative is best understood as incorporative union (Harris 123). The shorter reading, Ἰησοῦ, has strong external support (א*, B, C[2], and D*). Metzger gives it an {A} rating and notes that the two longer variants are interpolations from verse 4 (455).

VERSE 2

ὁ γὰρ νόμος τοῦ πνεύματος τῆς ζωῆς ἐν Χριστῷ Ἰησοῦ

The reason (*γάρ*) there is no condemnation is the domain of new life produced by the Spirit (cf. 7:6). Both Dunn (416) and Schreiner (400) argue that *ὁ νόμος* refers to the Torah, but Cranfield notes six additional possibilities and settles on "the authority and constraint exercised on the believer by the Holy Spirit" (375–76; cf. Moo 475). Τοῦ πνεύματος is a genitive of apposition that clarifies *ὁ νόμος* and refers to the Holy Spirit. Τῆς ζωῆς is a genitive of product (cf. Wallace 106). The concatenation of genitives explains the presence of the definite articles with each noun in the phrase. Although Cranfield (375), Dunn (418), and Schreiner (401) take ἐν Χριστῷ Ἰησοῦ with the following verb, Jewett takes it with the preceding noun phrase as referring to the domain in which "the law of the Spirit of life" functions (481). The absence of a definite article suggests a connection to the entire noun phrase rather than to any one of the nouns in it (cf. Kuss 2:490).

ἠλευθέρωσέν σε ἀπὸ τοῦ νόμου τῆς ἁμαρτίας καὶ τοῦ θανάτου

Of the four variant readings, two (ἡμᾶς and no object) "can be safely dismissed since they are slightly supported in the manuscript tradition" (Schreiner 408). Both *με* (א, B) and *σε* (A, D) are well-supported, but commentators tend to view the latter as the more difficult reading (e.g., Dunn 414; Moo 470 n. 11) and argue that *με* would be expected after the prominence of the first person in 7:14–25 (e.g., Schreiner 408). Ἠλευθέρωσεν (3 sg. aor. act. indic. of ἐλευθερόω, "set free") is a constative aorist referring to past conversion (Jewett 481). The second person singular pronoun (*σε*) individualizes the truth and applies it to all believers (Cranfield 377). Ἀπό + ablative regularly denotes separation after ἐλευθερόω (cf. 6:18). *Τοῦ νόμου* parallels the idea of authority in the first half of the verse; *τῆς ἁμαρτίας* clarifies *τοῦ νόμου* as a genitive of apposition; *τοῦ θανάτου* also depends on *τοῦ νόμου* (Moo 476 n. 31) and functions as a genitive of product.

VERSE 3

τὸ γὰρ ἀδύνατον τοῦ νόμου

The explanation (*γάρ*) for how we are set free from sin and death lies in God's action of sending Christ. First, however, Paul highlights what could not set us free. Robertson sets out five possible grammatical analyses of the phrase *τὸ ἀδύνατον τοῦ νόμου* (491). Moo (477 n. 37) and Schreiner (401) understand it as anacoluthon; Moule (35), Porter (91), Cranfield (378), and Jewett (482) understand it as standing in apposition to the main clause that follows. The article with *ἀδύνατον* allows the adjective to function as a noun (R 654); Turner suggests that it is *par excellence* (13). Dunn concludes that the effective distinction between "unable" and "impossible" as translations for *ἀδύνατον* is not very great (419). EVV uniformly choose the former ("could not do"). In contrast to the preceding verse, *τοῦ νόμου* refers to the Mosaic law (Moo 478); the genitive is subjective. Blass suggests that the phrase is an ellipsis for *ὅ τῷ νόμῳ ἀδύνατος ἦν* (§480.6).

ἐν ᾧ ἠσθένει διὰ τῆς σαρκός

Paul further explains the preceding phrase and reiterates his previous contention that we, rather than the law, are the problem (7:13–25). Ἐν ᾧ is causal (R 978; T 253; BDF §219.2; cf. 5:12); *ἠσθένει* (3 sg. impf. act. indic. of ἀσθενέω, "be weak") is a progressive imperfect used for vividness; *διά* + genitive denotes instrumentality. Moo describes *σάρξ* as "the 'this-worldly' orientation that all people share" (478; cf. 7:5).

ὁ θεὸς τὸν ἑαυτοῦ υἱὸν πέμψας ἐν ὁμοιώματι σαρκὸς ἁμαρτίας καὶ περὶ ἁμαρτίας

The article with *θεός* is monadic; the article with *υἱός* is also monadic and functions as a possessive pronoun ("his unique son"); the reflexive pronoun *ἑαυτοῦ* ("his own") is emphatic (Cranfield 379). The participle *πέμψας* (nom. sg. masc. of aor. act. ptc. of πέμπω, "send") is adverbial of means (cf. Longenecker 695; Schreiner 402). Two connected (*καί*) prepositional phrases modify the participle. Ἐν + dative indicates sphere; περί + genitive indicates reference; the objects of both prepositions are anarthrous and qualitative. Cranfield (379–81) sets out five possible understandings for ἐν ὁμοιώματι σαρκὸς ἁμαρτίας ("in the likeness of sinful flesh"). Jewett concludes that ὁμοίωμα, -τος, τό points to total identity and involvement rather than mere similarity (484; cf. Schreiner 403). Σαρκός is a genitive of material ("consisting of"); ἁμαρτίας is an attributed genitive ("sinful flesh"). Dunn provides LXX evidence that περὶ ἁμαρτίας should be understood as "a sin offering" (422; cf. Moo 480 n. 48).

κατέκρινεν τὴν ἁμαρτίαν ἐν τῇ σαρκί

Κατέκρινεν (3 sg. aor. act. indic. of κατακρίνω, "condemn") supplies the verb of which ὁ θεός is the subject; Cranfield defines the action as both the sentence and its execution that break sin's power (382; cf. Moo 480; Schreiner 402). Τὴν ἁμαρτίαν is accusative of direct object; the article is anaphoric. The prepositional phrase ἐν τῇ σαρκί modifies κατέκρινεν and indicates the sphere where God's judgment was carried out (Cranfield 382; Schreiner 403). The definite article should be understood as a personal pronoun referring to Christ ("in his [i.e., Christ's] flesh"; cf. CEV, NIRV).

VERSE 4

ἵνα τὸ δικαίωμα τοῦ νόμου πληρωθῇ ἐν ἡμῖν

The purpose (ἵνα + subjunc.) of God condemning sin relates directly to believers. Moo lists three options for τὸ δικαίωμα in this context and decides for "right or just requirement," by which he understands the summary of what the law demands of God's people (481–83; cf. Cranfield 384; Jewett 485). Νομός refers to the Mosaic law (Dunn 423); the genitive indicates source or origin. Πληρωθῇ (3 sg. aor. pass. subjunc. of πληρόω, "fulfill") is a constative aorist, and the passive voice places emphasis on the subject (τὸ δικαίωμα). Although Jewett understands ἐν ἡμῖν as "among us," that is, "within house and tenement churches" (485), it more likely describes individual followers of Christ (cf. Cranfield 385). Commentators differ on exactly how the righteous requirement of the law is fulfilled in believers. Moo argues that it happens through incorporation into Christ (484);* Schreiner argues for the actual obedience of believers due to God's work in believers (405). Cranfield is careful to clarify that the latter understanding does not imply that believers fulfill the law's requirement perfectly (384).

τοῖς μὴ κατὰ σάρκα περιπατοῦσιν ἀλλὰ κατὰ πνεῦμα

The dative definite article accompanies περιπατοῦσιν (dat. pl. masc. of pres. act. ptc. of περιπατέω, "walk") and brackets the participial phrase, which functions substantivally and stands in apposition to ἡμῖν (R 778). Μή "almost invariably" accompanies participles (T 285) and establishes a strong contrast with ἀλλά. The parallel prepositional phrases (κατά + acc.) denote both standard and control. Moo suggests "directed by" in the sense of "living under the control of and according to the values of" (485).

According to Harris, *κατὰ σάρκα* and *κατὰ πνεῦμα* designate "diametrically opposed patterns of conduct and thinking." The former describes life lived under the control of the unregenerate human nature; the latter describes life lived under the domination of the Spirit (151).

VERSE 5

οἱ γὰρ κατὰ σάρκα ὄντες τὰ τῆς σαρκὸς φρονοῦσιν

Having established the contrast between life lived *κατὰ σάρκα* and the life lived *κατὰ πνεῦμα*, Paul provides the reason (*γάρ*) the righteous requirement of the law is fulfilled in believers (Dunn 425). The definite article accompanies *ὄντες* (nom. pl. masc. of pres. act. ptc. of *εἰμί*) and brackets the substantival participial phrase. Schreiner argues that ontology is in view (410–12; cf. Jewett 486; Moo 486), although Cranfield (385) and Dunn (425) disagree. The article allows the descriptive genitive, *τῆς σαρκός*, to function as a substantive that Robertson translates as "the affairs of the flesh" (767). The basic meaning of *φρονέω* is "give careful attention to something" (BDAG 1066a). Similar uses in Phil 2:5 and 3:19 suggest the nuance of orientation, mindset, or attitude (Jewett 486). The present tense is customary.

οἱ δὲ κατὰ πνεῦμα τὰ τοῦ πνεύματος

In contrast (*δέ*) to those whose basic orientation is toward the flesh, are *οἱ κατὰ πνεῦμα*. The participle *ὄντες* is understood as is the verb *φρονοῦσιν*. *Πνεῦμα* refers to the Holy Spirit (Dunn 426); *τὰ τοῦ πνεύματος* ("the affairs of the Spirit") is parallel to *τὰ τῆς σαρκός* in the preceding line.

VERSE 6

τὸ γὰρ φρόνημα τῆς σαρκὸς θάνατος

Although Moo (487) and Schreiner (412) understand *γάρ* as continuative, explanatory ("for") is more likely (Cranfield 386). *Φρόνημα, -τος, τό* denotes a way of thinking and focusing with strong intent (BDAG 1066a). Dunn notes that the *–μα* suffix denotes the result of an action (426), which supports the understanding of *τῆς σαρκός* as a subjective genitive (Cranfield 386). The article with both nouns is common when one is in the genitive (R 780). *'Εστίν* is understood; *θάνατος* is a predicate nominative. Cranfield describes *τὸ φρόνημα τῆς σαρκός* as the "outlook, assumptions, values, desires, and purposes, which those who take the side of the flesh share" (386).

τὸ δὲ φρόνημα τοῦ πνεύματος ζωὴ καὶ εἰρήνη

The adversative conjunction *δέ* ("but") continues Paul's antithetic parallelism. See 2:7 for *ζωή* and 1:7 for *εἰρήνη*. Together, the nouns describe an objective reality rather than a subjective state of mind (Moo 488; cf. 5:1).

VERSE 7

διότι τὸ φρόνημα τῆς σαρκὸς ἔχθρα εἰς θεόν

Verses 7 and 8 provide the reason (*διότι*) the mindset of the flesh leads to death. See verse 6 for *τὸ φρόνημα τῆς σαρκός*. The verb *ἐστίν* is understood; *ἔχθρα* is a predicate adjective. *ἔχθρα, ας, ἡ* describes active hostility (cf. 5:10); *εἰς* + accusative denotes disadvantage ("against God").

τῷ γὰρ νόμῳ τοῦ θεοῦ οὐχ ὑποτάσσεται οὐδὲ γὰρ δύναται

Paul explains (*γάρ*) the hostility of the mind of the flesh more fully in terms of its inability. *Τῷ νόμῳ τοῦ θεοῦ* (indir. obj.) is the Torah (Dunn 427). *Ὑποτάσσεται* (3 sg. pres. mid. indic. of *ὑποτάσσω*, "subject") is a gnomic present and a direct middle. The verb carries the idea of voluntarily submitting oneself, usually to a superior authority (Jewett 488; cf. BDAG 1042a). *Οὐδέ* is ascensive ("not even"); *γάρ* is explanatory; Blass notes that each conjunction retains its own force and translates the combination as "for it cannot either" (§452.3). *Δύναται* (3 sg. pres. mid. indic. of dep. *δύναμαι*, "be able") is a gnomic present and describes the capability for doing something (BDAG 262a).

VERSE 8

οἱ δὲ ἐν σαρκὶ ὄντες θεῷ ἀρέσαι οὐ δύνανται

Paul continues (*δέ*) with a summary that reinforces his point (Dunn 427). The participial phrase *οἱ ἐν σαρκὶ ὄντες* echoes verse 5, with *ἐν σαρκί* equivalent to *κατὰ σάρκα* (Cranfield 387). The "backward" word order of the remainder of the clause calls attention to Paul's statement. See verse 7 for *δύνανται*; *οὐ* regularly negates indicative verbs; *ἀρέσαι* (aor. act. inf. of *ἀρέσκω*, "please") is a complementary infinitive that regularly takes a dative of person (R 540; cf. BDAG 129d). For the idea of *θεῷ ἀρέσαι* see Romans 12:1–2; 14:18; 1 Corinthians 7:32; 2 Corinthians 5:9; Ephesians 5:10; Philippians 4:18; Colossians 3:20; 1 Thessalonians 4:1 (cf. Cranfield 387).

VERSE 9

ὑμεῖς δὲ οὐκ ἐστὲ ἐν σαρκὶ ἀλλ' ἐν πνεύματι

The readers are different from (*δέ*) those Paul has just described. The pronoun *ὑμεῖς* is emphatic (Moo 489 n. 93), addresses the readers directly (Cranfield 387), and particularizes the argument of 8:5–8 (Dunn 438). Jewett notes that the combination *ὑμεῖς δέ* opens a sentence only here in Romans (489). *Οὐκ . . . ἀλλά* establishes a strong contrast between the spheres of *ἐν σαρκί* and *ἐν πνεύματι* and places the readers unambiguously in the latter. Robertson understands *ἐν* + dative as manner (589), and Blass understands it as local (§219.4). Dunn, however, suggests that *ἐν πνεύματι* captures "a sense of immediacy and communion with God and of enabling in daily conduct" (428).

εἴπερ πνεῦμα θεοῦ οἰκεῖ ἐν ὑμῖν

The strengthened form εἴπερ ("if indeed," cf. NASB, NKJV, NET) adds emphasis to the truth assumed for the sake of argument (R 1154); Longenecker translates the conjunction as "since" and sees it as adding a note of assurance (698). Both nouns in the anarthrous combination πνεῦμα θεοῦ are definite (Wallace 252) and denote one-of-a-kind (R 795). The use of θεοῦ without the article is common as the proper name for God (R 761). Οἰκεῖ (3 sg. pres. act. indic. of οἰκέω, "dwell") is a progressive present. Ἐν ὑμῖν ("in you") denotes sphere of reference and highlights the fellowship between the believer and Christ (Harris 125). S-H describe the combination as "a settled permanent penetrative influence" (196); NJB translates the clause "since the Spirit of God has made a home in you."

εἰ δέ τις πνεῦμα Χριστοῦ οὐκ ἔχει, οὗτος οὐκ ἔστιν αὐτοῦ

Δέ is connective (cf. NEB), and Cranfield takes the remainder of the verse as parenthetical (388). Εἰ + present indicative establishes a first class condition (R 1008); the indefinite pronoun τις marks the condition as general rather than particular (Wallace 706). Πνεῦμα Χριστοῦ is synonymous with πνεῦμα θεοῦ in the preceding clause; ἔχει is a progressive present. Dunn notes that ἔχω occurs elsewhere as the language of possession of long duration, both demonic in other writers (e.g., Matt 11:18; Mark 3:30; 7:15; Luke 4:33; Acts 8:7; 16:16) and positively in Paul (1 Cor 7:40; 2 Cor 4:13). The demonstrative pronoun οὗτος is resumptive (R 698); the pronoun αὐτοῦ is a possessive genitive.

VERSE 10

εἰ δὲ Χριστὸς ἐν ὑμῖν

In contrast (δέ) to the general condition just discussed is the particular first class condition (εἰ) in which the readers find themselves. All three clauses of the sentence assume the verb ἐστίν. Χριστός is synonymous with πνεῦμα θεοῦ and πνεῦμα Χριστοῦ (Dunn 430). See the preceding verse for ἐν ὑμῖν.

τὸ μὲν σῶμα νεκρὸν διὰ ἁμαρτίαν

The correlative μέν functions concessively (Cranfield 389; cf, NEB, ESV; contra Longenecker, who sees it as affirmative/emphatic, 700) so that this clause is subordinate to the one that follows (Moo 492). The article with σῶμα marks it as the subject; νεκρόν is the predicate adjective. Cranfield suggests that Paul uses νεκρός ("dead") instead of θνητός ("mortal") for the sake of vividness (389). Although Dunn views σῶμα as the embodiment of human existence (431), Moo's view that it refers to the physical body is more likely (491 n. 104). Διά + accusative is causal (Moule 195; cf. 4:25); the death "because of sin" is physical death.

τὸ δὲ πνεῦμα ζωὴ διὰ δικαιοσύνην

RSV and ESV leave the correlative δέ untranslated. Τὸ πνεῦμα refers to the Holy Spirit rather than to the human spirit (Cranfield 390; Dunn 431; Moo 492; Schreiner 415). See 1:17 for ζωή. Διά + accusative is causal ("because of"); δικαιοσύνη is Christ's righteousness imputed to the believer (Moo 492; cf. Cranfield 390).

VERSE 11

εἰ δὲ τὸ πνεῦμα τοῦ ἐγείραντος τὸν Ἰησοῦν ἐκ νεκρῶν οἰκεῖ ἐν ὑμῖν

The conjunction δέ ("and"; cf. NIV, NJB, ESV) is resumptive (Schreiner 415); εἰ + indicative establishes another first class condition (R 1009). The article accompanies πνεῦμα because the genitive participle that follows also has an article. The second article marks ἐγείραντος (gen. sg. masc. of aor. act. ptc. of ἐγείρω, "raise") as substantival; the aorist is constative; the genitive is possessive. Τὸν Ἰησοῦν is the object of the participle; the article is anaphoric. See 1:4 for the ablative ἐκ νεκρῶν and 8:9 for οἰκεῖ ἐν ὑμῖν.

ὁ ἐγείρας Χριστὸν ἐκ νεκρῶν ζῳοποιήσει καὶ τὰ θνητὰ σώματα ὑμῶν

Ὁ ἐγείρας Χριστὸν ἐκ νεκρῶν repeats the idea of the preceding line. Turner notes that the use of the predictive future (ζῳοποιήσει) in the apodosis points to definiteness that makes the protasis "almost causal" (115). See 4:17 for ζῳοποιέω; καί is adjunctive ("also"). The article accompanies σώματα because of the possessive pronoun that follows. Placing the adjective in the first predicate position gives it greater emphasis than the noun. See 6:12 for θνητός. Jewett agrees with Calvin that ζῳοποιήσει refers to the present work of the indwelling Spirit who enhances the life of those currently in Christ (492–93). Cranfield (391), Dunn (432), Moo (493), and Schreiner (416) all understand it as a reference to the final resurrection.

διὰ τοῦ ἐνοικοῦντος αὐτοῦ πνεύματος ἐν ὑμῖν

Both Moo (471 n. 12) and Schreiner (417) have good discussions of the textual choice between διά + genitive and διά + accusative. Metzger prefers the genitive on the basis of the combination of Alexandrian, Palestinian, and Western text-types (456), and the genitive of agency is more consistently Pauline (cf. 5:5; 7:4; 8:37; 2 Tim 1:14). Cranfield provides four reasons supporting the genitive reading (391–92). The definite article accompanies πνεύματος and brackets both the adjectival participle (gen. sg. neut. of pres. act. ptc. of ἐνοικέω, "live/dwell in") and the possessive pronoun (αὐτοῦ). The prefix ἐν strengthens οἰκέω and reinforces ἐν ὑμῖν. ESV translates the phrase literally as "through his Spirit who dwells in you," while NEB takes a simpler approach: "through his indwelling Spirit."

VERSE 12

Ἄρα οὖν, ἀδελφοί, ὀφειλέται ἐσμέν

Paul next moves to the implications of being indwelt by the Spirit. The first implication (v. 12–13) addresses the believer's relation to the flesh. See 5:18 for ἄρα οὖν (cf. 7:3, 25), 1:13 for ἀδελφοί (cf. 7:1, 4), and 1:14 for ὀφειλέται (nom. pl. masc. of ὀφειλέτης, -ου, ὁ, "debtor"). Placing ὀφειλέται before ἐσμέν (1 pl. pres. act. indic. of εἰμί) gives the predicate nominative emphasis.

οὐ τῇ σαρκὶ τοῦ κατὰ σάρκα ζῆν

The particle οὐ negates τῇ σαρκί; Robertson suggests that the dative is equivalent to a genitive following ὀφειλέται (537); Turner views it as a dative of disadvantage (238). Moo argues that "flesh" refers to "all that is characteristic of this life in its rebellion against God" (494). Τοῦ . . . ζῆν (pres. act. infin. of ζάω) is understood variously as an appositional modifier of ὀφειλέται (Porter 198), purpose (T 141), result (Cranfield 394), or epexegetical (R 996, 1067, 1087).* Moo opts for the latter and suggests the translation "debtors to the flesh, so as to live by it" (493 n. 116). See 8:4 for κατὰ σάρκα. Cranfield argues that the position of οὐ suggests Paul intended to continue with a contrasting statement (e.g., ἀλλὰ τῳ πνεύματι τοῦ κατὰ πνεῦμα ζῆν) but forgot to complete his thought after inserting verse 13 (394). That explanation seems unlikely (cf. Schreiner 419), although the contrast is implicit.

VERSE 13

εἰ γὰρ κατὰ σάρκα ζῆτε μέλλετε ἀποθνήσκειν

Paul sets out the rationale (γάρ) for not living according to the flesh in two parallel conditional constructions. Εἰ + indicative establishes a first class condition; κατὰ σάρκα ζῆτε echoes the end of the preceding verse; ζῆτε (2 pl. pres. act. indic. of ζάω) is a customary present. Dunn notes that the change to second plural increases the note of warning (448). Μέλλω has a future nuance inherent in its lexical meaning ("to take place at a future point in time," BDAG 628b); ἀποθνήσκειν (pres. act. infin. of ἀποθνήσκω, "die") is a complementary infinitive (Wallace 599). Cranfield describes the construction as a periphrastic future that emphasizes the consequence as necessary and certain (394). Schreiner highlights the eschatological nature of the death (420).

εἰ δὲ πνεύματι τὰς πράξεις τοῦ σώματος θανατοῦτε ζήσεσθε

Life lived by the Spirit is in direct contrast (δέ) to life lived according to the flesh. Πνεύματι is an instrumental dative (T 240) and is brought forward for emphasis. Πρᾶξις, -εως, ἡ denotes the performance of some deed, often evil or disgraceful (BDAG 860a; cf. 1:32); σώματος is a subjective genitive. Cranfield equates σῶμα with σάρξ (395), but Moo suggests that the phrase describes "deeds worked out through the body under the influence of the flesh" (495; cf. Schreiner 421). Θανατοῦτε (2 pl. pres.

act. indic. of θανατόω, "put to death"; cf. 7:4; Col 3:5) is a customary present; ζήσεσθε (2 pl. fut. mid. indic. of ζάω) is a predictive future (Dunn 449; cf. 1:17).

VERSE 14

ὅσοι γὰρ πνεύματι θεοῦ ἄγονται, οὗτοι υἱοὶ θεοῦ εἰσιν

The second implication (v. 14–15) addresses the believer's relation to God. It is common for a correlative pronoun to have no expressed antecedent (R 732). Ὅσοι (nom. pl. masc. of ὅσος, -η, -ον, "as many as") has an inclusive sense (NEB, "all who"; cf. Dunn 450), and Wallace notes that it introduces an implied condition (685). Πνεύματι is an instrumental dative (Moule 44); see verse 9 for πνεῦμα θεοῦ. Ἄγονται (3 pl. pres. pass. indic. of ἄγω, "lead") is a customary present and a simple passive; the verb denotes control and governing rather than guidance (Schreiner 422). The demonstrative pronoun οὗτοι (nom. pl. masc.) is resumptive (R 698) and emphatic (Jewett 496). Both nouns in the combination υἱοὶ θεοῦ are definite; the genitive of θεοῦ is possessive.

VERSE 15

οὐ γὰρ ἐλάβετε πνεῦμα δουλείας πάλιν εἰς φόβον

Paul sets out the rationale (γάρ) for being confident in our status as God's children in two contrasting statements (οὐ . . . ἀλλά). Ἐλάβετε (2 pl. aor. act. indic. of λαμβάνω, "receive") is a constative aorist that points to the beginning of the Christian life (Schreiner 423). Πνεῦμα δουλείας has been understood as either the human spirit (e.g., S-H 202–03) or the Holy Spirit. The latter is preferred (see Cranfield 396; contra Longenecker, who understands it as "the activating or essential principle influencing a person" 703). Δουλεία, -ας, ἡ describes a state or condition of being subservient (BDAG 259b); Dunn suggests that the genitive is ambiguous, describing either what the Spirit effects or expresses (452). Πάλιν ("again") points to a return to a previous activity (BDAG 752c) and should be taken with the prepositional phrase that follows (Moo 500). Εἰς + accusative denotes purpose (R 595); Jewett understands φόβον as "fear of failing to come up to the mark of acceptability" (498). Schreiner describes the use of πνεῦμα as "rhetorical" (Schreiner 424), and GNB translates the clause as "For the Spirit God has given you does not make you slaves and cause you to be afraid" (cf. NEB).

ἀλλʼ ἐλάβετε πνεῦμα υἱοθεσίας

Ἀλλά introduces the second half of the contrast, with ἐλάβετε repeated from the first line and πνεῦμα υἱοθεσίας ("a Spirit of adoption") contrasted with πνεῦμα δουλείας. See Schreiner for the Jewish background of υἱοθεσία (425) and Cranfield for Greco-Roman background (397–98; cf. *TDNT* 8.399 and Longenecker 703–705). Elsewhere in Paul υἱοθεσία occurs in Romans 8:23; 9:4; Galatians 4:5; Ephesians 1:5.

ἐν ᾧ κράζομεν· αββα ὁ πατήρ

Cranfield sets out three reasons to connect this relative clause with what precedes (398). The Spirit is also the means ("by whom") we are able to call God "Father" (Schreiner 425). Κράζω describes fervent, rather than loud, speech (BDAG 564a); Longenecker writes that it denotes "urgent prayer" (705, following Cranfield); Schreiner concludes that the verb connotes "gladness and joy inexpressible" (426). Αββα was originally an Aramaic term of endearment that became a title and personal name (BDAG 1d; cf. Cranfield 399–400). Ὁ πατήρ is a nominative used as a vocative; the article frequently occurs with the vocative (R 465).

VERSE 16

αὐτὸ τὸ πνεῦμα συμμαρτυρεῖ τῷ πνεύματι ἡμῶν ὅτι ἐσμὲν τέκνα θεοῦ

Although asyndetic (BDF §463), verses 16 and 17 reiterate and clarify what precedes (Jewett 500). The intensive use of αὐτό ("the Spirit himself"; cf. Porter 120) makes it clear Paul is talking about the Holy Spirit as distinct from the human spirit (Moo 504 n. 39). Συμμαρτυρεῖ (3 sg. pres. act. indic. of συμμαρτυρέω, "bear witness with"; cf. 2:15) is a progressive present. Jewett writes that the verb "is typically used to depict co-witnessing of some sort" (500). Similarly, Robertson (529), Dunn (454), Moo (504 n. 40), and Schreiner (426) all understand τῷ πνεύματι as a dative of association ("with our spirit"),* while Cranfield (403) and Wallace (160–61) understand it as a dative of indirect object ("to our spirit"). The spirit in question is our human spirit (Moo 503 n. 37; cf. 1:9). Ὅτι is declarative (R 1035); τέκνα θεοῦ ("children of God") is synonymous with υἱοὶ θεοῦ (Moo 504 n. 41; Dunn 455; contra Jewett 501).

VERSE 17

εἰ δὲ τέκνα, καὶ κληρονόμοι

Δέ is continuative ("and") rather than adversative; εἰ introduces an elliptical first class condition; καί is adjunctive ("also"). See 4:13 for κληρονόμος. Cranfield has an extended discussion on the language of inheriting in Paul (405–407).

κληρονόμοι μὲν θεοῦ, συγκληρονόμοι δὲ Χριστοῦ

The correlative conjunctions μέν . . . δέ provide a rhetorical expansion on the idea of inheritance. Jewett notes that first, κληρονόμοι is stated without qualification in the absolute sense; then, κληρονόμοι θεοῦ makes clear the source of the inheritance; finally, συγκληρονόμοι Χριστοῦ clarifies the relational nature of the inheritance (501). Θεοῦ is a subjective genitive ("heirs of what God promises"); Χριστοῦ is a genitive of association ("co-heirs with Christ"). Συγκληρονόμος occurs elsewhere in Ephesians 3:6, Hebrews 11:9, and 1 Peter 3:7.

εἴπερ συμπάσχομεν ἵνα καὶ συνδοξασθῶμεν

Cranfield (407) and Jewett (502) view εἴπερ as stating a fact (cf. "because," CEV); Dunn (456) and Schreiner (428) view it as stating a condition not yet fulfilled (cf. NJB, "provided that").* Συμπάσχομεν (1 pl. pres. act. indic. of συμπάσχω, "suffer with") is a progressive present. Ἵνα + subjunctive denotes purpose (Moo 506 n. 51); καί is adjunctive. Συνδοξασθῶμεν (1 pl. aor. pass. subjunc. of συνδοξάζω, "share in glory with") is a constative aorist and a divine passive; the verb completes the theme of inheritance by pointing to the eschatological glory believers ultimately receive (Schreiner 428; cf. 8:18–25).

FOR FURTHER STUDY

50. Holy Spirit (8:5)

Bloesch, D. G. *The Holy Spirit: Works and Gifts*. Downers Grove, IL: InterVarsity, 2000.
Blomberg, C. L. *EDBT* 344–48.
Carson, D. A. *Showing the Spirit*. Grand Rapids: Baker, 1987.
Caulley, T. S. *EDT* 521–27.
Fee, G. D. *Paul, the Spirit, and the People of God*. Peabody, MA: Hendrickson, 1996.
________. *God's Empowering Presence: The Holy Spirit in the Letters of Paul*. Peabody, MA: Hendrickson, 1994.
Ferguson, S. *The Holy Spirit*. Downers Grove, IL: InterVarsity, 1996.
Green, M. B. *I Believe in the Holy Spirit*. Grand Rapids: Eerdmans, 1989.
Harvey, J. D. *Anointed with the Spirit and Power: The Holy Spirit's Empowering Presence*. Phillipsburg, NJ: P&R, 2008.
Horn, F. W. *ABD* 3.260–80.
Meyer, P. "The Holy Spirit in the Pauline Letters: A Contextual Exploration." *Int* 33 (1979): 3–18.
Müller, H. *NIDNTT* 3.689–709.
Paige, T. *DPL* 404–13.
Schweizer, E. *TDNT* 6.332–455.
Thomas, R. "The Seal of the Spirit and the Religious Climate of Ephesus." *ResQ* (2001): 155–59.
Woodstock, E. "The Seal of the Holy Spirit." *BSac* 155 (1998): 139–50.

51. Adoption (8:15)

Brown, W. E. *EDBT* 11–12.
Braumann, G. *NIDNTT* 1.287–90.
Burke, T. J. *Adopted into God's Family: Exploring a Pauline Metaphor*. Downers Grove, IL: InterVarsity, 2006.
Ciampa, R. E. *NDBT* 376–78.
Cook, J. I. "The Concept of Adoption in the Theology of Paul." Pages 133–44 in *Saved by Hope: Essays in Honor of Richard C. Oudersluys*. Edited by J. L. Cook. Grand Rapids: Eerdmans, 1978.
Hodge C. E. J. *If Sons, then Heirs: A Study of Kinship and Ethnicity in the Letters of Paul*. Oxford: New York, 2007.

Knobloch, F. W. *ABD* 1.76–79.
Lindsay, H. *Adoption in the Roman World*. Cambridge: Cambridge University Press, 2009.
Lyall, F. *Slaves, Citizens, Sons: Legal Metaphors in the Epistles*. Grand Rapids: Zondervan, 1984.
________. "Roman Law in the Writings of Paul—Adoption." *JBL* 88 (1969): 458–66.
Peterson, R. A. *Adopted by God: From Wayward Sinners to Cherished Children*. Phillipsburg, NJ: P&R, 2001.
Rossell, W. H. "New Testament Adoption—Graeco-Roman or Semitic?" *JBL* 71 (1952); 233–34.
________. "Roman Law in the Writings of Paul—Adoption." *JBL* 88 (1969): 458–66.
Scott, J. M. *Adoption as Sons of God: An Exegetical Investigation into the Background of ΥΙΟΘΕΣΙΑ in the Pauline Corpus*. Tübingen: Mohr Siebeck, 1992.
________. *DPL* 15–18.
Theron, D. J. "'Adoption' in the Pauline Corpus." *EvQ* 28 (1956): 6–14.
v. Murtitz W., and E. Schweizer. *TDNT* 8.397–99.

HOMILETICAL SUGGESTIONS

The Role of the Indwelling Spirit (8:1–17)

1. Status: No condemnation (οὐδὲν ἄρα νῦν κατάκριμα, 8:1)
2. Reasons (8:2–11)
    a. The Spirit sets free from sin and death (γάρ, 8:2–4)
        1) Law is unable (8:3a)
        2) God condemned sin (8:3b)
            a) By sending his son as a sin offering (8:3c)
            b) In order to fulfill requirement of law (8:4)
    b. Those in the Spirit are oriented to spiritual affairs (γάρ, 8:5–8)
        1) The mindset of the Spirit is life and peace (8:6b)
        2) The mindset of the flesh is death (8:6a)
            a) It is hostile to God (8:7a)
            b) It is not subject to God's law (8:7b)
            c) It cannot please God (8:8)
    c. Those in the Spirit are indwelt by the Spirit (ὑμεῖς δέ, 8:9–11)
        1) The body is dead because of sin (8:10a)
        2) The spirit is alive because of righteousness (8:10b)
        3) The Spirit will give life to the body (8:11)
3. Implications (ἄρα οὖν, ἀδελφοί, 8:12–17)
    a. No longer debtors to the flesh (8:12–13)
        1) Living according to the flesh leads to death (8:13a)
        2) Putting to death deeds of flesh by the Spirit leads to life (8:13b)
    b. Now children of God (8:14–17)
        1) They are led by the Spirit (8:14)
        2) They received the Spirit of adoption (8:15)
        3) The Spirit witnesses to their status (8:16–17)

What the Holy Spirit Does (8:1–17)

1. The Spirit enables us to fulfill the law (8:4)
2. The Spirit sets our minds on spiritual things (8:5)
3. The Spirit indwells us (8:9)
4. The Spirit puts to death the deeds of the flesh (8:13)
5. The Spirit leads us (8:14)
6. The Spirit testifies to our adoption (8:16)

b. Who Gives Us Hope of Glory (8:18–30)

STRUCTURE

The idea of suffering and its connection to glory (8:17) leads Paul to embark on a longer discussion of that relationship. After stating his thesis (8:18), the discussion divides into four parts (8:19–21; 8:22–25; 8:26–27; 8:28–30). The first focuses on "creation" (κτίσις, three times); the second shifts to believers (first person plural) and focuses on "hope" (ἐλπίς/ἐλπίζω, five times). The third explains the Holy Spirit's role in the process (πνεῦμα, three times), and the fourth shifts to the divine perspective and concludes with the well-known climax of verses 29–30. The idea of "glory" (δόξα/δοξάζω) brackets the paragraph (8:18, 30). Jewett notes the stylistic unity created by eight verbs that are ἀπο- compounds, nine verbs that are συν- compounds, and five words that are προ- compounds (506).

Λογίζομαι γὰρ ὅτι οὐκ ἄξια τὰ παθήματα τοῦ νῦν καιροῦ πρὸς τὴν μέλλουσαν δόξαν
ἀποκαλυφθῆναι εἰς ἡμᾶς.

ἡ γὰρ ἀποκαραδοκία τῆς κτίσεως τὴν ἀποκάλυψιν τῶν υἱῶν τοῦ θεοῦ ἀπεκδέχεται.
τῇ γὰρ ματαιότητι ἡ κτίσις ὑπετάγη,
οὐχ ἑκοῦσα
ἀλλὰ διὰ τὸν ὑποτάξαντα,
ἐφ᾽ ἑλπίδι ὅτι καὶ αὐτὴ ἡ κτίσις ἐλευθερωθήσεται ἀπὸ τῆς δουλείας τῆς
φθορᾶς εἰς τὴν ἐλευθερίαν τῆς δόξης τῶν τέκνων τοῦ θεοῦ.

οἴδαμεν γὰρ ὅτι πᾶσα ἡ κτίσις συστενάζει καὶ συνωδίνει ἄχρι τοῦ νῦν·
οὐ μόνον δέ, ἀλλὰ καὶ αὐτοὶ τὴν ἀπαρχὴν τοῦ πνεύματος ἔχοντες, ἡμεῖς καὶ αὐτοὶ ἐν
ἑαυτοῖς στενάζομεν υἱοθεσίαν ἀπεκδεχόμενοι, τὴν ἀπολύτρωσιν τοῦ σώματος ἡμῶν.
τῇ γὰρ ἐλπίδι ἐσώθημεν·
ἐλπὶς δὲ βλεπομένη οὐκ ἔστιν ἐλπίς·
ὃ γὰρ βλέπει τίς ἐλπίζει;
εἰ δὲ ὃ οὐ βλέπομεν ἐλπίζομεν, δι᾽ ὑπομονῆς ἀπεκδεχόμεθα.

Ὡσαύτως δὲ καὶ τὸ πνεῦμα συναντιλαμβάνεται τῇ ἀσθενείᾳ ἡμῶν·
τὸ γὰρ τί προσευξώμεθα καθὸ δεῖ οὐκ οἴδαμεν,
ἀλλ᾽ αὐτὸ τὸ πνεῦμα ὑπερεντυγχάνει στεναγμοῖς ἀλαλήτοις·
ὁ δὲ ἐραυνῶν τὰς καρδίας οἶδεν τί τὸ φρόνημα τοῦ πνεύματος,
ὅτι κατὰ θεὸν ἐντυγχάνει ὑπὲρ ἁγίων.

οἴδαμεν δὲ ὅτι τοῖς ἀγαπῶσιν τὸν θεὸν πάντα συνεργεῖ εἰς ἀγαθόν, τοῖς κατὰ
πρόθεσιν κλητοῖς οὖσιν.

ὅτι οὓς προέγνω, καὶ προώρισεν συμμόρφους τῆς εἰκόνος τοῦ υἱοῦ αὐτοῦ,
εἰς τὸ εἶναι αὐτὸν πρωτότοκον ἐν πολλοῖς ἀδελφοῖς·
οὓς δὲ προώρισεν, τούτους καὶ ἐκάλεσεν·
καὶ οὓς ἐκάλεσεν, τούτους καὶ ἐδικαίωσεν·
οὓς δὲ ἐδικαίωσεν, τούτους καὶ ἐδόξασεν.

VERSE 18

Λογίζομαι γὰρ ὅτι οὐκ ἄξια τὰ παθήματα τοῦ νῦν καιροῦ

To explain (γάρ) his statement in verse 17, Paul declares his "firm conviction reached by rational thought" (Cranfield 408). See 3:8 for λογίζομαι; ὅτι is declarative (R 1035). Οὐκ negates the predicate adjective ἄξια; see 1:32 for ἄξιος; ἔστιν is understood. Cranfield suggests the translation "bear no comparison with" (408). Although πάθημα, -τος, τό carries the meaning "passions" in 7:5 (cf. Gal 5:24), the more common Pauline meaning of "sufferings" applies here (2 Cor 1:5–7; Phil 3:10; Col 1:24; 2 Tim 3:11). Τοῦ καιροῦ is a subjective genitive; the adverb νῦν functions as an adjective. Moo suggests the translation "the present evil age" (512 n. 18).

πρὸς τὴν μέλλουσαν δόξαν ἀποκαλυφθῆναι εἰς ἡμᾶς

Although the genitive usually accompanies πρός in a comparison (Cranfield 409), here πρός + accusative introduces a technical comparison that is equivalent to the dative (R 626; cf. BDF §239.8). Blass notes that it is unusual for the participle μέλλουσαν (acc. sg. fem. of pres. act. ptc. of μέλλω) to be separated from its adjuncts (§474.5a; cf. 1 Pet 5:1), and several solutions have been proposed. Turner suggests that Paul is using a stereotyped phrase (358). Moule concludes that μέλλω exerts a "disturbing influence" (169–70). Jewett argues that τὴν μέλλουσαν δόξαν should be separated from the infinitive and translated as "the future glory," making the infinitive epexegetical rather than complementary (510). Regardless, the combination emphasizes the future nature of the event (Cranfield 409 n. 2; cf. R 878). See 1:23 for δόξα and 1:17–18 for ἀποκαλύπτω. Schreiner notes that "glory" is the eschatological inheritance of believers (434), and Jewett highlights the OT background of divine radiance (510). Robertson (535) understands εἰς ἡμᾶς as a pure dative (ESV, "to us"; NJB, "for us,"); Cranfield (410) and Longenecker (718) understand it as local (NIV, "in us"); Schreiner (434) understands it as "[bestowed] upon us" (cf. Moo 512 n. 21).

VERSE 19

ἡ γὰρ ἀποκαραδοκία τῆς κτίσεως τὴν ἀποκάλυψιν τῶν υἱῶν τοῦ θεοῦ ἀπεκδέχεται

The first reason (γάρ) behind Paul's conviction is found in creation's expectation of deliverance. Cranfield sets out eight interpretations of "creation" in this context and decides on the totality of non-human creation, both animate and inanimate (411; cf. Dunn 469; Jewett 511; Longenecker 719–22; Schreiner 435). The references to creation in verses 19–22, therefore, should be understood as personification (Schreiner 434; e.g., Ps 65:12; Isa 24:4; Jer 4:28; 12:4). Ἀποκαραδοκία, -ας, ἡ describes eager, confident expectation (BDAG 112c; cf. *TNDT* 1.393; Phil 1:30); Cranfield notes the image of stretching the neck or craning forward (410). The genitive of τῆς κτίσεως is subjective. Bringing ἀποκάλυψιν forward gives it emphasis and connects it with the infinitive of the previous verse. Τῶν υἱῶν is an objective genitive; τοῦ θεοῦ is a possessive genitive; the concatenation of genitives explains the repeated articles. Ἀπεκδέχεται (3 sg. pres. mid. indic. of dep. ἀπεκδέχομαι, "await eagerly") is a progressive present, and the compound form is intensive. Paul uses the verb five times (Rom 8:19, 23, 25; 1 Cor 1:7; Phil 3:20), "always of the eager awaiting of Christian hope" (Dunn 470; cf. Heb 9:28; 1 Pet 3:20). Phillips paraphrases the verb as "is on tiptoe."

VERSES 20–21

τῇ γὰρ ματαιότητι ἡ κτίσις ὑπετάγη

Paul sets out his explanation (γάρ) of why creation is on tiptoe in an "overloaded" sentence that encompasses verses 20–21 (Schreiner 436). Τῇ ματαιότητι (dat. of manner) is moved forward for emphasis; the article accompanies the abstract noun; the noun itself carries the idea of being unable to fulfill a purpose (Cranfield 413). The article with κτίσις is anaphoric. Ὑπετάγη (3 sg. aor. pass. indic. of ὑποτάσσω, "put in subjection") is constative aorist pointing to a particular event (Cranfield 413) as well as a divine passive (Dunn 470). Commentators agree on an allusion to the curse God placed on the earth in Genesis 3:17–19 (cf. 4 Ezra 7.1).

οὐχ ἑκοῦσα ἀλλὰ διὰ τὸν ὑποτάξαντα, ἐφ' ἑλπίδι

Three adverbial phrases modify ὑπετάγη, with the first two set in strong contrast (οὐχ . . . ἀλλά). Ἑκοῦσα (nom. sg. fem. of ἑκων, -οῦσα, -όν, "of one's own free will") is an adjective used adverbially to indicate manner (R 550); NEB translates the phrase as "not of its own choice." Διά + accusative denotes cause (Cranfield 414); the substantival participle ὑποτάξαντα (acc. sg. masc. of aor. act. ptc. of ὑποτάσσω) supplies the agent who put creation in subjection (R 584) and most naturally refers to God (Moo 516). Dunn suggests that Paul is alluding to Psalm 8:7 (471), but the idea of a judicial decision is more natural (Cranfield 414). Cranfield (414), Moo (516 n. 43), and Schreiner (436) all agree that ἐφ' ἑλπίδι should be taken with ὑπετάγη; Harris classifies ἐπι + dative as circumstance (i.e., "in hope," 138; cf. EVV).

ὅτι καὶ αὐτὴ ἡ κτίσις ἐλευθερωθήσεται ἀπὸ τῆς δουλείας τῆς φθορᾶς

Although the variant reading διότι is supported by ℵ and D*, it can be explained by dittography of the final two letters of ἐλπίδι in the preceding verse (Metzger 456). The combination of 𝔓[46], A, B, C, D[2], and 33 is stronger (Schreiner 400), and ὅτι is the more likely original reading. It introduces the content ("that") of the hope Paul has just mentioned (Moo 516 n. 45). The article is normal with the intensive construction αὐτὴ ἡ κτίσις ("creation itself"). Ἐλευθερωθήσεται (3 sg. fut. pass. indic. of ἐλευθερόω, "set free") is a predictive future and a divine passive; see 5:18 for ἀπό + ablative following ἐλευθερόω and 8:15 for δουλεία. Jewett (515), Moo (517 n. 47) and Moule (175) classify τῆς φθορᾶς as an objective genitive ("slavery to corruption"); Turner (213) classifies it as a genitive of quality ("corrupting slavery"); Schreiner (436) concludes that an appositional genitive ("slavery which is corruption") adds the least meaning and, therefore, is to be preferred.*

εἰς τὴν ἐλευθερίαν τῆς δόξης τῶν τέκνων τοῦ θεοῦ

The goal (εἰς + acc.) of creation being set free is "freedom" (ἐλευθερίαν). The concatenation of genitives that follows explains the repeated articles, but the relationships among the nouns has been variously understood. Beginning from the end, τοῦ θεοῦ is a possessive genitive; τῶν τέκνων is an objective genitive; τῆς δόξης is a subjective genitive (contra Wallace who sees it as an attributed genitive, 878; cf. "glorious freedom" in most EVV). The resulting combination would be "the freedom resulting from the glory bestowed on God's children."

VERSE 22

οἴδαμεν γὰρ ὅτι πᾶσα ἡ κτίσις συστενάζει καὶ συνωδίνει ἄχρι τοῦ νῦν

The second reason (γάρ) behind Paul's premise (8:18) is found in the hope believers have. See 2:2 for οἴδαμεν ὅτι, which introduces a truth generally known among Christians (Cranfield 416; Longenecker 724). Πᾶσα ἡ κτίσις is the normal construction to say "the whole creation" (Jewett 516; cf. R 772). Συστενάζει (3 sg. pres. act. indic. of συστενάζω, "groan together with"; cf. BDAG 979a) is a progressive present; the συν- prefix carries the idea of "in harmony" (Schreiner 437). Καί adds a second progressive present; συνωδίνω carries the idea of letting out a groan in common pain (BDAG 977a). Ἄχρι + genitive denotes a period of time "up to" a given point (R 639; cf. 5:13); the article with νῦν allows the adverb to function as a noun (cf. 1:13); the same construction in Phil 1:5 suggests long continuance. CEV translates the clause as "all creation is still groaning and is in pain, like a woman about to give birth." See Cranfield for a concise analysis (416–17) and the OT background (416 n. 2).

VERSE 23

οὐ μόνον δέ, ἀλλὰ καὶ αὐτοὶ τὴν ἀπαρχὴν τοῦ πνεύματος ἔχοντες

Paul connects to (οὐ μόνον δέ) and builds on (ἀλλὰ καί) the truth of creation's groaning by introducing the groaning believers also experience. The combination of the intensive pronoun αὐτοί ("ourselves") followed by ἡμεῖς καὶ αὐτοί ("even we ourselves") in the next line is "extremely emphatic" (Cranfield 417). Τὴν ἀπαρχήν (acc. sg. fem.) is the object of the participle that follows; τοῦ πνεύματος is a genitive of apposition (Cranfield 418; R 408; Schreiner 438); GNB translates the phrase as "the Spirit as the first of God's gifts." Ἀπαρχή, -ῆς, ἡ is commonly translated "firstfruits" (e.g., NIV, ESV); Robertson suggests "receipt in full" (577); BDAG suggests "birth-certificate" (98c); Dunn has an extended discussion of the OT background in which he rejects the latter idea (473–74). Jewett (578) understands ἔχοντες (nom. pl. masc. of pres. act. ptc. of ἔχω) as adjectival, and Käsemann (237) argues for adverbial of concession. Adverbial of cause is more likely (cf. Dunn 473; Moo 520; Schreiner 438).

ἡμεῖς καὶ αὐτοὶ ἐν ἑαυτοῖς στενάζομεν υἱοθεσίαν ἀπεκδεχόμενοι

Paul reinforces the change in subject focus by stacking a personal pronoun (ἡμεῖς), an ascensive conjunction (καί), and an intensive pronoun (αὐτοί). 'Εν ἑαυτοῖς is both emphatic (Schreiner 438) and denotes location (GNB, "within ourselves"; NIV, "inwardly,"). Στενάζομεν (1 pl. pres. act. indic. of στενάζω, "sigh, groan") is the simple form of the verb in verse 22 (cf. Job 31:38 [LXX]). The omission of υἱοθεσίαν in 𝔓[46] and D simplifies the grammatical construction by making τὴν ἀπολύτρωσιν τοῦ σώματος ἡμῶν the obvious object of the participle (Cranfield 419 n. 1) and resolves the apparent theological contradiction with 8:12–14 (Jewett 505 n. i). Its inclusion, however, has stronger manuscript support (א, A, B, C, 33) and is the more difficult reading (Schreiner 441). 'Απεκδεχόμενοι (nom. pl. masc. of pres. mid. ptc. of dep. ἀπεκδέχομαι) is adverbial of time; see 8:15 for υἱοθεσία and 8:19 for ἀπεκδέχομαι.

τὴν ἀπολύτρωσιν τοῦ σώματος ἡμῶν

Τὴν ἀπολύτρωσιν (acc. sg. fem.) stands in apposition to υἱοθεσίαν; the article accompanies the abstract noun; see 3:24 for ἀπολύτρωσις. Τοῦ σώματος is an objective genitive (Moo 521 n. 67); ἡμῶν is a possessive genitive. Turner notes the use of the singular σώματος (gen. sg. neut.) to refer to a group (24).

VERSE 24

τῇ γὰρ ἐλπίδι ἐσώθημεν

Hope explains (γάρ) our eager waiting (8:23). Longenecker suggests that the article with ἐλπίδι functions as a mild demonstrative ("this hope," 727). Robertson concedes that the dative τῇ ἐλπίδι is ambiguous (543), and it has been classified in different ways (Moo 521 n. 72). Although GNB and CEV translate it as means ("by hope"; cf. R 531), most EVV (e.g., NEB, NIV, NJB, ESV) translate it as manner ("in hope" cf. T 241), which is more likely (cf. 8:20). 'Εσώθημεν (1 pl. aor. pass. indic. of σῴζω) is a constative aorist that refers to a completed past event (Jewett 520; cf. Moo 521 n. 71) and a divine passive. See 4:18 for ἐλπίς/ἐλπίζω and 1:16 for σωτηρία/σῴζω.

ἐλπὶς δὲ βλεπομένη οὐκ ἔστιν ἐλπίς

The second sentence adds to (δέ) the first by clarifying the nature of hope: it is focused on the unseen. Βλεπομένη (nom. sg. fem. of pres. pass. ptc. of βλέπω, "see") is an anarthrous atttibutive participle (R 1105) that modifies the preceding noun. The present tense is gnomic and states a general truth; the simple passive maintains focus on the subject.

ὃ γὰρ βλέπει τίς ἐλπίζει;

Paul uses a rhetorical question to explain further (γάρ) the statement he has just made. The relative clause (ὃ βλέπει) is the object of ἐλπίζει. Both verbs are gnomic presents. Of the four textual variants, the interrogative pronoun τίς is consistent with other Pauline questions and is the shortest reading, which suggests its originality (Schreiner 441). Metzger views the other readings as expansions (457). Ἐλπίζει makes better sense contextually than ὑπομένει (Schreiner 441) and has early and diverse manuscript support (𝔓[46], ℵ[2], C, D, 33).

VERSE 25

εἰ δὲ ὃ οὐ βλέπομεν ἐλπίζομεν, δι' ὑπομονῆς ἀπεκδεχόμεθα

Hope contrasts (δέ) with what is seen because it requires perseverance. Εἰ + indicative introduces a first class condition. The relative clause (ὃ οὐ βλέπομεν) is the object of ἐλπίζομεν (1 pl. pres. act. indic.). Διά + genitive denotes manner (NJB, "with persevering confidence"; cf. T 267). See 5:3 for ὑπομονή and 8:19 for ἀπεκδέχομαι. All three present tenses are gnomic.

VERSE 26

Ὡσαύτως δὲ καὶ τὸ πνεῦμα συναντιλαμβάνεται τῇ ἀσθενείᾳ ἡμῶν

In further support of his premise (8:18), Paul adds (δέ) a third reason that focuses on the help the Holy Spirit provides. The comparison he draws ("likewise also") relates more naturally to our need for perseverance in verse 25 (Jewett 521; Moo 523) than to our groaning with creation in verses 22–23 (Cranfield 421; Dunn 476). The article with πνεῦμα is anaphoric and connects this work of the Spirit to the others earlier in the chapter. Συναντιλαμβάνεται (3 sg. pres. mid. indic. of dep. συναντιλαμβάνομαι, "come to the aid of") is a progressive present and a deponent middle, although with intensive force (Schreiner 442). Robertson (573) suggests that the double prefix carries the idea of the Spirit laying hold with us (συν-) and carrying the burden facing us (ἀντι-), although commentators tend to minimize the lexical significance of the prefixes (e.g., Cranfield 421). The use of the same verb in Psalm 88:22 (LXX) supports the simpler idea of "helps/assists" and suggests that τῇ ἀσθενείᾳ ἡμῶν, although influenced by the συν- prefix, is most likely a dative of direct object (NASB, "helps our weakness").

τὸ γὰρ τί προσευξώμεθα καθὸ δεῖ οὐκ οἴδαμεν

The explanation (γάρ) of our need for the Spirit's help begins with our own ignorance (οὐκ οἴδαμεν). The definite article introduces the clause that stands as the object of οἴδαμεν (pf. with pres. force); Longenecker notes that construction reflects the classical use of the article to introduce an indirect question (732). The interrogative pronoun (τί) introduces an indirect question (R 739) and refers to the object of prayer (ESV, "what to pray for") rather than to its manner (NJB, "how to pray"). The aorist tense of προσευξώμεθα (1 pl. aor. mid. subjunc. of dep. προσεύχομαι, "pray") is common with deliberative subjunctives. Καθό is a contracted form of the prepositional phrase καθ' ὅ (cf. R 722), is equivalent to καθώς (T 320), and denotes standard (Moule 59); δεῖ (3 sg. pres. act. indic. of δέω, "bind") is impersonal ("it is necessary"); most EVV translate the phrase "as we should/ought."

ἀλλ' αὐτὸ τὸ πνεῦμα ὑπερεντυγχάνει στεναγμοῖς ἀλαλήτοις

The Spirit's work stands in contrast (ἀλλά) to our ignorance. The article regularly occurs with the intensive pronoun ("the Spirit himself"; cf. Porter 120). The reading ὑπερεντυγχάνει (3 sg. pres. act. indic. of ὑπερεντυγχάνω, "intercede for") is the shortest and is "decisively supported" by ℵ*, A, B, D (Metzger 457). The ὑπέρ- prefix carries the sense "in behalf of" (R 629); see Dunn for background (478; cf. *TDNT* 5.810–11). The two variants that include ὑπὲρ ἡμῶν make the reading easier and more explicit, which suggests they are secondary. The dative of στεναγμοῖς (dat. pl. masc. of στεναγμός, -οῦ, ὁ) denotes manner ("with groanings"); the noun is cognate with the verbs in verses 22–23 and describes an involuntary expression of great concern or stress (BDAG 942c). Following Moo (524), Longenecker translates the phrase as "with groans that words cannot express" (734). Schreiner suggests that the adjective ἀλαλήτοις (dat. pl. masc. of ἀλάλητος, -ον, "unspoken/wordless") describes "unutterable longings [in the hearts of believers] to conform their lives to the will of God," which the Spirit "takes . . . and presents . . . before God in an articulate form" (446). Most commentators reject the contention (cf. Käsemann 224) that the phrase refers to glossolalia (cf. Cranfield 423; Dunn 478; Schreiner 444–45).

VERSE 27

ὁ δὲ ἐραυνῶν τὰς καρδίας οἶδεν τί τὸ φρόνημα τοῦ πνεύματος

A further aspect (δέ) of the Spirit's intercessory work highlights the close relationship between the Spirit and the Father. The article identifies the substantival participle ἐραυνῶν (nom. sg. masc. of pres. act. ptc.) as the subject. Ἐραυνάω describes the action of making a careful, thorough effort to learn something (BDAG 341d; cf John 5:39; 1 Pet 1:10–11); Paul uses it in 1 Corinthians 2:10–16 to describe the Spirit's activity in searching the deep things of God. The article with καρδίας functions as a possessive pronoun (NIV, "our hearts"); οἶδεν is a perfect with present force; τί ("what") introduces an indirect question (cf. R 1046). Τὸ φρόνημα τοῦ πνεύματος echoes 8:6–7. The genitive of πνεύματος is subjective (CEV, "how the Spirit thinks"); although Moo argues for a possessive genitive, he concludes that φρόνημα has "something of a verbal force" (526 n. 100).

ὅτι κατὰ θεὸν ἐντυγχάνει ὑπὲρ ἁγίων

Ὅτι is causal ("because"; cf. EVV; Longenecker 735); κατά + accusative denotes standard (Moule 59); ἐντυγχάνει (3 sg. pres. act. indic.) is a progressive present.

Ἐντυγχάνω describes the act of making an earnest request through contact with the person approached (BDAG 341d); ὑπέρ + genitive denotes representation ("on behalf of"); see 1:7 for ἁγίοι. NEB translates the clause "because he pleads for God's people in God's own way."

VERSE 28

οἴδαμεν δὲ ὅτι τοῖς ἀγαπῶσιν τὸν θεὸν

Paul introduces the fourth reason in support of his premise (8:18) with the disclosure formula οἴδαμεν δὲ ὅτι ("Now we know that . . ."; cf. 2:2; 3:19; 7:14). The dative participial phrase is brought forward for emphasis. Τοῖς ἀγαπῶσιν is a substantival participle; the present tense is gnomic; the dative denotes advantage. Τὸν θεόν is the object of the participle; the article is monadic. See Cranfield for the OT background of loving God (424 n. 4).

πάντα συνεργεῖ εἰς ἀγαθόν

𝔓[46], A, and B include ὁ θεός after συνεργεῖ, but Robertson views the addition as "more than doubtful" (477). Metzger concludes that it is a natural explanatory addition that should be rejected in favor of the shorter reading that has broader and more diversified support (458). Cranfield sets out eight possibilities for understanding this clause and concludes that πάντα is the subject (425–27; cf. Cranfield, "Romans 8:28," *SJT* 19 [1066]: 204–15).* Longenecker concludes that πάντα is the object and is placed first for emphasis (738). The natural antecedent of πάντα (nom. pl. neut. of πᾶς, πᾶσα, πᾶν) is the sufferings of the present age (8:18), although Moo argues that the scope should not be too tightly restricted (529). Συνεργεῖ (3 sg. pres. act. indic. of συνεργέω, "work with") has been variously understood as "work together" (most EVV), "assist" (Cranfield 428; Moo 529 n. 120), or "cooperate with" (Jewett 523; cf. NEB). Dunn incorporates εἰς + accusative (purpose) to arrive at "contribute toward" (481). Ἀγαθόν is an adjective used as a noun and is best understood as "benefit" or "advantage" (cf. 13:4).

τοῖς κατὰ πρόθεσιν κλητοῖς οὖσιν.

The substantival participle τοῖς . . . οὖσιν (dat. pl. masc. of pres. act. ptc. of εἰμί) stands in apposition to and clarifies τοῖς ἀγαπῶσιν τὸν θεόν (Schreiner 450). Κατά + accusative denotes standard (Moo 531); the prepositional phrase should be taken with κλητοῖς rather than the participle. Four of Paul's other five uses of πρόθεσις, -εως, ἡ ("that which is planned in advance"; cf. BDAG 869d) denote God's divine purpose (Rom 9:11; Eph 1:11; 3:11; 2 Tim 1:9); see Cranfield for the OT background (430 n. 2). See 1:1 for κλητός. By clarifying "those who love God" with "those who are called according to [his] purpose," Paul makes it clear that our love for God has its source in his calling of us (cf. John 4:19).

VERSE 29

ὅτι οὓς προέγνω, καὶ προώρισεν συμμόρφους τῆς εἰκόνος τοῦ υἱοῦ αὐτοῦ

God's plan and purpose is the reason (ὅτι) all things contribute toward our benefit (8:28). The relative pronoun (οὕς) is the direct object of προέγνω (3 sg. aor. act. indic. of προγινώσκω, "know beforehand") and incorporates an embedded demonstrative (GNB, "those whom"; cf. Wallace 339–40) that is the understood object of an object-complement construction. Προγινώσκω occurs in 11:2 and three other times in the NT (Acts 26:5; 1 Pet 1:20; 2 Pet 3:17), but its background is in the OT where the idea (*yada'*) describes God's special knowledge of a person (e.g., Gen 18:19; Jer 1:5; Amos 3:2; cf. Cranfield 431) rather than a prior knowledge of how a person will respond to God (cf. Moo 532–33). The adjunctive καί ("also") introduces the main clause. Προώρισεν (3 sg. aor. act. indic. of προορίζω, "decide beforehand") occurs in the next verse and four other times in the NT (Acts 4:28; 1 Cor 2:7; Eph 1:5, 11) and stresses "the preordained plan of God that will certainly come to pass in accordance with his will" (Schreiner 453). In the case of both verbs, the προ- prefix refers to actions that took place "before the foundation of the world" (Eph 1:4; 1 Pet 1:20; cf. Cranfield 431). Συμμόρφους (acc. pl. masc. of σύμμορφος, -ον, "participating in the form of"; cf. BDF §182.1) is the object complement related to προώρισεν (cf. R 480). Although it occurs with the dative in Phil 3:21, τῆς εἰκόνος is a genitive of association here (R 528). Moo concludes that Paul uses εἰκών both to emphasize Christ (τοῦ υἱοῦ αὐτοῦ) as the "pattern" for believers and to invite comparison with Adam who was created in God's image (534 n. 151). The context of this verse and the next supports a focus on eschatological glory (cf. 8:18).

εἰς τὸ εἶναι αὐτὸν πρωτότοκον ἐν πολλοῖς ἀδελφοῖς

The purpose (εἰς τό + inf.) of being conformed to Christ's glorious image is Christocentric: "in order that he might be the firstborn among many brothers" (ESV). Αὐτόν is the subject of the infinitive (Wallace 195); πρωτότοκον is the predicate accusative; ἐν + dative denotes location ("among"; cf. Harris 118). Πρωτότοκος, -ον highlights the unique status and privileges associated with being the "firstborn" (BDAG 894a; *NIDNTT* 1.667–69; *TDNT* 6.865–82; cf. Col 1:15, 18; Heb 1:6; 11:28; 12:25). See also P. T. O'Brien, *DPL* 301–303. Πολλοῖς (dat. pl. masc. of πολύς, πολλή, πολύ, "many") includes both Jews and Gentiles and most likely alludes to the Abrahamic covenant (Gen 12:3; cf. Schreiner 453).

VERSE 30

οὓς δὲ προώρισεν, τούτους καὶ ἐκάλεσεν

Paul continues (δέ) his chain of verbs by repeating προώρισεν and following the basic pattern established at the beginning of verse 28. Blass notes the resulting rhetorical climax (§493.3). In this verse, οὕς has an expressed demonstrative pronoun (τούτους) as its antecedent, which serves to place emphasis on the recipients (Jewett 530; Wallace 330). An adjunctive καί stands immediately before each main verb. See 4:17 for καλέω.

καὶ οὓς ἐκάλεσεν, τούτους καὶ ἐδικαίωσεν

See 3:20 for δικαιόω.

οὓς δὲ ἐδικαίωσεν, τούτους καὶ ἐδόξασεν

See 8:18 for δοξάζω.

FOR FURTHER STUDY

52. Suffering (8:18)

Becker, J. C. *Suffering and Hope: The Biblical Vision and the Human Predicament*. Grand Rapids: Eerdmans, 1994.
Black, D. A. *Paul, Apostle of Weakness:* Astheneia *and Its Cognates in the Pauline Literature*. Revised edition. Eugene, OR: Wipf & Stock, 2012.
Bloomquist, L. G. *The Function of Suffering in Philippians*. Sheffield: Sheffield Academic Press, 1993.
Carson, D. A. *How Long, O Lord? Reflections on Suffering and Evil*. Grand Rapids: Baker, 1990.
Gärtner, B. *NIDNTT* 3.719–26.
Gerstenberger E., and W. Schrage. *Suffering*. Nashville: Abingdon, 1980.
Hafemann, S. J. *DPL* 919–21.
Hicks, P. *The Message of Evil and Suffering: Light into Darkness*. Nottingham: InterVarsity, 2006.
Hornbury, W., and B. McNeil, eds. *Suffering and Martyrdom in the New Testament*. Cambridge: Cambridge University Press, 1981.
Michaelis, W. *TDNT* 4.904–39.
Simudson, D. J. *Faith under Fire: Biblical Interpretation and Suffering*. Minneapolis: Fortress, 1980.
Sproul, R. C. *Surprised by Suffering*. Downers Grove, IL: Tyndale, 1989.
Talbert, C. H. *Learning through Suffering: The Educational View of Suffering in the New Testament and Its Milieu*. Collegeville, MN: Liturgical Press, 1991.

53. Deliverance of Creation (8:20)

Beker, J. C. "Suffering and Triumph in Paul's Letter to the Romans." *HBT* 7 (1985): 105–19.
Benoit, P. "'We Too Groan Inwardly . . .' (Romans 8:23)." Pages 40–50 in *Jesus and the Gospel*. Volume 2. London: Darton, 1974.
Bindemann, W. *Die Hoffnung der Schöpfung: Römer 8:18–27 und die Frage einer Theologie der Befreiung von Mensch und Natur*. Neukirchen: Neukirchener, 1983.
Braaten, L. J. "The Groaning Creation: The Biblical Background for Romans 8:22." *BR* 50 (2005): 19–39.

Cranfield, C. E. B. "The Creation's Promised Liberation: Some Observations on Romans 8:19–21." Pages 94–104 in *The Bible and Christian Life*. Edinburgh: T & T Clark, 1985.
Denton, D. R. "Ἀποκαραδοκία." *ZNW* 73 (1982): 138–40.
Folarin, G. O. "From Primordial Curse to Eschatological Restoration: Ecological Challenges from Genesis 3:14–20 and Romans 8:18–25." *Verbum et Ecclesia* 32 (2011): 492–97.
Gerber, U. "Röm 8:18ff als exegetisches Problem der Dogmatik." *NovT* 8 (1966): 58–81.
Gibbs, J. G. *Creation and Redemption: A Study in Pauline Theology*. Leiden: Brill, 1971.
Jackson, T. R. *New Creation in Paul's Letters: A Study of the Historical and Social Setting of a Pauline Concept*. Tübingen: Mohr Siebeck, 2010.
Lampe, G. W. H. "The New Testament Doctrine of *Ktisis*." *SJT* 17 (1964): 449–62.
Schlier, H. "Das, Worauf Alles Wartet: Eine Auslegung von Römer 8:18–30." Pages 599–616 in *Interpretation der Welt*. Edited by H. Kuhn. Würzburg: Echter, 1965.
Swetnam, J. "On Romans 8:23 and the 'Expectation of Sonship.'" *Bib* 48 (1967): 102–108.

54. Predestination and Election (8:29)

Allen, L. C. "The Old Testament Background of (Προ) Ὁρίζειν in the New Testament." *NTS* (1970–71): 1–32.
Basinger D., and R. Basinger, eds. *Predestination and Free Will: Four Views of Divine Sovereignty and Human Freedom*. Downers Grove, IL: InterVarsity, 1986.
Carson, D. A. *The Difficult Doctrine of the Love of God*. Wheaton, IL: Crossway, 2000.
________. *Divine Sovereignty and Human Responsibility: Biblical Perspectives in Tension*. Grand Rapids: Baker, 1994.
Caird, G. B. "Expository Problems: Predestination—Romans ix–xi." *ExpTim* 68 (1956–57): 324–27.
Coenen, I. *NIDNTT* 1.533–43.
Davidson, F. *Pauline Predestination*. London: Tyndale, 1946.
Eckert, J. *EDNT* 1.416–19.
Elwell, W. A. *DPL* 225–29.
________. *EDBT* 199–201.
Geisler, N. *Chosen but Free: A Balanced View of Divine Election*. Minneapolis: Bethany, 2001.
Grayson, K. "The Doctrine of Election in Rom 8:28–30." Pages 574–83 in *Studia Evangelica*, volume 2. Edited by F. L. Cross. Berlin: Akademie, 1964.
Jewett, P. *Election and Predestination*. Grand Rapids: Eerdmans, 1985.
Kaminsky, J. S. *Yet I Loved Jacob: Reclaiming the Biblical Concept of Election*. Nashville: Abingdon, 2007.
Klein, W. W. *The New Chosen People: A Corporate View of Election*. Grand Rapids: Zondervan, 1990.
MacDonald, W. G. "The Biblical Doctrine of Election." Pages 219–26 in *The Grace of God, the Will of Man*. Edited by C. H. Pinnock. Grand Rapids: Zondervan, 1989.
Peterson, R. A. *Election and Free Will: God's Gracious Choice and Our Responsibility*. Phillipsburg, NJ: P&R, 2007.
Piper, J. *The Justification of God: An Exegetical and Theological Study of Romans 9:1–23*. Grand Rapids: Eerdmans, 1983.
Rowley, H. H. *The Biblical Doctrine of Election*. Cambridge: Lutterworth, 1950.
Schrenk, G., and G. Quell. *TDNT* 4.144–92.

Schreiner, T. R. *NDBT* 450–54.
________., and B. A. Ware, eds. *Still Sovereign: Contemporary Perspectives on Election, Foreknowledge, and Grace*. Grand Rapids: Baker, 2000.
Shank, R. *Elect in the Son: A Study of the Doctrine of Election*. Springfield, MO: Westcott, 1970.
Sproul, R. C. *Chosen by God*. Wheaton, IL: Tyndale House, 1986.
Wilk, F., and J. R. Wagner, eds. *Between Gospel and Election: Explorations in the Interpretation of Romans 9–11*. Tübingen: Mohr Siebeck, 2010.

HOMILETICAL SUGGESTIONS

The Hope of Glory (8:18–30)

1. Conviction: Revelation of future glory (λογίζομαι, 8:18)
2. Reasons (8:19–30)
   a. Creation waits for deliverance (γάρ, 8:19–21)
      1) It was subjected in futility (8:20a–c)
      2) It was subjected in hope (8:20d–21)
   b. Believers hope for final redemption (οἴδαμεν γὰρ ὅτι, 8:22–25)
      1) We groan with creation (8:22, 23b)
         a) Because we have the firstfruits of the Spirit (8:23a)
         b) While we wait for the redemption of the body (8:23c)
      2) We were saved in hope (8:24)
      3) We wait with perseverance (8:25)
   c. The Spirit helps our weakness (ὡσαύτως δὲ καί, 8:26–27)
      1) The Spirit intercedes for us with wordless groanings (8:26b)
         a) Because we do not know what to pray (8:26a)
      2) God knows the Spirit's mind (8:27a)
         a) Because the Spirit intercedes according to God's will (8:27b)
   d. God accomplishes his purpose (οἴδαμεν δὲ ὅτι, 8:28–30)
      1) All things work together for good (8:28b)
         a) For those who love God (8:28a)
         b) For those whom God calls (8:28c)
         c) Because God glorifies those whom he foreknows (8:29–30)

The Nature of Christian Hope (8:18–30)

1. It endures suffering (8:18)
2. It waits expectantly (8:23)
3. It looks for things not seen (8:24)
4. It perseveres (8:25)
5. It relies on God's faithfulness (8:29–30)

5. God's Righteousness Results in Victory (8:31–39)

STRUCTURE

Paul concludes both chapter 8 and the second major segment of the letter body (5:1–8:39) with what Robertson calls "a brilliant oratorical passage" (1198). Jewett notes the parallels between this paragraph and 5:1–11 (535). Most commentators divide the paragraph into either two (e.g., Moo 538: 8:31–34; 8:35–39) or four (e.g., Dunn 497: 8:31–32; 8:33–34; 8:35–37; 8:38–39) fairly equal parts. More natural, however, is a longer question section (8:31–36) and a shorter answer section (8:37–39). After a rhetorical question that draws an inference from what precedes (8:31a), Paul asks and answers four more specific questions (8:31b–32; 8:33; 8:34; 8:35–36). He then answers the initial question with an emphatic declaration of victory in Christ. The sixth occurrence of the repeated refrain, "through/in our lord Jesus Christ" closes the paragraph (Harvey 125; cf. 5:1, 11, 21; 6:23; 7:24).

Τί οὖν ἐροῦμεν πρὸς ταῦτα;
    εἰ ὁ θεὸς ὑπὲρ ἡμῶν, τίς καθ' ἡμῶν;
        ὅς γε τοῦ ἰδίου υἱοῦ οὐκ ἐφείσατο ἀλλ' ὑπὲρ ἡμῶν πάντων παρέδωκεν αὐτόν,
        πῶς οὐχὶ καὶ σὺν αὐτῷ τὰ πάντα ἡμῖν χαρίσεται;

    τίς ἐγκαλέσει κατὰ ἐκλεκτῶν θεοῦ;
        θεὸς ὁ δικαιῶν·

    τίς ὁ κατακρινῶν;
        Χριστὸς [Ἰησοῦς] ὁ ἀποθανών, μᾶλλον δὲ ἐγερθείς,
            ὃς καί ἐστιν ἐν δεξιᾷ τοῦ θεοῦ,
            ὃς καὶ ἐντυγχάνει ὑπὲρ ἡμῶν.

    τίς ἡμᾶς χωρίσει ἀπὸ τῆς ἀγάπης τοῦ Χριστοῦ;
        θλῖψις ἢ στενοχωρία ἢ διωγμὸς
        ἢ λιμὸς ἢ γυμνότης
        ἢ κίνδυνος ἢ μάχαιρα;
            καθὼς γέγραπται ὅτι Ἕνεκεν σοῦ θανατούμεθα ὅλην τὴν ἡμέραν,
                ἐλογίσθημεν ὡς πρόβατα σφαγῆς.

ἀλλ' ἐν τούτοις πᾶσιν ὑπερνικῶμεν διὰ τοῦ ἀγαπήσαντος ἡμᾶς.
πέπεισμαι γὰρ ὅτι οὔτε θάνατος οὔτε ζωὴ
    οὔτε ἄγγελοι οὔτε ἀρχαὶ
    οὔτε ἐνεστῶτα οὔτε μέλλοντα
    οὔτε δυνάμεις
    οὔτε ὕψωμα οὔτε βάθος
    οὔτε τις κτίσις ἑτέρα δυνήσεται ἡμᾶς χωρίσαι ἀπὸ τῆς ἀγάπης
        τοῦ θεοῦ
            τῆς ἐν Χριστῷ Ἰησοῦ τῷ κυρίῳ ἡμῶν.

VERSE 31

Τί οὖν ἐροῦμεν πρὸς ταῦτα;

See 4:1 for τί οὖν ἐροῦμεν. Πρός + accusative expresses the idea of estimation ("in view of"; cf. Harris 189; Moule 53)* or response ("in response to"; Longenecker 749–50); ταῦτα (acc. pl. neut.) is retrospective (Wallace 334), pointing back to 8:28–30 (Meyer 2:97), 8:18–30 (Murray 322), 5:1–8:30 (Longenecker 751; Schreiner 458),* or 1:18–8:30 (Dunn 499). Jewett presents a strong argument for 5:1–8:30 (535). Paul develops this initial question by asking four more specific questions.

εἰ ὁ θεὸς ὑπὲρ ἡμῶν τίς καθ' ἡμῶν;

Paul's first specific question uses the language of opposition. Εἰ introduces a fact about which Paul "is altogether convinced" (Cranfield 435); the article with θεός is anaphoric and monadic. Ὑπέρ + genitive denotes advantage ("on the side of"); κατά + genitive denotes opposition ("against"); see Mark 9:40 for the same combination.

VERSE 32

ὅς γε τοῦ ἰδίου υἱοῦ οὐκ ἐφείσατο

Although framed as a question, this sentence functions as an answer to the preceding question. God is the understood antecedent of ὅς and has causal force (NJB, "since he"; cf. R 725); γε is emphatic ("indeed"; cf. Wallace 673), draws special attention to the clause (Cranfield 436), and adds an emotional nuance (Longenecker 754). The genitive τοῦ ἰδίου υἱοῦ is the direct object of φείδομαι (verb of emotion; R 509); the adjective ἰδίου highlights the subject's participation ("his very own son"; BDAG 467d). Ἐφείσατο (3 sg. aor. mid. indic. of dep. φείδομαι, "spare") is a constative aorist and a deponent middle with intensive force (Porter 71). See Dunn's discussion of the likely allusion to Genesis 22:16 (501; cf Longenecker 753).

ἀλλ' ὑπὲρ ἡμῶν πάντων παρέδωκεν αὐτόν

Ἀλλά ("but") establishes a strong contrast with οὐκ; ὑπέρ ἡμῶν denotes representation ("on our behalf"; cf. 8:27); πάντων incorporates both Jews and Gentiles (Dunn 501); see 1:24 for παραδίδωμι (cf. 4:25; Isa 53:6, 12 [LXX]).

πῶς οὐχὶ καὶ σὺν αὐτῷ τὰ πάντα ἡμῖν χαρίσεται;

Πῶς οὐκὶ καί (ESV, "how not also"; cf. 2 Cor 3:8) introduces a question that expects a "yes" answer; Jewett suggests "surely, most certainly" (538). Σὺν αὐτῷ ("with him") denotes sharing in what is freely given: Harris sees the phrase as a brachyology for "in Christ's person who is God's supreme gift" (202). Moo argues that τὰ πάντα refers to all blessings, both spiritual and material (541); Robertson suggests "the sum of all things" (773), which would correspond with Ephesians 1:10, 22–23 (cf. Dunn 502). Ἡμῖν ("to us") is the indirect object of χαρίσεται (3 sg. fut. mid. indic. of dep. χαρίζομαι, "give freely"). Paul uses the verb elsewhere to describe what God gives graciously and freely (e.g., Phil 1:29; 2:9; Phlm 22; cf. Schreiner 460).

VERSE 33

τίς ἐγκαλέσει κατὰ ἐκλεκτῶν θεοῦ;

Paul's second specific question moves from the language of opposition (8:31b) to the language of accusation. Although the verb (ἐγκαλέω) is judicial, Jewett cautions against emphasizing the imagery of eschatological judgment (539–40; contra Schreiner 462). Ἐγκαλέσει (3 sg. fut. act. indic. of ἐγκαλέω, "bring charges against") is a deliberative future that questions the possibility of the action considered (cf. Wallace 370). The verb occurs elsewhere with the idea of laying charges against someone (Acts 19:38, 40; 23:29, 38; 26:2, 7); Jewett highlights the idea of impeachment and possible disqualification (540). Κατά + genitive denotes opposition ("against"); the adjective ἐκλεκτῶν (gen. pl. masc. of ἐκλεκτός, -ή, -όν, "elect") is used as a noun (R 652) and describes those who have been selected (BDAG 306b); θεοῦ is a genitive of agency (Wallace 450). See Moo for a discussion of punctuation possibilities in verses 33–34 (541 n. 27, 28).

θεὸς ὁ δικαιῶν

Moving θεός (pred. nom.) forward gives it emphasis; ἔστιν is understood; ὁ δικαιῶν (nom. sg. masc. of pres. act. ptc. of δικαιόω, "declare righteous") is a substantival participle (R779); the present tense is gnomic (Schreiner 462). See 3:20 for δικαιόω; this occurrence of the verb is the last in the letter (Cranfield 438 n. 4).

VERSE 34

τίς ὁ κατακρινῶν;

Paul's third specific question is a follow-up to his second and moves from accusation to condemnation (cf. Moo 542). See 2:1 for κατακρίνω, which echoes Paul's initial declaration in 8:1. UBS[5] accents the participle as future (nom. sg. masc. of fut. act. ptc.; cf. R 878; Jewett 541); if it is accented as present, the present tense is gnomic (Moo 542 n. 33).* The article identifies the participle as substantival and equivalent to a relative clause ("the one who will accuse"; cf. Moule 103). Paul provides four answers; the first and second use participles, the third and fourth use relative clauses.

Χριστὸς [Ἰησοῦς] ὁ ἀποθανών, μᾶλλον δὲ ἐγερθείς

The manuscript support for the three textual variants is so evenly balanced that Metzger gives it a {C} rating and includes Ἰησοῦς in brackets (458). Schreiner notes the scribal tendency to add names, but concludes that the context suggests "Christ Jesus" as the likely reading (467). Ἀποθανών (nom. sg. masc. of aor. act. ptc. of ἀποθνήσκω, "die") is another substantival participle; the aorist tense is constative. The combination μᾶλλον δέ (NEB, "and more than that") highlights the addition of ἐγερθείς (nom. sg. masc. of aor. pass. ptc. of ἐγείρω, "raise"), which is also substantival despite being anarthrous.

ὅς καί ἐστιν ἐν δεξιᾷ τοῦ θεοῦ

Χριστὸς Ἰησοῦς is the antecedent for the relative pronoun; καί is adjunctive ("also"); ἐν + dative is locative ("at"). Ἐν δεξιᾷ is Paul's preferred form (Harris 107), and Moo explains the absence of an article with δεξιᾷ as possibly reflecting the Hebrew construct state (542 n. 37). Although δεξιός, -ά, -όν is an adjective, it is frequently used substantivally to denote the position at the right hand as a sign of prestige, power, relationship, and trust (BDAG 306b); Turner notes that χείρ is frequently omitted (17). See Dunn on the significance of the allusion to Ps 110:1.

ὃς καὶ ἐντυγχάνει ὑπὲρ ἡμῶν

See the preceding clause for ὅς καί and 8:27 for ἐντυγχάνει ὑπέρ. Jewett provides additional background (542).

VERSE 35

τίς ἡμᾶς χωρίσει ἀπὸ τῆς ἀγάπης τοῦ Χριστοῦ;

Paul's fourth specific question leads to a list of seven possible forms of suffering believers might encounter. Moo and most EVV translate the interrogative pronoun "who" (543; cf. NIV, ESV),* although Jewett argues for "what" as referring to any conceivable opponent, whether personal or impersonal (543; cf. NEB, NJB). Ἡμᾶς is brought forward for emphasis (Jewett 543); χωρίσει (3 sg. fut. act. indic. χωρίζω, "separate") is a deliberative future; ἀπό + ablative reinforces the separation; the genitive of τοῦ Χριστοῦ is subjective ("the love Christ has for us," Wallace 74). Both Χριστοῦ (C, D, 33) and θεοῦ (א) are equally short readings. The longer reading (θεοῦ τῆς ἐν Χριστῷ Ἰησοῦ) is most likely a harmonization with 8:39 (Schreiner 468), and θεοῦ is probably a partial echo of the same verse (Metzger 458).

θλῖψις ἢ στενοχωρία ἢ διωγμὸς

Jewett provides a helpful table comparing this list of sufferings with 2 Corinthians 11:23–29 and 1 Corinthians 4:10–13 (544; cf. Dunn 498). The disjunctive conjunction ἤ ("or") connects the seven forms of suffering listed. See 2:9 for θλῖψις ("tribulation") and στενοχωρία ("distress"). Διωγμός, -ου, ὁ ("persecution") describes a program or process designed to harass or oppress (BDAG 253d; cf. 1 Cor 4:12; 2 Cor 4:19; 12:10; Gal 5:11).

ἢ λιμὸς ἢ γυμνότης ἢ κίνδυνος ἢ μάχαιρα;

Λιμός -ου, ὁ ("famine/hunger") and γυμνότης -ητος, ἡ ("nakedness") form a natural pair, both with a connotation of destitution. Κίνδυνος -ου, ὁ ("danger") and μάχαιρα,

–ης, ἡ ("sword") likewise form a natural pair, the latter possibly referring to death or public execution.

VERSE 36

καθὼς γέγραπται ὅτι

See 1:17 and 3:10 for the introductory formula. The rabbis applied Psalm 44:22 (LXX 43:23) to the death of martyrs (Moo 544 n. 42); Paul makes a similar statement in 2 Corinthians 4:11. Jewett thinks Paul is countering the argument that the suffering Christians in Rome were experiencing somehow disqualified them from being true followers of Christ (548).

Ἕνεκεν σοῦ θανατούμεθα ὅλην τὴν ἡμέραν

Ἕνεκεν + genitive provides the cause or reason for something (BDAG 334d); θανατούμεθα (1 pl. pres. pass. indic. of θανατόω, "put to death") is a progressive present and a simple passive (ESV, "are being put to death"); ὅλην τὴν ἡμέραν is the normal construction to indicate "all day long" (GNB, NJB).

ἐλογίσθημεν ὡς πρόβατα σφαγῆς

Ἐλογίσθημεν (1 pl. aor. pass. indic. of dep. λογίζομαι, "consider") is gnomic aorist and a true passive (NIV, "we are considered"); the conjunction ὡς ("as") functions in a way equivalent to εἰς + accusative (BDF §157.5); σφαγῆς (gen. sg. fem. of σφαγή, -ῆς, ἡ, "slaughter") is an objective genitive (R 501, "doomed to slaughter").

VERSE 37

ἀλλ' ἐν τούτοις πᾶσιν ὑπερνικῶμεν διὰ τοῦ ἀγαπήσαντος ἡμᾶς

In stark contrast (ἀλλά) to the potential sufferings we might encounter is the reality of our "ultimate victory" (NEB). Ἐν τούτοις πᾶσιν ("in all these things") echoes πρὸς ταῦτα in 8:31 and introduces the final answer to Paul's initial question. Ὑπερνικῶμεν (1 pl. pres. act. indic. of ὑπερνικάω, "be completely victorious") is an intensified form of νικάω that describes winning in the face of every obstacle (BDAG 1034a). The agent (διά + gen.) through whom we are victorious is "the one who loved us" (CEV). The substantival participle ἀγαπήσαντος (gen. sg. masc. of aor. act. ptc. of ἀγαπάω) points to a particular historical act (Jewett 549) and most naturally refers to Christ and his death on the cross (Moo 544 n. 46).

VERSE 38

πέπεισμαι γὰρ ὅτι

The reason (γάρ) Paul is certain of victory is a firm and settled conviction introduced by a confidence formula (cf. 14:14; 15:14; Gal 5:10; Phil 1:6, 25; 2:24; 2 Thess 3:4; 2 Tim 1:5, 21; Phlm 21). Πέπεισμαι (1 sg. pf. pass. indic. of πείθω, "convince/persuade") is an intensive perfect that emphasizes Paul's present conviction (R 895); the passive voice implies that God is the unstated agent; ὅτι introduces content ("that"). See also S. N. Olson, "Pauline Expressions of Confidence in His Addressees," *CBQ* 47 (1985): 282–95.

οὔτε θάνατος οὔτε ζωὴ

The correlatives οὔτε . . . οὔτε ("neither . . . nor") in verses 38–39 are more forceful than the disjunctives (ἤ) in verse 35 (Dunn 506). Eight of the ten hostile forces listed occur in pairs. Θάνατος repeats the idea of death (θανατόω) from the OT quotation in verse 36. Together, death and life encompass the full range of human existence (cf. Jewett 550–51).

οὔτε ἄγγελοι οὔτε ἀρχαὶ

Ἄγγελοι ("angels") refers to spiritual beings who function as intermediaries between heaven and earth (cf. Gal 1:8; 4:14; 1 Cor 4:9; 1 Thess 1:7); ἀρχαί ("rulers") also refers to cosmic forces rather than to political authorities (cf. Eph 1:21; 2:2; 3:10; 6:12; Col 1:16; 2:15). Together, the pair encompasses the whole range of cosmic spiritual powers (cf. Dunn 507).

οὔτε ἐνεστῶτα οὔτε μέλλοντα οὔτε δυνάμεις

Four different sequences appear in manuscripts:

ἐνεστῶτα	μέλλοντα	δυνάμεις		(𝔓[27], 𝔓[46], ℵ, A, B)
δυνάμεις	ἐνεστῶτα	μέλλοντα		(Ψ)
ἐξουσίαι	ἐνεστῶτα	μέλλοντα	δυνάμεις	(C, D)
ἐξουσίαι	δυνάμεις	ἐνεστῶτα	μέλλοντα	(436, 1852)

The first reading has the strongest external support. The second appears to move δυνάμεις forward in an attempt to keep the angelic powers together (Schreiner 468). The addition of ἐξουσίαι in the third is probably influenced by similar combinations elsewhere in Paul (Jewett 532 n. m; cf. Eph 1:21; 6:12; Col 1:16; 2:10, 15). The fourth reading conflates the second and third. Metzger gives the first reading an {A} rating (458).

Both ἐνεστῶτα ("things present") and μέλλοντα (ESV, "things to come") are anarthrous substantival participles. The first (nom. pl. neut. of pf. act. ptc. of ἐνίστημι) is a perfect with present force and describes what is present at the time of speaking (BDAG 337b); the second (nom. pl. neut. of pres. act. ptc. of μέλλω) describes what is future. Together, the pair encompasses "the world as it is or the world as it shall be" (NEB). Δυνάμεις ("powers") stands alone, breaks the pattern of pairs, and refers to transcendent beings (BDAG 263c; cf. 1 Cor 15:30).

VERSE 39

οὔτε ὕψωμα οὔτε βάθος

Ὕψωμα, -τος, τό ("height") refers to the world above (BDAG 1046c), and βάθος, -ους, τό ("depth") refers to the world below (BDAG 162c). Cranfield suggests "neither heaven nor hell" (443). Together, the pair encompasses the entirety of the created order (Schreiner 465).

οὔτε τις κτίσις ἑτέρα

The final item in the list ("any other creation/creature") also stands alone and makes it clear that Paul intends to be comprehensive in excluding every possibility. Τις is an adjectival use of the indefinite pronoun (Wallace 347); Jewett notes that κτίσις can refer to individual creatures as well as the sum of everything created (554); Moo concludes that ἑτέρα (nom. fem. sg.) should be understood simply as "other" rather than as "wholly different" (546 n. 70; cf. T 197).

δυνήσεται ἡμᾶς χωρίσαι ἀπὸ τῆς ἀγάπης τοῦ θεοῦ

These words echo Paul's question in 8:35. Δυνήσεται (3 sg. fut. mid. indic. of dep. δύναμαι, "be able to") is a gnomic future; ἡμᾶς is the object of the infinitive; χωρίσαι (aor. act. inf. of χωρίζω) is a complementary infinitive. See verse 35 for ἀπὸ τῆς ἀγάπης; τοῦ θεοῦ is a subjective genitive (cf. 8:35).

τῆς ἐν Χριστῷ Ἰησοῦ τῷ κυρίῳ ἡμῶν

See 5:1, 11, 21; 6:23; 7:25 for previous uses of the same phrase. The definite article allows the phrase to function as an adjectival modifier of ἀγάπης (R 782). Ἐν + dative is locative and clarifies that God's love "is focused in" Christ Jesus (Harris 124). The article is repeated with κυρίῳ for emphasis (BDF §269.2) and because the possessive pronoun follows.

FOR FURTHER STUDY

55. The Binding of Isaac (8:32)

Dahl, N. A. "The Atonement—An Adequate Reward for the Akedah? (Rom 8:32)." Pages 15–29 in *Neotestamentica et Semitica*. Edited by E. E. Ellis and M. Wilcox. Edinburgh: T & T Clark, 1969.

Davies, P. R., and B. D. Chilton. "The Aqedah: A Revised Tradition History." *CBQ* 40 (1978): 514–46.

Schoeps, H. J. "The Sacrifice of Isaac in Paul's Theology." *JBL* 65 (1946): 385–92.

Segal, A. F. "'He Who did Not Spare His Own Son . . .': Jesus, Paul, and the Akedah." Pages 169–84 in *From Jesus to Paul*. Edited by P. Richardson and J. C. Hurd. Waterloo, ON: Wilfrid Laurier University, 1984.

Swetnam, J. *Jesus and Isaac*. Rome: Pontifical Biblical Institute, 1981.

HOMILETICAL SUGGESTIONS

Total Victory! (8:31–39)

1. Question Section (τί οὖν ἐροῦμεν πρὸς ταῦτα, 8:31–36)
   a. General rhetorical question (8:31a)
   b. Specific question #1: Who will oppose us? (τίς καθ' ἡμῶν, 8:31b–32)
   c. Specific question #2: Who will accuse us? (τίς ἐγκαλέσει, 8:33)
   d. Specific question #3: Who will condemn us? (τίς ὁ κατακρινῶν, 8:34)
   e. Specific question #4: What will separate us? (τίς ἡμᾶς χωρίσει, 8:35–36)
      1) Seven possible forms of suffering (8:35b)
      2) OT support (8:36)
2. Answer Section (ἀλλ' ἐν τούτοις πᾶσιν, 8:37–39)
   a. Declaration: We are more than conquerors (8:37)
   b. Conviction: Nothing can separate us from God's love in Christ (8:38–39)

C. THE VINDICATION OF GOD'S RIGHTEOUSNESS (9:1–11:36)

1. Paul's Concern for Israel (9:1–5)

STRUCTURE

Paul begins the next major section of his letter with an introductory paragraph in which he expresses his deep concern over Israel's lack of responsiveness to the gospel he preaches. The paragraph consists of two sentences (9:1–2; 9:3–5). In the first sentence, Paul affirms the truth of what he is writing and the depth of his pain. The second sentence provides the reason behind his distress and uses a series of relative clauses to itemize the multiple blessings God has bestowed on his "kinsmen according to the flesh" (ESV).

Ἀλήθειαν λέγω ἐν Χριστῷ, οὐ ψεύδομαι,
συμμαρτυρούσης μοι τῆς συνειδήσεώς μου ἐν πνεύματι ἁγίῳ,
    ὅτι λύπη μοί ἐστιν μεγάλη
    καὶ ἀδιάλειπτος ὀδύνη τῇ καρδίᾳ μου.

ηὐχόμην γὰρ ἀνάθεμα εἶναι αὐτὸς ἐγὼ ἀπὸ τοῦ Χριστοῦ
    ὑπὲρ τῶν ἀδελφῶν μου τῶν συγγενῶν μου κατὰ σάρκα,
        οἵτινές εἰσιν Ἰσραηλῖται,
        ὧν ἡ υἱοθεσία   καὶ ἡ δόξα
                         καὶ αἱ διαθῆκαι
                         καὶ ἡ νομοθεσία
                         καὶ ἡ λατρεία
                         καὶ αἱ ἐπαγγελίαι,
        ὧν οἱ πατέρες
καὶ ἐξ ὧν ὁ Χριστὸς τὸ κατὰ σάρκα,
                ὁ ὢν ἐπὶ πάντων
                θεὸς εὐλογητὸς εἰς τοὺς αἰῶνας, ἀμήν.

VERSE 1

Ἀλήθειαν λέγω ἐν Χριστῷ, οὐ ψεύδομαι

The asyndeton with which Paul begins the paragraph (R 444) suggests a pause before Paul begins a new major section of the letter (Dunn 523). Jewett notes the use of ἀλήθειαν λέγω in classical oratory (557); Paul uses the same phrase in 1 Timothy 2:7 (cf. 2 Cor 12:6); Longenecker classifies it as an "attestation statement" (781). See 1:18 for ἀλήθεια, which is qualitative and brought forward for emphasis; λέγω is a progressive present (Wallace 519). The phrase ἐν Χριστῷ (cf. 2 Cor 2:17; 12:19) qualifies the verb (Schreiner 478; contra Harris 122) and highlights the authoritative basis of Paul's statement (Harris 130; cf. Jewett 557); Cranfield writes that it establishes Christ as "the absolute guarantor of the truth" (452). Ψεύδομαι (1 sg. pres. mid. indic. of dep. ψεύδομαι, "lie, tell a falsehood") is a progressive present and a deponent middle. The parenthetical statement underlines Paul's truthfulness (Schreiner 478; cf. 2 Cor 11:31; Gal 1:20).

συμμαρτυρούσης μοι τῆς συνειδήσεώς μου ἐν πνεύματι ἁγίῳ

A second, longer parenthetical comment adds a second and a third witness in support of Paul's veracity (cf. Deut 17:6; 19:7). Συμμαρτυρούσης (gen. sg. fem. of pres. act. ptc. of *συμμαρτυρέω*) is a genitive absolute of time (R 1132), with *τῆς συνειδήσεώς μου* as its subject. See 2:15 for *συμμαρτυρέω* and *συνείδησις*. Moo describes *συνείδησις* as "an inborn faculty that monitors a person's conformity to a moral standard" (556). Μοι is an associative dative (Cranfield 452; cf. NASB); ἐν + dative is instrumental (Moo 556 n. 7; cf. NIV). Jewett explains the anarthrous form *πνεύματι ἁγίῳ* (cf. Rom 14:17; 1 Cor 12:3; 2 Cor 6:6; 1 Thess 1:5) as a Semitic idiom (558 n. 37) that certifies the witness of Paul's conscience (559).

VERSE 2

ὅτι λύπη μοί ἐστιν μεγάλη καὶ ἀδιάλειπτος ὀδύνη τῇ καρδίᾳ μου

A declarative *ὅτι* ("that") introduces the content of *ἀλήθειαν* in the preceding verse (Schreiner 479); the dative *μοί* is possessive; *καί* is connective ("and"); the dative of *καρδίᾳ* is local ("in my heart"). Λύπη, -ης, ἡ denotes pain of mind or spirit (BDAG 605a); *ὀδύνη, -ης, ἡ* denotes mental pain or distress (BDAG 692c). The combination intensifies the sense of emotion (Dunn 523), but Moo draws no clear distinction between the two nouns (557 n. 10). Μεγάλη (nom. sg. fem. of *μέγας, μεγάλη, μέγα*, "great") describes something that is above average in intensity; BDAG suggests "profound" (624c). Ἀδιάλειπτος, -ον describes something that is constant or unceasing (BDAG 19d; cf. the cognate adverb in 1:19). See 1:21 for *καρδία*. Wallace (310 n. 46) notes that the adjectival constructions can be understood as either attributive ("there is great grief and unceasing anguish in my heart") or predicate ("my grief is great and the anguish in my heart is unceasing"). With the exception of GNB, EVV choose the former.

VERSE 3

ηὐχόμην γὰρ ἀνάθεμα εἶναι αὐτὸς ἐγὼ ἀπὸ τοῦ Χριστοῦ

The reason (*γάρ*) behind Paul's distress is Israel's failure to recognize the blessings God has bestowed on them (Schreiner 482). His concern for his countrymen is so great it has led him to an extreme prayer. Ηὐχόμην (1 sg. impf. mid. indic of dep. *εὔχομαι*, "wish, pray") retains its middle sense (Porter 71), but its imperfect tense raises multiple interpretive issues (cf. Cranfield 454–6). Jewett (560) views it as describing actual prayers prior to the time of writing ("I used to pray"). Dunn (524) views it as a genuine desire that is not specific as to whether it is realizable ("I could pray"; cf. most EVV). Cranfield (456), Moo (558), and Schreiner (480) view it as a prayer that is unattainable or impermissible ("I would pray [if it were permissible for me so to pray and if the fulfillment of such a prayer could benefit them]"; cf. NLT).* Ἀνάθεμα, -τος, τό (cf. 1 Cor 12:3; 16:22; Gal 1:8, 9) is the predicate accusative and denotes something delivered over to the divine wrath of eschatological judgment (Schreiner 480). Εἶναι (pres. act. inf. of εἰμί) is a complementary infinitive; the nominative *αὐτὸς ἐγώ* ("I myself") is an exception to the more common accusative (T 146) but is not uncommon in a personal construction (R 1038). Ἀπό + ablative denotes alienation (BDF §211); the article with Χριστοῦ gives it the titular sense of "Messiah" (Moo 557 n. 13); the phrase points to exclusion from Messiah's presence (Cranfield 458).

ὑπὲρ τῶν ἀδελφῶν μου τῶν συγγενῶν μου κατὰ σάρκα

Ὑπέρ + genitive ("on behalf of") carries a substitutionary sense (Moule 64; cf. 5:6, 7, 8; 8:27, 31, 34). Although Paul uses *ἀδελφοί* elsewhere to refer to fellow Christians, he uses the appositive *τῶν συγγενῶν μου* to qualify his reference in this context. Συγγενής, -ές describes individuals who belong to the same people group (BDAG 950c); *κατὰ σάρκα* ("according to the flesh") denotes natural lineage (cf. 1:3).

VERSE 4

οἵτινές εἰσιν Ἰσραηλῖται

The indefinite relative pronoun *οἵτινες* introduces the first of the benefits God has bestowed. The pronoun is qualitative and focuses on essence ("who by their very nature"; cf. Porter 133); Moo notes that it also has a causal nuance (560 n. 27). Ἰσραηλίτης, -ου, ὁ highlights the special position of the Jewish people as God's people (Cranfield 460; cf. Moo's extended note, 561 n. 30).

ὧν ἡ υἱοθεσία καὶ ἡ δόξα καὶ αἱ διαθῆκαι

The possessive relative pronoun *ὧν* (gen. pl. masc.) introduces a list of six benefits that are divided into two sets of three; the verb *εἰσιν* is understood. The fivefold use of *καί* (polysyndeton) "gives solemn dignity" to the list (R 427); definite articles accompany each of the abstract nouns. Although Paul has used *υἱοθεσία* previously in connection with individuals (cf. 8:15, 23), the focus in this context is corporate and refers to God's gracious adoption of the Jewish nation as his son (Cranfield 461; cf. Exod 4:22; Jer 31:9; Hos 11:1). Moo notes that Israel's adoption brought with it all the rights and privileges included within the old covenant but does not imply salvation for every single Israelite (562). See 1:23 for *δόξα*, which in this context refers to the outward sign of God's presence with Israel (Cranfield 461; cf. Exod 16:7; Lev 9:6; Num 14:10). The plural, *διαθῆκαι* (א, C, 33), is the more difficult reading (Schreiner 489), and there would have been no good reason to change a singular to the plural (Metzger 459; cf. Longenecker 785). BDAG notes that the biblical concept of "covenant" denotes the declaration of one person's initiative rather than the result of an agreement between two persons and has no parallel in extrabiblical sources (228b). The reference in this verse is to all the biblical covenants recorded in the OT (Moo 563).

καὶ ἡ νομοθεσία καὶ ἡ λατρεία καὶ αἱ ἐπαγγελίαι

Νομοθεσία, -ας, ἡ can refer to the act of giving the law (Moo 564) or the collection of laws that were given (Cranfield 463); the majority of EVV choose the former (e.g., ESV). Λατρεία, -ας, ἡ can refer to the temple service in general (Cranfield 463), the sacrificial system more narrowly (Moo 564), or service more broadly (Jewett 565; Longenecker 786; cf. 1:9, 25; 12:1; 15:16); EVV choose the first (e.g., CSB). See 4:13 for *ἐπαγγελία*; the plural extends the referent beyond the specific promise to Abraham to include the promises given to the fathers (cf. 15:8; Gal 3:16, 21) and, most likely, other individuals mentioned in the OT (Jewett 565). The context suggests eschatological and messianic promises in particular (Cranfield 464).

VERSE 5

ὧν οἱ πατέρες

The repetition of *ὧν* with the next two benefits gives them special emphasis (Jewett 566); the appropriate form of εἰμί is understood in both relative clauses. "The fathers" refers at least to Abraham, Isaac, Jacob (Schreiner 486), and perhaps to David (Murray 2:6).

καὶ ἐξ ὧν ὁ Χριστὸς τὸ κατὰ σάρκα

The connective *καί* adds the ninth and final benefit: the Messiah derives (ἐκ + gen.) his natural lineage from Israel (Jewett 566). See verse 3 for the article with Χριστός. The article with *κατὰ σάρκα* allows the phrase to qualify Χριστός (R 766; T 15); Jewett translates the phrase "insofar as the material side is concerned" (566).

The punctuation of the remainder of verse 5 has generated extensive discussion. Metzger (459–62) and Dunn (528–29) place a full stop after *σάρκα* and understand the remainder of the verse as an independent doxology to God: "God who is over all be blessed forever" (cf. RSV, NEB, GNB, CEV). Jewett (567–69) places commas after *σάρκα* and θεός, which establishes Christ as "the one who is God over all" (cf. NIV, CSB). Cranfield (464–78), Moo (565–68), and Schreiner (486–89) place commas after *σάρκα* and *πάντων*, which declares Christ to be both "the one who is over all" and "God blessed forever" (cf. KJV, NASB, JB, NRSV, ESV, NET). Longenecker simply places a comma after *σάρκα* and translates as "who is supreme over all as God blessed forever" (788–91).* It is more natural to connect the second half of the sentence to Christ (Jewett, Cranfield, Moo, Schreiner, Longenecker) than to understand it as an independent element (Metzger, Dunn).

ὁ ὢν ἐπὶ πάντων

The substantive participle ὢν (nom. sg. masc. of pres. act. ptc. of εἰμί) stands in apposition to ὁ Χριστός (R 1108); ἐπί + genitive is positional (Porter 161). The idea of Christ being "the one who is over all things" aligns with 10:12 (cf. 14:9; 1 Cor 8:6; Eph 1:10, 21–22; Phil 2:10; Col 2:10)

θεὸς εὐλογητὸς εἰς τοὺς αἰῶνας, ἀμήν

Whether θεός stands in apposition to the participle (Moo 568) or is its predicate is a close call, but the latter is preferable. Jewett's note that εὐλογητός ("blessed") appears first in other blessing formulas is at least suggestive (cf. Luke 1:68; 2 Cor 1:3; Eph 1:3); his comment that the adjective is always directed toward God affirms Christ's deity on either reading (567). Harris explains that εἰς τοὺς αἰῶνας is idiomatic for "to all eternity/eternally/forever" (95). See 1:25 for ἀμήν.

FOR FURTHER STUDY

56. Punctuation of Romans 9:5

Bartsch, H.-W. "Rom 9:5 und 1 Clem 32:4. Eine notwendige Konjektur im Römerbrief." *TZ* 21 (1965): 401–409.

Harris, M. J. "God Blessed Forever (Romans 9:5)." Pages 143–72 in *Jesus as God: The New Testament Use of Theos in Reference to Jesus*. Grand Rapids: Baker, 1992.

Kuss, O. "Zu Römer 9:5." Pages 291–303 in *Rechtfertigung*. Edited by J. Friedrich et al. Tübingen: Mohr, 1976.

Lorimer, W. L. "Romans IX.3–5." *NTS* 13 (1966–67): 385–86.

Metzger, B. M. "The Punctuation of Rom 9:5." Pages 95–112 in *Christ and Spirit in the New Testament: In Honour of Charles Francis Digby Moule*. Edited by B. Lindars and S. S. Smalley. Cambridge: Cambridge University Press, 1973.

HOMILETICAL SUGGESTIONS

Paul's Grief over Israel (9:1–5)

1. The intensity of his grief (ἀλήθειαν λέγω, 9:1–2)
   a. Triple witness (9:1)
      1) Christ
      2) Conscience
      3) Spirit
   b. Double anguish (9:2)
      1) Great grief
      2) Unceasing sorrow
2. The reason for his grief (γάρ, 9:3–5)
   a. Kinsmen alienated from Messiah (9:3)
      1) Despite divinely-bestowed privileges (9:4–5)

God's Gifts to the Jews (9:4–5)

1. Special status (Ἰσραηλῖται)
2. Adoption (ἡ υἱοθεσία)
3. God's glory (ἡ δόξα)
4. Covenants (αἱ διαθῆκαι)
5. God's law (ἡ νομοθεσία)
6. Temple worship (ἡ λατρεία)
7. God's promises (ἐπαγγελίαι)
8. Patriarchs (οἱ πατέρες)
9. Messiah (ὁ Χριστός)

The Truth About the Messiah (9:5b)

1. He is sovereign (ὁ ὢν ἐπὶ πάντων)
2. He is divine (θεός)
3. He is eternal (εὐλογητὸς εἰς τοὺς αἰῶνας)

2. God's Righteousness Is Vindicated by His Sovereign Working (9:6–29)

a. According to His Sovereign Calling (9:6–13)

STRUCTURE

After expressing his deep concern for Israel (9:1–5), Paul states his thesis for this portion of the letter (9:6–29): Israel's lack of responsiveness to the gospel does not mean that God's word of promise has failed (9:6a). The remainder of the paragraph supports that thesis using the examples of Isaac (9:6b–9) and Jacob (9:10–13).

Οὐχ οἷον δὲ ὅτι ἐκπέπτωκεν ὁ λόγος τοῦ θεοῦ.

οὐ γὰρ πάντες οἱ ἐξ Ἰσραὴλ οὗτοι Ἰσραήλ·
    οὐδ' ὅτι εἰσὶν σπέρμα Ἀβραὰμ πάντες τέκνα,
        ἀλλ', Ἐν Ἰσαὰκ κληθήσεταί σοι σπέρμα.
    τοῦτ' ἔστιν,
        οὐ τὰ τέκνα τῆς σαρκὸς ταῦτα τέκνα τοῦ θεοῦ
        ἀλλὰ τὰ τέκνα τῆς ἐπαγγελίας λογίζεται εἰς σπέρμα.
    ἐπαγγελίας γὰρ ὁ λόγος οὗτος,
        Κατὰ τὸν καιρὸν τοῦτον ἐλεύσομαι καὶ ἔσται τῇ Σάρρᾳ υἱός.

οὐ μόνον δέ, ἀλλὰ καὶ
        Ῥεβέκκα ἐξ ἑνὸς κοίτην ἔχουσα, Ἰσαὰκ τοῦ πατρὸς ἡμῶν·
        μήπω γὰρ γεννηθέντων μηδὲ πραξάντων τι ἀγαθὸν ἢ φαῦλον,
            ἵνα ἡ κατ' ἐκλογὴν πρόθεσις τοῦ θεοῦ μένῃ,
                οὐκ ἐξ ἔργων
                ἀλλ' ἐκ τοῦ καλοῦντος,
    ἐρρέθη αὐτῇ ὅτι Ὁ μείζων δουλεύσει τῷ ἐλάσσονι,
        καθὼς γέγραπται, Τὸν Ἰακὼβ ἠγάπησα, τὸν δὲ Ἠσαῦ ἐμίσησα.

VERSE 6

Οὐχ οἷον δὲ ὅτι ἐκπέπτωκεν ὁ λόγος τοῦ θεοῦ

The unusual denial form οὐχ οἷον δέ introduces a negative corrollary to what Paul has just written. Blass suggests that the normal phrase is οἷον τέ ἐστιν (§304); ὅτι is epexegetical (R 1034). Cranfield proposes the translation "but what I have just said . . . is not to be understood as meaning that . . ." (472). Ἐκπέπτωκεν (3 sg. pf. act. indic. of ἐκπίπτω, "fail") is an extensive perfect ("has failed") that emphasizes the completion of a process from which a present state emerges (cf. Wallace 577); the verb describes something that has become inadequate for its function (BDAG 308a). Ὁ λόγος τοῦ θεοῦ is monadic and could denote God's OT word (Moo 573), the gospel (Jewett 573), or God's declared purpose (Cranfield 473). The list of privileges in verses 4–5 suggests the third as it relates to Israel.

οὐ γὰρ πάντες οἱ ἐξ Ἰσραὴλ οὗτοι Ἰσραήλ

Paul explains (γάρ) the dynamic that lies behind his thesis—God works selectively according to his promise—by stating the principle negatively. The particle οὐ negates the first phrase rather than the second (R 752; contra Moo 573 n. 19). The article allows the prepositional phrase to function as a noun; Harris suggests that ἐκ + genitive signifies "belonging to" or "members of" and translates the phrase "Israelites" (109). The demonstrative pronoun οὗτοι ("these") is resumptive (R 698): "For not all the ones belonging to Israel (these) are Israel."

VERSE 7

οὐδ᾽ ὅτι εἰσὶν σπέρμα Ἀβραὰμ πάντες τέκνα

Paul continues his argument with the first of two specific examples. Οὐδ᾽ ὅτι should be taken together as parallel to the beginning of verse 6 (Moo 575 n. 25; cf. Schreiner 295). The contrasting clause that follows makes it clear that σπέρμα Ἀβραάμ ("Abraham's seed") is the selective term as is the second Ἰσραήλ in the preceding clause as are both τέκνα τοῦ θεοῦ ("children of God") and τὰ τέκνα τῆς ἐπαγγελίας ("children of the promise") in verse 8 (cf. Cranfield 473). See 1:3 for σπέρμα and 8:16 for τέκνα. The clause should be translated "And [it is] not that all children are Abraham's seed."

ἀλλ᾽, Ἐν Ἰσαὰκ κληθήσεταί σοι σπέρμα

Ἀλλ᾽ establishes a strong contrast; ἐν Ἰσαάκ ("through Isaac"; cf. Jewett 576) is brought forward for emphasis; the passive voice of κληθήσεταί (3 sg. fut. pass. indic. of καλέω, "call") reinforces the emphasis. Σοι is a dative of possession; placing the subject (σπέρμα) last frames the compound sentence. The quotation of Genesis 21:12 matches the LXX exactly and is the first of four OT quotations in the paragraph.

VERSE 8

τοῦτ᾽ ἔστιν, οὐ τὰ τέκνα τῆς σαρκὸς ταῦτα τέκνα τοῦ θεοῦ

The explanatory formula τοῦτ᾽ ἔστιν ("that is") introduces a further discussion of the true "seed" (Jewett 576) that is framed as another strong contrast (οὐ . . . ἀλλά). The article commonly occurs with both nouns in a genitive phrase; the genitive of σαρκός is possessive (Moo 576 n. 32). Ταῦτα (nom. pl. neut.) is resumptive; ἐστιν is understood (R 701); the article with θεοῦ is monadic; the genitive is possessive. Moo notes that "children of God" denotes those who belong to God and participate in salvation (577; cf. 8:11, 17, 21; Eph 5:1; Phil 2:5).

ἀλλὰ τὰ τέκνα τῆς ἐπαγγελίας λογίζεται εἰς σπέρμα

The genitive of ἐπαγγελίας is possessive ("the children who belong to the promise"); see 2:3 for λογίζεται (3 sg. pres. pass. indic.), which is a true passive in this verse

(T 58); the use of a singular verb with a neuter plural subject is classical (T 313). Εἰς + accusative after λογίζομαι occurs frequently (cf. 2:26; 4:5, 22) and is equivalent to a predicate nominative (Harris 37).

VERSE 9

ἐπαγγελίας γὰρ ὁ λόγος οὗτος

Paul explains (γάρ) the promise by introducing a paraphrase of Genesis 18:10. The descriptive genitive ἐπαγγελίας is brought forward for emphasis (Cranfield 476) and to make an explicit connection to what precedes. The article regularly accompanies a noun to indicate the attributive use of a demonstrative pronoun (cf. Wallace 241). Dunn translates, "For this word is one of promise" (541).

Κατὰ τὸν καιρὸν τοῦτον ἐλεύσομαι καὶ ἔσται τῇ Σάρρᾳ υἱός

Κατά + accusative is temporal; the attributive demonstrative (τοῦτον) again occurs with an articular noun. The entire phrase points to the future, and Cranfield suggests "at this time next year" (476). Ἐλεύσομαι (1 sg. fut. mid. indic. of dep. ἔρχομαι, "come") is a predictive future and highlights God's intervention (Moo 578 n. 40). Καί is connective, and τῇ Σάρρᾳ is a possessive dative (GNB, "and Sarah will have a son").

VERSE 10

οὐ μόνον δέ, ἀλλὰ καὶ

A general transitional phrase (cf. 5:3, 11; 8:23; 2 Cor 8:19) introduces what Paul considers a more conclusive argument (Schreiner 492): the example of Jacob.

Ῥεβέκκα ἐξ ἑνὸς κοίτην ἔχουσα, Ἰσαὰκ τοῦ πατρὸς ἡμῶν

Ῥεβέκκα (nom. sg. fem.) is a pendant nominative that Paul replaces with the pronoun αὐτῇ in verse 12 (cf. Wallace 51). Ἐκ + genitive denotes source; κοίτη, -ης, ἡ describes engaging in sexual relations (BDAG 554b); ἔχουσα (nom. sg. fem. of pres. act. ptc. of ἔχω, "have") is adverbial of time (NEB). Ἰσαάκ (indecl.) stands in apposition to ἑνός, and τοῦ πατρὸς ἡμῶν stands in apposition to Ἰσαάκ. Cranfield (477), Dunn (542), and Moo (579) all conclude that Paul intends ἐξ ἑνός to refer not only to the same father but to the same act of conception and even the same sperm.

VERSE 11

μήπω γὰρ γεννηθέντων μηδὲ πραξάντων τι ἀγαθὸν ἢ φαῦλον

The connection intended by γάρ ("for") is difficult to establish. Cranfield suggests that it relates to an unexpressed thought in Paul's mind (477); Robertson writes that it is hard to draw the line in 9:11 between parenthesis or anacoluthon (434). It is perhaps best to understand everything from μήπω in verse 11 through καλοῦντος in verse 12b as parenthetical. Regardless, Paul inserts two genitive absolutes (Moo 580 n. 49) to describe the circumstances in which the promise was given to Rebecca and to make the point that God's act of selection is independent of all human effort. Μήπω ("not yet") strengthens the negative (R 1173); μηδέ ("nor/and not") is disjunctive (BDF §466). The participles γεννηθέντων (gen. pl. masc. of aor. pass. ptc. of γεννάω, "be born") and πραξάντων (gen. pl. masc. of aor. act. ptc. of πράσσω, "do") are adverbial of time. The implied subjects of the participles are Jacob and Esau (Jewett 578). The indefinite pronoun τι (acc. sg. neut.) is adjectival, modifying both ἀγαθόν and φαῦλον ("any good or bad thing," cf. NKJV). Φαῦλος, -η, -ον describes something base or morally substandard (BDAG 1050d).

ἵνα ἡ κατ' ἐκλογὴν πρόθεσις τοῦ θεοῦ μένῃ

This purpose clause (ἵνα + subjunc.) also modifies the giving of the promise in verse 12b (Cranfield 478). Paul moves it forward for emphasis (BDF §478). The definite article with πρόθεσις brackets the prepositional phrase ("according to election"), which serves as an attributive adjunct (Porter 117); the genitive of θεοῦ is subjective (T 268); see 8:28 for πρόθεσις. NEB translates the phrase as "God's selective purpose." Μένῃ (3 sg. pres. act. subjunc. of μένω, "remain") is a perfective present. Dunn (543) and Schreiner (500) suggest that μένω is the antithesis of ἐκπίπτω in verse 6.

VERSE 12

οὐκ ἐξ ἔργων ἀλλ' ἐκ τοῦ καλοῦντος

The cause (ἐκ + gen.) behind God's selective purpose is not (οὐκ) human works (ἔργων) but (ἀλλ') divine calling (cf. 8:30). The article enables the participle (gen. sg. masc. of pres. act. ptc. of καλέω, "call") to function substantivally and highlight God as the one who calls.

ἐρρέθη αὐτῇ ὅτι Ὁ μείζων δουλεύσει τῷ ἐλάσσονι

'Ερρέθη (3 sg. aor. pass. indic. of λέγω, "say") is a constative aorist; the passive voice avoids the use of the divine name (Cranfield 479). Jewett notes that apart from this verse and 9:26, this form of λέγω occurs elsewhere only as an introductory formula in Matthew (5:21, 27, 31, 37, 38, 43). The feminine dative pronoun αὐτῇ ("to her") reintroduces Rebecca from verse 10 (Moo 580 n. 47); ὅτι is recitative, introducing the third OT quotation (Gen 25:23). Μείζων, -ον and ἐλάσσων, -ον are both normal uses of comparative adjectives (Wallace 299); the articles with both adjectives allow them to function substantivally. The pairing "greater/smaller" to mean "younger/older" is idiomatic (Dunn 544). Δουλεύσει (3 sg, fut. act. indic. of δουλεύω, "serve") is a predictive future; τῷ ἐλάσσονι is a dative of direct object.

VERSE 13

καθὼς γέγραπται, Τὸν Ἰακὼβ ἠγάπησα τὸν δὲ Ἠσαῦ ἐμίσησα

See 1:17 for the formula καθὼς γέγραπται that introduces the fourth OT quotation (Mal 1:2–3). Since both Ἰακώβ ("Jacob") and Ἠσαῦ ("Esau") are indeclinable (R 760), the accusative articles clarify their function as direct objects; δέ is adversative ("but"). Both ἠγάπησα (1 sg. aor. act. indic.) and ἐμίσησα (1 sg. aor. act. indic.) are constative aorists. See 8:28 for ἀγαπάω and 7:15 for μισέω. Cranfield concludes that "hate" should not be understood as a lesser degree of "love," but rather as "rejection" in contrast to "election" (480; cf. *TDNT* 4.687).

FOR FURTHER STUDY

See For Further Study §§ 29 ("Flesh"), 37 ("Promise"), 38 ("Seed"), 54 ("Predestination and Election")

HOMILETICAL SUGGESTIONS

God's Sovereign Promise (9:6–13)

1. Thesis: God's word of promise has not failed (9:6a)
2. Principle: Not every Israelite is "Israel" (9:6b)
   a. First Example: Isaac (9:7–9)
      1) Not all of Abraham's children are his "seed" (9:7)
      2) The children of promise are considered "seed" (9:8)
      3) God's promise involved Sarah's son (9:9)
         a) OT support: Genesis 18:10
   b. Second Example: Jacob (9:10–13)
      1) Esau and Jacob were both conceived from the same act (9:10)
      2) Neither had done any good or evil thing (9:11a)
      3) God's purpose stands according to his call (9:11b–12a)
      4) God's promise involved Rebecca's younger son (9:12b–13)
         a) OT support: Malachi 1:2–3

b. Out of His Sovereign Mercy (9:14–18)

STRUCTURE

The discussion of the selectivity at work in connection with God's promise could lead to the false conclusion that God's actions are unfair—an idea Paul emphatically rejects (9:14). He then appeals to two OT passages and draws a conclusion from each (9:15–16; 9:17–18). In both instances, the conclusion is that God's actions are rooted in his sovereign mercy.

Τί οὖν ἐροῦμεν;
μὴ ἀδικία παρὰ τῷ θεῷ;

μὴ γένοιτο.
τῷ Μωϋσεῖ γὰρ λέγει, Ἐλεήσω ὃν ἂν ἐλεῶ
καὶ οἰκτιρήσω ὃν ἂν οἰκτίρω.
ἄρα οὖν οὐ τοῦ θέλοντος
οὐδὲ τοῦ τρέχοντος
ἀλλὰ τοῦ ἐλεῶντος θεοῦ.

λέγει γὰρ ἡ γραφὴ τῷ Φαραὼ ὅτι Εἰς αὐτὸ τοῦτο ἐξήγειρά σε
ὅπως ἐνδείξωμαι ἐν σοὶ τὴν δύναμίν μου
καὶ ὅπως διαγγελῇ τὸ ὄνομά μου ἐν πάσῃ τῇ γῇ.
ἄρα οὖν ὃν θέλει ἐλεεῖ,
ὃν δὲ θέλει σκληρύνει.

VERSE 14

Τί οὖν ἐροῦμεν; (See 3:1; 6:1; 7:7)

μὴ ἀδικία παρὰ τῷ θεῷ;

The particle μή expects a negative answer (R 917). See 1:18 for ἀδικία; Jewett notes that using the noun instead of an adjective shifts the focus of the question from God's character to his actions (581). Παρά + dative is associative ("with regard to God"; cf. Harris 172); the article with θεῷ is anaphoric and monadic.

μὴ γένοιτο (See 3:4)

VERSE 15

τῷ Μωϋσεῖ γὰρ λέγει

God's words to Moses (Exod 33:19b) provide the first reason (γάρ) to reject the possible conclusion that his actions are unfair. Μωϋσεῖ (dat. sg. masc.) is the indirect object; the article marks Moses as well known; λέγει (3 sg. pres. act. indic.) is a perfective present used in an introductory formula (Wallace 533).

Ἐλεήσω ὃν ἂν ἐλεῶ

Ἐλεήσω (1 sg. fut. act. indic. of ἐλεέω, "show mercy") is a gnomic future; the verb denotes the act of having pity on someone in need (BDAG 315d). The indefinite relative ὃν ἄν embeds a demonstrative pronoun in the clause (NJB, "to those to whom"); ἐλεῶ (1 sg. pres. act. subjunc.) is a gnomic present.

καὶ οἰκτιρήσω ὃν ἂν οἰκτίρω

Καί is continuative ("and"); οἰκτιρήσω (1 sg. fut. act. indic. of οἰκτίρω, "have compassion"; cf. BDAG 700d) is a gnomic future; the indefinite relative again embeds a demonstrative pronoun; οἰκτίρω (1 sg. pres. act. subjunc.) is a gnomic present.

VERSE 16

ἄρα οὖν οὐ τοῦ θέλοντος

The conclusion (ἄρα οὖν) Paul draws is that God's mercy does not depend on human will or effort. Cranfield suggests supplying "God's mercy" as a subject (484). Οὐ introduces the first in a series of three participles. The article establishes θέλοντος (gen. sing. masc. of pres. act. ptc. of θέλω, "will, wish") as a substantival participle ("the one who is willing"); the present tense is gnomic, denoting a general principle (Moo 593); see 1:13 for θέλω. The genitive indicates source, and NEB translates the idea as "It does not depend on man's will" (cf. Wallace 110).

οὐδὲ τοῦ τρέχοντος

The disjunctive οὐδέ ("and not") adds a second substantival participle (gen. sg. masc. of pres. act. ptc. of τρέχω, "run"). Τρέχω is a more intense way of describing human effort than περιπατέω and should be understood "as a reference to the lifestyle of the devout Jew in the intensity of his devotion" (Dunn 553). The present tense and the genitive case follow those of the first participle.

ἀλλὰ τοῦ ἐλεῶντος θεοῦ

Ἀλλά ("but") draws a strong contrast with the first two participles in the series. Τοῦ ἐλεῶντος (gen. sg. masc. of pres. act. ptc. of ἐλεέω) is also substantival; the present tense and genitive case follow those of the first participle; see verse 15 for ἐλεέω. Θεοῦ (gen. sg. masc.) stands in apposition to the participle and is emphatic.

VERSE 17

λέγει γὰρ ἡ γραφὴ τῷ Φαραὼ ὅτι

God's words to Pharaoh (Exod 9:16) provide the second reason (γάρ) to reject the possible conclusion that his actions are unfair. Λέγει (3 sg. pres. act. indic.) is a perfective present used in an introductory formula (Wallace 533); see 4:3 for ἡ γραφή. Φαραώ (indecl.) is the indirect object; the dative article clarifies the case and marks Pharaoh as well known; ὅτι is recitative. Jewett views Pharaoh as the archetype of cruel oppression and hardness of heart (583).

Εἰς αὐτὸ τοῦτο ἐξήγειρά σε

ESV captures the classical idiom of purpose (εἰς αὐτὸ τοῦτο) by translating the phrase "For this very purpose." Ἐξήγειρά (1 sg. aor. act. indic. of ἐξεγείρω, "bring into being") is a constative aorist; σε is the direct object. Dunn translates the verb "cause to appear" (554); Moo suggests the connotation of "appoint to a significant role in salvation history" (595).

ὅπως ἐνδείξωμαι ἐν σοὶ τὴν δύναμίν μου

Ὅπως ἐνδείξωμαι (1 sg. aor. mid. subjunc. of ἐνδείκνυμι) specifies the purpose anticipated in the previous clause (Porter 232–33); see 2:15 for ἐνδείκνυμι. Ἐν σοί is instrumental ("through you"; Moo 595 n. 41); δύναμιν replaces ἰσχύν (LXX) and points to God's saving power (Cranfield 487; cf. 1:4, 16, 20). That change is one of four variations from the LXX that Cranfield notes "[bring] out more sharply . . . the sovereignty of the divine purpose" (485–87).

καὶ ὅπως διαγγελῇ τὸ ὄνομά μου ἐν πάσῃ τῇ γῇ

Ὅπως διαγγελῇ (3 sg. aor. pass. subjunc. of διαγγέλλω, "proclaim") adds a second purpose; the passive voice keeps the focus on the subject (God's name/reputation); διαγγέλλω describes the act of making something known far and near (BDAG 227a). See 1:5 and 2:24 for τὸ ὄνομά μου. Ἐν + dative specifies the universal sphere of God's redemptive purpose: "in all the earth" (NIV).

VERSE 18

ἄρα οὖν ὃν θέλει ἐλεεῖ

The conclusion (ἄρα οὖν) Paul draws is that God exercises his mercy as he wills. The accusative pronoun (ὅν) introduces a relative clause that embeds a demonstrative and functions as the direct object. Both present tenses are gnomic; see 1:13 for θέλω and verse 15 for ἐλεέω.

ὃν δὲ θέλει σκληρύνει

Δέ is continuative (EVV); the relative pronoun functions in the same way as the preceding occurrence; the present tenses are again gnomic. Σκληρύνω describes the act of causing something to be unyielding (BDAG 930c); it occurs fourteen times in the LXX version of the Exodus account. Moo says the verb "is consistently used in Scripture to depict a spiritual condition that renders one unreceptive and disobedient to God and his word" (596).

FOR FURTHER STUDY

57. God's Mercy (9:15)

Andersen, F. I. "Yahweh, the Kind and Sensitive God." Pages 41–88 in *God, Who Is Rich in Mercy: Essays Presented to Dr. D. B. Knox*. Edited by P. T. O'Brien and D. G. Peterson. Homebush West, NSW: Lancer, 1986.
Bultmann, R. *TDNT* 2.477–87.
Eastman, S. G. "Israel and the Mercy of God: A Re-reading of Galatians 6.16 and Romans 9–11." *NTS* 56 (2010): 367–95.
Esser, H.-H. *NIDNTT* 2.593–97.
Gupta, N. K. "What 'Mercies of God'? *Oiktirmos* in Romans 12:1 against Its Septuagintal Background." *BBR* 22 (2012): 81–96.
Karris, R. J. "God's Boundary-Breaking Mercy." *BibT* 24 (1986): 24–29.
Morris, L. *DPL* 601–02.
Neyrey, J. H. "Hope Against Hope." *Way* 27 (1987): 264–73.
Nowell, I. "Sinfulness and Divine Mercy." *BibT* 47 (2009): 193–97.
Ryan, J. M. "God's Fidelity to Israel and Mercy to All." *BibT* 35 (1997): 89–93.
Segal, A. F. "Paul's Experience and Romans 9–11." *Princeton Seminary Bulletin Supplement* 1 (1990): 56–70.
Tamez, E. "God's Election, Exclusion and Mercy: A Bible Study of Romans 9–11." *International Review of Mission* 82 (1993): 29–37.
Thielman, F. "Unexpected Mercy: Echoes of a Biblical Motif in Romans 9–11." *SJT* 47 (1994): 169–81.
Towner, P. H. *EDBT* 520–23.

HOMILETICAL SUGGESTIONS

God's Sovereign Mercy (9:14–18)

1. False Conclusion: God's actions are unfair (9:14a)
2. Emphatic Negation: Never! (9:14b)
3. First Reason: God's word to Moses (γάρ, 9:15)
   a. Conclusion: His mercy does not depend on human will or effort (ἄρα οὖν, 9:16)
4. Second Reason: God's word to Pharaoh (γάρ, 9:17)
   a. Conclusion: He exercises his mercy as he wills (ἄρα οὖν, 9:18)

c. Under His Sovereign Authority (9:19–29)

STRUCTURE

Paul returns to the diatribe style, phrasing a potential objection as two questions (9:19). He responds to the objection with three counter-questions (9:20–21), using a technique Jewett labels *anteisagoge* (589). An intentionally incomplete sentence (*anantapodoton*; cf. Jewett 589) follows and concludes with a relative clause that calls attention to the fact that God's mercy extends to both the Jews and the Gentiles (9:22–24). A series of four OT quotations—two from Hosea and two from Isaiah—provides support for Paul's argument (9:25–29).

Ἐρεῖς μοι οὖν, Τί [οὖν] ἔτι μέμφεται;
τῷ γὰρ βουλήματι αὐτοῦ τίς ἀνθέστηκεν;

ὦ ἄνθρωπε, μενοῦνγε σὺ τίς εἶ ὁ ἀνταποκρινόμενος τῷ θεῷ;
μὴ ἐρεῖ τὸ πλάσμα τῷ πλάσαντι, Τί με ἐποίησας οὕτως;
ἢ οὐκ ἔχει ἐξουσίαν ὁ κεραμεὺς τοῦ πηλοῦ ἐκ τοῦ αὐτοῦ φυράματος
    ποιῆσαι ὃ μὲν εἰς τιμὴν σκεῦος ὃ δὲ εἰς ἀτιμίαν;

εἰ δὲ θέλων ὁ θεὸς ἐνδείξασθαι τὴν ὀργὴν καὶ γνωρίσαι τὸ δυνατὸν αὐτοῦ
    ἤνεγκεν ἐν πολλῇ μακροθυμίᾳ σκεύη ὀργῆς κατηρτισμένα εἰς ἀπώλειαν,
    καὶ ἵνα γνωρίσῃ τὸν πλοῦτον τῆς δόξης αὐτοῦ ἐπὶ σκεύη ἐλέους
    ἃ προητοίμασεν εἰς δόξαν;
    οὓς καὶ ἐκάλεσεν ἡμᾶς οὐ μόνον ἐξ Ἰουδαίων ἀλλὰ καὶ ἐξ ἐθνῶν,

ὡς καὶ ἐν τῷ Ὡσηὲ λέγει,
    Καλέσω τὸν οὐ λαόν μου λαόν μου
        καὶ τὴν οὐκ ἠγαπημένην ἠγαπημένην·
    καὶ ἔσται ἐν τῷ τόπῳ οὗ ἐρρέθη αὐτοῖς, Οὐ λαός μου ὑμεῖς,
        ἐκεῖ κληθήσονται υἱοὶ θεοῦ ζῶντος.

Ἠσαΐας δὲ κράζει ὑπὲρ τοῦ Ἰσραήλ,
    Ἐὰν ᾖ ὁ ἀριθμὸς τῶν υἱῶν Ἰσραὴλ ὡς ἡ ἄμμος τῆς θαλάσσης, τὸ ὑπόλειμμα σωθήσεται·
        λόγον γὰρ συντελῶν καὶ συντέμνων ποιήσει κύριος ἐπὶ τῆς γῆς.

καὶ καθὼς προείρηκεν Ἠσαΐας,
    Εἰ μὴ κύριος Σαβαὼθ ἐγκατέλιπεν ἡμῖν σπέρμα,
        ὡς Σόδομα ἂν ἐγενήθημεν καὶ ὡς Γόμορρα ἂν ὡμοιώθημεν.

VERSE 19

Ἐρεῖς μοι οὖν, Τί [οὖν] ἔτι μέμφεται;

Paul introduces a potentially false conclusion with ἐρεῖς μοι οὖν, which Jewett describes as an overstatement that allows the audience to engage the argument (591). Οὖν is inferential; ἐρεῖς (2 sg. fut. act. indic. of λέγω) is a deliberative future; μοι is an indirect object ("to me"). The neuter interrogative pronoun τί ("Why?") introduces the first of two questions; the postpositive οὖν is transitional ("then"). Μέμφεται (3 sg. pres. mid. indic. of dep. μέμφομαι, "find fault") is a progressive present and retains its intensive middle sense (Porter 71) in this verb of mental action (R 812). The verb occurs elsewhere in the NT in Mark 7:2 and Hebrews 8:8 (cf. Sir 11:7; 41:7; 2 Macc 2:7).

τῷ γὰρ βουλήματι αὐτοῦ τίς ἀνθέστηκεν;

A second question (τίς) supports (γάρ) the first (Cranfield 489). The definite article (τῷ) regularly accompanies a possessive pronoun (αὐτοῦ); the dative βουλήματι (dat. sg. neut. of βούλημα, -τος, τό, "will") is a direct object; Jewett suggests "purpose/intention" (591; cf. *TDNT* 1.636–67). Ἀνθέστηκεν (3 sg. pf. act. indic. of ἀνθίστημι, "resist") is a gnomic perfect (Moo 600 n. 62) with a middle sense ("set oneself against," Dunn 556; cf. BDAG 80a).

VERSE 20

ὦ ἄνθρωπε, μενοῦνγε σὺ τίς εἶ ὁ ἀνταποκρινόμενος τῷ θεῷ;

The introductory ὦ ἄνθρωπε, μενοῦνγε σὺ τίς εἶ (NJB, "But you—who do you think you, a human being, are?") is "very emphatic" (R 678) and "deeply emotive" (Jewett 592). Wallace notes that ὦ occurs with the vocative (ἄνθρωπε) in contexts where deep emotion is present (68; contra T 33). Μενοῦνγε can be either resumptive ("indeed") to heighten (cf. Phil 3:8) or adversative ("on the contrary") to correct (cf. Rom 10:18); the context here suggests the latter. The personal pronoun σύ ("you") is emphatic both by its inclusion and by its position (Moo 601 n. 69). The articular substantival participle ὁ ἀνταποκρινόμενος (nom. sg. masc. of pres. mid. ptc. of dep. ἀνταποκρίνομαι, "answer in turn") depends on the personal pronoun (T 153). The present tense is progressive; the double compound strengthens the implication that a reply is unwarranted (Dunn 556). Τῷ θεῷ is monadic and a dative of direct object; it offers a strong contrast to ὦ ἄνθρωπε; Moo concludes that it highlights "the subordinate, creaturely status of the objector" (601).

μὴ ἐρεῖ τὸ πλάσμα τῷ πλάσαντι, Τί με ἐποίησας οὕτως;

Μή anticipates a "no" answer (Moule 156); ἐρεῖ (3 sg. fut. act. indic. of λέγω) is a deliberative future; τὸ πλάσμα (nom. sg. neut.) is the subject; τῷ πλάσαντι (dat. sg. masc. of aor. act. ptc. of πλάσσω, "mold, form") is a substantival participle that functions as the indirect object. The cognate verb πλάσσω and noun πλάσμα, -τος, τό refer to the act of molding a soft surface and that which is formed by that act, respectively (BDAG 832a). The verb also occurs in 1 Timothy 2:13; Cranfield provides OT background on the imagery of the potter and his work (491; cf. Job 1:9; Ps 2:9; Isa 29:16; 41:25; 45:9; 61:8; Jer 18:1–12). The interrogative *τί* ("why") introduces a question in direct discourse; *με* is the direct object; *ἐποίησας* (2 sg. aor. act. indic. of *ποιέω*, "make") is a constative aorist; *οὕτως* (GNB, "like this") is an adverb used predicatively (T 226; cf. R 545).

VERSE 21

ἢ οὐκ ἔχει ἐξουσίαν ὁ κεραμεὺς τοῦ πηλοῦ

The disjunctive *ἤ* ("or") introduces a third counter-question that expects a "yes" answer (Moule 156); *ἔχει* (3 sg. pres. act. indic. of *ἔχω*) is a gnomic present. Moving the direct object *ἐξουσίαν* (acc. sg. fem.) forward gives it emphasis and separates it from the genitive of subordination (*τοῦ πηλοῦ*; ESV, "over the clay") that depends on it (cf. R 503). *Ὁ κεραμεύς* ("the potter") makes explicit the imagery of the previous verse (cf. Wis 15:7).

ἐκ τοῦ αὐτοῦ φυράματος ποιῆσαι ὃ μὲν εἰς τιμὴν σκεῦος ὃ δὲ εἰς ἀτιμίαν;

Ἐκ + genitive denotes source ("from, out of"); *αὐτοῦ* is intensive ("the same lump"); *φύραμα, -τος, τό* describes the doughlike mixture from which a potter makes his wares (BDAG 1069b). Placing the prepositional phrase first emphasizes the single source of what is produced. The epexegetical infinitive *ποιῆσαι* (aor. act. inf. of *ποιέω*) qualifies *ἐξουσίαν* earlier in the sentence; Robertson suggests "power for making" (1062). The correlative combination *ὃ μέν . . . ὃ δέ* ("one . . . another") sets out contrasting purposes (*εἰς* + acc.) for the vessel (*σκεῦος*) the potter forms. See 2:7 for *τιμή* and 1:26 for *ἀτιμία*; a similar contrast occurs in 2 Timothy 2:20. ESV translates "to make out of the same lump one vessel for honored use and another for dishonorable use."

VERSE 22

εἰ δὲ θέλων ὁ θεὸς ἐνδείξασθαι τὴν ὀργὴν καὶ γνωρίσαι τὸ δυνατὸν αὐτοῦ

Paul's argument moves from his three counter-questions to an incomplete construction that extends through verse 24. Cranfield suggests that the transitional conjunction *δέ* ("now/but") "indicates an element of opposition and implies that [Paul] regards his illustration as inadequate" (493). *Εἰ* introduces the protasis of a first class condition, but no apodosis follows (Moo 604). Similar constructions occur in John 6:62 and Acts 23:9 and lead many EVV to translate as a question beginning with "What if . . .?" (KJV, NASB, NIV, ESV, NET, CSB). *Θέλων* (nom. sg. masc. of pres. act. ptc. of *θέλω*) is adverbial of cause (Moo 605); moving the participle ahead of the clause's subject (*ὁ θεός*) reinforces God's sovereignty (cf. 9:14–18). *Ἐνδείξασθαι* (aor. mid. inf. of *ἐνδείκνυμι*, "show") and *γνωρίσαι* (aor. act. inf. of *γνωρίζω*, "make known") are complementary infinitives; the middle voice of ἐνδείξασθαι is indirect ("show for himself"). The article with ὀργήν is a mild possessive ("his wrath") that corresponds to the possessive pronoun that accompanies τὸ δυνατὸν αὐτοῦ ("his power"); the neuter singular adjective functions as an abstract noun (BDF § 263.2).

ἤνεγκεν ἐν πολλῇ μακροθυμίᾳ σκεύη ὀργῆς κατηρτισμένα εἰς ἀπώλειαν

The primary verb of the "if" clause, ἤνεγκεν (3 sg. aor. act. indic. of φέρω, "bear"), is delayed to this point; it carries the idea of "bear patiently" or "put up with" (BDAG 1052b). The manner (ἐν + dat.) of God's forbearance is πολλῇ μακροθυμίᾳ ("much patience"); see 2:4 for μακροθυμία. Moo suggests that the purpose of God's patience is "to allow the rebellion of his creation to gain force and intensity . . . to give opportunity for him to bestow his mercy on those he has chosen for his own" (606). The objects of his patience are σκεύη ὀργῆς; the genitive of ὀργῆς denotes either quality ("wrathful vessels"; cf. T 215) or, more likely, purpose ("vessels destined for wrath"; cf. Wallace 101). The adjectival participle κατηρτισμένα (acc. pl. neut. of pf. pass. ptc. of καταρτίζω, "prepare for a purpose") modifies σκεύη; the perfect tense is extensive ("have been prepared"); the passive (cf. Wallace 417) is a divine passive (Dunn 560) that maintains the focus on the subject (Cranfield 496). The purpose (εἰς + acc.) for which the vessels have been prepared is destruction. Ἀπώλεια, -ας, ἡ denotes annihilation or ruin (BDAG 127a); elsewhere it refers to final destruction (Phil 1:28; 3:9; 2 Thess 2:3; 1 Tim 6:9).

VERSE 23

καὶ ἵνα γνωρίσῃ τὸν πλοῦτον τῆς δόξης αὐτοῦ ἐπὶ σκεύη ἐλέους

The connective καί ("and") has strong manuscript support (𝔓[46], ℵ, A, D, 33), and UBS[5] gives the reading an {A} rating. Metzger suggests that B might have omitted the conjunction to simplify the construction (462). It adds a purpose (ἵνα + subjunc.) for God's action to the previously-stated cause (θέλων); γνωρίσῃ is an aorist subjunctive; the verb denotes the action of causing information to become known (BDAG 203b). See 2:4 for πλοῦτος and 1:23 for δόξα. The genitive of τῆς δόξης is either apposition ("riches which are glory")* or partitive ("riches that are part of glory"); the same idea occurs in Ephesians 1:18; Colossians 1:28; and Philippians 4:19 (cf. Moo 608 n. 99). The objects upon whom (ἐπί + gen.) the riches of glory are bestowed are σκεύη ἐλέους ("vessels destined for mercy"); compare σκεύη ὀργῆς in the preceding verse; see 9:15 for the cognate verb ἐλεέω.

ἃ προητοίμασεν εἰς δόξαν;

The relative pronoun ἅ (acc. pl. neut.) introduces a clause that further describes the "vessels of mercy." Προητοίμασεν (3 sg. aor. act. indic. of προετοιμάζω, "prepare beforehand") is a constative aorist; the other NT occurrence of the verb is in Ephesians 2:10. In this context, the purpose (εἰς + acc.) of God's prior action is glory.

VERSE 24

οὓς καὶ ἐκάλεσεν ἡμᾶς οὐ μόνον ἐξ Ἰουδαίων ἀλλὰ καὶ ἐξ ἐθνῶν

Although Dunn (570), Jewett (598), Moo (611), Schreiner (535), and some EVV (NEB, GNB, CEV, NLT) see this relative clause as starting a new paragraph, Cranfield (498), Murray (2:33), Robertson (438), and most EVV take this relative clause with verses 22–23. The latter understanding is preferred. NKJV and ESV punctuate all of verses 22–24 as a single question.* NIV, NET, and CSB punctuate verses 23–24 as a separate question; NASB punctuates them as a statement.

Moo observes that the mention of "calling" returns to the theme of verses 6–13 (610); Dunn notes that the "awkwardness of the phrasing" calls fresh attention to Paul's argument (570). The relative pronoun οὕς (acc. pl. masc.) incorporates the antecedent (R 718), and the change from neuter to masculine reflects the real gender (cf. R 713); καί is adjunctive ("also"). Ἐκάλεσεν (3 sg. aor. act.indic. of καλέω) takes a double accusative (Moo 611 n. 3; cf. 1 Cor. 12:28), and ἡμᾶς personalizes the application. See 1:32; 4:16; 5:3, 11; 8:23; 9:10 for οὐ μόνον . . . ἀλλὰ καί ("not only . . . but also"); ἐκ + genitive ("out of") indicates separation from a larger group (Dunn 570). See 1:16 for Ἰουδαίος and 1:5 for ἔθνος.

VERSE 25

ὡς καὶ ἐν τῷ Ὡσηὲ λέγει

Jewett notes that ὡς καί ("as also") establishes a loose connection to what precedes (599); together, verses 25–29 provide scriptural support for Paul's argument. BDF classifies ἐν + dative as local (§219.1); the construction matches Mark 1:2; GNB translates as "in the book of Hosea"; Moo notes that the phrase corresponds to a rabbinic introductory formula (611 n. 6). Λέγει (3 sg. pres. act. indic.) is a perfective present used in an introductory formula (cf. 9:15, 17).

Καλέσω τὸν οὐ λαόν μου λαόν μου

Καλέσω (1 sg. fut. act. indic. of καλέω) is a predictive future that forms an *inclusio* with κληθήσονται at the end of verse 26. Jewett includes a chart that compares Paul's double quotation with the LXX of Hosea 2:23 (2:25) and 1:10 respectively (599). The article allows οὐ λαόν μου (NJB, "those who were not my people") to function as the object while λαόν μου ("my people") functions as the complement in the object-complement construction following a verb of calling.

καὶ τὴν οὐκ ἠγαπημένην ἠγαπημένην

Καί is connective ("and"); ἠγαπημένην (acc. sg. fem. of pf. pass. ptc. of ἀγαπάω) is an intensive perfect and a divine passive. The article allows οὐκ ἠγαπημένην ("the unloved nation," NEB) to function as the object, while the second participle ("my beloved") functions as the complement in a second object-complement construction.

The use of οὐκ with the first participle is unusual (Moule 105) but comes from the LXX quotation (R 1138).

VERSE 26

καὶ ἔσται ἐν τῷ τόπῳ οὗ ἐρρέθη αὐτοῖς, Οὐ λαός μου ὑμεῖς

Καί is continuative ("and"); ἔσται is a predictive future; ἐν + dative is local; the article is mildly demonstrative ("in the very place," NEB); see 9:12 for ἐρρέθη (3 sg. aor. pass. indic. of λέγω, "say"); αὐτοῖς is the indirect object. BDAG translates the clause idiomatically as "instead of their being told . . ." (1012a). Οὐ λαός μου repeats the wording of the preceding quotation; ἐστε is understood.

ἐκεῖ κληθήσονται υἱοὶ θεοῦ ζῶντος

The adverb ἐκεῖ ("there") is a theological rather than a geographical reference (Jewett 601; cf. Cranfield 499–501). Κληθήσονται (3 pl. fut. pass. indic. of καλέω) is a predictive future and a divine passive; it forms an *inclusio* with the beginning of the previous quotation. Because the passive form functions as an equative verb (cf. Wallace 436), the nominative υἱοί follows it; θεοῦ is possessive; ζῶντος (gen. sg. masc. of pres. act. ptc. of ζάω, "live") is adjectival. EVV translate the clause "sons of the living God" (EVV). See Moo for the OT background of "sons of God" (499).

VERSE 27

Ἠσαΐας δὲ κράζει ὑπὲρ τοῦ Ἰσραήλ

The mildly adversative δέ (Jewett 601) shifts the focus of the OT support from the Gentiles to Israel, beginning with Isaiah 10:22–23. Κράζει suggests a degree of urgency (Dunn 572); ὑπέρ + genitive denotes reference ("concerning"; cf. R 367); the article clarifies the case of the indeclinable noun Ἰσραήλ.

Ἐὰν ᾖ ὁ ἀριθμὸς τῶν υἱῶν Ἰσραὴλ ὡς ἡ ἄμμος τῆς θαλάσσης

Ἐάν ᾖ (3 sg. pres. act. subjunc. of εἰμί) introduces a third class condition; ἀριθμός, -ου, ὁ designates a non-specific number (BDAG 131a); the genitive τῶν υἱῶν Ἰσραήλ is partitive. Ἡ ἄμμος τῆς θαλάσσης ("the grains of sand along the beach," CEV) were considered to be innumerable (BDAG 442a).

τὸ ὑπόλειμμα σωθήσεται

Ὑπόλειμμα, -τος, τό ("remnant") denotes a relatively small surviving group (BDAG 1038d); σωθήσεται (3 sg. fut. pass. indic.) is a predictive future and a divine passive; see 1:16 for the cognate noun σωτηρία.

VERSE 28

λόγον γὰρ συντελῶν καὶ συντέμνων ποιήσει κύριος ἐπὶ τῆς γῆς

𝔓[46], ℵ*, A, and B omit the longer reading following *συντέμνων* that is present in many manuscripts (ℵ[c], D, 33). Metzger (462), Moo (609 n. 1), and Schreiner (530) all conclude that the longer reading is the result of a scribe assimilating the text to the LXX wording. Cranfield writes, "The Hebrew of Isa 10:23 is difficult, and the LXX translators were apparently baffled by the details. Nevertheless . . . Paul's abbreviation . . . [gives] the general idea of the original quite correctly" (502). *Γάρ* is causal; *λόγον* is the direct object; *συντελῶν* (nom. sg. masc. of pres. act. ptc. *συντελέω*, "carry out") and *συντέμνων* (nom. sg. masc. of pres. act. ptc. of *συντέμνω*, "cut short") are both adverbial of manner; *ποιήσει* (3 sg. fut. act. indic.) is a predictive future; *ἐπί* + genitive is local. NLT suggests "For the Lord will carry out his sentence upon the earth quickly and with finality."

VERSE 29

καὶ καθὼς προείρηκεν Ἠσαΐας

The connective *καί* adds Isaiah 1:9 as the fourth and final OT quotation. The comparative *καθώς* ("just as") introduces a variation on the more common introductory formula *καθὼς γέγραπται* (cf. 1:17). Paul uses *προείρηκεν* (3 sg. pf. act. indic. of *προλέγω*, "tell beforehand") elsewhere in 2 Corinthians 13:2; Galatians 5:21; 1 Thessalonians 3:4; although not in an introductory formula. Jewett writes that the extensive perfect makes Isaiah's statement directly relevant for the present situation (604).

Εἰ μὴ κύριος Σαβαὼθ ἐγκατέλιπεν ἡμῖν σπέρμα

Εἰ μή ("except") followed by the past tense introduces the protasis of a second class condition (Wallace 696); *κύριος Σαβαώθ* occurs as a title thirty-eight times in the LXX; *ἐγκατέλιπεν* (3 sg. aor. act. indic. of *εγκαταλείπω*, "leave") describes the act of causing something to remain (BDAG 273b); *ἡμῖν* is the indirect object; see 1:3 and 9:7 for *σπέρμα*.

ὡς Σόδομα ἂν ἐγενήθημεν καὶ ὡς Γόμορρα ἂν ὡμοιώθημεν

The particle *ἄν* followed by the past tense introduces the double apodosis of the second class condition; *καί* connects the parallel ideas; the comparative phrases *ὡς Σόδομα* and *ὡς Γόμορρα* are brought forward for emphasis. *Ἐγενήθημεν* (1 pl. aor. pass. indic. of dep. *γίνομαι*) and *ὡμοιώθημεν* (1 pl. aor. pass. indic. of *ὁμοιόω*, "cause to resemble") are constative aorists and divine passives; both have a causative sense, reflecting the original Hebrew hiphil tense.

FOR FURTHER STUDY

See For Further Study §§ 13 ("God's Wrath"), 17 ("God's Glory"), 57 ("God's Mercy")

HOMILETICAL SUGGESTIONS

God's Sovereign Authority (9:19–29)

1. Objection: Why does God find fault with what he brings about? (9:19)
2. First Response: The audacity of human presumption (9:20–21)
   a. Question #1: Who are humans to question God? (9:20a)
   b. Question #2: Who is the creation to question the creator? (9:20b)
   c. Question #3: Who is the pot to question the potter? (9:21)
3. Second Response: The nature of divine forbearance (9:22–24)
   a. Cause: Desire to show wrath and power (9:22a)
   b. Purpose: Make known riches of grace toward vessels of mercy (9:23–24)
4. Third Response: The support of OT Scripture (9:25–29)
   a. Regarding the Gentiles (9:25b–26)
      1) Hosea 2:23
      2) Hosea 1:10
   b. Regarding the Jews (9:27–29)
      1) Isaiah 10:22–23
      2) Isaiah 1:9

Vessels of Honor and Dishonor (9:21–24; cf. 2 Tim. 2:20–21)

1. Vessels of Dishonor
   a. Created by God (9:21)
   b. Recipients of God's patience and forbearance (9:22b)
   c. Objects of God's wrath and power (9:22a)
   d. Destined for destruction (9:22c)
2. Vessels of Honor
   a. Created by God (9:21)
   b. Objects of God's mercy (9:23a)
   c. Destined for glory (9:23b)
   d. From both Jews and Gentiles (9:24)

3. God's Righteousness Is Vindicated Despite Israel's Unresponsiveness (9:30–10:21)

a. Reflected in Their Failed Pursuit (9:30–10:4)

STRUCTURE

Paul uses another rhetorical question (τί οὖν ἐροῦμεν;) to introduce the conclusion he wants to draw from the preceding discussion of God's sovereign authority (9:19–29). A change in the word-chain from λογός (3x) and ἐπαγγελία (3x) in 9:6–29 to δικαιοσύνη (11x) and πίστις/πιστεύω (13x) in 9:30–10:21 accompanies the shift in the argument (cf. Harvey 131). The paragraph divides into two parts (9:30–33; 10:1–4). The first is structured around two questions (9:31, 33); the second proceeds logically by the triple use of γάρ (10:2, 3, 4). Schreiner notes the points of correspondence between the sections (542).

Τί οὖν ἐροῦμεν;
ὅτι ἔθνη τὰ μὴ διώκοντα δικαιοσύνην κατέλαβεν δικαιοσύνην,
δικαιοσύνην δὲ τὴν ἐκ πίστεως,
Ἰσραὴλ δὲ διώκων νόμον δικαιοσύνης εἰς νόμον οὐκ ἔφθασεν.
διὰ τί;
ὅτι οὐκ ἐκ πίστεως ἀλλ' ὡς ἐξ ἔργων·
προσέκοψαν τῷ λίθῳ τοῦ προσκόμματος,
καθὼς γέγραπται, Ἰδοὺ τίθημι ἐν Σιὼν λίθον προσκόμματος καὶ πέτραν σκανδάλου,
καὶ ὁ πιστεύων ἐπ' αὐτῷ οὐ καταισχυνθήσεται.

Ἀδελφοί, ἡ μὲν εὐδοκία τῆς ἐμῆς καρδίας καὶ ἡ δέησις πρὸς τὸν θεὸν ὑπὲρ αὐτῶν εἰς σωτηρίαν.
μαρτυρῶ γὰρ αὐτοῖς ὅτι ζῆλον θεοῦ ἔχουσιν ἀλλ' οὐ κατ' ἐπίγνωσιν·
ἀγνοοῦντες γὰρ τὴν τοῦ θεοῦ δικαιοσύνην καὶ τὴν ἰδίαν [δικαιοσύνην]
ζητοῦντες στῆσαι,
τῇ δικαιοσύνῃ τοῦ θεοῦ οὐχ ὑπετάγησαν·
τέλος γὰρ νόμου Χριστὸς εἰς δικαιοσύνην παντὶ τῷ πιστεύοντι.

VERSE 30

Τί οὖν ἐροῦμεν;

The sixth occurrence of τί οὖν ἐροῦμεν is the final one in the letter. Three times it introduces a potentially false conclusion others might raise; each time, that false conclusion is refuted by μὴ γένοιτο (6:1–2; 7:7; 9:14). Three times it introduces a positive conclusion Paul himself wants to make (4:1; 8:31; 9:30).

ὅτι ἔθνη τὰ μὴ διώκοντα δικαιοσύνην κατέλαβεν δικαιοσύνην

Paul answers his own question with a noun clause (ὅτι) that functions as the object ("that") of an understood repetition of ἐροῦμεν (Moo 621 n. 20). The anarthrous ἔθνη (nom. pl. neut.) is definite and generic; it specifies those Gentiles who have responded to the gospel (Schreiner 536 n. 6; cf. Longenecker 839). The definite article accompanies the adjectival participle διώκοντα (nom. pl. neut. of pres. act. ptc. of διώκω, "pursue"), which is negated by μή. The present tense is conative (GNB, "were not trying to [pursue]"); the verb denotes the act of following in haste in order to find something (BDAG 254a). The first occurrence of δικαιοσύνην (acc. sg. fem.) is the object of the participle and is qualitative. Κατέλαβεν (3 sg. aor. act. indic. of καταλαμβάνω, "attain") is a consummative aorist that emphasizes the end of the action. The second occurrence of δικαιοσύνην denotes that which is attained and refers to righteous status in God's sight (cf. 1:17). Compare Philippians 3:12–14 for the combination of διώκω and καταλαμβάνω.

δικαιοσύνην δὲ τὴν ἐκ πίστεως

The ascensive conjunction δέ ("even") intensifies δικαιοσύνην, which is repeated for emphasis (R 1184; BDF §447.8). The article adds clarity (BDF §272) and allows the prepositional phrase to function adjectivally (T 221). Ἐκ + genitive denotes the basis on which the righteousness rests (Harris 99); see 1:5 for πίστις.

VERSE 31

Ἰσραὴλ δὲ διώκων νόμον δικαιοσύνης εἰς νόμον οὐκ ἔφθασεν

Israel's experience stands in contrast (δέ) to that of the Gentiles. The participle διώκων (nom. sg. masc. of pres. act. ptc.) is adjectival, and the present tense is conative. Dunn writes that διώκω describes "a committed lifestyle" both in this and the preceding verse (581). The anarthrous noun νόμον is indefinite, qualitative, and refers to the Mosaic law (Moo 624; Longenecker 841). Schreiner sets out five possible options for the genitive of δικαιοσύνης (537); the statements in 2:13 and 10:5 support the idea of "the law which promises righteousness" (cf. Cranfield 508 n. 1);* Longenecker argues for "a 'legalistic' or 'nomistic' form of righteousness" (841). Εἰς + accusative denotes destination; νόμον is definite although anarthrous; ἔφθασεν (3 sg. aor. act. indic. of φθάνω, "arrive") is a consummative aorist with a sense similar to καταλαμβάνω in the preceding verse.

VERSE 32

διὰ τί;

Dunn suggests "Why so?" for the question that opens the second part of the section and writes that "the abruptness of the interrogative indicates a strength of feeling" that acknowledges the "shock effect" of 9:31 (582). The same question occurs in 2 Corinthians 11:11.

ὅτι οὐκ ἐκ πίστεως ἀλλ' ὡς ἐξ ἔργων

A causal ὅτι introduces the reason Israel did not attain what they were pursuing (R 965). The elliptical construction understands ἐδίωξαν νόμον δικαιοσύνης (Cranfield 509) and highlights the strong contrast (οὐκ . . . ἀλλ') between the two ways (ἐκ + gen.) in which righteousness can be pursued: faith or works (cf. Schreiner 539). Dunn (583), Jewett (610), Moo (626 n. 43), and Schreiner (439) all conclude that ὡς ("as if," Longenecker 842) highlights Israel's subjective attitude toward the law. Ἔργων (without νόμου) is the shorter and more difficult reading (Schreiner 548) and is supported by 𝔓[46], ℵ*, A, and B.

προσέκοψαν τῷ λίθῳ τοῦ προσκόμματος

Cranfield notes that the asyndeton at the beginning of this clause "gives special solemnity" to it (510); Schreiner suggests that "therefore" is implicit (540). Προσέκοψαν (3 pl. aor. act. indic. of προσκόπτω, "stumble") is a constative aorist; the literal sense of the verb is "strike against, stumble" (Dunn 583; cf. Ps 91:12); BDAG suggests a more figurative sense of "to take offense at, feel repugnance for, reject" (882b). Τῷ λίθῳ is a dative of reference; τοῦ προσκόμματος (gen. sg. neut. of πρόσκομμα, -τος, τό, "that which causes stumbling, offense") is a genitive of product (CEV, "the stone that makes people stumble").

VERSE 33

καθὼς γέγραπται (see 1:17)

Ἰδοὺ τίθημι ἐν Σιὼν

As scriptural support Paul quotes a combination of Isaiah 28:16 and 8:14 (cf. 1 Pet 2:6–8). Τίθημι (1 sg. pres. act. indic.) is a perfective present that emphasizes the continuing results of God's action; Schreiner writes that it also "emphasizes divine predestination" (540). Ἐν + genitive is local.

λίθον προσκόμματος καὶ πέτραν σκανδάλου

This section of the quotation is taken from Isaiah 8:14. See verse 32 for λίθον προσκόμματος ("stone of stumbling," ESV); the connective καί adds a parallel genitive construction, πέτραν σκανδάλου (ESV, "rock of offense"). Σκάνδαλον, -ου, τό describes an action or circumstance that leads a person to act contrary to a proper course of action or set of beliefs (BDAG 926c). See Longenecker for a discussion of the OT "stone" imagery (842–44).

καὶ ὁ πιστεύων ἐπ' αὐτῷ οὐ καταισχυνθήσεται

The connective καί returns the quotation to Isaiah 28:16. The variant that adds πᾶς (33) is an assimilation to 10:11 (Moo 620 n. 15); the shorter reading is strongly supported by ℵ, A, B, D. The present tense of the substantival participle ὁ πιστεύων highlights continuing belief (Wallace 621); ἐπί + dative of personal object emphasizes reliance upon (Moule 50; cf. 4:24). Καταισχυνθήσεται (3 sg. fut. pass. indic. of καταισχύνω, "put to shame") is a predictive future and a divine passive; see 5:5 for καταισχύνω. Schreiner suggests that the idea is "vindicated in the [final] judgment" (541; cf. Dunn 585).

VERSE 1

Ἀδελφοί, ἡ μὲν εὐδοκία τῆς ἐμῆς καρδίας

Direct address (ἀδελφοί) occurs frequently at points of transition throughout Romans (Moo 631 n. 3), but despite the absence of a conjunction, the transition here is to another perspective on the same topic. The conjunction μέν without its correlative δέ is emphatic ("indeed") and affirms what Paul has said previously in 9:1–3 (Longenecker 845). Εὐδοκία, -ας, ἡ denotes desire that is directed toward something that causes satisfaction or favor (BDAG 404d; cf. *TDNT* 2.746–48; Dunn 585). The article is normal with the possessive pronoun (Porter 131); the genitive denotes source; see 1:21 for καρδία.

καὶ ἡ δέησις πρὸς τὸν θεὸν ὑπὲρ αὐτῶν εἰς σωτηρίαν

Καί is connective; δέησις, -εως, ἡ describes an urgent request to meet a need and is exclusively addressed to God (BDAG 213d); πρός + accusative is spatial ("toward"); ὑπέρ + genitive denotes reference (Harris 209); the antecedent of αὐτῶν is Israel collectively (9:31). The variant readings that supply ἐστιν and τοῦ Ἰσραήλ ἐστιν appear to be later attempts at clarification (Cranfield 513 n. 6; cf. Schreiner 549; Metzger 463). Εἰς + accusative indicates aim or goal (Cranfield 513); see 1:16 for σωτηρία.

VERSE 2

μαρτυρῶ γὰρ αὐτοῖς ὅτι ζῆλον θεοῦ ἔχουσιν ἀλλ' οὐ κατ' ἐπίγνωσιν

Paul provides the reason (γάρ) for his prayer with a public affirmation (μαρτυρῶ αὐτοῖς); ὅτι introduces the content of his testimony. According to Dunn, ζῆλον θεοῦ describes "a passionate consuming zeal focused on God, as evidenced by an overwhelming desire to do his will" (586). The present tense of ἔχουσιν (3 pl. pres. act. indic. of ἔχω) describes an act that began in the past and continues into the present (cf. Wallace 519). Ἀλλ' ("but") is adversative; οὐ negates the prepositional phrase that follows it; κατά + accusative denotes correspondence ("according to"); see 1:28 for ἐπίγνωσις. The phrase describes a lack of comprehension (Cranfield 514).

VERSE 3

ἀγνοοῦντες γὰρ τὴν τοῦ θεοῦ δικαιοσύνην

Paul explains (γάρ) the Jews' lack of knowledge in the terms of righteousness. First, they are ignorant of God's righteousness. The adverbial participle of cause ἀγνοοῦντες (nom. pl. masc. of pres. act. ptc. of ἀγνοέω, "be ignorant") is a customary present. The genitive τοῦ θεοῦ denotes source (Wallace 110); placing it between the article and the noun it modifies adds emphasis (cf. Wallace 306). The combination of the definite article with δικαιοσύνην plus the adjunct τοῦ θεοῦ makes the entire phrase monadic ("the one-of-a-kind righteousness that comes from God").

καὶ τὴν ἰδίαν [δικαιοσύνην] ζητοῦντες στῆσαι

Second (continuative καί), they seek to establish their own righteousness. Cranfield notes that ἰδίαν ("their own") highlights status of the Jews' own earning (515). Placing the noun phrase first gives it emphasis. The participle ζητοῦντες (nom. pl. masc. of pres. act. ptc. of ζητέω, "seek") is again causal; the present tense is conative, describing a "deliberate and sustained intention" (Dunn 587). The infinitive στῆσαι (aor. act. inf. of ἵστημι, "establish") is complementary; Jewett suggests the translation "validate" (617).

τῇ δικαιοσύνῃ τοῦ θεοῦ οὐχ ὑπετάγησαν

The result is that they refuse to subject themselves to God's righteousness. Placing τῇ δικαιοσύνῃ first gives it emphasis; the dative indicates the person or thing to which someone is subject; τοῦ θεοῦ is a subjective genitive; the phrase is again monadic. Ὑπετάγησαν (3 pl. aor. pass. indic. of ὑποτάσσω, "put/be in subjection") is a constative aorist (Moo 633 n. 18) with a middle sense (Schreiner 543; cf. Jewett 618).

VERSE 4

τέλος γὰρ νόμου Χριστὸς εἰς δικαιοσύνην παντὶ τῷ πιστεύοντι

The final explanatory step (γάρ) in Paul's argument has been the focus of considerable scholarly discussion, beginning with the meaning of the emphatically-placed predicate nominative τέλος (Cranfield 515; Schreiner 544), which is definite although anarthrous (Wallace 264). Moo provides a concise summary of the LXX and NT uses of τέλος (639 n. 41), and Cranfield (515–20) sets out three interpretations for the word: fulfillment (Eusebius), goal (Chrysostom), or termination (Irenaeus). Jewett argues for fulfillment (619), and Cranfield argues for "the goal, the aim, the intention, the real meaning and substance" (519). Murray's argument for termination is most likely correct (2:49–50; cf. Dunn 597; Longenecker 850; Moo 641; Schreiner 545). Νόμου refers to the OT law (Moo 636), and the genitive is objective (GNB, "for Christ has brought the law to an end"); Χριστός is the subject. Εἰς δικαιοσύνην is best understood as modifying νόμου and denoting general reference (Schreiner 547; cf. Longenecker

850); the substantival participle πιστεύοντι (dat. sg. masc. of pres. act. ptc. of πιστεύω) is a dative of advantage; the present tense emphasizes continuing belief (Wallace 621). The basic idea of Paul's statement, therefore, is that Christ brings a termination to the OT law's promise of righteousness (cf. 9:31) for the benefit of everyone who places his/her continuing reliance on him.

FOR FURTHER STUDY

58. "Christ Is the End of the Law" (10:4)

Badenas, R. *Christ the End of the Law: Romans 10:4 in Pauline Perspective*. Sheffield: *JSOT*, 1985.

Bechtler, S. R. "Christ, the Τέλος of the Law: The Goal of Romans 10:4." *CBQ* 56 (1994): 288–308.

Campbell, W. S. "Christ the End of the Law: Romans 10:4." Pages 73–81 in *Studia Biblica*. Volume 3. Edited by E. A. Livingstone. Sheffield: *JSOT*, 1980.

Edgar, C. F. "Paul and the Law: A Narrative Analysis of the Pentateuch and Its Significance for Understanding Romans 9:30–10:4." *Sewanee Theological Review* 39 (1996): 269–84.

Flückinger, F. "Christus, des Gesetzes τέλος." *TZ* 11 (1955): 153–57.

Getty, E. A. "An Apocalyptic Perspective on Rom 10:4." *HBT* 4 (1982): 79–131.

Heil, J. P. "Christ, the Termination of the Law (Romans 9:30–10:8)." *CBQ* 63 (2001): 484–98.

Hills, J. V. "'Christ was the Goal of the Law . . .' (Romans 10: 4)." *JTS* 44 (1993): 585–92.

Howard, G. E. "Christ the End of the Law: The Meaning of Romans 10:4." *JBL* 88 (1969): 331–37.

Jolivet, I. "Christ the *telos* in Romans 10:4 as Both Fulfillment and Termination of the Law." *ResQ* 51 (2009): 13–30.

Linns, W. C. "Exegesis of *Telos* in Romans 10:4." *BR* 33 (1988): 5–12.

Meyer, P. W. "Romans 10:4 and the 'End' of the Law." Pages 59–78 in *The Divine Helmsman: Studies on God's Control of Human Events, Presented to Lou H. Silberman*. Edited by J. L. Crenshaw and S. Sandmel. New York: Ktav, 1980.

Mussner, F. "Christus (ist) des Gesetzes Ende zur Gerechtigkeit für jeden der glaubt (Röm 10:4)." Pages 31–44 in *Paulus—Apostat oder Apostel*? Regensburg: Pustet, 1977.

Refoulé, F. "Romains X,4: Encore une fois." *RB* 91 (1984): 321–50.

Rhyne, C. T. "*Nomos Dikaiosynēs* and the Meaning of Romans 10:4." *CBQ* 47 (1985): 486–99.

Schreiner, T. R. "Paul's View of the Law in Romans 10:4–5." *WTJ* 55 (1993): 113–35.

Stuhlmacher, P. "Das Ende des Gesetzes: Über Ursprung und Ansatz der paulinischen Theologie." *ZTK* 67 (1970): 14–39.

Uchida, K. "Is Christ the End of the Law? Romans 10:4 Reconsidered." *Exegetica* 12 (2001): 75–106.

HOMILETICAL SUGGESTIONS

Israel's Failed Pursuit (9:30–10:4)

1. They focus on the wrong goal (9:30–33)

a. They pursue the law for righteousness (9:31)
b. They pursue works for righteousness (9:32a)
c. Explanation: They stumbled over Christ (9:32b–33)
2. They use the wrong approach (10:1–4)
a. They have zeal without knowledge (10:2)
b. They do not subject themselves to God's righteousness (10:3c)
1) Because they are ignorant of God's righteousness (10:3a)
2) Because they seek to establish their own righteousness (10:3b)
c. Explanation: Christ is the end of the law (10:4)

"Christ, the End of the Law" (10:4)

1. Christ
2. The end of the law
3. For righteousness
4. To everyone who believes

b. Rooted in Their Flawed Understanding (10:5–13)

STRUCTURE

Paul develops his statement about Christ as the end of the law (10:4) with a three-part paragraph that clarifies the correct understanding of righteousness by faith. The first part (10:5–8) contrasts righteousness by law (summarized by Lev 18:5) with righteousness by faith (summarized by Deut 30:12–14). The second (10:9–10) further explains the dynamics of righteousness by faith. The third (10:11–13) provides the scriptural proof (Isa 28:16; Joel 2:32) that righteousness by faith is available to all who believe in and call upon the name of the Lord.

Μωϋσῆς γὰρ γράφει τὴν δικαιοσύνην τὴν ἐκ [τοῦ] νόμου ὅτι
ὁ ποιήσας αὐτὰ ἄνθρωπος ζήσεται ἐν αὐτοῖς.
ἡ δὲ ἐκ πίστεως δικαιοσύνη οὕτως λέγει,
Μὴ εἴπῃς ἐν τῇ καρδίᾳ σου, Τίς ἀναβήσεται εἰς τὸν οὐρανόν;
τοῦτ᾽ ἔστιν Χριστὸν καταγαγεῖν·
ἤ, Τίς καταβήσεται εἰς τὴν ἄβυσσον;
τοῦτ᾽ ἔστιν Χριστὸν ἐκ νεκρῶν ἀναγαγεῖν.
ἀλλὰ τί λέγει; Ἐγγύς σου τὸ ῥῆμά ἐστιν
ἐν τῷ στόματί σου καὶ ἐν τῇ καρδίᾳ σου,
τοῦτ᾽ ἔστιν τὸ ῥῆμα τῆς πίστεως ὃ κηρύσσομεν.

ὅτι ἐὰν ὁμολογήσῃς ἐν τῷ στόματί σου κύριον Ἰησοῦν
καὶ πιστεύσῃς ἐν τῇ καρδίᾳ σου ὅτι ὁ θεὸς αὐτὸν ἤγειρεν ἐκ νεκρῶν, σωθήσῃ·
καρδίᾳ γὰρ πιστεύεται εἰς δικαιοσύνην,
στόματι δὲ ὁμολογεῖται εἰς σωτηρίαν.

λέγει γὰρ ἡ γραφή,
Πᾶς ὁ πιστεύων ἐπ᾽ αὐτῷ οὐ καταισχυνθήσεται.
οὐ γάρ ἐστιν διαστολὴ Ἰουδαίου τε καὶ Ἕλληνος,
ὁ γὰρ αὐτὸς κύριος πάντων, πλουτῶν εἰς πάντας τοὺς ἐπικαλουμένους αὐτόν·
Πᾶς γὰρ ὃς ἂν ἐπικαλέσηται τὸ ὄνομα κυρίου σωθήσεται.

VERSE 5

Μωϋσῆς γὰρ γράφει τὴν δικαιοσύνην τὴν ἐκ [τοῦ] νόμου ὅτι

The explanation (γάρ) of why Christ is the end of the law begins with what Moses says. Γράφει (3 sg. pres. act. indic. of γράφω) is a perfective present used in an introductory formula; the choice of γράφει rather than λέγει (cf. 9:15, 17, 25; 10:6) is not significant (cf. Moo 650 n. 25). Δικαιοσύνην is an accusative of respect (Wallace 105); the second definite article adds the prepositional phrase as an adjectival adjunct; ἐκ + genitive denotes source; the article with νόμου is anaphoric; ὅτι introduces content ("that"). Moo provides three possible interpretations of "the righteousness based on the law" and concludes that it has the negative connotation of the attempt to obey the law perfectly as a means of attaining righteousness (645–47).

ὁ ποιήσας αὐτὰ ἄνθρωπος ζήσεται ἐν αὐτοῖς

The definite article brackets the noun phrase; ποιήσας (nom. sg. masc. of aor. act. ptc. of ποιέω) is adjectival; the aorist tense ("the one who does them") is used generically (Wallace 615); ζήσεται (3 sg. fut. mid. indic. of ζάω) is a gnomic future; the middle is deponent; ἐν + dative is instrumental ("by them"). The statement is best understood as an expression of how the Jews understood righteousness (Dunn 601; contra Cranfield 521).

VERSE 6

ἡ δὲ ἐκ πίστεως δικαιοσύνη οὕτως λέγει

Righteousness by faith, however, stands in contrast (δέ) to righteousness by law. A definite article brackets the noun phrase; the prepositional phrase ἐκ πίστεως is adjectival and denotes source. The adverb οὕτως ("in this way") is emphatic; see 9:15 for λέγει. Schreiner notes that the NT writers often demonstrated that the understanding of a given text is incorrect by introducing a second text (555).

Μὴ εἴπῃς ἐν τῇ καρδίᾳ σου

Paul begins his OT proof with a verbatim quote from Deuteronomy 8:17 and 9:4 (Jewett 625). Μή + aorist subjunctive (εἴπῃς) is the normal way of stating a prohibition (Wallace 469); ἐν + dative is local.

Τίς ἀναβήσεται εἰς τὸν οὐρανόν;

Paul then moves to Deuteronomy 30 for the substance of his proof, beginning with verse 12. Ἀναβήσεται (3 sg. fut. mid. indic. of ἀναβαίνω, "ascend") is a deliberative future and a deponent middle; εἰς + accusative indicates destination; the article is monadic. See 1:18 for οὐρανός.

τοῦτ᾽ ἔστιν Χριστὸν καταγαγεῖν

Τοῦτ᾽ ἔστιν ("that is") is common terminology in Jewish exegesis (Cranfield 534) and introduces Paul's interpretation (cf. 9:8). Χριστόν is the object of the infinitive and is moved forward for emphasis; καταγαγεῖν (aor. act. infin. of κατάγω, "bring down") is an infinitive of purpose (T 135) and a constative aorist.

VERSE 7

ἤ, Τίς καταβήσεται εἰς τὴν ἄβυσσον;

Paul continues with Deuteronomy 30:13, adding the disjunctive ἤ ("or") but departing from the LXX reading. The result is wording that echoes LXX Psalm 106:26 (Jewett 627) and establishes a clear contrast between the heights and the depths. Καταβήσεται (3 sg. fut. mid. indic. of καταβαίνω, "descend") is a deliberative future and a deponent middle; εἰς + accusative indicates destination; the article is monadic. Ἄβυσσος, -ου, ἡ ("abyss") refers to the transcendent place associated with the dead and hostile powers (BDAG 2d).

τοῦτ' ἔστιν Χριστὸν ἐκ νεκρῶν ἀναγαγεῖν

See verse 6 for τοῦτ' ἔστιν; Χριστόν is again brought forward for emphasis; ἐκ νεκρῶν denotes origin; ἀναγαγεῖν (aor. act. infin. of ἀνάγω, "bring up") is an infinitive of purpose and a constative aorist.

VERSE 8

ἀλλὰ τί λέγει;

Deuteronomy 30:14 stands in strong contrast (μή . . . ἀλλά) to the idea of *doing* in verses 12–13. Instead, it introduces the idea of "the word of faith" (see below). See 9:15 and 10:5 for λέγει. Cranfield argues that the understood subject of the question is ἡ ἐκ πίστεως δικαιοσύνη from verse 6 (525).

Ἐγγύς σου τὸ ῥῆμά ἐστιν ἐν τῷ στόματί σου καὶ ἐν τῇ καρδίᾳ σου

The prepositional phrase ἐγγύς σου ("near you") serves as the predicate (R 394) and is brought forward for emphasis (Jewett 628). The article is *par excellence*; ῥῆμα, -τος, τό denotes that which is spoken or said (BDAG 905b; cf. Jewett 629); ἐν + dative is local ("in your mouth and in your heart"). See 3:14 for στόμα and 1:21 for καρδία.

τοῦτ' ἔστιν τὸ ῥῆμα τῆς πίστεως ὃ κηρύσσομεν

See verse 6 for τοῦτ' ἔστιν. Since ῥῆμα occurs in the OT quotation (cf. 10:18), Paul uses it in his interpretive comment (cf. 10:17) and adds two qualifiers to explain the gospel message (cf. Cranfield 526). Τῆς πίστεως is an objective genitive ("the word that calls for faith"; Moo 657 n. 52); the definite article accompanies the abstract noun; see 1:17 for πίστις. The relative clause ὃ κηρύσσομεν ("that we are preaching") further explains ῥῆμα; the present tense of κηρύσσομεν (1 pl. pres. act. indic.) is customary; see 2:21 for κηρύσσω.

VERSE 9

ὅτι ἐὰν ὁμολογήσῃς ἐν τῷ στόματί σου κύριον Ἰησοῦν

KJV, NASB, and NIV punctuate the end of verse 8 with a comma or colon, translate ὅτι as "that," and understand verses 9–10 as the content of "the word of faith." NEB and GNB punctuate the end of verse 8 with a period and leave ὅτι untranslated. RSV and ESV translate ὅτι as "because", and understand verses 9–10 as the reason "the word is near you." The best approach is to translate ὅτι as "for" and understand what follows as an explanation of verse 8 as a whole (cf. Cranfield 526; Moo 657; Schreiner 559). Ἐάν introduces a third class condition (Wallace 699) in which the tense is usually aorist (R 1019); ὁμολογήσῃς (2 sg. aor. act. subjunc. of ὁμολογέω, "confess") describes the act of professing allegiance, ordinarily in public (BDAG 708d); ἐν + dative is instrumental ("with your mouth," Moo 657 n. 55). Κύριον Ἰησοῦν is a double accusative in which κύριον is the complement and Ἰησοῦν is the object (Wallace 187–88; cf. 1 Cor 12:3; 2 Cor 4:5; Phil 2:11; Col 2:6). Cranfield writes that for Paul the statement acknowledges that "Jesus shares the name and nature, the holiness, the authority, power, majesty, and eternity of the one true God" (539).

καὶ πιστεύσῃς ἐν τῇ καρδίᾳ σου ὅτι ὁ θεὸς αὐτὸν ἤγειρεν ἐκ νεκρῶν, σωθήσῃ

Καί adds a second protasis to the condition. Wallace notes that both elements of a compound protasis do not necessarily bear the same relationship to the apodosis and concludes that in this case the first (ὁμολογήσῃς ἐν τῷ στόματί σου) provides the evidence while the second (πιστεύσῃς ἐν τῇ καρδίᾳ σου) establishes the cause (686). The order of the two elements reflects the order of the OT quotation in verse 8a. The aorist tense of πιστεύσῃς (2 sg. aor. act. subjunc. of πιστεύω) parallels the aorist of ὁμολογήσῃς in the first protasis; ἐν + dative is local ("in your heart"); ὅτι indicates the content of belief (Harris 233). The article with θεός is monadic; αὐτόν is the direct object; the aorist indicative of ἤγειρεν (3 sg. aor. act. indic. of ἐγείρω, "raise") describes "a unique, once-for-all act" (Cranfield 530); ἐκ νεκρῶν denotes origin. The future of σωθήσῃ (2 sg. fut. pass. indic. of σῴζω) is predictive; the passive is a divine passive; the verb denotes eschatological salvation (Cranfield 530).

VERSE 10

καρδίᾳ γὰρ πιστεύεται εἰς δικαιοσύνην

Paul reverses the sequence of believing and confessing to reflect the natural order: "inward belief coming to expression in spoken word" (Dunn 609). Καρδίᾳ (dat. sg. fem.) is instrumental; γάρ is causal (Cranfield 530); εἰς + accusative denotes result (Moule 70). Πιστεύεται (3 sg. pres. pass. indic.) is a gnomic present; the passive voice highlights the subject's participation in the action; the construction is indefinite (BDF §130.3; cf. NASB, "a person").

στόματι δὲ ὁμολογεῖται εἰς σωτηρίαν

Δέ is connective ("and"); *στόματι* (dat. sg. neut.) is instrumental; *ὁμολογεῖται* (3 sg. pres. pass. indic.) parallels *πιστεύεται* in the first line; *εἰς* + accusative denotes result (Harris 43).

VERSE 11

λέγει γὰρ ἡ γραφή, Πᾶς ὁ πιστεύων ἐπ' αὐτῷ οὐ καταισχυνθήσεται

The proof (*γάρ*) of Paul's explanation is found in the OT (*ἡ γραφή*; cf. 4:3; 9:17). See 9:15 for *λέγει*; Paul adds *πᾶς* to highlight the universal scope of the promise in Isaiah 28:16; the antecedent of *αὐτῷ* is Christ (verse 9). See 9:33 for the wording of the quotation.

VERSE 12

οὐ γάρ ἐστιν διαστολὴ Ἰουδαίου τε καὶ Ἕλληνος

The explanation (*γάρ*) for the universal scope of the promise is God's impartiality—he deals equally with both Jew and Greek. See 3:22 for *οὐ ἐστιν διαστολή*; see 1:16 for *Ἰουδαῖος τε καὶ Ἕλλην* (cf. 2:9, 10; 3:9); the genitives carry the sense of "between" (ESV; cf. Wallace 135).

ὁ γὰρ αὐτὸς κύριος πάντων

The reason (*γάρ*) God deals impartially with all is that he is Lord of all. *Αὐτός* is intensive ("same"); *ἐστιν κύριος* is understood (NIV, "the same lord [is lord] of all"); *πάντων* is an objective genitive. Compare Peter's statement in Acts 10:36.

πλουτῶν εἰς πάντας τοὺς ἐπικαλουμένους αὐτόν

Πλουτῶν (nom. sg. masc. of pres. act. ptc. of *πλουτέω*, "be rich") is an adjectival participle that modifies *κύριος*; the present tense is gnomic; see 2:4 for the cognate noun *πλοῦτος*, which Dunn notes refers to spiritual wealth (610). Εἰς + accusative is the equivalent of a dative of advantage (R 594; cf. Luke 12:21); *πάντας* reiterates the universal scope; the substantival participle *ἐπικαλουμένους* (acc. pl. masc. of pres. mid. ptc. of *ἐπικαλέω*, "call upon") is a customary present and an indirect middle. The verb describes calling upon a deity for any purpose (BDAG 373a; cf. Dunn 610); Jewett notes that it occurs where the allegiance of converts is in view (633; cf. Acts 9:14, 21; 1 Cor. 1:2).

VERSE 13

Πᾶς γὰρ ὃς ἂν ἐπικαλέσηται τὸ ὄνομα κυρίου σωθήσεται

Paul adds a second OT proof (γάρ) from Joel 2:32 (MT 3:5). Πᾶς again reiterates universal scope; the indefinite combination ὃς ἄν ("whoever") is the equivalent of a third class condition (Wallace 479); Moule suggests the translation "if anyone" (151). Ἐπικαλέσηται (3 sg. aor. mid. subjunc.) functions as the link word that connects verses 12–14; see 1:5; 2:24; 9:17 for other combinations with ὄνομα; see 9:27 for σωθήσεται.

FOR FURTHER STUDY

See For Further Study §§ 10 ("Righteousness"), 11 ("Faith"), 16 ("Heart"), 24 ("Paul and the Law"), 47 ("Honor and Shame in Paul's World")

HOMILETICAL SUGGESTIONS

Israel's Flawed Understanding (10:5–13)

1. They misunderstand the simplicity of righteousness by faith (10:5–8)
   a. The righteousness based on law (10:5; cf. Lev. 18:5)
   b. The righteousness based on faith (10:6–8: cf. Deut 30:12–14)
2. They misunderstand the dynamics of righteousness by faith (10:9–10)
   a. Cause: Believing in heart (10:9b, 10a)
   b. Evidence: Confessing with mouth (10:9a, 10b)
   c. Object: Christ's lordship and resurrection (10:9a; 9b)
   d. Result: Salvation (10:9b, 10b)
3. They misunderstand the universal scope of righteousness by faith (10:11–13)
   a. The OT proof (γάρ, 10:11, 13; cf. Isa 28:16; Joel 2:32)
   b. The theological explanation (γάρ, 10:12)
      1) Divine impartiality (10:12a)
      2) Divine generosity (10:12b)

How Righteousness by Faith Works (10:9–10)

1. Requirement: We believe that God raised Christ (10:9b)
2. Immediate Result: God bestows righteousness based on faith (10:10a)
3. Response: We confess Christ as Lord (10:9a)
4. Ultimate Result: God delivers us from final judgment (10:10b)

c. Resulting in Their Frustrating Disobedience (10:14–21)

STRUCTURE

Paul concludes his explanation of Israel's unresponsiveness with a two-part paragraph that incorporates six OT quotations in support of his argument. The first part (10:14–17) comprises a syllogism (Jewett 635) that begins with series of rhetorical questions leading to a climax (cf. 5:3–5; 8:29–30) and ends with a carefully-constructed summarizing conclusion. The second part (10:18–21) is structured around two questions (10:18, 19). The OT answers to those questions confirm that although Israel has both heard (10:18) and known about (1:19–20) the gospel, they have rejected it (10:21).

Πῶς οὖν ἐπικαλέσωνται εἰς ὃν οὐκ ἐπίστευσαν;
πῶς δὲ πιστεύσωσιν οὗ οὐκ ἤκουσαν;
πῶς δὲ ἀκούσωσιν χωρὶς κηρύσσοντος;
πῶς δὲ κηρύξωσιν ἐὰν μὴ ἀποσταλῶσιν;
    καθὼς γέγραπται,
        Ὡς ὡραῖοι οἱ πόδες τῶν εὐαγγελιζομένων [τὰ] ἀγαθά.
Ἀλλ' οὐ πάντες ὑπήκουσαν τῷ εὐαγγελίῳ.
    Ἠσαΐας γὰρ λέγει,
        Κύριε, τίς ἐπίστευσεν τῇ ἀκοῇ ἡμῶν;
ἄρα ἡ πίστις ἐξ ἀκοῆς, ἡ δὲ ἀκοὴ διὰ ῥήματος Χριστοῦ.

ἀλλὰ λέγω, μὴ οὐκ ἤκουσαν;
    μενοῦνγε·
        Εἰς πᾶσαν τὴν γῆν ἐξῆλθεν ὁ φθόγγος αὐτῶν
        καὶ εἰς τὰ πέρατα τῆς οἰκουμένης τὰ ῥήματα αὐτῶν.
ἀλλὰ λέγω, μὴ Ἰσραὴλ οὐκ ἔγνω;
    πρῶτος Μωϋσῆς λέγει,
        Ἐγὼ παραζηλώσω ὑμᾶς ἐπ' οὐκ ἔθνει,
        ἐπ' ἔθνει ἀσυνέτῳ παροργιῶ ὑμᾶς.
    Ἠσαΐας δὲ ἀποτολμᾷ καὶ λέγει,
        Εὑρέθην [ἐν] τοῖς ἐμὲ μὴ ζητοῦσιν,
        ἐμφανὴς ἐγενόμην τοῖς ἐμὲ μὴ ἐπερωτῶσιν.
    πρὸς δὲ τὸν Ἰσραὴλ λέγει,
        Ὅλην τὴν ἡμέραν ἐξεπέτασα τὰς χεῖράς μου πρὸς λαὸν ἀπειθοῦντα καὶ ἀντιλέγοντα.

VERSE 14

Πῶς οὖν ἐπικαλέσωνται εἰς ὃν οὐκ ἐπίστευσαν;

Paul transitions (οὖν) to a new stage in his argument by beginning a rhetorical climax with the link word ἐπικαλέω that occurs in verses 12–13. The interrogative particle πῶς ("how?") introduces a rhetorical question that uses the deliberative subjunctive ἐπικαλέσωνται (3 pl. aor. mid. subjunc. of ἐπικαλέω). The demonstrative τοῦτον is incorporated into the relative pronoun of the prepositional phrase εἰς ὅν (R 706); εἰς + accusative with ἐπίστευσαν (3 pl. aor. act. indic. of πιστεύω) "depicts the commitment of one's self to the person of Christ . . . something more than an intellectual acceptance of the message of the gospel or a recognition about the truth of Christ" (Harris 236; cf. Gal 2:16; Phil 1:29). Dunn notes that the aorist of πιστεύω denotes the act of commitment that expresses itself in ἐπικαλέω (620).

πῶς δὲ πιστεύσωσιν οὗ οὐκ ἤκουσαν;

The connective δέ adds a second rhetorical question that also begins with πῶς followed by the deliberative subjunctive πιστεύσωσιν (3 pl. aor. act. subjunc.); the demonstrative pronoun τούτῳ is incorporated into the genitive relative pronoun οὗ. When the genitive follows ἀκούω, it usually denotes the person who is heard rather than what is heard (BDAG 37d), and Moo suggests that Christ is heard speaking in the gospel (663 n. 12).

πῶς δὲ ἀκούσωσιν χωρὶς κηρύσσοντος;

A third rhetorical question follows the pattern of the first two with ἀκούσωσιν (3 pl. aor. act. subjunc.) as the deliberative subjunctive. Paul regularly uses χωρίς ("without/apart from") as a preposition (3:21, 28; 4:6; 7:8, 9); κηρύσσοντος (gen. sg. masc. of pres. act. ptc. of κηρύσσω) is an anarthrous substantival participle (R 1106); NIV translates "without someone preaching."

VERSE 15

πῶς δὲ κηρύξωσιν ἐὰν μὴ ἀποσταλῶσιν;

The final rhetorical question continues the pattern with κηρύξωσιν (3 pl. aor. act. subjunc. of κηρύσσω) as the deliberative subjunctive. Ἐὰν μή is idiomatic (ESV, "unless"); the subjunctive ἀποσταλῶσιν (3 pl. aor. pass. subjunc. of ἀποστέλλω) naturally follows the conditional conjunction ἐάν; the passive is a divine passive, and Jewett notes that the sender is assumed to be Christ (638; cf. 1:5). The verb ἀποστέλλω describes the act of dispatching someone for the achievement of an objective (BDAG 120d); Cranfield writes that it refers to "men who are authorized and commissioned by God" (534). The intentional repetitions of verbs (ἐπικαλέω, πιστεύω, ἀκούω, κηρύσσω) throughout the chain (*epanadiplosis*) is "decidedly rhetorical" (BDF §493.3), and the overall impact of the chain would lead the readers to conclude "Of course, it is impossible!" (Jewett 638).

καθὼς γέγραπται (See 1:17)

Ὡς ὡραῖοι οἱ πόδες τῶν εὐαγγελιζομένων [τὰ] ἀγαθά

The particle *ὡς* ("how") intensifies the adjective *ὡραῖοι* (nom. pl. masc. of *ὡραῖος, -α, -ον*), which can denote something that is either attractive or opportune (BDAG 1103c). Most EVV choose "beautiful" (e.g., NIV, NJB, ESV; cf. Schreiner 568), although Dunn (621), Jewett (640), and Moo (664) choose "timely" or "opportune" (cf. NEB, "welcome"). The reading *πόδες* is preferred because it is shorter and supported by 𝔓[46], ℵ*, A, and B. The addition of *τῶν εὐαγγελιζομένων εἰρήνην* (ℵ[2] D, 33; cf. KJV) was most likely an attempt to match the LXX of Isaiah 52:7 (Metzger 463). The substantival participle *τῶν εὐαγγελιζομένων* (gen. pl. masc. of pres. mid. ptc.) is a possessive genitive. The definite article accompanies the substantival adjective *ἀγαθά*, which is the object of the participle; Schreiner notes that the article "is probably original since its omission would harmonize the text with Isa 52:7 LXX" (576). See 1:15 for *εὐαγγελίζω* and 2:7 for *ἀγαθός*.

VERSE 16

Ἀλλ' οὐ πάντες ὑπήκουσαν τῷ εὐαγγελίῳ

The minor premise of verse 16 stands in contrast (*ἀλλ'*) to the major premise of verses 14–15 (Jewett 640). Schreiner classifies *οὐ πάντες* ("not all") as an instance of *meiosis* to indicate "the majority" (569; cf. Cranfield 536); Moo classifies it as an instance of *litotes* to indicate "only a few" (664). Dunn, however, views it simply as a contrast to *πᾶς* in verse 13 without specifying how many (622). *Ὑπήκουσαν* (3 pl aor. act. indic. of *ὑπακούω*, "obey") is a word play on *ἀκούω* in verse 13 and *ἀκοή* in this and the following verse; see 6:12 for *ὑπακούω*, which takes a dative direct object (*τῷ εὐαγγελίῳ*).

Ἠσαΐας γὰρ λέγει

The OT support (*γάρ*) for Paul's statement comes from Isaiah 53:1. See 9:15 for *λέγει* (cf. Wallace 633).

Κύριε, τίς ἐπίστευσεν τῇ ἀκοῇ ἡμῶν;

Κύριε ("Lord") is a vocative; *ἐπίστευσεν* (3 sg. aor. act. indic.) is a constative aorist; *τῇ ἀκοῇ* is a dative of direct object. *Ἀκοή, -ῆς, -ἡ* describes that which is heard (BDAG 60c; cf. Moo 665 n. 27) and is regularly translated "report" (KJV, NASB, NET) or "message" (NEB, NJB, NIV). ESV suggests "what he has heard from us," which makes the genitive of *ἡμῶν* subjective.

VERSE 17

ἄρα ἡ πίστις ἐξ ἀκοῆς

The conclusion of the syllogism provides a concise summary of verses 14–15a. Although *ἄρα* is postpositive in classical Greek (T 330), placing it first is "widespread" in the NT (Porter 206). The article accompanies the abstract noun *πίστις*; *ἐστιν* is understood; *ἐκ* + genitive denotes source; in this context *ἀκοῆς* describes the act of hearing (Dunn 623).

ἡ δὲ ἀκοὴ διὰ ῥήματος Χριστοῦ.

Δέ is connective (contra Jewett 642); the article with *ἀκοή* is anaphoric; *ἐστιν* is understood; *διά* + genitive denotes source (Jewett 642); Harris concludes that the change from *ἐκ* is a stylistic variation (113). *Ῥήματος* is definite although anarthrous and echoes verse 8; *Χριστοῦ* is an objective genitive (Schreiner 567, "the word about Christ"). The reading *ῥήματος Χριστοῦ* is more difficult, since it occurs only here in the NT, while *ῥῆμα θεοῦ* is more common (cf. Luke 3:2; John 3:34; Eph 6:17; Heb 6:5; 11:3); it also has strong manuscript support (𝔓[46], ℵ*, C, D*). Schreiner notes that the omission of any genitive (F, G) possibly reflects the same construction in 10:8 (576).

VERSE 18

ἀλλὰ λέγω, μὴ οὐκ ἤκουσαν;

Paul moves to the final stage of his argument by raising an objection of his own (*ἀλλὰ λέγω*) that might be a possible excuse for Israel (Jewett 643); compare 9:19; 10:19; 11:1, 11 for similar uses of the first person; *λέγω* is an instantaneous present. Although *μή* with a question normally expects a "no" answer (R 1175), when the verb is negated (*οὐκ ἤκουσαν*), the anticipated answer is "yes" (Dunn 623; cf. BDF §427.2; Longenecker 856). Robertson suggests "Did they all fail to hear?" (1174); Jewett writes that the audience must answer "Yes, they must have heard!" (643).

μενοῦνγε

The triple compound *μενοῦνγε* can correct or confirm. In 9:20 it corrects; here it confirms (GNB, "of course they did").

Εἰς πᾶσαν τὴν γῆν ἐξῆλθεν ὁ φθόγγος αὐτῶν

A quotation of Psalm 19:4 (LXX 18:5) provides OT support and highlights the transcendent witness of God's revelation, both general and special (Dunn 624). The prepositional phrase is moved forward for emphasis; *εἰς* + accusative denotes destination; *πᾶσαν τὴν γῆν* ("all the earth") makes explicit the universal scope of the witness. For *ἐξῆλθεν* (3 sg. aor. act. indic. of *ἐξέρχομαι*, "go out"), BDAG suggests "rang out" (348c), while NEB translates "sounded." *Φθόγγος, -ου , ὁ* describes a clear or distinct sound or voice (BDAG 1054c; cf. Dunn 624).

καὶ εἰς τὰ πέρατα τῆς οἰκουμένης τὰ ῥήματα αὐτῶν

Καί ("and") adds a second description of the extent of the witness (εἰς + acc.); πέρας, -ατος, τό denotes a set point at the farthest point of a space; τῆς οἰκουμένης (gen. sg. fem.) is a descriptive genitive; NEB translates the phrase "to the bounds of the inhabited world." Οἰκουμενή, -ης, ἡ describes the earth as an inhabited area (BDAG 699d) and is often used to describe the Roman Empire (cf. Luke 2:1; Acts 11:28; 17:6; 19:27; 24:5). Its use here is probably intended to denote a large number of people, both Jew and Gentile (Moo 667).

VERSE 19

ἀλλὰ λέγω, μὴ Ἰσραὴλ οὐκ ἔγνω;

See verse 18 for ἀλλὰ λέγω. The double negative again anticipates a "yes" answer. Although implicit throughout the paragraph, Ἰσραήλ is now explicitly mentioned as the subject of Paul's discussion (Moo 668). Οὐκ ἔγνω (3 sg. aor. act. indic. of γινώσκω) echoes οὐ κατ' ἐπίγνωσιν in 10:2 and parallels ἀγνοέω in 10:3. Cranfield captures the idea well: "They have been the recipients of God's special revelation, and yet they have been uncomprehending" (538).

πρῶτος Μωϋσῆς λέγει

Πρῶτος ("first") places Moses at the head of the line of OT witnesses (Moo 668 n. 42); see 9:15 for λέγει. Longenecker translates as "Moses is the first one who says" (857).

Ἐγὼ παραζηλώσω ὑμᾶς ἐπ' οὐκ ἔθνει

Ἐγώ is emphatic (Jewett 645) and provides subject focus (Wallace 323); παραζηλώσω (1 sg. fut. act. indic. of παραζηλόω, "make jealous") is a predictive future; Jewett suggests "provoke to zealous rage" (646). Ἐπί + dative denotes cause; οὐκ ἔθνει (NIV, "not a nation") echoes the quotation of Hosea in 9:25–26 and refers to the Gentiles (Moo 669; contra Jewett).

ἐπ' ἔθνει ἀσυνέτῳ παροργιῶ ὑμᾶς

The prepositional phrase ἐπ' ἔθνει ἀσυνέτῳ is brought forward for emphasis in a chiastic construction; see 1:21 for ἀσύνετος. Παροργιῶ (1 sg. fut. act. indic. of παροργίζω, "make angry") is a predictive future; Jewett translates "provoke to wrath" (634); Longenecker suggests "provoke to jealous anger" (858).

VERSE 20

Ἠσαΐας δὲ ἀποτολμᾷ καὶ λέγει

Isaiah is the next OT witness Paul cites (ESV, "then"); ἀποτολμᾷ (3 sg. pres. act. indic. of ἀποτολμάω, "be bold") is a verb used adverbially (R 551; cf. T 156); see 9:15 for λέγει; NIV translates "Isaiah boldly says."

Εὑρέθην [ἐν] τοῖς ἐμὲ μὴ ζητοῦσιν

Εὑρέθην (1 sg. aor. pass. indic. of εὑρίσκω, "find") is a constative aorist and a simple passive; ἐν + dative denotes agent (BDF §191.3; 220.1). The article accompanies the substantival participle ζητοῦσιν (dat. pl. masc. of pres. act. ptc. of ζητέω) and brackets the participial phrase; the present tense is progressive.

ἐμφανὴς ἐγενόμην τοῖς ἐμὲ μὴ ἐπερωτῶσιν

The adjective ἐμφανής, -ές pertains to being known (BDAG 325d); most EVV translate ἐγενόμην (1 sg. aor. mid. indic. of dep. γίνομαι, "be, become") is a constative aorist and a deponent middle (NASB, "I became manifest"). The article accompanies the substantival participle ἐπερωτῶσιν (dat. pl. masc. of pres. act. ptc. of ἐπερωτάω, "ask") and brackets the participial phrase; the present tense is progressive; the dative denotes an indirect object; GNB translates "to those who were not asking for me."

VERSE 21

πρὸς δὲ τὸν Ἰσραὴλ λέγει

What Isaiah has said about the Gentiles in 65:1 stands in contrast to (δέ) what he says concerning (πρός + acc.) Ἰσραήλ in the next verse; the article accompanies the indeclinable noun to specify the accusative case.

Ὅλην τὴν ἡμέραν ἐξεπέτασα τὰς χεῖράς μου

The accusative of ὅλην τὴν ἡμέραν (ESV, "all day long") denotes extent of time; the phrase is moved forward for emphasis; Jewett views it as a Semiticism meaning "without pause" and suggests that it points to "the extraordinary steadfastness of God's mercy" (649). Ἐξεπέτασα (1 sg. aor. act. indic. of ἐκπετάννυμι, "stretch out") is a constative aorist; "stretch out my hands" is a gesture of welcome and friendship (Cranfield 541; cf. Ps 143:6).

πρὸς λαὸν ἀπειθοῦντα καὶ ἀντιλέγοντα

Πρός + accusative is spatial ("toward"); λαόν is indefinite ("a people"). Ἀπειθοῦντα (acc. sg. masc. of pres. act. ptc. of ἀπειθέω, "disobey") and ἀντιλέγοντα (acc. sg. masc. of pres. act. ptc. of ἀντιλέγω, "oppose") are adjectival participles; both are progressive presents. Jewett suggests that ἀπειθέω carries the idea of "disobey truth," while ἀντιλέγω carries the idea of "speak against truth" (649). BDAG translates as "a disobedient and obstinate people" (cf. NASB); CSB captures the alliteration with "a disobedient and defiant people."

FOR FURTHER STUDY

See For Further Study §§ 3 ("Gospel"), 12 ("Paul's Use of the Old Testament")

HOMILETICAL SUGGESTIONS

Israel's Frustrating Disobedience (10:14–21)

1. Theological Syllogism (10:14–17)
   a. Major premise: God sends preachers with the message of salvation (10:14–15)
      1) OT Proof: Isaiah 52:7
   b. Minor premise: Not all believe the message (ἀλλ', 10:16)
      1) OT Proof: Isaiah 53:1
   c. Conclusion: Salvation comes from hearing and believing the message (ἄρα, 10:17)
2. OT Proof
   a. Israel has heard the message (10:18)
      1) OT Proof: Psalm 19:4
   b. Israel has known about the message (10:19–20)
      1) OT Proof: Deuteronomy 32:21; Isaiah 65:1
   c. Israel has rejected the message (10:21)
      1) OT Proof: Isaiah 65:2

4. God's Righteousness Is Vindicated by His Plan for Salvation History (11:1–32)

a. To Preserve a Jewish Remnant (11:1–10)

STRUCTURE

Does Israel's disobedient and defiant rejection of the gospel result in God's rejection of Israel? Paul raises that question in a two-part transitional paragraph that provides a bridge from his discussion of Israel's present (9:30–10:21) to a discussion of Israel's future (11:11–32). The first part of the paragraph (11:1–6) makes it clear that God still has a remnant within Israel; the second part (11:7–10) makes it equally clear that God has hardened the rest of Israel. Paul supports both parts of his argument with OT Scripture—first from 1 Kings 19, then from Deuteronomy 29, Isaiah 29, and Psalm 69 (LXX 68).

Λέγω οὖν, μὴ ἀπώσατο ὁ θεὸς τὸν λαὸν αὐτοῦ;
μὴ γένοιτο·
καὶ γὰρ ἐγὼ Ἰσραηλίτης εἰμί, ἐκ σπέρματος Ἀβραάμ, φυλῆς Βενιαμίν.
οὐκ ἀπώσατο ὁ θεὸς τὸν λαὸν αὐτοῦ ὃν προέγνω.
ἢ οὐκ οἴδατε ἐν Ἠλίᾳ τί λέγει ἡ γραφή,
ὡς ἐντυγχάνει τῷ θεῷ κατὰ τοῦ Ἰσραήλ;
Κύριε, τοὺς προφήτας σου ἀπέκτειναν,
τὰ θυσιαστήριά σου κατέσκαψαν,
κἀγὼ ὑπελείφθην μόνος
καὶ ζητοῦσιν τὴν ψυχήν μου.
ἀλλὰ τί λέγει αὐτῷ ὁ χρηματισμός;
Κατέλιπον ἐμαυτῷ ἑπτακισχιλίους ἄνδρας,
οἵτινες οὐκ ἔκαμψαν γόνυ τῇ Βάαλ.
οὕτως οὖν καὶ ἐν τῷ νῦν καιρῷ λεῖμμα κατ' ἐκλογὴν χάριτος γέγονεν·
εἰ δὲ χάριτι, οὐκέτι ἐξ ἔργων,
ἐπεὶ ἡ χάρις οὐκέτι γίνεται χάρις.

τί οὖν;
ὃ ἐπιζητεῖ Ἰσραήλ, τοῦτο οὐκ ἐπέτυχεν,
ἡ δὲ ἐκλογὴ ἐπέτυχεν·
οἱ δὲ λοιποὶ ἐπωρώθησαν,
καθὼς γέγραπται,
Ἔδωκεν αὐτοῖς ὁ θεὸς πνεῦμα κατανύξεως,
ὀφθαλμοὺς τοῦ μὴ βλέπειν
καὶ ὦτα τοῦ μὴ ἀκούειν,
ἕως τῆς σήμερον ἡμέρας.
καὶ Δαυὶδ λέγει,
γενηθήτω ἡ τράπεζα αὐτῶν εἰς παγίδα καὶ εἰς θήραν καὶ εἰς
σκάνδαλον καὶ εἰς ἀνταπόδομα αὐτοῖς,
σκοτισθήτωσαν οἱ ὀφθαλμοὶ αὐτῶν τοῦ μὴ βλέπειν καὶ τὸν νῶτον
αὐτῶν διὰ παντὸς σύγκαμψον.

VERSE 1

Λέγω οὖν, μὴ ἀπώσατο ὁ θεὸς τὸν λαὸν αὐτοῦ;

Paul draws an inference (οὖν) from 9:30–10:21 in the form of another rhetorical question. Λέγω is an instantaneous present (cf. 10:18, 19) that NEB and GNB translate as "ask" (cf. Jewett 653 n. 9). Μή introduces a question that expects a "no" answer (R 1175); ἀπώσατο (3 sg. aor. mid. indic. of ἀπωθέω, "reject") is an indirect middle that highlights the subject's involvement in the action (R 810); the verb occurs regularly in the OT with the sense of God rejecting his people (Dunn 634). The article with θεός is monadic; the use of λαός to describe Israel as God's people has occurred previously in 9:25 and 10:21 (cf. Dunn 634). The variant that substitutes τὴν κληρονομίαν for τὸν λαόν is supported only by 𝔓[46] and most likely represents an assimilation to the LXX of Psalm 93:14 (Moo 670 n. 1).

μὴ γένοιτο (cf. 3:4)

καὶ γὰρ ἐγὼ Ἰσραηλίτης εἰμί, ἐκ σπέρματος Ἀβραάμ, φυλῆς Βενιαμίν

As support (γάρ) for his emphatic denial, Paul points to himself: he is an Israelite, with his origin (ἐκ + gen.) in Abraham's seed and Benjamin's tribe. Καί is adjunctive (NJB, "too"); ἐγώ is emphatic (ESV, "I myself"); φυλή, -ῆς, ἡ ("tribe") denotes a subgroup of a nation characterized by a distinctive blood line (BDAG 1069a). See 9:4 for Ἰσραηλίτης and 9:7 for σπέρμα. Paul also cites his heritage in 2 Corinthians 11:22 and Philippians 3:3–6. He does so here as a specific instance of God's faithfulness to Israel in calling out a remnant for salvation (Schreiner 578; contra Cranfield 544).

VERSE 2

οὐκ ἀπώσατο ὁ θεὸς τὸν λαὸν αὐτοῦ ὃν προέγνω

Paul answers his own question by rewording it as a statement of fact, which Cranfield says makes his answer "solemn . . . explicit . . . [and] emphatic" (545). The relative pronoun ὅν (acc. sg. masc.) introduces an adjectival clause that further qualifies the description of God's people (Porter 248). See 8:29 for προέγνω (3 sg. aor. act. indic. of προγινώσκω), which highlights the ideas of God's foreknowledge and foreordination, functions as the antonym of ἀπωθέω ("rejected'), and carries the sense of "selected" (Schreiner 580).

ἢ οὐκ οἴδατε ἐν Ἠλίᾳ τί λέγει ἡ γραφή,

The disjunctive ἤ ("or") raises a point of antithesis (Jewett 655; cf. 3:29). See 6:9 for οὐκ οἴδατε, which assumes familiarity with the idea it introduces and expects a "yes" answer. Ἐν Ἠλίᾳ is local (BDF §219.1; T 261) and is best translated as "in the section about Elijah" (Moo 675; cf. 9:25). See 4:3 for τί λέγει ἡ γραφή (cf. 9:17; 10:11).

ὡς ἐντυγχάνει τῷ θεῷ κατὰ τοῦ Ἰσραήλ;

Ὡς introduces the manner ("how") of Elijah's action; ἐντυγχάνει (3 sg. pres. act. indic. of ἐντυγχάνω, "plead, appeal") describes an earnest request (BDAG 341d; cf. 8:27, 34); the present is the equivalent of a historical present (NIV, "appealed") even though it does not occur in a narrative passage. Τῷ θεῷ is a dative of destination with an intransitive verb (NIV, "to God"; cf. Wallace 147) rather than association ("with God"; contra R 529); κατά + genitive denotes opposition ("against Israel"; cf. Jewett 655); the genitive article with Ἰσραήλ (indecl.) specifies the case.

VERSE 3

Κύριε, τοὺς προφήτας σου ἀπέκτειναν, τὰ θυσιαστήριά σου κατέσκαψαν

Jewett compares Paul's wording with the LXX of 1 Kings 19:10 (655). Κύριε is a vocative of direct address (Wallace 68); "your prophets" and "your altars" are moved forward in their respective clauses for emphasis; ἀπέκτειναν (3 pl. aor. act. indic. of ἀποκτείνω, "kill") and κατέσκαψαν (3 pl. aor. act. indic. of κατασκάπτω, "destroy") are constative aorists. See 1:2 for προφήτης and 7:11 for ἀποκτείνω. Θυσιαστήριον, -ου, τό describes a structure on which sacrifices are offered (BDAG 463b); κατασκάπτω carries the idea of razing to the ground (BDAG 526d).

κἀγὼ ὑπελείφθην μόνος καὶ ζητοῦσιν τὴν ψυχήν μου

Κἀγώ is connective and emphatic ("and I"); the passive of ὑπελείφθην (1 sg. aor. pass. indic. of ὑπολείπω, "leave remaining") does not imply agency (cf. Wallace 436); the verb echoes the "remnant" idea of 9:27–29 (cf. 11:4–5). Μόνος is adjectival, modifying ἐγώ; GNB translates the clause as "I am the only one remaining." Καί is connective ("and"); ζητοῦσιν (3 pl. pres. act. indic.) is a progressive present retained from the direct discourse of 1 Kings 19. See 2:9 for ψυχή.

VERSE 4

ἀλλὰ τί λέγει αὐτῷ ὁ χρηματισμός;

God's response (1 Kgs 19:18) contrasts (ἀλλά) with Elijah's complaint. Λέγει is a perfective present (cf. 9:15); αὐτῷ is the indirect object ("to him"), referring to Elijah. Χρηματισμός, -οῦ, ὁ denotes an "authoritative divine answer" (Moo 676 n. 27) or an "oracular response" (Cranfield 546). The noun occurs in 2 Maccabees 2:4; the cognate verb occurs in Matthew 2:12, 22; Luke 2:26; Acts 10:22.

Κατέλιπον ἐμαυτῷ ἑπτακισχιλίους ἄνδρας

Κατέλιπον (1 sg. aor. act. indic. of καταλείπω, "leave behind") continues the remnant theme; Cranfield notes that the aorist denotes a divine decision (546). The reflexive pronoun ἐμαυτῷ (dat. sg. of ἐμαυτοῦ, -ῆς, "myself") substitutes for the reflexive middle (Wallace 414) and provides special emphasis (Cranfield 547). The adjective ἑπτακισχιλίους (acc. pl. masc. of ἑπτακισχίλιοι, -αι, -α, "seven thousand") modifies ἄνδρας; the number denotes completeness (Dunn 637).

οἵτινες οὐκ ἔκαμψαν γόνυ τῇ Βάαλ

The indefinite relative pronoun οἵτινες (nom. pl. masc.) is qualitative ("who indeed") and highlights what is special about the 7,000; they did not pay homage to Baal. EVV translate the aorist of ἔκαμψαν (3 pl. aor. act. indic. of κάμπτω, "bow") as a perfect (e.g., ESV, "have not bowed the knee"). The feminine of τῇ Βάαλ most likely reflects the OT practice of substituting the word "shame" to avoid the name Βάαλ; the Greek equivalent is the feminine noun αἰσχύνη (Moule 183).

VERSE 5

οὕτως οὖν καὶ ἐν τῷ νῦν καιρῷ λεῖμμα κατ' ἐκλογὴν χάριτος γέγονεν·

The tripling of οὕτως οὖν καί occurs only here in Paul (Dunn 638). The inferential οὖν ("therefore") draws a conclusion from Elijah's encounter with God; the combination οὕτως καί ("in this way also") makes it clear that Elijah's experience is a typical example of how God works (Dunn 638). See 3:26 and 8:18 for ἐν τῷ νῦν καιρῷ and 9:27 for λεῖμμα. Κατά + accusative is causal (GNB, "because of his grace"); the genitive of χάριτος is descriptive ("an election characterized by grace" cf. Moo 677 n. 35); the perfect of γέγονεν (3 sg. pf. act. indic. of dep. γίνομαι) is intensive and emphasizes the situation that is still in effect (Jewett 660).

VERSE 6

εἰ δὲ χάριτι, οὐκέτι ἐξ ἔργων

Δέ is transitional ("now"); εἰ introduces a first class condition; the contrast with ἐξ ἔργων (NIV, "by works") suggests that χάριτι is a dative of means ("by grace"; contra Moo 678 n. 37); οὐκέτι ("no longer") is logical rather than temporal (Dunn 639); ἐστίν is understood. Schreiner suggests that "election" is the implied subject (582).

ἐπεὶ ἡ χάρις οὐκέτι γίνεται χάρις

Ἐπεί ("for otherwise"; cf. T 318; BDF §456.3) supplies the reason election cannot be by works: such a situation would invalidate grace. Robertson notes that a conditional protasis is suppressed (1025); Moo suggests "for if it were otherwise . . ." (678). The article with χάρις not only marks it as the subject but also identifies it as the grace that brings about election (cf. Jewett 660); οὐκέτι is again logical (Schreiner 583); NEB translates "grace would cease to be grace" (cf. Jewett 660). The reading that concludes with χάρις alone as the predicate nominative is supported by 𝔓[46], א*, and D and is the shorter reading. There does not appear to be a reason to delete the additional words of the longer reading if it were original (Metzger 464).

VERSE 7

τί οὖν;

Schreiner notes that this rhetorical question draws a comprehensive conclusion from 9:30–11:6 (585; cf. 3:9 for τί οὖν). The three clauses that follow summarize the situations of three groups—two that have been part of the discussion so far—Israel and the elect—along with a third Paul now introduces: the rest (Moo 679).

ὃ ἐπιζητεῖ Ἰσραήλ, τοῦτο οὐκ ἐπέτυχεν

Ἰσραήλ designates the corporate entity that has pursued righteousness in the wrong way and, consequently, has not attained it (9:30–10:4). The relative pronoun ὅ incorporates a demonstrative ("that which"); ἐπιζητεῖ (3 sg. pres. act. indic. of ἐπιζητέω, "seek") describes a strong desire or serious intent (BDAG 371c). Jewett views the present tense as progressive and implies that Israel continues its pursuit (661), but Porter concludes that Paul has chosen the present tense to highlight the verb by contrasting it with the surrounding aorists (*Verbal Aspect* 197). Schreiner concludes that τοῦτο refers to righteousness by faith (585). Moule notes that the accusative of thing with ἐπέτυχεν (3 sg. aor. act. indic. of ἐπιτυγχάνω) is common in classical Greek (37); the verb describes being successful in achieving or gaining what one seeks (BDAG 385c).

ἡ δὲ ἐκλογὴ ἐπέτυχεν

In contrast (δέ) with Israel as a whole are the elect—the remnant according to the election of grace that Paul has just been discussing (11:2–6). Cranfield notes that the use of the abstract noun (ἡ ἐκλογή) places special emphasis on God's action (548). "The small group that God chose" (GNB) gained what they were seeking (ἐπέτυχεν).

οἱ δὲ λοιποὶ ἐπωρώθησαν

In further contrast (δέ) with the elect are οἱ λοιποί ("the rest"; cf. 1:13), whom God has hardened (cf. 11:25). Ἐπωρώθησαν (3 pl. aor. pass. indic. of πωρόω, "harden") is a constative aorist and a divine passive (Schreiner 587); the verb describes causing someone to have difficulty in comprehending or understanding (BDAG 900d; cf. *TDNT* 5.1024–32). Dunn provides helpful background (640) and concludes that the verb is synonymous with σκληρύνω in 9:18 (640; contra Jewett 661).

VERSE 8

καθὼς γέγραπται (see 1:17)

Ἔδωκεν αὐτοῖς ὁ θεὸς πνεῦμα κατανύξεως

Jewett analyzes the OT quotation, which combines Deuteronomy 29:4 and Isaiah 29:10 (662). The indirect object αὐτοῖς (= Israel) is brought forward for emphasis; the anarthrous noun πνεῦμα is indefinite; κατανύξεως (gen. sg. fem. of κατάνυξις, -εως, ἡ, "numbness") is an attributive genitive (Wallace 88). NJB translates as "God has infused them with a spirit of lethargy."

ὀφθαλμοὺς τοῦ μὴ βλέπειν καὶ ὦτα τοῦ μὴ ἀκούειν

Both articular infinitives are adjectival (R 1061); μή is the normal negative; the present tense is customary. NIV accurately reflects the nuance of result (BDF §400.2; T 141; Wallace 592): "Eyes so that they could not see and ears so that they could not hear."

ἕως τῆς σήμερον ἡμέρας

Ἕως + genitive is temporal ("until"); τῆς σήμερον ἡμέρας carries the idea of "this very day" (Jewett 663; cf. Matt 28:15; 2 Cor 3:14). Cranfield notes the OT use of the phrase to denote permanence, although perhaps with a limit suggested by 11:25–27 (550).

VERSE 9

καὶ Δαυὶδ λέγει

To Moses's rebuke Paul adds (καί) an extended section from one of David's impreccatory psalms (Ps 69:22–23). See 9:15 for λέγει.

Γενηθήτω ἡ τράπεζα αὐτῶν εἰς παγίδα καὶ εἰς θήραν καὶ εἰς σκάνδαλον καὶ εἰς ἀνταπόδομα αὐτοῖς

Γενηθήτω (3 sg. aor. pass. impv. of γίνομαι) is a pronouncement ("may [it] be") in imperative form (Wallace 440, 493); ἡ τράπεζα αὐτῶν ("their table") should be understood as a general reference rather than as referring to the Jewish cultic table (cf. Schreiner 588); εἰς + accusative substitutes for the predicate nominative (Wallace 47). Παγίς, -ίδος, ἡ denotes a snare; θήρα, -ας, ἡ denotes a trap; ἀνταπόδομα, -τος, τό ("recompense") describes that which is given in return for a behavior (BDAG 87b); see 9:33 for σκάνδαλον. Cranfield concludes, "The general sense is . . . no doubt a wish that even the good things which these enemies enjoy may prove to be a cause of disaster for them" (551).

VERSE 10

σκοτισθήτωσαν οἱ ὀφθαλμοὶ αὐτῶν τοῦ μὴ βλέπειν καὶ τὸν νῶτον αὐτῶν διὰ παντὸς σύγκαμψον

Σκοτισθήτωσαν (3 pl. aor. pass. impv. of σκοτίζω, "become dark") is a pronouncement in imperative form; see verse 8 for ὀφθαλμοὶ . . . τοῦ μὴ βλέπειν. Νῶτος, -ου, ὁ denotes the back from the neck to the pelvis; διὰ παντός is idiomatic for "continually" (Dunn 643; Jewett 665); σύγκαμψον (2 sg. aor. act. impv. of συγκάμπτω, "bend") is a third pronouncement. Suggestions on this latter pronouncement include being burdened by the law, being oppressed by grief or fear, groping on the ground because of blindness (Cranfield 552), but Schreiner concludes that the imagery should not be pressed (589 n. 9).

FOR FURTHER STUDY

59. Remnant (11:5)

Clements, R. E. "'A Remnant Chosen by Grace' (Romans 11:5)." Pages 106–21 in *Pauline Studies: Essays Presented to Professor F. F. Bruce on His Seventieth Birthday*. Edited by D. A. Hagner and M. J. Harris. Grand Rapids: Eerdmans, 1980.

Donaldson, T. L. "Jewish Christianity, Israel's Stumbling and the Sonderweg Reading of Paul." *JSNT* 29 (2006): 27–54.

Gadenz, P. T. "'The Lord Will Accomplish His Word': Paul's Argumentation and Use of Scripture in Romans 9:24–29." *Letter & Spirit* 2 (2006): 141–58.

Guenther, W. and H. Krienke. *NIDNTT* 3.247–54.

Heil, J. P. "From Remnant to Seed of Hope for Israel: Romans 9:27–29." *CBQ* 64 (2002): 703–20.

Herntrich, V. and G. Schrenk. *TDNT* 4.194–214

Litwak, K. "One or Two Views of Judaism: Paul in Acts 28 and Romans 11 on Jewish Unbelief." *TynBul* 57 (2006): 229–49.

Martens, E. A. *EDBT* 669–71.

Sibley, J. R. "Christianity Vis-à-Vis Judaism." *SwJT* 44 (2002): 24–43.

Sneen, D. "The Root, the Remnant, and the Branches." *Word & World* 6 (1986): 398–409.

Tanner, J. P. "The New Covenant and Paul's Quotations from Hosea in Romans 9:25–26." *BSac* 162 (2005): 95–110.

Watts, J. W. "The Remnant Theme: A Survey of New Testament Research, 1921–1987." *Perspectives in Religious Studies* 15 (1988): 109–29.

HOMILETICAL SUGGESTIONS

Rejected, Selected, or Hardened? (11:1–10)

1. God has not rejected Israel (11:1)
    a. Proof: Paul's experience (1:1b)
        1) Israelite
        2) Abraham's seed
        3) Benjamin's tribe
2. God has preserved a remnant (11:2–6)
    a. Proof: Elijah's experience (11:2–4)
        1) 1 Kings 19:10
        2) 1 Kings 19:18
    b. Contemporary application (11:5–6)
3. God has hardened the rest (11:7–10)
    a. Proof: Moses's and David's rebukes (11:8–10)
        1) Deuteronomy 29:4
        2) Psalm 69:22–23

b. To Bring Salvation to the Gentiles (11:11–24)

STRUCTURE

If Paul's (primarily Gentile) audience is to grasp God's plan to restore Israel, they must first understand that Israel's hardening results in salvation coming to the Gentiles (11:11–15), is not a reason for them to boast (11:16–21), and can be reversed (11:22–24). An opening rhetorical question and an emphatic response establish Paul's thesis for the paragraph (11:11). A carefully framed section explains how Paul uses Gentile responsiveness to the gospel to provoke Israel to a similar response (11:12–15). An extended olive tree metaphor reminds the Gentiles that they must maintain a proper perspective on God's kindness to them (11:16–21). The paragraph closes with an elegant summary of God's kindness and severity in his dealings with both Jews and Gentiles (11:22–24).

Λέγω οὖν, μὴ ἔπταισαν ἵνα πέσωσιν;
μὴ γένοιτο·
ἀλλὰ τῷ αὐτῶν παραπτώματι ἡ σωτηρία τοῖς ἔθνεσιν εἰς τὸ παραζηλῶσαι αὐτούς.

εἰ δὲ τὸ παράπτωμα αὐτῶν πλοῦτος κόσμου καὶ τὸ ἥττημα αὐτῶν πλοῦτος ἐθνῶν,
πόσῳ μᾶλλον τὸ πλήρωμα αὐτῶν.
Ὑμῖν δὲ λέγω τοῖς ἔθνεσιν·
ἐφ' ὅσον μὲν οὖν εἰμι ἐγὼ ἐθνῶν ἀπόστολος,
τὴν διακονίαν μου δοξάζω,
εἴ πως παραζηλώσω μου τὴν σάρκα καὶ σώσω τινὰς ἐξ αὐτῶν.
εἰ γὰρ ἡ ἀποβολὴ αὐτῶν καταλλαγὴ κόσμου,
τίς ἡ πρόσλημψις εἰ μὴ ζωὴ ἐκ νεκρῶν;

εἰ δὲ ἡ ἀπαρχὴ ἁγία, καὶ τὸ φύραμα·
καὶ εἰ ἡ ῥίζα ἁγία, καὶ οἱ κλάδοι.
Εἰ δέ τινες τῶν κλάδων ἐξεκλάσθησαν,
σὺ δὲ ἀγριέλαιος ὢν ἐνεκεντρίσθης ἐν αὐτοῖς
καὶ συγκοινωνὸς τῆς ῥίζης τῆς πιότητος τῆς ἐλαίας ἐγένου,
μὴ κατακαυχῶ τῶν κλάδων·
εἰ δὲ κατακαυχᾶσαι οὐ σὺ τὴν ῥίζαν βαστάζεις ἀλλ' ἡ ῥίζα σέ.

ἐρεῖς οὖν, Ἐξεκλάσθησαν κλάδοι ἵνα ἐγὼ ἐγκεντρισθῶ.
καλῶς· τῇ ἀπιστίᾳ ἐξεκλάσθησαν, σὺ δὲ τῇ πίστει ἕστηκας.
μὴ ὑψηλὰ φρόνει ἀλλὰ φοβοῦ·
εἰ γὰρ ὁ θεὸς τῶν κατὰ φύσιν κλάδων οὐκ ἐφείσατο, [μή πως] οὐδὲ σοῦ φείσεται.
ἴδε οὖν χρηστότητα καὶ ἀποτομίαν θεοῦ·
A ἐπὶ μὲν τοὺς πεσόντας ἀποτομία,
B ἐπὶ δὲ σὲ χρηστότης θεοῦ,
B ἐὰν ἐπιμένῃς τῇ χρηστότητι, ἐπεὶ καὶ σὺ ἐκκοπήσῃ.
A κἀκεῖνοι δέ, ἐὰν μὴ ἐπιμένωσιν τῇ ἀπιστίᾳ, ἐγκεντρισθήσονται·
δυνατὸς γάρ ἐστιν ὁ θεὸς πάλιν ἐγκεντρίσαι αὐτούς.

B εἰ γὰρ <u>σὺ</u> ἐκ τῆς κατὰ φύσιν ἐξεκόπης ἀγριελαίου καὶ παρὰ φύσιν ἐνεκεντρίσθης εἰς καλλιέλαιον,
A πόσῳ μᾶλλον <u>οὗτοι</u> οἱ κατὰ φύσιν ἐγκεντρισθήσονται τῇ ἰδίᾳ ἐλαίᾳ.

VERSE 11

λέγω οὖν, μὴ ἔπταισαν ἵνα πέσωσιν;

The next question Paul raises is whether Israel's hardening (11:7–10) means they have no hope. See 11:1 for λέγω οὖν; μή anticipates a negative answer; the subject of the question is οἱ λοιποί in verse 7 (Cranfield 554); ἵνα πέσωσιν (3 pl. aor. act. subjunc. of πίπτω) may be understood either as purpose (ESV; cf. Porter 236) or result (NIV; cf. R 998).* Although προσκόπτω is the more common word for "stumble" (cf. 9:32; 14:21), πταίω is probably chosen as word play with πίπτω (Jewett 672), which describes a fall that leads to irreversible ruin (Cranfield 555; cf. 11:22; 14:4; 1 Cor. 10:12). The idea of stumbling echoes 9:32–33.

μὴ γένοιτο· (See 3:4)

ἀλλὰ τῷ αὐτῶν παραπτώματι ἡ σωτηρία τοῖς ἔθνεσιν

On the contrary (ἀλλά), Israel's trespass is the cause of the Gentiles' salvation. Τῷ παραπτώματι is a dative of cause (Moo 687 n. 19); the article with σωτηρία is anaphoric, referring back to 10:1, 10 (Jewett 674); τοῖς ἔθνεσιν is the indirect object; Moo notes that most commentators supply a verb like γέγονεν (687 n. 21). See 5:15–21 for παράπτωμα, which denotes a serious lapse that can be overcome (Jewett 673); σωτηρία again denotes eschatological deliverance.

εἰς τὸ παραζηλῶσαι αὐτούς

Further, the divine purpose (εἰς τό + infin.) behind salvation coming to the Gentiles is to provoke the Jews to jealousy. See 10:19 for παραζηλῶσαι (aor. act. inf.); αὐτούς is the object of the infinitive.

VERSE 12

εἰ δὲ τὸ παράπτωμα αὐτῶν πλοῦτος κόσμου

Paul transitions (δέ) from his thesis in verse 11 to what Jewett describes as "an eloquent oral ellipse" in verse 12 with the verbs understood, parallelism in the first two lines, and the parechesis of παράπτωμα . . . ἥττημα . . . πλήρωμα (675). Εἰ introduces the first in a string of conditional clauses that unify the logic of Paul's argument (11:14, 15, 16, 17). The anarthrous noun πλοῦτος (cf. 2:4) is qualitative; the genitive of κόσμου is objective (NJB, "great gain to the world"). See the preceding verse for παράπτωμα. Jewett notes that "riches" can describe both material (2 Cor 8:2) or spiritual (Col 1:27) wealth and prosperity (676); its use here anticipates Paul's hymn of praise in 11:33–36.

καὶ τὸ ἥττημα αὐτῶν πλοῦτος ἐθνῶν

Paul adds (*καί*) a second protasis in synonymous parallelism to the first. EVV translate *ἥττημα, -τος, τό* variously as "diminishing" (KJV), "falling off" (NEB), "poverty" (GNB), "loss" (NJB), and "defeat" (NET), but the parallelism with *παράπτωμα* suggests "failure" (NASB, ESV). See the preceding line for *πλοῦτος*; Turner notes that *ἐθνῶν* is especially likely to be anarthrous (181); the genitive is again objective.

πόσῳ μᾶλλον τὸ πλήρωμα αὐτῶν

Πόσῳ μᾶλλον ("how much more") is qualitative (Porter 138) and a variation on *πολλῷ μᾶλλον* (cf. 5:9, 11, 15, 17). Cranfield provides four interpretations for *πλήρωμα, -τος, τό* and decides for "full and completed number" (558; cf. Moo 690 n. 35; Schreiner 598). Cranfield also raises the question of the antecedent for the three uses of *αὐτῶν*. He argues for the hardened majority (i.e., *οἱ λοιποί* in 11:7c), while most commentators appear to assume the corporate entity of Israel (i.e., *Ἰσραήλ* in 11:7a). In light of 11:25 (*τὸ πλήρωμα τῶν ἐθνῶν*), the full number of elect Israelites (i.e., *ἡ ἐκλογή* in 11:7b) seems likely in this line.

VERSE 13

Ὑμῖν δὲ λέγω τοῖς ἔθνεσιν

Verses 13–14 form a parenthesis in which Paul specifically addresses Gentile believers (*ὑμῖν . . . τοῖς ἔθνεσιν*), a practice he resumes in 11:17–24. The indirect object *ὑμῖν* is brought forward for emphasis (Dunn 655); *δέ* is slightly adversative (NASB; cf. Cranfield 558); *λέγω* is an instantaneous present; *τοῖς ἔθνεσιν* stands in apposition to *ὑμῖν*.

ἐφ' ὅσον μὲν οὖν εἰμι ἐγὼ ἐθνῶν ἀπόστολος, τὴν διακονίαν μου δοξάζω

Ἐφ' ὅσον is better understood as degree ("to the degree that"; cf. Matt. 25:40, 45) than as time ("as long as"; cf. Rom. 7:1). Since there is no subsequent *δέ*, it is best to take *μέν οὖν* together as a summarizing transition ("indeed then"; cf. Longenecker 887); *εἰμι ἐγώ* is emphatic (Jewett 678); *ἐθνῶν* is attributive even though it precedes the noun it modifies (BDF §474.4); *ἀπόστολος* is indefinite (RSV, "an apostle"). *Διακονία, -ας, ἡ* ("service") describes a role that functions in the interest of a larger public (BDAG 230b); see 15:15–21 for Paul's description of his apostolic service. See 1:21 for *δοξάζω*; here it suggests the concrete act of wholehearted and unreserved commitment (Dunn 656; cf. Cranfield 560); the present tense is customary.

VERSE 14

εἴ πως παραζηλώσω μου τὴν σάρκα καὶ σώσω τινὰς ἐξ αὐτῶν

Πως (GNB,"perhaps") introduces a sense of "hesitant expectation" into the first class condition (εἴ + fut. indic.; Wallace 707). See 10:19 and 11:11 for παραζηλώσω (1 sg. fut. act. indic. of παραζηλόω); μου τὴν σάρκα ("my flesh") is equivalent to τῶν συγγενῶν μου κατὰ σάρκα in 9:3; Cranfield suggests "convert" for σώσω (1 sg. fut. act. indic. of σῴζω); ἐξ αὐτῶν is partitive (ESV, "some of them").

VERSE 15

εἰ γὰρ ἡ ἀποβολὴ αὐτῶν καταλλαγὴ κόσμου

Paul's explanation (γάρ) of his ministry returns to the elliptical construction of verse 12. Ἀποβολή, -ῆς, ἡ describes a temporary casting away (Cranfield 562; cf. Acts 27:22); αὐτῶν is an objective genitive (GNB, "for when they were rejected"). See 5:10–11 for καταλλαγή; κόσμου is an objective genitive (cf. 11:12).

τίς ἡ πρόσλημψις εἰ μὴ ζωὴ ἐκ νεκρῶν;

Paul frames the protasis as a rhetorical question. Πρόσλημψις, -εως, ἡ describes the acceptance into a relationship (BDAG 883c); εἰ μή is idiomatic for "except"; ζωή is qualitative; ἐκ + genitive denotes origin; νεκρῶν is definite. "Life from the dead" is best understood as the final resurrection (Cranfield 563; Dunn 658; contra Schreiner 599).

VERSE 16

εἰ δὲ ἡ ἀπαρχὴ ἁγία, καὶ τὸ φύραμα

Paul continues his elliptical style (R 1023) to create a "proverb-like statement" (Cranfield 563) that serves as a transition (δέ) to the extended olive tree metaphor that follows in verses 17–24. Εἰ introduces a first class condition, καί is adjunctive ("also") and summarizes the protasis (R 1181). See 8:23 for ἀπαρχή ("firstfruits"); 1:2 for ἅγιος, -α, - ον, and 9:21 for φύραμα ("lump"). Jewett provides OT background on the Jewish practice of firstfruits (681–82; cf. Num 15:17–21).

καὶ εἰ ἡ ῥίζα ἁγία, καὶ οἱ κλάδοι

Paul adds (καί) a second conditional statement, with ῥίζα ("root") parallel to ἀπαρχή and κλάδοι ("branches") parallel to φύραμα. Schreiner summarizes four interpretations of Paul's imagery and concludes that ἀπαρχή and ῥίζα both refer to the Jewish patriarchs, while φύραμα and κλάδοι both refer to Israel as a whole (600–601; contra Cranfield 564, who views ἀπαρχή as Jewish Christians). Paul's point is clear enough: God's promises to the patriarchs mean that Israel is still set apart in his sight. The lessons to be drawn from that fact follow in verses 17–24, where Robertson writes that "Paul is very earnest" (482).

VERSE 17

Εἰ δέ τινες τῶν κλάδων ἐξεκλάσθησαν

Εἰ δέ ("now if") continues the logical progress of Paul's argument by introducing an extended metaphor (contra Jewett, who considers it an allegory, 668–69) that uses the second person singular (σύ) to enhance the liveliness and directness of his appeal (Cranfield 566). The compound protasis of the first extended sentence includes the three lines of verse 17, with the apodosis in the first line of verse 18. Τινες τῶν κλάδων ("some of the branches") makes it clear that Paul is talking about part of Israel (partitive gen.); ἐξεκλάσθησαν (3 pl. aor. pass. indic. of ἐκκλάω, "break off") is a divine passive highlighting God's role in the action (Dunn 660). Longenecker has a concise analysis of Paul's imagery in 11:17–24 (892–94).

σὺ δὲ ἀγριέλαιος ὢν ἐνεκεντρίσθης ἐν αὐτοῖς

The second person pronoun σύ ("you," i.e., a Gentile Christian in a representative sense; R 678; cf. 11:13) adds subject emphasis (Porter 297) and stands in contrast (δέ) to "the branches" (i.e., Israel). NIV and ESV understand ὤν (nom. sg. masc. of pres. act. ptc. of εἰμί) as an adverbial participle of concession ("although you are"), while NASB, NKJV, and NET understand it as adjectival ("[you] who are"); the difference is not significant. Ἀγριέλαιος ("wild olive") describes "a small, scraggly bush that produces nothing useful" (Jewett 684); ἐνεκεντρίσθης (2 sg. aor. indic. of εγκεντρίζω, "graft") is another divine pass. (Dunn 661); ἐν αὐτοῖς is local; Dunn suggests "among [the remaining] branches" (661).

καὶ συγκοινωνὸς τῆς ῥίζης τῆς πιότητος τῆς ἐλαίας ἐγένου

A second (καί) aspect of God's work on behalf of the Gentiles is that they have become (ἐγένου, 2 sg. aor. mid. indic. of dep. γίνομαι) participants (συγκοινωνός) in the blessings that accrue to God's people (cf. Schreiner 605, who argues that the olive tree is best understood as God's people, composed of both Jews and Gentiles). The concatenation of genitives, τῆς ῥίζης τῆς πιότητος τῆς ἐλαίας (literally, "the root of the richness of the olive tree"), is complicated by a textual variant. The reading in UBS[5] (א*, B) is the more difficult and best explains the others, which appear to be attempts to clarify the awkward combination (Schreiner 609). Τῆς ῥίζης is an objective genitive, denoting the thing shared (Cranfield 567); τῆς πιότητος (gen. sg. fem. of πιότης, -ητος, ἡ, "richness") is a genitive of product; τῆς ἐλαίας (gen. sg. fem. of ἐλαία, -ας, ἡ, "olive tree") is a genitive of source (Moo 702 n. 28). The resulting translation is "the root that produces the richness that comes from the olive tree." Dunn notes that the olive tree was noted for its richness (661; cf. Judg 9:9).

VERSE 18

μὴ κατακαυχῶ τῶν κλάδων

The apodosis of Paul's extended sentence is a prohibition (μή + impv.). Κατακαυχῶ (2 sg. pres. mid. impv. of dep. κατακαυχάομαι, "boast against") is a customary present and a deponent middle; Dunn writes that the verb denotes an element of competitive superiority expressed in boasting (661); Moo writes that it combines the ideas of sinful pride and arrogant superiority (703). The genitive of τῶν κλάδων is required by the nuance of opposition ("against") resulting from the κατά- prefix.

εἰ δὲ κατακαυχᾶσαι οὐ σὺ τὴν ῥίζαν βαστάζεις ἀλλ' ἡ ῥίζα σέ

Δέ is adversative ("but"); εἰ introduces another first class condition; κατακαυχᾶσαι (2 sg. pres. mid. indic. of dep. κατακαυχάομαι) is a deponent middle. Blass proposes a brachyology: "But you should know that if you boast . . ." (483). The apodosis is constructed to be memorable: οὐ . . . ἀλλά establishes a strong contrast; σύ is emphatic (Dunn 662); τὴν ῥίζαν . . . ἡ ῥίζα σέ is chiastic. Βαστάζεις (2 sg. pres. act. indic. of βαστάζω, "bear, carry") is a gnomic present; Dunn suggests that the verb denotes both sustaining a burden and bearing fruit (662).

VERSE 19

ἐρεῖς οὖν, Ἐξεκλάσθησαν κλάδοι ἵνα ἐγὼ ἐγκεντρισθῶ

Ἐρεῖς οὖν ("Therefore you will say") begins a new sub-section of the paragraph (11:19–21) as Paul continues his diatribe style. See 9:19, where a similar construction introduces a question; here it draws a logical inference from what precedes (Jewett 687); see verse 17 for ἐξεκλάσθησαν κλάδοι. Ἵνα + subjunctive denotes purpose; ἐγώ is emphatic (Moo 705 n. 42) and "highlights a note of presumption" (Dunn 663); ἐγκεντρισθῶ (1 sg. aor. pass. subjunc. of ἐγκεντρίζω) is a divine passive (Cranfield 568).

VERSE 20

καλῶς· τῇ ἀπιστίᾳ ἐξεκλάσθησαν, σὺ δὲ τῇ πίστει ἕστηκας

Jewett suggests four possible ways of understanding Paul's one-word answer (καλῶς): a flat rejection ("No, thank you!"), an ironic concession ("Well, well!"; cf. R 1199), a qualified acceptance ("Alright, but!"), or an acceptance of the point ("Well said!"). He decides on the fourth (687), which seems to be the best choice. Τῇ ἀπιστίᾳ is a dative of cause (BDF §196; R 532; T 242); see 11:17 for ἐξεκλάσθησαν. Σύ is again emphatic; δέ is adversative; τῇ πίστει is also a dative of cause (Cranfield 569). Ἕστηκας (2 sg. pf. act. indic. of ἵστημι, "stand") is an intensive perfect that emphasizes the continuing state resulting from a past action (cf. Dunn 663); Moo notes that Paul uses the word elsewhere to describe a person's spiritual state (705 n. 46), which aligns well with his emphasis on the role of faith (cf. Rom 5:2; 2 Cor 1:24).

μὴ ὑψηλὰ φρόνει ἀλλὰ φοβοῦ

Although they currently stand by faith, Gentile Christians must guard their attitude. Μὴ ὑψηλὰ φρόνει (2 sg. pres. act. impv. of φρονέω) is a second prohibition parallel to μὴ κατακαυχῶ in verse 18; ὑψηλός, -ή, όν denotes an attitude of arrogance, haughtiness, or pride (BDAG 1044d; cf. 12:16; 1 Tim 6:17). In contrast (ἀλλά) to being proud, they should adopt an attitude of profound respect for God and his working (cf. Cranfield 569 n. 4); φοβοῦ (2 sg. pres. mid. impv. of dep. φοβέομαι) is an imperative of command and a deponent middle.

VERSE 21

εἰ γὰρ ὁ θεὸς τῶν κατὰ φύσιν κλάδων οὐκ ἐφείσατο

The reason (γάρ) to fear God is that he is "the ultimate source of status assignment" (Jewett 688): what he did to the Jews, he can also do to the Gentiles. Εἰ introduces yet another first class condition (R 1012); the article with θεός is monadic; the genitive direct object τῶν κλάδων is brought forward for emphasis. The prepositional phrase κατὰ φύσιν functions as an attributive modifier (T 221) best translated here as "natural" (e.g., NIV); see 1:26 for this phrase and its opposite, παρὰ φύσιν (cf. also 11:24). Robertson writes that the negative οὐκ is "very emphatic" (1012); ἐφείσατο (3 sg. aor. mid. indic. of dep. φείδομαι, "spare"; cf. 8:32) is a constative aorist and a deponent middle.

[μή πως] οὐδὲ σοῦ φείσεται

Although the reading that inserts μή πως before οὐδέ reflects typical Pauline phraseology and has solid Western manuscript support (𝔓[46], D, 33), commentators view it as secondary (e.g., Cranfield 569 n. 4; Schreiner 610). The shorter reading has strong Alexandrian manuscript support (א, A, B) and is more likely original (Moo 697 n. 2). Σοῦ ("you") is a genitive of direct object and is moved forward for emphasis; φείσεται (3 sg. fut. mid. indic.) is a gnomic future (Jewett 689).

VERSE 22

ἴδε οὖν χρηστότητα καὶ ἀποτομίαν θεοῦ

Paul draws his argument to a conclusion (οὖν) with a statement of God's kindness and severity in dealing with both the Jews ("those who fall") and the Gentiles ("you"). Ἴδε ("Pay attention!" Jewett 689) calls Paul's audience to consider carefully the implications of what he has just written. See 2:4 for χρηστότης. Dunn notes that the etymology of ἀποτομία relates to the idea of "cutting off," continues the imagery Paul has been using, and is best understood as "judicial strictness" (664; cf. the cognate adverb in 2 Cor 10:13; Titus 1:13). Θεοῦ is a genitive of source.

ἐπὶ μὲν τοὺς πεσόντας ἀποτομία

The correlative μέν ("on the one hand") begins an elegant ABBABA sequence that extends through verse 24. "Severity" (ἀποτομία) has come upon (ἐπί + acc.) unbelieving Jews (τοὺς πεσόντας; cf. 11:11). Demonstrative pronouns replace the substantival participle (acc. pl. masc. of aor. act. ptc. of πίπτω) in verse 23 (κἀκεῖνοι) and verse 24 (οὗτοι).

ἐπὶ δὲ σὲ χρηστότης θεοῦ

"On the other hand" (δέ) God's kindness (χρηστότης θεοῦ) has come upon (ἐπί + acc.) believing Gentiles (σέ).

ἐὰν ἐπιμένῃς τῇ χρηστότητι, ἐπεὶ καὶ σὺ ἐκκοπήσῃ

The Gentiles, though, should not presume on God's kindness. What is expected under normal circumstances (ἐάν + subjunc.) is that they will continue (2 sg. pres. act. subjunc. of ἐπιμένω) in that kindness (local dat.). If they do not, they also will be cut off. See 11:6 for ἐπεί; καί is adjunctive ("also"); σύ is emphatic; ἐκκοπήσῃ (2 sg. fut. pass. indic. of ἐκκόπτω) is a divine passive. A similar conditional statement occurs in Colossians 1:23 (εἴ γε ἐπιμενετε τῇ πίστει), and Cranfield suggests that the use here of τῇ χρηστότητι "brings out the true nature of faith as living from God's kindness" (570).

VERSE 23

κἀκεῖνοι δέ, ἐὰν μὴ ἐπιμένωσιν τῇ ἀπιστίᾳ, ἐγκεντρισθήσονται

With κἀκεῖνοι δέ ("but those also") Paul makes an emphatic subject change to the unbelieving Jews (Moo 707 n. 58). Ἐάν introduces a parallel third class condition; μή is normal with the subjunctive; ἐπιμένωσιν (3 pl. pres. act. subjunc. of ἐπιμένω) balances verse 22; τῇ ἀπιστίᾳ ("in unbelief") is a local dative (R 524); ἐγκεντρισθήσονται (3 pl. fut. pass. indic. of ἐγκεντρίζω) is a divine passive (cf. 11:17; Dunn notes that in this verse as well as in the preceding verse "it is not a once-for-all refusal of belief (or act of faith) which is decisive for condemnation (or salvation) but the persistence in that attitude" (665).

δυνατὸς γάρ ἐστιν ὁ θεὸς πάλιν ἐγκεντρίσαι αὐτούς

The reason (γάρ) it is possible for Israel to be grafted in is that God is able to do it. See 4:21 for δυνατός, which is brought forward for emphasis; the article with θεός is monadic; see 8:15 for πάλιν ("again"). Ἐγκεντρίσαι (aor. act. inf. of ἐγκεντρίζω) is an epexegetic infinitive that explains δυνατός; αὐτούς is the object of the infinitive. Jewett notes the connection to God's power in 1:16–17 as well as the similar connection between God's grace and his power in 2 Corinthians 9:8 (692).

VERSE 24

εἰ γὰρ σὺ ἐκ τῆς κατὰ φύσιν ἐξεκόπης ἀγριελαίου

As a further explanation (γάρ) Paul offers a concluding "from lesser to greater" argument (εἰ . . . πόσῳ μᾶλλον; cf. 11:12) that appeals to God's work on behalf of the Gentiles (σύ). The word order of ἐκ τῆς κατὰ φύσιν ἐξεκόπης ἀγριελαίου is awkward. Ἐξεκόπης (2 sg. aor. pass. indic. of ἐκκόπτω) is a divine passive; ἐκ τῆς . . . ἀγριελαίου denotes the wild olive tree from which the Gentiles have been cut (Moo 708 n. 63). Κατὰ φύσιν ("according to nature") can be understood as describing the wild olive tree (e.g., NIV, "a tree that is wild by nature") or the relation of the branch to the tree (e.g., CSB, "your native wild olive tree"). The latter is to be preferred (cf. Cranfield 571; Jewett 692).

καὶ παρὰ φύσιν ἐνεκεντρίσθης εἰς καλλιέλαιον

Similarly, παρὰ φύσιν ("contrary to nature," Harris 172) does not describe the process of engrafting as unnatural but, rather, the fact that the branches do not naturally belong to the cultivated olive tree. Ἐνεκεντρίσθης (2 sg. aor. pass. indic. of ἐγκεντρίζω) is a divine passive; εἰς + accusative is a substitute for a simple dative (Harris 33); καλλιέλαιος, -ου, ἡ ("cultivated olive tree") implies the superiority of Jewish spiritual heritage (Dunn 661) and so undermines any Gentile sense of pride (cf. 20).

πόσῳ μᾶλλον οὗτοι οἱ κατὰ φύσιν ἐγκεντρισθήσονται τῇ ἰδίᾳ ἐλαίᾳ.

See 11:12 for πόσῳ μᾶλλον. Οὗτοι (ESV, "these") is emphatic and refers to the Jews; οἱ κατὰ φύσιν ("the natural [branches]") is substantival and stands in apposition to the demonstrative pronoun; ἐγκεντρισθήσονται (3 pl. fut. pass. indic. of ἐγκεντρίζω) is a predictive future and a divine passive; τῇ ἰδίᾳ ἐλαίᾳ is a local dative (R 524); ἴδιος, -α, ον highlights the special relation of the branches to the tree ("their very own olive tree"). Just as God has grafted the Gentiles into the olive tree of God's people, so he will be able to do the same for the Jews if he so chooses.

FOR FURTHER STUDY

60. Fullness (11:12, 25)

Bruce, F. F. *EDT* 432.
Delling, G. *TDNT* 6.283–311.
Ernst, J. *Pleroma und Pleroma Christi*. Geschichte und Deutung eines Begriffs der paulinischen Antilegomena. Regensburg: Pustet, 1970.
Farrell, H. K. *EDBT* 278–79.
Lim, D. S. *DPL* 319–20.
Moule, C. F. D. "'Fulness' and 'Fill' in the New Testament." *SJT* 4 (1951): 79–86.
Overfield, P. D. "*Pleroma*: A Study in Content and Context." *NTS* 25 (1979): 384–96.
Schippers, R. *NIDNTT* 1.733–41.
Yates, R. "A Re-Examination of Ephesians 1:23." *ExpTim* 83 (1972): 146–51.

61. Ministry, Minister (11:13)

Beyer, H. W. *TDNT* 2.81–93.
Brown, C. "Ministry in the New Testament." Pages 10–22 in *Ministry in the Seventies*. Edited by J. C. Porthouse. London: Falcon, 1970.
Giles, K. *Patterns of Ministry among the First Christians*. Melbourne: Collins Dove, 1989.
Hess, K. *NIDNTT* 3.544–49.
Kruse, C. G. *DPL* 602–08.
________. *New Testament Models for Ministry: Jesus and Paul*. Nashville: Nelson, 1985.
Perkins, P. *Ministering in the Pauline Churches*. New York: Paulist, 1982.
Toon, P. *EDBT* 530–31.

62. Olive Tree Metaphor (11:17–24)

Baxter, A. G. and J. A. Ziesler. "Paul and Arboriculture: Romans 11.17–24." *JSNT* 24 (1985): 25–32.
Bourke, M. M. *A Study of the Metaphor of the Olive Tree in Romans 11*. Washington, DC: Catholic University of America, 1947.
Campbell, W. S. *DPL* 642–44.
Davies, W. D. "Paul and the Gentiles: A Suggestion Concerning Romans 11:13–24." Pages 153–63, 356–60 in *Pauline and Jewish Studies*. Philadelphia: Fortress, 1984.
Esler, P. F. "Ancient Oleiculture and Ethnic Differentiation: The Meaning of the Olive-Tree Image in Romans 11." *JSNT* 26 (2003): 103–24.
Havemann, J. C. T. "Cultivated Olive—Wild Olive: The Olive Tree Metaphor in Romans 11:16–24." *Neot* 31 (1997): 87–106.
Maartens, P. J. "Inference and Relevance in Paul's Allegory of the Wild Olive Tree." *TS* 53 (1997): 1000–29.
Nanos, M. D. "Romans 11 and Christian-Jewish Relations: Exegetical Options for Revisiting the Translation and Interpretation of This Central Text." *CTR* 9 (2012): 3–21.
Papworth, C. "Paul, the Olive Tree, and the Wild Olive Branch." *Center for Hermeneutical Studies Protocol* 60 (1990): 54–59.
Rengstorf, K. H. "Das Ölbaum-Gleichnis in Röm 11:16ff." Pages 127–64 in *Donum Gentilicum: New Testament Studies in Honor of David Daube*. Edited by E. Bammel, C. K. Barrett, and W. D. Davies. Oxford: Clarendon, 1978.
Zeigan, H. "Die Wurzel des Ölbaums (Röm 11,18): Ein alternative Perspektive." *Protokolle zur Bibel* 15 (2006): 119–32.

HOMILETICAL SUGGESTIONS

Lessons from Israel's Hardening (11:11–24)

1. It has universal impact (11:11–15)
    a. It brings salvation to the Gentiles (11:11–12)
    b. It provokes the Jews to jealousy and salvation (11:13–14)
    c. It promises global reconciliation and life (11:15)
2. It is not a reason for Gentile arrogance (11:16–21)
    a. Prohibition against boasting (11:16–18)
        1) Because they are dependent on the root (11:18b)
    b. Prohibition against pride (11:19–21)

        2) Because they are not immune from being cut off (11:21)
3. It demonstrates God's kindness (11:22–24)
    a. He currently exercises kindness to persevering Gentiles (11:22)
    b. He is able to exercise kindness to repenting Jews (11:23–24)
        1) On the model of his kindness to the Gentiles (11:24a)

c. To Restore Israel (11:25–32)

STRUCTURE

Paul concludes his discussion of Israel's future by disclosing a mystery that makes clear God has not yet finished with Israel. The paragraph consists of two parts. The first part summarizes God's plan to restore Israel and provides OT proof of that plan (11:25–27). The second part provides a theological explanation of that plan and includes a carefully constructed statement of the interaction between human unbelief and divine mercy (11:28–32).

Οὐ γὰρ θέλω ὑμᾶς ἀγνοεῖν, ἀδελφοί, τὸ μυστήριον τοῦτο,
    ἵνα μὴ ἦτε [παρ'] ἑαυτοῖς φρόνιμοι,
ὅτι πώρωσις ἀπὸ μέρους τῷ Ἰσραὴλ γέγονεν
    ἄχρι οὗ τὸ πλήρωμα τῶν ἐθνῶν εἰσέλθῃ
καὶ οὕτως πᾶς Ἰσραὴλ σωθήσεται,
    καθὼς γέγραπται,
        Ἥξει ἐκ Σιὼν ὁ ῥυόμενος,
            ἀποστρέψει ἀσεβείας ἀπὸ Ἰακώβ.
        καὶ αὕτη αὐτοῖς ἡ παρ' ἐμοῦ διαθήκη,
            ὅταν ἀφέλωμαι τὰς ἁμαρτίας αὐτῶν.

κατὰ μὲν τὸ εὐαγγέλιον ἐχθροὶ δι' ὑμᾶς,
κατὰ δὲ τὴν ἐκλογὴν ἀγαπητοὶ διὰ τοὺς πατέρας·
    ἀμεταμέλητα γὰρ τὰ χαρίσματα καὶ ἡ κλῆσις τοῦ θεοῦ.

A   ὥσπερ γὰρ ὑμεῖς ποτε ἠπειθήσατε τῷ θεῷ,
B   νῦν δὲ ἠλεήθητε τῇ τούτων ἀπειθείᾳ,
A   οὕτως καὶ οὗτοι νῦν ἠπείθησαν τῷ ὑμετέρῳ ἐλέει,
B   ἵνα καὶ αὐτοὶ [νῦν] ἐλεηθῶσιν·
A   συνέκλεισεν γὰρ ὁ θεὸς τοὺς πάντας εἰς ἀπείθειαν,
B   ἵνα τοὺς πάντας ἐλεήσῃ.

VERSE 25

οὐ γὰρ θέλω ὑμᾶς ἀγνοεῖν, ἀδελφοί, τὸ μυστήριον τοῦτο

The disclosure formula raises an emphasis of special importance (cf, 1:13). Τὸ μυστήριον τοῦτο ("this mystery") points forward to the subsequent ὅτι clause (Cranfield 574). Μυστήριον, -ου, τό denotes a secret too profound for human ingenuity (BDAG 662b). Paul uses it elsewhere to describe the bodily change at the resurrection (1 Cor 15:51), the principle of lawlessness embodied in the anti-Christ (2 Thess 2:7), the basic tenets of the Christian faith (1 Tim 3:9, 16), unspecified divine secrets (1 Cor 4:1; 13:2; 14:2), and the eternal council of God eschatologically fulfilled in Christ (1 Cor

2:1; Eph 1:9; 3:3–4, 9; 6:19; Col 1:26–27; 2:2; 4:3). Here, it describes God's three-step plan for the restoration of Israel.

ἵνα μὴ ἦτε [παρ'] ἑαυτοῖς φρόνιμοι

Paul's purpose (ἵνα + subjunc.) in disclosing the mystery repeats his prohibition in 11:20b: the Gentiles must not be "wise in [their] own conceits" (ESV). Μή is the expected negative with ἦτε (2 pl. pres. act. subjunc. of εἰμί). Although the inclusion of παρ' before ἑαυτοῖς is supported by א, C, D, 33 and the inclusion of ἐν is supported by A, B, the reading that omits a preposition (𝔓[46]) best explains the others (Jewett 694 n. a; Moo 711 n. 1; Schreiner 623). The reflexive pronoun ἑαυτοῖς (dat. of advantage; cf. T 238) in combination with φρόνιμοι ("prudent/wise," BDAG 1066c) "implies . . . an unacceptable measure of arrogance" (Jewett 699).

ὅτι πώρωσις ἀπὸ μέρους τῷ Ἰσραὴλ γέγονεν

The first step in God's plan is the present hardening of Israel. Ὅτι ("that") introduces the content of the mystery (Moo 715); see 11:7 for πώρωσις ("hardening"); τῷ Ἰσραήλ is a dative of disadvantage; γέγονεν (3 sg. pf. act. indic. of dep. γίνομαι) is an intensive perfect that highlights the result of an action continuing into the present. EVV take ἀπὸ μέρους (BDAG 633d, "in part") either with πώρωσις (e.g., NASB, NIV, ESV, NET, "a partial hardening") or with τῷ Ἰσραήλ (e.g., NJB, CEV, NLT, "part of Israel"). Elsewhere in Paul, though, the phrase is adverbial (cf. Rom 15:15, 24; 2 Cor 1:14; 2:5; cf. R 550), which suggests that it should be taken with γέγονεν ("has partially come"; cf. Moo 717 n. 25).

ἄχρι οὗ τὸ πλήρωμα τῶν ἐθνῶν εἰσέλθῃ

The second step is the bringing in of the Gentiles. Ἄχρι οὗ is adverbial of time ("until"; cf. Dunn 680) and is short for ἄχρι τοῦ χρόνου οὗ; Moo concludes that the phrase denotes "a period of time that will come to an end and be followed by a change of circumstances" (717 n. 30). The basic meaning of πλήρωμα, -τος, τό is "full number" (BDAG 829d); τῶν ἐθνῶν is a partitive genitive. Εἰσέλθῃ (3 sg. aor. act. subjunc. of dep. εἰσέρχομαι, "come in") denotes "a punctiliarly conceived future event preceded in time by the action of the main verb" (T 111); Jewett notes that the verb is a technical term for "entering the kingdom"and has an eschatological sense (701). The phrase "fullness of the Gentiles" is best understood as "the full number of the elect from among the Gentiles" (Cranfield 575; cf. Jewett 700; Moo 719); Dunn's suggestion (680) that Paul "intended to indicate that the incoming of the Gentiles would be [numerically] equivalent to that of Israel" seems unlikely.

VERSE 26

καὶ οὕτως πᾶς Ἰσραὴλ σωθήσεται

The third step is the salvation of all Israel. Καὶ οὕτως ("and so") denotes the next natural event in the sequence (Cranfield 574–75); πᾶς Ἰσραήλ ("all Israel") specifies the class as a whole (Wallace 253); σωθήσεται (3 sg. fut. pass. indic. of σῴζω) is a divine passive and refers to an eschatological event (Cranfield 575). There are at least six different understandings of "all Israel"—(1) all Jews throughout history, including those who have been hardened (S-H 335; cf. Jewett 702); (2) the nation of Israel as a whole, but not necessarily including every individual member (Cranfield 577); (3) the corporate entity of the nation of Israel as it exists at a particular point in time (Moo 723); (4) "spiritual Israel," consisting of all elect Jews and Gentiles throughout time (e.g., Calvin; cf. Schreiner 614 n. 7); (5) all elect Jews throughout all time (Ridderbos, *Paul: An Outline of His Theology* 358–59); and (6) a large number of elect ethnic Jews near the end of history (Longenecker 897; Schreiner 619). The last understanding is the most likely (1) because Paul has used "Israel" to refer to ethnic Israel throughout chapters 9–11; (2) because Paul has emphasized God's gracious election throughout chapters 9–11; and (3) because the sequence of events Paul has outlined in 11:25–26 specifies an eschatological timeframe for Israel's salvation. Further, the entire context of Romans 9–11 presupposes that this future salvation will come through faith in Christ rather than through some sort of "special way"unique to Israel. See Moo (725–62) and Schreiner (616) for refutations of that suggestion, including the significance of the quotation from Isa 50:20 that follows.

καθὼς γέγραπται *(see 1:17)*

Ἥξει ἐκ Σιὼν ὁ ῥυόμενος

Jewett analyzes the OT quotation, which combines Isaiah 50:20–21 with Isaiah 27:9 (702–04). Ἥξει (3 sg. fut. act. indic. of ἥκω, "come") is a predictive future; ἐκ Σιών denotes origin; the substantival participle ὁ ῥυόμενος (nom. sg. masc. of pres. mid. ptc. of dep. ῥύομαι, "rescue") is a deponent middle. The rescuer who comes is Christ (cf. 7:24; 1 Thess 1:10); "out of Zion" may indicate that Christ originates from the Jewish people (cf. 9:5) or that he comes from the heavenly Zion (cf. Heb 12:22). If the latter, Moo views it as an indication that the salvation of "all Israel" will come at Christ's parousia (728; cf. Jewett 704).

ἀποστρέψει ἀσεβείας ἀπὸ Ἰακώβ

Paul omits the καί from the LXX original to improve the parallelism (Jewett 704); ἀποστρέψει (3 sg. fut. act. indic. of ἀποστρέψω, "turn away") is a predictive future; see 1:18 for ἀσεβείας ("ungodliness"), which is qualitative; ἀπό + genitive denotes separation ("from Jacob"). Dunn suggests that ἀποστρέψω carries the sense of "remove" (683); Jewett points to 1 Thessalonians 2:15–16 as a partial list of the Jews' ungodly acts (704).

VERSE 27

καὶ αὕτη αὐτοῖς ἡ παρ' ἐμοῦ διαθήκη

Καί is connective ("and"); the demonstrative pronoun αὕτη ("this") agrees with the predicate nominative (διαθήκη) and is prospective; αὐτοῖς is an associative dative ("with them"); ἐστίν is understood. The article with διαθήκη allows the prepositional phrase to function as an attributive adjective (R 782). Robertson categorizes παρ' ἐμοῦ as ablative with the sense "from the side of" (R 615); Jewett suggests "my very own covenant" (705).

ὅταν ἀφέλωμαι τὰς ἁμαρτίας αὐτῶν

The final line of the quotation comes from Isaiah 27:9 (cf. Jer 31:34c) and interprets the covenant as forgiveness of sins. Ὅταν + subjunctive is temporal ("whenever"); Jewett (706) concludes that the aorist of ἀφέλωμαι (1 sg. aor. mid. subjunc. of ἀφαιρέω, "take away") is best translated as a future ("when I shall take away their sins"; cf. NLT); see 3:9 for ἁμαρτία.

VERSE 28

κατὰ μὲν τὸ εὐαγγέλιον ἐχθροὶ δι' ὑμᾶς

The correlative pronouns μέν . . . δέ establish an antithetic parallelism (Moule 195) that forms "a deliberate and strong rhetorical structure" (Dunn 684). Κατά + accusative denotes respect ("with respect to"; cf. Dunn 684); the definite article is anaphoric (cf. 10:16). See 1:1 for εὐαγγέλιον; in this context the focus is on the activity of preaching the gospel rather than on the message itself (Jewett 707; cf. Cranfield 579). See 5:10 for ἐχθρός; in this context, the idea is passive with the sense of "under God's wrath" (Schreiner 625; contra Jewett 707). Διά + accusative denotes advantage ("for the sake of"; cf. Moo 731); the antecedent of ὑμᾶς is the Gentiles.

κατὰ δὲ τὴν ἐκλογὴν ἀγαπητοὶ διὰ τοὺς πατέρας

Κατά + accusative denotes respect ("with respect to"; cf. Dunn 684); the definite article is anaphoric (cf. 11:5, 7). See 8:33 for the cognate adjective for ἐκλεκτός; the parallelism with εὐαγγέλιον suggests that the noun describes God's electing work (Schreiner 625). See 1:7 for ἀγαπητός; the idea is passive with the sense of "objects of God's love." Διά + accusative denotes cause ("because of"; Moo 731); see 9:5 for τοὺς πατέρας.

VERSE 29

ἀμεταμέλητα γὰρ τὰ χαρίσματα καὶ ἡ κλῆσις τοῦ θεοῦ.

The reason (γάρ) Israel is beloved resides in "the unbreakable nature of God's gifts and calling" (Schreiner 626). Ἀμεταμέλητα (nom. pl. neut. of ἀμεταμέλητος, -ον, "irrevocable") is moved forward to give it "the greatest possible emphasis" (Cranfield 582); it describes something that one does not take back (Dunn 686). The definite article accompanies the abstract χαρίσματα (nom. pl. neut. of χάρισμα, -τος, τό, "gift"); see 1:11 for the noun; καί is connective ("and"). The combination of the definite article with κλῆσις plus the adjunct τοῦ θεοῦ makes the noun phrase monadic. See 1:1 for the cognate adjective κλητός; the noun describes an invitation to experience a special privilege and responsibility (BDAG 549a); θεοῦ is a subjective genitive (NLT, "God's gifts and his call").

VERSE 30

ὥσπερ γὰρ ὑμεῖς ποτε ἠπειθήσατε τῷ θεῷ

As a concluding explanation (γάρ), Paul pens "the most carefully constructed formulation [he] ever produced" (Cranfield 687). The chiasm of ἠλεήθητε . . . ἀπειθείᾳ . . . ἠπείθησαν . . . ἐλέει is artistically woven into the alternating ABABAB pattern of the verbs ἀπειθέω and ἐλεέω. The adverb ὥσπερ ("just as") is balanced by οὕτως καί ("so also") in the next verse (cf. 5:19, 21; 6:4). Ὑμεῖς (i.e., the Gentiles) is emphatic and provides subject focus; the adverb ποτε ("formerly") is balanced by νῦν ("now") in the next clause. Ἠπειθήσατε (2 pl. aor. act. indic.) is a constative aorist; see 2:8 for ἀπειθέω; τῷ θεῷ is a dative of direct object (CSB, "disobeyed God").

νῦν δὲ ἠλεήθητε τῇ τούτων ἀπειθείᾳ

Δέ is adversative; νῦν highlights the present era of salvation history; see 3:21; 6:22; 7:6; 17 for the combination "but now." Ἠλεήθητε (2 pl. aor. pass. indic. of ἐλεέω) is a constative aorist and a divine passive; see 9:15 for ἐλεέω; τῇ τούτων ἀπειθείᾳ is a dative of cause (R 532; BDF §196; cf. ESV). Ἀπείθεια, -ας, ἡ describes disobedience with a connotation of disbelief (BDAG 99c); the Jews are the antecedent of the demonstrative pronoun τούτων.

VERSE 31

οὕτως καὶ οὗτοι νῦν ἠπείθησαν τῷ ὑμετέρῳ ἐλέει

The demonstrative pronoun οὗτοι again refers to the Jews and provides subject focus; see verse 30 for νῦν. Ἠπείθησαν (3 pl. aor. act. indic. of ἀπειθέω) is a constative aorist; τῷ ὑμετέρῳ ἐλέει is a dative of cause (Wallace 168) and is best understood as modifying the preceding verb (Dunn 688; Moo 734; Schreiner 628; contra Cranfield 585). See 9:23 for ἔλεος; the possessive pronoun ὑμετέρῳ (2 sg. dat. of ὑμέτερος, -α, ου, "your") is emphatic (BDF §284.2) and objective (ESV, "the mercy shown to you"; cf. R 685).

ἵνα καὶ αὐτοὶ [νῦν] ἐλεηθῶσιν

The divine purpose (ἵνα + subjunc.) of the Jews' disobedience is that God may also extend his mercy to them. Καί is adjunctive ("also"); αὐτοί ("they") is emphatic; see verse 30 for νῦν ("now"); ἐλεηθῶσιν (3 pl. aor. pass. subjunc. of ἐλεέω) is a divine passive. Moo concludes that arguments in favor of including νῦν "slightly outweigh those for omitting it" and notes three: it has early attestation (א, B, D*), it fits the balanced structure of the sentence, and it is the more difficult reading (711 n. 2; cf. Jewett 694 n. f).

VERSE 32

συνέκλεισεν γὰρ ὁ θεὸς τοὺς πάντας εἰς ἀπείθειαν

Paul's explanation (γάρ) of verses 30–31 summarizes both chapter 11 and chapters 9–11 as a whole (Schreiner 629). Συνέκλεισεν (3 sg. aor. act. indic. of συγκλείω, "make a prisoner"; cf. Cranfield 586 n. 7) is a consummative aorist (NASB, "has shut up"). The article with θεός is monadic; including θεός at this point makes God's role explicit. Τοὺς πάντας (GNB, "all people"; i.e., both Jews and Gentiles) is a substantival use of the adjective; the reading has strong manuscript support (א, A, B, D^2, 33), while the alternate reading (τὰ πάντα) most likely reflects an assimilation to Galatians 3:22 (Metzger 465). Εἰς ἀπείθειαν ("in disobedience") denotes the state in which all human beings are imprisoned (cf. Jewett 711).

ἵνα τοὺς πάντας ἐλεήσῃ

God's purpose (ἵνα + subjunc.) in shutting up all in sin is to extend his mercy to all. See the preceding line for τοὺς πάντας; ἐλεήσῃ (3 sg. aor. act. subjunc. of ἐλεέω) concludes the discussion with a final emphasis on God's sovereign mercy (cf. 9:14–18).

FOR FURTHER STUDY

63. Mystery (11:25)

Bockmuehl, M. N. *Revelation and Mystery in Ancient Judaism and Pauline Christianity.* Tübingen: Mohr Siebeck, 1990.

Bornkamm, G. *TDNT* 4.819–28.

Brown, R. E. *The Semitic Background of the Term "Mystery" in the New Testament.* Philadelphia: Fortress, 1968.

Cohen, J. "The Mystery of Israel's Salvation: Romans 11:25–26 in Patristic and Medieval Exegesis." *HTR* 98 (2005): 247–81.

Coppens, J. "'Mystery' in the Theology of St. Paul and Its Parallels at Qumran." Pages 132–58 in *Paul and Qumran.* Edited by J. Murphy-O'Connor. London: Chapman, 1968.

Creaney, M. "A Mystery Thriller: Paul's Use of the Term 'Mystery' in the New Testament." *ExpTim* 114 (2003): 296–99.
Finkenrath, G. *NIDNTT* 3.501–506.
Harrington, D. J. *Paul on the Mystery of Israel.* Collegeville, MN: Liturgical Press, 1992.
Harvey, A. E. "The Use of Mystery Language in the Bible." *JTS* 81 (1980): 320–36.
Kim, S. "The 'Mystery' of Rom 11.25–26 Once More." *NTS* 43 (1997): 412–29.
Malpan, V. "'Mystery' in Saint Paul." *Hekima Review* 39 (2008): 8–19.
O'Brien, P. T. *DPL* 621–23.
Spencer, F. S. "Metaphor, Mystery and the Salvation of Israel in Romans 9–11: Paul's Appeal to Humility and Doxology." *RevExp* 103 (2006): 113–38.
Thielman, F. *EDBT* 546–47.

64. "All Israel Will be Saved" (11:26)

Bloesch, D. G. "'All Israel Will Be Saved': Supersessionism and the Biblical Witness." *Int* 43 (1989): 130–42.
Cohen, J. "The Mystery of Israel's Salvation: Romans 11:25–26 in Patristic and Medieval Exegesis." *HTR* 98 (2005): 247–81.
Glancy, J. "Israel vs. Israel in Romans 11:25–32." *USQR* 45 (1991): 191–203.
Hahn, F. "Um Verständnis von Römer 11:26a '. . . und so wird ganz Israel gerettet werden.'" Pages 221–36 in *Paul and Paulinism: Essays in Honor of C. K. Barrett.* Edited by M. D. Hooker and S. G. Wilson. London: SPCK 1982.
Harrington, D. J. "Israel's Salvation according to Paul." *Bible Today* 26 (1988): 304–08.
Hofius, O. "'All Israel Will be Saved': Divine Salvation and Israel's Deliverance in Romans 9–11." *Princeton Seminary Bulletin Supplement* 1 (1990):19–39.
House, H. W. "The Future of National Israel." *BSac* 166 (2009): 463–81.
Ito, A. "'All Israel Will Be Saved!'" *Exegetica* 13 (2002): 55–72.
Keller, W. *Gottes Treue—Israels Heil. Röm 11,25–27: Die These vom 'Sonderweg' in der Diskussion.* Stuttgart: Katholisches Bibelwerk, 1998.
Kim, D. "Reading Paul's *kai outos pas Israel sothesetai* (Rom. 11:26a) in the Context of Romans." *CTJ* 45 (2010): 317–34.
Kim, S. "The 'Mystery' of Rom 11.25–26 Once More." *NTS* 43 (1997): 412–29.
Longenecker, B. W. "Different Answers to Different Issues: Israel, the Gentiles and Salvation History in Romans 9–11." *JSNT* 36 (1989): 95–123.
Merkle, B. L. "Romans 11 and the Future of Ethnic Israel." *JETS* 43 (2000): 709–21.
Räisänen, H. "Paul, God and Israel: Romans 9–11 in Recent Research." Pages 178–206 in *The Social World of Formative Christianity and Judaism: Essays in Tribute to Howard Clark Kee.* Edited by J. Neusner. Philadelphia: Fortress, 1988.
Stuhlmacher, P. "Zur Interpretation von Röm 11:25–32." Pages 555–70 in *Probleme biblisher Theologie: Gerhard von Rad zum 70. Geburtstag.* Edited by H. W. Wolfe. Munich: Kaiser, 1971.
van der Horst, P. W. "'Only Then Will All Israel Be Saved': A Short Note on the Meaning of *kai outos* in Romans 11:26." *JBL* 119 (2000): 521–25.
van Houwelingen, P. H. R. "The Redemptive-Historical Dynamics of the Salvation of 'All Israel' (Rom. 11:26a)." *CTJ* 46 (2011): 301–14.
Vanlaningham, M. G. "Romans 11:25–27 and the Future of Israel in Paul's Thought." *Master's Seminary Journal* 3 (1992): 141–74.
Vasholz, R. "The Character of Israel's Future in Light of the Abrahamic and Mosaic Covenants." *TJ* 25 (2004): 39–59.

Voorwinde, S. "Rethinking Israel: An Exposition of Romans 11:25–27." *Vox Reformata* 68 (2003): 4–48.

Zoccali, C. "'And So All Israel Will Be Saved': Competing Interpretations of Romans 11.26 in Pauline Scholarship." *JSNT* 30 (2008): 289–318.

65. Call, Calling (11:29)

Bieder, W. *Die Berufung im Neuen Testament.* Zürich: Zwingli, 1961.

Coenen, L. *NIDNTT* 1.271–76.

Condon, K. "*Klesis*—Call and Calling." *IBS* 6 (1984): 71–84.

Dietzelbinger, C. *Der Berufung des Paulus als Ursprung seiner Theology.* Neukirchen-Vluyn: Neukirchener, 1985.

Kruse, C. G. *DPL* 84–85.

Moyter, S. *EDBT* 80–81.

Packer, J. I. *EDT* 184.

Schmidt, K. L. *TDNT* 3.487–536.

Sievers, J. "How Irrevocable? Interpreting Romans 11:29 from the Church Fathers to the Second Vatican Council." *Gregorianum* 87 (2006): 748–61.

HOMILETICAL SUGGESTIONS

The Mystery of Salvation History (11:25–32)

1. The mystery disclosed (11:25–26a)
   a. Israel partially hardened (11:25c)
   b. Full number of Gentiles brought in (11:25d)
   c. All Israel saved (11:26a)
2. The mystery supported (11:26b–27)
   a. Isaiah 59:20–21
   b. Isaiah 27:9
3. The mystery explained (11:28–32)
   a. The Jews' status (11:28–29)
   b. Human disobedience and divine mercy (11:30–32)

5. Paul's Praise to God (11:33–36)

STRUCTURE

A three-part "exuberant rhapsody" of praise (Harris 73) closes chapters 9–11. Jewett notes the points of correspondence with 9:1–5 and explores possible layers of redaction in the passage (713–15). The progression of thought moves from an exclamation of amazement at God's riches, wisdom, and knowledge (11:33) to human inability to comprehend his ways (11:34–35; cf. Isa 40:13; Job 41:11) to doxological praise of his absolute sovereignty (11:36).

Ὦ βάθος πλούτου καὶ σοφίας καὶ γνώσεως θεοῦ·
ὡς ἀνεξεραύνητα τὰ κρίματα αὐτοῦ
καὶ ἀνεξιχνίαστοι αἱ ὁδοὶ αὐτοῦ.

Τίς γὰρ ἔγνω νοῦν κυρίου;
ἢ τίς σύμβουλος αὐτοῦ ἐγένετο;
ἢ τίς προέδωκεν αὐτῷ, καὶ ἀνταποδοθήσεται αὐτῷ;

ὅτι ἐξ αὐτοῦ καὶ δι' αὐτοῦ καὶ εἰς αὐτὸν τὰ πάντα·
αὐτῷ ἡ δόξα εἰς τοὺς αἰῶνας, ἀμήν.

VERSE 33

Ὦ βάθος πλούτου καὶ σοφίας καὶ γνώσεως θεοῦ

The interjection ὦ ("O!") suggests strong emotion (BDF §146.2; cf. Longenecker 908); the anarthrous nouns that follow are abstract, qualitative, and definite. Βάθος (nom. sg. neut., "depth") is a nominative absolute (Porter 85); Cranfield suggests that the noun denotes "profundity and immensity" (589). See 11:12 for πλοῦτος; σοφία, -ας, ἡ denotes the transcendent wisdom of God (BDAG 935a); see 2:20 for γνῶσις. The genitives of the three abstract nouns describe content and carry more weight than the nominative βάθος on which they depend (Wallace 92–94); Θεοῦ is a subjective genitive (Schreiner 633); Robertson notes that θεοῦ is anarthrous because it denotes one who is "without comparison" (795).

ὡς ἀνεξεραύνητα τὰ κρίματα αὐτοῦ

The exclamatory use of ὡς intensifies the adjectives that follow (R 1032; cf. 10:15). Ἀνεξεραύνητος, -ον ("unsearchable") is extremely rare, and Moo suggests that it might be a Hellenistic variation of the classical word that means "not to be searched out" (742 n. 14). Τὰ κρίματα ("judgments") describes God's execution of his judgment (Cranfield 590; cf. 2:2); αὐτοῦ is a subjective genitive.

καὶ ἀνεξιχνίαστοι αἱ ὁδοὶ αὐτοῦ

Ἀνεξιχνίαστος, -ον ("untraceable") describes something that cannot be tracked out (BDAG 77c; cf. Eph. 3:8) and describes God's greatness in Job (5:9; 9:10; 34:24). Αἱ ὁδοί ("ways") describes the ways God takes in accomplishing his purposes (Cranfield 590); αὐτοῦ is a possessive genitive. Together, the synonymous parallelism "points to the truth that God's judgments and ways 'cannot be judged from a higher vantage point, but are to be discerned as right only in subjection to them as the affairs and ways of God'" (Cranfield 590, quoting Barth).

VERSES 34–35

Τίς γὰρ ἔγνω νοῦν κυρίου;

Jewett analyzes the quotations of Isaiah 40:13 (718) and Job 41:3 (719). The reason (γάρ) God's work in the world is unsearchable and untraceable is that no one can know his mind, give him advice, or cause him to be in their debt. The three questions are "obviously rhetorical, expecting the answer 'no one'" (Moo 743). The use of the disjunctive ἤ ("or") to separate the questions intensifies the impossibility of anyone meeting the conditions described (cf. Jewett 718). The verbs are gnomic (cf. GNB). See 1:28 for νοῦς; κυρίου is a possessive genitive. The verb ἔγνω (3 sg. aor. act. indic. of γινώσκω) raises the possibility that the first question relates to "knowledge" (γνῶσις) in verse 33a.

ἢ τίς σύμβουλος αὐτοῦ ἐγένετο;

Σύμβουλος, -ου, ὁ describes an advisor or counselor (BDAG 957c); αὐτοῦ is an objective genitive (GNB, "Who is able to give him advice?"). It is possible to see the second question relating to "wisdom" (σοφία) in verse 33a.

ἢ τίς προέδωκεν αὐτῷ, καὶ ἀνταποδοθήσεται αὐτῷ;

Προέδωκεν (3 sg. aor. act. indic. of προδίδωμι) describes the act of paying in advance (Dunn 701; cf. BDAG 867c); αὐτῷ is a dative of advantage in both clauses; the passive of ἀνταποδοθήσεται (3 sg. fut. pass. indic. of ἀνταποδίδωμι, "repay") maintains a focus on the subject; the verb describes the act of paying back an obligation (BDAG 87b). The idea that it is impossible to repay God suggests a relationship to "riches" (πλοῦτος) in verse 33a (cf. Harvey 135 on the inverted structure)

VERSE 36

ὅτι ἐξ αὐτοῦ καὶ δι' αὐτοῦ καὶ εἰς αὐτὸν τὰ πάντα

Ὅτι is causal ("because"); ἐξ αὐτοῦ denotes source ("from him"); δι' αὐτοῦ denotes agency ("through him"); εἰς αὐτὸν denotes goal ("to him"); τὰ πάντα describes "the sum of all things" (R 773; cf. BDF §275.7, "the universe"). See Harris for details on the prepositional phrases (73); the use of καί το join the three phrases serves to set off each one as distinct. NEB translates as "Source, Guide, and Goal of all that is!"

αὐτῷ ἡ δόξα εἰς τοὺς αἰῶνας, ἀμήν.

Αὐτῷ ("to him") is the indirect object; the verb εἴη ("may [it] be") is understood; ἡ δόξα is the glory due solely to God (R 759); εἰς τοὺς αἰῶνας is idiomatic for "to all eternity," "eternally," or "forever" (Harris 95; cf, 9:5); see 1:25 and 9:5 for ἀμήν. For similar doxologies, see Romans 16:27; Galatians 1:5; Ephesians 3:21; Philippians 4:20; 1 Timothy 1:17; 2 Timothy 4:18.

FOR FURTHER STUDY

66. Benedictions and Doxologies (11:36)

Bailey, J. L., and L. D. Vander Broek. *Literary Forms in the New Testament: A Handbook.* Louisville, KY: Westminster/John Knox, 1992.

Barth, M. "Theologie—ein Gebet (Röm 11,33–36)." *TZ* 41 (1985): 330–48.

Champion, L. G. *Benedictions and Doxologies in the Epistles of Paul.* Oxford: Kemp Hall, 1934.

Cummings, G. J. "Service-Endings in the Epistles." *NTS* 22 (1975–76): 110–13.

Dugmore, C. W. "Jewish and Christian Benedictions." Pages 145–52 in *Mélanges offerts à Marcel Simon.* Paris: de Boccard, 1978.

Hoeck, A. "2 Cor 3:17a Unlocks Paul's Dyadic Doxologies." *Estudios Bíblicos* 69 (2011): 217–28.

Jewett, R. "The Form and Function of the Homiletic Benediction." *AThR* 51 (1969): 18–34.

Mullins, T. Y. "Benediction as a NT Form." *AUSS* 15 (1977): 59–64.

O'Brien, P. *DPL* 68–71.

Westermann, C. *Blessing in the Bible and the Life of the Church.* Philadelphia: Fortress, 1978.

HOMILETICAL SUGGESTIONS

Paul's Praise to God (11:33–36)

1. Praise of God's plan (11:33)
   a. Its depth (11:33a)
   b. Its unsearchability (11:33b)
   c. Its untraceability (11:33c)
2. OT support (11:34–35)
   a. Isaiah 40:13
   b. Job 41:11
3. Confession and doxology (11:36)

In Praise of God's Riches, Wisdom, and Knowledge (11:33–36)

1. They are beyond measure (11:33a)
2. They are beyond understanding (11:33b–c)
3. They are beyond knowing (11:34)
4. They are beyond anticipating (11:35)

D. THE PRACTICE OF GOD'S RIGHTEOUSNESS (12:1–15:13)

1. God's Righteousness Is Practiced in Christian Living (12:1–13:14)

a. By Giving Ourselves Wholly to God (12:1–2)

STRUCTURE

This paragraph forms the introduction to the next section of the letter (12:1–15:13) and provides the thesis for that section. It consists of two sentences. The first (12:1) uses a request formula to lend earnestness to Paul's exhortation. The second (12:2) uses a strong contrast to reinforce the means by which his readers should carry out his exhortation.

Παρακαλῶ οὖν ὑμᾶς, ἀδελφοί, διὰ τῶν οἰκτιρμῶν τοῦ θεοῦ
παραστῆσαι τὰ σώματα ὑμῶν
θυσίαν ζῶσαν ἁγίαν εὐάρεστον τῷ θεῷ,
τὴν λογικὴν λατρείαν ὑμῶν·
καὶ μὴ συσχηματίζεσθε τῷ αἰῶνι τούτῳ,
ἀλλὰ μεταμορφοῦσθε τῇ ἀνακαινώσει τοῦ νοὸς
εἰς τὸ δοκιμάζειν ὑμᾶς τί τὸ θέλημα τοῦ θεοῦ,
τὸ ἀγαθὸν καὶ εὐάρεστον καὶ τέλειον.

VERSE 1

Παρακαλῶ οὖν ὑμᾶς, ἀδελφοί, διὰ τῶν οἰκτιρμῶν τοῦ θεοῦ

The inferential conjunction οὖν introduces the implications of what precedes (Porter 305). Most commentators see the connection to all of chapters 1–11 (e.g., Moo 748; contra Dunn 708). Paul uses παρακαλῶ formulas elsewhere both to introduce major sections of letters (1 Cor 1:10; 2 Cor 10:1; Eph 4:1; 1 Thess 4:1) and to address discrete topics (Rom 15:30; 16:17; 1 Cor 4:16; 16:15; Phlm 10; 1 Tim 2:1); see C. J. Bjerkelund, *Parakalo: Form, Funktion und Sinn der parakalo-Satze in der paulinischen Briefen*. Oslo: Universitetsforlaget, 1967.

Παρακαλῶ (1 sg. pres. act. indic.) is an instantaneous present; the verb carries the sense of earnestness, urgency, and authority (Cranfield 697; cf. Moo 748) and is best translated "exhort" (NET). Ὑμᾶς and ἀδελφοί highlight the family ethos of Paul's appeal (Jewett 727); see 1:13 for the latter. The basis (διά + gen.; cf. Schreiner 643) for Paul's exhortation is God's compassion; οἰκτιρμός, -οῦ, ὁ denotes a display of concern over another's misfortune (BDAG 700c); the plural of οἰκτιρμῶν reflects the classical use for a class of an abstract concept; Longenecker concludes that the phrase refers to a number of deeds of divine mercy (920); the article with θεοῦ is monadic.

παραστῆσαι τὰ σώματα ὑμῶν θυσίαν ζῶσαν ἁγίαν εὐάρεστον τῷ θεῷ

The infinitive *παραστῆσαι* (aor. act. inf. of *παρίστημι*, "present") introduces indirect discourse (Wallace 604); the aorist is constative; the infinitive has an imperatival sense. The verb carries the sense of "to offer, place at the disposal of" (Cranfield 598 n. 1; cf. *TDNT* 5.771–98); see also 6:13, 16, 19. *Τὰ σώματα ὑμῶν* ("your bodies") is a synecdoche for the whole person (Schreiner 644) and is the object in an object-complement structure; Longenecker translates as "yourselves" (920). The anarthrous noun *θυσίαν* ("sacrifice") is qualitative and the complement in the object-complement structure. The three modifiers are best understood as parallel and define the character of the sacrifice. *Ζῶσαν* (acc. sg. fem. of pres. act. ptc. of *ζάω*, "living") highlights both the continuing efficacy of the sacrifice (Moo 751) and its implications for daily living (Dunn 710). *Ἁγίαν* ("holy") highlights both the fact that the sacrifice belongs to God (Cranfield 599) and that it involves ethical content (601). *Εὐάρεστον* ("pleasing, acceptable") specifies the sacrifice as one that is "true and proper . . . which is desired by God and which he will accept" (Cranfield 601; cf. Phil 4:18); the adjective is regularly followed by the dative (*τῷ θεῷ*).

τὴν λογικὴν λατρείαν ὑμῶν

The noun phrase stands in apposition to the entire preceding infinitival clause (R 1205; BDF §480.6; Moule 601). See 9:4 for *λατρεία*. The article regularly occurs in conjunction with a possessive pronoun; the placement of the adjective gives it greater emphasis. Cranfield includes an extended discussion of *λογικήν* (acc. sg. fem. of *λογικός, -ή, -όν*) and decides on "consistent with a proper understanding of the truth of God revealed in Christ" (602–605); Schreiner prefers "eminently reasonable" (645); Moo explores four options and suggests "true" (752–53; cf. TEV). Longenecker reviews translation options and suggests "this is your proper act of worship as rational people" (920–21).

VERSE 2

καὶ μὴ συσχηματίζεσθε τῷ αἰῶνι τούτῳ

Although *καί* is most frequently continuative ("and"), Moo argues that it introduces the means for carrying out the exhortation in verse 1 (754). *Μή* introduces an imperative of prohibition; *συσχηματίζεσθε* (2 pl. pres. pass. impv. of *συσχηματίζω*, "conform") is a gnomic present (Wallace 525) and a causative/permissive passive (cf. Wallace 441; contra Longenecker, who understands the voice as middle, 922). The verb denotes the action of being formed according to a pattern or mold (BDAG 979b). Cranfield suggests "stop allowing yourselves to be conformed" (609). *Τῷ αἰῶνι τούτῳ* is a dative of rule that specifies the standard of conduct to which someone or something conforms (GNB, "to the standard of this [age]"). "This age" regularly carries a negative connotation (1 Cor 1:20; 2:6, 8; 3:18; 2 Cor 4:4).

ἀλλὰ μεταμορφοῦσθε τῇ ἀνακαινώσει τοῦ νοός

The Majority Text adds ὑμῶν after νοός, but the shorter reading has good early manuscript support (𝔓[46], A, B, D). The longer reading is most likely a secondary addition to fill out the sense and create a parallel to τὰ σώματα ὑμῶν in the preceding verse (Dunn 707; Metzger 466). Ἀλλά establishes a strong contrast between the command in this line with the preceding prohibition; μεταμορφοῦσθε (2 pl. pres. pass. impv. of μεταμορφόω, "transform") is a gnomic present and a causative/permissive passive. The verb describes an inward change in fundamental character or conduct (BDAG 640a); commentators tend to see little distinction in meaning between μεταμορφόω and συσχηματίζω (e.g., Cranfield 607; Dunn 712). Τῇ ἀνακαινώσει (dat. sg. fem.) is instrumental (T 240); τοῦ νοός (gen. sg. masc.) is objective; the article with νοός implies possession (NIV, "by the renewing of your mind"). See *TDNT* 3.452–53 for ἀνακαίνωσις (cf. 2 Cor 4:16; Eph 4:23; Col 3:10; Titus 3:5) and 1:28 for νοῦς.

εἰς τὸ δοκιμάζειν ὑμᾶς τί τὸ θέλημα τοῦ θεοῦ

Εἰς τό + infinitive most frequently denotes purpose (Cranfield 609), can possibly denote result (Harris 90), and might well indicate purpose/result in this context. The present tense infinitive is common in such constructions (R 891) and probably has a futuristic nuance (e.g., NIV, GNB, NEB). Schreiner writes that the verb "signifies that which is approved after a process of testing and examining" (648). Ὑμᾶς is the subject of the infinitive (Wallace 196); the phrase τὸ θέλημα τοῦ θεοῦ is monadic (cf. 1:10) and functions as the object. See 2:18 for the combination of δοκιμάζω and θέλημα.

τὸ ἀγαθὸν καὶ εὐάρεστον καὶ τέλειον.

Three substantival adjectives stand in apposition to θέλημα (Cranfield 610); the article and double use of καί unite the three characteristics, although they are distinct (cf. Wallace 286). Ἀγαθός describes that which is morally good (Cranfield 610); εὐάρεστος describes that which is theocentric; τέλειος describes that which has attained its purpose (Dunn 715).

FOR FURTHER STUDY

67. Sacrifice (12:1)

Averbeck, R. F. *EDBT* 374–81.
Behm, H. *TDNT* 3.280–90.
Best, E. "Spiritual Sacrifice: General Priesthood in the New Testament." *Int* 14 (1960): 280–90.
Ferguson, E. "Spiritual Sacrifice in Early Christianity and Its Environment." Pages 1115–89 in *Aufstieg und Niedergang der Römischen Welt* 2.32.2. Berlin: DeGruyter, 1997.
Kendall, E. L. *A Living Sacrifice*. London: SCM, 1960.
Kim, S. "Paul's Common Paraenesis (1 Thess. 4–5; Phil. 2–4; and Rom. 12–13): The Correspondence between Romans 1:18–32 and 12:1–2, and the Unity of Romans 12–13." *TynBul* 62 (2011): 109–39.
Kiuchi, N. "A Living Sacrifice (Rom 12:1)." *Exegetica* 11 (2000): 21–51.
Morris, L. *DPL* 856–58.

Ridgway, J. K. "'By the Mercies of God . . .'—Mercy and Peace in Romans 12." *IBS* 14 (1992): 170–91.
Roetzel, C. J. "Sacrifice in Romans 12–15." *Word & World* 6 (1986): 410–19.
Thiele, F., and C. Brown. *NIDNTT* 3.415–38.
Thyen, H. *EDNT* 2.161–63.
Viagulamuthu, X. P. B. *Offering Our Bodies as a Living Sacrifice to God: A Study in Pauline Spirituality Based on Romans 12,1*. Rome: Editrice Pontificia Università Gregoriana, 2002.

68. Worship in the New Testament (12:1)

Aune, D. E. *ABD* 6.973–89.
Block, D. I. *For the Glory of God: Recovering a Biblical Theology of Worship*. Grand Rapids: Baker, 2014.
Borchert, G. L. *Worship in the New Testament: Divine Mystery and Human Response*. St. Louis: Chalice, 2008.
Cabaniss, A. *Patterns in Early Christian Worship*. Macon, GA: Mercer, 1989.
Carson, D. A., ed. *Worship by the Book*. Grand Rapids: Zondervan, 2002.
Cranfield, C. E. B. "Divine and Human Action: The Biblical Concept of Worship." *Int* 22 (1958): 387–98.
Cullman, O. *Early Christian Worship*. Translated by A. S. Todd and J. B. Torrance. London: SCM, 1953.
Delling, G. *Worship in the New Testament*. Translated by P. Scott. Philadelphia: Westminster, 1962.
Driscoll, J. "Worship in the Spirit of Logos: Romans 12:1–2 and the Source and Summit of Christian Life." *Letter & Spirit* 5 (2009): 77–101.
Greeven, H. *TDNT* 6.758–66.
Hahn, F. *The Worship of the Early Church*. Translated by D. E. Green. Edited by J. Reumann. Philadelphia: Fortress, 1973.
Hess, F. *NIDNTT* 3.544–53.
Humphrey, E. *Grand Entrance: Worship on Earth as in Heaven*. Grand Rapids: Eerdmans, 1998.
Hurtado, L. W. *At the Origins of Christian Worship: The Context and Character of Earliest Christian Devotion*. Grand Rapids: Eerdmans, 2000.
Malan, F. S. "Church Singing according to Pauline Epistles." *Neot* 32 (1998): 509–24.
Martin, R. P. *DPL* 982–91.
________. "Patterns of Worship in New Testament Churches." *JSNT* 37 (1989): 59–95.
________. *The Worship of God*. Grand Rapids: Eerdmans, 1982.
________. "Some Reflections on New Testament Hymns." Pages 173–97 in *Christ the Lord: Studies in Christology Presented to Donald Guthrie*. Edited by H. H. Rowdon. Downers Grove, IL: InterVarsity, 1982.
Moule, C. F. D. *Worship in the New Testament*. Richmond: John Knox, 1961.
Peterson, D. "Worship and Ethics in Romans 12." *TynBul* 44 (1993): 271–88.
________. *Engaging with God: A Biblical Theology of Worship*. Grand Rapids: Eerdmans, 1992.
Schönweiss, H., and C. Brown. *NIDNTT* 2.875–79.
Webber, R. E. *Worship: Old and New*. Grand Rapids: Eerdmans, 1982.

HOMILETICAL SUGGESTIONS

Total Commitment to God (12:1–2)

1. Present yourselves as living sacrifices (12:1)
   a. On the basis of God's compassion
   b. Because it is reasonable
2. Do not be conformed to this age (12:2a)
3. Be transformed (12:2b)
   a. By renewing the mind
   b. Because it validates God's will

b. By Humbly Exercising Spiritual Gifts (12:3–8)

STRUCTURE

Paul provides the first concrete instance of how God's righteousness is practiced in Christian living by turning to the exercise of spiritual gifts. The paragraph divides into three parts (12:3, 4–5, 6–8). A saying formula introduces the first part, which uses an example of *annominatio* (four occurrences of φρονεῖν and compounds) to call attention to the importance of a proper attitude. The second uses the analogy of the human body to highlight the importance of both unity and diversity. The third sets out seven spiritual gifts that illustrate the diversity present within God's grace.

Λέγω γὰρ διὰ τῆς χάριτος τῆς δοθείσης μοι παντὶ τῷ ὄντι ἐν ὑμῖν
    μὴ <u>ὑπερφρονεῖν</u>
        παρ' ὃ δεῖ <u>φρονεῖν</u>
    ἀλλὰ <u>φρονεῖν</u>
        εἰς τὸ <u>σωφρονεῖν</u>,
        ἑκάστῳ ὡς ὁ θεὸς ἐμέρισεν μέτρον πίστεως.

καθάπερ γὰρ ἐν ἑνὶ σώματι πολλὰ μέλη ἔχομεν,
    τὰ δὲ μέλη πάντα οὐ τὴν αὐτὴν ἔχει πρᾶξιν,
οὕτως οἱ πολλοὶ ἓν σῶμά ἐσμεν ἐν Χριστῷ,
    τὸ δὲ καθ' εἷς ἀλλήλων μέλη.

ἔχοντες δὲ χαρίσματα κατὰ τὴν χάριν τὴν δοθεῖσαν ἡμῖν διάφορα,
    εἴτε προφητείαν κατὰ τὴν ἀναλογίαν τῆς πίστεως,
    εἴτε διακονίαν ἐν τῇ διακονίᾳ,
    εἴτε ὁ διδάσκων ἐν τῇ διδασκαλίᾳ,
    εἴτε ὁ παρακαλῶν ἐν τῇ παρακλήσει·
    ὁ μεταδιδοὺς ἐν ἁπλότητι,
    ὁ προϊστάμενος ἐν σπουδῇ,
    ὁ ἐλεῶν ἐν ἱλαρότητι.

VERSE 3

Λέγω γὰρ διὰ τῆς χάριτος τῆς δοθείσης μοι παντὶ τῷ ὄντι ἐν ὑμῖν

Moo suggests that the explanatory conjunction γάρ introduces the first of a series of "concrete instances of the transformed way of life to which the believer is called" (760). Paul adds weight to his next set of instructions (λέγω) by referring to the apostolic grace God has given him (cf. 15:15; 1 Cor 3:10; Gal 2:9; Eph 3:2, 7). Διά + genitive carries the sense "by virtue of" (BDF §223.4); the article with χάριτος is well-known. The attributive adjectival participle δοθείσης (gen. sg. fem. of aor. pass. ptc. of δίδωμι) is a constative aorist and a divine passive. Παντί (dat. sg. masc.) is emphatic (Dunn 720); ὄντι (dat. sg. masc. of pres. act. ptc. of εἴμι) is substantival; the locative ἐν ὑμῖν should be translated "among you." The phrase is stronger than *πᾶσιν ὑμῖν* (Cranfield 612) and makes it clear that none is exempt (Schreiner 651).

μὴ ὑπερφρονεῖν παρ' ὃ δεῖ φρονεῖν

Paul again uses indirect discourse to phrase his instructions. Μὴ ὑπερφρονεῖν (pres. act. inf.) functions as a prohibition; ὑπερφρονέω describes the act of thinking highly of oneself (BDAG 1034d). Παρ' ὃ is comparative ("than"; cf. Porter 167, 238); see 8:26 for δεῖ; φρονεῖν (pres. act. inf.) is a complementary infinitive; the present tenses are gnomic. NIV translates "Do not think of yourself more highly than you ought."

ἀλλὰ φρονεῖν εἰς τὸ σωφρονεῖν

Ἀλλά places the imperatival infinitive (φρονεῖν) in strong contrast to the preceding prohibition; see 8:5 for φρονέω. Εἰς τό + infinitive is best understood as purpose (T 143; Porter 153). Σωφρονεῖν (pres. act. inf. of σωφρονέω) describes being prudent with a focus on self-control (BDAG 986d; cf. *TDNT* 7.1098–1100); Schreiner notes that self-control was one of the primary virtues in the Greek world (651).

ἑκάστῳ ὡς ὁ θεὸς ἐμέρισεν μέτρον πίστεως

The dative of ἑκάστῳ is attracted to παντὶ τῷ ὄντι at the beginning of the verse; Moo suggests that it is short for ἕκαστος ὡς αὐτῷ (760 n. 13); Cranfield proposes a "more correct" reading for the entire clause (613). Ὡς indicates manner ("as"); ἐμέρισεν (3 sg. aor. act. indic. of μερίζω, "assign") is a consummative aorist that emphasizes continuing results. Μέτρος, -ου, ὁ denotes the result of measuring (BDAG 644a); it can indicate standard (Cranfield 616) or quantity (Schreiner 652);* πίστεως is most likely a genitive of apposition (e.g., NLT, "the faith God has given you"). Cranfield (613–16) and Moo (761) conclude that Paul is referring to the common gift of faith God has given to all believers; Dunn (721–22), Jewett (742) and Schreiner (652–53) conclude that he is referring to the unique gifts of faith God gives to each believer. The explanation (γάρ) that follows in verses 4–8 suggests the latter is to be preferred.

VERSE 4

καθάπερ γὰρ ἐν ἑνὶ σώματι πολλὰ μέλη ἔχομεν

Καθάπερ ("just as") establishes an extended comparison that continues into verse 5. Ἐν + dative is locative ("in one body"); see 1 Corinthians 12:12–30 for a fuller example of the body metaphor; πολλὰ μέλη ("many members") is the direct object; ἔχομεν is a gnomic present that states what Paul and his readers already know generally to be the case (Moo 762 n. 22).

τὰ δὲ μέλη πάντα οὐ τὴν αὐτὴν ἔχει πρᾶξιν

Δέ is adversative ("but"); τὰ μέλη πάντα is better translated as "all the members" (NASB) rather than "the members . . . all" (e.g., NIV); οὐ negates ἔχει (gnomic present) which intervenes in the noun phrase (Porter 292) and gives πρᾶξιν emphasis; αὐτήν is intensive ("the same function").

VERSE 5

οὕτως οἱ πολλοὶ ἓν σῶμά ἐσμεν ἐν Χριστῷ

The correlative οὕτως ("so") introduces the second half of the comparison; the definite article allows the adjective πολλοί to function substantivally (R 774); ἓν σῶμά is the predicate nominative. Harris views ἐν Χριστῷ as indicating mode: "by our union with Christ" (124); Schreiner suggests cause: "because [we] are united with [Christ]" (654).*

τὸ δὲ καθ' εἷς ἀλλήλων μέλη

Δέ is continuative ("and"); the article allows the prepositional phrase to function as a noun (766). Κατά is distributive (Moule 60 n. 1); εἷς is nominative (R 294); the idiomatic phrase should be translated "each one" (Moo 762 n. 25). The reciprocal pronoun ἀλλήλων (gen. pl.) denotes mutual relationship (Porter 132); the genitive is descriptive; placing the genitive before its head noun gives it emphasis.

VERSE 6

ἔχοντες δὲ χαρίσματα κατὰ τὴν χάριν τὴν δοθεῖσαν ἡμῖν διάφορα

Paul transitions (δέ) to a new sentence (Cranfield 618) that provides specific examples of diversity within the body of Christ. Robertson understands ἔχοντες (nom. pl. masc. of pres. act. ptc.) as imperatival (946); Wallace understands it as equivalent to an indicative (653; cf. NIV, NET, CSB); it is also possible to understand the participle as adverbial of cause and supply a verb (e.g., NASB, "Since we have . . . each of us is to exercise"; cf. Moo 764; Schreiner 654).* See 1:11 for χαρίσματα (acc. pl. neut.), which provides a word play with χάρις and denotes a special endowment for service (Cranfield 619). Κατά + accusative denotes standard; the article with χάριν is well known; see verse 3 for the adjectival participle (δοθεῖσαν); ἡμῖν reflects the distribution of gifts to all believers. The adjective διάφορα (acc. pl. neut. of διάφορος, -ον, "different") modifies χαρίσματα, is placed emphatically (Jewett 745), and focuses on distinctiveness (BDAG 239d).

εἴτε προφητείαν κατὰ τὴν ἀναλογίαν τῆς πίστεως

Moo notes that the seven gifts in Paul's list do not correspond linguistically to those on other gift lists (cf. 1 Cor 12:7–10, 28; Eph 4:11), although there might be overlap in function (764). Longenecker provides a concise definition of the gifts (929). Schreiner notes that the emphasis falls on the manner in which the gifts are to be exercised rather than on the gifts themselves (650). The correlative chain εἴτε . . . εἴτε . . . εἴτε . . . εἴτε ("whether . . . or . . . or . . . or") joins the first four gifts. Προφητεία, -ας, ἡ describes the gift of interpreting the divine will or purpose (BDAG 889d); Schreiner suggests that it is spontaneous and directed to specific situations (655). Κατά + accusative denotes standard (Cranfield 621); ἀναλογία, -ας, ἡ ("analogy") refers to relation and proportion (Dunn 727; cf. BDAG 67c); πίστεως is a genitive of apposition; the article accompanies the abstract noun. The phrase parallels κατὰ τὴν χάριν τὴν δοθεῖσαν ἡμῖν διάφορα in the first line of the verse and is best understood as individual faith (cf. v. 3); NEB translates "in proportion to a man's faith."

VERSE 7

εἴτε διακονίαν ἐν τῇ διακονίᾳ

See 11:13 for διακονία; in this context, the gift is best understood as practical service to those in need (Cranfield 622). In this line and the two that follow, ἐν + dative denotes sphere; the articles with the dative nouns denote what is well known (BDF §258.1). According to Schreiner, Paul's main point is that those who possess each gift "should devote themselves to the gift that they have received" (657).

εἴτε ὁ διδάσκων ἐν τῇ διδασκαλίᾳ

Ὁ διδάσκων (nom. sg. masc. of pres. act. ptc.) is a substantival participle and a gnomic present ("the one who teaches"), as are those that follow. See 2:20–21 for διδάσκω/διδασκαλία. Moo suggests that teaching differs from prophecy in that the latter "involves the passing on of the truth of the gospel as it has been preserved in the church" (767). Schreiner highlights the study and effort involved in teaching (658).

VERSE 8

εἴτε ὁ παρακαλῶν ἐν τῇ παρακλήσει

See 12:1 for παρακαλέω/παράκλησις. BDAG notes that the noun describes the act of emboldening another in a belief or course of action (766a); in this context, "encourage" is a good translation (e.g., GNB, NJB). Cranfield suggests that the gift involves the pastoral application of the gospel (624).

ὁ μεταδιδοὺς ἐν ἁπλότητι

Μεταδίδωμι describes the act of sharing something with someone (BDAG 638b; cf. 1:11); in this context, that act involves the distribution of what is one's own (Schreiner 659). In this line and the two that follow ἐν + dative denotes manner; the omission of the article highlights the quality of the action. Ἁπλότης, -ητος, ἡ is variously translated "simplicity, sincerity, uprightness, frankness" (BDAG 104b; cf *TDNT* 1.386–7); the use of the word in similar contexts related to money (cf. 2 Cor 8:2; 9:11, 13) suggests that "generosity" is the best choice (e.g., NIV, ESV, CSB).

ὁ προϊστάμενος ἐν σπουδῇ

Προΐστημι denotes the exercise of leadership (BDAG 870c) and elsewhere depicts the ministry of elders (1 Tim 5:17; cf. 1 Thess 5:12; 1 Tim 3:4, 5, 12); σπουδή, -ῆς, ἡ ("earnestness, eagerness, diligence") describes earnest commitment in the discharge of an obligation or in the context of a relationship (BDAG 939d; cf. 2 Cor 7:11–12; 8:7–8).

ὁ ἐλεῶν ἐν ἱλαρότητι

This verse is the only NT instance in which ἐλεέω refers to human mercy; see 9:15 for divine mercy. Cranfield suggests that concrete examples of this gift would include tending the sick, relieving the needs of the poor, and caring for the aged (627). Ἱλαρότης, -ητος, ἡ ("cheerfulness, gladness, wholeheartedness") describes a quality or state of cheerfulness that contrasts with an attitude of being under stress (BDAG 473d).

FOR FURTHER STUDY

69. Body of Christ (12:4)

Best, E. *One Body in Christ*. London: SPCK, 1955.

Bosch, J. S. "Le Corps du Christ et les charismes dans l'épître aux Romains." Pages 51–72 in *Dimensions de la vie chrétienne*. Edited by I. de Lorenzi. Rome: Abbey of St. Paul, 1979.

Breed, J. L. "The Church as the 'Body of Christ': A Pauline Analogy." *Near East School of Theology Theological Review* 6 (1985): 9–32.

Daines, B. "Paul's Use of the Analogy of the Body of Christ." *EvQ* 50 (1978): 71–78.

Dunn, J. D. G. "'The Body of Christ' in Paul." Pages 146–62 in *Worship, Theology and Ministry in the Early Church: Essays in Honor of Ralph P. Martin*. Edited by M. J. Wilkins and T. Paige. Sheffield: Academic Press, 1992.

Field, B. "The Discourses Behind the Metaphor 'the Church is the Body of Christ' as Used by St Paul and the 'Post-Paulines.'" *Asia Journal of Theology* 6 (1992): 88–107.

Fung, R. Y. K. *DPL* 76–82.

Hultgren, A. J. "The Church as the Body of Christ: Engaging an Image in the New Testament." *Word & World* 22 (2002): 124–32.

Judge, E. A. "Demythologizing the Church: What is the Meaning of 'The Body of Christ'?" *Interchange* 11 (1972): 155–67.

Käsemann, E. "The Theological Problem Presented by the Motif of the Body of Christ." Pages 102–21 in *Perspectives on Paul*. Philadelphia: Fortress, 1971.

McVay, J. K. *DPL* 377–78.

Minear, P. S. *Images of the Church in the New Testament*. Philadelphia: Westminster, 1960.

Pelser, G. M. M. "Once more the body of Christ in Paul." *Neot* 32 (1998): 525–45.

Perriman, A. "'His body, which is the church . . .': Coming to Terms with Metaphor." *EvQ* 62 (1990): 123–42.

Robinson, J. A. T. *The Body: A Study in Pauline Theology*. London: SCM, 1952.

Schweizer, R. E. *ABD* 1.770–72.

Yorke, G. *The Church as the Body of Christ in the Pauline Corpus: A Re-examination*. Lanham, MD: University Press, 1991.

70. Spiritual Gifts (12:6)

Berding, K. *What Are Spiritual Gifts: Rethinking the Conventional View*. Grand Rapids: Kregel, 2006.

Carson, D. A. *Showing the Spirit: A Theological Exposition of 1 Corinthians 12–14*. Grand Rapids: Baker, 1987.

Conzelmann, H. *TDNT* 9.402–06.

Dunn, J. D. G. *Jesus and the Spirit*. Philadelphia: Westminster, 1975.

Ellis, E. E. "'Spiritual' Gifts in the Pauline Community." *NTS* 20 (1974): 128–44.

Fee, G. D. *DPL* 339–47.

________. *God's Empowering Presence: The Holy Spirit in the Letters of Paul*. Peabody, MA: Hendrickson, 1993.

Fung, R. Y. K. "Ministry, Community and Spiritual Gifts." *EvQ* 56 (1984): 3–20.

Hemphill, K. S. *Spiritual Gifts: Empowering the New Testament Church*. Nashville: Broadman, 1988.

Kilgallen, J. J. "Reflections on Charisma(ta) in the New Testament." *Studia Missionalia* 41 (1992): 289–323.

Koenig, J. *Charismata: God's Gifts for God's People*. Philadelphia: Westminster John Knox, 1978.

MacGorman, J. W. *The Gifts of the Spirit*. Nashville: Broadman, 1974.

Martin, R. P. *The Spirit and the Congregation*. Grand Rapids: Eerdmans, 1984.

Nijru, P. K. *Charisms and the Holy Spirit's Activity in the Body of Christ: An Exegetical-Theological Study of 1 Corinthians 12,4–11 and Romans 12,6–8*. Rome: Editrice Pontificia Università Gregoriana, 2002.

Schartzmann, S. *A Pauline Theology of Charismata*. Peabody, MA: Hendrickson, 1986.

HOMILETICAL SUGGESTIONS

The Exercise of Spiritual Gifts (12:3–8)

1. The right attitude: You ought to think soberly about yourselves (12:3)
    a. Not more highly than is proper
    b. As God has given each one faith
2. The right perspective: You are members of one body (12:4–5)
    a. Many members
    b. One body
3. The right manner: You should exercise your gifts as God intended (12:6–8)
    a. Prophecy
    b. Serving
    c. Teaching
    d. Encouragement
    e. Giving
    f. Leading
    g. Showing mercy

c. By Pursuing Total Transformation (12:9–21)

STRUCTURE

Paul continues with an extended list of loosely related instructions that incorporate adjectives, imperatival participles, true imperatives, and imperatival infinitives. The paragraph divides into three general parts (12:9–13, 14–16, 17–21). The first includes twelve adjectives and imperatival participles arranged 2–3–2–3–2. The second combines three true imperatives, two imperatival infinities, and three imperatival participles. The third consists of two three-line instructions followed by a tightly constructed summary. See Black ("The Pauline Love Command," *FilNeot* 1 [1989]: 3–21) for a slightly different understanding of the overall structure. Miller argues that Paul's use of participles, adjectives, and infinitives communicates more politely than imperatives. (See N. F. Miller, "The Imperativals of Romans 12." Pages 162–82 in *Linguistics and New Testament Interpretation: Essays in Discourse Analysis*. Edited by D. A. Black, K. Barnwell, and S. Levinsohn. Nashville: Broadman, 1992.) She suggests that the participles introduce appeals to reason (ethical actions), the adjectives introduce appeals to emotion (ideal attitudes), the infinitives introduce appeals to conscience (moral duties), and the imperatives introduce appeals to will (volitional choices).

Ἡ ἀγάπη ἀνυπόκριτος.
    ἀποστυγοῦντες τὸ πονηρόν,
    κολλώμενοι τῷ ἀγαθῷ,
        τῇ φιλαδελφίᾳ εἰς ἀλλήλους φιλόστοργοι,
        τῇ τιμῇ ἀλλήλους προηγούμενοι,
        τῇ σπουδῇ μὴ ὀκνηροί,
    τῷ πνεύματι ζέοντες,
    τῷ κυρίῳ δουλεύοντες,
        τῇ ἐλπίδι χαίροντες,
        τῇ θλίψει ὑπομένοντες,
        τῇ προσευχῇ προσκαρτεροῦντες,
    ταῖς χρείαις τῶν ἁγίων κοινωνοῦντες,
    τὴν φιλοξενίαν διώκοντες.

εὐλογεῖτε τοὺς διώκοντας [ὑμᾶς],
    εὐλογεῖτε καὶ μὴ καταρᾶσθε.
χαίρειν μετὰ χαιρόντων,
    κλαίειν μετὰ κλαιόντων.
τὸ αὐτὸ εἰς ἀλλήλους φρονοῦντες,
    μὴ τὰ ὑψηλὰ φρονοῦντες
    ἀλλὰ τοῖς ταπεινοῖς συναπαγόμενοι.
μὴ γίνεσθε φρόνιμοι παρ' ἑαυτοῖς.

μηδενὶ κακὸν ἀντὶ κακοῦ ἀποδιδόντες,
προνοούμενοι καλὰ ἐνώπιον πάντων ἀνθρώπων·

εἰ δυνατὸν τὸ ἐξ ὑμῶν, μετὰ πάντων ἀνθρώπων εἰρηνεύοντες·
μὴ ἑαυτοὺς ἐκδικοῦντες, ἀγαπητοί,
ἀλλὰ δότε τόπον τῇ ὀργῇ,
γέγραπται γάρ, Ἐμοὶ ἐκδίκησις, ἐγὼ ἀνταποδώσω, λέγει κύριος.
ἀλλ᾽ ἐὰν πεινᾷ ὁ ἐχθρός σου, ψώμιζε αὐτόν·
ἐὰν διψᾷ, πότιζε αὐτόν·
τοῦτο γὰρ ποιῶν ἄνθρακας πυρὸς σωρεύσεις ἐπὶ τὴν κεφαλὴν αὐτοῦ.
μὴ νικῶ ὑπὸ τοῦ κακοῦ
ἀλλὰ νίκα ἐν τῷ ἀγαθῷ τὸ κακόν.

VERSE 9

Ἡ ἀγάπη ἀνυπόκριτος

The lack of a connecting conjunction (asyndeton) and the change in syntax suggests the start of a new section (cf. Dunn 739). The article with the abstract noun ἀγάπη marks it as well-known (Moo 775); placing the adjective in the second predicate position gives slightly more emphasis to the noun (Wallace 308). Ἀνυπόκριτος, -ον ("unhypocritical") pertains to something that is sincere and without pretense (BDAG 91d); elsewhere, it describes qualities or virtues that are genuine and not counterfeit (2 Cor 6:6; 1 Tim 1:5; 2 Tim 1:5; Jas 3:17; 1 Pet 1:22).

ἀποστυγοῦντες τὸ πονηρόν

Ἀποστυγοῦντες (nom. pl. masc. of pres. act. ptc. of ἀποστυγέω, "abhor") is the first of ten imperatival participles (Wallace 650–51); Turner classifies the participles as durative, carrying the nuance "always" (343). The verb denotes strong dislike for something (BDAG 123b); Dunn suggests "hate violently" (740). Τὸ πονηρόν ("that which is evil") is a substantival adjective describing something that is evil/wicked and morally worthless (BDAG 852a).

κολλώμενοι τῷ ἀγαθῷ

Κολλώμενοι (nom. pl. masc. of pres. mid. ptc. of dep. κολλάομαι, "hold on to") describes the act of clinging to someone or something in close association; the dative naturally follows κολλάω (cf. BDAG 556b). The deponent middle has an indirect nuance. See 2:7, 10 for ἀγαθός.

VERSE 10

τῇ φιλαδελφίᾳ εἰς ἀλλήλους φιλόστοργοι

Τῇ φιλαδελφίᾳ (dat. sg. fem. of φιλαδελφία, -ας, ἡ, "brotherly love") is the first of three datives of reference (Moo 777 n. 32); εἰς + accusative denotes relationship ("toward one another"; cf. Harris 93; Moo 782); the adjective φιλόστοργοι (nom. pl. masc. of φιλόστοργος, -ον, "devoted") is "virtually a participle" (Moule 156). Both the noun and the adjective are "family words" denoting belongingness that transcends natural or ethnic bonds (Dunn 741).

τῇ τιμῇ ἀλλήλους προηγούμενοι

See 2:7, 10 for τιμή; ἀλλήλους ("one another") is the object of the participle προηγούμενοι (nom. pl. masc. of pres. mid. ptc. of dep. προηγέομαι, "esteem highly"). Suggested translations for προηγέομαι include "preferring" (Schreiner 664; cf. NASB, NKJV),* "leading the way" (Dunn 741), and "surpassing" (Moo 777).

VERSE 11

τῇ σπουδῇ μὴ ὀκνηροί

See verse 8 for σπουδή; the adjective ὀκνηροί (nom. pl. masc. of ὀκνηρός, -ά, -όν, "lazy") has an imperatival sense (R 1172), which explains the use of μή. Schreiner notes that ὀκνηρός can denote laziness (665; cf. Matt 25:26); NAB translates "not lagging behind in diligence"; NLT suggests "never be lazy."

τῷ πνεύματι ζέοντες

The dative τῷ πνεύματι is locative (R 524); commentators agree that the reference is to the Holy Spirit (e.g., Moo 778); ζέω describes being stirred up emotionally (BDAG 426d); Dunn suggests the idea of burning passion (742); Luke applies the description to Apollos in Acts 18:25.

τῷ κυρίῳ δουλεύοντες

The substitution of καιρῷ for κυρίῳ (D*, F, G) is more difficult (Dunn 737) but would give the instruction a negative connotation (Moo 769 n. 1) and is most likely "simply a visual error" (Jewett 755 n. b; cf. Metzger 466). The reading κυρίῳ has earlier and more diversified support ($\mathfrak{P}^{46}$, ℵ, A, B, D^2, 33). The dative direct object regularly follows δουλεύω; see 6:6; 7:6 for the verb.

VERSE 12

τῇ ἐλπίδι χαίροντες

The dative τῇ ἐλπίδι could be locative (Moo 779 n. 48) or causal (BDF §186); Schreiner thinks local, causal, and instrumental are all included (666). Χαίροντες (nom. pl. masc. of pres. act. ptc. of χαίρω, "rejoice") continues the string of imperatival participles.

τῇ θλίψει ὑπομένοντες

The same possible categories apply to the dative τῇ θλίψει. See 5:3 for θλῖψις; ὑπομένω describes the action of maintaining a belief or course of action in the face of opposition (BDAG 1039b).

τῇ προσευχῇ προσκαρτεροῦντες

The dative of τῇ προσευχῇ naturally follows προσκαρτεροῦντες (nom. pl. masc. of pres. act. ptc. of προσκαρτερέω, "be devoted to"; cf. BDAG 881d). See 1:9 for προσευχή; for προσκαρτερέω, compare Acts 1:14; 2:42; 6:4; Ephesians 6:18; Colossians 4:2; 1 Thessalonians 5:17.

VERSE 13

ταῖς χρείαις τῶν ἁγίων κοινωνοῦντες

The dative ταῖς χρείαις (dat. pl. fem. of χρεία, -ας, ἡ, "need") naturally follows κοινωνοντες (nom. pl. masc. of pres. act. ptc. of κοινωνέω, "contribute"; cf. BDAG 552c); τῶν ἁγίων is a possessive genitive. Κοινωνέω denotes practical assistance, usually financial or material (Rom 15:26; Gal 6:6; Phil 4:15; 1 Tim 6:18; Heb 13:16); Moo notes that the other occurrences of χρείαις (pl.) refer to material needs such as food, clothing, and shelter (779 n. 52).

τὴν φιλοξενίαν διώκοντες

The article with φιλοξενία ("hospitality"; cf. 1 Tim 3:2; Titus 1:8; Heb 13:3; 1 Pet 4:9) marks a virtue that is well known; see 9:30–31 for διώκω. Schreiner suggests the instruction is to take the initiative in providing hospitality (666).

VERSE 14

εὐλογεῖτε τοὺς διώκοντας [ὑμᾶς], εὐλογεῖτε καὶ μὴ καταρᾶσθε

The inclusion or omission of ὑμᾶς after διώκοντας makes little difference to the sense of the first command (Moo 770 n. 2), and the readings are evenly supported (Metzger 466). Commentators conclude that the addition is secondary (Dunn 737; Schreiner 670). Εὐλογεῖτε (2 pl. pres. act. impv. of εὐλογέω, "bless") is a gnomic present of command (Wallace 535); the verb describes the act of calling on God to bestow his favor (Dunn 744; cf. BDAG 408a). Τοὺς διώκοντας (acc. pl. masc. of pres. act. ptc.) is a substantival participle; in this context the verb denotes persecution (GNB, "those who persecute you"). The prohibition μὴ καταρᾶσθε (2 pl. pres. mid. impv. of dep. καταράομαι, "curse") is a gnomic present and a deponent middle. In contrast to εὐλογέω, καταράομαι describes the act of calling on God to withhold his favor.

VERSE 15

χαίρειν μετὰ χαιρόντων, κλαίειν μετὰ κλαιόντων

Χαίρειν (pres. act. inf. of χαίρω, "rejoice") and κλαίειν (pres. act. inf. of κλαίω, "weep") are infinitives of command (Moule 126; Porter 202); Turner notes that such commands are always in the present tense (78). Μετά + genitive denotes association ("with"). The anarthrous substantival participles χαιρόντων (gen. pl. masc. of pres. act. ptc.) and κλαιόντων (gen. pl. masc. of pres. act. ptc.) are indefinite (R 1106) and describe members of a class ("those who rejoice/weep"). Both clauses include instances of *annominatio* (R 1201) and *homoioteleuton* (BDF §488.3).

VERSE 16

τὸ αὐτὸ εἰς ἀλλήλους φρονοῦντες

Τὸ αὐτό is the intensifying use of the personal pronoun ("the same [thing]"); see verse 10 for εἰς ἀλλήλους ("toward one another"); φρονοῦντες (nom. pl. masc. of pres. act. ptc. of φρονέω) resumes the use of imperatival participles. The idea of "being of the same mind toward one another" (NASB) occurs elsewhere in Romans 15:5; 2 Corinthians 13:11; Philippians 2:2; 4:2.

μὴ τὰ ὑψηλὰ φρονοῦντες ἀλλὰ τοῖς ταπεινοῖς συναπαγόμενοι

Μή . . . ἀλλά establishes a strong contrast between the attitudes of pride and humility. See 11:20 for μὴ ὑψηλὰ φρονοῦντες (cf. 1 Tim 6:17). Τοῖς ταπεινοῖς is a dative of association (Moo 784 n. 73); ταπεινός, -ή, όν describes someone or something of low status (BDAG 989c). Συναπαγόμενοι (nom. pl. masc. of pres. mid. ptc. of dep. συναπάγομαι, "associate") denotes the act of adjusting to a condition or set of circumstances (BDAG 965d); the deponent middle has an indirect nuance. Commentators are divided on whether the sense is "associate with the humble [persons]" (Cranfield 644; e.g., NIV) or "be carried away with the humble [tasks]" (Murray 2:136; e.g., GNB). See Moo's discussion, in which he concludes that both options fit the context well and both have parallels elsewhere in the NT (783).

μὴ γίνεσθε φρόνιμοι παρ' ἑαυτοῖς

The predicate adjective φρόνιμοι (nom. pl. masc.) provides the third element in the word-chain; see 11:25 for φρόνιμος. The explicit prohibition μὴ γίνεσθε (2 pl. pres. mid. impv. of dep. γίνομαι) stands out against the participles and infinitives that dominate the passage. Παρά + dative is locative (R 614); Moo translates the phrase "in your own eyes" (784; cf. Moule 52).

VERSE 17

μηδενὶ κακὸν ἀντὶ κακοῦ ἀποδιδόντες

Μηδενί (dat. sg. masc. of *μηδείς*, *μνδεμία*, *μηδέν*, "no one") is the indirect object; *κακός* describes something that is socially or morally reprehensible (cf. 1:29); *ἀντί* + genitive denotes exchange ("in return for"; cf. Harris 50); see 2:6 for *αποδίδωμι*.

προνοούμενοι καλὰ ἐνώπιον πάντων ἀνθρώπων

Variant readings that include expansions before *ἐνώπιον πάντων* are most likely influenced by Proverbs 3:4 and 2 Corinthians 8:21 (Metzger 466). Schreiner concludes that the reading *ἐνώπιον πάντων* is "surely original" (676). Προνοούμενοι (nom. pl. masc. of pres. mid. ptc. of *προνοέω*, "give careful thought to") is an indirect middle; see 7:16 for *καλός*, which contrasts sharply with *κακός* in the previous line; *ἐνώπιον* + genitive denotes presence ("before/in the sight of"; cf. 3:20). See 2 Corinthians 8:21 for a nearly identical exhortation.

VERSE 18

εἰ δυνατὸν τὸ ἐξ ὑμῶν, μετὰ πάντων ἀνθρώπων εἰρηνεύοντες

Εἰ introduces a first class condition; see 4:21 for *δυνατός*; a neuter article accompanies the adverbial prepositional phrase (T 14), which Moule understands as idiomatic of reference/respect (33). NIV translates the clause "If it is possible, as far as it depends on you." Μετά + genitive is associative ("with all men"); *εἰρηνεύοντες* (nom. pl. masc. of pres. act. ptc. of *εἰρηνεύω*, "be at peace") echoes Jesus's command in Mark 9:50 as well as Psalm 33:15 (cf. 2 Cor 13:11; 1 Thess 5:13).

VERSE 19

μὴ ἑαυτοὺς ἐκδικοῦντες, ἀγαπητοί, ἀλλὰ δότε τόπον τῇ ὀργῇ

Μή . . . *ἀλλά* establishes a strong contrast between two approaches to being wronged. The reflexive pronoun *ἑαυτούς* (acc. pl. masc.) is the object of the participle; *ἐκδικοῦντες* (nom. pl. masc. of pres. act. ptc. of *ἐκδικέω*, "avenge") describes the act of procuring justice for someone (BDAG 300d); see 1:13 for *ἀγαπητοί*. Δότε (2 pl. aor. act. impv. of *δίδωμι*) is an imperative of command; *τόπος, -ου, ὁ* describes the favorable circumstances for doing something (BDAG 1012a). The article with *ὀργῇ* (dat. sg. fem.) is well known (T 173); the dative denotes reference; the wrath is God's (Cranfield 647; Dunn 749; Moo 786; Schreiner 673). NIV translates "leave room for God's wrath"; ESV renders "leave it to the wrath of God."

γέγραπται γάρ (See 1:17)

Ἐμοὶ ἐκδίκησις, ἐγὼ ἀνταποδώσω, λέγει κύριος

In support of his instruction, Paul quotes Deuteronomy 32:35. Ἐμοί is a dative of possession ("mine") and is placed first for emphasis; ἐκδίκησις denotes the process of procuring justice; ἐστιν is understood. Ἐγώ provides subject focus and is emphatic; ἀνταποδώσω (1 sg. fut. act. indic. of ἀνταποδίδωμι, "repay"; cf. 11:9, 35) is a predictive future. Λέγει is a perfective present; see 1:4 for κύριος.

VERSE 20

ἀλλʼ ἐὰν πεινᾷ ὁ ἐχθρός σου, ψώμιζε αὐτόν

Paul continues with a quotation from Proverbs 25:21–22a that follows the LXX exactly; the addition of ἀλλά contrasts the quotation with the initial prohibition of verse 19. Ἐάν πεινᾷ (3 sg. pres. act. subjunc. of πεινάω, "be hungry") introduces a third class condition; see 5:10 for ἐχθρός. Ψώμιζε (2 sg. pres. act. impv. of ψωμίζω, "feed") is an imperative of command and takes an accusative of person (R 484).

ἐὰν διψᾷ, πότιζε αὐτόν

Ἐὰν διψᾷ (3 sg. pres. act. subjunc. of διψάω, "be thirsty") introduces another third class condition; πότιζε (2 sg. pres. act. impv. of ποτίζω, "give to drink") is an imperative of command. Schreiner suggests that the two specific instructions stand for doing every kind of good (674).

τοῦτο γὰρ ποιῶν ἄνθρακας πυρὸς σωρεύσεις ἐπὶ τὴν κεφαλὴν αὐτοῦ

The final line of the quotation provides the reason (γάρ) for responding with good when wronged. Τοῦτο (acc. sg. neut.) refers retrospectively to the preceding two lines; ποιῶν (nom. sg. masc. of pres. act. ptc. of ποιέω) is adverbial of means (Wallace 630); πυρός is an attributive genitive, which leads to the translation "fiery coals." Σωρεύσεις (2 sg. fut. act. indic. of σωρεύω, "pile up"); ἐπὶ τὴν κεφαλὴν αὐτοῦ ("upon his head") denotes spatial rest. The idea is more likely one of bringing God's judgment upon someone (Schreiner 674–75, with OT references) than one of bringing burning pangs of shame and contrition (Moo 788–89; cf. Longenecker 941). See Cranfield for the possible origin of the expression (650).

VERSE 21

μὴ νικῶ ὑπὸ τοῦ κακοῦ

Paul summarizes verses 17–20 with a concise statement framed as antithetic parallelism; μή . . . ἀλλά strengthens the contrast. Turner understands νικῶ (2 sg. pres. pass. impv. of νικάω) as a perfective present (62; cf. R 881); Dunn suggests that the present tense indicates dedicated persistence (751); see 3:4 for νικάω. Ὑπό + genitive denotes direct agency (R 532); the article with the substantival adjective κακοῦ is generic (R 763).

ἀλλὰ νίκα ἐν τῷ ἀγαθῷ τὸ κακόν

Νίκα (2 sg. pres. act. impv. of νικάω) is an imperative of command; ἐν + dative denotes intermediate agency (R 534); the articles with the substantival adjectives are generic; τὸ κακόν is the direct object and forms an *inclusio* with verse 17.

FOR FURTHER STUDY

71. Paraenesis (12:9)

Bradley, D. G. "The Topos as a Form in the Pauline Paraenesis." *JBL* 72 (1953): 238–46.
Coetzer, W. C. "The Literary Genre of Paraenesis in the Pauline Letters." *TE* 17 (1984): 36–42.
Kim, S. "Paul's Common Paraenesis (1 Thess. 4–5; Phil. 2–4; and Rom. 12–13): The Correspondence between Romans 1:18–32 and 12:1–2, and the Unity of Romans 12–13." *TynBul* 62 (2011): 109–39.
Malherbe, A. J. *Moral Exhortation. A Greco-Roman Sourcebook*. Philadelphia: Westminster, 1986.
Onwu, N. "Mimetes Hypothesis: A Key to the Understanding of Pauline Paraenesis." *African Journal of Biblical Studies* 1 (1986): 95–112.
Roetzel, C. J. *The Letters of Paul: Conversations in Context*. Atlanta: John Knox, 1982.
Schroeder, D. *IDBSup* 643.
Sensing, T. "Towards a Definition of Paraenesis." *Restoration Quarterly* 38 (1996): 145–58.
Stowers, S. K. *Letter Writing in Greco-Roman Antiquity*. Philadelphia: Westminster, 1986.
Thompson, M. B. *DPL* 922–23.

72. Hospitality (12:13)

Bietenhard, H. *NIDNTT* 1.686–90.
Carroll, M. "A Biblical Approach to Hospitality." *RevExp* 108 (2011): 519–26.
Duke, R. K. *EDBT* 359–61.
Fitzgerald, J. T. *DNTB* 522–25.
Koenig, J. *New Testament Hospitality: Partnership with Strangers as Promise and Mission*. Philadelphia: Fortress, 1985.
Stählin, G. *TDNT* 5.1–36.
Trakatellis, D. "Love and Care for Strangers: Philoxenia in Christian Tradition." *Bulletin of the Boston Theological Institute* 12 (2013): 4–7.

73. Coals of Fire (12:19)

Day, J. N. "'Coals of Fire' in Romans 12:19–20." *BSac* 160 (2003): 414–20.
Klassen, W. *Love of Enemies: The Way to Peace*. Eugene, OR: Wipf & Stock, 2002.
________. "Coals of Fire: Sign of Repentance or Revenge?" *NTS* 9 (1962–63): 337–50.

Martens, J. W. "Burning Questions in Romans 12:20: What Is the Meaning and Purpose of 'Coals of Fire'?" *CBQ* 76 (2014): 291–305.
Morenz, S. "Feurige Kohlen auf dem Haupt." *TLZ* 78 (1953): 187–92.
Scaer, D. P. *EDBT* 796–98.
Schottroff, L. "Non-violence and the Love of Enemies." Pages 9–39 in *Essays on the Love Commandment*. Editor R. H. Fuller. Philadelphia: Fortress, 1978.
Segert, S. "'Live Coals Heaped on the Head'." Pages 159–64 in *Love and Death in the Ancient Near East: Essays in Honor of Marvin H. Pope*. Edited by J. H. Marks and R. M. Good. Guilford, CT: Four Quarters, 1987.
Stendahl, K. "Hate, Non-Retaliation, and Love." *HTR* 55 (1962): 343–55.
Wilson, W. T. *Love without Pretense: Romans 12:9–21 and Hellenistic-Jewish Wisdom Literature*. Tübingen: Mohr, 1991.
Zerbe, G. M. *Non-Retaliation in Early Jewish and New Testament Texts: Ethical Themes in Social Contexts*. Sheffield: *JSOT*, 1993.

HOMILETICAL SUGGESTIONS

Total Transformation (three-part series)

Evidence of a Transformed Mind (12:9–13)

A transformed mind . . .

1. Practices sincere love and goodness (12:9)
2. Practices brotherly love and honor (12:10)
3. Practices diligent zeal and service (12:11)
4. Practices joyful endurance and prayer (12:12)
5. Practices active assistance and hospitality (12:13)

Evidence of a Transformed Heart (12:14–16)

A transformed heart . . .

1. Deals graciously with those who oppose (12:14)
2. Identifies with others' joys and sorrows (12:15)
3. Lives with others in harmony and humility (12:16)

Evidence of a Transformed Will (12:17–21)

A transformed will . . .

1. Chooses to be at peace with others (12:17–18)
2. Chooses to trust in God's justice (12:19)
3. Chooses to do good to enemies (12:20)
4. Chooses to overcome evil with good (12:21)

d. By Being Subject to Authorities (13:1–7)

STRUCTURE

Paul continues his series of loosely connected *topoi* by turning to the believer's relationship to governing authorities. The paragraph consists of two parts (13:1–4, 5–7). The first begins with a command (13:1a) followed by two reasons (13:1b–2, 3–4); the second provides a summary of verses 1–4 (13:5–6) followed by four obligations owed to governing authorities (13:7). Moo provides an overview of seven interpretations of the paragraph (806–10); Jewett refutes the theory that the paragraph is a non-Pauline interpolation (782–84). See Longenecker for a discussion of the paragraph's occasion and purpose (949–54).

Πᾶσα ψυχὴ ἐξουσίαις ὑπερεχούσαις ὑποτασσέσθω.

οὐ γὰρ ἔστιν ἐξουσία εἰ μὴ ὑπὸ θεοῦ, αἱ δὲ οὖσαι ὑπὸ θεοῦ τεταγμέναι εἰσίν.
    ὥστε ὁ ἀντιτασσόμενος τῇ ἐξουσίᾳ τῇ τοῦ θεοῦ διαταγῇ ἀνθέστηκεν,
    οἱ δὲ ἀνθεστηκότες ἑαυτοῖς κρίμα λήμψονται.

οἱ γὰρ ἄρχοντες οὐκ εἰσὶν φόβος τῷ ἀγαθῷ ἔργῳ ἀλλὰ τῷ κακῷ.
    θέλεις δὲ μὴ φοβεῖσθαι τὴν ἐξουσίαν· τὸ ἀγαθὸν ποίει, καὶ ἕξεις ἔπαινον ἐξ αὐτῆς·
        θεοῦ γὰρ διάκονός ἐστιν σοὶ εἰς τὸ ἀγαθόν.
    ἐὰν δὲ τὸ κακὸν ποιῇς, φοβοῦ·
        οὐ γὰρ εἰκῇ τὴν μάχαιραν φορεῖ·
        θεοῦ γὰρ διάκονός ἐστιν ἔκδικος εἰς ὀργὴν τῷ τὸ κακὸν πράσσοντι.

διὸ ἀνάγκη ὑποτάσσεσθαι,
    οὐ μόνον διὰ τὴν ὀργὴν
    ἀλλὰ καὶ διὰ τὴν συνείδησιν.
διὰ τοῦτο γὰρ καὶ φόρους τελεῖτε·
    λειτουργοὶ γὰρ θεοῦ εἰσιν εἰς αὐτὸ τοῦτο προσκαρτεροῦντες.

ἀπόδοτε πᾶσιν τὰς ὀφειλάς,
    τῷ τὸν φόρον τὸν φόρον,
    τῷ τὸ τέλος τὸ τέλος,
    τῷ τὸν φόβον τὸν φόβον,
    τῷ τὴν τιμὴν τὴν τιμήν.

VERSE 1

Πᾶσα ψυχὴ ἐξουσίαις ὑπερεχούσαις ὑποτασσέσθω

Metzger (467) gives the UBS[5] reading an {A} rating based on what Schreiner describes as "superior manuscript support" (688; ℵ, A, B, D[c], 33). The alternate reading has mainly Western support (𝔓[46], D*), and Moo notes that the meaning is not significantly affected by either reading (790 n. 1). Asyndeton (R 444) and a shift to the third person mark a change of topic. Πᾶσα ψυχή ("every soul") is a Semiticism that designates the whole person (Moo 794). Longenecker (956) concludes that the phrase refers to "every Christian (in Rome)." Ἐξουσίαις designates beings who exercise authority; the dative is natural with ὑποτάσσω (cf. 8:7, 20; 10:3). Ὑπερεχούσαις (dat. pl. fem. of pres. act. ptc. of ὑπερέχω, "govern, have power over") is an adjectival participle; the verb denotes holding a position of authority (Moo 796 n. 23). Jewett notes that the phrase "governing authorities" encompasses a variety of imperial and local offices (788); according to Longenecker (959) the phrase refers to "governing authorities (of the empire's capital city)." Ὑποτασσέσθω (3 sg. pres. mid./pass. impv. of ὑποτάσσω, "put in subjection/submission") is a gnomic present (Wallace 535) and an imperative of command; the voice may be understood either as middle (NIV, "submit oneself"; cf. Dunn 760) or as passive (ESV, "be subject"; cf. Moo 797 n. 24). The verb denotes the recognition that a person holds a subordinate place in a hierarchy (Moo 797); Paul uses it in connection with a variety of relationships (1 Cor 14:32; 16:16; Eph 5:21, 24; Col 3:18; Titus 2:5, 9; 3:1).

οὐ γὰρ ἔστιν ἐξουσία εἰ μὴ ὑπὸ θεοῦ

The first reason (γάρ) to be subject to governing authorities is that they are divinely ordained. Εἰ μή ("except") is idiomatic (cf. Porter 209); ὑπό + genitive specifies the ultimate agent (Wallace 433). The concept of divinely appointed human authorities has OT roots (2 Sam 12:8; Jer 25:6–7; Dan 2:21, 37; 4:17, 25, 32; 5:21).

αἱ δὲ οὖσαι ὑπὸ θεοῦ τεταγμέναι εἰσίν

Δέ is connective ("and"); the substantival participle αἱ οὖσαι (nom. pl. fem. of pres. act. ptc. of εἰμί) is used redundantly (T 152). Τεταγμέναι (nom. pl. fem. of pf. pass. ptc. of τάσσω, "appoint") is a periphrastic participle; the perfect tense is intensive (Wallace 575). The verb describes the action of bringing about order by arranging (BDAG 991c); Cranfield suggests that the statement relates particularly to the Roman emperor and his representatives with whom the Roman church had to deal (663).

VERSE 2

ὥστε ὁ ἀντιτασσόμενος τῇ ἐξουσίᾳ τῇ τοῦ θεοῦ διαταγῇ ἀνθέστηκεν

The nature of divinely ordained authority has consequences (ὥστε): resistance to those authorities is actually resistance to God. The substantival participle ἀντιτασσόμενος (nom. sg. masc. of pres. mid. ptc. of ἀντιτάσσω, "oppose") is a gnomic present and a direct middle (R 807); the verb occurs only here in Paul and connotes resistance to duly constituted authority (Jewett 790). Τῇ ἐξουσίᾳ is a dative of disadvantage, and Cranfield suggests "to set oneself against" (663); the article is anaphoric. Τῇ διαταγῇ (dat. sg. fem. of διαταγή, -ῆς, ἡ, "ordinance") is the object of ἀνθίστημι; τοῦ θεοῦ is a subjective genitive (Wallace 114). Cranfield notes that διαταγή is rare (cf. Acts 7:53), occurs only once in the LXX, and focuses on the action of the subject (663 n. 4).

Ἀνθέστηκεν (3 sg. pf. act. indic. of ἀνθίστημι, "resist, oppose") is an intensive perfect that emphasizes the existing state of resistance (Moo 799 n. 36); the verb is virtually synonymous with ἀντιτάσσω (Jewett 790).

οἱ δὲ ἀνθεστηκότες ἑαυτοῖς κρίμα λήμψονται

Δέ is connective ("and"); οἱ ἀνθεστηκότες (nom. pl. masc. pf. act. ptc. of ἀνθίστημι) is a substantival participle; Dunn notes that the perfect tense denotes a "determined and established policy" (762). Ἑαυτοῖς is a dative of disadvantage (BDF §188.2; cf. NIV, "on themselves"). To "receive judgment" is Semitic (Dunn 762; cf. Mark 12:40); the placement of κρίμα is emphatic; λήμψονται (3 pl. fut. mid. indic. of λαμβάνω, "receive") is a predictive future and a deponent middle. Schreiner concludes that the judgment is inflicted by the divinely ordained human authorities rather than by God (683; contra Cranfield and Dunn).

VERSE 3

οἱ γὰρ ἄρχοντες οὐκ εἰσὶν φόβος τῷ ἀγαθῷ ἔργῳ ἀλλὰ τῷ κακῷ

The second reason (γάρ) to be subject to governing authorities is that they are rewarders of good and avengers of evil. Οἱ ἄρχοντες (nom. pl. masc. of ἄρχων, -οντος, ὁ, "ruler") describes someone who has administrative authority (BDAG 140d); in this context, it denotes human rulers in general (Dunn 763) and public officials in particular (Jewett 792). Φόβος refers to "that which arouses fear" rather than an emotional response (Dunn 763); the articles with ἔργῳ and κακῷ are generic (T 14, 22); the datives denote reference. The adjective ἀγαθῷ is in the first predicate position and, therefore, carries more emphasis than ἔργῳ; οὐκ . . . ἀλλά establishes a strong contrast between "good" and "evil"; NIV translates "[not] for those who do right, but for those who do wrong."

θέλεις δὲ μὴ φοβεῖσθαι τὴν ἐξουσίαν

Δέ is transitional ("now"); θέλεις (2 sg. pres. act. indic. of θέλω) is a progressive present; μή is natural with the complementary infinitive φοβεῖσθαι (pres. mid. inf. of dep. φοβέομαι); the article with ἐξουσίαν is anaphoric. The clause functions as the protasis of a condition (BDF §471.3); NJB translates "So, if you want to live with no fear of authority." Most EVV understand τὴν ἐξουσίαν as "the one in authority" (e.g., ESV).

τὸ ἀγαθὸν ποίει, καὶ ἕξεις ἔπαινον ἐξ αὐτῆς

The article with ἀγαθόν allows the adjective to function as a noun and is anaphoric; ποίει is imperative (2 sg. pres. act. impv.) rather than indicative; καί is connective; ἕξεις (2 sg. fut. act. indic. of ἔχω) is a predictive future. See 2:29 for ἔπαινος, which refers to public commendation (Dunn 763; cf. *TDNT* 2.586); the anarthrous noun is qualitative; ἐκ + genitive denotes source; the antecedent of αὐτῆς (gen. sg. fem.) is ἐξουσία in the preceding clause.

VERSE 4

θεοῦ γὰρ διάκονός ἐστιν σοὶ εἰς τὸ ἀγαθόν

The reason (γάρ) for the promise in verse 3 is that the one in authority is God's servant. The objective genitive θεοῦ (Wallace 119) is emphatic; διάκονος ("minister") describes one who serves as an intermediary in an action (BDAG 230c); in this context it denotes a civil official (Schreiner 684; cf. Esth 1:10; 2:2; 6:3). Σοί is a dative of advantage dependent on διάκονος (Moo 801 n. 52) and refers to the person who is doing good (Cranfield 666); εἰς τὸ ἀγαθόν states the purpose of God's minister, who is "working for your good" (NEB).

ἐὰν δὲ τὸ κακὸν ποιῇς, φοβοῦ

In contrast (δέ) to the positive purpose of the one in authority is that individual's negative role. Ἐάν . . . ποιῇς (2 sg. pres. act. subjunc. of ποιέω) establishes a third class condition; the article with κακόν is generic; φοβοῦ (2 sg. pres. mid. impv. of dep. φοβέομαι, "fear") is a deponent imperative of command (R 1019).

οὐ γὰρ εἰκῇ τὴν μάχαιραν φορεῖ

The government's role in punishing evil explains (γάρ) why the one who does evil should fear. The adverb εἰκῇ carries the idea of "without cause, in vain, to no avail, to no purpose" (Dunn 764); the article with μάχαιραν is generic (Wallace 229); the noun describes the military sword, and Jewett suggests that it was "the classic symbol for government coercion" (795). Φορεῖ (3 sg. pres. act. indic. of φορέω, "hold the power of") is "the frequentative of φέρω" (Dunn 764) and describes action that is customary or habitual (Jewett 795). Cranfield understands the statement to describe the government's possession of military power (667), while Schreiner understands it as the broader judicial function of the state, including capital punishment (684).

θεοῦ γὰρ διάκονός ἐστιν ἔκδικος εἰς ὀργὴν τῷ τὸ κακὸν πράσσοντι

The reason (γάρ) for the warning is, again, that the one in authority is God's servant. See the first line of this verse for θεοῦ διάκονος. Ἔκδικος, -ου, ὁ describes one who does justice so as to punish a wrong (BDAG 301b); Dunn (764) and Schreiner (685) suggest "avenger" (cf. 1 Thess 4:6). Εἰς ὀργήν denotes purpose (Cranfield 665); the dative of the substantival participle τῷ πράσσοντι (dat. sg. masc. of pres. act. ptc.) denotes disadvantage; see 1:32 for πράσσω; τὸ κακόν is the object of the participle. Schreiner concludes that the "wrath" is God's wrath exercised through the ruling authorities (685 n. 24); Longenecker views it as referring to punishment (cf. 965–66).

VERSE 5

διὸ ἀνάγκη ὑποτάσσεσθαι

Elsewhere, Paul uses the inferential conjunction διό ("therefore") to draw a conclusion in the middle of his argument (e.g., 1:24; 4:22); in this case, it introduces a summary of verses 1–4 (Moo 802). The verb ἐστιν is frequently omitted in impersonal constructions (BDF §127.2; cf. Matt 18:7; Heb 9:16, 23). Ἀνάγκη, -ης, ἡ describes a constraint that is inherent in the nature of things (BDAG 61a); Dunn concludes that it carries the idea of a divine necessity (765); Jewett suggests "indispensable" (796). Ὑποτάσσεσθαι (pres. pass. infin. of ὑποτάσσω) is an epexegetical infinitive; the present tense is gnomic; the passive voice echoes verse 1.

οὐ μόνον διὰ τὴν ὀργὴν ἀλλὰ καὶ διὰ τὴν συνείδησιν

See 1:32 for the stereotyped phrase οὐ μόνον . . . ἀλλὰ καί (cf. 4:16; 5:3, 11; 8:23; 9:10, 24); διά + accusative denotes cause (Cranfield 668). The first prepositional phrase summarizes verses 3–4 and the state's role as God's minister; see verse 4 for ὀργή, which Longenecker views as referring to "punishment" in this context (965–66); the article is anaphoric. The second phrase summarizes verses 1b–2 and the state's status as divinely ordained; the article functions as a personal pronoun (Jewett 796, "your conscience"); συνείδησις "signifies a sense of moral responsibility and obligation to conform to what is required" (Schreiner 685).

VERSE 6

διὰ τοῦτο γὰρ καὶ φόρους τελεῖτε

The sequence διὰ τοῦτο γάρ occurs nowhere else in the NT (Moo 804 n. 69). Διὰ τοῦτο ("because of this") is causal (cf. 4:16; 5:12) and retrospective (Cranfield 668; cf. 1:26), pointing back to the double reason in verse 5. Most EVV (e.g., NASB) understand γάρ as explanatory ("for"), although Paul's tendency to multiply conjunctions for emphasis (e.g., Phil 3:8; 1 Thess 4:8) suggests that γάρ might possibly be emphatic ("indeed"); καί is adjunctive ("also"). See verse 7 for φόρους (acc. pl. masc. of φόρος, -ου, ὁ, "tax, tribute"); τελεῖτε (2 pl. pres. act. indic. of τελέω, "fulfill, complete, pay") is indicative (Dunn 766), the present tense is customary.

λειτουργοὶ γὰρ θεοῦ εἰσιν εἰς αὐτὸ τοῦτο προσκαρτεροῦντες

Γάρ is causal and introduces a reason parallel to those in verse 4; λειτουργοί is placed emphatically; θεοῦ is an objective genitive; εἰσιν is used independently (Moo 805 n. 75). Λειτουργός, -οῦ, ὁ ("minister") is synonymous with διάκονος, refers to public service (Dunn 767), and carries a sense of solemnity and dignity (Cranfield 668). Εἰς αὐτὸ τοῦτο (ESV, "to this very thing") replaces the dative that more commonly accompanies προσκαρτερέω (Cranfield 669 n. 1; cf. 12:12); προσκαρτεροῦντες (nom. pl. masc.

of pres. act. ptc.) is an adjectival participle; NIV translates "who give their full time to governing."

VERSE 7

ἀπόδοτε πᾶσιν τὰς ὀφειλάς

Jewett notes the lack of a conjunction (asyndeton) and characterizes this verse as "a highly compressed gnomic saying that summarizes the basic contention of the passage" (193). The aorist imperative ἀπόδοτε commands the action as a whole; see 2:6 for ἀποδίδωμι. Πᾶσιν is the indirect object and can refer to "everyone, everywhere" or to every category of government official (Jewett 801); the latter seems more likely. The article accompanies the abstract noun ὀφειλάς (acc. pl. fem.); the noun describes a financial debt or obligation (BDAG 743a). NASB translates the command "Render to all what is due them." Cranfield notes the probable connection between this command and Jesus's statement in Mark 12:17 (cf. Matt 22:24; Luke 22:25).

τῷ τὸν φόρον τὸν φόρον, τῷ τὸ τέλος τὸ τέλος

The four specific obligations are elliptical (cf. BDF §481); ἀπόδοτε is understood from the preceding command; it is possible to supply something like ὀφειλόμενῳ as the indirect object in each instance (e.g., "To the one who is being owed tribute {pay} tribute."); the articles particularize the nouns (Porter 104). Schreiner (686) concludes that φόρος refers to direct "tribute" paid by subject nations and from which Roman citizens were exempt (cf. Luke 20:22; 23:2), while τέλος refers to indirect "tax" levied on goods and paid by all (cf. Matt 17:25). Longenecker suggests that φόρος refers to city taxes and τέλος to tolls and government revenues (966).

τῷ τὸν φόβον τὸν φόβον, τῷ τὴν τιμὴν τὴν τιμήν

Jewett (803) argues that φόβος refers to "respect" that acknowledges the jurisdiction of the king (Prov 24:21) and other government officials,while τιμή refers to "honor" that recognizes superior status and good performance (Philo, *Legat.* 10.140). Longenecker suggests that φόβος is a general term, while τιμή refers specifically to the city officials of Rome (966).

FOR FURTHER STUDY

74. Christians and Government (13:1)

Bammel, E. "Romans 13. Pages 365–83 in *Jesus and the Politics of His Day*. Edited by E. Bammel and C. F. D. Moule. Cambridge: Cambridge University Press, 1984.

Barrett, C. K. "The New Testament Doctrine of Church and State." Pages 1–19 in *New Testament Essays*. London: SPCK, 1972.

Borg, M. "A New Context for Romans 13." *NTS* (1972–73): 205–18.

Bruce, F. F. "Paul and 'the Powers that be.'" *BJRL* 66 (1983–84): 78–96.

Delling, G. *Röm 13:1–7 innerhalb der Briefe des Paulus*. Berlin: Evangelische Verlagsanstalt, 1962.
Dunn, J. D. G. "Romans 13:1–7—A Charter for Political Quietism?" *Ex Auditu* 2 (1986): 55–68.
Heiligenthal, R. "Strategien conformer Ethik im Neuen Testament am Beispiel von Röm 13:1–7." *NTS* 29 (1983): 55–61.
Käsemann, E. "Principles of the Interpretation of Romans 13." Pages 196–216 in *New Testament Questions of Today*. Translated by W. J. Montague. Philadelphia: Fortress, 1969.
Koenig, J. *Charismata: God's Gifts for God's People*. Philadelphia: Westminster, 1978.
McDonald, J. I. H. "Romans 13:1–7: A Test Case for New Testament Interpretation." *NTS* 35 (1989): 540–49.
Porter, S. E. "Romans 13:1–7 as Pauline Political Rhetoric." *FilNeot* 3 (1990): 115–39.
Stein, R. H. "The Argument of Romans 13:1–7." *NovT* 31 (1989): 325–43.
Tellbe, M. *Paul Between Synagogue and State: Christians, Jews, and Civic Authorities in 1 Thessalonians, Romans, and Philippians*. Stockholm: Almqvist and Wiksell, 2001.
Wright, N. T. "Paul's Gospel and Caesar's Empire." Pages 160–83 in *Paul and Politics*. Edited by R. A. Horsley. Harrisburg, PA: Trinity Press International, 2000.

HOMILETICAL SUGGESTIONS

The Christian and Government (13:1–7)

1. Command: Be subject to governing authorities (13:1a)
   a. First Reason: They are ordained by God (γάρ, 13:1b–2)
   b. Second Reason: They are rewarders of good and avengers of evil (γάρ, 13:3–4)
2. Conclusion: It is necessary to be subject (διό, 13:5)
   a. Explanation: They are the reason to pay taxes (διὰ τοῦτο, 13:6a)
   b. Reason: They are God's ministers (γάρ, 13:6b)
3. Categories: Four specific obligations (13:7)
   a. Tribute
   b. Tax
   c. Respect
   d. Honor

e. By Loving One Another (13:8–10)

STRUCTURE

Paul returns to the topic of love (cf. 12:9–10), using the verb ἀγαπάω four times and the noun ἀγάπη twice. The concise paragraph of three sentences begins with a command (13:8a) supported by a reason (13:8b). An explanation brings together commandments from Exodus 20:13–17 and Leviticus 19:18 (13:9). A concluding statement is framed by *inclusio* (13:10). Longenecker views this paragraph as explaining how the "love ethic" of 12:9–21 is fulfilled in the Mosaic law (978).

Μηδενὶ μηδὲν ὀφείλετε εἰ μὴ τὸ ἀλλήλους ἀγαπᾶν·
    ὁ γὰρ ἀγαπῶν τὸν ἕτερον νόμον πεπλήρωκεν.

τὸ γὰρ Οὐ μοιχεύσεις,
    Οὐ φονεύσεις,
    Οὐ κλέψεις,
    Οὐκ ἐπιθυμήσεις,
    καὶ εἴ τις ἑτέρα ἐντολή,
ἐν τῷ λόγῳ τούτῳ ἀνακεφαλαιοῦται
[ἐν τῷ] Ἀγαπήσεις τὸν πλησίον σου ὡς σεαυτόν.

ἡ ἀγάπη τῷ πλησίον κακὸν οὐκ ἐργάζεται·
πλήρωμα οὖν νόμου ἡ ἀγάπη.

VERSE 8

Μηδενὶ μηδὲν ὀφείλετε εἰ μὴ τὸ ἀλλήλους ἀγαπᾶν

The verb ὀφείλω serves as a link-word to τὰς ὀφειλάς in the preceding paragraph (Moo 810), although there is no conjunction to make the connection (asyndeton). The double negative μηδενὶ μηδέν is placed emphatically and intensifies the command (R 1173); the present imperative ὀφείλετε (2 pl. pres. act. impv. of ὀφείλω, "owe") commands a continuing action; the verb describes the state of being under obligation to meet moral expectations (BDAG 743b; cf. *TDNT* 5.559–61). Εἰ μή ("except") introduces a sub-category of condition (Porter 209); the article introduces a quotation (Moo 812 n. 9); see 12:5 for ἀλλήλους ("one another") and 8:28 for ἀγαπᾶν (pres. act. inf.). CSB translates as "Do not owe anyone anything, except to love one another." Schreiner believes the command applies primarily to other believers (691), while Cranfield (675) and Dunn (776) view it as all-embracing.*

ὁ γὰρ ἀγαπῶν τὸν ἕτερον νόμον πεπλήρωκεν

The reason (γάρ) for loving others is that doing so fulfills the law. The present tense substantival participle (nom. sg. masc. of pres. act. ptc. of ἀγαπάω) emphasizes continuing action; τὸν ἕτερον ("the other") is the object of the participle (Cranfield

675) and is equivalent to τὸν πλησίον ("the neighbor") in verse 9 (R 748); the article particularizes: "*each* man whom God presents to one as one's neighbor" (Dunn 776). Νόμον is the Mosaic law (Schreiner 692), as will become clear in the next verse, and the object of πεπλήρωκεν (3 sg. pf. act. indic. of πληρόω, "fulfill"). The perfect tense is gnomic (R 897; cf Porter 42); the verb carries the idea of performing something properly (Dunn 777).

VERSE 9

τὸ γὰρ Οὐ μοιχεύσεις, Οὐ φονεύσεις, Οὐ κλέψεις, Οὐκ ἐπιθυμήσεις

Commentators view the addition of οὐ ψευδομαρτυρήσεις (א) as an assimilation to Exodus 20:15–17 and Deuteronomy 5:19–21 (Cranfield 677 n. 2; Moo 810 n. 1, Schreiner 695). The patristic quotations that omit one or more of the commandments are most likely the result of *homoeoteleuton* (Metzger 467). The UBS[5] reading is strongly supported by 𝔓[46], A, B, D, and 33. Γάρ introduces an explanation of how loving others fulfills the law (Moo 813); the article introduces a quotation (T 182); the four prohibitions (cf. Exod 20:13–15, 17) use the future indicative of command, which Wallace describes as "quite emphatic" (452). The order of the first three commandments differs from Exodus 20 and Deuteronomy 5 but agrees with Luke's version of the rich young ruler's answer (18:20). See 2:22 for μοιχεύω, 2:21 for κλέπτω, and 7:7 for ἐπιθυμέω; φονεύω describes the act of committing murder (BDAG 1063c).

καὶ εἴ τις ἑτέρα ἐντολή

Paul adds (καί) a conditional qualifier (εἴ) that makes the scope of his explanation all-embracing (Dunn 778); ἐστιν is understood; τις ἑτέρα ἐντολή functions as a single phrase (ESV, "any other commandment"); see 7:8–13 for ἐντολή.

ἐν τῷ λόγῳ τούτῳ ἀνακεφαλαιοῦται

Ἐν τῷ λόγῳ τούτῳ denotes the impersonal means by which the action of the passive verb is accomplished ("by this word"); see 9:6, 9, 28 for the use of λόγος to refer to the OT. Ἀνακεφαλαιοῦται (3 sg. pres. pass. indic. of ἀνακεφαλαιόω, "sum up") is a perfective present; the verb describes the act of recapitulation (cf. Eph 1:20; *TDNT* 3.681–82); BDAG suggests the translation "is summed up completely" (65c).

[ἐν τῷ] Ἀγαπήσεις τὸν πλησίον σου ὡς σεαυτόν

Ἐν τῷ refers back to λόγῳ and introduces the quotation of Leviticus 19:18. Jewett notes that including ἐν τῷ is the more difficult reading because of the redundancy it creates (804 n. f).; Ἀγαπήσεις (2 sg. fut. act. indic. of ἀγαπάω) is a future of command; τὸν πλησίον σου ("your neighbor") describes a fellow human being (BDAG 830b); ὡς is comparative; see 2:1 for the reflexive pronoun σεαυτόν (acc. sg. masc.).

VERSE 10

ἡ ἀγάπη τῷ πλησίον κακὸν οὐκ ἐργάζεται

The placement of ἡ ἀγάπη is emphatic (Jewett 814), and the article accompanies the abstract noun; the dative article allows the preposition πλησίον ("near") to function as the indirect object; the anarthrous direct object κακόν ("evil") is qualitative; ἐργάζεται (3 sg. pres. mid. indic. of dep. ἐργάζομαι) is a gnomic present and a deponent middle.

πλήρωμα οὖν νόμου ἡ ἀγάπη

The inferential conjunction οὖν ("therefore") introduces Paul's conclusion to the paragraph (Cranfield 678). See 11:12, 25 for πλήρωμα; most commentators agree that the sense in this context is "fulfilling" (Dunn 786; Moo 817; Schreiner 693); νόμου is an objective genitive (NLT, "love fulfills the requirements of God's law"); ἡ ἀγάπη forms an *inclusio* with the first word in the verse.

FOR FURTHER STUDY

75. Love of Neighbor (13:10)

Falkenroth, U. *NIDNTT* 1.258–59.
Furnish, V. P. *The Love Command in the New Testament*. Nashville: Abingdon, 1972.
Greeven, H., and J. Fichtner. *TDNT* 6.317–18.
McKnight, S. *EDBT* 556–57.
________. *The Jesus Creed: Loving God, Loving Others*. Brewster, MA: Paraclete, 2004.
Mohrlang, R. *DPL* 575–78.
Montefiore, H. W. "Thou Shalt Love Thy Neighbour as Thyself." *NovT* 5 (1902): 157–70.
Perkins, P. *Love Commands in the New Testament*. New York: Paulist, 1982.
Piper, J. *Love Your Enemies: Jesus' Love Command in the Synoptic Gospels and the Early Christian Paraenesis*. Reprint edition. Wheaton, IL: Crossway, 2012.

HOMILETICAL SUGGESTIONS

Love and the Law (13:8–10)

1. Command: Owe no one anything except love (13:8a)
   a. Reason: Loving your neighbor fulfills the law (γάρ, 13:8b)
2. Explanation: The command to love your neighbor summarizes the law (γάρ, 13:9)
   a. Exodus 20:13–15, 17
   b. Leviticus 19:18
3. Conclusion: Because love does no evil to your neighbor, it fulfills the law (οὖν, 13:10)

f. By Living in Light of Jesus's Return (13:11–14)

STRUCTURE

Christ's return is the focus of Paul's final paragraph on practicing God's righteousness in daily living. He begins with a call to action (13:11a) supported by a reminder of the nearness of "the day" (13:11b–12a). He then offers three specific responses to his call to action (13:12b–14). Jewett adopts the suggestion that verses 11b–12 (ὥρα . . . ἤγγικεν) are an early Christian hymn (817). Longenecker views this paragraph as explaining how the ethic of 12:9–12 is lived out in "this present age" (978).

Καὶ τοῦτο εἰδότες τὸν καιρόν,
ὅτι ὥρα ἤδη ὑμᾶς ἐξ ὕπνου ἐγερθῆναι,
    νῦν γὰρ ἐγγύτερον ἡμῶν ἡ σωτηρία ἢ ὅτε ἐπιστεύσαμεν.
    ἡ νὺξ προέκοψεν, ἡ δὲ ἡμέρα ἤγγικεν.

ἀποθώμεθα οὖν τὰ ἔργα τοῦ σκότους,
ἐνδυσώμεθα [δὲ] τὰ ὅπλα τοῦ φωτός.

ὡς ἐν ἡμέρᾳ εὐσχημόνως περιπατήσωμεν,
    μὴ κώμοις καὶ μέθαις,
    μὴ κοίταις καὶ ἀσελγείαις,
    μὴ ἔριδι καὶ ζήλῳ.

ἀλλ' ἐνδύσασθε τὸν κύριον Ἰησοῦν Χριστὸν
καὶ τῆς σαρκὸς πρόνοιαν μὴ ποιεῖσθε εἰς ἐπιθυμίας.

VERSE 11

Καὶ τοῦτο εἰδότες τὸν καιρόν

Καὶ τοῦτο has prompted several explanations. Robertson (1134) and Jewett (818) suggest adding the imperative ποιεῖτε (cf. NASB, NET); BDF suggests adding the indicative λέγω (§480.5); Schreiner sees τοῦτο as gathering up all of 12:1–13:10 (697). Wallace's argument (335) that the phrase is adverbial with no antecedent for τοῦτο ("and especially") is similar to Cranfield's conclusion that it is a classical idiom "serving to introduce an additional circumstance heightening the force of what has been said" (680). The independent participle εἰδότες (nom. pl. masc. of pf. act. ptc. of οἶδα) is a perfect tense with present force (cf. Wallace 579) and functions as an indicative (ESV, "you know the time"; cf. Jewett 818). See 3:26 and 8:18 for the eschatological force of καιρός.

ὅτι ὥρα ἤδη ὑμᾶς ἐξ ὕπνου ἐγερθῆναι

The vowel exchange between ὑμᾶς (א*, A, B) and ἡμᾶς (𝔓[46], א[c], D, 33) is common (Moo 817 n. 1). Metzger gives ὑμᾶς a {B} rating (467), and most commentators view ἡμᾶς as a change to parallel ἡμῶν in the second line of the verse (e.g., Cranfield 680 n.

2; Schreiner 701; contra Jewett 816 n. a). Ὅτι ("that") explains τὸν καιρόν; ὥρα is also eschatological (Moo 821 n. 23), especially in John's writings (John 4:23; 5:25; 12:34; 1 John 2:18; Rev 3:3, 10); ἤδη ("already") adds a sense of urgency (Dunn 785) and is best taken with ὥρα (Moo 820 n. 17); Cranfield suggests "it is high time" (681). Ὑμᾶς is the subject of the infinitive; ἐξ ὕπνου ("from sleep") denotes separation; ἐγερθῆναι (aor. pass. inf. of ἐγείρω) is a constative aorist and a divine passive; the infinitive stands in apposition to ὥρα (R 1059). Paul uses the metaphor of rising from sleep elsewhere in Ephesians 5:14 and 1 Thessalonians 5:6–8; Cranfield writes that sleep describes a state "which is altogether opposed to that of readiness for the imminent crisis" (681).

νῦν γὰρ ἐγγύτερον ἡμῶν ἡ σωτηρία ἢ ὅτε ἐπιστεύσαμεν

The reason (γάρ) for rising from sleep is the nearness of our ultimate salvation. Νῦν ("now") is eschatological (cf. 3:21; 5:9); ἐγγύτερον is a comparative adjective (acc. sg. neut. of ἐγγύς, "near") used as an adverb (R 298). Ἡμῶν is best taken with σωτηρία (Dunn 787; contra Cranfield 681), which refers to future salvation as the completion of God's work at the time of Christ's return (Moo 822; Schreiner 697). Ἤ is comparative (R 666; "than"); ὅτε is temporal ("when"); ἐπιστεύσαμεν (1 pl. aor. act. indic. of πιστεύω) is an ingressive aorist (Schreiner 698) that highlights the initial act of commitment (Dunn 786).

VERSE 12

ἡ νὺξ προέκοψεν, ἡ δὲ ἡμέρα ἤγγικεν

Ἡ νύξ ("night") describes a time that contrasts with the time of eschatological fulfillment (BDAG 682d); προέκοψεν (3 sg. aor. act. indic. of προκόπτω, "advance") is a proleptic aorist that NJB translates as "is nearly over"; δέ is connective ("and"); see 2:5, 16 for ἡ ἡμέρα ("the day"); ἤγγικεν (3 sg. pf. act. indic. of ἐγγίζω, "draw near") is a perfect with present force that NASB translates as "is near." The contrast between "night" and "day" occurs elsewhere in Paul (2 Cor 6:14; Eph 5:8; 1 Thess 5:4–5), with the former referring to the present age and the latter to the coming age (cf. Cranfield 682; Schreiner 698). Moo provides both Paul's use of "the day" and the OT background of "the day of the Lord" (821 n. 20).

ἀποθώμεθα οὖν τὰ ἔργα τοῦ σκότους

𝔓[46] and D* read ἀποβαλώμεθα instead of ἀποθώμεθα (ℵ, A, B, C, D[c], 33). The latter reading better fits Paul's style (cf. Eph 4:22, 25; Col 3:8). Ἀποβαλώμεθα occurs nowhere else in Paul (Moo 818 n. 2) and, therefore, is the more difficult reading (Cranfield 685 n. 3; Jewett 816 n. b). As Dunn notes, "the sense is hardly affected" (784 n. b). The nearness of "the day" calls for three responses (οὖν), the first of which uses the imagery of "putting off" and "putting on" (cf. Eph 4:22, 24; Col 3:8, 12). Ἀποθώμεθα (1 pl. aor. mid. subjunc. of ἀποτίθημι, "lay aside") is a constative aorist that views the action as a whole, an indirect middle (cf. Wallace 417), and a hortatory subjunctive (Wallace 465). Τὰ ἔργα is the direct object; τοῦ σκότους (gen. sg. neut.) is a descriptive genitive ("the works that are characteristic of the darkness").

ἐνδυσώμεθα [δὲ] τὰ ὅπλα τοῦ φωτός

Δέ is connective ("and"); ἐνδυσώμεθα (1 pl. aor. mid. subjunc. of ἐνδύω, "put on") is a constative aorist, an indirect middle, and a hortatory subjunctive. Τὰ ὅπλα carries the sense of "armor" (Jewett 822; cf. ESV) or "weapons" (Moo 824 n. 37; cf. GNB); τοῦ φωτός (gen. sg. neut.) is a descriptive genitive ("the weapons that are characteristic of the light").

VERSE 13

ὡς ἐν ἡμέρᾳ εὐσχημόνως περιπατήσωμεν

Cranfield discusses four suggested interpretations of ὡς ἐν ἡμέρᾳ (686). EVV translate the phrase as manner ("as in the day/daylight"),* although BDF (§425.4), Robertson (1140), and Turner (159) all suggest that a participle should be understood. Turner suggests ὡς ἡμεράς οὔσης, which he analyzes as temporal (243). Ἡμέρᾳ is definite although anarthrous (R 792) and is best understood as referring to the eschatological "day" in the preceding verse (Moo 824). The idea reflects Paul's "already/not yet" perspective (Schreiner 700), and Käsemann suggests "[while] you stand under the sign of the new day" (363). Paul uses the adverb εὐσχημόνως elsewhere in 1 Corinthians 14:40 and 1 Thessalonians 4:12; it describes conduct that is decent, proper, and presentable in responsible society (Dunn 789); περιπατήσωμεν (1 pl. aor. act. subjunc. of περιπατέω, "walk") is an ingressive aorist (R 850) that contrasts with previous conduct (BDF §337.1) and a hortatory subjunctive.

μὴ κώμοις καὶ μέθαις, μὴ κοίταις καὶ ἀσελγείαις, μὴ ἔριδι καὶ ζήλῳ

This "mini-vice list" (Schreiner 699) consists of three paired nouns that are best understood as instances of hendiadys. The datives denote manner; the plurals indicate frequency (Schreiner 699). Κῶμος, -ου, ὁ describes excessive carousing; μέθη, -ης, ἡ describes drunkenness; the composite idea may be understood as "drunken orgies" (Dunn 789). Κοίτη, -ης, ἡ refers to sexual impurity; ἀσέλγεια, -ας, ἡ describes a lack of self-restraint that results in excess (BDAG 141d); the composite idea may be understood as "unrestrained promiscuity." Ἔρις, -ιδος, ἡ describes quarrels (cf. 1:29); ζῆλος, -ου, ὁ describes jealousy (cf. 10:2); the composite idea may be understood as "jealous strife" (Cranfield 687).

VERSE 14

ἀλλ' ἐνδύσασθε τὸν κύριον Ἰησοῦν Χριστόν

Ἀλλά draws a strong contrast with the preceding list (Jewett 827); ἐνδύσασθε (2 pl. aor. mid. impv. of ἐνδύω) is a constative aorist, an indirect middle, and an imperative of command (NLT, "clothe yourselves with"); Ἰησοῦν Χριστόν stands in apposition to τὸν κύριον (Wallace 199). Paul uses the title "Lord Jesus" three times (Rom 10:9; 2 Cor 4:14; Phlm 5) and "Lord Jesus Christ" twice (Rom 13:14; Phil 3:20). Moo suggests that Paul's command is to "embrace Christ in such a way that his character is manifest in all we do and say" (825).

καὶ τῆς σαρκὸς πρόνοιαν μὴ ποιεῖσθε εἰς ἐπιθυμίας

Τῆς σαρκός is an objective genitive and is moved forward for emphasis; πρόνοια, -ας, ἡ suggests planning, foresight, or provision (BDAG 873a); σάρξ describes the principle and power of life in this age (cf. 7:5). Μή makes it clear that ποιεῖσθε is an imperative; the middle voice is customary with πρόνοια (Moo 826 n. 52); εἰς ἐπιθυμίας denotes purpose (ESV, "to gratify its desires"); see 1:24 for ἐπιθυμία.

FOR FURTHER STUDY

76. Day of the Lord (13:12)

Baird, W. "Pauline Eschatology in Hermeneutical Perspective." *NTS* 17 (1970–71): 314–27.

Beker, J. C. "Paul and Jewish Apocalyptic Eschatology." Pages 169–90 in *Apocalyptic and the New Testament: Essays in Honor of J. Louis Martyn*. Edited by J. Marcus and M. L. Soards. Sheffield: Academic Press, 1989.

Blaising, C. A. "The Day of the Lord: Theme and Pattern in Biblical Theology." *BSac* 169 (2012): 3–19.

Brauman G., and C. Brown. *NIDNTT* 2.887–91.

Everson, A. J. *IDBSup* 209–10.

Keck, L. "Paul and Apocalyptic Theology." *Int* 38 (1984): 229–41.

Kreitzer, L. J. *DPL* 253–69.

Martens, E. A. *EDBT* 146–49.

von Rad, G. "The Origin on the Concept of the Day of Yahweh." *Journal of Semitic Studies* 4 (1959): 97–108.

________ and G. Delling. *TDNT* 2.943–53.

Vos, G. *The Pauline Eschatology*. Princeton: University Press, 1930.

HOMILETICAL SUGGESTIONS

Waiting for the Day of the Lord (13:11–14)

1. Call to Action: Rise from sleep (13:11a)
   a. Reason: The nearness of "the day" (γάρ, 13:11b–12a)
2. Implications (οὖν, 13:12b–14)
   a. First Response: Put on the weapons of light (13:12b)
   b. Second Response: Walk properly (13:13)
   c. Third Response: Make no provision for the flesh (13:14)

2. God's Righteousness Is Practiced in Christian Liberty (14:1–15:13)

a. By Accepting One Another (14:1–12)

STRUCTURE

Paul moves to the next major aspect of practicing God's righteousness by relating it to the topic of Christian liberty (14:1–15:13). Longenecker concludes that the discussion in 14:1–15:15 addresses issues specific to the congregations in Rome, while 12:1–13:14 addresses more general issues (995). The first paragraph forms an A-B-A′ structure in which 14:1–3 (A) and 14:10–12 (A′) are linked by the verbs ἐξουθενέω and κρίνω and frame the central panel of 14:4–9 (B). The opening admonition (14:1–3) is further framed by an inclusion using προσλαμβάνω. The central panel (14:4–9) provides four guiding principles for accepting one another. The closing section (14:10–12) draws a conclusion (ἄρα οὖν) that includes OT support (Isa 45:23).

Τὸν δὲ ἀσθενοῦντα τῇ πίστει προσλαμβάνεσθε, μὴ εἰς διακρίσεις διαλογισμῶν.

ὃς μὲν πιστεύει φαγεῖν πάντα,
ὁ δὲ ἀσθενῶν λάχανα ἐσθίει.
ὁ ἐσθίων τὸν μὴ ἐσθίοντα μὴ ἐξουθενείτω,
ὁ δὲ μὴ ἐσθίων τὸν ἐσθίοντα μὴ κρινέτω,
ὁ θεὸς γὰρ αὐτὸν προσελάβετο.

σὺ τίς εἶ ὁ κρίνων ἀλλότριον οἰκέτην;
τῷ ἰδίῳ κυρίῳ στήκει ἢ πίπτει·
σταθήσεται δέ, δυνατεῖ γὰρ ὁ κύριος στῆσαι αὐτόν.

ὃς μὲν [γὰρ] κρίνει ἡμέραν παρ' ἡμέραν,
ὃς δὲ κρίνει πᾶσαν ἡμέραν·
ἕκαστος ἐν τῷ ἰδίῳ νοῒ πληροφορείσθω.

ὁ φρονῶν τὴν ἡμέραν κυρίῳ φρονεῖ·
καὶ ὁ ἐσθίων κυρίῳ ἐσθίει, εὐχαριστεῖ γὰρ τῷ θεῷ·
καὶ ὁ μὴ ἐσθίων κυρίῳ οὐκ ἐσθίει καὶ εὐχαριστεῖ τῷ θεῷ.

οὐδεὶς γὰρ ἡμῶν ἑαυτῷ ζῇ καὶ οὐδεὶς ἑαυτῷ ἀποθνῄσκει·
ἐάν τε γὰρ ζῶμεν, τῷ κυρίῳ ζῶμεν, ἐάν τε ἀποθνῄσκωμεν, τῷ κυρίῳ ἀποθνῄσκομεν.
ἐάν τε οὖν ζῶμεν ἐάν τε ἀποθνῄσκωμεν, τοῦ κυρίου ἐσμέν.
εἰς τοῦτο γὰρ Χριστὸς ἀπέθανεν καὶ ἔζησεν, ἵνα καὶ νεκρῶν καὶ ζώντων κυριεύσῃ.

σὺ δὲ τί κρίνεις τὸν ἀδελφόν σου;
ἢ καὶ σὺ τί ἐξουθενεῖς τὸν ἀδελφόν σου;
πάντες γὰρ παραστησόμεθα τῷ βήματι τοῦ θεοῦ,
γέγραπται γάρ, Ζῶ ἐγώ, λέγει κύριος,
ὅτι ἐμοὶ κάμψει πᾶν γόνυ

καὶ πᾶσα γλῶσσα ἐξομολογήσεται τῷ θεῷ.

ἄρα [οὖν] ἕκαστος ἡμῶν περὶ ἑαυτοῦ λόγον δώσει [τῷ θεῷ].

VERSE 1

Τὸν δὲ ἀσθενοῦντα τῇ πίστει προσλαμβάνεσθε

Paul transitions (δέ) to a new topic with a command to "accept the one who is weak in faith" (NASB). Commentators have debated at great length both the identity of the "weak" and the "strong" and the nature of the problem Paul is addressing. Cranfield sets out six possible interpretations and concludes that the parties held opposing positions on the role of obedience to the Jewish ceremonial law (690–98). Moo concurs and specifically identifies the two groups as Jewish ("weak") and Gentile ("strong") Christians (826–33). The substantival participle ἀσθενοῦντα (acc. sg. masc. of pres. act. ptc. of ἀσθενέω, "be weak") is emphatic; the article is generic (T 22); see 4:19 for ἀσθενέω. Jewett suggests that the verb describes someone who is "excessively observant in a religion" and could include ascetics in pagan religions (834–35). Τῇ πίστει is most likely a dative of reference (Moo 835 n. 36); the article points out faith that is well known. Cranfield argues at some length that "faith" throughout the section refers to "the assurance that one is permitted by one's faith to do some particular thing" (697–98). Moo notes the parallel to 1 Corinthians 8–10, where Paul uses "conscience" instead of "faith" (836 n. 43). Schreiner, however, concludes that there is no reason to deviate from the usual idea of saving faith (cf. 4:19) and suggests that the weak believed a person would be a better Christian if he/she observed the Jewish ceremonial laws (712; cf. Dunn 798). Προσλαμβάνεσθε (2 pl. pres. mid. impv. of προσλαμβάνω, "welcome, receive") is a gnomic present, an indirect middle, and an imperative of command. LXX uses the verb to describe God's gracious acceptance of human beings (1 Sam 12:22; Ps 17:17; 26:10; 64:4; 72:24); Paul uses it elsewhere to describe the act of welcoming someone into a circle of acquaintances and treating that person as a brother or sister (Phlm 17; cf. Jewett 835).

μὴ εἰς διακρίσεις διαλογισμῶν

Paul qualifies his command with the phrase "not for judging scruples" (ASV; cf. Cranfield 700). Εἰς + accusative indicates purpose, and the genitive of διαλογισμῶν is objective (Moo 836 n. 44 and 45). Διάκρισις, -εως, ἡ describes the act of engaging in verbal conflict because of differing viewpoints (BDAG 231d); see for 1:21 for διαλογισμός, -οῦ, ὁ (cf. Phil 2:14; 1 Tim 2:8). Jewett suggests "disputes over opinions" (836). Dunn describes Paul's pastoral concern in this way: "that newcomers should not be subjected to demanding discussion about their common faith and its outworking . . . and that the majority should not seek to impose their views and practice" (798; cf. Schreiner 716).

VERSE 2

ὃς μὲν πιστεύει φαγεῖν πάντα

Paul sets the theme for his extended instructions by raising a specific instance of differing practices (v. 2) and following it with a pair of specific prohibitions related to those practices (v. 3). The correlative conjunctions (μέν . . . δέ) establish two contrasting groups; the more common NT construction occurs with a definite article (ὁ μέν; cf. R 695); the relative pronoun (ὅς) incorporates an embedded demonstrative ("the one who"). Πιστεύει (3 sg. pres. act. indic. of πιστεύω) is a gnomic present; see verse 1 for the discussion of "faith/believe." Φαγεῖν (aor. act. inf. of ἐσθίω, "eat") is the direct object (T 137); πάντα (acc. pl. neut.) is the object of the infinitive. On the basis of Acts 15:11, Jewett suggests the gloss "believes that it is legitimate to eat all things" (837).

ὁ δὲ ἀσθενῶν λάχανα ἐσθίει

The article allows the participle ἀσθενῶν (nom. sg. masc. of pres. act. ptc. of ἀσθενέω) to function substantivally ("the one who is weak"); see 4:19 for ἀσθενέω. Λάχανον, -ου, ὁ refers to edible green herbs (BDAG 587c); ἐσθίει (3 sg. pres. act. indic. of ἐσθίω) is a gnomic present. Jewett provides background on vegetarianism and argues that both positions (omnivore and vegetarian) are hyperbole (837–38); Dunn describes Jewish dietary rules (800–801).

VERSE 3

ὁ ἐσθίων τὸν μὴ ἐσθίοντα μὴ ἐξουθενείτω

The substantival participle ὁ ἐσθίων (nom. sg. masc. of pres. act. ptc. of ἐσθίω) functions as the subject ("the one who is eating"); τὸν μὴ ἐσθίοντα (acc. sg. masc. of pres. act. ptc.) functions as the direct object ("the one who is not eating"); both present tenses are gnomic. Ἐξουθενείτω (3 sg. pres. act. impv. of ἐξουθενέω, "despise") is an imperative of command and a gnomic present; Wallace suggests that, as a third person imperative, it would best be translated as "must not despise" (486). Ἐξουθενέω describes the act of showing by attitude or manner of treatment that someone has no merit or worth (BDAG 352b).

ὁ δὲ μὴ ἐσθίων τὸν ἐσθίοντα μὴ κρινέτω

Δέ is connective ("and"); the negatives are reversed ("the one who is not eating . . . the one who is eating"); the grammar of the participles is identical to the previous line. Κρινέτω (3 sg. pres. act. impv. of κρίνω, "judge") is an imperative of command and a gnomic present. The verb carries the nuance of "censor" in this context (Cranfield 702); Paul uses it with a variety of nuances throughout chapter 14 (cf. Moo 838 n. 51).

ὁ θεὸς γὰρ αὐτὸν προσελάβετο

The reason (γάρ) believers should neither despise nor condemn one another (cf. 14:1) is that God has already accepted both the weak and the strong. The article with θεός is monadic. Dunn believes αὐτόν refers to the weak (803); Moo believes it refers to the strong (839 n. 53); Jewett's conclusion that it refers to both groups is most likely correct (841). Προσελάβετο (3 sg. aor. mid. indic. of προσλαμβάνω) is a constative aorist and an indirect middle (R 810). The verb forms an *inclusio* with 14:1 to round off the first panel of the paragraph.

VERSE 4

σὺ τίς εἶ ὁ κρίνων ἀλλότριον οἰκέτην;

Σὺ τίς εἶ ("Who are you?") is "very emphatic" (R 678); Jewett notes that the question has its roots in diatribe and may be viewed as a "put-down question" (841 n. 113; cf. 9:20). The articular participle ὁ κρίνων (nom. sg. masc. of pres. act. ptc. of κρίνω) depends on σύ (T 153) and is equivalent to a relative clause (BDF §412.5); the present tense is customary. The adjective ἀλλότριος, -α, -ον describes something that belongs to someone else (BDAG 47c); it is a more emphatic form and a natural antonym to ἴδιος (Moo 839 n. 58); it refers to Christ rather than to a human master (Cranfield 702 n. 3). Οἰκέτης, -ου, ὁ should be understood more broadly than simply a household slave. Jewett concludes that it can describe all the members of a typical household, including children, house slaves, freed persons, clients, and spouses (842; cf. Eph 2:19).

τῷ ἰδίῳ κυρίῳ στήκει ἢ πίπτει

Placing τῷ ἰδίῳ κυρίῳ at the beginning of the clause gives it emphasis; ἰδίῳ (dat. sg. masc. of ἴδιος, -α, -ον, "one's own") is in the first attributive position and has greater emphasis than κυρίῳ, which refers to Christ. The dative of κυρίῳ may be means ("by his own master's judgment," Barrett 258), advantage ("to his own master's benefit," R 539; T 238; BDF §188.2), or reference ("with reference to his own master," Dunn 804; Jewett 842; Moo 840 n. 59; Schreiner 718 n. 14); the third is most likely. Στήκει (3 sg. pres. act. indic. of στήκω, "stand") is a gnomic present, as is πίπτει (3 sg. pres. act. indic. of πίπτω, "fall"); ἤ is disjunctive ("or"). "Standing" and "falling" are best understood as referring to persevering and falling away resulting in eschatological acceptance and judgment (Cranfield 703 n. 5; Jewett 843; Schreiner 719).

σταθήσεται δέ, δυνατεῖ γὰρ ὁ κύριος στῆσαι αὐτόν

Δέ is continuative ("and"); σταθήσεται (3 sg. fut. pass. indic. of ἵστημι, "stand") is a gnomic future and a passive with active meaning ("he will stand"; cf. T 57; Cranfield 703; Dunn 804; contra Jewett 843). The reason (γάρ) the individual will stand resides in Christ's ability (3 sg. pres. act. indic. of δυνατέω, "be able") to cause him or her (αὐτόν) to stand (aor. act. inf. of ἵστημι). Κύριος has strong manuscript support ($\mathfrak{P}^{46}$, ℵ, A, B, C), while θεός is most likely influenced by verse 3 (Metzger 468).

VERSE 5

ὃς μὲν [γὰρ] κρίνει ἡμέραν παρ' ἡμέραν

Manuscript evidence is divided on whether to include γάρ, with 𝔓[46], ℵ[c], B, and 33 omitting the conjunction, while ℵ* and A include it. The former reading is shorter, but the latter is more difficult (cf. Schreiner 724). Moo (833 n. 27) and Schreiner (724) choose to include the conjunction;* Cranfield (704), Dunn (796 n. d), and Jewett (830 n. f) choose to omit it. Metzger gives it a {C} rating (468), and UBS[5] includes it in brackets to reflect the divided internal and external evidence. Moo (842 n. 67) and Schreiner (724) suggest that γάρ has a continuative sense; EVV leave it untranslated (e.g., NIV, ESV). The correlative combination ὃς μέν . . . ὃς δέ establishes another contrast that CEV translates "one person . . . another person." Κρίνει is a gnomic present and carries the nuance "prefer" (BDAG 567d; cf. Cranfield 704 n. 5; Jewett 844). Both occurrences of ἡμέραν ("day") are indefinite; παρά + accusative is comparative ("more than," Harris 172; cf. R 616).

ὃς δὲ κρίνει πᾶσαν ἡμέραν

The phrase ὃς δέ introduces the second half of the contrast; see the preceding line for κρίνει; πᾶσαν ἡμέραν ("every day") is the direct object. The sentence is elliptical; Moo supplies "to be the same" (842 n. 70). Dunn provides background on Jewish feast days (805); Cranfield concludes that the discussion focuses on days of the OT ceremonial law (705); Moo (842) and Schreiner (715) argue that the focus is the Jewish Sabbath; Jewett views the discussion as generic, perhaps related to several issues (844). It is difficult to be precise on the identity of the "day" in question, but the difference in practice is clear.

ἕκαστος ἐν τῷ ἰδίῳ νοῒ πληροφορείσθω

Ἕκαστος ("each one") applies the argument to each member of the congregation (Cranfield 705). Ἐν + dative is local; ἰδίῳ (dat. sg. masc.) is equivalent to ἑαυτῷ (R 692); placing it in the first attributive position gives it more emphasis than νοΐ (dat. sg. masc. of νοῦς, νοός, ὁ, "mind"). Πληροφορείσθω (3 sg. pres. pass. impv. of πληροφορέω, "convince fully") is a gnomic present, a passive with no agency implied, and an imperative of command ("must be fully convinced," NASB); see 4:21 for πληροφορέω. Wallace notes that a third person command "is stronger than a mere option, engaging the volition and placing a requirement on the individual" (486 n. 97).

VERSE 6

ὁ φρονῶν τὴν ἡμέραν κυρίῳ φρονεῖ

Paul next goes behind the differing practices to address the common motivation: both groups are characterized by their focus on Christ and their attitude of thanksgiving. The substantival participle ὁ φρονῶν (nom. sg. masc. of pres. act. ptc. of φρονέω) is a gnomic present; φρονέω has the sense of "be concerned about" (Moo 843). The article with ἡμέραν is anaphoric; κυρίῳ is a dative of reference (Jewett 846); φρονεῖ (3 sg. pres. act. indic. of φρονέω is also a gnomic present.

καὶ ὁ ἐσθίων κυρίῳ ἐσθίει, εὐχαριστεῖ γὰρ τῷ θεῷ

Καί is continuative; ὁ ἐσθίων functions as the subject; κυρίῳ is a dative of reference; both ἐσθίων and ἐσθίει are gnomic presents. The explanation (γάρ) for the practice of observing days and eating more than vegetables lies in the motivation of giving thanks (εὐχαριστεῖ); τῷ θεῷ is a dative of direct object, reflecting personal relationship (cf. Wallace 171–72).

καὶ ὁ μὴ ἐσθίων κυρίῳ οὐκ ἐσθίει καὶ εὐχαριστεῖ τῷ θεῷ

The first occurrence of καί is continuative ("and"); the second is equivalent to "also" (Jewett 847). Μή negates the participle; οὐκ negates the indicative. The remainder of the grammar in this line is identical to the preceding line.

VERSE 7

οὐδεὶς γὰρ ἡμῶν ἑαυτῷ ζῇ καὶ οὐδεὶς ἑαυτῷ ἀποθνῄσκει

Jewett suggests that verses 7–9 constitute a formal syllogism (847). Together, the verses elaborate (γάρ) on what it means to do all things "to the Lord" (Schreiner 721). The genitive ἡμῶν is partitive ("no one of us"; cf. Wallace 85); Cranfield notes that the reference is to Christians in particular rather than to human beings in general (707). Dunn notes that to "live for oneself" (ἑαυτῷ ζῇ) is to live selfishly (807; cf. Cranfield 707 n. 3). Both ζῇ (3 sg. pres. act. indic. of ζάω, "live") and ἀποθνῄσκει (3 sg. pres. act. indic. of ἀποθνῄσκω, "die") are gnomic presents, since the statement sets forth a general maxim.

VERSE 8

ἐάν τε γὰρ ζῶμεν, τῷ κυρίῳ ζῶμεν

Verse 8 explains (γάρ) why no Christian lives or dies "for him/herself" (Moo 844). 'Εάν + subjunctive introduces a third class condition; τέ (untranslated) is the first of four occurrences that links the lines in this verse and establishes a "somewhat closer link" than καί (R 1179); τῷ κυρίῳ is a dative of reference. The first occurrence of ζάω is subjunctive (1 pl. pres. act. subjunc.); the second is indicative (1 pl. pres. act. indic.).

ἐάν τε ἀποθνῄσκωμεν, τῷ κυρίῳ ἀποθνῄσκομεν

'Εάν + subjunctive introduces another third class condition; τέ continues the connection between lines; τῷ κυρίῳ is a dative of reference. The first occurrence of ἀποθνῄσκω is subjunctive (1 pl. pres. act. subjunc.); the second is indicative (1 pl. pres. act. indic.).

ἐάν τε οὖν ζῶμεν ἐάν τε ἀποθνῄσκωμεν, τοῦ κυρίου ἐσμέν

Οὖν ("therefore") summarizes the preceding explanation; ἐάν τε . . . ἐάν τε is equivalent to εἴτε . . . εἴτε ("whether . . . or"; cf. R 1189). Τοῦ κυρίου refers to Christ (Moo 845 n. 86) and is moved forward for emphasis; the possessive genitive highlights the believer's total possession by and union with Christ (Moo 844).

VERSE 9

εἰς τοῦτο γὰρ Χριστὸς ἀπέθανεν καὶ ἔζησεν

Of the four variant readings of this line, Metzger gives ἀπέθανεν καὶ ἔζησεν an {A} rating (468). It has solid manuscript support (א*, A, B, C) and is one of the two shorter readings. It is also more difficult than ἀπέθανεν καὶ ἀνέστη (א², D), which is most likely influenced by 1 Thessalonians 4:14 (Schreiner 724). Jewett concludes that the reading is "undoubtedly original" (830 n. 11; cf. Cranfield 708 n. 1). The reason (γάρ) underlying Paul's argument is Christological. Εἰς τοῦτο (NLT, "for this very purpose") points forward to the next clause (Moo 845 n. 87), stands in apposition to it (R 699), and creates double emphasis (Dunn 808). Ἀπέθανεν (3 sg. aor. act. indic. of ἀποθνῄσκω) is a consummative aorist; καί is continuative; ἔζησεν (3 sg. aor. act. indic. of ζάω) is an ingressive aorist (R 834; T 71; Moule 10). Murray suggests that Paul also uses ζάω to refer to Christ's resurrection in Romans 5:10 and 2 Corinthians 4:10 (2:182).

ἵνα καὶ νεκρῶν καὶ ζώντων κυριεύσῃ

The purpose (ἵνα + subjunc.) of Christ's death and resurrection was that he might establish his complete lordship (Dunn 808). Καί . . . καί ("both . . . and") is equivalent to τε . . . καί (Porter 216; contra Moo 845 n. 94). Νεκρῶν (gen. pl. masc. of νεκρός, -ά, -όν) and ζώντων (gen. pl. masc. of pres. act. ptc. of ζάω) are genitives of direct object; both anarthrous forms are substantival, definite, and generic, referring to classes of individuals (NET, "both the living and the dead"). Κυριεύσῃ (3 sg. aor. act. subjunc. of κυριεύω) is an ingressive aorist (Cranfield 708 n. 3; Jewett 849 n. 193); see 6:9 for κυριεύω.

VERSE 10

σὺ δὲ τί κρίνεις τὸν ἀδελφόν σου; ἢ καὶ σὺ τί ἐξουθενεῖς τὸν ἀδελφόν σου;

The verbs κρίνεις (2 sg. pres. act. indic.) and ἐξουθενεῖς (2 sg. pres. act. indic.) echo 14:3 and serve to introduce the third panel of the paragraph. Δέ is adversative (Jewett 850); the emphatic uses of σύ echo 14:4 (Moo 846), as do the questions introduced by τί ("Why?"). Ἤ is disjunctive ("or"); καί is adjunctive ("also"). The double use of τὸν ἀδελφόν σου ("your brother") strengthens Paul's appeal by reminding members of both groups that they are dealing with fellow believers (Cranfield 709).

πάντες γὰρ παραστησόμεθα τῷ βήματι τοῦ θεοῦ

The explanation (γάρ) for why the weak should not judge and the strong should not despise is that everyone will stand before God for judgment. Παραστησόμεθα (1 pl. fut. mid. indic. of παρίστημι, "stand before, be present") is a predictive future and an indirect middle; πάντες (nom. pl. masc. of πᾶς, πᾶσα, πᾶν) is emphatic (Jewett 850) and rules out any exceptions (Dunn 809). Παρίστημι occurs elsewhere in the NT to describe the act of standing before a ruler or judge (Acts 27:24; 1 Cor 8:8; 2 Cor 4:14; 2 Tim 4:11; cf. Moo 846 n. 103). Βῆμα, -τος, τό describes a platform that required steps to ascend (BDAG 175b); elsewhere in the NT it denotes a secular place of judgment (Matt 27:19; John 19:13; Acts 7:5; 12:21; 18:12, 16, 17; 25:6, 10, 17). Τῷ βήματι is a local dative; τοῦ θεοῦ is a possessive genitive; the articles with both nouns make the phrase monadic (Wallace 224). The concluding θεοῦ is strongly supported (א*, A, B, C*, D), while the variant reading Χριστοῦ is most likely influenced by 2 Corinthians 5:10 (Metzger 468).

VERSE 11

γέγραπται γάρ, Ζῶ ἐγώ, λέγει κύριος

Paul provides OT support (γέγραπται γάρ; cf. 1:17) for his preceding statement and gives it authority by introducing it with "a typical prophetic oath formula" from Isa 49:18 (Jewett 851). EVV translate ζῶ ἐγώ with "as I live"; λέγει is an instantaneous present (cf. 9:25; 10:8; 11:9); κύριος refers to God the Father (Cranfield 710; Moo 848).

ὅτι ἐμοὶ κάμψει πᾶν γόνυ

Ὅτι is recitative ("that") and introduces a solemn oath (R 1034; BDF §454.5); ἐμοί is a dative of advantage ("to me"); κάμψει (3 sg. fut. act. indic. of κάμπτω, "bend") is a predictive future. Κάμπτω γόνυ describes the act of paying homage (cf. 11:4); πᾶν continues the inclusiveness of verse 10.

καὶ πᾶσα γλῶσσα ἐξομολογήσεται τῷ θεῷ

Καί is continuative ("and"); πᾶσα γλῶσσα ("every tongue") is the third instance of inclusive language; ἐξομολογήσεται (3 sg. fut. mid. indic. of ἐξομολογέω, "confess") is a predictive future and an indirect middle; τῷ θεῷ is a dative of indirect object (contra BDF §188.2). Ἐξομολογέω usually carries the sense of "acknowledge/confess" but with the accompanying dative is better translated "praise" (Moo 847 n. 106; cf. 2 Sam 22:50; 1 Chron 29:13; Ps 85:12).

VERSE 12

ἄρα [οὖν] ἕκαστος ἡμῶν περὶ ἑαυτοῦ λόγον δώσει [τῷ θεῷ]

Paul concludes the paragraph with a clear statement of personal application. See 5:18; 7:3, 25; 8:12; 9:16, 18 for ἄρα οὖν (ESV, "so then"). Metzger does not address the question of whether οὖν is original, and manuscript evidence is divided. Inclusion seems more likely based on Paul's use of the combination elsewhere in the letter, but Schreiner notes that the meaning is not affected if οὖν is omitted (725; cf. Dunn 796 n. i). Ἕκαστος ἡμῶν ("each one of us") is emphatic (Jewett 852) and sounds a note of individual accountability (Harris 193); ἡμῶν is a partitive genitive (cf. Wallace 85). Περί ἑαυτοῦ denotes reference ("concerning himself"); δώσει (3 sg. fut. act. indic. of δίδωμι, "give") is a predictive future. In this context, λόγον carries the sense of "formal accounting" (BDAG 600c); coupled with δίδωμι it describes the settling of accounts (cf. Matt 12:36; Luke 16:2; Acts 19:40; Heb 13:17; 1 Pet 4:5). Τῷ θεῷ ("to God") has strong manuscript support (א, A, B, C*, D, 33), but commentators are divided on whether to include it. Because omitting the noun is both the shorter and the more difficult reading, Jewett chooses to omit it (831 n. q; cf. Schreiner 725). Dunn includes it because of the strong manuscript support (796 n. j), and Moo argues that without τῷ θεῷ, the sequence ends unsatisfactorily (834 n. 30). Cranfield's conclusion that "the originality [of τῷ θεῷ] is highly probable" (711 n. 3) is most likely correct.

FOR FURTHER STUDY

77. Strong and Weak (14:1–15:13)

Black, D. A. *Paul, Apostle of Weakness: Astheneia and Its Cognates in the Pauline Literature.* Revised edition. Eugene, OR: Pickwick Publications, 2012.

de Lorenzi, I., ed. *Freedom and Love: The Guide for Christian Life* (1 Co 8–11; Rm 14–15). Rome: St. Paul's Abbey, 1981.

Gathercole, S. "Romans 1–5 and the 'Weak' and the 'Strong': Pauline Theology, Pastoral Rhetoric, and the Purpose of Romans." *RevExp* 100 (2003): 35–51.

Karris, R. J. "Romans 14:1–15:13 and the Occasion of Romans." *CBQ* 35 (1973): 155–78.

Meeks, W. "Judgment and the Brother: Romans 14:1–15:13." Pages 290–300 in *Tradition and Interpretation in the New Testament. Festschrift for E. Earle Ellis*. Edited by G. F. Hawthorne and O. Betz. Grand Rapids: Eerdmans, 1987.

Omanson, R. L. "The 'Weak' and the 'Strong' and Paul's Letter to the Roman Christians."*BT* 33 (1982): 106–14.

Pitta, A. "The Strong, the Weak, and the Mosaic law in the Christian Communities of Rome (Rom. 14:1–15:13)." Pages 96–107 in *Christians as a Religious Minority in a Multicultural City. Modes of Interaction and Identity Formation in Early Imperial Rome*. London: T & T Clark, 2004.

Reasoner, M. *The Strong and the Weak. Romans 14:1–15:13 in Context*. Cambridge: Cambridge University Press, 1999.

Sampley, J. P. "The Weak and the Strong: Paul's Careful and Crafty Rhetorical Strategy in Romans 14:1–15:13." Pages 41–52 in *The Social World of the First Christians: Essays*

in Honor of Wayne A. Meeks. Edited by L. M. White and O. L. Yarbrough. Minneapolis: Augsburg Fortress, 1995.
Simmons, W. A. *EDBT* 748–49.
Sobanaraj, S. "Paul's Theology of Convergence in Conflict Situations: An Inquiry into Romans 14:1–15:13." *Bangalore Theological Forum* 42 (2010): 1–43
Spitaler, P. "Household Disputes in Rome (Romans 14:1–15:13)." *RB* 116 (2009): 44–69.
Thompson, M. B. *DPL* 916–18.
________. *Clothed with Christ: The Example and Teaching of Jesus in Romans 12:1–15:13*. Sheffield: *JSOT*, 1991.
Watson, F. "The Two Roman Congregations: Romans 14:1–15:13." Pages 203–15 in *The Romans Debate*. Edited by K. P. Donfried. Peabody, MA: Hendrickson, 1991.

HOMILETICAL SUGGESTIONS

To Eat or Not to Eat, Part 1 (14:1–12)

1. Admonition (14:1–3)
    a. General command: Accept one another (14:1a)
        1) Specification: No disputes over opinions (14:1b)
    b. Issue: Dietary practices (14:2)
    c. Specific prohibitions: Do not despise or condemn (14:3a–b)
1) Reason: God has accepted both (γάρ, 14:3c)
2) Explanation (14:4–9)
    a. Each is responsible to his/her master (14:4)
    b. Each must be assured in his/her mind (14:5)
    c. Each gives thanks to God (14:6)
    d. Each lives or dies to Christ (14:7–8)
        1) Reason: Christ is lord over the dead and the living (γάρ, 14:9)
3. Conclusion (14:10–12)
    a. All will stand before God's judgment seat (14:10)
        1) OT Proof: Isaiah 45:23 (14:11)
    b. Each will give account to God (ἄρα οὖν, 14:12)

b. By Pursuing Peace with One Another (14:13–23)

STRUCTURE

The second paragraph (14:13–23) consists of four parts (14:13–15; 14:16–18; 14:19–21; 14:22–23) and is framed by uses of the verb κρίνω and cognates (14:13, 22b, 23a). The conjuction οὖν introduces each of the first three parts, and each issues a call to action (exhortation, prohibition, exhortation). The structure of the first and third parts are generally parallel, with a qualified slogan embedded in each (14:14b, 20b). The fourth (14:22–23) provides concluding advice.

Μηκέτι οὖν ἀλλήλους κρίνωμεν·
ἀλλὰ τοῦτο κρίνατε μᾶλλον, τὸ μὴ τιθέναι πρόσκομμα τῷ ἀδελφῷ ἢ σκάνδαλον.
        οἶδα καὶ πέπεισμαι ἐν κυρίῳ Ἰησοῦ ὅτι οὐδὲν κοινὸν δι᾽ ἑαυτοῦ,
        εἰ μὴ τῷ λογιζομένῳ τι κοινὸν εἶναι, ἐκείνῳ κοινόν.
    εἰ γὰρ διὰ βρῶμα ὁ ἀδελφός σου λυπεῖται, οὐκέτι κατὰ ἀγάπην περιπατεῖς·
    μὴ τῷ βρώματί σου ἐκεῖνον ἀπόλλυε ὑπὲρ οὗ Χριστὸς ἀπέθανεν.

μὴ βλασφημείσθω οὖν ὑμῶν τὸ ἀγαθόν.
    οὐ γάρ ἐστιν ἡ βασιλεία τοῦ θεοῦ βρῶσις καὶ πόσις
    ἀλλὰ δικαιοσύνη καὶ εἰρήνη καὶ χαρὰ ἐν πνεύματι ἁγίῳ·
    ὁ γὰρ ἐν τούτῳ δουλεύων τῷ Χριστῷ εὐάρεστος τῷ θεῷ καὶ δόκιμος τοῖς ἀνθρώποις.

ἄρα οὖν τὰ τῆς εἰρήνης διώκωμεν καὶ τὰ τῆς οἰκοδομῆς τῆς εἰς ἀλλήλους.
μὴ ἕνεκεν βρώματος κατάλυε τὸ ἔργον τοῦ θεοῦ.
        πάντα μὲν καθαρά,
        ἀλλὰ κακὸν τῷ ἀνθρώπῳ τῷ διὰ προσκόμματος ἐσθίοντι.
    καλὸν τὸ μὴ φαγεῖν κρέα μηδὲ πιεῖν οἶνον μηδὲ ἐν ᾧ ὁ ἀδελφός σου προσκόπτει.

σὺ πίστιν [ἣν] ἔχεις κατὰ σεαυτὸν ἔχε ἐνώπιον τοῦ θεοῦ.
    μακάριος ὁ μὴ κρίνων ἑαυτὸν ἐν ᾧ δοκιμάζει·
    ὁ δὲ διακρινόμενος ἐὰν φάγῃ κατακέκριται, ὅτι οὐκ ἐκ πίστεως·
    πᾶν δὲ ὃ οὐκ ἐκ πίστεως ἁμαρτία ἐστίν.

VERSE 13

Μηκέτι οὖν ἀλλήλους κρίνωμεν

The conjunction οὖν ("therefore") draws a conclusion from verses 10–12 (Dunn 817) using the link-word κρίνω from 14:10. The adverb μηκέτι is temporal ("no longer"); ἀλλήλους (acc. pl. masc.) is the direct object; κρίνωμεν (1 pl. pres. act. subjunc. of κρίνω) is a customary present and a hortatory subjunctive (Porter 222).

ἀλλὰ τοῦτο κρίνατε μᾶλλον

The adversative ἀλλά ("but") establishes a strong contrast with the first clause (Jewett 856). Τοῦτο (acc. sg. neut.) is prospective; the aorist imperative κρίνατε (2 pl.

aor. act. impv. of κρίνω) issues a summary command; the adverb μᾶλλον is best translated "instead" (Cranfield 712). ESV translates κρίνω as "decide" (cf. BDAG 568b); NASB chooses "determine"; NIV translates "make up your mind." Jewett concludes that the verb reflects a specific judgment both the weak and strong make (857); Moo notes that the change from first to second plural and present to aorist tense lends urgency to the command (851 n. 9).

τὸ μὴ τιθέναι πρόσκομμα τῷ ἀδελφῷ ἢ σκάνδαλον

The articular infinitive τὸ μὴ τιθέναι ("not to put") stands in apposition to τοῦτο (R 1059; T 140; Wallace 607). See 9:32 for πρόσκομμα (cf. Moo 851 n. 10), which is the object of the infinitive (acc. sg. neut.). Τῷ ἀδελφῷ is a local dative (NET, "before a brother"); the article is generic (Jewett 857 n. 10); ἤ is disjunctive ("or"). See 9:33 for σκάνδαλον. Jewett identifies πρόσκομμα ἢ σκάνδαλον as an instance of hendiadys (858); Dunn describes σκάνδαλον as "the more emotive word" (818).

VERSE 14

οἶδα καὶ πέπεισμαι ἐν κυρίῳ Ἰησοῦ

Οἶδα καὶ πέπεισμαι also occurs in Galatians 5:10, Philippians 2:22, and 2 Thessalonians 3:4. With the addition of ἐν κυρίῳ Ἰησοῦ the combination is "strikingly emphatic" (Cranfield 712) and denotes "an extraordinary level of conviction" (Jewett 859). Οἶδα (1 sg. pf. act. indic. of οἶδα) is a perfect with present force and suggests a rational, theoretical conviction (Jewett 859; cf. 2:2; 6:9; 8:27). Πέπεισμαι (1 sg. pf. pass. indic. of πείθω, "persuade") is an intensive perfect and suggests persuasion by proof (Jewett 859; cf. 8:38; 15:14; 2 Tim 1:5, 12). Ἐν κυρίῳ Ἰησοῦ ("in the Lord Jesus") establishes the "authoritative basis" for Paul's conviction (cf. NAB, JB, NLT); Longenecker argues for an instrumental sense (1007); Harris provides twenty-seven translations (130); Moo sets out three interpretations (852–53).

ὅτι οὐδὲν κοινὸν δι' ἑαυτοῦ

Ὅτι is recitative ("that"); οὐδέν (nom. sg. neut.) is the subject and refers to the resources of the created world (Cranfield 713); ἐστιν is understood; κοινόν (nom. sg. neut.) is the predicate adjective. In general, κοινός, -ή, -όν denotes something that is of little value ("common, ordinary"); more narrowly, it describes something that is ceremonially impure (BDAG 552a) or "ritually unclean" (Moo 852 n. 14; cf. 1 Macc 1:62; Acts 10:14; 11:8–9). Διά + genitive is local/spatial (NIV, "in itself").

εἰ μὴ τῷ λογιζομένῳ τι κοινὸν εἶναι, ἐκείνῳ κοινόν

Dunn suggests that εἰ μή ("except") is equivalent to ἀλλά (820); Turner views it as a strong positive (333). The substantival participle τῷ λογιζομένῳ (dat. sg. masc. of pres. mid. ptc. of dep. λογίζομαι) is the indirect object; see 2:3 for λογίζομαι; BDF suggests "be of the opinion" (§397.2). The indefinite pronoun τι ("something, anything") is the object of the participle; κοινόν is the complement; εἶναι (pres. act. infin. of εἰμί) makes the construction clear (NASB, "to him who thinks anything to be unclean"). The demonstrative pronoun ἐκείνῳ (dat. sg. masc.) is redundant, adds emphasis (Dunn 826), functions substantivally (T 46), and refers back to the participle. Ἐστιν is understood; κοινόν is the predicate adjective.

VERSE 15

εἰ γὰρ διὰ βρῶμα ὁ ἀδελφός σου λυπεῖται

Cranfield (714), Jewett (860), and Schreiner (726) all view verse 14 as parenthetical, which means γάρ ("for") provides the explanation for verse 13. Εἰ introduces a first class condition; διά + accusative denotes agency; see 14:10 for βρῶμα; λυπεῖται (3 sg. pres. pass. indic. of λυπέω, "grieve") is a gnomic present. Λυπέω describes being sad or distressed (BDAG 604d). Cranfield suggests that it denotes a "specially strong" sense of grief (714); *EDNT* concludes that it indicates "terrible worry and fearful distress" (2.363); Dunn argues for grievous hurt in which the integrity of a person's faith is destroyed and his/her salvation is put at risk (820).

οὐκέτι κατὰ ἀγάπην περιπατεῖς

Κατά + accusative denotes conduct; Harris suggests "governed by" (134); see 1:7 for ἀγαπή; περιπατεῖς (2 sg. pres. act. indic. of περιπατέω, "walk") carries the nuance of daily conduct (cf. 6:4; 8:14; 13:13).

μὴ τῷ βρώματί σου ἐκεῖνον ἀπόλλυε ὑπὲρ οὗ Χριστὸς ἀπέθανεν

Μή naturally accompanies the subsequent imperative; τῷ βρώματί σου is causal (NASB, NIV, NET, "because of your food"); ἐκεῖνον (acc. sg. masc.) is emphatic (Jewett 861). The present imperative ἀπόλλυε (2 sg. pres. act. impv. of ἀπόλλυμι, "destroy") denotes an ongoing processs (Moo 854 n. 26); Dunn (821), Moo (854 n. 28), and Schreiner (734) conclude that the verb describes final eschatological ruin (contra Jewett 861). Ὑπέρ + genitive denotes representation (Harris 216); the antecedent of the relative pronoun οὗ (gen. sg. masc.) is ἐκεῖνον (R 708); ἀπέθανεν (3 sg. aor. act. indic. of ἀποθνῄσκω, "die") is a consummative aorist. The relative clause echoes 5:6–8.

VERSE 16

μὴ βλασφημείσθω οὖν ὑμῶν τὸ ἀγαθόν

The inferential conjunction οὖν ("therefore") introduces the second part of the paragraph and draws a conclusion from verses 13–15 (Moo 855). Βλασφημείσθω (3 sg. pres. pass. impv. of βλασφημέω) is an iterative present, a permissive passive (Wallace 441), and an imperative of command; it carries the sense of "allow to be slandered" (Jewett 862). Ὑμῶν is possessive rather than emphatic (T 189); τὸ ἀγαθόν (GNB, "what you regard as good') has been understood as the freedom of the strong (Jewett 862; Moo 855; cf. NLT), the entirety of covenant blessings in Christ (Dunn 821), or the gospel (Cranfield 717; Schreiner 727).

VERSE 17

οὐ γάρ ἐστιν ἡ βασιλεία τοῦ θεοῦ βρῶσις καὶ πόσις

The reason (γάρ) not to let eating or not eating be a cause for slander resides in a correct understanding of God's kingdom. Ἡ βασιλεία τοῦ θεοῦ is comparatively rare in Paul's letters (cf. 1 Cor 4:20; 6:20; 15:50; Gal 5:21; Eph 5:5; Col 4:11; 2 Thess 1:5) and usually refers to a future state—except here and in 1 Corinthians 4:20 (Moo 857 n. 40); τοῦ θεοῦ is most likely possessive* but could possibly be subjective; the entire phrase is monadic (Wallace 224). Βρῶσις καὶ πόσις ("eating and drinking") is a conventional phrase (Wallace 419).

ἀλλὰ δικαιοσύνη καὶ εἰρήνη καὶ χαρὰ ἐν πνεύματι ἁγίῳ

Ἀλλά establishes a strong contrast with οὐ in the preceding line. See 1:17 for δικαιοσύνη and 1:7 for εἰρήνη; χαρά ("joy") completes the triad; all three abstract nouns are anarthrous (Moule 112). Δικαιοσύνη denotes the state of being righteous, while εἰρήνη denotes the state of being reconciled (Cranfield 718; Moo 857). Ἐν πνεύματι ἁγίῳ is an adjectival prepositional phrase (Wallace 784) that modifies all three of the preceding nouns (Moo 857 n. 46; cf. Schreiner 741; contra Cranfield 718 and Jewett 863); ἐν + dative most likely denotes agency (cf. ἐδικαιώθη ἐν πνεύματι in 1 Tim. 3:16); GNB translates as "which the Holy Spirit gives."

VERSE 18

ὁ γὰρ ἐν τούτῳ δουλεύων τῷ Χριστῷ εὐάρεστος τῷ θεῷ καὶ δόκιμος τοῖς ἀνθρώποις

Paul continues with a further explanation (γάρ) of verse 17. The substantival participle ὁ δουλεύων (nom. sg. masc. of pres. act. ptc. of δουλεύω, "serve") is a customary present; τῷ Χριστῷ is a dative of direct object; the article makes Χριστῷ titular ("the Messiah"). The referent of the adverbial prepositional phrase ἐν τούτῳ ("in this") is ambiguous. Cranfield connects it to "righteousness, and peace and joy in the Holy Spirit" (719); Dunn suggests that it is simply adverbial of manner (824; cf. T 252); Jewett understands it to refer to the general topic under discussion (864). Moo agrees with Jewett and connects the idea specifically to the kingdom-focused manner of service set out in verse 17 (858). This last understanding corresponds to Wallace's category of "conceptual antecedent" (333–34) and is preferable. Ἐστιν is understood; see 12:1 for εὐάρεστος ("acceptable/pleasing"); τῷ θεῷ ("to God") is a dative of indirect object. Καί is connective ("and"); see 1:28 for δόκιμος; Moo suggests "respected" (858 n. 50) while Jewett suggests "esteemed" (864); τοῖς ἀνθρώποις ("by men") is a dative of agency (Wallace 165); the definite article is generic (Jewett 864).

VERSE 19

ἄρα οὖν τὰ τῆς εἰρήνης διώκωμεν καὶ τὰ τῆς οἰκοδομῆς τῆς εἰς ἀλλήλους

There are three variant readings of the verb in this sentence: διώκωμεν (pres. subjunc.), διώκομεν (pres. indic.), and διώκετε (pres. impv.). The important manuscript evidence is divided between the first two, with support for the indicative reading (ℵ, A, B) somewhat stronger than for the subjunctive reading (C, D, 33). Metzger notes that elsewhere in the letter ἄρα οὖν is always followed by the indicative (469); both Dunn (816 n. f) and Jewett (853 n. g) view the indicative reading as the more likely original. On the other hand, Cranfield believes that the hortatory subjunctive makes for a better transition (721), and Moo concludes that the subjunctive better fits the imperatives in verses 13, 15, 16, 20, and 22 (849 n. 1).* UBS[5] gives the subjunctive a rating of {D}.

The double inferential ἄρα οὖν (cf. 5:18; 7:3, 25; 8:12; 9:16, 18; 12:1) introduces the third part of the paragraph and the conclusion to Paul's argument (Longenecker 1008; Schreiner 727). The neuter plural article substantizes the genitive (R 767) and creates a periphrasis (T 16) for which BDF suggests the translation "what makes for peace" (§266.3; cf. ESV); the "peace" involved is peace with other Christians (Cranfield 721). If διώκωμεν (1 pl. pres. act. subjunc. of διώκω, "pursue") is the original reading, it is a customary present and a hortatory subjunctive (Moo 859 n. 58); the idea of pursuing peace occurs elsewhere in Psalm 33:14, Hebrews 12:14, and 1 Peter 3:11. Καί is continuative; τὰ τῆς οἰκοδομῆς ("what makes for edification") is parallel to τὰ τῆς εἰρήνης; the article allows εἰς ἀλλήλους to function as an adjective modifying οἰκοδομῆς (Moo 859 n. 60); εἰς + accusative denotes advantage. Οἰκοδομή, -ῆς, ἡ describes the process of edifying or building up (BDAG 696d; cf, *TDNT* 5.139–51); it contrasts with ἀπόλλυμι (14:15) and καταλύω (14:20) and refers to the collective strengthening of the church as a whole (Moo 859 n. 61).

VERSE 20

μὴ ἕνεκεν βρώματος κατάλυε τὸ ἔργον τοῦ θεοῦ

Μή naturally accompanies the imperative; ἕνεκεν + genitive is causal; see 14:15 for βρῶμα. Κατάλυε (2 sg. pres. act. impv. of καταλύω, "destroy") is a gnomic present and an imperative of command; καταλύω describes the act of tearing down or causing ruin and is the natural antonym to οἰκοδομέω (Dunn 825). Τὸ ἔργον τοῦ θεοῦ ("the work of God") is best understood as God's work in the entire congregation (Jewett 866; contra Cranfield 723); the genitive of θεοῦ is subjective.

πάντα μὲν καθαρά, ἀλλὰ κακὸν τῷ ἀνθρώπῳ τῷ διὰ προσκόμματος ἐσθίοντι

Μέν is concessive (Jewett 867 n. 160; cf. NASB) and introduces a slogan that echoes Luke 11:41. Πάντα (nom. pl. neut.) is the subject; ἐστιν is understood; καθαρά (nom. pl. neut. of καθαρός, -ά, -όν, "clean") is the predicate adjective, denotes something that is ceremonially pure (BDAG 489c), and is the opposite of κοινός (14:14). Ἀλλά introduces a sharp contrast (R 1152) that qualifies the preceding slogan. Τὸ ἐσθιεῖν ἐστιν is understood (Moo 860 n. 65); κακόν (NIV, ESV, NET, CSB, "wrong") is the predicate accusative; τῷ ἀνθρώπῳ is a dative of disadvantage; the adjectival participle τῷ ἐσθίοντι (dat. sg. masc. of pres. act. ptc. of ἐσθίω, "eat") modifies ἀνθρώπῳ. Moule (112) and most EVV (e.g., NIV, NET) understand διὰ προσκόμματος as causal ("in a way that causes stumbling");* Robertson (583), Turner (267), and BDF (§223.3) understand it as manner (KJV, "with offense"); most commentators understand it as attendant circumstance (Cranfield 723 n. 7; Dunn 826; Jewett 867; Moo 860 n. 65) as does NASB ("who eats and gives offense").

VERSE 21

καλὸν τὸ μὴ φαγεῖν κρέα μηδὲ πιεῖν οἶνον μηδὲ ἐν ᾧ ὁ ἀδελφός σου προσκόπτει

Cranfield (724) describes this asyndetic statement as "an authoritative pronouncement" commending action that is καλόν ("good") in contrast to what is κακόν (14:20). Jewett notes the parallel to 1 Corinthians 7:1 and provides OT examples (867). The placement of καλόν (pred. adj.) is emphatic; the compound infinitival phrase that follows is the subject. The aorist infinitives φαγεῖν (aor. act. infin. of ἐσθίω, "eat") and πιεῖν (aor. act. infin. of πίνω, "drink") are constative (R 858). Dunn argues that the aorist tense points to a specific instance (826; cf. BDF §338.1); Moo nuances the argument for application to specific situations based on 1 Corinthians 10:23–11:1 rather than on the aorist tense (861 n. 70). Μηδὲ ἐν ᾧ is elliptical (BDF §480.1), with the antecedent of ᾧ (dat. sg. neut.) understood; ἐν + dative is instrumental (R 978; contra T 253); see 9:32 for προσκόπτει (3 sg. pres. act. indic.); NASB translates as "or do anything by which your brother stumbles." Adding the third element highlights the comprehensive scope of Paul's conclusion (Cranfield 725). Instead of προσκόπτει (ℵ[1], A, C), the original hand of ℵ reads λυπειται, which is most likely an assimilation to verse 15 (Schreiner 743). The Majority Text has a longer reading (προσκόπτει ἤ σκανδαλίζεται ἤ ασθενεῖ) that Moo concludes is "almost certainly a secondary expansion" (849 n. 2).

VERSE 22

σὺ πίστιν [ἣν] ἔχεις κατὰ σεαυτὸν ἔχε ἐνώπιον τοῦ θεοῦ

The fourth part of the paragraph offers concluding advice and begins with an emphatic σύ ("as for you," Moo 861) that applies the discussion to each member of the community (Jewett 870). See 14:1 on πίστις in the context of this section of the letter. The relative pronoun ἥν (acc. sg. fem.) has good Alexandrian support (ℵ, A, B, C). Moo concludes that the pronoun is "probably original" because omitting it would be a stylistic improvement to smooth the reading (849 n. 3; cf. Jewett 854 n. n). Κατά + accusative denotes reference; ἔχε (2 sg. pres. act. impv. of ἔχω, "have") is an imperative of command; ἐνώπιον + genitive is local ("in the presence of God"); the article is monadic.

μακάριος ὁ μὴ κρίνων ἑαυτὸν ἐν ᾧ δοκιμάζει

See 4:7–8 for μακάριος ("blessed"); the gnomic substantival participle ὁ μὴ κρίνων (nom. sg. masc. of pres. act. ptc.) begins a triple word-play (κρίνων . . . διακρινόμενος . . . κατακέκριται) that, along with 14:13, frames the paragraph. Ἑαυτόν (acc. sg. masc.) is the object of the participle; ἐν ᾧ denotes reference (T 265) with the demonstrative τούτῳ understood (cf. R 706); δοκιμάζει (3 sg. pres. act. indic. of δοκιμάζω, "approve") is a gnomic present; see 1:28 for δοκιμάζω. The blessing described in this statement is best understood as applying to both the weak and the strong (Jewett 871; Moo 862). NLT translates, "Blessed are those who don't feel guilty for doing something they have decided is right."

VERSE 23

ὁ δὲ διακρινόμενος ἐὰν φάγῃ κατακέκριται, ὅτι οὐκ ἐκ πίστεως

Δέ is adversative ("but"); the substantival participle ὁ διακρινόμενος (nom. sg. masc. of pres. mid. ptc. of διακρίνω) is an indirect middle (Jewett 871); see 4:20 for διακρίνω; Cranfield suggests "waver" (727 n. 14). Ἐάν introduces a third class condition; the subjunctive φάγῃ (3 sg. aor. act. subjunc. of ἐσθίω, "eat") reflects the implicit uncertainty of who might eat. Κατακέκριται (3 sg. pf. pass. indic. of κατακρίνω, "condemn") is a proleptic (future) perfect (Wallace 581; BDF §344) and a divine passive; see 2:1 for κατακρίνω. Ὅτι is causal; ἐστιν is understood; ἐκ + genitive denotes source; see 14:1 for πίστις.

πᾶν δὲ ὃ οὐκ ἐκ πίστεως ἁμαρτία ἐστίν

Δέ ("and") continues the discussion of οὐκ ἐκ πίστεως. Πᾶν (nom. sg. neut.) gathers up the matters at issue between the weak and strong (Cranfield 728; contra Schreiner 738); ὃ οὐκ ἐκ πίστεως qualifies πᾶν; GNB translates the phrase as "anything that is not based on faith." Ἁμαρτία refers to "sin" as act (Moo 863 n. 85) rather than state (3:9) or disposition (7:20). Cranfield writes that it describes "the conduct of the Christian who does a particular action in spite of the fact that he has not received the inner freedom to do it" (729).

The question of the doxology that appears in different manuscripts after 14:23, after 15:33, or after 16:23 will be addressed at the end of chapter 16.

FOR FURTHER STUDY

78. Stumbling Block (14:13)

Giesen, H. *EDNT* 3.248–50.
Guhrt, J. *NIDNTT* 2.705–10.

Moulton, J. H. "Σκάνδαλον." *ExpTim* 26 (1914–15): 331–32.
Müller, K. *Anstoss und Gericht: Eine Studie zum jüdischen Hintergrund des paulinischen Skandalon-Begriffs*. Munich: Kösel, 1969.
Stählin, G. *TDNT* 7.339–58.
Thompson, M. B. *DPL* 918–19.

79. Ritual Purity/Impurity (14:14)

Chilton, B. D. *DNTB* 874–82.
Dunnett, W. M. *EDBT* 660–61.
Neusner, J. *The Idea of Purity in Ancient Judaism*. Leiden: Brill, 1973.
Newton, M. *The Concept of Purity at Qumran and in the Letters of Paul*. Cambridge: Cambridge University Press, 1985.
Paschen, W. *Rein und Unrein: Untersuchung zur biblischen Wortgeschichte*. Munich: Kösel, 1970.
Reasoner, M. *DPL* 775–76.

80. The Kingdom Concept in Paul (14:17)

Donfried, K. P. "The Kingdom of God in Paul." Pages 175–90 in *The Kingdom of God in Twentieth-Century Interpretation*. Edited by W. Willis. Peabody, MA: Hendrickson, 1987.
Haufe, G. "Reich Gottes bei Paulus und in der Jesus tradition." *NTS* 31 (1985): 467–72.
Johnson, G. "'Kingdom of God' Sayings in Paul's Epistles." Pages 143–56 in *From Jesus to Paul: Studies in Honor of Francis Wright Beare*. Edited by P. Richardson and J. C. Hurd. Ontario: Wilfred Laurier University, 1984.
Kennedy, H. A. A. *St. Paul's Conceptions of the Last Things*. London: Hodder, 1961.
Kreitzer, L. J. *DPL* 524–26.
________. *Jesus and God in Paul's Eschatology*. Sheffield: Academic Press, 1987.
Lewis, J. P. "'The Kingdom of God . . . Is Righteousness, Peace, and Joy in the Holy Spirit' (Rom 14:17): A Survey of Interpretation." *Restoration Quarterly* 40 (1998): 53–68.
López, R. A. "Views on Paul's Vice Lists and Inheriting the Kingdom." *BSac* 168 (2011): 81–97.
________. "A Study of Pauline Passages on Inheriting the Kingdom. *BSac* 168 (2011): 443–59.
Shires, H. M. *The Eschatology of Paul in the Light of Modern Scholarship*. Philadelphia: Westminister, 1966.
Shogren, G. S. "'Is the Kingdom of God about Eating and Drinking or Isn't It?' (Romans 14:17)." *NovT* 42 (2000): 238–56.
Vos, G. *The Pauline Eschatology*. Princeton: University Press, 1930.

HOMILETICAL SUGGESTIONS

To Eat or Not to Eat, Part 2 (14:13–23)

1. Exhortation: Determine not to cause stumbling (οὖν, 14:13–15)
   a. Slogan: Nothing is unclean in itself (14:14a)
      1) Qualification: Except to the one who considers it to be (14:14b)

b. Explanation: Grieving another destroys Christ's work (γάρ, 14:15)

2. Command: Your good must not be blasphemed (οὖν, 14:16–18)
   a. Explanation: The kingdom of God is not eating or drinking (γάρ, 14:17)
   b. Explanation: Obedience is pleasing to God and respected by others (γάρ, 14:18)
3. Exhortation: Pursue peace and edification (ἄρα οὖν, 14:19–21)
   a. Slogan: All things are good (14:20b)
      1) Qualification: Except to the one who eats with stumbling (14:20c)
   b. Explanation: Abstaining is good if it forestalls stumbling (14:21)
4. Concluding Advice: Maintain your convictions before God (14:22–23)
   a. The one who does not judge himself is blessed (14:22b)
   b. The one who doubts is condemned (14:23a)
   c. What is not of faith is sin (14:23b)

c. By Pleasing One Another (15:1–6)

STRUCTURE

The third paragraph on practicing Christian liberty begins with a general statement of obligation (15:1), moves to a specific command (15:2) supported by the example of Christ (15:3–4), and concludes with a prayer-wish (15:5–6; cf. Longenecker 1013–14).

Ὀφείλομεν δὲ ἡμεῖς οἱ δυνατοὶ τὰ ἀσθενήματα τῶν ἀδυνάτων βαστάζειν
καὶ μὴ ἑαυτοῖς ἀρέσκειν.

ἕκαστος ἡμῶν τῷ πλησίον ἀρεσκέτω εἰς τὸ ἀγαθὸν πρὸς οἰκοδομήν·
καὶ γὰρ ὁ Χριστὸς οὐχ ἑαυτῷ ἤρεσεν,
  ἀλλὰ καθὼς γέγραπται, Οἱ ὀνειδισμοὶ τῶν ὀνειδιζόντων σε ἐπέπεσαν ἐπ' ἐμέ.

  ὅσα γὰρ προεγράφη, εἰς τὴν ἡμετέραν διδασκαλίαν ἐγράφη,
    ἵνα διὰ τῆς ὑπομονῆς καὶ διὰ τῆς παρακλήσεως τῶν γραφῶν τὴν ἐλπίδα
    ἔχωμεν.

ὁ δὲ θεὸς τῆς ὑπομονῆς καὶ τῆς παρακλήσεως δῴη ὑμῖν τὸ αὐτὸ φρονεῖν ἐν ἀλλήλοις
κατὰ Χριστὸν Ἰησοῦν,
  ἵνα ὁμοθυμαδὸν ἐν ἑνὶ στόματι δοξάζητε τὸν θεὸν καὶ πατέρα τοῦ κυρίου ἡμῶν
  Ἰησοῦ Χριστοῦ.

VERSE 1

Ὀφείλομεν δὲ ἡμεῖς οἱ δυνατοὶ τὰ ἀσθενήματα τῶν ἀδυνάτων βαστάζειν

Moo (865) notes the shift in style and vocabulary as Paul transitions (δέ) from his extended discussion of eating and drinking (14:1–23) to Christ's example of how to practice liberty (15:1–13). Ὀφείλομεν (1 pl. pres. act. indic. of ὀφείλω) is a gnomic present and a potential indicative (Wallace 452); ὀφείλω + infinitive denotes moral obligation (*TDNT* 5.559–64; cf. Jewett 876). The substantival adjective οἱ δυνατοί (nom. pl. masc.) stands in apposition to ἡμεῖς, which is emphatic (Dunn 837); δυνατός, -ά, -όν identifies Paul with the "strong" (contra Jewett 876). Τὰ ἀσθενήματα (acc. pl. neut of ἀσθένημα, -τος, τό, "weakness") is the object of the infinitive; the noun denotes the conscientious scruples caused by weakness of faith (BDAG 142d; cf. 14:1); the substantival adjective τῶν ἀδυνάτων (gen. pl. masc. of ἀδύνατος, -ον) is a possessive genitive and describes the "weak" in contrast to the "strong." The complementary infinitive βαστάζειν (pres. act. inf. of βαστάζω, "bear") is a gnomic present; the same verb occurs in Gal 6:2 and carries a sense stronger than simply "tolerate" (Schreiner 746; cf. Moo 866 n. 10).

καὶ μὴ ἑαυτοῖς ἀρέσκειν

The connective καί adds a second complementary infinitive as a negative (μή) injunction. Ἑαυτοῖς (dat. pl. masc.) is a dative of direct object; EVV translate as "ourselves" (e.g., ESV); the present tense infinitive is gnomic; see 8:8 for ἀρέσκω, which links verses 1–3.

VERSE 2

ἕκαστος ἡμῶν τῷ πλησίον ἀρεσκέτω εἰς τὸ ἀγαθὸν πρὸς οἰκοδομήν

Ayndeton calls attention to the next command. Ἕκαστος ("each one") replaces the expected ἀνήρ (R 746); ἡμῶν is a partitive genitive; the combination includes both groups (Jewett 878). Τῷ πλησίον is a dative of direct object; the definite article functions as a possessive pronoun ("his neighbor"); see 13:9 for πλησίον. Ἀρεσκέτω (3 sg. pres. act. impv.) is a gnomic present, an imperative of command, and is best translated "must please" (cf. Wallace 486). Εἰς + accusative denotes purpose; the article with ἀγαθόν functions as a possessive pronoun (e.g., NASB). Πρός + accusative denotes a second purpose that interprets the first (Schreiner 746); Moule suggests "leading to" (53); see 14:19 for οἰκοδομή (cf. 1 Thess 5:11); Jewett notes that the word is always used of congregational life (878).

VERSE 3

καὶ γὰρ ὁ Χριστὸς οὐχ ἑαυτῷ ἤρεσεν

Compare 11:1 for καὶ γάρ (R 1191); γάρ is causal ("because"); καί is ascensive ("even"). The article with Χριστός is titular (e.g., Porter 107); οὐχ . . . ἀλλά establishes a strong contrast between this statement and the introductory formula that follows; ἑαυτῷ is a dative of direct object and is moved forward for emphasis; ἤρεσεν (3 sg. aor. act. indic. of ἀρέσκω) is a constative aorist (T 72); BDF suggests "in his whole earthly life" (§332.13).

ἀλλὰ καθὼς γέγραπται (See 1:17)

Οἱ ὀνειδισμοὶ τῶν ὀνειδιζόντων σε ἐπέπεσαν ἐπ' ἐμέ

Paul's quotation of Psalm 68:10 follows LXX exactly (Jewett 879). Ὀνειδισμός, -οῦ, ὁ describes an act of disparagement that results in disgrace (BDAG 720d); Paul uses it in 1 Timothy 3:7 in parallel with "the snare of the devil"; Moo discusses the cognate verb ὀνειδίζω (860 n. 30). The present tense of τῶν ὀνειδιζόντων (gen. pl. masc. of pres. act. ptc.) is iterative; the genitive is subjective. The pronoun σε is best understood as referring to God (Cranfield 733; Schreiner 747 n. 6; contra Jewett 880). Ἐπέπεσαν (3 pl. aor. act. indic. of ἐπιπίπτω, "happen, befall") can denote extraordinary events and misfortunes (BDAG 377b); the aorist tense is constative; ἐπί + accusative is spatial ("upon me").

VERSE 4

ὅσα γὰρ προεγράφη, εἰς τὴν ἡμετέραν διδασκαλίαν ἐγράφη

Paul's parenthetical explanation (γάρ) highlights the importance of the OT and paves the way for the multiple quotations in the next paragraph (Schreiner 748). The relative adjective ὅσα (nom. pl. neut.) draws a comparison ("as many [things] as"); προεγράφη (3 sg. aor. pass. indic. of προγράφω, "write before") is a constative aorist and a divine passive. Εἰς + accusative denotes purpose; the possessive adjective ἡμετέραν (acc. sg. fem.) is in the first attributive position, which gives it more emphasis than the noun it modifies; Robertson notes that the accusative is objective (685); see 12:7 for διδασκαλία (cf. Moo 869 n. 32); see 4:23 for ἐγράφη (3 sg aor. pass. indic.).

ἵνα διὰ τῆς ὑπομονῆς καὶ διὰ τῆς παρακλήσεως τῶν γραφῶν τὴν ἐλπίδα ἔχωμεν

The purpose (ἵνα + subjunc.) of OT instruction is to give us hope. The double διά phrases may be understood as attendant circumstance + instrumental (Moo 870 n. 36–37), both causal (Schreiner 749), or both instrumental (most EVV); the third option seems most likely. The articles accompany ὑπομονῆς and παρακλήσεως because of the genitive of source (Schreiner 748) that follows and modifies both nouns (Jewett 882). See 2:7 for ὑπομονή, 12:8 for παράκλησις, and 1:2 for γραφή. The direct object τὴν ἐλπίδα is moved forward for emphasis; the definite article specifies; see 4:18 for ἐλπίς. Ἔχωμεν (1 pl. pres. act. subjunc.) is a customary present that "indicates the maintenance and sustaining of hope" (Moo 869 n. 34).

VERSE 5

ὁ δὲ θεὸς τῆς ὑπομονῆς καὶ τῆς παρακλήσεως δῴη ὑμῖν

A connective δέ ("and") introduces the prayer-wish that closes the paragraph (cf. 1 Thess 5:23; 2 Tim 1:16, 18; Heb 13:20–21; cf. Cranfield 736; Jewett prefers "homiletic benediction," 883). God is the source of endurance and encouragement (Schreiner 749); the definite article with θεός is monadic; the genitives that follow denote product (Wallace 107); the genitive definite articles are anaphoric, pointing back to verse 4. Δῴη (3 sg. aor. act. opt. of δίδωμι, "give") is a voluntative optative (Wallace 483; R 940); ὑμῖν is a dative of indirect object; Schreiner concludes that the pronoun refers to both the strong and the weak (804).

τὸ αὐτὸ φρονεῖν ἐν ἀλλήλοις κατὰ Χριστὸν Ἰησοῦν

The substantival infinitive phrase is the direct object of δῴη. Τὸ αὐτό is the intensifying use of the personal pronoun ("the same [thing]"); see 14:6 for φρονεῖν (pres. act. inf. of φρονέω); the idea of "to have the same point of view" (GNB) occurs elsewhere in Romans 12:16; 2 Corinthians 13:11; Philippians 2:2; 4:2. Ἐν ἀλλήλοις is locative (R 692) and is best translated "among one another" (Jewett 884). Κατά + accusative denotes standard ("in accordance with"); Schreiner concludes that the phrase refers both to Christ's example and his will (750); Dunn suggests "modeled on and obedient to" (840).

VERSE 6

ἵνα ὁμοθυμαδὸν ἐν ἑνὶ στόματι δοξάζητε τὸν θεὸν καὶ πατέρα τοῦ κυρίου ἡμῶν Ἰησοῦ Χριστοῦ

The purpose (ἵνα + subjunc.) of having the same point of view is that believers may glorify God. The adverb ὁμοθυμαδόν ("with one mind," BDAG 706c; cf. *TDNT* 5.185) describes the "powerful unity" (Jewett 884) that "characterized the first Spirit-filled church" (Moo 872 n. 53). Ἐν ἑνὶ στόματι (EVV, "with one voice") is instrumental (Moo 872, n. 54; contra T 252); δοξάζητε (2 pl. pres. act. subjunc.) is a customary present; see 1:21 for δοξάζω. Τὸν θεὸν καὶ πατέρα (NET, "the God and Father") is an example of the Granville Sharp rule (Wallace 274; cf. 2 Cor 1:3; 11:31; Eph 1:3, 17; 1 Pet 1:3); τοῦ κυρίου ἡμῶν is a genitive of relationship (descendant); Ἰησοῦ Χριστοῦ is a genitive in simple apposition.

FOR FURTHER STUDY

See For Further Study §§ 8 ("Prayer in Paul"), 17 ("God's Glory"), 75 ("Love of Neighbor")

HOMILETICAL SUGGESTIONS

Put Your Brother/Sister First (15:1–6)

1. Statement of Obligation (15:1)
    a. Positive: Bear others' weaknesses (15:1a)
    b. Negative: Do not please yourselves (15:1b)
2. Command: Please your neighbor (15:2–4)
    a. Purpose: The good of edification (εἰς, 15:2b)
    b. Cause: Christ did not please himself (γάρ, 15:3a)
        1) OT Proof: Psalm 69:9 (15:3b)
        2) NT Application: Our instruction (15:4)
        3) Prayer-Wish: Think the same thing (15:5–6)
    c. Purpose: Glorify God with one accord (ἵνα, 15:6)

d. By Following Christ's Example (15:7–13)

STRUCTURE

Paul concludes his discussion of Christian liberty with a paragraph that expands on the example of Christ as a model for practicing God's righteousness in relationship with others (cf. 15:3). The double use of προσλαμβάνω in verse 7 brings the discussion full circle from 14:1–3. A "solemn declaration" (Cranfield 740) introduces the example of Christ (15:8–12), which includes God's purpose for "all the peoples" and incorporates OT quotations from the law (Deut 32:43), the writings (Ps 18:49; 117:1), and the prophets (Isa 11:10). Paul closes both the paragraph and the entire topic with a prayer-wish (15:13).

Διὸ προσλαμβάνεσθε ἀλλήλους,
καθὼς καὶ ὁ Χριστὸς προσελάβετο ὑμᾶς
εἰς δόξαν τοῦ θεοῦ.

λέγω γὰρ Χριστὸν διάκονον γεγενῆσθαι περιτομῆς ὑπὲρ ἀληθείας θεοῦ,
εἰς τὸ βεβαιῶσαι τὰς ἐπαγγελίας τῶν πατέρων,
τὰ δὲ ἔθνη ὑπὲρ ἐλέους δοξάσαι τὸν θεόν,

καθὼς γέγραπται, Διὰ τοῦτο ἐξομολογήσομαί σοι ἐν ἔθνεσιν
καὶ τῷ ὀνοματί σου ψαλῶ.

καὶ πάλιν λέγει, Εὐφράνθητε, ἔθνη, μετὰ τοῦ λαοῦ αὐτοῦ.

καὶ πάλιν, Αἰνεῖτε, πάντα τὰ ἔθνη, τὸν κύριον
καὶ ἐπαινεσάτωσαν αὐτὸν πάντες οἱ λαοί.

καὶ πάλιν Ἠσαΐας λέγει, Ἔσται ἡ ῥίζα τοῦ Ἰεσσαί,
καὶ ὁ ἀνιστάμενος ἄρχειν ἐθνῶν,
ἐπ' αὐτῷ ἔθνη ἐλπιοῦσιν.

ὁ δὲ θεὸς τῆς ἐλπίδος πληρώσαι ὑμᾶς πάσης χαρᾶς καὶ εἰρήνης ἐν τῷ πιστεύειν,
εἰς τὸ περισσεύειν ὑμᾶς ἐν τῇ ἐλπίδι ἐν δυνάμει πνεύματος ἁγίου.

VERSE 7

διὸ προσλαμβάνεσθε ἀλλήλους

Paul uses the inferential conjunction διό (R 888) to introduce his conclusion to 14:1–15:6 (Schreiner 753); see 14:1 for προσλαμβάνεσθε (2 pl. pres. mid. impv. of προσλαμβάνω), which echoes the beginning of the entire section; the direct object ἀλλήλους ("one another") includes both the strong and the weak (Jewett 888).

καθὼς καὶ ὁ Χριστὸς προσελάβετο ὑμᾶς εἰς δόξαν τοῦ θεοῦ.

Καθὼς καί (NASB, "just as also") is more naturally understood as comparative (Jewett 889 n. 18; Dunn 846) than causal (Cranfield 739; Moo 875); the article with Χριστός is titular (Moo 875 n. 10); προσελάβετο (3 sg. aor. mid. indic. of προσλαμβάνω) is an indirect middle and a consummative aorist. Ὑμᾶς has strong manuscript support (ℵ, A, C, D², 33) and is preferable on internal grounds because it would include both the weak and the strong, whereas ἡμᾶς would have a limiting effect (Jewett 886 n. a; cf. Cranfield 739). Εἰς + accusative denotes purpose (Harris 92); δόξαν is definite as the object of the preposition; τοῦ θεοῦ is an objective genitive; the entire phrase is monadic (cf. 3:23; 5:3); GNB translates "that God will be given the glory." Cranfield (739), Jewett (889), and Moo (875) all connect the prepositional phrase to the initial command rather than to the comparative clause.

VERSE 8

λέγω γὰρ Χριστὸν διάκονον γεγενῆσθαι περιτομῆς ὑπὲρ ἀληθείας θεοῦ

Paul provides the explanation (γάρ) for his command in verse 7a with what Cranfield describes as "a solemn doctrinal declaration" (740); λέγω is an instantaneous present that Jewett translates "I declare" (890). The accusative + infinitive construction expresses the content of Paul's declaration (indirect discourse, R 909). Γεγενῆσθαι (pf. mid. inf. of dep. γίνομαι) is an intensive perfect ("has become") that emphasizes continuing result beyond Jesus's earthly life and ministry (Moo 877). Χριστός (Messiah) is the accusative subject; διάκονον is the predicate accusative (cf. Wallace 195); περιτομῆς is an objective genitive that modifies διάκονον and refers to the Jewish people (cf. 3:30; 4:12). Ὑπέρ + genitive might denote advantage (Porter 176; e.g., NASB, NET, "on behalf of"), although Moo (877) and Schreiner (755) argue for purpose (e.g., ESV, "to show").* Ἀληθείας θεοῦ refers to God's covenant faithfulness (Dunn 847; cf. 3:7); the genitive of θεοῦ is subjective.

εἰς τὸ βεβαιῶσαι τὰς ἐπαγγελίας τῶν πατέρων

Εἰς τό + infinitive introduces the purpose (Cranfield 741) of γεγενῆσθαι (R 1040); βεβαιῶσαι (aor. act. inf. of βεβαιόω, "confirm") is a legal term (Schreiner 755) that describes the act of putting something beyond doubt (BDAG 173a); Dunn (847) and Jewett (892) suggest "guarantee." Τὰς ἐπαγγελίας is the object of the infinitive; τῶν πατέρων is an objective genitive; NASB translates "the promises given to the fathers." See 4:13 for βεβαιόω and 4:16 for ἐπαγγελία.

VERSE 9

τὰ δὲ ἔθνη ὑπὲρ ἐλέους δοξάσαι τὸν θεόν

Δέ is best understood as continuative (Jewett 892, "and at the same time"), adding δοξάσαι (aor. act. inf. of δοξάζω) as a second purpose infinitive to the εἰς τό construction in the preceding line (Jewett 892; Moo 876; Schreiner 755; contra Cranfield 743). Τὰ ἔθνη is the subject of the infinitive, is the first of six occurrences in verses 9–12, and anticipates the discussion of Paul's mission and travel plans in 15:14–29. Ὑπὲρ ἐλέους parallels ὑπὲρ ἀληθείας in verse 8 and reintroduces the theme of God's mercy extended to both Gentiles and Jews (9:22–29). Moo notes the possible connection to the OT combination of "truth" and "mercy" (878 n. 32). Τὸν θεόν is the object of the infinitive; the definite article is monadic; see 1:21 for δοξάζω.

καθὼς γέγραπται (See 1:17)

Διὰ τοῦτο ἐξομολογήσομαί σοι ἐν ἔθνεσιν

Paul's quotation is from the LXX of Psalm 17:49 (Moo 878 n. 36) or 2 Samuel 22:50 (Schreiner 757); the wording is identical in both OT verses. See 1:26; 4:16; 5:12; 13:6 for διὰ τοῦτο; see 14:11 for ἐξομολογήσομαι (1 sg. fut. mid. indic. of ἐξομολογέω); ἐν ἔθνεσιν is locative (CSB, "among the Gentiles"). The speaker may be understood as David (Schreiner 757), Christ (Moo 879), or Paul (Jewett 894). Regardless, God's plan has always included both Jews (verse 8b) and Gentiles (verse 9a).

καὶ τῷ ὀνόματί σου ψαλῶ

Καί is connective; τῷ ὀνόματί σου is a dative of advantage; ψαλῶ (1 sg. fut. act. indic. of ψάλλω, "sing praise") describes singing of psalms or hymns of praise, with or without accompaniment (BDAG 1096b).

VERSE 10

καὶ πάλιν λέγει

Καί is connective ("and"); πάλιν ("again") adds a second OT quotation; ἡ γραφή is the understood subject (Moo 879 n. 39; cf. 4:3; 9:17; 10:11; 11:2); λέγει is a perfective present used in an introductory formula (cf. 9:15).

Εὐφράνθητε, ἔθνη, μετὰ τοῦ λαοῦ αὐτοῦ

Paul's second quotation comes from the LXX of Deuteronomy 32:43. Εὐφράνθητε (2 pl. aor. pass. impv. of εὐφραίνω, "rejoice") is a constative aorist, a passive with active meaning, and an imperative of command; the verb describes the act of expressing admiration or approval for someone or something (BDAG 357a; cf. Cranfield 746 n. 1; *TDNT* 2.770–73). Ἔθνη is direct address; μετά + genitive denotes association (NASB, "with his people").

VERSE 11

καὶ πάλιν (See 15:10)

Αἰνεῖτε, πάντα τὰ ἔθνη, τὸν κύριον

Paul's third quotation is a slightly altered version of the LXX of Psalm 116:1 (Jewett 895). Αἰνεῖτε (2 pl. pres. act. impv. of αἰνέω, "praise") is a gnomic present and an imperative of command. Πάντα τὰ ἔθνη is direct address; the use of πᾶς "stresses the fact that no people is to be excluded from this common praise of God" (Cranfield 746). Τὸν κύριον is the direct object and refers to God.

καὶ ἐπαινεσάτωσαν αὐτὸν πάντες οἱ λαοί

Καί is connective; ἐπαινεσάτωσαν (3 pl. pres. act. impv. of ἐπαινέω, "celebrate") is a gnomic present and an imperative of command; the third person imperative is best translated as "must celebrate." Αὐτόν is the direct object and, again, refers to God; πάντες οἱ λαοί (NET, "all the peoples") is the subject and includes the Jews (Jewett 895).

VERSE 12

καὶ πάλιν Ἠσαΐας λέγει (See 9:25 and 15:10)

Ἔσται ἡ ῥίζα τοῦ Ἰεσσαί

Paul's final quotation is taken verbatim from the LXX of Isaiah 11:10; see Dunn for the frequency with which Paul quotes Isaiah (850). Ἔσται (3 sg. fut. mid. indic. of εἰμί) is a predictive future; ῥίζα, -ης, ἡ describes a shoot that springs from a root (BDAG 906a); Moo provides the messianic background for the term (880 n. 45); τοῦ Ἰεσσαί is a genitive of relationship (progenitor).

καὶ ὁ ἀνιστάμενος ἄρχειν ἐθνῶν

Καί is ascensive (ESV, "even"); the substantival participle ὁ ἀνιστάμενος (nom. sg. masc. of pres. mid. ptc. of ἀνίστημι, "rise, arise") includes a possible allusion to Christ's resurrection (Moo 880 n. 44); ἄρχειν (pres. act. inf. of ἄρχω, "rule") denotes purpose; ἐθνῶν is a genitive of direct object (Wallace 134); BDF notes that the anarthrous noun occurs frequently (§254.3).

ἐπ' αὐτῷ ἔθνη ἐλπιοῦσιν

Ἐπ' αὐτῷ is moved forward for emphasis; ἔθνη is the subject; ἐλπιοῦσιν (3 pl. fut. act. indic.) is a predictive future. Paul uses ἐν + dative (1 Cor 15:19; Eph 1:12), εἰς + accusative (2 Cor 1:10; 1 Tim 5:5), and ἐπί + dative (1 Tim 4:10; 6:17) interchangeably to designate the object of hope.

VERSE 13

ὁ δὲ θεὸς τῆς ἐλπίδος πληρώσαι ὑμᾶς πάσης χαρᾶς καὶ εἰρήνης ἐν τῷ πιστεύειν

A connective δέ ("and") introduces the prayer-wish that closes the paragraph (cf. 15:5); ὁ θεός is the source of hope; the definite article is monadic; the genitive of τῆς ἐλπίδος denotes product; the article is anaphoric, pointing back to verse 12. See Longenecker for a helpful comment on three aspects of "the God of hope" (1016). Πληρώσαι (3 sg. aor. act. opt. of πληρόω, "fill") is a voluntative optative (Wallace 483);

ὑμᾶς is the direct object; πάσης χαρᾶς καὶ εἰρήνης ("with all joy and peace") is a verbal genitive of content (cf. Wallace 94). Jewett notes that "the peculiarity" of the phrase ἐν τῷ πιστεύειν "gives weight to its importance" (898). BDF (§404.1) and Moo (880 n. 50) view it as temporal (e.g., NIV, "as you believe");* Wallace (598) views it as means (e.g., GNB, "by believing"); Turner (145) views it as causal (e.g., NLT, "because you trust"). Jewett settles for "in having faith" (cf. KJV, NASB, ESV).

εἰς τὸ περισσεύειν ὑμᾶς ἐν τῇ ἐλπίδι ἐν δυνάμει πνεύματος ἁγίου

Εἰς τό + infinitive denotes the purpose of being filled with joy and peace (Jewett 899); ὑμᾶς is the accusative subject of περισσεύειν (pres. act. inf. of περισσεύω, "abound"); ἐν τῇ ἐλπίδι denotes reference (T 265); the article is anaphoric; ἐν δυνάμει is instrumental (Schreiner 757 n. 17; cf. NASB); πνεύματος ἁγίου is a subjective genitive and refers to the Holy Spirit; the anarthrous nouns are qualitative.

FOR FURTHER STUDY

See For Further Study §§ 5 ("Gentiles"), 8 ("Prayer in Paul"), 12 ("Paul's Use of the Old Testament"), 17 ("God's Glory"), 26 ("Circumcision"), 40 ("Peace"), 41 ("Hope")

HOMILETICAL SUGGESTIONS

Christ's Example of Acceptance (15:7–13)

1. Concluding Command: Accept one another (15:7)
    a. Comparison: As Christ accepted you (15:7b)
    b. Purpose: For God's glory (15:7c)
2. Christological Explanation: Christ's ministry to the circumcision (γάρ, 15:8–12)
    a. Purpose: Confirm the promises to the fathers (15:8b)
    b. Purpose: Gentiles praise God (15:9a)
        1) OT Proof (15:9b–12)
            a) Psalm 18:49 (15:9b)
            b) Deuteronomy 32:43 (15:10)
            c) Psalm 117:1 (15:11)
            d) Isaiah 11:10 (15:12)
3. Closing Prayer-Wish: Fill with joy and peace (15:13)
    a. Purpose: To abound in hope (15:13b)

III. Letter Closing (15:14–16:27)

A. PAUL'S MISSION (15:14–21)

STRUCTURE

Having completed his discussion of God's righteousness, Paul now moves to the first of eight epistolary sections that close the letter. As is true in seven of the other letters he writes to churches (1 Cor 1:10–4:21; 2 Cor 1:12–6:10; Gal 1:11–2:21; Eph 3:1–13; Phil 1:12–26; Col 1:24–2:5; 1 Thess 2:1–10), Paul includes a discussion of his ministry as an apostle (the "apostolic apologia"; cf. Harvey, *Interpreting the Pauline Letters* 37). This paragraph gives the readers an overview of Paul's mission and divides into three parts. The first expresses his confidence in the Romans (15:14); the second explains the apostolic authority with which he writes (15:15–16); the third describes the nature, scope, and strategy of his apostolic ministry (16:17–21).

Πέπεισμαι δέ, ἀδελφοί μου, καὶ αὐτὸς ἐγὼ περὶ ὑμῶν
    ὅτι καὶ αὐτοὶ μεστοί ἐστε ἀγαθωσύνης,
        πεπληρωμένοι πάσης [τῆς] γνώσεως,
        δυνάμενοι καὶ ἀλλήλους νουθετεῖν.

τολμηρότερον δὲ ἔγραψα ὑμῖν ἀπὸ μέρους
    ὡς ἐπαναμιμνήσκων ὑμᾶς διὰ τὴν χάριν τὴν δοθεῖσάν μοι ὑπὸ τοῦ θεοῦ
    εἰς τὸ εἶναί με λειτουργὸν Χριστοῦ Ἰησοῦ εἰς τὰ ἔθνη,
    ἱερουργοῦντα τὸ εὐαγγέλιον τοῦ θεοῦ,
    ἵνα γένηται ἡ προσφορὰ τῶν ἐθνῶν εὐπρόσδεκτος,
        ἡγιασμένη ἐν πνεύματι ἁγίῳ.

ἔχω οὖν [τὴν] καύχησιν ἐν Χριστῷ Ἰησοῦ τὰ πρὸς τὸν θεόν·
οὐ γὰρ τολμήσω τι λαλεῖν
    ὧν οὐ κατειργάσατο Χριστὸς δι' ἐμοῦ εἰς ὑπακοὴν ἐθνῶν,
        λόγῳ καὶ ἔργῳ,
        ἐν δυνάμει σημείων καὶ τεράτων,
        ἐν δυνάμει πνεύματος [θεοῦ]·

ὥστε με ἀπὸ Ἰερουσαλὴμ καὶ κύκλῳ μέχρι τοῦ Ἰλλυρικοῦ πεπληρωκέναι τὸ εὐαγγέλιον τοῦ Χριστοῦ,
οὕτως δὲ φιλοτιμούμενον εὐαγγελίζεσθαι οὐχ ὅπου ὠνομάσθη Χριστός,
ἵνα μὴ ἐπ' ἀλλότριον θεμέλιον οἰκοδομῶ,
ἀλλὰ καθὼς γέγραπται, Οἷς οὐκ ἀνηγγέλη περὶ αὐτοῦ ὄψονται,
καὶ οἳ οὐκ ἀκηκόασιν συνήσουσιν.

VERSE 14

Πέπεισμαι δέ, ἀδελφοί μου, καὶ αὐτὸς ἐγὼ περὶ ὑμῶν

Paul begins with an expanded confidence formula (Jewett 903). Δέ is transitional ("now"); see 8:38 for πέπεισμαι (1 sg. pf. pass. indic. of πείθω); ἀδελφοί introduces a new topic (Moo 887; cf. 1:13; 7:1; 12:1); μου adds special warmth (Cranfield 752). Καί is ascensive ("indeed"); αὐτὸς ἐγώ (NIV, "I myself") is emphatic and highlights personal commitment (Dunn 857); περὶ ὑμῶν denotes reference (NASB, "concerning you").

ὅτι καὶ αὐτοὶ μεστοί ἐστε ἀγαθωσύνης

The content (ὅτι) of Paul's confidence is the Romans' character, which consists of three qualities, beginning with their goodness. Καί is adjunctive ("also"); αὐτοί is emphatic ("you yourselves") and contrasts sharply with αὐτὸς ἐγώ in the previous line (R 686); the predicate adjective μεστοί (nom. pl. masc. of μεστός, -ή, -όν, "full") describes being fully characterized by something (BDAG 686a) and is moved forward for emphasis; ἀγαθωσύνης (gen. sg. fem. of ἀγαθωσύνη, -ης, ἡ, "goodness") is a genitive of content that describes a positive moral quality characterized by an interest in the welfare of others (BDAG 4c).

πεπληρωμένοι πάσης [τῆς] γνώσεως

The second quality is their knowledge. Πεπληρωμένοι (nom. pl. masc. of pf. pass. ptc. of πληρόω, "fill") is an adjectival participle; the perfect tense carries present force (cf. R 909; cf Burton §154). See 15:13 for πληρόω and 2:28 for γνῶσις. Dunn suggests that in this context γνώσεως carries the idea of insight into God's saving purpose (858); πάσης (gen. sg. fem.) highlights comprehensiveness (Schreiner 763); the article is anaphoric (cf. 11:33).

δυνάμενοι καὶ ἀλλήλους νουθετεῖν

The third quality is their ability to admonish one another. Δυνάμενοι (nom. pl. masc. of pres. mid. ptc. of dep. δύναμαι) is an adjectival participle; καί is adjunctive ("also"); ἀλλήλους is the object of the infinitive. Νουθετεῖν (pres. act. inf. of νουθετέω, "admonish, warn") is a complementary infinitive; the verb describes the act of counseling someone about avoiding or stopping an improper course of conduct (BDAG 679d; cf. *TDNT* 4.1019).

VERSE 15

τολμηρότερον δὲ ἔγραψα ὑμῖν ἀπὸ μέρους

Δέ is adversative (Moo 888 n. 21); τολμηρότερον is an adverb from the comparative of the adjective τολμηρός, -ά, -όν (R 298, 665); Cranfield suggests "somewhat boldly," although BDAG prefers "more/rather boldly" (1010c; cf. Jewett 905). Ἔγραψα (1 sg. aor. act. indic. of γράφω) is an epistolary aorist (R 846; Wallace 563; contra Moo 888 n. 32) that refers to what Paul has written earlier in the letter (T 73; BDF §334); ὑμῖν is the indirect object. Ἀπὸ μέρους is best understood as modifying the verb (Cranfield 753); elsewhere the phrase carries the sense of "partially" (cf. 11:25; 15:24; 2 Cor 1:14; 2:5; cf. Jewett 905); Schreiner's suggestion of "on some points" is apt (765; cf. NASB).

ὡς ἐπαναμιμνῄσκων ὑμᾶς διὰ τὴν χάριν τὴν δοθεῖσάν μοι ὑπὸ τοῦ θεοῦ

Most EVV understand ὡς as indicating purpose (e.g., NASB, NET, "so as to remind"; cf. Schreiner 766; contra ESV and Moo 888 n. 25); the participle ἐπαναμιμνῄσκων (nom. sg. masc. of pres. act. ptc. of ἐπαναμιμνῄσκω, "cause to remember") is adverbial and a progressive present; ὑμᾶς is the object of the participle. Διά + accusative is causal (Harris 73); the article is anaphoric; see 12:3 for χάρις. The article with δοθεῖσάν (acc. sg. fem. of aor. pass. ptc. of δίδωμι) marks the participle as adjectival; the aorist is constative; the agent of the passive voice is indicated by ὑπὸ τοῦ θεοῦ (Wallace 433); μοι is the indirect object.

VERSE 16

εἰς τὸ εἶναί με λειτουργὸν Χριστοῦ Ἰησοῦ εἰς τὰ ἔθνη, ἱερουργοῦντα τὸ εὐαγγέλιον τοῦ θεοῦ

The purpose (εἰς τὸ εἶναί) of God's gift of grace to Paul was that he might be a "minister" (cf. 13:6) of Christ Jesus. Με is the subject of the infinitive; λειτουργόν is the predicate accusative (Wallace 192); Χριστοῦ Ἰησοῦ is a possessive genitive; εἰς + accusative is equivalent to a dative (R 544; cf. NASB, NIV, "to the Gentiles"). Although Jewett prefers to translate λειτουργός as "ambassador" (906–07), the context suggests the nuance of a priestly function (Schreiner 766; see also his discussion of cultic terms in this verse). Ἱερουργοῦντα (acc. sg. masc. of pres. act. ptc. of ἱερουργέω, "serve as a priest") is an adjectival participle modifying λειτουργόν; the present tense is customary; the verb describes engaging in a sacred capacity and performing holy service as a priest (BDAG 471d; cf. *TDNT* 3.251–2). See 1:1 for τὸ εὐαγγέλιον τοῦ θεοῦ.

ἵνα γένηται ἡ προσφορὰ τῶν ἐθνῶν εὐπρόσδεκτος

The purpose (ἵνα + subjunc.) of Paul's priestly ministry is that the offering of the Gentiles might be acceptable to God. Προσφορά, -ᾶς, ἡ describes something that is brought as a voluntary gift or offering (BDAG 887a; cf. Eph 5:2); τῶν ἐθνῶν is a genitive of simple apposition (Schreiner 767; cf. R 498); εὐπρόσδεκτος, -ον describes something that is capable of eliciting favorable acceptance (BDAG 411a).

ἡγιασμένη ἐν πνεύματι ἁγίῳ

Ἡγιασμένη (nom. sg. fem. of pf. pass. ptc. of ἁγιάζω, "sanctify") is an adjectival participle that adds a second description of the offering of the Gentiles (cf. Wallace 618); the perfect tense is intensive. Ἁγιάζω describes the act of including someone or something in the inner circle of what is holy (BDAG 10a; cf. *TDNT* 1.90–91); Paul uses the idea frequently (1 Cor 1:2; 6:11; 7:14; Eph 5:26; 1 Thess 5:23; 1 Tim 4:5; 2 Tim 2:21). Ἐν + dative denotes agency (Schreiner 767, "by"); πνεύματι ἁγίῳ is definite although anarthrous and refers to the Holy Spirit.

VERSE 17

ἔχω οὖν [τὴν] καύχησιν ἐν Χριστῷ Ἰησοῦ τὰ πρὸς τὸν θεόν

Οὖν is inferential ("therefore") and introduces the topic of Paul's apostolic ministry that follows logically from the role God has given him. Ἔχω is a customary present that describes an ongoing state (cf. Wallace 521); the article with καύχησιν (cf. 3:27) functions as a demonstrative adjective ("this boasting") that refers back to verse 16 (Cranfield 757). Ἐν + dative identifies the object of Paul's boasting (Harris 133; cf. NLT, "about all Christ Jesus has done"). The definite article substantizes the prepositional phrase (Moo 891 n. 43), which functions as an adverbial accusative of reference (T 221; BDF §160); πρός + accusative also indicates reference (BDAG 875b, "as far as . . . is concerned"; cf. NASB, NET, "pertaining to God").

VERSE 18

οὐ γὰρ τολμήσω τι λαλεῖν

What Cranfield describes as a "decidedly clumsy sentence" explains (γάρ) how Paul's boasting is truly "in Christ Jesus" (757). See 5:7 and 10:15 for τολμήσω (1 sg. fut. act. indic. of τολμάω, "dare/be bold"), which is a gnomic future; the indefinite pronoun τι is the object of the infinitive; λαλεῖν (pres. act. infin. of λαλέω, "speak") is a complementary infinitive and a gnomic present.

ὧν οὐ κατειργάσατο Χριστὸς δι' ἐμοῦ εἰς ὑπακοὴν ἐθνῶν, λόγῳ καὶ ἔργῳ

The relative pronoun ὧν has an embedded antecedent (R 720); Cranfield suggests that Paul wanted to give greater emphasis to his statement and that ὧν οὐ is equivalent to ἐκείνων ἃ οὐ (758). Κατειργάσατο (3 sg. aor. mid. indic. of dep. κατεργάζομαι) is a constative aorist and a deponent middle; in this context, the idea is "achieve" or "accomplish" (Dunn 862). Χριστός is the subject; δι' ἐμοῦ ("through me") is instrumental (Jewett 909); εἰς ὑπακοήν denotes result (Schreiner 767); ἐθνῶν is a subjective genitive (cf. 1:5). Λόγῳ and ἔργῳ are comprehensive terms describing "speech" and "action" (Cranfield 759; cf. 2 Cor 10:11; Col 3:7; 2 Thess 2:17); the datives denote means (Jewett 910).

VERSE 19

ἐν δυνάμει σημείων καὶ τεράτων

Ἐν + dative denotes means (Dunn 863); see 1:4 for δύναμις; the genitives of σημείων and τεράτων denote product; both anarthrous nouns are qualitative. See 4:11 for σημεῖον, -ου, τό; τέρας, -ατος, τό describes something transcendent that astounds (BDAG 999d; cf. *TDNT* 7.199–261; 8.113–127). The combination also appears in 2 Corinthians 12:12 where it attests to the truth of the gospel and 2 Thessalonians 2:9 where it describes the works of Satan; Dunn suggests that Paul has the miracles of Exodus in mind (862).

ἐν δυνάμει πνεύματος [θεοῦ]

Ἐν δυνάμει again denotes means; πνεύματος is a genitive of source (Jewett 911); θεοῦ is a possessive genitive; both anarthrous nouns are definite referring to the Holy Spirit's enabling (Cranfield 759). The shortest reading (πνεύματος) has the weakest manuscript support (B), although Cranfield (758 n. 5) and Jewett (901 n. u) prefer it. Paul uses πνεύματος ἁγίου (A, D^{*}, 33) five other times in his letters (Rom 5:5; 15:13; 1 Thess 1:6; 2 Tim 1:14; Titus 3:5) and πνεύματος θεοῦ ($\mathfrak{P}^{46}$, ℵ, D^{1}) nowhere else, which makes the latter reading the more difficult. Πνεύματος θεοῦ is the most likely original reading, with πνεύματος ἁγίου an assimilation to 15:13 (cf. Schreiner 772).

ὥστε με ἀπὸ Ἰερουσαλὴμ καὶ κύκλῳ μέχρι τοῦ Ἰλλυρικοῦ

The result (ὥστε + infin.) of the Spirit's enabling has been Paul's ministry throughout the eastern Mediterranean region. Με is the subject of the infinitive; ἀπὸ Ἰερουσαλήμ describes the easternmost extent of Paul's preaching (NIV, "from Jerusalem"); καί is continuative ("and"); the adverb κύκλῳ describes the completing of a circuit (BDAG 574a; NASB, "round about"); μέχρι τοῦ Ἰλλυρικοῦ describes the westernmost extent of Paul's preaching (NET, "as far as Illyricum"). Moo provides background on the details of Paul's "circuitous route" (894–95).

πεπληρωκέναι τὸ εὐαγγέλιον τοῦ Χριστοῦ

Πεπληρωκέναι (pf. act. infin. of πληρόω, "fulfill") completes the result construction and is an extensive perfect (R 909); Cranfield concludes that the verb refers to pioneer preaching (762); see 1:1 for εὐαγγέλιον; τοῦ Χριστοῦ is an objective genitive (GNB, "the good news about Christ").

VERSE 20

οὕτως δὲ φιλοτιμούμενον εὐαγγελίζεσθαι οὐχ ὅπου ὠνομάσθη Χριστός

Δέ is adversative (Moo 896 n. 79); the adverb *οὕτως* (NET, "in this way") points forward to the description of Paul's missionary strategy (Cranfield 763). *Φιλοτιμούμενον* (acc. sg. masc. of pres. act. ptc. of dep. *φιλοτιμέομαι*, "make it one's aim") is an adverbial participle of means (Moo 896 n. 80), a customary present, and a deponent middle; *εὐαγγελίζεσθαι* (cf. 1:15) is a complementary infinitive. The negative *οὐχ* is emphatic (Dunn 865); the adverb *ὅπου* marks position in space ("where"; cf. BDAG 717b). The aorist of *ὠνομάσθη* (3 sg. aor. pass. indic. of *ὀνομάζω*, "name") points to an event that would precede Paul's preaching (cf. Burton §52–54); the absence of an agent maintains subject focus on *Χριστός*; Cranfield suggests that the verb has the sense of "be named in worship" (764; cf. Schreiner 770).

ἵνα μὴ ἐπ' ἀλλότριον θεμέλιον οἰκοδομῶ

Jewett notes that by stating his purpose negatively (*ἵνα μή* + subjunc.) and following it with *ἀλλά* in the next line, Paul "brings into contrast preaching where churches have already been established and preaching to those who have not yet heard" and focuses on Gentiles who have not yet had access to the gospel (916). *Ἐπί θεμέλιον* is spatial ("on a foundation"); see 14:4 for *ἀλλότριον*; *οἰκοδομῶ* (1 sg. pres. act. subjunc. of *οἰκοδομέω*, "build") denotes constructing in a transcendent sense (BDAG 696b). Compare 1 Corinthians 3:10–12 for the imagery of laying a foundation (cf. Heb 6:1).

VERSE 21

ἀλλὰ καθὼς γέγραπται (See 1:17)

Οἷς οὐκ ἀνηγγέλη περὶ αὐτοῦ ὄψονται

Moo provides three likely reasons Paul quoted Isaiah 52:15 at this point (897; cf. Jewett 916). The dative relative pronoun *οἷς* lacks an antecedent (R 720) and is the indirect object ("to whom"); *ἀνηγγέλη* (3 sg. aor. pass. indic. of *ἀναγγέλλω*, "proclaim") is a consummative aorist; the agent is most likely suppressed for rhetorical effect (cf. Wallace 437); *περὶ αὐτοῦ* ("concerning him") denotes reference; *ὄψονται* (3 pl. fut. mid. indic. of dep. *ὁράω*, "see") is a predictive future and a deponent middle.

καὶ οἳ οὐκ ἀκηκόασιν συνήσουσιν

Καί is continuative; *οἳ οὐκ ἀκηκόασιν* (nom. pl. masc. of pf. act. indic. of *ἀκούω*, "hear") is a substantival participle (NIV, "those who have not heard"); the perfect tense is intensive; *συνήσουσιν* (3 pl. fut. act. indic. of *συνίημι*, "understand"; cf. 3:11) is a predictive future.

FOR FURTHER STUDY

81. Letter Closings (15:14–16:27)

Bahr, G. J. "The Subscriptions in the Pauline Letters." *JBL* 87 (1968): 27–41.

Cumming, G. J. "Service-Endings in the Epistles." *NTS* 22 (1976): 110–13.

Weima, J. A. D. *Neglected Endings: The Significance of the Pauline Letter Closings.* Sheffield: Academic Press, 1994.

82. Signs and Wonders (15:19)

Hofius, O. *NIDNTT* 2.626–35.

Jervell, J. "The Signs of an Apostle: Paul's Miracles." Pages 77–95 in *The Unknown Paul.* Minneapolis: Augsburg, 1984.

Moule, C. F. D. ed. *Miracles: Cambridge Studies in their Philosophy and History.* London: Mowbry, 1965.

Praeder, S. M. "Miracle Worker and Missionary: Paul in the Acts of the Apostles." Pages 107–29 in *Society of Biblical Literature Seminar Papers, 1983.* Atlanta: Scholars Press, 1982.

Stolz, F. "Zeichen und Wunder. Die prophetischen Legitimation und ihre Geschichte." *ZTK* (1972): 125–44.

Rengstorf, K. H. *TDNT* 7.200–61.

________. *TDNT* 8.113–26.

Twelftree. G. H. *DPL* 875–77.

HOMILETICAL SUGGESTIONS

Paul's Basis for Writing to the Romans (15:14–21)

1. His confidence in the Romans (15:14)
    a. Full of goodness (15:14b)
    b. Filled with knowledge (15:14c)
    c. Able to admonish one another (15:14d)
2. His apostolic authority (15:15–16)
    a. The source: God's grace (15:15)
    b. The role: Minister of Jesus Christ to the Gentiles (15:16a)
    c. The task: Priestly service to the gospel (15:16b)
    d. The purpose: Well-pleasing offering of the Gentiles (15:16c)
3. His apostolic ministry (15:17–21)
    a. The enabling: Christ's working and the Spirit's power (15:17–19a)
    b. The scope: Jerusalem to Illyricum (15:19b)
    c. The strategy: Pioneer preaching (15:20–21)
        1) OT support: Isaiah 52:12

B. PAUL'S TRAVEL PLANS (15:22–29)

STRUCTURE

In ten of his other letters, Paul includes a sub-unit in which he seeks to make his "presence" felt (1 Cor 4:19–21; 2 Cor 13:1–10; Eph 6:20–22; Phil 2:19–30; Col 4:7–9; 1 Thess 2:17–3:13; 1 Tim 3:14–16; 2 Tim 4:9–15; Titus 3:12–14; Phlm v. 21–22). One of the elements of such an "apostolic parousia" is a discussion of travel plans (cf. Funk 250–55). In this paragraph of Romans, Paul discusses his desire to visit Rome (15:22–24), his need to visit Jerusalem (15:25–27), and his plans to visit Spain (15:28–29).

Διὸ καὶ ἐνεκοπτόμην τὰ πολλὰ τοῦ ἐλθεῖν πρὸς ὑμᾶς·
νυνὶ δὲ μηκέτι τόπον ἔχων ἐν τοῖς κλίμασι τούτοις, ἐπιποθίαν δὲ ἔχων τοῦ ἐλθεῖν πρὸς ὑμᾶς ἀπὸ πολλῶν ἐτῶν, ὡς ἂν πορεύωμαι εἰς τὴν Σπανίαν·

> ἐλπίζω γὰρ διαπορευόμενος θεάσασθαι ὑμᾶς καὶ ὑφ' ὑμῶν προπεμφθῆναι ἐκεῖ ἐὰν ὑμῶν πρῶτον ἀπὸ μέρους ἐμπλησθῶ.

νυνὶ δὲ πορεύομαι εἰς Ἰερουσαλὴμ διακονῶν τοῖς ἁγίοις.
εὐδόκησαν γὰρ Μακεδονία καὶ Ἀχαΐα κοινωνίαν τινὰ ποιήσασθαι εἰς τοὺς πτωχοὺς τῶν ἁγίων τῶν ἐν Ἰερουσαλήμ.
εὐδόκησαν γὰρ καὶ ὀφειλέται εἰσὶν αὐτῶν·
εἰ γὰρ τοῖς πνευματικοῖς αὐτῶν ἐκοινώνησαν τὰ ἔθνη, ὀφείλουσιν καὶ ἐν τοῖς σαρκικοῖς λειτουργῆσαι αὐτοῖς.

τοῦτο οὖν ἐπιτελέσας καὶ σφραγισάμενος αὐτοῖς τὸν καρπὸν τοῦτον, ἀπελεύσομαι δι' ὑμῶν εἰς Σπανίαν·
οἶδα δὲ ὅτι ἐρχόμενος πρὸς ὑμᾶς ἐν πληρώματι εὐλογίας Χριστοῦ ἐλεύσομαι.

VERSE 22

Διὸ καὶ ἐνεκοπτόμην τὰ πολλὰ τοῦ ἐλθεῖν πρὸς ὑμᾶς

The conjunction διό ("therefore") draws an inference from what precedes; καί is adjunctive ("also"); ἐνεκοπτόμην (1 sg. impf. pass. indic. of ἐγκόπτω, "hinder") is an iterative imperfect (Moo 899 n. 5) modified by the adverbial accusative of time τὰ πολλά (R 470; cf. Moule 108; EVV, "often"). Ἐγκόπτω describes the act of making progress slow or difficult (BDAG 274b). The absence of an agent for the passive voice leads commentators to different conclusions. Jewett notes that Paul uses ἐγκόπτω elsewhere to refer to Satanic opposition (1 Thess 2:18; cf. Gal 5:7) and concludes that the connection is to verses 20–21 (922). Schreiner argues that ἐνεκοπτόμην is a divine passive (774), and along with Cranfield (766) and Moo (899), concludes that what hindered Paul was the work God had for him in the eastern Mediterranean (cf. 15:19). Verse 23 seems to support the latter conclusion. Τοῦ ἐλθεῖν (aor. act. infin. of dep. ἔρχομαι, "come") has an ablative sense (EVV, "hindered from coming"; R 996; Moo 899 n. 7); πρὸς ὑμᾶς is spatial ("to you").

VERSE 23

νυνὶ δὲ μηκέτι τόπον ἔχων ἐν τοῖς κλίμασιν, τούτοις

See 3:21 for the temporal contrast of νυνὶ δέ ("but now"), which the adverb μηκέτι ("no longer") reinforces. Τόπον (acc. sg. masc. of τόπος, -ου, ὁ, "place") is best translated "opportunity" here (Moo 899 n. 9); ἔχων (nom. sg. masc. of pres. act. ptc.) is an adverbial participle of cause (Cranfield 768); ἐν τοῖς κλίμασιν τούτοις denotes location (NASB, "in these regions"; cf. BDAG 549c).

ἐπιποθίαν δὲ ἔχων τοῦ ἐλθεῖν πρὸς ὑμᾶς ἀπὸ πολλῶν ἐτῶν

The continuative conjunction δέ ("and") adds a second adverbial participle of cause (ἔχων) with ἐπιποθίαν (acc. sg. fem. of ἐπιποθία, -ας, ἡ, "longing, desire"; cf. BDAG 377d); τοῦ ἐλθεῖν (aor. act. infin. of dep. ἔρχομαι, "come") is a substantival infinitive that stands in apposition to ἐπιποθίαν (Wallace 607); πρὸς ὑμᾶς ("to you") is spatial; ἀπὸ πολλῶν ἐτῶν is equivalent to an accusative of extent (Moo 900 n. 12); Jewett translates as "for many years" (923).

VERSE 24

ὡς ἂν πορεύωμαι εἰς τὴν Σπανίαν·

Ὡς ἄν introduces an indefinite temporal clause (Moule 133) that modifies ἔχων (Cranfield 768; contra Moo 900). BDF equates the combination with ὅταν (§455.2; cf. NASB, "whenever"); πορεύωμαι (1 sg. pres. mid. subjunc. of dep. πορεύομαι, "go") is a present subjunctive of definite action in the future (T 112) and a deponent middle; εἰς + accusative is spatial (NET, "to Spain"). Σπανίαν is shorter, has strong manuscript support (𝔓[46], ℵ*, A, B, D), and is the more likely original reading. The longer variant was probably added to remedy the anacoluthon that exists without it (Schreiner 779). See Dunn for Paul's reasons to visit Spain (872).

ἐλπίζω γὰρ διαπορευόμενος θεάσασθαι ὑμᾶς καὶ ὑφ' ὑμῶν προπεμφθῆναι ἐκεῖ

Although most EVV smooth out the syntax of the remainder of the verse (e.g., NIV), it is best to follow NASB and understand the second and third lines as parenthetical (cf. Cranfield 766; Dunn 871; Jewett 924). Γάρ is explanatory ("for"); the present tense of ἐλπίζω is progressive; see 4:18 for the idea of "hope." Διαπορευόμενος (nom. sg. masc. of pres. mid. ptc. of dep. διαπορεύομαι, "pass through") is adverbial of time, a futuristic present, and a deponent middle; θεάσασθαι (aor. mid. infin. of dep. θεάομαι, "visit"; cf. BDAG 445d) is a complementary infinitive; ὑμᾶς is the object of the infinitive. Καί ("and") adds a second complement to ἐλπίζω; ὑφ' ὑμῶν ("by you") is the ultimate agent; προπεμφθῆναι (aor. pass. infin. of προπέμπω, "send on one's way") is a constative aorist and a simple passive; the adverb ἐκεῖ ("there") refers to Spain. Προπέμπω describes the act of assisting someone in making a journey (BDAG 873d); it occurs elsewhere in referring to missionary support (Acts 15:3; 20:38; 21:5; 1 Cor

16:6; 2 Cor 1:16; Titus 3:13; cf. Dunn 872); GNB translates "helped by you to go [to Spain]."

ἐὰν ὑμῶν πρῶτον ἀπὸ μέρους ἐμπλησθῶ

Ἐάν + subjunctive introduces a third class condition; ὑμῶν is a genitive of agency ("by you"; cf. Wallace 126); πρῶτον ἀπὸ μέρους is best taken together as temporal (Jewett 926, "first for a time"); ἐμπλησθῶ (1 sg. aor. pass. subjunc. of ἐμπίπλημι, "fill, satisfy") is a proleptic aorist and a simple passive ("I might be filled"); the subjunctive completes the conditional clause. Ἐμπίπλημι may be translated "have one's fill of something" or "enjoy someone or something" (BDAG 324d). EVV (e.g., CSB) commonly translate the clause with a variation of "once I have first enjoyed your company for a while."

VERSE 25

νυνὶ δὲ πορεύομαι εἰς Ἰερουσαλὴμ διακονῶν τοῖς ἁγίοις

Νυνὶ δέ ("but now") repeats the wording of verse 24a (anaphoric ring-composition) to introduce Paul's need to visit Jerusalem before he comes to Rome on his way to Spain. Πορεύομαι is a present with future meaning (Dunn 873) and a deponent middle; εἰς Ἰερουσαλήμ is spatial ("to Jerusalem"); διακονῶν (nom. sg. masc. of pres. act. ptc. of διακονέω) is an adverbial participle of purpose (Wallace 637); τοῖς ἁγίοις is a dative of direct object; the definite article is kataphoric, pointing forward to the saints in Jerusalem (15:26). In this context, διακονέω describes the role of functioning as an intermediary (BDAG 229d) and is shorthand for Paul's task of delivering the Jerusalem collection (Jewett 927). See Dunn's discussion of the possible reasons the collection was important to Paul (873–74; cf. Schreiner 776).

VERSE 26

εὐδόκησαν γὰρ Μακεδονία καὶ Ἀχαΐα κοινωνίαν τινὰ ποιήσασθαι

The explanation (γάρ) for Paul's travel to Jerusalem relates to the action the churches in Macedonia and Achaia "considered a good and worthy choice" (BDAG 404b). Εὐδόκησαν (3 pl. aor. act. indic. of εὐδοκέω, be pleased; cf. 1:32) is a constative aorist; εὐδοκέω + accusative and infinitive indicates choice or preference (Dunn 874). The absence of articles with Μακεδονία and Ἀχαΐα is an exception to common practice (T 170); the regional names stand for the members of the churches in those regions (Cranfield 772). The indefinite pronoun τινά is used adjectivally to modify κοινωνίαν (ESV, "some contribution"); the middle voice of ποιήσασθαι (aor. mid. infin. of ποιέω, "make") is reciprocal and highlights the shared nature of the decision (cf. Moo 903 n. 36). Κοινωνία, -ας, ἡ denotes a sign of fellowship or proof of unity (BDAG 553b); in this context it refers to the collection Paul was carrying to Jerusalem (Dunn 875; cf, 2 Cor 8:4; 9:13; contra Jewett 928–29).

εἰς τοὺς πτωχοὺς τῶν ἁγίων τῶν ἐν Ἰερουσαλήμ

Εἰς + accusative denotes advantage (NET, "for the poor"); πτωξός, -ή, όν describes individuals who are economically disadvantaged (BDAG 896b); τῶν ἁγίων is a partitive genitive (R 502; T 209; NASB, "among the saints"); the article allows ἐν Ἰερουσαλήμ to function adjectivally; ἐν + dative is local ("in Jerusalem").

VERSE 27

εὐδόκησαν γὰρ καὶ ὀφειλέται εἰσὶν αὐτῶν

The repetition of εὐδόκησαν γάρ reinforces the voluntary decision of the Macedonian and Achaian congregations (Cranfield 773); καί is ascensive ("indeed"); the predicate nominative ὀφειλέται (nom. pl. masc. of ὀφειλέτης, -ου, ὁ, "debtor"; cf. 1:14) carries the nuance of moral debt (Schreiner 778); αὐτῶν refers back to the saints in Jerusalem; the genitive with ὀφειλέτης identifies the person(s) to whom the debt is owed (Moo 904 n. 45).

εἰ γὰρ τοῖς πνευματικοῖς αὐτῶν ἐκοινώνησαν τὰ ἔθνη

Paul further explains (γάρ) the Gentiles' indebtedness in terms of salvation blessings (Schreiner 778). Εἰ introduces a first class condition (R 1009); the dative of τοῖς πνευματικοῖς denotes sphere (Porter 99). Cranfield concludes that τά πνευματικά "refers to those spiritual good things which have been mediated to the Gentiles through the original Jerusalem church" and that ἐκοινώνησαν (3 pl. aor. act. indic. of κοινωνέω, "share, participate") carries the idea of "receive a share in" (773). NLT translates "the Gentiles received the spiritual blessings of the Good News from the believers in Jerusalem."

ὀφείλουσιν καὶ ἐν τοῖς σαρκικοῖς λειτουργῆσαι αὐτοῖς

Ὀφείλουσιν (3 pl. pres. act. indic. of ὀφείλω, "be obligated"; cf. 13:8; 15:1) is a gnomic present; καί is adjunctive ("also"); ἐν + dative denotes sphere; the definite article is the equivalent of a possessive pronoun; σαρκικός, -ή, -όν describes something belonging to the physical realm (NCV, "their material possessions"). Λειτουργῆσαι (aor. act. infin. of λειτουργέω, "serve") is a gnomic aorist and a complementary infinitive; in this context, λειτουργέω describes the act of doing material service (cf. BDAG 591b); αὐτοῖς is the dative object of the infinitive (cf. Acts 13:2).

VERSE 28

τοῦτο οὖν ἐπιτελέσας καὶ σφραγισάμενος αὐτοῖς τὸν καρπὸν τοῦτον

The inferential conjunction οὖν ("therefore") summarizes Paul's statement of his plans (Cranfield 774); τοῦτο (acc. sg. neut. of οὗτος, αὕτη, τοῦτο) is retrospective and the object of the participle; ἐπιτελέσας (nom. sg. masc. of aor. act. ptc. of ἐπιτελέω, "finish/bring to an end") is an adverbial participle of time and a consummative aorist

(NIV, "after I have completed") as is σφραγισάμενος (nom. sg. masc. of aor. mid. ptc. of σφραγίζω, "seal"); καί is continuative ("and have sealed"). Σφραγίζω carries the idea of preparing something for delivery (Jewett 931–32; cf. BDAG 980c); Cranfield discusses five possible options and concludes that the verb refers to confirmation of the collection's significance and integrity (774–75; cf. Moo 907 n. 62); αὐτοῖς is the indirect object; τὸν καρπὸν τοῦτον ("this fruit") refers to the collection (Dunn 877).

ἀπελεύσομαι δι' ὑμῶν εἰς Σπανίαν

Ἀπελεύσομαι (1 sg. fut. mid. indic. of dep. ἀπέρχομαι, "depart, leave") is a predictive future and a deponent middle; δι' ὑμῶν describes extension through (Moule 55); Robertson translates as "through your city" (582); εἰς Σπανίαν is spatial (NASB, "to Spain").

VERSE 29

οἶδα δὲ ὅτι ἐρχόμενος πρὸς ὑμᾶς

Δέ is continuative; οἶδα is a perfect with present force; Cranfield notes that the verb describes "firm confidence" (775); ὅτι introduces content ("that"); ἐρχόμενος (nom. sg. masc. of pres. mid. ptc. of dep. ἔρχομαι) is an adverbial participle of time (Moule 134; cf. NIV, "when I come"), a futuristic present, and a deponent middle; πρὸς ὑμᾶς is spatial ("to you").

ἐν πληρώματι εὐλογίας Χριστοῦ ἐλεύσομαι

Ἐν + dative denotes accompanying circumstance (R 589; cf. Moo 907 n. 63); see 11:12 for πλήρωμα; εὐλογίας (gen. sg. fem.) is a genitive of content; Χριστοῦ is a genitive of source; ἐλεύσομαι (1 sg. fut. mid. indic. of dep. ἔρχομαι) is a predictive future and a deponent middle. The variant reading, Χριστοῦ, is shorter, has strong manuscript support (𝔓[46], ℵ*, A, B, D), and is the more likely original reading. Cranfield describes του εὐαγγελίου τοῦ Χριστοῦ as "an unnecessary attempted improvement" (774 n. 4).

FOR FURTHER STUDY

83. Apostolic Parousia (15:22–29)

Aus, R. D. "Paul's Travel Plans to Spain and the 'Full Number of the Gentiles' of Rom 11:25." *NovT* 21 (1979): 232–62.

Bowers, P. "Fulfilling the Gospel: The Scope of the Pauline Mission." *JETS* 30 (1987): 185–98.

Funk, R. W. "The Apostolic 'Parousia': Form and Significance." Pages 249–68 in *Christian History and Interpretation: Studies Presented to John Knox*. Edited by W. R. Farmer, C. F. D. Moule, and R. R. Niebuhr. Cambridge: Cambridge University Press, 1967.

Knox, J. "Romans 15:14–23 and Paul's Conception of His Apostolic Mission." *JBL* 83 (1964): 1–11.

Jervis, L. A. *The Purpose of Romans: A Comparative Letter Structure Investigation.* Sheffield: Academic Press, 1991.
Knox, J. "Rom 15:14–33 and Paul's Conception of His Apostolic Mission." *JBL* 83 (1964): 1–11.
Miller, J. C. "The Jewish Context of Paul's Gentile Mission." *TynBul* 58 (2007): 101–15.
Mullins, T. Y. "'Visit Talk' in the NT Letters." *CBQ* 35 (1973): 350–58.

84. Spanish Mission (15:24, 28)

Bowers, W. P. "Jewish Communities in Spain in the Time of Paul the Apostle." *JTS* 26 (1975): 395–402.
Chappie, A. "Why Spain? Paul and His Mission Plans." *Journal for the Study of Paul and His Letters* 1 (2011): 193–212.
Das, A. A. "Paul of Tarshish: Isaiah 66.19 and the Spanish Mission of Romans 15.24, 28." *NTS* 54 (2008): 60–73.
Dewey, A. J. "Εἰς τὴν Σπανίαν: The Future and Paul." Pages 321–49 in *Religious Propaganda and Missionary Competition in the New Testament World: Essays Honoring Dieter Georgi*. Edited by L. Bormann. Leiden: Brill, 1994.

85. Jerusalem and the Collection (15:25–26)

Bartsch, H.-W. ". . . wenn ich ihnen diese Frucht versiegelt habe. Röm 15:28." *ZNW* 63 (1972): 95–107.
Batey, R. A. *DNTB* 559–61.
Berger, K. "Almosen für Israel; zum historischen Kontext der paulinischen Kollekte." *NTS* 23 (1976–77): 180–204.
Bruce, F. F. "Paul and Jerusalem." *TynBul* 19 (1968): 3–25.
Georgi, D. *Remembering the Poor. The History of Paul's Collection for Jerusalem.* Translated by I. Racz. Nashville: Abingdon, 1992.
Hurtado, L. W. "The Jerusalem Collection and the Book of Galatians." *JSNT* 5 (1979): 46–62.
Jeremias, J. *Jerusalem in the Time of Jesus*. Philadelphia: Fortress, 1969.
Joubert, S. *Paul as Benefactor: Reciprocity, Strategy and Theological Reflection in Paul's Collection.* Tübingen: Mohr Siebeck, 2000.
Keck, L. E. "The Poor among the Saints in the New Testament." *ZNW* 56 (1965): 100–29.
________. "'The Poor among the Saints' in Jewish Christianity and Qumran." *ZNW* 57 (1966): 54–78.
Knox, W. L. *St. Paul and the Church of Jerusalem*. Cambridge: Cambridge University Press, 1925.
McKnight, S. *DPL* 143–47.
Nickle, K. F. *The Collection. A Study in Paul's Strategy*. London: SCM, 1966.
Purvis, J. D. *Jerusalem, The Holy City: A Bibliography*. Metuchen: Scarecrow, 1991.
Stein, R. H. *DPL* 463–74.
Wright, N. T. "Jerusalem in the New Testament." Pages 53–77 in *Jerusalem: Past and Present in the Purposes of God*. Edited by P. W. L. Walker. Cambridge: Tyndale House, 1992.

HOMILETICAL SUGGESTIONS

Paul's Travel Plans (15:22–29)

1. His Desire to Visit Rome (15:22–24)
   a. Past circumstances: Often hindered (15:22)
   b. Present circumstances: "No more room" in the East (15:23–24a)
   c. Purpose: Help for journey (15:24b)
2. His Need to Visit Jerusalem (15:25–27)
   a. Purpose: To minister to the saints (15:25)
   b. Reason: Macedonia's and Achaia's contribution (15:26)
   c. Explanation: Reciprocal obligation (15:27)
3. His Plan to Visit Spain (15:28–29)
   a. His route: Through Rome to Spain (15:28)
   b. His confidence: The full blessing of Christ (15:29)

C. PAUL'S PRAYER REQUEST (15:30–33)

STRUCTURE

His upcoming visit to Jerusalem (15:25–27) leads Paul to request prayer from his readers. He uses an extended request formula to ask the Romans to pray with him (15:30). His request involves two petitions (15:31) directed toward a specific purpose (15:32). He closes the brief paragraph with his own prayer-wish for the Romans (15:33).

Παρακαλῶ δὲ ὑμᾶς [,ἀδελφοι,] διὰ τοῦ κυρίου ἡμῶν Ἰησοῦ Χριστοῦ καὶ διὰ τῆς ἀγάπης τοῦ πνεύματος συναγωνίσασθαί μοι ἐν ταῖς προσευχαῖς ὑπὲρ ἐμοῦ πρὸς τὸν θεόν,
ἵνα ῥυσθῶ ἀπὸ τῶν ἀπειθούντων ἐν τῇ Ἰουδαίᾳ
καὶ ἡ διακονία μου ἡ εἰς Ἰερουσαλὴμ εὐπρόσδεκτος τοῖς ἁγίοις γένηται,
ἵνα ἐν χαρᾷ ἐλθὼν πρὸς ὑμᾶς διὰ θελήματος θεοῦ συναναπαύσωμαι ὑμῖν.

ὁ δὲ θεὸς τῆς εἰρήνης μετὰ πάντων ὑμῶν, ἀμήν.

VERSE 30

Παρακαλῶ δὲ ὑμᾶς [,ἀδελφοι,] διὰ τοῦ κυρίου ἡμῶν Ἰησοῦ Χριστοῦ καὶ διὰ τῆς ἀγάπης τοῦ πνεύματος

Although 𝔓[46] and B omit *ἀδελφοί*, all other manuscripts include it, and it fits well with similar request formulas in the letter (cf. 12:1; 16:17). Δέ is transitional ("now") and introduces a new paragraph; *παρακαλῶ* is an instantaneous present; *διά* + genitive provides the basis for Paul's request and invokes divine authority (Cranfield 776; Moo 909); compare 5:1 for *διὰ τοῦ κυρίου ἡμῶν Ἰησοῦ Χριστοῦ*. The continuative *καί* adds a second basis (*διά* + gen.); *τοῦ πνεύματος* is a genitive of source (Moo 909 n. 12, "love that the Spirit inspires"). Invoking both Christ and the Spirit reinforces the urgency of the request.

συναγωνίσασθαί μοι ἐν ταῖς προσευχαῖς ὑπὲρ ἐμοῦ πρὸς τὸν θεόν

Συναγωνίσασθαί (aor. mid. infin. of dep. *συναγωνίζομαι*, "contend along with") is a complementary infinitive, a constative aorist, and an indirect middle. The verb describes the act of joining with someone in a common effort (BDAG 964a; cf. Col 4:12); Jewett suggests that it involves an urgent need for assistance (939); Longenecker defines the word as "a combat in company with another person or people" (1048). Μοι is associative (NASB, "with me"); *ἐν* + dative is temporal ("during"); the article is the equivalent of a possessive pronoun (KJV, ESV, "your prayers"); see 1:10 for *προσευχή*. Ὑπέρ + genitive denotes advantage (NET, CSB, "on my behalf"); *πρός* + accusative denotes direction (EVV, "to God.").

VERSE 31

ἵνα ῥυσθῶ ἀπὸ τῶν ἀπειθούντων ἐν τῇ Ἰουδαίᾳ

Ἵνα introduces the twofold content of Paul's prayer request (Jewett 935). First, he asks the Romans to pray that he will be delivered from unbelievers in Judea. Ῥυσθῶ (1 sg. aor. pass. subjunc. of dep. ῥύομαι, "rescue, deliver") is a divine passive; see 7:24 for the verb, which carries the nuance here of deliverance from serious danger (Cranfield 778; Dunn 878). Ἀπό + genitive denotes separation (cf. 2 Thess 3:2); τῶν ἀπειθούντων (gen. pl. masc. of pres. act. ptc. of ἀπειθέω, "disobey"; cf. 2:8) is a customary present; the substantival participle is best translated "unbelievers" (Moo 910); ἐν + dative denotes location (Jewett 936); Robertson notes the absence of the definite article with the adjectival prepositional phrase (783).

καὶ ἡ διακονία μου ἡ εἰς Ἰερουσαλὴμ εὐπρόσδεκτος τοῖς ἁγίοις γένηται

Paul's second request (καί) is that the saints in Jerusalem will be pleased with the gift he will deliver. Διακονία has strong manuscript support (𝔓[46], ℵ, A, D[2], 33) and was probably viewed as harsh by some scribes (Metzger 474). Since δωροφορία (B, D*) occurs nowhere else in the NT, Jewett concludes that it was a correction for ecclesiastical purposes (920 n. t). The article with διακονία is anaphoric (cf. 15:25) and refers to the collection (Moo 910); the second article allows the prepositional phrase to function adjectivally; εἰς + accusative denotes advantage (NASB, ESV, "for Jerusalem"). See 15:16 for εὐπρόσδεκτος, which regularly has the dative following it (NET, "acceptable to the saints"); placing the predicate adjective and the dative noun before the verb gives them emphasis; the subjunctive verb γένηται (3 sg. aor. mid. subjunc. of dep. γίνομαι) concludes the compound ἵνα clause.

VERSE 32

ἵνα ἐν χαρᾷ ἐλθὼν πρὸς ὑμᾶς διὰ θελήματος θεοῦ συναναπαύσωμαι ὑμῖν

The purpose (ἵνα + subjunc.; cf. Cranfield 779; Jewett 937; Moo 911) of Paul's prayer is that he might enjoy a refreshing time with the Romans. That purpose is qualified in three ways: ἐν χαρᾷ (ESV, "with joy") describes manner; ἐλθὼν πρὸς ὑμᾶς (nom. sg. masc. of aor. act. ptc. of dep. ἔρχομαι) is adverbial of time ("when I come to you"); διὰ θελήματος θεοῦ (NET, "by God's will") denotes intermediate agency (Wallace 434 n. 79). See 1:10 for θελήματος θεοῦ; both nouns are definite although anarthrous. Συναναπαύσωμαι (1 sg. aor. mid. subjunc. of dep. συναναπαύομαι, "rest with") is a direct middle; ὑμῖν is an associative dative (R 529); the verb describes the refreshment that comes from relaxing in someone's company (BDAG 965b).

Metzger notes that Paul always speaks of the will of God rather than the will of Christ Jesus, or the will of Jesus Christ (474). Of the five variant readings, 𝔓[46], ℵ[2], A, C, D*, and 33 support θελήματος θεοῦ (Schreiner 784), which narrows the options to three. Of those, the two readings that include the subjunctive ἔλθω are easier than the one that includes the participle ἐλθών (Moo 908 n. 3). These considerations suggest that the UBS[5] reading is probably original.

VERSE 33

ὁ δὲ θεὸς τῆς εἰρήνης μετὰ πάντων ὑμῶν, ἀμήν

See 15:5–6 and 15:13 for similar prayer-wishes. Δέ is transitional ("now"); ὁ θεός is the source of peace; the genitive of τῆς εἰρήνης denotes product; the optative εἴη is understood (Wallace 396); μετά + genitive denotes presence (Harris 168). See 1:7 for εἰρήνη and 1:25 for ἀμήν. Although the variants that omit ἀμήν (𝔓[46], A) are shorter and might have tempted scribes to add it, the reading that includes ἀμήν has stronger manuscript support (א, B, D, 33). The omission most likely arises from versions of the letter that add 16:25–27 at this point. Longenecker views this verse as marking the beginning of the letter closing and, so, treats it with what follows (1062).

FOR FURTHER STUDY

See For Further Study §§ 8 ("Prayer in Paul"), 40 ("Peace"), 61 ("Ministry, Minister")

HOMILETICAL SUGGESTIONS

Paul's Prayer Request (15:30–33)

1. Request for urgent prayer (15:30–32)
   a. Petition #1: Rescue from unbelievers (15:31a)
   b. Petition #2: Acceptable service to the saints (15:31b)
   c. Purpose: Opportunity to visit Rome (ἵνα, 15:32)
2. Prayer-Wish (15:33)

D. COMMENDATION OF PHOEBE (16:1–2)

STRUCTURE

Jewett notes that this paragraph follows the basic structure of other recommendations in Paul's letters (Jewett 942; cf. Phil 4:2–3; 1 Cor 16:15–18; 1 Thess 5:12–13a; Phlm 10–17): an introduction (16:1a), credentials (16:1b), and a desired action (16:2a–b). To these standard elements, Paul adds a rationale to support the desired action (16:2c). (See also C. W. Keyes, "The Greek Letter of Introduction," *American Journal of Philology* 56 (1935): 28–44 and C.-H. Kim, *Form and Structure of the Familiar Greek Letter of Recommendation*. Missoula, MT: University of Montana, 1972.)

Συνίστημι δὲ ὑμῖν Φοίβην τὴν ἀδελφὴν ἡμῶν,
οὖσαν [καὶ] διάκονον τῆς ἐκκλησίας τῆς ἐν Κεγχρεαῖς,
    ἵνα αὐτὴν προσδέξησθε ἐν κυρίῳ ἀξίως τῶν ἁγίων
    καὶ παραστῆτε αὐτῇ ἐν ᾧ ἂν ὑμῶν χρῄζῃ πράγματι·
    καὶ γὰρ αὐτὴ προστάτις πολλῶν ἐγενήθη καὶ ἐμοῦ αὐτοῦ.

VERSE 1

Συνίστημι δὲ ὑμῖν Φοίβην τὴν ἀδελφὴν ἡμῶν

The transitional δέ ("now") argues against these verses as a separate letter (Jewett 941). Συνίστημι (1 sg. pres. act. indic. of *συνίστημι*, "commend") is an instantaneous present (Wallace 518); the verb was regularly used to commend someone to someone else (BDAG 972d; cf. *TDNT* 7.897) and occurs five times in 2 Corinthians (3:1; 5:12; 6:4; 10:12, 18). Ὑμῖν is the indirect object ("to you"); Φοίβην is the direct object; τὴν ἀδελφὴν ἡμῶν stands in apposition to Φοίβην and denotes a member of the Christian community (Cranfield 780; cf. Phlm 2). Phoebe was a Gentile from Cenchrea (Moo 913) and was most likely a freed slave (Cranfield 780). She held a prominent role in the church, which might have met in her residence (Jewett 944). It is probable that she carried the letter to Rome (Dunn 866).

οὖσαν [καὶ] διάκονον τῆς ἐκκλησίας τῆς ἐν Κεγχρεαῖς

Οὖσαν (acc. sg. fem. of pres. act. ptc. of *εἰμί*) is an adjectival participle; *καί* is adjunctive ("also"); *διάκονον* is the predicate accusative (Wallace 191); *τῆς ἐκκλησίας* is a genitive of subordination; the article with ἐν Κεγχρεαῖς allows the prepositional phrase to function adjectivally (R 782). Although Schussler-Fiorenza suggests that *διάκονος, ου, ὁ* designates a traveling missionary (*In Memory of Her* 171), it more likely refers to either a definite office (e.g., "deacon"; Cranfield 781; Schreiner 787) or a semi-official role (e.g., "minister"; Dunn 887; Moo 914 n. 11) in the church in Cenchrea, the eastern port of Corinth (Acts 18:18; cf. Jewett 943).

VERSE 2

ἵνα αὐτὴν προσδέξησθε ἐν κυρίῳ ἀξίως τῶν ἁγίων

Paul has a double purpose (ἵνα + subjunc.) in commending Phoebe to the Roman church (Moo 915 n. 12). The first is to receive her favorably (BDAG 877a; cf. Phil 2:29). Προσδέξησθε (2 pl. aor. mid. subjunc. of dep. προσδέχομαι, "welcome") is a constative aorist and a deponent middle; αὐτήν is the direct object; ἐν κυρίῳ denotes personal relationship (Harris 129) and a degree of intimacy (Dunn 887). The genitive regularly follows the adverb ἀξίως (R 505); Cranfield suggests that the phrase "worthily of the saints" introduces a motive of self-respect (782); Jewett concludes that it describes honors suitable to her role in the church in Cenchrea and her contribution to the Christian mission (945).

καὶ παραστῆτε αὐτῇ ἐν ᾧ ἂν ὑμῶν χρῄζῃ πράγματι

A continuative καί adds a second purpose: to help Phoebe with whatever need she might have. Παραστῆτε (2 pl. aor. act. subjunc. of παρίστημι) carries the idea of standing by to help (Dunn 888; cf. 2 Tim 4:17); αὐτῇ (dat. sg. fem.) denotes the person helped (BDAG 778c). Although Robertson (718, 721) and Moule (130) claim that the antecedent of the relative pronoun (ᾧ) is omitted, Moo's understanding that πράγματι (dat. sg. neut. of πρᾶγμα, -ατος, τό, "matter") is the antecedent is preferable (915 n. 15; cf. T 265). Ἐν + dative denotes reference (T 265); ὑμῶν is the equivalent of a dative of source (NET, "from you"); the use of χρῄζῃ (3 sg. pres. act. subjunc. of χρῄζω, "need") in an indefinite relative clause (ἐν ᾧ ἄν) is equivalent to a third class condition (more probable future). Paul most likely uses a conditional form "because appropriate measures are more easily decided by the recipient than by the letter writer" (Jewett 946). Πρᾶγμα is a general word for a task or undertaking (BDAG 859a; cf. Dunn 888); Moo suggests that a legal dispute is involved (915 n. 18); Jewett connects the need to the Spanish mission (947).

καὶ γὰρ αὐτὴ προστάτις πολλῶν ἐγενήθη καὶ ἐμοῦ αὐτοῦ

The rationale (γάρ) for the action Paul requests is Phoebe's role as his patroness. Καί is ascensive (CSB, "indeed"); αὐτή is intensive (NASB, "she herself"); προστάτις (nom. sg. fem.) is the predicate nominative; πολλῶν (gen. pl. masc. of πολύς, πολλή, πολύ, "much, many") is an objective genitive (NCV, "she has helped . . . many others"); ἐγενήθη (3 sg. aor. pass. indic. of dep. γίνομαι) is a deponent passive (Jewett 946). Καί is continuative, linking ἐμοῦ to πολλῶν as a second objective genitive; αὐτοῦ is intensive (R 687). Προστάτις, -ιδος, ἡ describes a woman in a supportive role (BDAG 885b). It can simply denote a "helper" (Cranfield 783; Schreiner 788), but in this context it more likely identifies Pheobe as a patroness (Dunn 888; Jewett 946; Moo 916 n. 21).

FOR FURTHER STUDY

86. Phoebe (16:1)

Arichea, D. C. "Who was Phoebe? Translating διάκονος in Romans 16.1." *BT* 39 (1988): 401–409.
Goodspeed, E. J. "Phoebe's Letter of Introduction." *HTR* 44 (1951): 55–57.
Jewett. R. "Paul, Phoebe, and the Spanish Mission." Pages 142–61 in *The Social World of Formative Christianiity and Judaism.* Edited by J. Neusner, E. S. Frerichs, P. Borgen, and R. Horsley. Philadelphia: Fortress, 1988.
Walters, J. C. "'Phoebe' and 'Junia(s)'—Rom 16:1–2, 7." Pages 176–90 in *Essays on Women in Earliest Christianity*. Edited by C. D. Osburn. Joplin, MO: College Press, 1993.
Whelan, C. F. "Amica Pauli: The Role of Phoebe in the Early Church." *JSNT* 49 (1993): 67–85.

87. Patron, Patronage (16:2)

Chow, J. K. *Patronage and Power: A Study of Social Networks in Corinth.* Sheffield: Academic, 1992.
Danker, F. W. *Benefactor: Epigraphic Study of a Greco-Roman and New Testament Semantic Field.* St. Louis: Clayton, 1982.
deSilva, D. A. *DNTB* 766–71.
________. *Honor, Patronage, Kinship and Purity: Unlocking New Testament Culture.* Downers Grove, IL: InterVarsity, 2000.
Moxnes, H. "Patron-Client Relations and the New Community in Luke-Acts." Pages 241–68 in *The Social World of Luke-Acts*. Edited by J. H. Neyrey. Peabody, MA: Hendrickson, 1991.
Saller, R. P. *Personal Patronage Under the Early Empire*. Cambridge: Cambridge University Press, 1982.
Winter, B. W. "The Public Honouring of Christian Benefactors: Romans 13:3–4 and 1 Peter 2:14–15." *JSNT* 34 (1988): 87–103.

HOMILETICAL SUGGESTIONS

Commendation of Phoebe (16:1–2)

1. Recommendation and credentials (16:1)
   a. Minister of the church in Cenchrea (16:1b)
2. Requests (ἵνα, 16:2a–b)
   a. Receive her (16:2a)
   b. Help her (16:2b)
3. Rationale: Her previous patronage (γάρ, 16:2c)

E. GREETINGS FROM PAUL (16:3–16)

STRUCTURE

Paul regularly includes greetings in his letters. In this paragraph, he greets twenty-six individuals. Fifteen appear to be close friends, while eleven appear to be house church leaders whom Paul knew less well (Jewett 952–53). Longenecker's suggestion that all twenty-six were Jewish believers who had left Rome because of Claudius's edict and returned (or migrated) to Rome after that edict was repealed seems unlikely (1066). Fifteen of the individuals have Greek cultural identities; seven have Jewish cultural identities; and four have Roman identities (Jewett 953). It appears that at least ten are slaves or freedmen (Moo 918 n. 8); nine are women. Paul also greets five groups, at least three of which (16:5a, 14b, 15b) are house churches (Moo 917). The purpose of the extended list is to secure a positive reception for the letter and, ultimately, for Paul (Dunn 890).

The paragraph consists of seventeen sentences. The first fifteen are greetings to individuals that begin with *ἀσπάσασθε* (2 pl. aor. mid. impv. of dep. *ἀσπάζομαι*, "greet"). Gamble notes that the imperative of command "functions here as a surrogate for the first person indicative form, and so represents a direct personal greeting of the writer himself to the addressees" (93). These fifteen greetings may be divided into two sections. The first section (16:3–7) includes four greetings to people identified with Paul's mission, while the second section (16:8–15) includes eleven greetings to other friends and acquaintances (Schreiner 789). A third section (16:16) consists of a call for mutual greeting and greetings from "all the churches in Christ."

Ἀσπάσασθε Πρίσκαν καὶ Ἀκύλαν
τοὺς συνεργούς μου ἐν Χριστῷ Ἰησοῦ,
οἵτινες ὑπὲρ τῆς ψυχῆς μου τὸν ἑαυτῶν τράχηλον ὑπέθηκαν,
οἷς οὐκ ἐγὼ μόνος εὐχαριστῶ ἀλλὰ καὶ πᾶσαι αἱ ἐκκλησίαι τῶν ἐθνῶν,
καὶ τὴν κατʼ οἶκον αὐτῶν ἐκκλησίαν.
ἀσπάσασθε Ἐπαίνετον
τὸν ἀγαπητόν μου,
ὅς ἐστιν ἀπαρχὴ τῆς Ἀσίας εἰς Χριστόν.
ἀσπάσασθε Μαριάν,
ἥτις πολλὰ ἐκοπίασεν εἰς ὑμᾶς.
ἀσπάσασθε Ἀνδρόνικον καὶ Ἰουνιᾶν
τοὺς συγγενεῖς μου καὶ συναιχμαλώτους μου,
οἵτινές εἰσιν ἐπίσημοι ἐν τοῖς ἀποστόλοις,
οἳ καὶ πρὸ ἐμοῦ γέγοναν ἐν Χριστῷ.

ἀσπάσασθε Ἀμπλιᾶτον
τὸν ἀγαπητόν μου ἐν κυρίῳ.
ἀσπάσασθε Οὐρβανὸν
τὸν συνεργὸν ἡμῶν ἐν Χριστῷ

καὶ Στάχυν
τὸν ἀγαπητόν μου.
ἀσπάσασθε Ἀπελλῆν
τὸν δόκιμον ἐν Χριστῷ.
ἀσπάσασθε τοὺς ἐκ τῶν Ἀριστοβούλου.
ἀσπάσασθε Ἡρῳδίωνα
τὸν συγγενῆ μου.
ἀσπάσασθε τοὺς ἐκ τῶν Ναρκίσσου
τοὺς ὄντας ἐν κυρίῳ.
ἀσπάσασθε Τρύφαιναν καὶ Τρυφῶσαν
τὰς κοπιώσας ἐν κυρίῳ.
ἀσπάσασθε Περσίδα τὴν ἀγαπητήν,
ἥτις πολλὰ ἐκοπίασεν ἐν κυρίῳ.
ἀσπάσασθε Ῥοῦφον
τὸν ἐκλεκτὸν ἐν κυρίῳ
καὶ τὴν μητέρα αὐτοῦ καὶ ἐμοῦ.
ἀσπάσασθε Ἀσύγκριτον, Φλέγοντα, Ἑρμῆν, Πατροβᾶν, Ἑρμᾶν
καὶ τοὺς σὺν αὐτοῖς ἀδελφούς.
ἀσπάσασθε Φιλόλογον καὶ Ἰουλίαν,
Νηρέα καὶ τὴν ἀδελφὴν αὐτοῦ,
καὶ . Ὀλυμπᾶν
καὶ τοὺς σὺν αὐτοῖς πάντας ἁγίους.

Ἀσπάσασθε ἀλλήλους ἐν φιλήματι ἁγίῳ.

Ἀσπάζονται ὑμᾶς αἱ ἐκκλησίαι πᾶσαι τοῦ Χριστοῦ.

VERSE 3

Ἀσπάσασθε Πρίσκαν καὶ Ἀκύλαν

Prisca (Priscilla) and Aquila were a married couple who were tentmakers/leatherworkers and are mentioned elsewhere in connection with Corinth (Acts 18:1–4, 18) and Ephesus (Acts 18:19, 24–28; 1 Cor 19:19; 2 Tim 4:19). See *NIDNTT* 3.812–13 for a discussion of σκηνοποιός (Acts 18:3); Longenecker suggests that the couple had "established a tentmaking and leatherworking firm at Rome, with branches . . . at Corinth and at Ephesus" (1067). Churches met in their homes in Ephesus (1 Cor 16:19) and in Rome (Rom 16:5a). Although both names were Latin (Jewett 953), Acts 18:2 identifies Aquila as a Jew from Pontus, and Cranfield concludes that Prisca was also Jewish (783). Jewett suggests that Aquila was a freed slave while Prisca was born free, which would give her a higher social status in Rome and might explain why she is mentioned first (955). See Longenecker's extended discussion (1066–68).

τοὺς συνεργούς μου ἐν Χριστῷ Ἰησοῦ

Συνεργός, -οῦ, ὁ describes another with whom someone works (BDAG 969c); for Paul, the term describes an itinerant missionary colleague (Jewett 956; Schreiner 790).

Paul uses it elsewhere to refer to his associates (1 Cor 3:9; 2 Cor 1:24; 8:23; Phil 2:25; 4:3; Col 4:11; 1 Thess 3:2; Phlm 1, 24). In this context, ἐν Χριστῷ Ἰησοῦ denotes location (NLT, "in the ministry of Christ Jesus").

VERSE 4–5A

οἵτινες ὑπὲρ τῆς ψυχῆς μου τὸν ἑαυτῶν τράχηλον ὑπέθηκαν

Οἵτινες (nom. pl. masc. of indef. rel. pron. ὅστις, ἥτις, ὅ τι) is qualitative ("who indeed"); ὑπέρ + genitive denotes reference; ψυχῆς should be translated "life" (Moo 920 n. 16; cf. 11:3); the reflexive pronoun ἑαυτῶν adds emphasis ("their own"); τράχηλον (acc. sg. masc. of τράχηλος, -ου, ὁ, "neck") is the direct object. Ὑπέθηκαν (3 pl. aor. act. indic. of ὑποτίθημι, "risk") is a constative aorist; the verb carries the idea of laying something down as an expression of service (BDAG 1042c). The most common suggestion on the incident to which Paul refers was the riot in Ephesus (Acts 19:23–40), although that understanding is by no means certain (Cranfield 785).

οἷς οὐκ ἐγὼ μόνος εὐχαριστῶ ἀλλὰ καὶ πᾶσαι αἱ ἐκκλησίαι τῶν ἐθνῶν

There is little semantic difference between οἵτινες in the preceding clause and οἷς (dat. pl. masc.) in this one (R 728). The dative regularly follows εὐχαριστέω, although here it designates the individuals "for whom" (rather than "to whom") thanks is offered. Οὐκ . . . ἀλλά establishes a sharp contrast; ἐγὼ μόνος is emphatic; see 1:8 for εὐχαριστέω. Καί is adjunctive ("also"); πᾶσαι αἱ ἐκκλησίαι ("all the churches") suggests that the couple is well known among the churches of the Gentile mission; τῶν ἐθνῶν is attributive ("Gentile churches").

καὶ τὴν κατ' οἶκον αὐτῶν ἐκκλησίαν

Καί is continuative; the article serves to bracket the noun phrase; κατά + accusative is local ("in"; Harris 155; Jewett 959; Moo 920 n. 20); αὐτῶν is a possessive genitive. Similar references to "house churches" occur in 1 Corinthians 16:9; Colossians 4:15; Philemon 2. Cranfield notes that the members of such congregations most likely included more than family members (786).

VERSE 5B

ἀσπάσασθε Ἐπαίνετον τὸν ἀγαπητόν μου

Epaenetus was a Greek (Dunn 893) and a freedman (Jewett 960) who was well known to Paul (Schreiner 790; cf. Jewett 952). Τὸν ἀγαπητόν μου stands in apposition to the proper name and further describes Epaenetus as "my beloved." The article regularly accompanies a noun modified by a genitive possessive pronoun. Commentators differ on the degree of personal relationship the phrase indicates. Jewett (960) and Schreiner (790) understand it as denoting particular affection and personal attachment;* Moo views it as a semi-formalized expression equivalent to ἀδελφός (920 n. 21); Dunn takes a middle position (893).

ὅς ἐστιν ἀπαρχὴ τῆς Ἀσίας εἰς Χριστόν

The relative clause introduced by ὅς (nom. sg. masc.) further describes Epaenetus, who is ἀπαρχὴ τῆς Ἀσίας ("the firstfruit of Asia"). See 8:23 and 11:26 for ἀπαρκή; the genitive of τῆς Ἀσίας is partitive (Porter 93); εἰς + accusative denotes advantage ("for Christ"; cf. Jewett 960). Epaenetus probably immigrated to Rome from Ephesus (Jewett 959), where he was one of Paul's first converts in the Roman province of Asia (Moo 920).

VERSE 6

ἀσπάσασθε Μαριάν, ἥτις πολλὰ ἐκοπίασεν εἰς ὑμᾶς

Mary was probably Jewish and came from a slave background (Jewett 961). Ἥτις (nom. sg. fem. of indef. rel. pron. ὅστις, ἥτις, ὅ τι) is qualitative ("who indeed"); πολλά (acc. pl. neut. of πολύς, πολλή, πολύ, "much, many") is an accusative of reference; ἐκοπίασεν (3 sg. aor. act. indic. of κοπιάω) carries the idea of exerting oneself physically or spiritually (BDAG 558c); εἰς + accusative is the equivalent of a dative of advantage (Moo 921 n. 27; cf. NLT, "for your benefit"). Jewett suggests that Mary worked as an evangelist in Rome after her conversion (961).

VERSE 7

ἀσπάσασθε Ἀνδρόνικον καὶ Ἰουνίαν

Moo writes that the manuscript support for Ἰουλίαν ($\mathfrak{P}^{46}$) is "too weak to consider seriously" (916 n. 1). Apart from accenting—which was not originally present—א, A, B, D, and 33 all support Ἰουνιαν, which can be either masculine (Ἰουνιᾶν) or feminine (Ἰουνίαν). Jewett notes that the masculine is not found elsewhere (950 n. h), and Moo notes that "commentators before the thirteenth century were unanimous in favor of the feminine identification" (922). It is probable that Andronicus and Junia were a second husband and wife team (Jewett 962). Andronicus is a Greek name, and Junia is a Latin name (Jewett 953), but they were most likely Hellenized Jews with slave origins (Dunn 894).

τοὺς συγγενεῖς μου καὶ συναιχμαλώτους μου

Συγγενής, -οῦς, ὁ describes a fellow Jew (Dunn 894; Jewett 962; Schreiner 791; cf. 9:3); συναιχμαλώτος, -ου, ὁ describes a fellow prisoner. Moo notes that we cannot know for certain whether Andronicus and Junia were imprisoned with Paul at the same time or only shared the experience of being imprisoned for Christ (923 n. 37). The article-noun-καί-noun construction applies both descriptors to Andronicus and Junia and is an example of the Granville Sharp rule.

οἵτινές εἰσιν ἐπίσημοι ἐν τοῖς ἀποστόλοις

Οἵτινες (nom. pl. masc. of indef. rel. pron. ὅστις, ἥτις, ὅ τι) is qualitative ("who indeed"); ἐν + dative is local; ἐπίσημος, -ον denotes someone or something of exceptional quality (BDAG 378b); ἀπόστολος, -ου, ὁ denotes an itinerant evangelist or missionary (Moo 924 n. 42) rather than one of the Twelve (cf. Acts 14:4, 14; 1 Cor 12:28; Eph 4:11; 1 Thess 2:7). There is considerable discussion over how best to understand the phrase ἐπίσημοι ἐν τοῖς ἀποστόλοις. Most commentators (Cranfield 789, Dunn 894, Jewett 963, Longenecker 1069, Moo 923, Schreiner 796) and EVV (ASV, RSV, NASB, NEB, GNB, NIV, NJB, NLT) understand the combination as local: "outstanding/prominent/esteemed/distinguished *among* the apostles." Murray (2:230) and a few EVV (ESV, NET) translate the phrase as idiomatic: "well-known *to* the apostles." The former seems the more natural understanding of ἐν + dative. For a detailed defense of the minority position see M. Burer, "'ΕΠΙΣΗΜΟΙ 'ΕΝ ΤΟΙΣ 'ΑΠΟΣΤΟΛΟΙΣ in Rom 16:7 as "Well-Known to the Apostles': Further Defense and New Evidence," *JETS* 58 (2015): 731–55.

οἳ καὶ πρὸ ἐμοῦ γέγοναν ἐν Χριστῷ

The relative pronoun οἵ (nom. pl. masc.) further qualifies Andronicus and Junia; καί is adjunctive ("also"; cf. Jewett 964); πρὸ ἐμοῦ ("before me") denotes priority in time (R 622); γέγοναν (3 pl. pf. act. indic. of dep. γίνομαι) is a consummative perfect, emphasizing completed action (Wallace 577). In this context, Harris concludes that ἐν Χριστῷ denotes sphere of reference and is equivalent to "Christian" (124).

VERSE 8

ἀσπάσασθε Ἀμπλιᾶτον τὸν ἀγαπητόν μου ἐν κυρίῳ

Ampliatus is a Latin name (Jewett 953) that was commonly given to slaves (Dunn 895). See 16:5b for τὸν ἀγαπητόν μου. Harris suggests that in this contect ἐν κυρίῳ denotes sphere of reference and is equivalent to "Christian" (130).

VERSE 9

ἀσπάσασθε Οὐρβανὸν τὸν συνεργὸν ἡμῶν ἐν Χριστῷ

Urbanus is a common Roman slave name (Dunn 895). Paul's greeting is probably addressed to a freedman who was "definitely known to Paul" as a missionary colleague (Jewett 965). See 16:3 for τὸν συνεργὸν ἡμῶν ἐν Χριστῷ. The use of ἡμῶν rather than μου might suggest that Paul knew Urbanus more by reputation than personally (Cranfield 791). Harris suggests that in this context ἐν Χριστῷ denotes "in the service of Christ" (124).

καὶ Στάχυν τὸν ἀγαπητόν μου

Little is known about Stachys. The name is Greek (Jewett 953) and probably reflects a slave background (Cranfield 791). See 16:5b for τὸν ἀγαπητόν μου.

VERSE 10

ἀσπάσασθε Ἀπελλῆν τὸν δόκιμον ἐν Χριστῷ

Apelles is a Greek name, but his social and ethnic status is uncertain (Jewett 965). Τὸν δόκιμον stands in apposition to the proper name; the definite article denotes that Apelles was well known for his proven character (R 759); δόκιμος, -ον carries the idea of "approved, genuine" (Moo 924 n. 49; cf. 14:18; 2 Cor 13:5–7). Ἐν Χριστῷ might denote personal relationship (NIRV, "as one who belonged to Christ") or agency (NLT, "whom Christ approves").

ἀσπάσασθε τοὺς ἐκ τῶν Ἀριστοβούλου

Aristobulus is a Greek name (Jewett 953). Paul's greeting, however, is addressed not to the individual with that name but to those of his household. Aristobulus might well have been the grandson of Herod the Great who lived in Rome and died AD 45–49 (Cranfield 791; cf. Moo 925). The definite article allows the prepositional phrase to function as the direct object. Ἐκ + genitive is partitive; the genitive itself denotes possession (T 169; BDF §162.3). The addressees, therefore, are most likely members of a house church consisting of some of the slaves in the household of Aristobulus. Jewett suggests that they were administrative slaves who enjoyed a measure of education and independence (966).

VERSE 11

ἀσπάσασθε Ἡρῳδίωνα τὸν συγγενῆ μου

Herodion is a Greek name, but συγγενῆ identifies him as "indisputably Jewish" (Jewett 967). He was most likely a slave or freedman in the services of the extended family of Herod (Dunn 896). Jewett suggests that Paul knew him by reputation rather than from personal contact (953). See 16:7 for τὸν συγγενῆ μου.

ἀσπάσασθε τοὺς ἐκ τῶν Ναρκίσσου τοὺς ὄντας ἐν κυρίῳ

Narcissus is a Greek name (Jewett 953). He has no apparent connection with Judaism (Jewett 968), and Cranfield concludes that he was a pagan (792). Paul's greeting, however, is addressed to those of his household. Ἐκ + genitive is partitive; the genitive itself denotes possession (T 169; BDF §162.3). The addressees, therefore, are most likely members of a house church consisting of some of the slaves in the household. Τοὺς ὄντας (acc. pl. masc. of pres. act. ptc. of εἰμί) is a substantival participle standing in apposition to Ναρκίσσου. In this context, ἐν κυρίῳ denotes personal relationship (GNB, "Christians").

VERSE 12

ἀσπάσασθε Τρύφαιναν καὶ Τρυφῶσαν τὰς κοπιώσας ἐν κυρίῳ

Tryphaena and Tryphosa are both Greek names (Jewett 953), and the *καί* that links the two names supports the conclusion that they were sisters (Jewett 968). Dunn suggests that they were freedwomen with a degree of independence (897). Τὰς κοπιώσας (acc. pl. fem. of pres. act. ptc. of *κοπιάω*) is a substantival participle standing in apposition to the sisters' names; see 16:6 for *κοπιάω*; in this context, ἐν κυρίῳ denotes location (Harris 130; cf. GNB, "in the Lord's service").

ἀσπάσασθε Περσίδα τὴν ἀγαπητήν, ἥτις πολλὰ ἐκοπίασεν ἐν κυρίῳ

Persis is a typical Greek slave name (Dunn 897). Moo notes that the name is derived from "Persia," which suggests she might have been a slave captured in that region (925 n. 56); See 16:5 for τὴν ἀγαπητήν, 16:6 for ἥτις πολλὰ ἐκοπίασεν, and the previous line for ἐν κυρίῳ.

VERSE 13

ἀσπάσασθε Ῥοῦφον τὸν ἐκλεκτὸν ἐν κυρίῳ καὶ τὴν μητέρα αὐτοῦ καὶ ἐμοῦ

Rufus is a Latin name (Dunn 897). He was probably a freeborn Gentile, possibly with considerable means (Jewett 969). Τὸν ἐκλεκτόν stands in apposition to the proper name; the definite article denotes that Rufus was well known for his "election" (cf. R 759). Ἐκλεκτός, -ή, -όν may describe Rufus as "chosen" for salvation (Schreiner 791; cf. 8:33) or for a special role or task (Dunn 897). If the former understanding is correct, ἐν κυρίῳ denotes agency (NLT, "whom the Lord picked out to be his very own");* if the latter is correct, it denotes location (GNB, "that outstanding worker in the Lord's service"). The fact that Paul identifies Rufus's mother (τὴν μητέρα αὐτοῦ) also as his own (καὶ ἐμοῦ) suggests at least previous hospitality and care (Moo 926) and perhaps her patronage (Jewett 969).

VERSE 14

ἀσπάσασθε Ἀσύγκριτον, Φλέγοντα, Ἑρμῆν, Πατροβᾶν, Ἑρμᾶν καὶ τοὺς σὺν αὐτοῖς ἀδελφούς

Asyncritus, Phlegon, Hermes, Patrobas, and Hermas are all Greek names (Jewett 953) usually given to slaves or freedman (Dunn 898). Καί is continuative; σύν + dative denotes association. Jewett suggests that ἀδελφούς implies an egalitarian ethos in which the five named individuals are collective leaders of a "tenement" church with no patron (971).

VERSE 15

ἀσπάσασθε Φιλόλογον καὶ Ἰουλίαν

In contrast to 16:7, the manuscript support for Ἰουλίαν in this verse is strong (א, A, B, D, 33). The variant reading Ἰουνιαν (C*) is most likely either an error of sight (Metzger 476) or an assimilation to 16:7 (Schreiner 799). The connective καί makes it likely that Philologus and Julia were a third husband and wife team (Moo 926). Philologus is a Greek name, while Julia is a Latin name (Jewett 953). Both names were common for slaves or freedmen, and Dunn suggests that this couple might have been slaves of the emperor's household (898).

Νηρέα κὶ τὴν ἀδελφὴν αὐτοῦ

Nereus is another Greek name (Jewett 953). He and his sister most likely came from a slave background (Dunn 898).

καὶ Ὀλυμπᾶν καὶ τοὺς σὺν αὐτοῖς πάντας ἁγίους

Olympas is a fifth Greek slave name, and Jewett suggests that the five named individuals were the collective leaders of a second tenement church (972). Σύν + dative denotes association; πάντας (acc. pl. masc.) is extensive (Porter 190 n. 3; cf. R 773,"the total number of"). Moule suggests that the substantival prepositional phrase is equivalent to πάντας τοὺς ἁγίους τοὺς σὺν αὐτοῖς (93 n. 3).

VERSE 16

Ἀσπάσασθε ἀλλήλους ἐν φιλήματι ἁγίῳ.

Ἀσπάσασθε (2 pl. aor. mid. impv. of dep. ἀσπάζομαι, "greet") is an imperative of command; the reciprocal pronoun ἀλλήλους ("one another") is the direct object; ἐν + dative denotes instrumentality ("by means of"). Moo notes that the kiss was a common form of greeting in the ancient world, including Judaism (926; cf. Matt 26:47–49); Paul issues the same command at the end of 1 Corinthians (16:20), 2 Corinthians (13:12), and 1 Thessalonians (5:26); Peter concludes his first letter in the same way (5:14). Dunn suggests that ἁγίῳ (dat. sg. neut. of ἅγιος, -α, -ον, "holy") adds solemnity (899).

Ἀσπάζονται ὑμᾶς αἱ ἐκκλησίαι πᾶσαι τοῦ Χριστοῦ

Ἀσπάζονται (3 pl. pres. mid. indic. of dep. ἀσπάζομαι, "greet") is an instantaneous present; ὑμᾶς is the direct object; αἱ ἐκκλησίαι πᾶσαι ("all the churches") most likely refers to the churches Paul has planted (Longenecker 1070; cf. 1 Cor 7:17; 14:33; 2 Cor 8:18; 11:28); τοῦ Χριστοῦ is a genitive of relationship (T 212; Moo 926 n. 66).

FOR FURTHER STUDY

88. Rome and Roman Christianity (16:3–16)

Brown, R. E. "Further Reflections on the Origins of the Church at Rome." Pages 98–115 in *The Conversation Continues: Studies in Paul and John. In Honor of J. Louis Martyn*. Edited by R. T. Fortna and B. R. Gaventa. Nashville: Abingdon, 1990.

________. and Meier, J. P. *Antioch and Rome: New Testament Cradles of Christianity*. New York: Paulist, 1982.

Edmundson, G. *The Church in Rome in the First Century*. London: Longmans, Green, 1913.

Ferguson, J. *The Religions of the Roman Empire*. Ithaca, NY: Cornell University Press, 1970.

Judge, E. A., and Thomas, G. S. R. "The Origin of the Church at Rome: A New Solution?" *RTR* 25 (1966): 81–94.

Lampe, P. "The Roman Christians of Romans 16." Pages 216–30 in *The Romans Debate*. Edited by Karl P. Donfried. Peabody, MA: Hendrickson, 1991.

Leon, H. J. *The Jews of Ancient Rome*. Philadelphia: Jewish Publication Society of America, 1960.

Porter, S. E. *DNTB* 1010–18.

Reasoner, M. *DPL* 850–55.

Wilken, M. H. *The Christians as the Romans Saw Them*. New Haven: Yale University Press, 1984.

89. Greetings (16:3–16; cf. 16:21–23)

Erbes, K. "Zeit und Ziel der Grüsse Röm 16,3–25 und der Mitteilungen 2 Tim 4,9–21." *ZNW* 19 (1909): 128–47, 195–218.

Horsley, G. H. R. "Personal News and Greetings in a Letter." *NewDocs* 1 (1981): 54–56.

Mullins, T. Y. "Greeting as a NT Form." *JBL* 87 (1968): 418–26.

Windisch, H. *TDNT* 1.496–502.

90. Women in Paul's Churches (16:3–15)

Abrahamsen, V. "Women at Philippi: The Pagan and Christian Evidence." *Journal of Feminist Studies in Religion* 3 (1987): 17–30.

Cotter, W. "Women's Authority Roles in Paul's Churches: Countercultural or Conventional?" *NovT* 36 (1994): 350–72.

D'Angelo, M. R. "Women Partners in the New Testament." *Journal of Feminist Studies in Religion* 6 (1990): 65–86.

Epp, E. J. *Junia: The First Woman Apostle*. Minneapolis: Fortress, 2005.

Fabrega, V. "War Junia(s) der hervorragende Apostel (Rom. 16,7) eine Frau?" *JAC* 27 (1984): 47–64.

Gerberding, K. A. "Women Who Toil in Ministry, Even as Paul." *Currents in Theology and Mission* 18 (1991): 285–91.

Gillman, F. M. "Early Christian Women at Philippi." *Journal of Gender and World Religions* 1 (1990): 59–79.

Keener, C. *Paul, Women and Wives: Marriage and Women's Ministry in the Letters of Paul*. Peabody, MA: Hendrickson, 1991.

Richardson, P. "From Apostles to Virgins: Romans 16 and the Roles of Women in the Early Church." *TJT* 2 (1986): 232–61.

Thorley, J. "Junia, A Woman Apostle." *NovT* 38 (1996): 18–29.

Trebilco, P. "Women as Co-workers and Leaders in Paul's Letters." *Journal of the Christian Brethren Research Fellowship* 122 (1990): 27–36.

Walters, J. C. "'Phoebe' and 'Junia(s)'—Rom 16:1–2, 7." Pages 176–90 in *Essays on Women in Earliest Christianity*. Edited by C. D. Osburn. Joplin, MO: College Press, 2003.

91. The House Church in the New Testament (16:5, 10, 11, 14, 15)

Bank, R. *Paul's Idea of Community: The Early House Churches in their Historical Setting*. Peabody, MA: Hendrickson, 1994.

Branick, V. P. *The House Church in the Writings of Paul*. Wilmington: Glazier, 1989.

Filson, F. V. "The Significance of the Early House Churches." *JBL* 58 (1939): 105–12.

Gielen, M. "Zur Interpretation der Formel ἡ κατ' οἶκον ἐκκλησία." *ZNW* 77 (1986): 109–25.

Jewett, R. "Tenement Churches and Communal Meals in the Early Church: The Implications of a Form-Critical Analysis of 2 Thess 3:10." *BR* 38 (1993): 23–43.

Klauck, H. J. *Hausgemeinde und Hauskirche im frühen Christentum*. Stuttgart: Katholische Bibelwerk, 1981.

Lorenzen, T. "Das Christliche Hauskirche." *TZ* 43 (1987): 333–52.

Malherbe. A. J. "House Churches and Their Problems." Pages 60–91 in *Social Aspects of Early Christianity*. Philadelphia: Fortress, 1983.

Peterson, J. M. "House-Churches in Rome." *Vigiliae Christianae* 25 (1969): 264–72.

92. Holy Kiss (16:16)

Benko, S. "The Kiss." Pages 79–102 in *Pagan Rome and the Early Christians*. Bloomington, IN: Indiana University Press, 1984.

Hofmann, K. M. *Phlma Hagion*. Gütersloh: Bertelsmann, 1938.

Klassen, W. "The Sacred Kiss in the New Testament." *NTS* 39 (1993): 122–35.

Kreider, E. "Let the Faithful Greet Each Other: The Kiss of Peace." *Conrad Grebel Review* 5 (1987): 28–49.

Löw, I. "Der Kuss." *MGWJ* 65 (1921): 253–76, 323–49.

Perella, N. J. *The Kiss: Sacred and Profane*. Berkeley: University of California Press, 1969.

Stählin, G. *TDNT* 9.119–27, 138–46.

Thraede, K. "Ursprünge und Formen des 'Heiligen Kusses in frühen Christentum." *JAC* 11/12 (1968/1969): 124–80.

Wünsche, A. *Der Kuss in Bibel, Talmud und Midrasch*. Breslau: Marcus, 1911.

HOMILETICAL SUGGESTIONS

Greetings from Paul (16:3–16)

1. To individuals
    a. To those who are coworkers (συνεργός)
        1) Prisca (Priscilla) and Aquila (16:3–4)

a) Who risked their necks for Paul (16:4a)
b) For whom all the Gentile churches give thanks (16:4b)
2) Urbanus (16:9a)
b. To those who are kinsmen (συγγενής)
1) Andronicus and Junia (16:7)
a) Who are Paul's fellow prisoners (16:7a)
b) Who are prominent among the apostles (16:7b)
c) Who were in Christ before Paul (16:7c)
2) Herodion (16:11a)
c. To those who are laborers (κοπιάω)
1) Mary (16:6)
2) Tryphaena and Tryphosa (16:12a)
3) Persis (16:12b)
d. To those who are beloved (ἀγαπητός)
1) Epaenetus (16:5b–c)
a) Who is the firstfruits of Asia (16:5c)
2) Ampliatus (16:8)
3) Stachys (16:9b)
4) Persis (16:12b)
e. To those who are proven (δόκιμος) and elect (ἐκλεκτός) ones
1) Apelles (16:10a)
2) Rufus and his mother (16:13)
2. To house churches
a. In the house of Prisca and Aquila (16:5a)
b. Those of Aristobulus's household (16:10b)
c. Those of Narcissus's household (16:11b)
d. Those with Asyneritus, Phlegon, Hermes, Patrobas, and Hermas (16:14)
e. Those with Philologus, Junia, Nereus, his sister, and Olympas (16:15)
3. To the whole church
a. Command to greet another with a holy kiss (16:16a)
b. Greetings from all the churches of Christ (16:16b)

The Women of Rome (16:3–15)

1. Rufus's mother, Julia, and Nereus's sister (16:13, 15)
a. Who they were
1) Rufus's mother: Gentile, freeborn
2) Julia: Gentile, slave, married to Philologos
3) Nereus's sister: Gentile, slave
b. What they did
1) Missionary patroness
2) House church leadership team members
2. Mary, Tryphaena, Tryphosa, and Persis (16:6, 12)
a. Who they were

            1) Mary: Jew, slave
            2) Tryphaena and Tryphosa: Gentile, freedwomen, sisters
            3) Persis: Gentile, slave
        b. What they did: labor (κοπιάω)
            1) Involvement: extensive (πολλά)
            2) Focus: others (εἰς ὑμᾶς)
            3) Motivation: Christ (ἐν κυρίῳ)
    3. Prisca (Priscilla) and Junia (16:3–5a, 7)
        a. Who they were
            1) Prisca (Priscilla): hellenized Jew, freeborn, married to Aquila
            2) Junia: hellenized Jew, slave, married to Andronicus
        b. What they did
            1) Paul's fellow workers (συνεργούς μου)
            2) Paul's fellow kinsmen (συγγενεῖς μου)
            3) Paul's fellow prisoners (συναιχμαλώτους μου)

F. FINAL ADVICE (16:17–20)

STRUCTURE

The change in tone and style of this paragraph as well as its place between two sets of greetings (16:3–16; 16:21–23) leads Jewett to view it as a non-Pauline interpolation (986–88). Elsewhere, however, Paul includes a final paragraph in his own hand (cf. 1 Cor 16:21–24; Gal 6:11–18; Col 4:18; 2 Thess 3:17), and he includes final advice in other letters (cf. 2 Cor 13:5–10; Eph 6:10–20; Phil 4:2–9; 1 Thess 5:12–22). It is probable that this paragraph reflects both of those practices. Paul opens with an exhortation to steer clear of false teachers (16:17–18), follows that warning with encouragement based on the Romans' acknowledged obedience (16:19–20a), and concludes with a grace benediction (16:20b).

Παρακαλῶ δὲ ὑμᾶς, ἀδελφοί, σκοπεῖν τοὺς τὰς διχοστασίας καὶ τὰ σκάνδαλα παρὰ τὴν διδαχὴν ἣν ὑμεῖς ἐμάθετε ποιοῦντας, καὶ ἐκκλίνετε ἀπ' αὐτῶν·
οἱ γὰρ τοιοῦτοι τῷ κυρίῳ ἡμῶν Χριστῷ οὐ δουλεύουσιν ἀλλὰ τῇ ἑαυτῶν κοιλίᾳ,
καὶ διὰ τῆς χρηστολογίας καὶ εὐλογίας ἐξαπατῶσιν τὰς καρδίας τῶν ἀκάκων.

ἡ γὰρ ὑμῶν ὑπακοὴ εἰς πάντας ἀφίκετο·
ἐφ' ὑμῖν οὖν χαίρω, θέλω δὲ ὑμᾶς σοφοὺς εἶναι εἰς τὸ ἀγαθόν, ἀκεραίους δὲ εἰς τὸ κακόν.
ὁ δὲ θεὸς τῆς εἰρήνης συντρίψει τὸν Σατανᾶν ὑπὸ τοὺς πόδας ὑμῶν ἐν τάχει.

ἡ χάρις τοῦ κυρίου ἡμῶν Ἰησοῦ μεθ' ὑμῶν.

VERSE 17

Παρακαλῶ δὲ ὑμᾶς, ἀδελφοί, σκοπεῖν τοὺς τὰς διχοστασίας καὶ τὰ σκάνδαλα παρὰ τὴν διδαχὴν ἣν ὑμεῖς ἐμάθετε ποιοῦντας

The transitional *δέ* ("now") argues against this section being an interpolation, while the vocative *ἀδελφοί* marks a shift in subject matter (Moo 929). See 12:1 and 15:30 for similar request formulas. *Σκοπεῖν* (pres. act. inf. of *σκοπέω*, "pay careful attention to") is a complementary infinitive. Although the verb can have a positive nuance (e.g., Phil 2:4; 3:17), in this context, it carries the idea of "mark so as to avoid" (Cranfield 798; cf. *TDNT* 7.414–5). The definite article (*τούς*) individualizes (R 758), accompanies the substantival participle (Moo 930 n. 17), and brackets the phrase. *Διχοστασίας* (acc. pl. fem. of *διχοστασία, -ας, ἡ*, "dissension") and *σκάνδαλα* (acc. pl. neut. of *σκάδαλον, -ου, τό*, "stumblingblock") are the objects of the participle; the definite articles are generic, indicating a class; *καί* is continuative. See BDAG 253d for *διχοστασία* and 9:33 for *σκάδαλον*. *Παρά* + accusative denotes opposition (R 616; cf. Gal 1:8; "contrary to"); the article denotes teaching that is well-known; Cranfield suggests that *διδακήν* refers to common Christian teaching (798). The relative clause introduced by *ἥν* (acc. sg. fem.) restricts *διδακήν*; *ὑμεῖς* is emphatic; *ἐμάθετε* (2 pl. aor. act. indic. of *μανθάνω*, "learn") is a constative aorist; the verb describes the process of gaining knowledge or skill by instruction (BDAG 615b); the present tense of ποιοῦντας (acc. pl. masc. of pres. act. ptc. of ποιέω) is customary.

καὶ ἐκκλίνετε ἀπ' αὐτῶν

Καί is continuative; ἐκκλίνετε (2 pl. pres. act. impv. of ἐκκλίνω, "avoid") is an imperative of command; the present tense suggests constant vigilance (Moo 930 n. 22; cf. 3:12); Jewett suggests the translation "steer clear" (990); ἀπό + genitive denotes separation (NASB, "turn away from them").

VERSE 18

οἱ γὰρ τοιοῦτοι τῷ κυρίῳ ἡμῶν Χριστῷ οὐ δουλεύουσιν ἀλλὰ τῇ ἑαυτῶν κοιλίᾳ

There are two reasons (γάρ) to steer clear of false teachers. First, such people serve themselves rather than Christ. Οἱ τοιοῦτοι (nom. pl. masc. of τοιοῦτος, -αύτη, -οῦτον, "of such kind") is qualitative (NLT, "such people"); τῷ κυρίῳ ἡμῶν Χριστῷ is dative of direct object following δουλεύουσιν (3 pl. pres. act. indic. of δουλεύω, "serve"). Οὐ . . . ἀλλά establishes a strong contrast; τῇ ἑαυτῶν κοιλίᾳ is a second dative of direct object; ἑαυτῶν ("their own") is emphatic. Although κοιλία, -ας, ἡ can refer to a person's stomach (BDAG 550d), here it is figurative, possibly referring to greed (Cranfield 800) but more likely to the false teachers' self-interest (Moo 931 n. 29; cf. Phil 3:19).

καὶ διὰ τῆς χρηστολογίας καὶ εὐλογίας ἐξαπατῶσιν τὰς καρδίας τῶν ἀκάκων

Second (καί), these false teachers deceive the unsuspecting. Διά + genitive denotes means; τῆς χρηστολογίας καὶ εὐλογίας is an example of the Granville Sharp rule (article-noun-καί-noun) in which the second noun is a subset of the first (Wallace 287); Dunn notes it as an example of hendiadys (903). Χρηστολογία, -ας, ἡ describes smooth or plausible speech (BDAG 1089d); εὐλογία, -ας, ἡ describes words that are well chosen but untrue (BDAG 408d). Dunn suggests "smooth speech and fine words" (903); Jewett suggests "sweet talk and well-chosen words" (992). Ἐξαπατῶσιν (3 pl. pres. act. indic. of ἐξαπατάω, "lead astray") is a customary present; τὰς καρδίας is the direct object; τῶν ἀκάκων is a possessive genitive; ἄκακος, -ον describes someone who is innocent, unsuspecting, or guileless (BDAG 34d; cf. Moo 931 n. 30). The identity of the false teachers is disputed and impossible to determine with certainty (Cranfield 801–02).

VERSE 19

ἡ γὰρ ὑμῶν ὑπακοὴ εἰς πάντας ἀφίκετο

Schreiner suggests that the reason (γάρ) for Paul's warning is that the Romans are well-known for their obedience, which would make them a special target for false teachers who would want to undermine that obedience (804). See 1:5 for ὑπακοή;

εἰς + accusative denotes reference (Harris 85); ἀφίκετο (3 sg. aor. mid. indic. of dep. ἀφικνέομαι, "reach") is a constative aorist and a deponent middle.

ἐφ' ὑμῖν οὖν χαίρω

The logical implication of their obedience (οὖν) is that Paul rejoices. Ἐπί + dative denotes cause (NCV, "because of you"); χαίρω is a progressive present.

θέλω δὲ ὑμᾶς σοφοὺς εἶναι εἰς τὸ ἀγαθόν, ἀκεραίους δὲ εἰς τὸ κακόν

Δέ is adversative ("but"); θέλω is a gnomic present (Wallace 526); ὑμᾶς is the subject of the infinitive; σοφούς is the predicate accusative; εἶναι (pres. act. infin. of εἰμί) is a complementary infinitive. Εἰς + accusative denotes reference (Harris 85; cf. Moo 932 n. 36); the article is generic (NIV, "what is good . . . what is evil"); δέ is adversative and adds a second predicate accusative; ἀκέραιος, -ον describes what is pure or innocent (BDAG 35d). See 2:9–10 for the contrast between ἀγαθός and κάκος. Paul's statement might be an echo of Jesus's saying in Matthew 10:16.

VERSE 20

ὁ δὲ θεὸς τῆς εἰρήνης συντρίψει τὸν Σατανᾶν ὑπὸ τοὺς πόδας ὑμῶν ἐν τάχει

A few EVV translate δέ as continuative (KJV, ASV, GNB, NKJV); most leave it untranslated (e.g., NASB, NIV, ESV). The article with θεός is monadic; τῆς εἰρήνης is a genitive of product (Wallace 106; cf. 15:33). Συντρίψει (3 sg. fut. act. indic. of συντρίβω, "crush") is a predictive future; the verb describes a complete subduing of someone (BDAG 976b; cf. 1 Macc 3:22; PsSol 17:24). Τὸν Σατανᾶν is the direct object; the article denotes well known; ὑπό + accusative is spatial ("under"); τάχος, -ους, τό denotes a relatively brief period of time; ἐν τάχει is temporal (NASB, "soon"). The background behind Paul's promise is most likely Genesis 3:15 (Schreiner 804–805).

ἡ χάρις τοῦ κυρίου ἡμῶν Ἰησοῦ μεθ' ὑμῶν

Although the manuscript support for omitting the entire benediction (16:20b) is limited (D), Jewett adopts that reading (7–8; cf. 16:23). The support for including it, however, is considerably stronger and is divided between the two other readings. Ἰησοῦ ($\mathfrak{P}^{46}$, ℵ, B) is shorter and older (Metzger 476), while Dunn views the addition of Χριστοῦ (A, 33) as "liturgical polishing" (901 n. d). Paul often concludes his letters with a grace benediction (1 Cor 16:23; 2 Cor 13:13; Gal 6:18; Phil 4:23; Col 4:18; 1 Thess 5:28; 2 Thess 3:18). The article with χάρις denotes well known (cf. 1:7); τοῦ κυρίου ἡμῶν is a genitive of source; Ἰησοῦ stands in apposition to κυρίου; the optative εἴη is understood; μετά + genitive denotes association (cf. 15:33).

FOR FURTHER STUDY

93. Satan (16:20)

Bietenhard, H., C. Brown, and J. S. Wright. *NIDNTT* 3.468–77.
Böcher, O. *EDNT* 1.297–98.
Brown, D. R. "The Devil in the Details: A Survey of Research on Satan in Biblical Studies." *Currents in Biblical Research* 9 (2011): 200–27.
________. "'The God of Peace Will Shortly Crush Satan under Your Feet': Paul's Eschatological Reminder in Romans 16:20a." *Neot* 44 (2010): 1–14.
Day, P. L. *An Adversary in Heaven: Satan in the Hebrew Bible*. Atlanta: Scholars, 1987.
Diebelius, M. *Die Geisterwelt im Glauben des Paulus*. Göttingen: Vandenhoeck & Ruprecht, 1909.
Elgvin, T. *DNTB* 153–57.
Foerster, W. *TDNT* 2.71–81.
________. *TDNT* 7.151–63.
Hamilton, V. P. *ABD* 5.985–89.
Hiers, R. H. "Satan, Demons and the Kingdom of God." *SJT* 27 (1974): 35–47.
Löfstedt, T. "Paul, Sin and Satan: The Root of Evil according to Romans." *Svensk Exegetisk Årsbok* 75 (2010): 109–34.
Reid, D. G. *DPL* 862–67.
Russell, J. B. *Satan: The Early Christian Tradition*. Ithaca, NY: Cornell University, 1981.
Twelftree, G. H. *DJG* 163–72.
Yates, R. "The Powers of Evil in the NT." *EvQ* 52 (1980): 97–111.

HOMILETICAL SUGGESTIONS

Paul's Final Advice (16:17–20)

1. Watch out for and avoid false teachers (16:17–18)
   a. Their impact: Dissension and doubt (16:17)
   b. Their means: Smooth speech and fine words (16:18b)
   c. Their victims: The unsuspecting (16:18c)
2. Maintain your obedience (16:19–20a)
   a. It is known to all (16:19a)
   b. It brings others joy (16:19b)
   c. It anticipates ultimate victory (16:20a)
3. Grace benediction (16:20b)

G. GREETINGS FROM OTHERS (16:21–23)

STRUCTURE

Since he includes greetings from others elsewhere in his letters (cf. 1 Cor 16:19–20a; 2 Cor 13:12b; Phil 4:22; Col 4:10–14; Titus 3:15a; Phlm 23–24), it is not surprising that Paul does so in Romans as well. Moo suggests that this set of greetings is separated from the previous set because the mention of "all the churches of Christ" (16:16b) led Paul to address his concern that the false teachers who had disrupted other churches might do the same in Rome (933). Tertius then added the second greeting list (cf. Dunn 908). The list itself includes eight names: four teammates (16:21), Tertius, to whom Paul dictated the letter (16:22), and three members of the church in Corinth (16:23). Longenecker views this set of greetings as complementary to the previous set in that the 16:3–16 highlights Paul's personal relationships, while 16:21–23 highlights Paul's apostolic authority (1083).

Ἀσπάζεται ὑμᾶς Τιμόθεος
ὁ συνεργός μου
καὶ Λούκιος
καὶ Ἰάσων
καὶ Σωσίπατρος
οἱ συγγενεῖς μου.

ἀσπάζομαι ὑμᾶς ἐγὼ Τέρτιος
ὁ γράψας τὴν ἐπιστολὴν ἐν κυρίῳ.

ἀσπάζεται ὑμᾶς Γάϊος
ὁ ξένος μου καὶ ὅλης τῆς ἐκκλησίας.
ἀσπάζεται ὑμᾶς Ἔραστος
ὁ οἰκονόμος τῆς πόλεως
καὶ Κούαρτος
ὁ ἀδελφός.

VERSE 21

Ἀσπάζεται ὑμᾶς Τιμόθεος ὁ συνεργός μου

Ἀσπάζεται (3 sg. pres. mid. indic. of dep. ἀσπάζομαι, "greet") is an instantaneous present; ὑμᾶς is the direct object; see 16:3 for ὁ συνεργός μου. Timothy was from Lystra in Asia Minor, the son of a Jewish mother and a Greek father (Acts 16:1–2). He was coauthor of 2 Corinthians (1:1), Philippians (1:1), 1 Thessalonians (1:1), 2 Thessalonians (1:1), Colossians (1:1), and Philemon (v. 1) and the addressee of 1–2 Timothy. He traveled between Thessalonica (Acts 17:14–15), Corinth (Acts 18:5; 20:4), Macedonia (Acts 19:22), and Ephesus (1 Tim 1:3) and is mentioned elsewhere in Paul's letters (1 Cor 4:17; 16:10–11; 2 Cor 1:19; Phil 2:19–24; 1 Thess 3:2, 6).

καὶ Λούκιος καὶ Ἰάσων καὶ Σωσίπατρος οἱ συγγενεῖς μου

Although Lucius is a Latin name, he was most likely a Jewish convert and a representative from one of the Pauline churches (Jewett 977). Jason was most likely Paul's host in Thessalonica (cf. Acts 17:5–9) and a Jewish convert (Jewett 978). Sosipater is a longer version of the Greek name Sopater (cf. Acts 20:4) and most likely was a Jewish convert from Berea (Jewett 978). See 16:7 for οἱ συγγενεῖς μου. These three hellenized Jewish colleagues from Macedonia most likely accompanied Paul as he delivered the Jerusalem collection.

VERSE 22

ἀσπάζομαι ὑμᾶς ἐγὼ Τέρτιος ὁ γράψας τὴν ἐπιστολὴν ἐν κυρίῳ

Ἀσπάζομαι (1 sg. pres. act. mid. of dep. ἀσπάζομαι, "greet") is an instantaneous present; ὑμᾶς is the direct object; ἐγώ is emphatic. Dunn notes that greetings in the first person are unusual (909). Tertius is a Latin name given to slaves or freedmen; Jewett suggests that he was a scribe who was a member of Phoebe's household (978–79). Ὁ γράψας (nom. sg. masc. of aor. act. ptc. of γράφω, "write") is a substantival participle that stands in apposition to Τέρτιος; the aorist is epistolary (cf. Wallace 562) and refers to the letter as a whole (cf. 15:15). The article with ἐπιστολήν is deictic (Wallace 221); ἐν κυρίῳ is best taken with ἀσπάζομαι (Cranfield 806) and denotes sphere of reference (NLT, "as one of the Lord's followers").

VERSE 23

ἀσπάζεται ὑμᾶς Γάϊος ὁ ξένος μου καὶ ὅλης τῆς ἐκκλησίας

See 16:21 for ἀσπάζεται ὑμᾶς. Gaius's Latin name suggests that he was a noble or a freedman and a Roman citizen (Jewett 980). His full name was most likely Gaius Titius Justus (Dunn 910), which would identify him as a leader in the church in Corinth (Acts 18:7; 1 Cor 1:14). Ξένος (nom. sg. masc. of ξένος, -η, -ον, "host") is a substantival adjective that describes someone who extends hospitality and treats a stranger as a guest (BDAG 684a). Καί is continuative; ὅλης τῆς ἐκκλησίας is best translated as "the whole church" (NIV); ἐκκλησίας is an objective genitive. Jewett examines three possible understandings of the phrase and concludes that Paul is referring to members of the worldwide church who might pass through Corinth (980; cf. Moo 935).

ἀσπάζεται ὑμᾶς Ἔραστος ὁ οἰκονόμος τῆς πόλεως καὶ Κούαρτος ὁ ἀδελφός

See 16:21 for ἀσπάζεται ὑμᾶς. Erastus is a Latin name; Jewett suggests that he was a rich freedman and a Roman citizen (982). Οἰκονόμος, -ου, ὁ refers to a financial officer (Dunn 910), most likely a public treasurer (BDAG 698d); τῆς πόλεως ("of the city") is a genitive of subordination; καί is continuative. Quartus is a Latin name that was common among slaves and freedmen (Dunn 911). Cranfield concludes that ὁ ἀδελφός designates a "fellow Christian" (808); Jewett (983) argues at length that the article should be translated as a personal pronoun referring to Quartus ("his [i.e., Quartus's] brother"). Similar constructions elsewhere (e.g., 1 Cor 1:1; 16:12; 2 Cor 2:1; Col 1:1; Phlm 1), however, suggest the translation "our brother" (e.g., NIV), in which case Quartus must have been known to at least some of the members of the Roman church.

𝔓^{46}, ℵ, A, and B all omit the benediction of 16:24, which leads Metzger to give the omission an {A} rating. Cranfield (808) and Moo (933 n. 1) view the benediction as "clearly a later addition,"* although Jewett believes it was part of 16:21–24, which originally concluded the letter (7–8).

FOR FURTHER STUDY

94. Paul and His Coworkers (16:21)

Banks, R. *Paul's Idea of Community*. Rev. Ed. Peabody, MA: Hendrickson, 1994.
Bruce, F. F. *The Pauline Circle*. Grand Rapids: Eerdmans, 1985.
Elllis, E. E. *DPL* 183–89.
______. "Paul and His Co-workers." *NTS* 17 (1970–71): 437–52.
Harrington, D. J. "Paul and Collaborative Ministry." *New Theology Review* 3 (1990): 62–71.
Hellerman, J. H. *Embracing Shared Ministry*. Grand Rapids: Kregel, 2013.
Hiebert. D. F. *Personalities around Paul*. Chicago: Moody, 1973.
Meggett, J. J. "The Social Status of Erastus (Rom. 16:23)." *NovT* 38 (1996): 218–23.
Ollrog, W. H. *Paulus und seine Mitarbeiter*. Neukirchen-Vluyn: Neukirchener, 1979.
Redlich, E. B. S. *Paul and His Companions*. London: Macmillan, 1913.
Seekings, H. S. *The Men of the Pauline Circle*. London: Kelly, 1914.

95. Amanuenses (16:21)

Bahnsen, G. L. "Autographs, Amanuenses and Restricted Inspiration." *EvQ* 45 (1973): 100–10.
Bahr, G. J. "Paul and Letter Writing in the First Century." *CBQ* 28 (1966): 465–77.
Elsner, I. J. "'I, Tertius': Secretary or Co-author of Romans." *AusBR* 56 (2008): 45–60.
Longenecker, R. N. "Ancient Amanuenses and the Pauline Epistles." Pages 218–97 in *New Dimensions in New Testament Study*. Edited by R. N. Longenecker and M. C. Tenney. Grand Rapids: Eerdmans, 1974.
McGuire, M. R. P. "Letters and Letter Carriers in Christian Antiquity." *Classical World* 53 (1960): 150–57.
Manus, C. U. "Amanuensis Hypothesis: A Key to the Understanding of Paul's Epistles in the New Testament." *Biblebhashyam* 10 (1984): 160–74.
Richards, E. R. *The Secretary in the Letters of Paul*. Tübingen: Mohr Siebeck, 1991.
______. *Paul and First-Century Letter Writing: Secretaries, Composition, and Collection*. Downers Grove, IL: InterVarsity, 2004.

HOMILETICAL SUGGESTIONS

Greetings from Others (16:21–23)

1. From Paul's teammates (16:21)

   a. Timothy, Paul's coworker (16:21a)
   b. Lucius, Jason, and Sosipater, Paul's kinsmen (16:21b)
2. From Tertius, who wrote the letter (16:22)
3. From members of the church in Corinth (16:23)
   a. Gaius, Paul's host (16:23a)
   b. Erastus, the city administrator (16:23b)
   c. Quartus, "the brother" (16:23c)

H. DOXOLOGY (16:25–27)

STRUCTURE

Jewett describes the doxology as "lumbering [and] somewhat redundant" (1004) with a "loose structure and lack of logical development" (997). It is a single incomplete sentence without a finite verb, in which four patterns of three are evident: (1) three datives referring to God, (2) three genitive participles qualifying *μυστηρίου*, (3) three prepositional phrases beginning with *κατά*, and (4) three prepositional phrases beginning with εἰς. The datives referring to God (16:25a, 27) frame an extended summary of the gospel (16:25b–26), the latter part of which is framed by two aorist passive participles in the genitive (*φανερωθέντος . . . γνωρισθέντος*). The logic of Paul's train of thought begins in verse 27 and moves to verses 25 and 26. (See the Homiletical Suggestions below.)

Τῷ δὲ δυναμένῳ ὑμᾶς στηρίξαι
κατὰ τὸ εὐαγγέλιόν μου καὶ τὸ κήρυγμα Ἰησοῦ Χριστοῦ,
κατὰ ἀποκάλυψιν μυστηρίου
χρόνοις αἰωνίοις
σεσιγημένου,
φανερωθέντος δὲ νῦν
διά τε γραφῶν προφητικῶν
κατ' ἐπιταγὴν τοῦ αἰωνίου θεοῦ
εἰς ὑπακοὴν πίστεως
εἰς πάντα τὰ ἔθνη
γνωρισθέντος,
μόνῳ σοφῷ θεῷ,
διὰ Ἰησοῦ Χριστοῦ,
ᾧ ἡ δόξα εἰς τοὺς αἰῶνας, ἀμήν.

TEXTUAL QUESTIONS

The textual questions about 16:25–27 extend beyond whether the doxology should be viewed as Pauline to a consideration of its original place in the letter. Jewett identifies fifteen variants (4–7). Moo summarizes six major combinations (6):

1:1–16:23	+	16:25–27				
1:1–14:23	+	16:25–27	+	15:1–16:23	+	16:25–27
1:1–14:23	+	16:25–27	+	15:1–16:24		
1:1–16:24						
1:1–14:23	+	16:24–27				
1:1–15:33	+	16:25–27	+	16:1–23		

In an attempt to explain these combinations, scholars have suggested three major solutions. Lake argued that an original circular letter consisted of chapters 1–14, and chapters 15–16 were added when the letter was subsequently sent to Rome. (See K. Lake, "The Epistle to the Romans." Pages 324–413 in *The Earlier Epistles of St. Paul: Their Motive and Origin*, 2nd edition. London: Rivingtons, 1914.) Manson argued that chapters 1–15 were originally sent to Rome, and chapter 16 was added when the letter was subsequently sent to Ephesus. (See W. T. Manson, "St. Paul's Letter to the Romans—and Others." Pages 3–15 in *The Romans Debate*, revised and expanded edition. Edited by K. P. Donfried. Peabody, MA: Hendrickson, 1991.). Lightfoot argued that chapters 1–16 were originally sent to Rome, and chapters 15–16 were subsequently deleted to create a circular letter. (See J. B. Lightfoot, "The Structure and Destination of the Epistle to the Romans." Pages 287–320 in *Biblical Essays*, reprint edition. Eugene, OR: Wipf & Stock, 2005.) The different locations of the doxology are then discussed in light of one or more of these explanations of the letter's complex textual history.

Jewett (998–1005) views 16:25–27 in its final form as a non-Pauline interpolation that developed in three stages from an original Hellenistic Jewish version and was added after 14:23 when Marcion shortened the letter. Cranfield (6–9) and Dunn (912–13) view 16:25–27 as a later addition. Longenecker (1085), Moo (936 n. 2), and Schreiner (810–11) view 16:25–27 as original and standing in its present location.* Three factors should be considered in making a decision: (1) Origen wrote that Marcion shortened the letter to chapters 1–14 (Com Rom 10.43), which explains the doxology standing after 14:23 in some manuscripts. (2) Other than 𝔓[46], there is no manuscript evidence that the doxology stood after 15:33, and 𝔓[46] includes 16:1–23 after the doxology. (3) The strongest manuscript evidence (א, A, B, D, 33) suggests that the doxology stood after 16:23. Although Metzger gives the UBS[5] reading a {C} rating (476), including the doxology after 1:1–16:23 seems to be the preferred reading.

VERSE 25

Τῷ δὲ δυναμένῳ ὑμᾶς στηρίξαι κατὰ τὸ εὐαγγέλιόν μου καὶ τὸ κήρυγμα Ἰησοῦ Χριστοῦ

Δέ is transitional ("now"); τῷ δυναμένῳ (dat. sg. masc. of pres. mid. ptc. of dep. δύναμαι, "be able") is a substantival participle functioning as the indirect object of the understood verb (cf. Eph 3:20; Jude 24); ὑμᾶς is the object of the complementary infinitive στηρίξαι (aor. act. inf. of στηρίζω, "strengthen"; cf. 1:11). Κατά + accusative denotes standard (R 609; Jewett 1006); see 1:1 for εὐαγγέλιόν; μου refers to the gospel Paul preached (Cranfield 810; cf. 2 Tim 2:8). Καί ("that is to say") is epexegetic (Cranfield 810; Dunn 914; Schreiner 811); κήρυγμα, -τος, τό describes something proclaimed aloud publicly, often by a herald sent by God (BDAG 543a) and is better understood as the content than the activity (Schreiner 812); Ἰησοῦ Χριστοῦ is an objective genitive describing the specific content that is preached (Dunn 914).

κατὰ ἀποκάλυψιν μυστηρίου χρόνοις αἰωνίοις σεσιγημένου

Κατά + accusative denotes cause (Harris 42; Schreiner 812) or basis (Moo 939);* see 1:17 for ἀποκάλυψις; see 11:25 for μυστηρίου (cf. 1 Cor 2:6–10; Col 1:26–27;

2 Tim 1:9–10; Titus 1:2–3); the genitive is objective; the prepositional phrase is best understood as modifying *κήρυγμα* (Moo 939). *Χρόνοις αἰωνίοις* (ESV, "for long ages") is a temporal dative (BDF §201) indicating duration (T 203; cf. Wallace 156) and modifies *σεσιγημένου* (gen. sg. neut. of pf. pass. ptc. of *σιγάω*, "keep secret"), which is an adjectival participle modifying *μυστηρίου*; the perfect is extensive; the passive is a divine passive (Dunn 915).

VERSE 26

φανερωθέντος δὲ νῦν

Δέ is adversative ("but"); *φανερωθέντος* (gen. sg. neut. of aor. pass. ptc. of *φανερόω*, "make known"; cf. 1:19; 3:21) is a second adjectival participle modifying *μυστηρίου*; the aorist tense is constative; the passive is a divine passive; *νῦν* ("now") establishes a sharp temporal contrast (R 1117).

διά τε γραφῶν προφητικῶν κατ' ἐπιταγὴν τοῦ αἰωνίου θεοῦ

The conjunction *τε* ("and") connects the next series of prepositional phrases to the participle that follows (Jewett 1009; Schreiner 813). *Διά* + accusative denotes instrument (Harris 42); *γραφῶν* is definite, although anarthrous; *προφητικός, -ή, -όν* describes something that pertains to the inspired interpretation of the divine will (BDAG 891b); the phrase "the prophetic Scriptures" (Schreiner 813) refers to the OT (Moo 940; cf. Dunn 915). *Κατά* + accusative denotes basis (CEV, "based on the command"); *ἐπιταγή, -ῆς, ἡ* describes an authoritative directive (BDAG 383b; cf. 1 Tim 1:1; Titus 1:3; 2:15); *τοῦ αἰωνίου θεοῦ* is a subjective genitive (NLT, "as the eternal God has commanded"); placing *αἰωνίου* in the first attributive position gives it emphasis.

εἰς ὑπακοὴν πίστεως εἰς πάντα τὰ ἔθνη γνωρισθέντος

Εἰς + accusative denotes purpose (Moo 940); see 1:5 for *ὑπακοή*; *πίστεως* is a genitive of source (NIV, "obedience that comes from faith"); *εἰς πάντα τὰ ἔθνη* ("to all the nations") identifies the audience of the revealed mystery. *Γνωρισθέντος* (gen. sg. neut. of aor. pass. ptc. of *γνωρίζω*, "make known"; cf. 9:22, 23) is the third adjectival participle modifying *μυστηρίου* in verse 25; the aorist is constative; the passive is a divine passive.

VERSE 27

μόνῳ σοφῷ θεῷ

Μόνος is frequently anarthrous (R 776) and should be taken with *σοφῷ* (Cranfield 814); *θεῷ* stands in apposition to *τῷ δυναμένῳ* at the beginning of verse 25 (Moo 940 n. 32). EVV regularly translate the phrase as "to the only wise God" (e.g., ESV; cf. Moo 940 n. 33).

διὰ Ἰησοῦ Χριστοῦ, ᾧ ἡ δόξα εἰς τοὺς αἰῶνας, ἀμήν

Διά + denotes agency (Harris 42) and is best taken with what follows (Moo 941 n. 35). The relative pronoun ᾧ (dat. sg. masc.) is resumptive (R 437) and has θεῷ as its antecedent (Dunn 916). The optative εἴη is understood; see 1:21 for δόξα; εἰς + accusative is temporal ("throughout the ages"). The manuscript evidence is split between αἰῶνας (𝔓[46], B, 33) and αἰῶνας τῶν αἰώνων (א, A, D). The former reading is shorter, and it seems probable that a scribe would conform it to the more common longer reading (cf. Gal 1:5; Phil 4:20; 1 Tim 1:17; 2 Tim 4:18). Schreiner views the shorter reading as "surely original" and the longer reading as "an obvious liturgical addition" (880; contra Cranfield 813 n. 3). See 1:25 for ἀμήν.

FOR FURTHER STUDY

96. Textual History of Romans (16:25–27)

Aland, K. "Der Schluss und die ursprungliche Gestalt des Römerbriefes." Pages 284–301 in *Neutestmentliche Entwürfe*. Munich: Kaiser, 1979.

Collins, R. F. "The Case of the Wandering Doxology: Rom 16,25–27." Pages 293–303 in *New Testament Textual Criticism and Exegesis. Festschrift J. Deloble*. Edited by A. Denaux. Leufen: Peeters, 2002.

Elliott, J. K. "The Language and Style of the Concluding Doxology to the Epistle to the Romans." *ZNW* 72 (1981): 124–30.

Gamble, H. G. *The Textual History of the Letter to the Romans*. Grand Rapids: Eerdmans, 1977.

Hort, F. J. A. "On the End of the Epistle to the Romans." Pages 321–51 in *Biblical Essays*. Edited by J. B. Lightfoot. London: Macmillan, 1893.

Hurtado, L. W. "The Doxology at the End of Romans." Pages 185–99 in *New Testament Textual Criticism: Its Significance for Exegesis. Essays in Honor of Bruce M. Metzger*. Edited by E. J. Epp and G. D. Fee. Oxford: Clarendon, 1981.

Lampe, P. "Zur Textgeschichte des Römerbriefes." *NovT* 27 (1985): 273–77.

McDonald, J. I. H. "Was Romans XVI a Separate Letter?" *NTS* 16 (1969–70): 369–72.

HOMILETICAL SUGGESTIONS

Soli Deo Gloria (16:25–27)

1. Call to give the only-wise God eternal glory (16:27a, c)
   a. Agent: Jesus Christ (16:27b)
   b. Reason: His ability to establish believers (16:25a)
      (1) Standard: The gospel Paul preaches (16:25b)
         (a) Character: Once hidden, now revealed (16:25c–26a)
            i. Instrument: The prophetic writings (16:26b)
            ii. Cause: God's command (16:26c)
            iii. Purpose: The obedience of faith (16:26d)
            iv. Sphere: All the Gentiles (16:26e)

God and the Gospel (16:25–27)

1. God
   a. He is powerful (16:25a)
   b. He is eternal (16:26c)
   c. He is wise (16:27a)
2. The Gospel
   a. It was once hidden (16:25c)
   b. It is now revealed (16:26a)
   c. It produces the obedience of faith (16:26d)

Exegetical Outline

- I. Letter Opening (1:1–17)
  - A. Salutation (1:1–7)
    1. The writer: the apostle Paul (1:1–5)
    2. The recipients: the saints in Rome (1:6–7a)
    3. The greeting: grace and peace (1:7b)
  - B. Thanksgiving (1:8–12)
    1. Paul thanks God for the Roman believers (1:8)
    2. Paul prays for the Roman believers (1:9–10)
    3. Paul longs to see the Roman believers (1:11–12)
  - C. Occasion for writing (1:13–15)
    1. Paul's intention to visit Rome (1:13)
    2. Paul's reason to visit Rome (1:14–15)
  - D. Thesis (1:16–17)
    1. The gospel is the expression of God's power (1:16)
    2. The gospel is the revelation of God's righteousness (1:17; cf. Hab 2:4)
- II. Letter Body (1:18–15:13)
  - A. The revelation of God's righteousness (1:18–4:25)
    1. God reveals his righteousness through wrath (1:18–3:20)
       - a. Because humankind suppresses God's truth (1:18–23)
         - i. Humankind unrighteously suppresses his truth (1:18–19)
         - ii. Humankind inexcusably ignores his power and divine nature (1:20–21)
         - iii. Humankind foolishly discards his glory (1:22–23)
       - b. Because the Gentiles practice unrighteousness (1:24–32)
         - i. God "hands them over" to perverted worship (1:24–25)
         - ii. God "hands them over" to perverted sex (1:26–27)
         - iii. God "hands them over" to perverted conduct (1:28–32)
       - c. Because the moral person judges others (2:1–16)
         - i. God's judgment is deserved (2:1–5)
           - (a) Because they practice what they judge (2:1–3)
           - (b) Because they despise God's goodness (2:4–5)

- ii. God's judgment is based on works (2:6–11)
- iii. God's judgment is impartially applied (2:12–16)
  - (a) To those who have the law (2:12–13)
  - (b) To those who do not have the law (2:14–16)

d. Because the Jews transgress the law (2:17–29)

- i. Possession of the law does not exempt from judgment (2:17–24)
  - (a) Four advantages of being instructed from the Mosaic law (2:17–18)
  - (b) Four obligations that result from possessing the Mosaic law (2:19–20)
  - (c) Four transgressions of the Mosaic law (2:21–23)
  - (d) Proof of guilt from the Mosaic law (2:24; cf. Isa 52:5)
- ii. Possession of circumcision does not exempt from judgment (2:25–29)
  - (a) The relation of circumcision to the law (2:25)
  - (b) The relation of uncircumcision to the law (2:26–27)
  - (c) The nature of true Jewishness and true circumcision (2:28–29)

e. Because God always acts righteously (3:1–8)

- i. Paul's teaching does not impugn God's covenant with Israel (3:1–2)
- ii. Paul's teaching does not impugn God's faithfulness (3:3–4; cf. Ps 51:4)
- iii. Paul's teaching does not impugn God's justice (3:5–6)
- iv. Paul's teaching does not impugn God's truth (3:7–8)

f. Because all are under sin (3:9–20)

- i. Thesis: Jews and Greeks are both under sin (3:9)
- ii. The support of OT Scripture (3:10–18; cf. Ps 13:1–3)
- iii. Implication: The law makes accountable and exposes sin (3:19–20)

2. God reveals his righteousness apart from law (3:21–31)

a. Through faith in Christ (3:21–26)

- i.. It is manifested in the new epoch (3:21–22b)
- ii. It is available to all (3:22c–24)
- iii. It is displayed in Jesus's propitiatory sacrifice (3:25–26)

b. Apart from works of law (3:27–31)

- i. It shuts the door on boasting (3:27–28)
- ii. It establishes God as the God of both Jew and Gentile (3:29–30)
- iii. It confirms the role of the law (3:31)

3. God reveals his righteousness in response to faith (4:1–25)

a. Apart from works or circumcision (4:1–12)

i. Question: How was Abraham declared righteous? (4:1–2)
ii. Answer #1: Abraham was declared righteous apart from works (4:3–5; cf. Gen 15:6)
iii. Answer #2: Abraham was declared righteous apart from circumcision (4:6–12; cf. Ps 32:1–2)

b. Apart from law (4:13–25)
i. The promise was not given to Abraham through the law (4:13–15)
(a) The law would nullify the promise (4:14)
(b) The law provokes wrath and reveals sin (4:15)
ii. The promise was given to Abraham on the basis of faith (4:16–22)
iii. The promise was given for our sakes (4:23–25)

B. The provision of God's righteousness (5:1–8:39)
1. God's righteousness is imputed in Christ (5:1–21)
a. Bringing peace, hope, and reconciliation (5:1–11)
i. The present results of justification (5:1–5)
(a) We have peace with God (5:1)
(b) We have access into grace (5:2a)
(c) We have hope in God's glory (5:2b–5)
ii. The past basis of justification: Christ's death for us (5:6–8)
(a) We were not righteous or good (5:7)
(b) We were weak, ungodly, and sinful (5:6, 8)
iii. The future promise of justification: Salvation from wrath (5:9–11)
(a) Because we are declared righteous by Christ's blood (5:9)
(b) Because we are reconciled through Christ's death (5:10)
b. Counteracting the effects of Adam's sin (5:12–21)
i. The impact of Adam's sin: Sin entered the world, and death passed to all (5:12)
ii. The period before the law: Sin was not charged, but death reigned (5:13–14)
iii. The differences between Adam and Christ (5:15–17)
(a) In Adam, many died; in Christ, grace abounds (5:15)
(b) In Adam, judgment led to condemnation; in Christ, grace leads to acquittal (5:16)
(c) In Adam, death reigned; in Christ, grace and righteousness reign (5:17)
iv. The impact of Christ's gift: Many are declared righteous (5:18–19)
v. The impact of the law: Sin increased, but grace increases even more (5:20–21)

2. God's righteousness is appropriated in Christ (6:1–23)
   a. By understanding our death with Christ (6:1–14)
      i. We were buried with Christ to walk in newness of life (6:1–4)
      ii. We died with Christ and were justified from sin (6:5–7)
      iii. We were made alive with Christ to live to God (6:8–11)
      iv. Application (6:12–14)
         (a) Sin must not reign in our bodies (6:12)
         (b) We must present our members to God and righteousness (6:13)
   b. By serving our new master (6:15–23)
      i. Obedience reveals our master (6:15–16)
      ii. We have been freed from sin and enslaved to God (6:17–19)
      iii. Slavery to sin leads to death; slavery to God leads to eternal life (6:20–23)
3. God's righteousness is not lived out according to the law (7:1–25)
   a. Because dying with Christ brings release from the law (7:1–6)
      i. Analogy from marital law: The law governs a person as long as he/she lives (7:1–3)
      ii. Practical application: Christ's death severed our obligation to the law (7:4–6)
   b. Because the law brings knowledge of sin (7:7–12)
      i. The law is not sin; it identifies sin (7:7)
      ii. Sin uses the law to deceive and kill (7:8–11)
      iii. The law, therefore, is holy, just, and good (7:12)
   c. Because sin uses the law to produce death (7:13–25)
      i. Issue: Sin uses the law to produce death (7:13)
      ii. First Explanation (7:14–17)
         (a) The law is spiritual, but human beings are fleshly (7:14–16)
         (b) Indwelling sin is responsible for producing detested acts (7:17)
      iii. Second Explanation (7:18–20)
         (a) No good dwells in the fleshly body (7:18–19)
         (b) Indwelling sin is responsible for producing evil (7:20)
      iv. Conclusion (7:21–25)
         (a) Evil is present despite the desire to do good (7:21–23)
         (b) Only Jesus Christ can deliver (7:24–25)
4. God's righteousness is lived out according to the Spirit (8:1–30)
   a. Who gives us life and assurance (8:1–17)
      i. The Spirit sets us free from condemnation, sin, and death (8:1–4)
      ii. The Spirit orients us to spiritual affairs (8:5–8)
      iii. The Spirit indwells us (8:9–11)

- iv. The Spirit enables us to put to death the deeds of the body (8:12–13)
- v. The Spirit bears witness that we are God's children (8:14–17)

b. Who gives us hope of glory (8:18–30)
- i. Creation waits for deliverance (8:18–21)
- ii. Believers hope for final redemption (8:22–25)
- iii. The Spirit helps our weakness (8:26–27)
- iv. God accomplishes his purpose (8:28–30)

5. God's righteousness results in victory (8:31–39)

a. Question section (8:31–36)
- i. Who will oppose us? (8:31–32)
- ii. Who will accuse us? (8:33)
- iii. Who will condemn us? (8:34)
- iv. What will separate us? (8:35–36)

b. Answer section (8:37–39)
- i. We are more than conquerors (8:37)
- ii. Nothing can separate us from God's love in Christ (8:38–39)

C. The vindication of God's righteousness (9:1–11:36)

1. Paul's concern for Israel (9:1–5)
   - a. The intensity of his grief (9:1–2)
   - b. The reason for his grief (9:3–5)

2. God's righteousness is vindicated by his sovereign working (9:6–29)

a. According to his sovereign calling (9:6–13)
- i. Not every Israelite is "Israel" (9:6)
- ii. First Example: Isaac (9:7–9; cf. Gen 18:10)
- iii. Second Example: Jacob (9:10–13; cf. Mal 1:2–3)

b. Out of his sovereign mercy (9:14–18)
- i. God's actions are never unfair (9:14)
- ii. God's mercy does not depend on human will or effort (9:15–16)
- iii. God exercises his mercy as he wills (9:17–18)

c. Under his sovereign authority (9:19–29)
- i. The audacity of human presumption (9:19–21)
- ii. The nature of divine forbearance (9:22–24)
- iii. The support of OT Scripture (9:25–29)
  - (a) Regarding the Gentiles (9:25b–26; cf. Hos 2:23; 1:10)
  - (b) Regarding the Jews (9:27–29; cf. Isa 10:22–23; 1:9)

3. God's righteousness is vindicated despite Israel's unresponsiveness (9:30–10:21)

a. Reflected in their failed pursuit (9:30–10:4)
- i. They focus on the wrong goal (9:30–33)
- ii. They use the wrong approach (10:1–4)

b. Rooted in their flawed understanding (10:5–13)

- i. They misunderstand the simplicity of righteousness by faith (10:5–8)
- ii. They misunderstand the dynamics of righteousness by faith (10:9–10)
- iii. They misunderstand the universal scope of righteousness by faith (10:11–13)

c. Resulting in their frustrating disobedience (10:14–21)

- i. Theological Syllogism (10:14–17)
  - (a) Major premise: God sends preachers with the message of salvation (10:14–15; cf. Isa 52:7)
  - (b) Minor premise: Not all believe the message (10:16; Isa 53:1)
  - (c) Conclusion: Salvation comes from hearing and believing the message (10:17)
- ii. The support of OT Scripture (10:18–21)
  - (a) Israel has heard the message (10:18; cf. Ps 19:4)
  - (b) Israel has known about the message (10:19–20; cf. Deut 32:21; Isa 65:1)
  - (c) Israel has rejected the message (10:21; cf. Isa 65:2)

4. God's righteousness is vindicated by his plan for salvation history (11:1–32)

a. To preserve a Jewish remnant (11:1–10)

- i. God has not rejected Israel (11:1)
- ii. God has preserved a remnant (11:2–6; cf. 1 Kgs 19:10, 18)
- iii. God has hardened the rest (11:7–10; cf. Deut 29:4; Ps 69:22–23)

b. To bring salvation to the Gentiles (11:11–24)

- i. Israel's hardening has universal impact (11:11–15)
  - (a) It brings salvation to the Gentiles (11:11–12)
  - (b) It provokes the Jews to jealousy and salvation (11:13–14)
  - (c) It promises global reconciliation and life (11:15)
- ii. Israel's hardening is not a reason for Gentile arrogance (11:16–21)
  - (a) Because they are dependent on the root (11:16–18)
  - (b) Because they are not immune from being cut off (11:19–21)
- iii. Israel's hardening demonstrates God's kindness (11:22–24)
  - (a) He currently exercises kindness to persevering Gentiles (11:22)
  - (b) He is able to exercise kindness to repenting Jews (11:23–24)

c. To restore Israel (11:25–32)

- i. The mystery disclosed (11:25–26a)

(a) Israel partially hardened (11:25c)
(b) Full number of Gentiles brought in (11:25d)
(c) All Israel saved (11:26a)
ii. The mystery supported (11:26b–27; cf. Isa 59:20–21; 27:9)
iii. The mystery explained (11:28–32)
(a) The Jews' status (11:28–29)
(b) Human disobedience and divine mercy (11:30–32)
5. Paul's praise to God (11:33–36)
a. Praise of God's plan (11:33)
b. The support of OT Scripture (11:34–35; Isa 40:13; Job 41:11)
c. Confession and doxology (11:36)
D. The practice of God's righteousness (12:1–15:13)
1. God's righteousness is practiced in Christian living (12:1–13:14)
a. By giving ourselves wholly to God (12:1–2)
i. Present yourselves as living sacrifices (12:1)
ii. Do not be conformed to this age, but be transformed (12:2)
b. By humbly exercising spiritual gifts (12:3–8)
i. The right attitude: You ought to think soberly about yourselves (12:3)
ii. The right perspective: You are members of one body (12:4–5)
iii. The right manner: You should exercise your gifts as God intended (12:6–8)
c. By pursuing total transformation (12:9–21)
i. Evidence of a transformed mind (12:9–13)
ii. Evidence of a transformed heart (12:14–16)
iii. Evidence of a transformed will (12:17–21)
d. By being subject to authorities (13:1–7)
i. Be subject to governing authorities (13:1–4)
(a) They are ordained by God (13:1–2)
(b) They are rewarders of good and avengers of evil (13:3–4)
ii. It is necessary to be subject (13:5–6)
(a) They are the reason to pay taxes (13:6a)
(b) They are God's ministers (13:6b)
iii. Four specific obligations (13:7)
e. By loving one another (13:8–10)
i. Owe no one anything except love (13:8)
ii. The command to love your neighbor summarizes the law (13:9; cf. Exod 20:13–15, 17; Lev 19:18)
iii. Because love does no evil to your neighbor, it fulfills the law (13:10)
f. By living in light of Jesus's return (13:11–14)
i. Rise from sleep, because "the day" is near (13:11–12a)
ii. Put on the weapons of light (13:12b)

iii. Walk properly (13:13)
iv. Make no provision for the flesh (13:14)
2. God's righteousness is practiced in Christian liberty (14:1–15:13)
a. By accepting one another (14:1–12)
i. Admonition (14:1–3)
(a) Accept one another (14:1–2)
(b) Do not despise or condemn (14:3)
ii. Explanation (14:4–9)
(a) Each is responsible to his/her master (14:4)
(b) Each must be assured in his/her mind (14:5)
(c) Each gives thanks to God (14:6)
(d) Each lives or dies to Christ (14:7–9)
iii. Conclusion (14:10–12)
(a) All will stand before God's judgment seat (14:10–11; cf. Isa 45:23)
(b) Each will give account to God (14:12)
b. By pursuing peace with one another (14:13–23)
i. Determine not to cause stumbling, because grieving another destroys Christ's work (14:13–15)
ii. Your good must not be blasphemed, because obedience is pleasing to God and respected by others (14:16–18)
iii. Pursue peace and edification, because abstaining is good if it forestalls causing others to stumble (14:19–21)
iv. Maintain your convictions before God, because what is not of faith is sin (14:22–23)
c. By pleasing one another (15:1–6)
i. Bear others' weaknesses (15:1)
ii. Please your neighbor (15:2–4; cf Ps 69:9)
iii. Think the same thing (15:5–6)
d. By following Christ's example (15:7–13)
i. Command: Accept one another as Christ accepted you (15:7)
ii. Explanation: Christ's ministry to the circumcision confirms God's promises to the fathers (15:8–12; cf. Ps 18:49; Deut 32:43; Ps 117.1, Isa 11:10)
iii. Prayer-wish (15:13)

III. Letter Closing (15:14–16:27)
A. Paul's mission (15:14–21)
1. His confidence in the Romans (15:14)
2. His apostolic authority (15:15–16)
3. His apostolic ministry (15:17–21; cf. Isa 52:12)
B. Paul's travel plans (15:22–29)
1. His desire to visit Rome (15:22–24)
2. His need to visit Jerusalem (15:25–27)

    3. His plan to visit Spain (15:28–29)
C. Paul's prayer request (15:30–33)
    1. Request for urgent prayer (15:30–32)
    2. Prayer-wish (15:33)
D. Commendation of Phoebe (16:1–2)
    1. Recommendation and credentials (16:1)
    2. Requests and rationale (16:2)
E. Greetings from Paul (16:3–16)
    1. To individuals (16:3–15)
    2. To house churches (16:5, 10, 11, 14, 15)
    3. To the whole church (16:16)
F. Final advice (16:17–20)
    1. Watch out for and avoid false teachers (16:17–18)
    2. Maintain your obedience (16:19–20a)
    3. Grace benediction (16:20b)
G. Greetings from others (16:21–23)
    1. From Paul's teammates (16:21)
    2. From Tertius, who wrote the letter (16:22)
    3. From members of the church in Corinth (16:23)
H. Doxology (16:25–27)

Grammar Index

C

D

E

F

G

H

I

M

N

O

P

Scripture Index

1 Corinthians

2 Corinthians

Galatians

Ephesians

2 Peter

1 John

Jude

Revelation